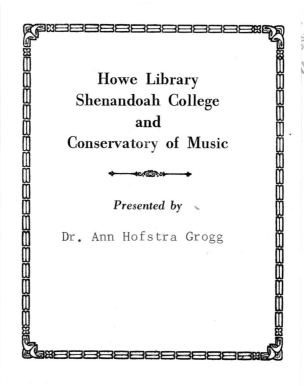

ESSAYS OF GEORGE ELIOT

ESSAYS OF
GEORGE ELIOT

EDITED BY

Thomas Pinney

New York: Columbia University Press

LONDON: ROUTLEDGE AND KEGAN PAUL

Copyright Thomas Pinney 1963

Library of Congress Catalog Card Number 63-20343

FIRST PRINTING 1963

SECOND PRINTING 1967

PRINTED IN THE UNITED STATES OF AMERICA

To

Gordon S. Haight

PREFACE

MOST of George Eliot's periodical articles were written between 1851 and 1857, when she was earning her living as a journalist in London. But she wrote a few articles in Coventry as early as 1846, and even after the success of *Scenes of Clerical Life* in 1857 she published an occasional review or essay, so that there are articles belonging to nearly every decade of her adult life. Shortly before her death she revised for republication five of the longer essays she had written during the 1850's and two from the 1860's, leaving instructions that no more of her published articles should be reprinted. The selection she authorized, published in 1884 as *Essays and Leaves from a Note-Book*, gives a very imperfect idea of the extent and variety of her periodical writings; even those she chose for reprinting have lost some of their liveliness through revision. Several editors, using the incomplete information contained in Cross's *Life of George Eliot* and other sources, have made collections of her articles to supplement the rigorously narrow authorized selection. But these editions were inevitably handicapped by the lack of full evidence about George Eliot's career as a journalist and could not be based on a knowledge of the entire range of what she wrote.

The identification of most of her anonymous articles, now established by Gordon S. Haight in *The George Eliot Letters*, has made it possible for the first time to provide a selection fully representative of her range as a journalist. Since more than sixty articles are positively attributed to her, it would not be practicable to reprint all of them. This edition reprints articles of every kind she wrote, from all but one of the periodicals to which she contributed anything besides fiction. The articles in the edition of 1884 are given here in their original form, before revision. Together with twenty others, they cover more than thirty years in George Eliot's life. Eleven of them have not been reprinted

vii

before; one, 'Notes on Form in Art', is here published for the first time.

The articles, arranged in the order of their publication, are reprinted without alteration, except that obvious misprints have been silently corrected; no attempt has been made to normalize the spellings, which differ in some periodicals. The irregular style of setting off quotations in the essays has in most cases been changed to follow the modern British usage. In one instance, the article on Carlyle, the long extracts which conclude the review have been omitted. The omission is clearly indicated and the source of the extracts identified in a note. Titles printed between square brackets have been supplied by the editor; otherwise, the titles are those under which the articles originally appeared. I have indicated all of George Eliot's substantive revisions by placing each altered passage in square brackets and describing the nature of the change in a note. The headnote to each article gives the circumstances of its composition, the history of its publication and reprinting (if any), and occasionally includes a brief commentary. I have tried to identify all quotations, except for those clearly taken from the work George Eliot is reviewing.

Although only one editor's name appears on the title page, a book of this kind is really a co-operative enterprise. I have drawn on the work of so many scholars that most of my acknowledgments must be confined to the notes. Among all my sources, however, there is one without which I could, quite literally, have done nothing: I mean Gordon S. Haight's edition of *The George Eliot Letters*. My dependence upon Professor Haight's knowledge and generosity is acknowledged in the dedication of this book, but I take this opportunity to thank him again, and the Yale University Press, for permission to print from the *Letters* the information that makes most of the substance of my notes.

I am grateful to the Yale University Library for making available to me George Eliot's MS. Journals and the text of the MS. essay, 'Notes on Form in Art', published in this edition. For permission to publish the essay I owe thanks to Mrs. E. Carrington Ouvry, G. H. Lewes's granddaughter, to whom the copyright belongs.

To Professor Walter E. Houghton and the invaluable *Wellesley Index to Victorian Periodicals* I am indebted for help in compiling the appendix of articles misattributed to George Eliot.

Finally, I should like to thank my former colleagues in the

department of English at Hamilton College, and especially Professor John M. Crossett, for help and encouragement throughout most of the time of my work on this edition. For all of that time I have had the generous assistance of my wife, Sherrill Ohman Pinney.

CONTENTS

CONTENTS

INTRODUCTION

GEORGE ELIOT wrote most of her articles in the 1850's, after she had outgrown the self-conscious awkwardness of her provincial days and before she took on the new self-consciousness of her fame. They have in consequence the freedom and occasional raciness typical of her mind in those years. The reader familiar only with the wide tolerance of her novels will discover in her articles a surprising severity of judgment, and sometimes, as in her attacks on Cumming and Young, a fierce gusto in denunciation. Despite the rather ponderously allusive style characteristic of almost all Victorian periodical writing, there are frequent moments of humour and real wit in her comments on books and men. The characteristic earnestness and seriousness of her articles are not defects in response to appropriately weighty subjects, and in George Eliot they may frequently flare up into passionate argument when she grapples with a theme that engages her deepest convictions. She had an accurately informed, wide-ranging intelligence, which, though it produces some heaviness, gives her articles the weight and strength that has made them endure far better than the ordinary run of Victorian journalism.

The most important of George Eliot's connections during her years as a working journalist was with the *Westminster Review*, founded originally as the voice of Philosophic Radicalism, and in her time still the organ of liberal opinion among the great quarterlies of the day. In 1851, the year in which she sent her first contribution to it, she became editor of the *Westminster*, keeping the position until 1854. She wrote no essays for the *Westminster* while she was its editor, and though she must certainly have contributed brief reviews to it, there is no evidence to identify more than a few of them. Only one review from the period of her editorship is reprinted here. Shortly after her union with G. H. Lewes in 1854 she began to contribute regularly to the *Westminster* and continued to do so until the beginning of 1857: her contributions to it during this period devoted entirely to professional journalism accounted for more than half of her income at the time.

The eight long articles she wrote for the *Westminster* are spacious reviews in the mode typical of the nineteenth-century quarterlies. Between the first and last of them we can see developing an increased confidence and freedom in her treatment of a subject, and a growing sense of power that helped to prepare her for the venture of creative writing. Though the earliest essay, the review of Mackay's *The Progress of the Intellect*, is an impressive display of learning and assured opinion, in it George Eliot stays close to her text, relying heavily upon quotation, paraphrase, and summary. 'Woman in France', too, is less an independent essay than a conscientious attempt to render the substance of the book for the reader's own judgment. But by the time of the article on Cumming, George Eliot has learned how to take advantage of the licence given the Victorian journalist to express himself with magisterial anonymity under pretext of noticing other men's books. She never loses sight of the works she is ostensibly reviewing, but in her later essays for the *Westminster* they serve as occasions to deliver something she herself particularly wants to say. This is especially true of the three slashing essays—'Evangelical Teaching', 'Silly Novels', and 'Worldliness and Other-Worldliness'—that set out to demolish their subjects. But when she finds herself in sympathy with her subject, as in the essays on Heine and Riehl, she can be equally effective. She preferred to admire rather than criticize, and her praise, based on understanding, independent judgment, and genuine liking, is distinguished. The essay on Heine is remarkable as one of the first recognitions in England of his greatness, and for the way in which George Eliot, unlike many Victorian critics, avoids letting her reservations about the artist's personal life influence her admiration for his art.

Her reviews for the *Westminster* regularly appeared in the section entitled 'Belles Lettres', which, between July, 1855, and January, 1857, was written entirely by George Eliot. Each section opened with a long discussion of the book she had selected to receive the most prominent notice for the quarter, and then passed on to notice as many as twenty-eight other titles at varying lengths, from several pages to several lines. Reviewing on such a heroic scale was bound to be uneven, but the opening review for each quarter was always carefully done, and usually there were three or four others that, for thoughtful analysis, deserved to be called more than mere notices. George Eliot's most interesting comments on her famous contemporaries are to be found in the 'Belles Lettres' articles; the reviews of Kingsley, Geraldine Jewsbury, Tennyson, Mrs. Stowe, Charles Reade, and Fredrika Bremer reprinted in this edition provide a good idea of her virtues and limitations as a practising critic of literature.

The most striking characteristic of her reviews is their desire to find something to praise; this explains why George Eliot regularly applies the method of isolating the beauties and faults of a book, for it permits her to lay a charitable stress on whatever 'beauties' she may discover. Alternatively, when she feels bound to condemn a work out of hand, as she does *Maud*, she begins with an extended tribute to Tennyson's greatness, and so, in intention at least, softens the blow. One is always aware in reading George Eliot's reviews that behind the letter of the published work she discerns a human being, towards whom her disposition is to be kind. If this is a weakness, it is surely an amiable one, nor does it prevent her from giving her genuine opinion of a book, whether good or bad.

Her judgments may seem at first to refer too much to the arguments rather than the formal qualities of the literature she reviews: *Maud*, for example, is scored on ethical and political grounds, and Geraldine Jewsbury is taken to task over a point of moral theory in her *Constance Herbert*. For George Eliot, as for Ruskin, an author's beliefs were inseparable from his art. She constantly uses the distinction between form and content in her discussions, and yet she is particularly effective in showing how the truth of action and character in literature may be vitiated by a too-narrow moral or doctrinal conviction.

Another distinctive element in her criticism appears in this observation from her review of Kingsley's *Westward Ho!*:

Poet and artist in a rare degree, his passionate impetuosity and theological prepossessions inexorably forbid that he should ever be a philosopher; he sees, feels, and paints vividly, but he theorizes illogically and moralizes absurdly. If he would confine himself to his true sphere, he might be a teacher in the sense in which every great artist is a teacher—namely, by giving us his higher sensibility as a

3

medium, a delicate acoustic or optical instrument, bringing home to our coarser senses what would otherwise be unperceived by us.

This belief, that art teaches not by preaching but by a sympathetic and imaginative presentation, is repeatedly affirmed in her articles and becomes one of the vital principles of her own novels. She is also free from the common Victorian notion that art must be confined within the limits of ordinary morality; she believes instead that the vision of the artist may reveal a truer and more comprehensive morality in virtue of its very freedom from orthodox restraints. Few of her contemporaries could have written, as she did in 'The Morality of Wilhelm Meister', that 'the line between the virtuous and vicious, so far from being a necessary safeguard to morality, is itself an immoral fiction'. It is the spirit of this utterance that flowered in the generous sympathy of George Eliot's novels.

Despite the fact that her reviews for the *Westminster* were written under the pressure of other regular work and covered far too many books, her opinions have, on the whole, stood the test of time remarkably well. Most of the titles she had to discuss were part of the undistinguished commerce of literature; of these she was content merely to say a few descriptive words, or to pronounce a succinct and deserved condemnation. A survey of the entire series of 'Belles Lettres' reviews would show her welcoming, among others, Matthew Arnold's *Poems, Second Series*, Browning's *Men and Women*, *Walden*, *Modern Painters*, and *The Shaving of Shagpat*. Rarely is she led into extravagant praise of the transient masterpiece that enjoys its short vogue before an early death. Few of her literary judgments would need much revision today: though her high estimate of Mrs. Stowe's *Dred*, shared by most of the novel's other reviewers, would not be supported now, nor her condemnation of *Maud*, there is little to modify in her analysis of Kingsley and Charles Reade, or of the lesser novelists and poets she discussed in her reviews.

After the *Westminster*, the periodical most important in George Eliot's career as a journalist was the *Leader*, a Radical weekly that G. H. Lewes had helped to found in 1850. When George Eliot met him in 1851 the original partnership had been dissolved, but he still wrote for the paper. Even before they left for Germany together she had occasionally helped him with his articles, and upon their return to England in 1855 she began contributing short reviews and miscellaneous articles. The books she reviewed for the *Leader* she was often able to notice a second time in her 'Belles Lettres' review for the *Westminster*; by this convenient device her work was made to yield double returns, though a comparison of her *Leader* and *Westminster* reviews of the same books shows that she was always careful to avoid repeating herself in form if not in substance.

Her articles for the weekly *Leader* were naturally more hastily done than those for the quarterly *Westminster*; a few are mere skeletons of comment fleshed out with a heavy padding of quotation. But the *Leader* articles are written on a wider range of subjects and have a more interesting variety than any other of her periodical writings. In the small part of her thirty-three articles for the *Leader* represented by the nine reprinted here, her range is from German philosophy to Greek tragedy, from Milton's Doctrine of Divorce to the art of translation and the question of women's rights. None of the *Leader* articles reprinted is negligible, and they show better than any other of her writings how the practice of journalism was developing her skill in expression. Even at their most desultory, they reveal the distinctiveness of thought and the complex, controlled style that contribute to the excellence of George Eliot the novelist. The style may not be notable for elegance of phrase or lightness of movement, but it has the virtue of analytic and expository precision.

The *Leader* and the *Westminster* were the only periodicals to which George Eliot contributed regularly, and between them they published more than half of all her articles. Before her success as a novelist, however, while she and Lewes were supporting themselves and Lewes's family solely by journalism, she published two articles in *Fraser's Magazine* and four brief reviews in the newly founded *Saturday Review*. Once the necessity for writing articles was gone she wrote only a few more: a series of four sketches for the new *Pall Mall Gazette* in 1865; two reviews for the new *Fortnightly Review* in 1865; and, at the request of her publisher, 'Address to Working Men, By Felix Holt', in *Blackwood's*, 1868.

Underneath the miscellaneous surface of her articles are a number of themes to which George Eliot often returns. Among the most important of these is the question of religious belief and its relation to moral practice, a subject which, as in the essays on Cumming and Young, inspires her most energetic and impassioned argument. The morality of sympathy, self-sacrifice, duty, and resignation that later determines the action and values of her novels is clearly defined and argued in her articles of the 1850's. Several other characteristic topics are best understood in relation to this central philosophic and ethical concern. Her conservative political beliefs, based on the conception of society as an organic and interdependent growth, and fully expressed in her essay on Riehl, are inseparably connected with her morality; both derive from the same recognition of the vast and intricately ordered system of things that enforces submission and the restraint of personal desire. The scientific and philosophical interests revealed in her articles are also intimately related to her moral ideas; in the first of her essays for the *Westminster* George Eliot wrote that the 'master key' to divine revelation

> is the recognition of the presence of undeviating law in the material and moral world—of that invariability of sequence which is acknowledged to be the basis of physical science, but which is still perversely ignored in our social organization, our ethics and our religion.

This idea is of fundamental importance to the analysis of conduct in the novels; Maggie Tulliver, to take a single example, is the victim of her confused aspirations because she was

> unhappily quite without that knowledge of the irreversible laws within and without her, which, governing the habits, becomes morality, and, developing the feelings of submission and dependence, becomes religion.[1]

The conception of irreversible but ultimately beneficent law as the unifying basis of morality, politics, and science underlies George Eliot's frequently misunderstood doctrine of consequences, her conservative view of society, and her meliorism.

As we should expect from the translator of Strauss and Feuerbach and the companion of Goethe's first English biographer, George Eliot wrote frequently on German literature and German culture. Always alertly responsive to the significant intellectual movements of the day, she had begun to study German in 1840,

[1] *The Mill on the Floss*, Book IV, Ch. 3.

when the influence of Carlyle was stimulating an eager interest in German thought. Though she shared Carlyle's 'awful sense of the mystery of existence', the Germany she discovered was not his: she found no messages of natural supernaturalism; she was attracted, not to the idealist philosophers, but to the historical critics of the Bible and the scholarly thoroughness and integrity they represented. The source of the attraction for her is given in 'A Word for the Germans', a half-bantering apology written in 1865, years after her first enthusiastic study of German historical scholarship. Without the Germans, she writes,

> historical criticism would have been simply nowhere; take away the Germans, with their patience, their thoroughness, their need for a doctrine which refers all transient and material manifestations to subtler and more permanent causes, and all that we most value in our appreciation of early history would have been wanting to us.

The need for such a doctrine as the German *Gelehrter* felt was no less urgent in George Eliot, and the promise of finding it in the scientifically applied principles of historical criticism was a powerful appeal. Like Dorothea Brooke's, 'her mind was theoretic, and yearned by its nature after some lofty conception of the world which might frankly include the parish of Tipton and her own rule of conduct there'.[2] But by the 1850's she had assimilated the lessons she had learned from German criticism into a wider current of ideas, and apart from a few passages in her review of Mackay she makes no doctrinaire display of her knowledge. Much more characteristic is her tactful summary, in 'Introduction to Genesis', of the various beliefs about Biblical inspiration. Her own position is made clear, but it is established without anger or a triumphant sense of superiority.

For George Eliot, one of the advantages of anonymity was the freedom it gave her to speak out on the question of woman's place in society. In her later years, because of her anomalous position, she scrupulously refrained from any public comment on the question, and though the problems of her heroines in the novels may touch it indirectly, they are concerned with a much wider range of issues than the status of women. In her articles, however, she was at liberty to say what she would. Her review of the 'Life and Opinions of Milton' urges her readers to reconsider Milton's

[2] *Middlemarch*, Ch. 1.

'calm and dignified' arguments for divorce—a suggestion she could not have dared to make in print after she became famous. In 'Woman in France', 'Margaret Fuller and Mary Wollstonecraft', and 'Silly Novels by Lady Novelists' she develops, directly or by implication, her mildly Radical conviction that the culture of women requires their admission 'to a common fund of ideas, to common objects of interest with men'; though she is fond of quoting *The Princess*, her measure of what is possible or appropriate for women is considerably wider than Tennyson's. But it is not very helpful to categorize George Eliot's opinions on the 'woman question', since they are particularly good illustrations of the mixed conservative and reforming tendencies of her mind. She never suggests that women deserve an equal social standing with men, and in this she is perhaps conservative; but she is persuaded that women require an equal moral and intellectual culture, not only for themselves but for the general good of society, and this is the basis of whatever is progressive in her opinions on the subject. The complexity of her attitude sets her comments above the level at which this discussion was usually carried on in her day; so does her refreshing scorn for the popular sentimental mystique of woman as a vestal guarding the purity of the community. 'If it were true,' she writes in 'Margaret Fuller and Mary Wollstonecraft', 'then there would be a case in which slavery and ignorance nourished virtue, and so far we should have an argument for the continuance of bondage.'

Perhaps even more interesting than her notion of an ideal culture for women are her observations on the kinds of women produced by actual institutions. Her articles contain many hints later developed in the novels; the seed of Rosamond and Lydgate's story, for example, is in this passage from 'Margaret Fuller and Mary Wollstonecraft' criticizing the masculine fear of the intelligent and cultured woman as likely to be 'obstinate':

> But surely, so far as obstinacy is concerned, your unreasoning animal is the most unmanageable of creatures, where you are not allowed to settle the question by a cudgel, a whip and bridle, or even a string to the leg. . . . Wherever weakness is not harshly controlled it must *govern*, as you may see when a strong man holds a little child by the hand, how he is pulled hither and thither, and wearied in his walk by his submission to the whims and feeble movements of his companion.

George Eliot's essays and reviews contain an unsystematic but sufficiently distinct theory of fiction that is of great interest in the study of her novels, especially the early ones. Her standard of value, defined in 'Silly Novels by Lady Novelists', 'The Natural History of German Life', and in the reviews of Fredrika Bremer, Charles Reade, and Kingsley, is literary realism. 'Art is the nearest thing to life', she affirms in 'The Natural History of German Life', and from this principle the rest of her theory is deduced. The argument developed in the review of Kingsley and 'The Morality of Wilhelm Meister', that the true mode of artistic teaching is simply to 'follow the stream of fact and of life', is a necessary consequence of her belief that a scene, character, or action truly observed will carry with it its own moral value; she has, in theory at least, a Wordsworthian sense of the sacredness and significance of fact. But her conception of realism stops well short of the naturalist extreme, and has ample room for frankly idealized elements if they can claim the authority of imaginative insight rather than of mere creative fancy—a distinction for which she suggests no sure test.

In her first novels George Eliot attempted to apply the ideal of 'truth to nature' expounded in her articles of the 1850's. Though 'truthfulness' always remained a cardinal point in her literary creed, she later came to interpret it more liberally. From the suggestions in her letters after 1860 and in 'Notes on Form in Art' it seems clear that she moved away from her early theory of realistic imitation towards a more formal theory of the novel as a highly stylized and patterned construction.

In the same articles defining her theory of fiction George Eliot defines the function of all art as the awakening of sympathy—'moral emotion'. What is true of art in general is true *a fortiori* of fiction, which is 'a mode of amplifying experience and extending our contact with our fellow-men beyond the bounds of our personal lot' ('The Natural History of German Life'). On this point the articles written before her career as a novelist express a conviction George Eliot never altered. The experience of the practising artist may have brought about some important shifts in her literary theory, but the purposes of the moralist were fixed.

This brief survey of George Eliot's articles only suggests the extent of their interest. They touch on most of the important questions of her day, and, as practice for her later writing and as a record of her reading, they contain much that is directly relevant

9

to the study of the novelist. George Eliot's powers as an essayist and reviewer can add nothing to her reputation, but her articles display, in lesser measure, the same intelligence and breadth of view that we have learned to appreciate in her novels. This is praise enough.

ABBREVIATIONS

Cross, *Life*   *George Eliot's Life as Related in Her Letters and Journals. Arranged and Edited by Her Husband J. W. Cross*, 3 vols., Edinburgh and London, William Blackwood and Sons, 1885.

Journal   George Eliot's MS. journal [1849]–1861 (Yale University Library).
George Eliot's MS. diary 1861–1877 (Tinker Collection, Yale University Library).

Letters   Gordon S. Haight, ed., *The George Eliot Letters*, 7 vols., New Haven, Yale University Press, 1954–1955.

1884   In the notes, refers to the revised text of George Eliot's essays published in *Essays and Leaves from a Note-Book*, Edinburgh and London, William Blackwood and Sons, 1884.

1

POETRY AND PROSE, FROM THE NOTEBOOK OF AN ECCENTRIC

Coventry *Herald and Observer*, 4 December 1846, p. 2b; 15 January 1847, p. 2b; 5 February 1847, p. 2bc; 12 February 1847, p. 2ab; 19 February 1847, p. 2ab

The sketches and impressions grouped together as 'Poetry and Prose, From the Notebook of an Eccentric' are George Eliot's first published original writing, except for the short poem entitled 'Farewell' that appeared in the *Christian Observer* for January, 1840. (Despite the title, no poetry was included in the 'Poetry and Prose' essays.) They are slight, awkward, and self-consciously literary, but the careful reader will discover in them the presence of ideas and attitudes that look forward to the preoccupations of George Eliot's mature work. It is interesting to note that in her last book, *Impressions of Theophrastus Such*, she returned to the form of these early essays: though they are separated by more than thirty years, her first and last published prose compositions are both *moralia*.

The five articles in 'Poetry and Prose' were republished in 1919 as *Early Essays by George Eliot*, privately printed by Major George Redway. The book contains an editor's note which, as Professor Haight observes, 'under the kindest interpretation must be called equivocal'.[1] It reads in part:

> At the time of George Eliot's death, or perhaps a few years later, the manuscript which is here printed was placed in my hands for publication. Ever since then it has lain among forgotten papers, and now, in

[1] *Letters*, I, 250, n. For information about Redway and his publishing practices, see John Carter and Graham Pollard, *The Firm of Charles Ottley, Landon & Co., Footnote to an Enquiry* (London and New York, 1948).

order to prevent the total loss of a literary treasure—for such I deem it—I am accepting the responsibility of printing a few copies.

Copies of the essays, clipped from the Coventry *Herald* and pasted in a Commonplace Book of George Eliot's friend Mrs. Bray, had been displayed at the Coventry Public Libraries on the occasion of George Eliot's centenary in 1919. No manuscript of the essays is known to exist, and the coincidence of the exhibit with Major Redway's reprint is difficult to overlook.

*   *   *

INTRODUCTORY

A WEEK ago, I stood sole mourner at the grave of my friend Macarthy. He lies in a village Church-yard;—not one of those peaceful green plots which seem to speak well for the influence of the Bishop's blessing, in which there is some spreading chesnut or yew of age immemorial, that seems to say to the world-weary, 'Come and rest under my shadow.' No. The Church-yard in which Macarthy lies looks not like a *Gottes-acker*, but a Vicar's acre, the profits of which (including the grazing of half-a-dozen sheep) go to eke out the Curate's yearly hundred, upon which he supports, or rather diets, the gentility of his wife and ten children. It is a thoroughfare for a materialized population, too entirely preoccupied with the needs of the living, to retain an Old Mortality's affectionate care for tomb-stones and epitaphs, or to offer to the graves that terrified veneration which hurries past them after sunset. They are in the strong grasp of giant Hunger, and fear no shadows. Not one of this plodding generation will long remember Macarthy, 'the sick gentleman that lodged at Widow Crowe's,' and when the grass is green and long upon his grave, it will seem to say of him as truly as of others—'I cover the forgotten.' But it is not so, Macarthy. With me thou wilt still live: my thoughts will seem to be all spoken to thee, my actions all performed in thy presence; for ours was a love passing the love of women.[2] My friend was one of whom the world proved itself not worthy, for it never made a true estimate of him. His soul was a lyre of exquisite structure, but men knew not how to play on it: it was a bird endowed with rich and varied notes, which it was ready to bestow on human hearers;

[2] George Eliot was fond of David's great lament for Saul and Jonathan, later choosing a line from it for the motto to *The Mill on the Floss*: 'In their death they were not divided.'

but their coarse fondling or brutal harshness scared it away, and the poor bird ceased to sing, save in the depths of the forest or the silence of night. To those who saw only the splendour of his genius, and the nobility of his sentiments, his childhood and youth seemed to promise a brilliant career; but any who were capable of a more discriminating estimate and refined analysis of his character, must have had a foreboding that it contained elements which would too probably operate as non-conductors, interposed between his highly-charged mind and the negatively electrified souls around him. The quality on which a good prophet would have pronounced my friend's fate to hang, was one which will be held to have placed him not above, but simply out of, the sphere of his fellow men. It was a morbid sensitiveness in his feeling of the beautiful, which I can compare to nothing but those alleged states of mesmeric lucidity, in which the patient obtains an unenviable cognizance of irregularities, happily imperceptible to us in the ordinary state of our consciousness. His ideal was not, as with most men, an enshrined object of worship, but a beautiful shadow which was ever floating before him, importunately presenting itself as a twin object with all realities, whether external or mental, and turning all their charms into mockery. He moved among the things of this earth like a lapidarian among false gems, which fetch high prices and admiration from others, but to him are mere counterfeits. He seemed to have a preternaturally sharpened vision, which saw knots and blemishes, where all was smoothness to others. The unsightly condition of the masses—their dreary ignorance—the conventional distortion of human nature in the upper classes—the absence of artistic harmony and beauty in the details of outward existence, were with him not merely themes for cold philosophy, indignant philippics, or pointed satire; but positively painful elements in his experience, sharp iron entering into his soul. Had his nature been less noble, his benevolence less God-like, he would have been a misanthropist, all compact of bitter sarcasm, and therefore no poet. As it was, he was a humourist,—one who sported with all the forms of human life, as if they were so many May-day mummings, uncouth, monstrous disguises of poor human nature, which has not discovered its dignity. While he laughed at the follies of men, he wept over their sorrows; and while his wit lashed them as with a whip of scorpions, there was a stream of feeling in the deep caverns of his soul, which was all the time murmuring,

'Would that I could die for thee, thou poor humanity!' From the age of twenty, I never knew him to form a particular predilection for any individual, or admit any new intimacy. He seemed to have learned by experience, that his sensibility was too acute for special friendship—that his sympathy with mankind was that of a being of analogous, rather than of identical race. Even animals, which usually attract those who are cut off by any material or immaterial barrier from their own kind, seemed to have a repulsion for him. He was their zealous protector, it is true, and I have known him walk back a hundred yards to give a consolatory pat on the head to an ugly cur, which he thought he had repulsed too unkindly; though all the while feeling the direst aversion to the ill-favoured brute. He seemed, indeed, to shrink from all organized existences. He was an ardent lover of Nature, but it was in her grand inorganic forms,—the blue sky, the stars, the clouds, the sea, mountains, rocks, and rivers,—in which she seems pregnant with some sublimer birth than the living races of this globe. He would lie on the grass gazing at the setting sun, with a look of intense yearning, which might have belonged to a banished Uriel. The roaring of the wind would produce in him an enthusiastic excitement, a spiritual intoxication. He felt a delight in the destructive power of the elements, which seemed to be in singular conflict with his angelic pity: had he been a witness of an earthquake, a city on fire, or the eruption of a volcano, I know not which would have predominated in him, bleeding compassion for the sufferers, or wild ecstacy at the triumphant fury of the forces of Nature. Such in part was Macarthy; and it is no wonder that before he had well attained manhood, he renounced all attempts at any profession, which must have made him one of the weary labourers in the treadmill of society. He thought the fetters of comparative poverty less heavy than those of wealth, and determined to content himself with his small hereditary property. This he considerably reduced by travelling in foreign countries, and by gifts which for him were lavish, so that when, at the age of forty, he sought his native village, in the belief that he was near his end, his means of support were contracted to the merest pittance. I was his earliest friend, and though we had been long separated, our hearts had been too closely entwined while their affections were yet young and tender, to have ever lost the loving bias by which they had formed one stem. He sent for me, implying that I was to receive his last wishes. I found

16

him in a poor little dwelling, the occupant of a widow's spare room. His emaciated figure confirmed the idea expressed in his letter, that it would not be much longer animated by that bright spirit which now gleamed with augmented intensity from his deep-set eyes, as if glowing at the prospect of deliverance from its captivity. When we had talked long and earnestly together, he pointed to a large trunk filled with manuscripts. 'When I am dead,' he said, 'take these as the only memorial I have to give, and use them as you will.' I refused to leave my friend until he was committed to his mother earth; and it then became my most interesting employment to examine the papers which contained the best history and image of his mind. I have found the results of profound thought and widely extended research—productions, some of which have been carefully meditated, others apparently thrown off with the rapidity of inspiration; but in all of them there is a strange mixture of wisdom and whimsicality, of sublime conception and stinging caricature, of deep melancholy and wild merriment. No publisher would venture to offer such caviare to the general; and my friend's writings are not old and musty enough to fall within the scheme of any publishing Club, so that the bulk of them will probably be their own tomb. Meanwhile, among his other manuscripts, I have discovered three thick little volumes, which were successively carried in his pocket, for the purpose of noting down casual thoughts, sketches of character, and scenes out of the common; in short, as receptacles of what would probably have evaporated in conversation, had my friend been in the habit of companionship. From these fragmentary stores, I shall now and then give a selection in some modest nook of an unpretending journal—not to the world, far be so ambitious an aspiration from me—but to the half-dozen readers who can be attracted by unsophisticated thought and feeling, even though it be presented to them in the corner of the weekly newspaper of their own petty town.

HOW TO AVOID DISAPPOINTMENT

One of my favourite lounges in Paris is the studio of an artist, who tolerates my presence on the score of a slight service which I happened to render him some years ago, and which he magnifies into a lasting claim on his gratitude. I soon acquire an almost passionate interest in the progress of a noble picture. I love to think how the perfect whole exists in the imagination of the artist, before his pencil has marked the canvass,—to observe how every minute stroke, every dismal-looking layer of colour, conduces to the ultimate effect, and how completely the creative genius which has conceived the result can calculate the necessary means. I love to watch the artist's eye, so wrapt and unworldly in its glance, scrupulously attentive to the details of his actual labour, yet keeping ever in view the idea which that labour is to fulfil. I say to myself,—this is an image of what our life should be,—a series of efforts directed to the production of a contemplated whole, just as every stroke of the artist's pencil has a purpose bearing on the conception which he retains in his mind's eye. We should all be painting our picture, whether it be a home scene, after Wilkie,[3] a Paul preaching at Athens, or a Brutus passing sentence on his son. We should all have a purpose in life as perfectly recognized and definite as the painter's idea of his subject. 'Indisputably,' says your man of the world, 'I have never for a moment swerved from the determination to make myself rich and respectable. I chose my wife with that object; I send my sons to the University, I give dinners, I go to balls, I go to Church,—all that I may be "respectable." Am not I a man of purpose?' Then there is the man of public spirit, who has devoted his life to some pet project, which is to be the grand catholicon for all the diseases of society. He has travelled, he has lectured, he has canvassed, he has moved heaven and earth, has become the victim of a fixed idea, and died disappointed. Doubtless, such men as these have a distinct purpose in life, but they are not the men of whom my artist reminds me—who seem to me to be painting a picture. The kind of purpose which makes life resemble a work of art in its isolated majesty or loveliness, is not the attempt to satisfy that inconvenient troop of wants which metamorphose themselves like the sprites of an enchantress, so that no sooner have we provided food for the linnet's beak, than a huge lion's maw gapes upon us. It is to live, not for our friends, not for those hostages to fortune, wives and children; not for any individual, any specific form; but for something which, while it dwells in these, has an existence beyond them. It is to live for the good, the true, the beautiful, which outlive every generation, and are all-pervading as the light which vibrates from the remotest

[3] David Wilkie (1785–1841), whose paintings of domestic and commonplace scenes George Eliot admired; they probably had an effect upon her own conception of the value of ordinary life as a subject for art.

nebula to our own sun. The spirit which has ascertained its true relation to these, can never be an orphan: it has its home in the eternal mind, from which neither things present nor to come can separate it. You may infallibly discern the man who lives thus. His eye has not that restless, irresolute glance, which tells of no purpose beyond the present hour: it looks as you might imagine the eye of Numa to have looked after an interview with Egeria; the earnest attention and veneration with which it gazed on the divine instructress still lingering in its expression. Such a man is not like the parasitic plants which crawl ignobly or climb aspiringly, just as accident has disposed the objects around them. He has a course of his own, like our forest trees, a fixed form of growth, which defies and hurls down the stones and mortar with which society attempts to bind him in. He loves individuals, he labours for specific objects, but only as transient forms of the abiding reality which he seeks; so that if the individual pass away, if the object be frustrated, his love and his labour are not essentially disappointed.

I said one day to my artist, when he was ardently engaged on a favourite picture, 'Adolphe, has your love of art ever been tested by any great misfortune?' He replied, 'I have suffered—I am suffering under a great calamity; not the blighting of ambition, not the loss of any loved one, but a far more withering sorrow; I have ceased to love the being whom I once believed that I must love while life lasted. I have cherished what I thought was a bright amethyst, and I have seen it losing its lustre day by day, till I can no longer delude myself into a belief that it is not valueless. But you see,' he said, turning to me and smiling, 'I love my pictures still; I should not like to die till I have worked up my chosen subjects.'

Who would not have some purpose in life as independent in its value as art is to the artist?

THE WISDOM OF THE CHILD

It may not be an original idea, but never mind, if it be a true one, that the proper result of intellectual cultivation is to restore the mind to that state of wonder and interest with which it looks on everything in childhood. Thus, Jean Jacques Rousseau, couched on the grass by the side of a plant, that he might examine its structure and appearance at his ease, would have seemed to a little child so like itself in taste and feeling, that it would have lain down by him, in full confidence of entire sympathy between them, in spite of his wizard-like Armenian attire. But I will extend the parallel, and say that true wisdom, which implies a moral as well as an intellectual result, consists in a return to that purity and simplicity which characterize early youth, when its intuitions have not been perverted. It is, indeed, a similarity with a difference; for the wonder of a child at the material world is the effect of novelty, its simplicity and purity of ignorance; while the wonder of the wise man is the result of knowledge disclosing mystery, the simplicity and purity of his moral principles, the result of wide experience and hardly-attained self-conflict. A truce to your philosophers whose elevation above their fellow-beings consists in their ability to laugh at the ties which bind women and children, who have looked just so far into the principles of ethics as to be able to disconcert a simple soul that talks of vice and virtue as realities. The child which abstains from eating plums, because grandmamma forbade, is their superior in wisdom; it exercises faith and obedience to law—two of the most ennobling attributes of humanity, which these philosophers have cast off. I have little more respect for those who have reached the stage of enlightenment in which virtue is another name for prudence, who give their sanctions to a system of morals as they do to a system of Police—to prevent inconvenience to themselves, and to society, as a necessary adjunct of themselves,—who would change their morals with their climate, and become lords of a harem in a country where such a position would be a title to respect, instead of infamy.

The true philosopher knows what these men knew, but he knows something more. He, too, has 'broken through the barriers of the heavens,' but it has been with a more powerful telescope than theirs. He gathers his rule of conduct, not from the suggestions of appetite, not from the dictates of expediency, but from the indications of man's highest destiny, to be found in those faculties of his nature which may be justly said to be more than human, since they might belong to conditions of being far less limited than those of man. Self-renunciation, submission to law, trust, benignity, ingenuousness, rectitude,—these are the qualities we delight most to witness in the child, and these are the qualities which most dignify the man. The true philosopher, then, constructs his moral code with a view to preserve these sentiments in that state of unsullied purity and freedom of exercise which he loves to see in a child. If he were to admit that all things were lawful to him, he would add, 'I will not be thought under the power of any; I will not circumscribe or bring into bondage the action of any one of my highest endowments.' He feels that in submitting to the restraint of a self-imposed law, he would be presenting humanity in its grandest aspect. But it is *only* the highest human state at which he aims—not anything superhuman. He seeks exercise for all the minor feelings—nay, he holds that these are the only nest in which the ever-aspiring eagle nature can be properly fledged and winged; but he baptizes and hallows them all with the chrism of the diviner soul within him, and regulates their indulgence by his consciousness of the degree in which they encourage or repress the impulses of his moral sentiments. He would be neither an angel, an anchorite, nor a saint, but a man in the most complete and lofty meaning of the name—a man to whom the 'child is father,'[4] perhaps in more senses than the poet thought; and who is no degenerate offspring, but a development of all the features impressed on that heaven-born parent.

A LITTLE FABLE WITH A GREAT MORAL

In very early times indeed, when no maidens had looking-glasses, except the mermaidens, there lived in a deep valley two beautiful Hamadryads. Now the Hamadryads are a race of nymphs that inhabit the forests. Whenever a little acorn, or a beech nut, or any other seed of a forest tree, begins to sprout, a little Hamadryad is born, and grows up, and lives and dies with the tree. So, you see, the Hamadryads, the daughters of the trees, live far longer than the daughters of men,—some of them even a thousand years; still, they do at last get old, and faded, and shrivelled. Now the two Hamadryads of whom I spoke lived in a forest by the side of a clear lake, and they loved better than anything to go down to the brink of the lake, and look into the mirror of waters; but not for the same reason. Idione loved to look into the lake because she saw herself there; she would sit on the bank, weaving leaves and flowers in her silken hair, and smiling at her own image all the day long, and if the pretty water-lilies or any other plants began to spread themselves on the surface below her, and spoil her mirror, she would tear them up in anger. But Hieria cared not to look at herself in the lake; she only cared about watching the heavens as they were

---

[4] Wordsworth, 'My Heart Leaps up when I Behold', 7.

reflected in its bosom—the foamy clouds on the clear blue by day, and the moon and the stars by night. She did not mind that the water-lilies grew below her, for she was always looking farther off, into the deep part of the lake; she only thought the lilies pretty, and loved them. So, in the course of time, these two Hamadryads grew old, and Idione began to be angry with the lake, and to hate it, because it no longer gave back a pleasant image of herself, and she would carry little stones to the margin, and dash them into the lake for vengeance; but she only tired herself, and did not hurt the lake. And as she was frowning and looking spiteful all the day, the lake only went on giving her an uglier and uglier picture of herself, till at last she ran away from it into the hollow of her tree, and sat there lonely and sad till she died. But Hieria grew old without finding it out, for she never looked for herself in the lake;—only as, in the centuries she had lived, some of the thick forests had been cleared away from the earth, and men had begun to build and to plough, the sky was less often obscured by vapours, so that the lake was more and more beautiful to her, and she loved better and better the water-lilies that grew below her. Until one morning, after she had been watching the stars in the lake, she went home to her tree, and lying down, she fell into a gentle sleep, and dreamed that she had left her mouldering tree, and had been carried up to live in a star, from which she could still look down on her lake that she had loved so long. And while she was dreaming this, men came and cut down her tree, and Hieria died without knowing that she had become old.

HINTS ON SNUBBING

It has been sagely said, that men reasoned before Aristotle was born; that animals used their limbs before anatomy was heard of; and that fingers were very efficient prehensile instruments long before the invention of forks; which ingenious observations are meant to illustrate the fact, that nature is beforehand with art and science. So the faculty of snubbing has been in exercise ever since the days of Cain and Abel, though the great intellect which is to trace out the laws by which its phenomena are governed, and lay down rules for the development of all its hidden resources, has not yet arisen. There have indeed been examples of snubbing genius, and it is in the nature of genius to transcend all rules,—rather, to furnish the type on which all rules are framed; nevertheless it is undeniable that for snubbing to attain its complete scope and potency as a moral agent, it must be reduced to an art accessible to the less intuitive mind of the many. A few crude suggestions towards this important end may not be unfruitful in the soil of some active intellect.

Hobbes defined laughter to be the product of a triumphant feeling of superiority:[5] substitute snubbing for laughter, and you have a more just definition. The idea of snubbing presupposes inferiority in the snubbed. You can no more snub your betters than you can patronize them; on the contrary, toadyism towards superiors is the invariable attendant on a large endowment of the snubbing faculty. Toadyism, in fact, is the beautiful concavity which corresponds to the snubbing convexity:—the angular posture of Baillie MacWheeble's body is a perfect illustration.[6] Snubbing is a generic term, comprehending many species; as the snub monarchical, the snub political, the snub social, the snub religious, and the snub domestic. Each of these varieties has its different and appropriate kind of language, from the delicate modifications of voice, the refined *nuances* of demeanour, the degrees of temperature indicated in the glance, which belong to the higher branches, down to those coarser manifestations of the snub social and domestic, familiarly known as the cut direct, tipping the cold shoulder, snapping off the nose, and the like. The monarchical species of snubbing is doubtless an interesting subject of investigation, but the urgent wants of society point rather to the social, political, religious, and domestic species. We throw out a few hints on these, as mere finger-posts to the rich mines below:

1. All men of a thousand-a-year, who can occasionally afford to give Champagne at their dinner parties, may feel authorized to snub any poorer genius of less magnitude than Dickens, especially if he live in the same town or neighbourhood, as in that case he can by no means be made available as a lion, to be served up to the company with the soups and venison.

[5] *Leviathan*, Part I, Ch. 6: 'Sudden glory is the passion which maketh those grimaces called *laughter*.'

[6] In Scott's *Waverley*, Ch. 11: '. . . either out of more respect, or in order to preserve that proper declination of person which showed a sense that he was in the presence of his patron, he sat upon the edge of his chair, placed at three feet distance from the table, and achieved a communication with his plate by projecting his person towards it in a line which obliqued from the bottom of his spine, so that the person who sat opposite to him could only see the foretop of his riding periwig.'

2. Men of great or small wit who have established a reputation as diners-out, may give additional zest to their condiments and wine, by snubbing any humbler aspirant to the applause of the company. Let them take Johnson as their model in this department.

3. Editors of country newspapers, who feel themselves and their cause in a precarious condition, and who, therefore, as Paley said of himself, cannot afford to keep a conscience,[7] may find a forlorn hope in snubbing. Let them choose for a victim any individual who presumes to avow an opinion in opposition to their own—and, what is more, to act upon it. We assure the dullest poor fellow of an editor, that he may put down such an upstart, and utterly ruin him in the esteem of the majority, by keeping a stock of epithets, like so many little missiles, to be hurled at him on every favourable occasion: such, for instance, as pseudo-philosopher, man of crotchets, infantine dreamer, &c. No matter how stale the epithets may be: paucity of invention is no disadvantage here; since the oftener a nick-name is repeated the better it will tell. Do we not know that two-thirds of mankind are influenced, not by facts or principles, but by associations about as appropriate as the connection between a bright summer's day and roast pig, in the mind of the ingenious Mrs. Nickleby?[8]

4. Any who have been elevated in society, whether by a migration from the thoroughfare of Gudgeon-street to the more genteel locality of the Olympian Villas, or by a still more brilliant transit, must not neglect the precious opportunity of snubbing their former familiars. We refer them to Shakespeare's Falconbridge:

'Good den, Sir Richard,—God a' mercy, fellow:
And if his name be George, I'll call him Peter:
For new-made honour doth forget men's names;
'Tis too respective and too sociable,
For your conversion.'[9]

[7] When Paley refused to sign a petition for relief from subscription to the articles of religion, even though he approved the petition's object, he was reported to have said 'I cannot afford to have a conscience.' See the 'Life of the Author' in the *Works of William Paley, D.D.* (Philadelphia, 1831), p. xii.

[8] *Nicholas Nickleby*, Ch. 41: ' "Kate, my dear," said Mrs. Nickleby; "I don't know how it is, but a fine warm summer day like this, with the birds singing in every direction, always puts me in mind of roast pig, with sage and onion sauce, and made gravy." '

[9] *King John*, I, i, 185–189.

5. Ladies who go to parties with the hope of being the belles of the evening, must on no account venture to snub any whose pretensions threaten to eclipse their own. This would look like envy. They must rather behave to such with a sweet condescending blandness, as if unconcious of the danger of rivalry. They may, however, repay themselves by snubbing the plain and ill-dressed; nay, if they can manage to secure a brisk flirtation for the evening with any one of the gentlemen tolerably well to pass, they may even produce a very good effect by snubbing the remainder.

6. But the chief empire of feminine talent lies in the snub religious. Anacreon tells us that nature has given weapons of defence to all creatures,—horns to bulls, hoofs to horses, &c., understanding to man, and to woman *beauty*.[10] But this is mere poet's flummery: he should have said *bigotry*, which is the far more generic attribute. All ladies of decidedly orthodox sentiments and serious habits, who, in short, form the public for whom young Clergymen print volumes of sermons, which may be compared to that popular specific, treacle and brimstone,—all such ladies, we say, may snub any man not marriageable, and any woman not an heiress, though as full of talents or of good works as a Sir Philip Sidney or a John Howard,[11] if he or she be suspected of diverging in opinion from that standard of truth which is lodged in the brain of the Rev. Amylatus Stultus, who keeps the key of these same ladies' consciences. But let every one beware of snubbing on religious grounds in quarters where there is wealth, or fashion, or influence. In such cases all aberrations from the standard are to be regarded as amiable eccentricities, which do not warrant an uncharitable construction. On the whole it must be admitted that the snub religious is a most valuable agent in society, resembling those compensating contrivances by which nature makes up for the loss of one organ by an extraordinary development of the functions of another. Now that we have no Star-Chamber, Pillory, Test Act, &c., what would become of society without this admirable refinement on the rougher measures of our ancestors? Do we not appeal to a stronger element in the minds of suspected heretics by silently putting a chalk hieroglyphic on their backs, than by hauling them off to Prison or to Smithfield?

---

[10] No. 24 of the Anacreontics in Bergk, *Lyrici Græci Poetæ.*
[11] 1726?–1790, the prison reformer.

7. As regards the snub domestic, gentlemen should by no means neglect one of the grand privileges of conjugal life, an unlimited power of snubbing their wives. Indeed, this may be said to be a sort of safety-valve for the masculine faculty of snubbing, which, as men are somewhat amenable for its exercise, and cannot, like women and priests, snub with impunity, might lead to no end of duels and horse-whippings, and thus reduce society to a horribly internecine state.

8. Ladies may take reprisals for their endurance in this matter, on such small deer as their governesses, servants, and such old maids of their acquaintance as are not useful in sewing or taking care of the children.

9. The servants, again, may snub the shoe-black or the vendor of hareskins. The shoe-black may snub the dog and cat in a variety of ingenious ways, and doubtless the beautiful chain, if we could trace it, descends to the lowest grades of existence. We have no warrant, however, to suppose that a faculty for snubbing is given to any other races than the terrestrial, since we have express authority for the fact, that the archangel Michael, on a very remarkable occasion, abstained from snubbing the devil.[12]

---

[12] See Jude 9.

2

[THE PROGRESS OF THE INTELLECT]

Westminster Review, LIV (January, 1851), 353–368

In 1850 John Chapman published in two volumes Robert William Mackay's *The Progress of the Intellect, as Exemplified in the Religious Development of the Greeks and Hebrews*. In October of that year the two men, publisher and author, meeting George Eliot at the home of her friend Charles Bray in Coventry, suggested to her that she review the book. The resulting article was George Eliot's first contribution to the *Westminster Review*, the quarterly in which her most important work as a journalist appeared. Within a year of the publication of her review, Chapman had purchased the *Westminster*, and George Eliot had gone to London to serve as its editor. The ability she had shown in her review of Mackay was certainly a part of the reason why Chapman eagerly sought her to take the position.

The review of *The Progress of the Intellect*, though much of it is merely quotation and paraphrase, is nevertheless of great interest as George Eliot's first sustained presentation of the conclusions she had reached on the religious, philosophical, historical, and moral questions that had engaged her mind during the decade of remarkable intellectual ferment that lay behind her, the period of her life in Coventry amid the Bray family and their friends.

'The Progress of the Intellect' has been reprinted once, in *Essays and Uncollected Papers*, vol. 22 of *The Writings of George Eliot*, Large Paper Edition (Boston and New York, 1908).

* * *

THERE are many, and those not the least powerful thinkers and efficient workers amongst us, who are prone to under-rate critical research into ancient modes of life and forms of thought, alleging that what it behoves us chiefly to ascertain is the truth which comes home to men's business and bosoms in these our days, and not by-gone speculations and beliefs which we can never fully comprehend, and with which we can only yet more imperfectly sympathise. Holding, with Auguste Comte,[1] that theological and metaphysical speculation have reached their limit, and that the only hope of extending man's sources of knowledge and happiness is to be found in positive science, and in the universal application of its principles; they urge that the thinkers who are in the van of human progress should devote their energies to the actual rather than to the retrospective.

There is, undeniably, truth in this view. It is better to discover and apply improved methods of draining our own towns, than to be able to quote Aristophanes in proof that the streets of Athens were in a state of unmacadamized muddiness—better to reason justly on some point of immediate concern, than to know the fallacies of the ancient sophists—better to look with 'awful eye'[2] at the starry heavens, and, under the teaching of Newton and Herschel, feel the immensity, the order, the sublimity of the universe, and of the forces by which it subsists, than to pore over the grotesque symbols, whereby the Assyrian or Egyptian shadowed forth his own more vague impressions of the same great facts. But it would be a very serious mistake to suppose that the study of the past and the labours of criticism have no important practical bearing on the present. Our civilization, and, yet more, our religion, are an anomalous blending of lifeless barbarisms, which have descended to us like so many petrifactions from distant ages, with living ideas, the offspring of a true process of development. We are in bondage to terms and conceptions which, having had their root in conditions of thought no longer existing, have ceased to possess any vitality, and are for us as spells which have lost their virtue. The endeavour to spread enlightened ideas is perpetually

---

[1] The earliest recorded allusion of George Eliot to Comte. Blanche Colton Williams, *George Eliot, a Biography* (New York, 1936), p. 82, says Herbert Spencer introduced George Eliot to Comte's work, but she did not meet Spencer until October, 1851, nearly a year after the date of the Mackay review (see *Letters*, I, 364). In any case, Spencer knew nothing of Comte at that time (*Letters*, II, 140). George Eliot's comments on the followers of Comte show that she already recognizes that, as she later said, Positivism is a 'one-sided' system (*Letters*, III, 439).

[2] Milton, 'On the Morning of Christ's Nativity', 59.

counteracted by these *idola theatri*, which have allied themselves, on the one hand with men's better sentiments, and on the other with institutions in whose defence are arrayed the passions and the interests of dominant classes. Now, though the teaching of positive truth is the grand means of expelling error, the process will be very much quickened if the negative argument serve as its pioneer; if, by a survey of the past, it can be shown how each age and each race has had a faith and a symbolism suited to its need and its stage of development, and that for succeeding ages to dream of retaining the spirit along with the forms of the past, is as futile as the embalming of the dead body in the hope that it may one day be resumed by the living soul.

But apart from this objective utility of critical research, it has certain highly advantageous influences on the mind which pursues it. There is so far justice in the common sarcasms against men of erudition *par excellence*, that they have rarely been distinguished for warmth of moral sympathy, or for fertility and grandeur of conception; but your eminently practical thinker is often beset by a narrowness of another kind. It may be doubted, whether a mind which has no susceptibility to the pleasure of changing its point of view, of mastering a remote form of thought, of perceiving identity of nature under variety of manifestation—a perception which resembles an expansion of one's own being, a pre-existence in the past—can possess the flexibility, the ready sympathy, or the tolerance, which characterizes a truly philosophic culture. Now and then, however, we meet with a nature which combines the faculty for amassing minute erudition with the largeness of view necessary to give it a practical bearing; a high appreciation of the genius of antiquity, with a profound belief in the progressive character of human development—in the eternal freshness of the founts of inspiration, a wonderful intuition of the mental conditions of past ages with an ardent participation in the most advanced ideas and most hopeful efforts of the present; a nature like some mighty river, which, in its long windings through unfrequented regions, gathers mineral and earthy treasures only more effectually to enrich and fertilize the cultivated valleys and busy cities which form the habitation of man.

Of such a nature, with valuable qualities thus 'antithetically mixt,'[3] we have evidence in the work before us. It exhibits an

[3] Byron, *Childe Harold*, Canto III, st. 36.

29

industry in research which reminds us of Cudworth, and for which, in recent literature, we must seek a parallel in Germany rather than in England, while its philosophy and its aims are at once lofty and practical. Scattered through its more abstruse disquisitions we find passages of pre-eminent beauty—gems into which are absorbed the finest rays of intelligence and feeling. We believe Mr. Mackay's work is unique in its kind. England has been slow to use or to emulate the immense labours of Germany in the departments of mythology and biblical criticism; but when once she does so, the greater solidity and directness of the English mind ensure a superiority of treatment.[4]

The series of subjects which Mr. Mackay has chosen as waymarks in tracing the 'Progress of the Intellect,' are—after an introductory chapter on Intellectual Religion—Ancient Cosmogony; the Metaphysical Idea of God; the Moral Notion of God; the Theory of Mediation; the Hebrew Theory of Retribution and Immortality; the Messianic Theory; Christian Forms and Reforms; and Speculative Christianity. In the introductory dissertation on Intellectual Religion, he develops his view concerning the true basis and character of religion and morals, and the relation between ancient and modern ideas on these subjects, and it is perhaps here that he presents himself to the greatest advantage; this preliminary chapter is a sort of lofty, airy vestibule, in which we gather breath and courage to descend with the author into the crypts of citation and conjecture, into which he is about to introduce us. It is Mr. Mackay's faith that divine revelation is not contained exclusively or pre-eminently in the facts and inspirations of any one age or nation, but is co-extensive with the history of human development, and is perpetually unfolding itself to our widened experience and investigation, as firmament upon firma-

---

[4] George Eliot is recalling David Strauss's praise of Charles Hennell and his *An Inquiry Concerning the Origin of Christianity* (1838). Strauss, in the preface he contributed to the German translation of Hennell's book, had complimented the author as 'an Englishman, a merchant, a man of the world [who] possesses, both by nature and by training, the practical insight, the sure tact, which lays hold on realities. The solution of problems over which the German flutters with many circuits of learned formulæ, our English author often succeeds in seizing at one spring' (quoted in Cross, *Life*, I, 102). George Eliot included Strauss's words in the account of Hennell's book that she wrote for *An Analytical Catalogue of Mr. Chapman's Publications* (1852).

ment becomes visible to us in proportion to the power and range of our exploring instruments. The master key to this revelation, is the recognition of the presence of undeviating law in the material and moral world—of that invariability of sequence which is acknowledged to be the basis of physical science, but which is still perversely ignored in our social organization, our ethics and our religion. It is this invariability of sequence which can alone give value to experience and render education in the true sense possible. The divine yea and nay, the seal of prohibition and of sanction, are effectually impressed on human deeds and aspirations, not by means of Greek and Hebrew, but by that inexorable law of consequences, whose evidence is confirmed instead of weakened as the ages advance; and human duty is comprised in the earnest study of this law and patient obedience to its teaching. While this belief sheds a bright beam of promise on the future career of our race, it lights up what once seemed the dreariest region of history with new interest; every past phase of human development is part of that education of the race in which we are sharing; every mistake, every absurdity into which poor human nature has fallen, may be looked on as an experiment of which we may reap the benefit. A correct generalization gives significance to the smallest detail, just as the great inductions of geology demonstrate in every pebble the working of laws by which the earth has become adapted for the habitation of man.[5] In this view, religion and philosophy are not merely conciliated, they are identical; or rather, religion is the crown and consummation of philosophy—the delicate corolla, which can only spread out its petals in all their symmetry and brilliance to the sun, when root and branch exhibit the conditions of a healthy and vigorous life. Mr. Mackay's preliminary chapter has an independent value, and would be read with interest by many who might not care to follow him in his subsequent inquiry. The dilemma of sensuousness and sentimentalism is thus excellently put:

[5] The illustration from geology suggests that in the argument of this passage George Eliot is thinking of Sir Charles Lyell's *Principles of Geology* (1830–1833), which set up the principle of uniformity in natural processes against the conception of catastrophic changes. The analogy between the gradual, uniform processes of character and action in George Eliot's novels and the uniformitarianism expounded by Lyell is a close one.

Religion often appears to be a mere sentiment, because the reason
by which it should be disciplined requires long cultivation, and can
only gradually assume its proper prominence and dignity. The
faculties are seldom combined in its avowed service; and from its
consequent misdirection has been inferred the impossibility of finding
within the limits of the mind an effectual religious guide. It has even
been said that religion has properly nothing to do with the head, but
is exclusively an exercise of the heart and feelings; that all the teaching
or education which can properly be called 'religious,' consists 'in the
formation of the temper and behaviour, the infusing of devotional
feeling, and the implanting of Christian principles.' In other words,
the highest faculty of the mind is not required in the service of him
who bestowed it. Through this narrow view the sentiments are over-
excited; the judgment becomes proportionately languid and incapable, the connexion between the theory of practice and duty is
unobserved, and dogmas are blindly learned without regard to their
origin or meaning. Superficial religion has everywhere the same
result; it fluctuates between the extremes of sensibility and superstition, and exhibits in this respect a curious parallel to the analogous
catastrophe of natural[6] philosophy. The uneducated feeling has only
the alternative of unquestioning credulity, or of sacrificing and abro-
gating itself. This is the universal dilemma of artificial creeds; their
votaries divide into formalists and sceptics, Pharisees and Sadducees;
Calvinism, in our own days, has swung back to rationalism, and the
symbolical forms of ancient religion are pronounced by a competent
observer to have generally led to these extremes.[7] The passage is easy
from one to the other. The devotional feeling of a Catholic of the
middle age might have been destroyed, if the doctrines of Copernicus
or Galileo had induced him to mistrust the infallibility of the Pope;
and in the days of Sir Thomas Browne, it may have been correct to
say that a disbelief in witchcraft implied 'a sort of atheism.' Horace
was startled out of his irreligious philosophy by a clap of thunder;
but if a heathen who saw an angry Hecate in the eclipsed moon could

[6] Mackay reads 'notional philosophy.' There are many variations
between the quotations and Mackay's text in George Eliot's review,
especially in punctuation. Some of these may be attributed to the compositors, but the occasional substantive differences between quotation and
original suggest that George Eliot, who was not very strict in such
matters, was responsible. Cross says that 'she could never trust herself to
write a quotation without verifying it' (*Life*, III, 422), but it is apparent
from her writings that as a rule she quoted without book. Even where, as
in the quotations from Mackay, she is obviously transcribing directly
from the text, she is not wholly reliable.
[7] Plutarch, 'Isis and Osiris', ch. 67 [Mackay's note].

have understood a modern almanack, he might at once have fallen into the impiety from which Horace was a convert.—Sec. 3, p. 9.

Admirable again is the section on Faith, from which we cannot resist giving a long extract:

Religion and science are inseparable. No object in nature, no subject of contemplation is destitute of a religious tendency and meaning. If religion be made to consist only in traditional and legendary forms, it is of course as distinguishable from science as the Mosaic cosmogony from geology; but if it be the *ascensio mentis in Deum per scalas creatarum rerum*, the evolving the grounds of hope, faith, and duty from the known laws of our being and the constitution of the universe; a religion may be said to include science as its minister, and antiquity, which beheld a divinity in all things, erred only in mistaking its intelligible character, and in making it a mere matter of mystic speculation. In a more limited sense, religion may be contrasted with science, as something beyond and above it; as beginning where science ends, and as a guide through the realms of the unknown. But the known and the unknown are intimately connected and correlative. A superstructure of faith can be securely built only on the foundations of the known. Philosophy and religion have one common aim; they are but different forms of answer to the same great question—that of man and his destination. . . . Faith is, to a great extent, involuntary; it is a law or faculty of our nature, operating silently and intuitively to supply the imperfections of our knowledge. The boundary between faith and knowledge is, indeed, hard to distinguish. We are said to know our own impressions; to believe in their reality, or in the existence of an external cause of them. It follows that the immediate as well as the more remote inferences from phenomena, are the blended fruit of faith and knowledge; and that though faith, properly speaking, is not knowledge, but the admission of certain inferences beyond knowledge, yet it is almost impossible, in tracing back the operations of the mind, to find any, even the most elementary inference, which is not in some degree a compound of both, and which may not ultimately be resolved into a consistent belief in the results of experience. Faith being thus the inseparable companion and offspring of knowledge, is, like it, liable to modification and correction; that which we call our knowledge of the ultimate purpose of existence being, in fact, only a belief or inference from experience, which would lose its rational value if it were supposed to be so complete and infallible as to exempt us from the necessity of further reflection. All human knowledge must partake of the imperfection of the faculties through which it is derived; and the limited and unsatisfactory

33

character of what we know leaves a wide and most important void to be filled up by our belief. But the more imperfect our knowledge, the more necessary it becomes to examine with suspicion the foundations of the faith so closely connected with it. Faith, as opposed to credulity, and to that blind submission to inexplicable power which usurped its name in the ancient East, is an allegiance of the reason; and as the 'evidence of things unseen,' stands on the verge of mysticism, its value must depend on the discretion with which it is formed and used. Like all the other faculties, the belief requires to be educated; as the feet are taught to walk, the lips and tongue to speak, so the capacity of belief must be taught how to build securely, yet not arrogantly, on the data of experience. Faith is not that belief of St. Augustine, whose merit increased with the absurdity of the proposition, nor that which attributed to the instigation of God the real or projected murder of an only son. An irrational faith grew out of the opposite extreme of incredulity, when men refused to believe the truth, unless authenticated by sensuous evidence that confounded their understandings. True faith is a belief in things probable; it is the assigning to certain inferences a hypothetical objectivity, and upon the conscious acknowledgment of this hypothetical character alone depends its advantage over fanaticism; its moral value and dignity. Between the opposite risks of credulity and scepticism, it must be guided by those broad principles of reason which all the faculties require for their regulation. Reason alone can in each case determine where credulity begins, and fix the limit beyond which the mind should cease to assign even a qualified objectivity to its own imaginations. In its advanced stages faith is a legitimate result of the calculation of probabilities; it may transcend experience, but can never absolutely contradict it. Faith and knowledge tend mutually to the confirmation and enlargement of each other; faith by verification being often transformed into knowledge, and every increase of knowledge supplying a wider and firmer basis of belief. Faith, as an inference from knowledge, should be consistently inferred from the whole of knowledge; since, when estranged and violated,[8] it loses its vitality, and the estrangement is as effectual when it is hastily and unfairly inferred as where it is wholly gratuitous. The same experience which is the source of knowledge being, therefore, the only legitimate foundation of faith, a sound faith cannot be derived from the anomalous and exceptional. It is the avidity for the marvellous, and the morbid eagerness for a cheap and easy solution of the mysteries of existence—a solution supposed to be implied in the conception of an arbitrary and unintelligible rule, which has ever retarded philosophy and stultified religion. Faith naturally arises out

[8] Mackay reads 'isolated'.

34

of the regular and undeviating. The same unerring uniformity, which alone made experience possible, was also the first teacher of the invisible things of God. It is this

> Elder Scripture, writ by God's own hand,
> Scripture authentic, uncorrupt by man,

which is set before every one, without note or comment, and which even Holy Writ points out as the most unquestionable authority by which, both in heaven and earth, the will of God is interpreted to mankind. If man is not permitted to solve the problem of existence, he is at least emboldened to hope, and to infer so much from its actual conditions as to feel confident as to its results. Faith takes up the problem exactly where knowledge leaves it, and, as from confounding the objects of the two have arisen the discords of sects and the puzzles of philosophy, so the discovery of their true relations and limits enables the mind to reconcile and account for the controversies of the past, and in some measure to penetrate the mysteries that occasioned them.—vol. i, p. 35.

Having thus indicated the ground on which he takes his stand, Mr. Mackay commences his survey and delineation of religious development, selecting that of the Hebrews and Greeks as the most typical and complete, and tracing it up to the period when the combination of the two modes of thought in the Alexandrian theosophy formed that web of metaphysical and religious dogma, which constitutes speculative Christianity. While the Hebrew and Greek religions are his main subject, he has not neglected the copious illustration to be drawn from the Persian, the Hindoo and the Northern mythologies, by indicating instances of analogy and of possible derivation, and thus the 'Progress of the Intellect', is, perhaps, the nearest approach in our language to a satisfactory natural history of religion. The third chapter on the 'Metaphysical Idea of God' is a rich mine of associated facts and ideas; but while admiring the range of learning which it exhibits, it is here that we begin to perceive the author's defects, or rather his redundances. Some of his pages read like extracts from his common-place book, which must be, as Southey said of his own, an urn under the arm of a river-god, rather than like a digested result of study, intended to inform the general reader. Only a devotedness of research such as his own, can give interest and significance to the mass of allusions and particulars with which Mr. Mackay overlays, rather than illustrates, his more general passages, which are usually at once profound and lucid. The popular lecturer on science comes before his audience with a selection of striking and apt experiments in readiness, and is silent as to the morning's preparation in the laboratory; and so the scholar, who would produce a work of general utility, must not drag his readers through the whole region of his own researches, but simply present them with an impressive *coup d'œil*. The occasional absence of this artistic working-up of materials diminishes the effectiveness of Mr. Mackay's admirable work.

The introduction of a truly philosophic spirit into the study of mythology—an introduction for which we are chiefly indebted to the Germans—is a great step in advance of the superficial Lucian-like tone of ridicule adopted by many authors of the eighteenth century, or the orthodox prepossessions of writers such as Bryant,[9] who saw in the Greek legends simply misrepresentations of the authentic history given in the book of Genesis. The enlarged acquaintance with Hindoo literature, and with the monumental records of other ancient nations, which the last half century has brought us, has rendered more possible that wide comparison which is a requisite for all true, scientific generalization. O. Müller[10] says, obviously enough, that if we possessed no other access to Grecian antiquity than its mythology, a systematic and philosophic explanation of the latter would be impossible; and so while the mythology of one nation is studied apart from that of others, or while what is really mythology in the records of any one nation is not recognized as such, but, though it presents the ordinary mythical elements, is accounted for by a special theory; we shall never arrive at a just and full estimate of this phase of man's religious tendencies.

[9] Jacob Bryant, *A New System, or an Analysis of Ancient Mythology*, 3 vols., 1774–1776. In Ch. 22 of *Middlemarch*, written more than twenty years after the review of Mackay, George Eliot has Will Ladislaw criticize Casaubon's ignorance of German scholarship, saying to Dorothea, 'Do you not see that it is no use now to be crawling a little way after men of the last century—men like Bryant—and correcting their mistakes?—living in a lumber-room and furbishing up broken-legged theories about Chus and Mizraim?' Readers of *Middlemarch* will recognize more than one hint for Casaubon's history in George Eliot's review of Mackay.

[10] Karl Otfried Müller (1798–1840), *Prolegomena zu einer wissenschaftlichen Mythologie* (1825).

Mr. Mackay holds, with Creuzer,[11] that the basis of all mythology was a nature-worship; that 'those interpreters are in the main
right, who held that the heathen Pantheon, in its infinite diversity
of names and personifications, was but a multitudinous, though in
its origin, unconscious allegory, of which physical phenomena, and
principally the heavenly bodies, were the fundamental types.' This
primitive period of the myth, in which sacerdotal influence was in
the ascendant, he thinks may be designated the Orphic or Cabiric,
in distinction from the Epic period, which was characterized by a
gradual merging of the mystic or religious feeling in the poetic. He
says: 'Between the life-like Epic and the sombre Orphic style,
between the picturesque and eventful romance, in which the gods
are the mere machinery of a human drama, and the mystical symbols of theological metaphysics, there must have been many
varieties in the treatment of religious legend, tending to reduce its
fragmentary materials to the consistent and positive forms in
which they are found in Homer.' In this theory, mythical conception, instead of being a step in advance of fetishism, is a decadence
of the religious sentiment from that monotheistic or pantheistic
impression to which it leaps by its first impulse; general ideas in
the process of transmission, or simply as a necessary result of the
laws of expression in the early stages of thought, resolve themselves into the crystalline forms of the legend. We will quote the
author's own presentation of his opinion. Under the head of
'Relation of Monotheism to Symbolism,' he says:

It is impossible to assume any period of time at which the vague
sense of Deity ceased to be a mere feeling and assumed a specific
form, or became an 'idea.' The notion of external power must have
been almost instantaneously associated with some external object;
and the diversified reflections of the Divine easily came to be looked
on as substantive and distinct divinities. But however infinite the
variety of objects which helped to develope the notion of Deity, and
eventually usurped its place, the notion itself was essentially a concentrated or monotheistic one. A vague monotheism resided in the
earliest exertions of thought, being nearly identical with that impression
of unity and connection in sensible phenomena, which in its simplest
form appears to rise independently of any effort of philosophical

[11] Georg Friedrich Creuzer (1771–1858), author of *Symbolik*, 4 vols.,
1810–1812, a history of ancient religions. According to Emery Neff, *The
Poetry of History* (New York, 1947), p. 106, Creuzer resembled Casaubon
in tracing all myths to a single source.

comparison. The power of generalization, or of seeing the one in the many, that first element both of science and of religion, is so nearly innate or instinctive as to have been termed by Plato a divine or Promethean gift; and the philosophical conception of the oneness of the universe and of its author, usually regarded as the last acquisition of civilization and reflection, appears to have been anticipated by a natural revelation, an indefinite dread of the aggregate of supersensuous nature; which is said to be common even among savages. In this indefinite feeling must be sought, if anywhere, that conceptional monotheism of primitive ages, which like the virtues of the golden age, makes every successive epoch, unless it be the present, appear only as a stage in the progress of degeneracy and aberration. The genius of religion . . . does not wait for the co-operation of science in order to commence her task, the powers of combination are at work long before the maturity of the reason eventually found necessary to guide them; nay, the origin of religion, like that of civilization, may be said to be free from many of the corruptions attending its onward progress, which arise from the mind's inability to deal unembarrassed with the multitude of sensuous analogies. Generalization begins before a sufficient basis has been prepared to make it legitimate, and every successive step in the research into particulars seems to be in mysterious contradiction to the first hurried conclusion. Hence the universal blending of monotheism with polytheism, and the impossibility of discovering historically, which of the two is older or more original.

Mr. Mackay's main proposition, that the substratum of religious symbolism was a worship or deification of the elements, is well sustained by the evidence; but he perhaps overstates the degree in which the monotheistic idea was originally coexistent with polytheistic personification. To the uncultured intellect, a plurality of divine agencies, analogous to the human, would seem, by their conflicting wills and influences, a natural explanation of physical and moral vicissitudes. As the impression of unity in nature gained force, these agencies would gradually become subordinate to a higher power, but that impression would at first be hardly more than a shadowy presentiment—one of those

> High instincts, before which our mortal nature
> Doth shudder like a guilty thing surprised.[12]

That allegorical elements exist to a considerable extent, in the divine, if not in the heroic myths of Greece, there is strong

[12] Wordsworth, 'Ode, Intimations of Immortality', 150–151.

evidence, both presumptive and internal; and the allegorical interpretation, on the lowest estimate of its soundness, is far superior to the pragmatical or semi-historical, which, in endeavouring to show a nucleus of fact in the myths, exhibits an utter blindness to the mental state in which they originated, and simply substitutes an unpoetical fable for a poetical one. But owing to the manysidedness of all symbols, there is a peculiarly seductive influence in allegorical interpretation; and we observe that all writers who adopt it, though they set out with the largest admissions as to the spontaneous and unconscious character of mythical allegory, and the manifold modifications which have obscured it, acquire a sort of fanatical faith in their rule of interpretation, and fall into the mistake of supposing that the conscious allegorizing of a modern can be a correct reproduction of what they acknowledge to be unconscious allegorizing in the ancients. We do not see what unconscious allegory can mean, unless it be personification accompanied with belief, and with the spontaneous, vivid conception of a symbol, as opposed to the premeditated use of a poetical figure; and this belief would lead to an elaboration of the myth, in harmony rather with the attributed personality than with the true physical characteristics of the object personified. As a painter, in treating an allegorical subject, is led on by his artistic feeling to add one detail after another, until the specific idea with which he began becomes subordinate to the general effect; so the exuberant religious imagination of the Greek, which set out with a personification of the sun or the ocean, would generate myths having relation rather to the human symbol than to the real phenomena of its cosmical prototype. Hence it appears to us, that any attempt extensively to trace consistent allegory in the myths must fail. Nor need we regret it, since our interest in the subject is of a different nature from that of the ancient philosophical interpreters, who, living at a period when the myths still constituted the popular religion, were under the necessity of bringing them into accordance with their own moral and religious views. It is enough for us if we have sufficient insight into the myths to form an approximate conception of the state of mind which produced them, and to assign them their true rank in the scale of religious development. Mr. Mackay has not escaped the influence of the allegorizing mania; he does not despair of finding the true cosmical meaning of the most natural human incidents in the Odyssey, or of the tragic conceptions of the dramatists; but if, like the alchymists, he is sometimes in quest of things not in *rerum naturâ*, he, like them, elicits much that is suggestive in his search. To criticise details would carry us beyond our limits, and we shall do a greater service to the reader by referring him to the work itself, which, open it where he may, will offer both food and stimulus to his thought.

While the poets of Greece were giving to its religious thought a more and more sensuous expression, its philosophers were working out an opposite result; and Mr. Mackay traces this subtilizing process until it reaches the Aristotelian theosophy, of which he gives a comprehensive and clear account.

It is in his theory concerning the religious development of the Hebrews, and in his treatment of their records, that Mr. Mackay departs the most widely from prevalent opinion. The idea that many parts of the Old Testament have a mythical character, an idea which was necessary to conciliate them, as well with the philosophic Hebrewism of Philo, as with the Christian morality of Origen, and which has long been familiar to German critics, is still startling to the English theological mind. No thinker of ordinary intelligence can fail to perceive, not merely difference in degree of completeness, but contrast, between the religious conceptions which represented the Deity as sanctioning or prescribing the cunning trickery of Jacob, or the savage cruelties of Joshua, and those which preside over the sublime remonstrances of the prophets; but the explanation is still sought in the theory of accommodation, that is, the puerile and unworthy religious conceptions invariably accompanying an absence of intellectual culture which in other nations are referred to the general principles of human development, are, in the case of the Hebrews, supposed to have been benevolent falsities on the part of the true God, whereby he allured a barbarous race to his recognition and worship. On this theory, because Abraham had but limited notions of honour and justice, God plagued Pharaoh and Abimelech for being misled by the falsehoods of the father of the faithful, and made those false-hoods redound to the temporal advantage of his chosen servant: because the Israelites were surrounded by examples of idolatrous and sacrificial observance, and had a strong propensity to imitate them, Jehovah, in condescension to their weakness, prescribed for them a ritual analogous in spirit and symbolism to that of their heathen neighbours: because they were a ferocious race, eager to 'eat of the prey and drink the blood of the slain,'[13] a suitable vent for their destructive energies was found in such requirements as the slaughter of three thousand in their own camp, and the war of extermination against the Canaanites, or in the especial injunction to Joshua to hough the enemy's horses. The only argument by which the theory of accommodation can be sustained is, that in conjunction with that divine countenance of human vice and weakness which it supposes, there were delivered and preserved certain elements of superhuman truth which attest the specifically divine origin of the religion—its distinctive character as a revelation. Now, while the mythical theory does not exclude that more enlarged idea of providential evolution, which sees in the peculiar religious and political history of the Hebrews, a preparation for ushering into the world a religion which anticipates and fulfils the yearnings of man's spiritual nature, it delivers the understanding from a heavy burthen of contradiction and absurdity, and the religious sentiment from the admission of painful anomalies. The fact, that the history of all other nations has a mythical period, urges a strong presumption, that the Hebrew records will not present an exception in this respect, and an unprejudiced examination confirms this presumption. We find there not only a generic similarity to the gentile myths, in a degrading conception of the divine attributes, with a corresponding crudeness and obliquity of moral views, in an ignorant interpretation of physical phenomena, a love of prodigy, and a lavish supposition of gratuitous miracle, but also a specific resemblance in symbolism. This is visible on a cursory glance, but a nearer investigation discloses overwhelming proof, that the Hebrew writings, far from meriting an exceptional confidence, require, from the evidence they exhibit that the Hebrew mind was peculiarly deficient in a true historical sense, special canons of caution in their interpretation. On applying the test of a critical analysis, the books of the Pentateuch resolve themselves into a compilation of distinct documents, differing in date and frequently in spirit and purpose, as may be seen from the variations and contradictions in their accounts of the same event; and the more ancient of these documents presents internal evidence, that it was not in existence earlier than the time of Samuel, about 400 years after Moses. The same artificial coherence, the same arbitrariness of classification and of titles, together with palpable inaccuracies

[13] Numbers 23:24.

and indications of partisanship, characterize large portions, not only of the remaining historical works, but also of the prophetic. Since these conclusions are denied by no competent critic uncommitted to the maintenance of certain tenets, it would be wise in our theological teachers, instead of struggling to retain a footing for themselves and their doctrine on the crumbling structure of dogmatic interpretation, to cherish those more liberal views of biblical criticism, which, admitting of a development of the Christian system corresponding to the wants and the culture of the age, would enable it to strike a firm root in man's moral nature, and to entwine itself with the growth of those new forms of social life to which we are tending. The spirit which doubts the ultimately beneficial tendency of inquiry, which thinks that morality and religion will not bear the broadest daylight our intellect can throw on them, though it may clothe itself in robes of sanctity and use pious phrases, is the worst form of atheism; while he who believes, whatever else he may deny, that the true and the good are synonymous, bears in his soul the essential element of religion. Viewed in this relation, the 'Progress of the Intellect' is a valuable addition to recent examples of plain speaking—of that παρρησια which Paul held to be the proper effect of confidence in the excellence of revelation,[14] whose manifestation was in the spirit, and not in the letter.

Before stating Mr. Mackay's theory concerning the Hebrew history and religion, we must express our regret that the force of his conclusions is weakened by his unduly insisting on details difficult of proof, by a frequently infelicitous citation, and by his not giving due value to a free poetical impulse in the figurative language of the Hebrews, a deficiency which sometimes leads him into an almost trivial literalness of interpretation. But notwithstanding these occasional defects, the chapters which treat principally of the Hebrews will repay a close study, both from their suggestiveness, and the soundness of their general views. Mr. Mackay holds that the original God of the Israelites was no other than the Nature-God, El or Ilus, worshipped in Arabia, Palestine, and Phœnicia, with licentious and sanguinary rites, under the double aspect of Baal and Moloch; and that the purer worship of Jehovah, inculcated by the prophets, and established by Josiah, was a religious reformation among the Hebrews, generated by the

---

[14] See, e.g., 2 Corinthians 3:12; 7:4.

growth in civilization consequent on an enlarged commercial intercourse with foreign nations, and contemporaneous with a movement of religious reform which took place throughout Asia, about
700 B.C., 'connected in India with the name of Buddha, in Persia
(or Media), with that of Zoroaster, and a century later extending
itself by Xenophanes and Heraclitus into Greece.' According to
this theory, the calf-worship in the wilderness and under the kings,
the altars in the high places, and the atrocities of the valley of
Hinnom, were not acts of apostasy, but of persistence in early
barbarism. In Mr. Mackay's opinion, the account of the Passover,
as it now stands, is the veil which the purer conceptions of later
Hebrews cast over the ancient custom of sacrificing first-born
children to the bloodthirsty El; the massacre of three thousand
Israelites, represented in Exodus as retributive, was probably
sacrificial—a huge offering to the same demon, the rather that
Aaron, the leader in the calf-worship, was not involved in the same
destruction; the command by which God is said to have tempted
Abraham, the vow of Jephthah, the slaughter of the seven descendants of Saul, whereby David sought to propitiate his God and
avert a famine, are indications that human sacrifices were familiar
to the Hebrews; above all, that 'passing of children through the
fire,'[15] recorded of so many kings, and indignantly denounced by
the prophets, as a practice habitual to the nation, is most probably
to be interpreted as an actual immolation. The somewhat obscure
passage, Amos v. 25, 26—'Have ye offered unto me sacrifices and
offerings in the wilderness forty years, O house of Israel? But ye
have borne the tabernacle of your Moloch and Chiun, your images,
the star of your God which ye made to yourselves'—Mr. Mackay
thinks important as conveying a denial of the early existence of a
pure, Jehovistic religion. A disputed passage is, of course, dubious
ground for an inference; but there is ample evidence of a less
questionable kind, that the early Hebrew God, whether identical
or not with any heathen deity, was of a character widely different
from the one proclaimed by Micah, as requiring nothing of man
but to do justly, to love mercy, and to walk humbly with God.

The original presiding Deity of Israel was, in Mr. Mackay's
words, 'emphatically the terrific God.' The Old Testament abounds
in pictures of Divine operations that cannot be regarded as true
delineations of the real character of Deity; but only distortions

[15] See, e.g., 2 Kings 16:3; 21:6; 23:10.

of it, analogous to those exhibited in the mythologies of other countries. The judicious reader of the Hebrew Scriptures, however orthodox his faith, cannot fail to perceive that they exhibit a progress from degrading to enlightened views of Divine nature and government. The writings of the prophets are full of protests against the conceptions of popular ignorance, and by continually expanding and purifying the Jewish ideas of Deity, prepared the way for the reception of the teachings of Christ. This view of the progressive character of 'revelation' does not depend for its evidence on minute points of criticism; it rests rather upon broad facts which are open to the apprehension of the most unlearned: and the 'Progress of the Intellect' abounds in statements which place them in the most forcible point of view. To a greater or less extent they are now recognized by Christians of all denominations, and it is impossible to take up the writings, or listen to the discourses of the leading men of any church or sect, without perceiving the influence which they have exerted upon their minds.

Mr. Mackay's analysis and history of the theory of Mediation, from its earliest mythical embodiments, those 'flowers which fancy strewed before the youthful steps of Psyche, when she first set out in pursuit of the immortal object of her love,' to its subtilization in philosophy—his delineation of the origin of Christianity as an expansion of the prophetic spiritualism, yet carrying within it certain elements of Jewish symbolism, which have arrested its true development and perverted its influence—his final sketch of the confluence of Greek Philosophy and Christianized Hebrewism—are admirable, both from their panoramic breadth and their richness in illustrative details. We can only recommend the reader to resort himself to this treasury of mingled thought and learning, and, as a further inducement, we will quote the concluding passage from the section of the 'Mediation of Philosophy'.

The true religious philosophy of an imperfect being is not a system of creed, but, as Socrates thought, an infinite search or approximation. Finality is but another name for bewilderment or defeat, the common affectation of indolence and superstition, a temporary suspension of the mind's health arising from prejudice, and especially from the old error of clinging too closely to notions found instrumental in assisting it after they have ceased to be serviceable, and striving rather to defend and retain them, than to make them more correct. A remnant of the mythical lurks in the very sanctuary of science. Forms

44

or theories ever fall short of nature, though they are ever tending to reach a position above nature, and may often be found really to include more than the maker of them at the time knew. To a certain extent they are reliable and complete; as a system of knowledge they are but intermediate and preparatory. As matter is the soul's necessary instrument, so ignorance, more or less mixed up with all its expressions and forms, may be said to be as it were the eyelid through which it gradually opens itself to the truth, admitting no more than it can for the time support, and, as through a veil, learning to support its lustre. The old religionists discovered a universal cause, personified it and prayed to it. The mere notion seemed not only to satisfy the religious feeling, but to solve all problems. Nations unanimously subscribed to the pious formula, which satisfied their imaginations, and pleased their vanity by cheating them into a belief that they were wise; but which, at the same time, supplanted nature by tradition, the sources of truth by artificial disguises, and at last paralysed the sentiment which gave birth to it. Science, unlike the rude expedient which stupified without nourishing the mind, gratifies the religious feeling without arresting it, and opening out the barren mystery of the one[16] into more explicit and manageable 'forms' expressing, not indeed his essence, but his will, feeds an endless enthusiasm by accumulating for ever new objects of pursuit. We have long experienced that knowledge is profitable; we are beginning to find out that it is moral, and shall at last discover it to be religious. Aristotle declared the highest and truest science to be that which is most disinterested; Bacon, treating science as separate from religion, asserted knowledge to be power, and held that truth must be tested by its fruits, that is, its instrumentality in promoting the right and the useful. Both assertions may be justified and reconciled by the fact that, while no real knowledge is powerless or fruitless, the fruits differ in refinement and value, the highest being unquestionably those disinterested gratifications which minister to the highest wants of the highest faculties, and which earned for philosophy the title of a divine love, realizing the mysterious longing of the soul, and promoting the accomplishment of its destiny,

> To rise in science as in bliss,
> Initiate in the secrets of the skies.

[16] Mackay reads 'One'.

45

3

[THE LIFE OF STERLING]

Westminster Review, LVII (January, 1852), 247–251

The notice of Carlyle's *Life of John Sterling* (1851) which opens the 'Contemporary Literature of England' section in the first number of the *Westminster* edited by George Eliot has long been attributed to her hand. There is no positive external evidence for the attribution, though W. M. W. Call assigned it to her as early as 1881 in his memorial article in the *Westminster*, and Cross identifies it as hers in the *Life*. George Eliot had read the book more than two months before the notice appeared, and her comments on it in a letter to the Brays are exactly in the spirit of the review:

> I have been reading Carlyle's life of Sterling with great pleasure—not for its presentation of Sterling but of Carlyle. There are racy bits of description in his best manner and exquisite touches of feeling. Little rapid characterizations of living men too—of Francis Newman for example, 'a man of fine university and other attainments, of the sharpest cutting and most restlessly advancing intellect, and of the mildest pious enthusiasm.' There is an inimitable description of Coleridge and his eternal monologue, 'To sit as a passive bucket and be pumped into, whether one like it or not, can in the end be exhilarating to no creature.'[1]

These points taken together, though they do not provide certain authority, make it overwhelmingly probable that the review is George Eliot's, and are supported by the evidence of style. It seems safe to conclude with Professor Haight that it is 'clearly GE's work'.[2]

The review has been reprinted as George Eliot's in Nathan Sheppard,

[1] *Letters*, I, 370.
[2] *Letters*, I, 378, n. 4. The attribution is reaffirmed in Haight's 'George Eliot's Theory of Fiction', *Victorian Newsletter*, No. 10 (Autumn, 1956), 1.

ed., *The Essays of 'George Eliot', Complete* (New York [1883]); in Mrs. S. B. Herrick, ed., *Essays and Reviews of George Eliot* (Boston, 1887); and in *Essays and Uncollected Papers.*

*   *   *

AS soon as the closing of the Great Exhibition afforded a reasonable hope that there would once more be a reading public, 'The Life of Sterling' appeared. A new work by Carlyle must always be among the literary births eagerly chronicled by the journals and greeted by the public. In a book of such parentage we care less about the subject than about its treatment, just as we think the 'Portrait of a Lord' worth studying if it comes from the pencil of a Vandyck. The life of John Sterling, however, has intrinsic interest, even if it be viewed simply as the struggle of a restless aspiring soul, yearning to leave a distinct impress of itself on the spiritual development of humanity, with that fell disease which, with a refinement of torture, heightens the susceptibility and activity of the faculties, while it undermines their creative force. Sterling, moreover, was a man thoroughly in earnest, to whom poetry and philosophy were not merely another form of paper currency or a ladder to fame, but an end in themselves—one of those finer spirits with whom, amidst the jar and hubbub of our daily life,

> The melodies abide
> Of the everlasting chime.[3]

But his intellect was active and rapid, rather than powerful, and in all his writings we feel the want of a stronger electric current to give that vigour of conception and felicity of expression, by which we distinguish the undefinable something called genius; while his moral nature, though refined and elevated, seems to have been subordinate to his intellectual tendencies and social qualities, and to have had itself little determining influence on his life. His career was less exceptional than his character: a youth marked by delicate health and studious tastes, a short-lived and not very successful share in the management of the *Athenæum*, a fever of sympathy with Spanish patriots, arrested before it reached a dangerous crisis by an early love affair ending in marriage, a fifteen months' residence in the West Indies, eight months of curate's duty at Herstmonceux, relinquished on the ground of failing

[3] John Keble, *The Christian Year*, 'St. Matthew', 27–28.

health, and through his remaining years a succession of migrations to the South in search of a friendly climate, with the occasional publication of an 'article', a tale, or a poem in 'Blackwood' or elsewhere,—this, on the prosaic background of an easy competence, was what made up the outer tissue of Sterling's existence. The impression of his intellectual power on his personal friends seems to have been produced chiefly by the eloquence and brilliancy of his conversation; but the mere reader of his works and letters would augur from them neither the wit, nor the *curiosa felicitas* of epithet and imagery, which would rank him with the men whose sayings are thought worthy of perpetuation in books of table-talk and 'ana'. The public, then, since it is content to do without biographies of much more remarkable men, cannot be supposed to have felt any pressing demand even for a single life of Sterling; still less, it might be thought, when so distinguished a writer as Archdeacon Hare had furnished this,[4] could there be any need for another. But, in opposition to the majority of Mr. Carlyle's critics, we agree with him that the first life is properly the justification of the second. Even among the readers personally unacquainted with Sterling, those who sympathized with his ultimate alienation from the Church, rather than with his transient conformity, were likely to be dissatisfied with the entirely apologetic tone of Hare's life, which, indeed, is confessedly an incomplete presentation of Sterling's mental course after his opinions diverged from those of his clerical biographer;[5] while those attached friends (and Sterling possessed the happy magic that secures many such) who knew him best during this latter part of his career, would naturally be pained to have it represented, though only by implication, as a sort of deepening declension ending in a virtual retraction. Of such friends Carlyle was the most eminent, and perhaps the most highly valued, and, as co-trustee with Archdeacon Hare of Sterling's

[4] *Essays and Tales by John Sterling, Collected and Edited, With a Memoir of His Life,* by *Julius Charles Hare,* 2 vols., 1848.

[5] In his prefatory 'Life of the Author', I, cxxxvi–cxxxvii, Hare wrote: 'Of Sterling's opinions during the latter part of his life, I cannot give so full an account as during the period of our greater intimacy and sympathy. For after some painful controversial letters on the subject of Strauss, in which it did not appear that any good was likely to accrue from our prolonging the controversy, our correspondence became much less frequent.' George Eliot, the translator of Strauss's *Life of Jesus,* would hardly have failed to notice this event in Sterling's history.

literary character and writings, he felt a kind of responsibility that
no mistaken idea of his departed friend should remain before the
world without correction. Evidently, however, his 'Life of
Sterling' was not so much the conscientious discharge of a trust as
a labour of love, and to this is owing its strong charm. Carlyle here
shows us his 'sunny side'. We no longer see him breathing out
threatenings and slaughter as in the Latter-Day Pamphlets, but
moving among the charities and amenities of life, loving and
beloved—a Teufelsdröckh still, but humanized by a Blumine
worthy of him.[6] We have often wished that genius would incline
itself more frequently to the task of the biographer,—that when
some great or good personage dies, instead of the dreary three or
five volumed compilations of letter, and diary, and detail, little to
the purpose, which two-thirds of the reading public have not the
chance, nor the other third the inclination, to read, we could have a
real 'Life', setting forth briefly and vividly the man's inward and
outward struggles, aims, and achievements, so as to make clear
the meaning which his experience has for his fellows. A few such
lives (chiefly, indeed, autobiographies) the world possesses, and
they have, perhaps, been more influential on the formation of
character than any other kind of reading.[7] But the conditions
required for the perfection of life writing,—personal intimacy, a
loving and poetic nature which sees the beauty and the depth of
familiar things, and the artistic power which seizes characteristic
points and renders them with life-like effect,—are seldom found
in combination. 'The Life of Sterling' is an instance of this rare
conjunction. Its comparatively tame scenes and incidents gather
picturesqueness and interest under the rich lights of Carlyle's
mind. We are told neither too little nor too much; the facts noted,
the letters selected, are all such as serve to give the liveliest conception of what Sterling was and what he did; and though the book
speaks much of other persons, this collateral matter is all a kind of
scene-painting, and is accessory to the main purpose. The portrait

[6] Both from Carlyle's *Sartor Resartus*.
[7] According to Mrs. Cash, reported in Cross's *Life*, New Edition (1887),
p. ĩo4, after George Eliot met Emerson in 1848 'she told us that he had
asked her what had first awakened her to deep reflection, and when she
answered, Rousseau's 'Confessions', he remarked that this was very
interesting, inasmuch as Carlyle had told him that very book had had the
same effect upon his mind.'

of Coleridge, for example, is precisely adapted to bring before us
the intellectual region in which Sterling lived for some time before
entering the Church. Almost every review has extracted this
admirable description, in which genial veneration and compassion
struggle with irresistible satire; but the emphasis of quotation
cannot be too often given to the following pregnant paragraph:

> The truth is, I now see Coleridge's talk and speculation was the
> emblem of himself. In it, as in him, a ray of heavenly inspiration
> struggled, in a tragically ineffectual degree, with the weakness of flesh
> and blood. He says once, he 'had skirted the howling deserts of
> infidelity.' This was evident enough; but he had not had the courage,
> in defiance of pain and terror, to press resolutely across said deserts to
> the new firm lands of faith beyond; he preferred to create logical
> *fata-morganas* for himself on this hither side, and laboriously solace
> himself with these.

The above-mentioned step of Sterling—his entering the Church
—is the point on which Carlyle is most decidedly at issue with
Archdeacon Hare. The latter holds that had Sterling's health
permitted him to remain in the Church, he would have escaped
those aberrations from orthodoxy, which, in the clerical view, are
to be regarded as the failure and ship-wreck of his career, apparently thinking, like that friend of Arnold's who recommended a
curacy as the best means of clearing up Trinitarian difficulties,[8]
that 'orders' are a sort of spiritual backboard, which, by dint of
obliging a man to look as if he were strait, end by making him so.
According to Carlyle, on the contrary, the real 'aberration' of
Sterling was his choice of the clerical profession, which was
simply a mistake as to his true vocation:

> Sterling [he says] was not intrinsically, nor had ever been in the
> highest or chief degree, a devotional mind. Of course all excellence in
> man, and worship as the supreme excellence, was part of the inherit-
> ance of this gifted man; but if called to define him, I should say
> artist, not saint, was the real bent of his being.

Again:

> No man of Sterling's veracity, had he clearly consulted his own
> heart, or had his own heart been capable of clearly responding, and

---

[8] The friend was Keble. See A. P. Stanley, *Life and Correspondence of
Thomas Arnold, D.D.*, 2nd American ed., (New York and Philadelphia,
1846), p. 36. Lytton Strachey tells the story in *Eminent Victorians* (New
York and London, 1918), pp. 208–209.

not been bewildered by transient fantasies and theosophic moonshine, could have undertaken this function. His heart would have answered, 'No, thou canst not. What is incredible to thee, thou shalt not, at thy soul's peril, attempt to believe! Elsewhither for a refuge, or die here. Go to perdition if thou must, but not with a lie in thy mouth; by the eternal Maker, no!'

From the period when Carlyle's own acquaintance with Sterling commenced, the Life has a double interest, from the glimpses it gives us of the writer, as well of his hero. We are made present at their first introduction to each other; we get a lively idea of their colloquies and walks together, and in this easy way, without any heavy disquisition or narrative, we obtain a clear insight into Sterling's character and mental progress. Above all, we are gladdened with a perception of the affinity that exists between noble souls, in spite of diversity in ideas—in what Carlyle calls 'the logical outcome' of the faculties. This 'Life of Sterling' is a touching monument of the capability human nature possesses of the highest love, the love of the good and beautiful in character, which is, after all, the essence of piety. The style of the work, too, is for the most part at once pure and rich; there are passages of deep pathos which come upon the reader like a strain of solemn music, and others which show that aptness of epithet, that masterly power of close delineation, in which, perhaps, no writer has excelled Carlyle.

We have said that we think this second 'Life of Sterling' justified by the first; but were it not so, the book would justify itself.

4

WOMAN IN FRANCE: MADAME DE SABLÉ

Westminster Review, LXII (October, 1854), 448–473

'Woman in France' marks the beginning of the second phase of George Eliot's association with the *Westminster*. In the spring of 1854 she had given up her editorship of the review, and in July went off to the Continent with Lewes to begin her new life with him. On 5 August 1854, while they were in Weimar, George Eliot noted in her Journal 'a letter from Mr. Chapman, proposing to me to write an art. on Victor Cousin's Mde. de Sablé'. The commission was a tangible sign of Chapman's genuine good will towards his former editor, even in her new circumstances, and led to the series of articles and reviews for the *Westminster* in the next two years. The record of her Journal shows that she worked on the article from the time of her receiving Chapman's letter until 8 September 1854, when she wrote: 'Sent off my article on Mme. de Sablé.'

Besides Victor Cousin's *Madame de Sablé: études sur les femmes illustres et la société du XVIIe siècle* (1854), 'Woman in France' nominally reviews Sainte-Beuve's *Portraits de femmes* (1844) and Jules Michelet's *Les femmes de la révolution* (1854).

'Woman in France' has been reprinted in Nathan Sheppard, *The Essays of 'George Eliot', Complete*; in Mrs. S. B. Herrick, *Essays and Reviews of George Eliot*; and in *Essays and Uncollected Papers*.

*　　　*　　　*

IN 1847, a certain Count Leopold Ferri died at Padua, leaving a library entirely composed of works written by women, in various languages, and this library amounted to nearly 32,000 volumes. We will not hazard any conjecture as to the proportion of these volumes which a severe judge, like the priest in Don Quixote, would deliver to the flames, but for our own part, most of those we should care to rescue would be the works of French women. With a few remarkable exceptions, our own feminine literature is made up of books which could have been better written by men; books which have the same relation to literature in general, as academic prize poems have to poetry: when not a feeble imitation, they are usually an absurd exaggeration of the masculine style, like the swaggering gait of a bad actress in male attire. Few English women have written so much like a woman as Richardson's Lady G.[1] Now, we think it an immense mistake to maintain that there is no sex in literature. Science has no sex: the mere knowing and reasoning faculties, if they act correctly, must go through the same process, and arrive at the same result. But in art and literature, which imply the action of the entire being, in which every fibre of the nature is engaged, in which every peculiar modification of the individual makes itself felt, woman has something specific to contribute. Under every imaginable social condition, she will necessarily have a class of sensations and emotions—the maternal ones—which must remain unknown to man; and the fact of her comparative physical weakness, which, however it may have been exaggerated by a vicious civilization, can never be cancelled, introduces a distinctively feminine condition into the wondrous chemistry of the affections and sentiments, which inevitably gives rise to distinctive forms and combinations.[2] A certain amount of psychological difference between man and woman necessarily arises out of the difference of sex, and instead of being destined to vanish before a complete development of woman's intellectual and moral nature, will be a permanent source of variety and beauty, as long as the tender light and dewy freshness of morning affect us differently from the strength and brilliancy of the mid-day sun. And those

[1] Charlotte, Lady Grandison, sister of Sir Charles. George Eliot read Richardson's novel in 1847 (*Letters*, I, 240). In 1852 she wrote: 'Like Sir Charles Grandison? I should be sorry to be the heathen that did not like that book. I don't like Harriet Byron much, she is too proper and insipid. Lady G. is the gem, with her marmoset' (*Letters*, II, 65).

[2] Cf. Lewes's 'The Lady Novelists', *Westminster Review*, LVIII (July, 1852), 129–141: 'Woman, by her greater affectionateness, her greater range and depth of emotional experience, is well fitted to give expression to the emotional facts of life, and demands a place in literature corresponding with that she occupies in society' (p. 132).

delightful women of France, who, from the beginning of the seventeenth to the close of the eighteenth century, formed some of the brightest threads in the web of political and literary history, wrote under circumstances which left the feminine character of their minds uncramped by timidity, and unstrained by mistaken effort. They were not trying to make a career for themselves; they thought little, in many cases not at all, of the public; they wrote letters to their lovers and friends, memoirs of their every-day lives, romances in which they gave portraits of their familiar acquaintances, and described the tragedy or comedy which was going on before their eyes. Always refined and graceful, often witty, sometimes judicious, they wrote what they saw, thought, and felt, in their habitual language, without proposing any model to themselves, without any intention to prove that women could write as well as men, without affecting manly views or suppressing womanly ones. One may say, at least with regard to the women of the seventeenth century, that their writings were but a charming accident of their more charming lives, like the petals which the wind shakes from the rose in its bloom. And it is but a twin fact with this, that in France alone woman has had a vital influence on the development of literature; in France alone the mind of woman has passed like an electric current through the language, making crisp and definite what is elsewhere heavy and blurred; in France alone, if the writings of women were swept away, a serious gap would be made in the national history.

Patriotic gallantry may perhaps contend that English women could, if they had liked, have written as well as their neighbours; but we will leave the consideration of that question to the reviewers of the literature that might have been. In the literature that actually is, we must turn to France for the highest examples of womanly achievement in almost every department. We confess ourselves unacquainted with the productions of those awful women of Italy, who held professional chairs, and were great in civil and canon law;[3] we have made no researches into the catacombs of female literature, but we think we may safely conclude that they would yield no rivals to that which is still unburied; and here, we suppose, the question of pre-eminence can only lie between England and France. And to this day, Madame de Sévigné

[3] George Eliot means such women as Cassandra Fedele (1465–1558), who is several times mentioned in *Romola*, e.g., Ch. 36.

remains the single instance of a woman who is supreme in a class
of literature which has engaged the ambition of men; Madame
Dacier still reigns the queen of blue-stockings, though women have
long studied Greek without shame;[4] Madame de Staël's name still
rises first to the lips when we are asked to mention a woman of
great intellectual power; Madame Roland is still the unrivalled type
of the sagacious and sternly heroic, yet lovable woman; George
Sand is the unapproached artist who, to Jean Jacques' eloquence
and deep sense of external nature, unites the clear delineation of
character and the tragic depth of passion. These great names,
which mark different epochs, soar like tall pines amidst a forest of
less conspicuous, but not less fascinating, female writers; and
beneath these again are spread, like a thicket of hawthorns,
eglantines, and honeysuckles, the women who are known rather
by what they stimulated men to write, than by what they wrote
themselves—the women whose tact, wit, and personal radiance,
created the atmosphere of the *Salon*, where literature, philosophy,
and science, emancipated from the trammels of pedantry and
technicality, entered on a brighter stage of existence.

What were the causes of this earlier development and more
abundant manifestation of womanly intellect in France? The
primary one, perhaps, lies in the physiological characteristics of the
Gallic race: the small brain and vivacious temperament which
permit the fragile system of woman to sustain the superlative
activity requisite for intellectual creativeness; while, on the other
hand, the larger brain and slower temperament of the English and
Germans are, in the womanly organization, generally dreamy and
passive. The type of humanity in the latter may be grander, but it
requires a larger sum of conditions to produce a perfect specimen.
Throughout the animal world, the higher the organization the more
frequent is the departure from the normal form; we do not often
see imperfectly-developed or ill-made insects, but we rarely see a
perfectly-developed, well-made man. And thus the *physique* of a
woman may suffice as the substratum for a superior Gallic mind,
but is too thin a soil for a superior Teutonic one. Our theory is
borne out by the fact, that among our own countrywomen, those

[4] Queen Christina, when Mme Dacier (then Mlle Le Fevre) sent her a
copy of her edition of 'Callimachus,' wrote in reply;— 'Mais vous, de
qui on m'assure que vous êtes une belle et agréable fille, n'avez vous pas
honte d'être si savante?' [George Eliot's note.]

who distinguish themselves by literary production, more frequently approach the Gallic than the Teutonic type; they are intense and rapid rather than comprehensive. The woman of large capacity can seldom rise beyond the absorption of ideas; her physical conditions refuse to support the energy required for spontaneous activity; the voltaic-pile is not strong enough to produce crystallizations; phantasms of great ideas float through her mind, but she has not the spell which will arrest them, and give them fixity. This, more than unfavourable external circumstances, is, we think, the reason why woman has not yet contributed any new form to art, any discovery in science, any deep-searching inquiry in philosophy. The necessary physiological conditions are not present in her. That under more favourable circumstances in the future, these conditions may prove compatible with the feminine organization, it would be rash to deny. For the present, we are only concerned with our theory so far as it presents a physiological basis for the intellectual effectiveness of French women.

A secondary cause was probably the laxity of opinion and practice with regard to the marriage-tie. Heaven forbid that we should enter on a defence of French morals, most of all in relation to marriage! But it is undeniable, that unions formed in the maturity of thought and feeling, and grounded only on inherent fitness and mutual attraction, tended to bring women into more intelligent sympathy with men, and to heighten and complicate their share in the political drama. The quiescence and security of the conjugal relation, are doubtless favourable to the manifestation of the highest qualities by persons who have already attained a high standard of culture, but rarely foster a passion sufficient to rouse all the faculties to aid in winning or retaining its beloved object— to convert indolence into activity, indifference into ardent partisanship, dulness into perspicuity. Gallantry and intrigue are sorry enough things in themselves, but they certainly serve better to arouse the dormant faculties of woman than embroidery and domestic drudgery, especially when, as in the high society of France in the seventeenth century, they are refined by the influence of Spanish chivalry, and controlled by the spirit of Italian causticity. The dreamy and fantastic girl was awakened to reality by the experience of wifehood and maternity, and became capable of loving, not a mere phantom of her own imagination, but a living man, struggling with the hatreds and rivalries of the political arena; she espoused his quarrels, she made herself, her fortune, and her influence, the stepping-stones of his ambition; and the languid beauty, who had formerly seemed ready to 'die of a rose,'[5] was seen to become the heroine of an insurrection. The vivid interest in affairs which was thus excited in woman, must obviously have tended to quicken her intellect, and give it a practical application; and the very sorrows—the heart-pangs and regrets which are inseparable from a life of passion—deepened her nature by the questioning of self and destiny which they occasioned, and by the energy demanded to surmount them and live on. No wise person, we imagine, wishes to restore the social condition of France in the seventeenth century, or considers the ideal programme of woman's life to be a *mariage de convenance* at fifteen, a career of gallantry from twenty to eight-and-thirty, and penitence and piety for the rest of her days. Nevertheless, that social condition had its good results, as much as the madly-superstitious Crusades had theirs.

But the most indisputable source of feminine culture and development in France was the influence of the *salons*; which, as all the world knows, were *réunions* of both sexes, where conversation ran along the whole gamut of subjects, from the frothiest *vers de société* to the philosophy of Descartes. Richelieu had set the fashion of uniting a taste for letters with the habits of polite society and the pursuits of ambition; and in the first quarter of the seventeenth century, there were already several hôtels in Paris, varying in social position from the closest proximity of the Court to the debatable ground of the aristocracy and the bourgeoisie, which served as a rendezvous for different circles of people, bent on entertaining themselves either by showing talent or admiring it. The most celebrated of these rendezvous was the Hôtel de Rambouillet, which was at the culmination of its glory in 1630, and did not become quite extinct until 1648, when, the troubles of the Fronde commencing, its *habitués* were dispersed or absorbed by political interests. The presiding genius of this *salon*, the Marquise de Rambouillet, was the very model of the woman who can act as an amalgam to the most incongruous elements; beautiful, but not preoccupied by coquetry or passion; an enthusiastic admirer of talent, but with no pretensions to talent on her own part; exquisitely refined in language and manners, but warm and generous withal; not given to entertain her guests with her own compositions, or to

[5] Pope, 'Essay on Man', I, 200.

paralyse them by her universal knowledge. She had once *meant* to learn Latin, but had been prevented by an illness; perhaps she was all the better acquainted with Italian and Spanish productions, which, in default of a national literature, were then the intellectual pabulum of all cultivated persons in France who were unable to read the classics. In her mild, agreeable presence was accomplished that blending of the high-toned chivalry of Spain with the caustic wit and refined irony of Italy, which issued in the creation of a new standard of taste—the combination of the utmost exaltation in sentiment with the utmost simplicity of language. Women are peculiarly fitted to further such a combination,—first, from their greater tendency to mingle affection and imagination with passion, and thus subtilize it into sentiment; and next, from that dread of what over-taxes their intellectual energies, either by difficulty or monotony, which gives them an instinctive fondness for lightness of treatment and airiness of expression, thus making them cut short all prolixity and reject all heaviness. When these womanly characteristics were brought into conversational contact with the materials furnished by such minds as those of Richelieu, Corneille, the Great Condé, Balzac, and Bossuet, it is no wonder that the result was something piquant and charming. Those famous *habitués* of the Hôtel de Rambouillet did not, apparently, first lay themselves out to entertain the ladies with grimacing 'small-talk,' and then take each other by the sword-knot to discuss matters of real interest in a corner; they rather sought to present their best ideas in the guise most acceptable to intelligent and accomplished women. And the conversation was not of literature only; war, politics, religion, the lightest details of daily news—everything was admissible, if only it were treated with refinement and intelligence. The Hôtel de Rambouillet was no mere literary *réunion*; it included *hommes d'affaires* and soldiers as well as authors, and in such a circle, women would not become *bas bleus* or dreamy moralizers, ignorant of the world and of human nature, but intelligent observers of character and events. It is easy to understand, however, that with the herd of imitators who, in Paris and the provinces, aped the style of this famous *salon*, simplicity degenerated into affectation, and nobility of sentiment was replaced by an inflated effort to outstrip nature, so that the *genre précieux* drew down the satire, which reached its climax in the *Précieuses Ridicules* and *Les Femmes Savantes*, the former of which appeared

58

in 1660, and the latter in 1673.[6] But Madelon and Caltros[7] are the lineal descendants of Mademoiselle Scudéry and her satellites, quite as much as of the Hôtel de Rambouillet. The society which assembled every Saturday in her *salon* was exclusively literary, and, although occasionally visited by a few persons of high birth, bourgeois in its tone, and enamoured of madrigals, sonnets, stanzas, and *bouts rimés*. The affectation that decks trivial things in fine language, belongs essentially to a class which sees another above it, and is uneasy in the sense of its inferiority; and this affectation is precisely the opposite of the original *genre précieux*.

Another centre from which feminine influence radiated into the national literature, was the Palais du Luxembourg, where Mademoiselle d'Orleans, in disgrace at court on account of her share in the Fronde, held a little court of her own, and for want of anything else to employ her active spirit, busied herself with literature. One fine morning, it occurred to this princess to ask all the persons who frequented her court, among whom were Madame de Sévigné, Madame de la Fayette, and La Rochefoucauld, to write their own portraits, and she at once set the example. It was understood that defects and virtues were to be spoken of with like candour. The idea was carried out; those who were not clever or bold enough to write for themselves employing the pen of a friend.

Such [says M. Cousin] was the pastime of Mademoiselle and her friends during the years 1657 and 1658: from this pastime proceeded a complete literature. In 1659, Ségrais revised these portraits, added a considerable number in prose and even in verse, and published the whole in a handsome quarto volume, admirably printed, and now become very rare, under the title, *Divers Portraits*. Only thirty copies were printed, not for sale, but to be given as presents by Mademoiselle. The work had a prodigious success. That which had made the fortune of Mademoiselle de Scudéry's romances—the pleasure of seeing one's portrait a little flattered, curiosity to see that of others, the passion which the middle class always have and will have for knowing what goes on in the aristocratic world, (at that time not very easy of access,) the names of the illustrious persons who were here for the first time described physically and morally with the utmost detail, great ladies transformed all at once into writers, and unconsciously

---

[6] I.e., 1659 and 1672.

[7] Presumably a misprint for Cathos; she and Madelon are the *précieuses ridicules* of Moliere's comedy.

inventing a new manner of writing, of which no book gave the slightest idea, and which was the ordinary manner of speaking of the aristocracy; this undefinable mixture of the natural, the easy, and at the same time of the agreeable, and supremely distinguished—all this charmed the court and the town, and very early in the year 1659 permission was asked of Mademoiselle to give a new edition of the privileged book for the use of the public in general.

The fashion thus set, portraits multiplied throughout France, until in 1688, La Bruyère adopted the form in his' Characters', and ennobled it by divesting it of personality. We shall presently see that a still greater work than La Bruyère's also owed its suggestion to a woman, whose salon was hardly a less fascinating resort than the Hôtel de Rambouillet itself.

In proportion as the literature of a country is enriched and culture becomes more generally diffused, personal influence is less effective in the formation of taste and in the furtherance of social advancement. It is no longer the coterie which acts on literature, but literature which acts on the coterie; the circle represented by the word *public*, is ever widening, and ambition, poising itself in order to hit a more distant mark, neglects the successes of the salon. What was once lavished prodigally in conversation, is reserved for the volume, or the 'article'; and the effort is not to betray originality rather than to communicate it. As the old coach-roads have sunk into disuse through the creation of railways, so journalism tends more and more to divert information from the channel of conversation into the channel of the Press: no one is satisfied with a more circumscribed audience than that very indeterminate abstraction 'the public', and men find a vent for their opinions not in talk, but in 'copy'. We read the 'Athenæum' askance at the tea-table, and take notes from the 'Philosophical Journal' at a soirée; we invite our friends that we may thrust a book into their hands, and presuppose an exclusive desire in the 'ladies' to discuss their own matters, 'that we may crackle the *Times*' at our ease. In fact, the evident tendency of things to contract personal communication within the narrowest limits makes us tremble lest some further development of electric telegraph should reduce us to a society of mutes, or to a sort of insects, communicating by ingenious antennæ of our own invention. Things were far from having reached this pass in the last century; but even then, literature and society had outgrown the nursing of coteries, and although many *salons* of that period were worthy successors of the Hôtel de Rambouillet, they were simply a recreation, not an influence. Enviable evenings, no doubt, were passed in them; and if we could be carried back to any of them at will, we should hardly know whether to choose the Wednesday dinner at Madame Geoffrin's, with d'Alembert, Mademoiselle de l'Espinasse, Grimm, and the rest, or the graver society which, thirty years later, gathered round Condorcet and his lovely young wife. The *salon* retained its attractions, but its power was gone: the stream of life had become too broad and deep for such small rills to affect it.

A fair comparison between the Frenchwomen of the seventeenth century and those of the eighteenth would, perhaps, have a balanced result, though it is common to be a partisan on this subject. The former have more exaltation, perhaps more nobility of sentiment, and less consciousness in their intellectual activity— less of the *femme auteur*, which was Rousseau's horror in Madame d'Epinay; but the latter have a richer fund of ideas—not more ingenuity, but the materials of an additional century for their ingenuity to work upon. The women of the seventeenth century, when love was on the wane, took to devotion, at first mildly and by halves, as English women take to caps, and finally without compromise; with the women of the eighteenth century, Bossuet and Massillon had given way to Voltaire and Rousseau; and when youth and beauty failed, then they were thrown on their own moral strength.

M. Cousin is especially enamoured of the women of the seventeenth century, and relieves himself from his labours in philosophy by making researches into the original documents which throw light upon their lives. Last year he gave us some results of these researches, in a volume on the youth of the Duchess de Longueville;[8] and he has just followed it up with a second volume, in which he further illustrates her career by tracing it in connexion with that of her friend, Madame de Sablé. The materials to which he has had recourse for this purpose, are chiefly two celebrated collections of manuscripts: that of Conrart, the first secretary to the French Academy, one of those universally curious people who seem made for the annoyance of contemporaries and the benefit of

---

[8] *La jeunesse de Mme. de Longueville: études sur les femmes illustres et la société du XVIIe siècle* . . . (1853), the first volume in the series of which *Madame de Sablé* is the second.

posterity; and that of Valant, who was at once the physician, the secretary, and general steward of Madame de Sablé, and who, with or without her permission, possessed himself of the letters addressed to her by her numerous correspondents during the latter part of her life, and of various papers having some personal or literary interest attached to them. From these stores M. Cousin has selected many documents previously unedited; and though he often leaves us something to desire in the arrangement of his materials, this volume of his on Madame de Sablé is very acceptable to us, for she interests us quite enough to carry us through more than three hundred pages of rather scattered narrative, and through an appendix of correspondence in small type. M. Cousin justly appreciates her character as 'un heureux mélange de raison, d'esprit, d'agrément, et de bonté'; and perhaps there are few better specimens of the woman who is extreme in nothing, but sympathetic in all things; who affects us by no special quality, but by her entire being; whose nature has no *tons criards*, but is like those textures which, from their harmonious blending of all colours, give repose to the eye, and do not weary us though we see them every day. Madame de Sablé is also a striking example of the one order of influence which woman has exercised over literature in France; and on this ground, as well as intrinsically, she is worth studying. If the reader agrees with us he will perhaps be inclined, as we are, to dwell a little on the chief points in her life and character.

Madeline de Souvré, daughter of the Marquis of Courtenvaux, a nobleman distinguished enough to be chosen as governor of Louis XIII., was born in 1599, on the threshold of that seventeenth century, the brilliant genius of which is mildly reflected in her mind and history. Thus, when in 1635, her more celebrated friend, Mademoiselle de Bourbon, afterwards the Duchess de Longueville, made her appearance at the Hôtel de Rambouillet, Madame de Sablé had nearly crossed that table-land of maturity which precedes a woman's descent towards old age. She had been married, in 1614, to Philippe Emanuel de Laval-Montmorency, Seigneur de Bois-Dauphin, and Marquis de Sablé, of whom nothing further is known than that he died in 1640, leaving her the richer by four children, but with a fortune considerably embarrassed. With beauty and high rank added to the mental attractions of which we have abundant evidence, we may well believe that

Madame de Sablé's youth was brilliant. For her beauty, we have the testimony of sober Madame de Motteville, who also speaks of her as having 'beaucoup de lumière et de sincérité'; and in the following passage very graphically indicates one phase of Madame de Sablé's character:

> The Marquise de Sablé was one of those whose beauty made the most noise when the Queen came into France. But if she was amiable, she was still more desirous of appearing so; this lady's self-love rendered her too sensitive to the regard which men exhibited towards her. There yet existed in France some remains of the politeness which Catherine de Medici had introduced from Italy, and the new dramas, with all the other works in prose and verse, which came from Madrid, were thought to have such great delicacy, that she (Madame de Sablé) had conceived a high idea of the gallantry which the Spaniards had learned from the Moors.
>
> She was persuaded that men can, without crime, have tender sentiments for women—that the desire of pleasing them led men to the greatest and finest actions—roused their intelligence, and inspired them with liberality, and all sorts of virtues; but, on the other hand, women, who were the ornament of the world, and made to be served and adored, ought not to admit anything from them but their respectful attentions. As this lady supported her views with much talent and great beauty, she had given them authority in her time, and the number and consideration of those who continued to associate with her, have caused to subsist in our day what the Spaniards call *finezas*.

Here is the grand element of the original *femme précieuse*, and it appears further, in a detail also reported by Madame de Motteville, that Madame de Sablé had a passionate admirer in the accomplished Duc de Montmorency, and apparently reciprocated his regard; but discovering (at what period of their attachment is unknown) that he was raising a lover's eyes towards the queen, she broke with him at once. 'I have heard her say,' tells Madame de Motteville, 'that her pride was such with regard to the Duc de Montmorency, that at the first demonstrations which he gave of his change, she refused to see him any more, being unable to receive with satisfaction attentions which she had to share with the greatest princess in the world.' There is no evidence, except the untrustworthy assertion of Tallement de Réaux, that Madame de Sablé had any other *liaison* than this; and the probability of the negative is increased by the ardour of her friendships. The strongest of these was formed early in life with Mademoiselle Dona d'Attichy, afterwards Comtesse de Maure; it survived the effervescence of youth and the closest intimacy of middle age, and was only terminated by the death of the latter in 1663. A little incident in this friendship is so characteristic in the transcendentalism which was then carried into all the affections, that it is worth relating at length. Mademoiselle d'Attichy, in her grief and indignation at Richelieu's treatment of her relative, quitted Paris, and was about to join her friend at Sablé, when she suddenly discovered that Madame de Sablé, in a letter to Madame de Rambouillet, had said, that her greatest happiness would be to pass her life with Julie de Rambouillet, afterwards Madame de Montausier. To Anne d'Attichy this appears nothing less than the crime of *lèse-amitié*. No explanations will appease her: she refuses to accept the assurance that the offensive expression was used simply out of unreflecting conformity to the style of the Hôtel de Rambouillet—that is was mere '*galimatias*'. She gives up her journey, and writes a letter, which is the only one Madame de Sablé chose to preserve, when, in her period of devotion, she sacrificed the records of her youth. Here it is:

I have seen this letter in which you tell me there is so much *galimatias*, and I assure you that I have not found any at all. On the contrary, I find everything very plainly expressed, and among others, one which is too explicit for my satisfaction—namely, what you have said to Madame de Rambouillet, that if you tried to imagine a perfectly happy life for yourself, it would be to pass it all alone with Mademoiselle de Rambouillet. You know whether any one can be more persuaded than I am of her merit; but I confess to you that that has not prevented me from being surprised that you could entertain a thought which did so great an injury to our friendship. As to believing that you said this to one, and wrote it to the other, simply for the sake of paying them an agreeable compliment, I have too high an esteem for your courage to be able to imagine that complaisance would cause you thus to betray the sentiments of your heart, especially on a subject in which, as they were unfavourable to me, I think you would have the more reason for concealing them, the affection which I have for you being so well-known to every one, and especially to Mademoiselle de Rambouillet, so that I doubt whether she will not have been more sensible of the wrong you have done me, than of the advantage you have given her. The circumstance of this letter falling into my hands, has forcibly reminded me of these lines of Bertaut:

'Malheureuse est l'ignorance
Et plus malheureux le savoir.'

Having through this lost a confidence which alone rendered life supportable to me, it is impossible for me to take the journey so much thought of. For would there be any propriety in travelling sixty miles in this season, in order to burthen you with a person so little suited to you, that after years of a passion without parallel, you cannot help thinking that the greatest pleasure of your life would be to pass it without her? I return, then, into my solitude, to examine the defects which cause me so much unhappiness, and unless I can correct them, I should have less joy than confusion in seeing you.

It speaks strongly for the charm of Madame de Sablé's nature that she was able to retain so susceptible a friend as Mademoiselle d'Attichy in spite of numerous other friendships, some of which, especially that with Madame de Longueville, were far from luke-warm—in spite too of a tendency in herself to distrust the affection of others towards her, and to wait for advances rather than to make them. We find many traces of this tendency in the affectionate remonstrances addressed to her by Madame de Longueville, now for shutting herself up from her friends, now for doubting that her letters are acceptable. Here is a little passage from one of these remonstrances which indicates a trait of Madame de Sablé, and is in itself a bit of excellent sense, worthy the consideration of lovers and friends in general: 'I am very much afraid that if I leave to you the care of letting me know when I can see you, I shall be a long time without having that pleasure, and that nothing will incline you to procure it me, for I have always observed a certain luke-warmness in your friendship after our *explanations*, from which I have never seen you thoroughly recover; and that is why I dread explanations, for however good they may be in themselves, since they serve to reconcile people, it must always be admitted, to their shame, that they are at least the effect of a bad cause, and that if they remove it for a time they *sometimes leave a certain facility in getting angry again*, which, without diminishing friendship, renders its intercourse less agreeable. It seems to me that I find all this in your behaviour to me; so I am not wrong in sending to know if you wish to have me today.' It is clear that Madame de Sablé was far from having what Saint-Beuve calls the one fault of Madame Necker—absolute perfection. A certain exquisiteness in her physical and moral nature was, as we shall see, the source of more than one weakness, but the perception of these weaknesses, which is indicated in Madame de Longueville's letters, heightens our idea of the attractive qualities which notwithstanding drew from her, at the sober age of forty, such expressions as these: 'I assure you that you are the person in all the world whom it would be most agreeable to me to see, and there is no one whose intercourse is a ground of truer satisfaction to me. It is admirable that at all times, and amidst all changes, the taste for your society remains in me; and, *if one ought to thank God for the joys which do not tend to salvation,* I should thank him with all my heart for having preserved that to me at a time in which he has taken away from me all others.'

Since we have entered on the chapter of Madame de Sablé's weaknesses, this is the place to mention what was the subject of endless raillery from her friends—her elaborate precaution about her health, and her dread of infection, even from diseases the least communicable. Perhaps this anxiety was founded as much on æsthetic as on physical grounds, on disgust at the details of illness as much as on dread of suffering: with a cold in the head or a bilious complaint, the exquisite *précieuse* must have been considerably less conscious of being 'the ornament of the world,' and 'made to be adored'. Even her friendship, strong as it was, was not strong enough to overcome her horror of contagion; for when Mademoiselle de Bourbon, recently become Madame de Longueville, was attacked by small-pox, Madame de Sablé for some time had not courage to visit her, or even to see Mademoiselle de Rambouillet, who was assiduous in her attendance on the patient. A little correspondence *à propos* of these circumstances so well exhibits the graceful badinage in which the great ladies of that day were adepts, that we are tempted to quote one short letter.

Mlle de Rambouillet to the Marquise de Sablé.

Mlle de Chalais (*dame de compagnie* to the Marquise) will please to read this letter to Mme la Marquise, *out of* a draught.
Madame,

I do not think it possible to begin my treaty with you too early, for I am convinced that between the first proposition made to me that I should see you, and the conclusion, you will have so many reflections to make, so many physicians to consult, and so many fears to surmount, that I shall have full leisure to air myself. The conditions which I offer to fulfil for this purpose are, not to visit you until I have been three days absent from the Hôtel de Condé (where Mme de Longueville was ill), to choose a frosty day, not to approach you within four paces, not to sit down on more than one seat. You may also have a great fire in your room, burn juniper in the four corners, surround yourself with imperial vinegar, with rue and wormwood. If you can feel yourself safe under these conditions, without my cutting off my hair, I swear to you to execute them religiously; and if you want examples to fortify you, I can tell you that the Queen consented to see M. Chaudebonne, when he had come directly from Mlle de Bourbon's room, and that Mme d'Aiguillon, who has good taste in such matters, and is free from reproach on these points, has just sent me word that if I did not go to see her, she would come to me.

Madame de Sablé betrays in her reply that she winces under this raillery, and thus provokes a rather severe though polite rejoinder, which, added to the fact that Madame de Longueville is convalescent, rouses her courage to the pitch of paying the formidable visit. Mademoiselle de Rambouillet, made aware, through their mutual friend Voiture, that her sarcasm has cut rather too deep, winds up the matter by writing that very difficult production, a perfectly conciliatory yet dignified apology. Peculiarities like this always deepen with age, and accordingly, fifteen years later, we find Madame D'Orleans, in her *Princesse de Paphlagonia*—a romance in which she describes her court, with the little quarrels and other affairs that agitated it—giving the following amusing picture, or rather caricature, of the extent to which Madame de Sablé carried her pathological mania, which seems to have been shared by her friend the Countess de Maure (Mademoiselle d'Attichy). In the romance, these two ladies appear under the names of the Princesse Parthénie and the Reine de Mionie.[9]

There was not an hour in the day in which they did not confer together on the means of avoiding death, and on the art of rendering themselves immortal. Their conferences did not take place like those of other people; the fear of breathing an air which was too cold or too warm, the dread lest the wind should be too dry or too moist—in short, the imagination that the weather might not be as temperate as they thought necessary for the preservation of their health, caused them to write letters from one room to the other. It would be extremely fortunate if these notes could be found, and formed into a

[9] I.e., *Reine de Misne*.

collection. I am convinced that they would contain rules for the regimen of life, precautions even as to the proper time for applying remedies, and also remedies which Hippocrates and Galen, with all their science, never heard of. Such a collection would be very useful to the public, and would be highly profitable to the faculties of Paris and Montpelier. If these letters were discovered, great advantages of all kinds might be derived from them, for they were princesses who had nothing mortal about them but the *knowledge* that they were mortal. In their writings might be learned all politeness in style, and the most delicate manner of speaking on all subjects. There is nothing with which they were not acquainted; they knew the affairs of all the States in the world, through the share they had in all the intrigues of its private members, either in matters of gallantry, as in other things on which their advice was necessary; either to adjust embroilments and quarrels, or to excite them, for the sake of the advantages which their friends could derive from them;—in a word, they were persons through whose hands the secrets of the whole world had to pass. The Princess Parthénie (Mme de Sablé) had a palate as delicate as her mind; nothing could equal the magnificence of the entertainments she gave; all the dishes were exquisite, and her cleanliness was beyond all that could be imagined. It was in their time that writing came into use; previously, nothing was written but marriage contracts, and letters were never heard of; thus it is to them that we owe a practice so convenient in intercourse.

Still later, in 1669, when the most uncompromising of the Port Royalists seemed to tax Madame de Sablé with lukewarmness that she did not join them at Port-Royal-des-Champs, we find her writing to the stern M. de Sévigny: 'En vérité, je crois que je ne pourrois mieux faire que de tout quitter et de m'en aller là. Mais que devendroient ces frayeurs de n'avoir pas de médecins à choisir, ni de chirurgien pour me saigner?'

Mademoiselle, as we have seen, hints at the love of delicate eating, which many of Madame de Sablé's friends numbered among her foibles, especially after her religious career had commenced. She had a genius in *friandise*, and knew how to gratify the palate without offending the highest sense of refinement. Her sympathetic nature showed itself in this as in other things: she was always sending *bonnes bouches* to her friends, and trying to communicate to them her science and taste in the affairs of the table. Madame de Longueville, who had not the luxurious tendencies of her friend, writes—'Je vous demande au nom de Dieu, que vous ne me prépariez aucun ragoût. Surtout ne me donnez point de festin. Au nom de Dieu, qu'il n'y ait rien que ce qu'on peut manger, car vous savez que c'est inutile pour moi; de plus j'en ai scrupule.' But other friends had more appreciation of her niceties. Voiture thanks her for her melons, and assures her that they are better than those of yesterday; Madame de Choisy hopes that her ridicule of Jansenism will not provoke Madame de Sablé to refuse her the receipt for salad; and La Rochefoucauld writes: 'You cannot do me a greater charity than to permit the bearer of this letter to enter into the mysteries of your marmalade and your genuine preserves, and I humbly entreat you to do everything you can in his favour. If I could hope for two dishes of those preserves, which I did not deserve to eat before, I should be indebted to you all my life.' For our own part, being as far as possible from fraternizing with those spiritual people who convert a deficiency into a principle, and pique themselves on an obtuse palate as a point of superiority, we are not inclined to number Madame de Sablé's *friandise* amongst her defects. M. Cousin, too, is apologetic on this point. He says:

It was only the excess of a delicacy which can be readily understood, and a sort of fidelity to the character of *précieuse*. As the *précieuse* did nothing according to common usage, she could not dine like another. We have cited a passage from Mme de Motteville, where Mme de Sablé is represented in her first youth at the Hôtel de Rambouillet, maintaining that woman is born to be an ornament to the world, and to receive the adoration of men. The woman worthy of the name, ought always to appear above material wants, and retain, even in the most vulgar details of life, something distinguished and purified. Eating is a very necessary operation, but one which is not agreeable to the eye. Mme de Sablé insisted on its being conducted with a peculiar cleanliness. According to her, it was not every woman who could with impunity be at table in the presence of a lover; the first distortion of the face, she said, would be enough to spoil all. Gross meals, made for the body merely, ought to be abandoned to *bourgeoises*, and the refined woman should appear to take a little nourishment merely to sustain her, and even to divert her, as one takes refreshments and ices. Wealth did not suffice for this; a particular talent was required. Mme de Sablé was a mistress in this art. She had transported the aristocratic spirit and the *genre précieux*, good breeding and good taste, even into cookery. Her dinners, without any opulence, were celebrated and sought after.

It is quite in accordance with all this, that Madame de Sablé should delight in fine scents, and we find that she did; for being threatened, in her Port Royal days, when she was at an advanced age, with the loss of smell, and writing for sympathy and information to Mère Agnès, who had lost that sense early in life, she receives this admonition from the stern saint: 'You would gain by this loss, my very dear sister, if you made use of it as a satisfaction to God, for having had too much pleasure in delicious scents.' Scarron describes her as

> La non pareille Bois-Dauphine,
> *Entre dames perle très fine,*

and the superlative delicacy implied by this epithet seems to have belonged equally to her personal habits, her affections, and her intellect.

Madame de Sablé's life, for anything we know, flowed on evenly enough until 1640, when the death of her husband threw upon her the care of an embarrassed fortune. She found a friend in Réné de Longueil, Seigneur de Maisons, of whom we are content to know no more than that he helped Madame de Sablé to arrange her affairs, though only by means of alienating from her family the estate of Sablé, that his house was her refuge during the blockade of Paris, in 1649, and that she was not unmindful of her obligations to him, when, subsequently, her credit could be serviceable to him at court. In the midst of these pecuniary troubles came a more terrible trial—the loss of her favourite son, the brave and handsome Guy de Laval, who, after a brilliant career in the campaigns of Condé, was killed at the siege of Dunkirk, in 1646, when scarcely four-and-twenty. The fine qualities of this young man had endeared him to the whole army, and especially to Condé, had won him the hand of the Chancellor Séguire's daughter, and had thus opened to him the prospect of the highest honours. His loss seems to have been the most real sorrow of Madame de Sablé's life. Soon after followed the commotions of the Fronde, which put a stop to social intercourse, and threw the closest friends into opposite ranks. According to Lenet, who relies on the authority of Gourville, Madame de Sablé was under strong obligations to the court, being in the receipt of a pension of 2000 crowns; at all events, she adhered throughout to the Queen and Mazarin, but being as far as possible from a fierce partisan, and given both by disposition and judgment to hear both sides of a question, she acted as a conciliator, and retained her friends of both parties. The Countess de Maure, whose husband was the most obstinate of *frondeurs*, remained throughout her most cherished friend, and she kept up a constant correspondence with the lovely and intrepid heroine of the Fronde, Madame de Longueville. Her activity was directed to the extinction of animosities, by bringing about marriages between the Montagues and Capulets of the Fronde—between the Prince de Condé, or his brother, and the niece of Mazarin, or between the three nieces of Mazarin and the sons of three noblemen who were distinguished leaders of the Fronde. Though her projects were not realized, her conciliatory position enabled her to preserve all her friendships intact, and when the political tempest was over, she could assemble around her in her residence, in the Place Royal, the same society as before. Madame de Sablé was now approaching her twelfth lustrum, and though the charms of her mind and character made her more sought after than most younger women, it is not surprising that, sharing as she did in the religious ideas of her time, the concerns of 'salvation' seemed to become pressing. A religious retirement, which did not exclude the reception of literary friends, or the care for personal comforts, made the most becoming frame for age and diminished fortune. Jansenism was then to ordinary Catholicism what Puseyism is to ordinary Church of Englandism in these days—it was a *récherché* form of piety unshared by the vulgar; and one sees at once that it must have special attractions for the *précieuse*. Madame de Sablé, then, probably about 1655 or 6, determined to retire to Port Royal, not because she was already devout, but because she hoped to become so; as, however, she wished to retain the pleasure of intercourse with friends who were still worldly, she built for herself a set of apartments at once distinct from the monastery and attached to it. Here, with a comfortable establishment, consisting of her secretary, Dr. Valant, Mademoiselle de Chalais, formerly her *dame de compagnie*, and now become her friend; an excellent cook; a few other servants, and for a considerable time a carriage and coachman; with her best friends within a moderate distance, she could, as M. Cousin says, be out of the noise of the world without altogether forsaking it, preserve her dearest friendships, and have before her eyes edifying examples—'vaquer enfin à son aise aux soins de son salut et à ceux de sa santé.'

We have hitherto looked only at one phase of Madame de Sablé's character and influence—that of the précieuse. But she was much more than this: she was the valuable, trusted friend of noble women and distinguished men; she was the animating spirit of a society whence issued a new form of French literature: she was the woman of large capacity and large heart, whom Pascal sought to please, to whom Arnauld submitted the Discourse prefixed to his Logic, and to whom La Rochefoucauld writes: 'Vous savez que je ne crois que vous etes sur de certains chapitres, et surtout sur les replis du cœur.' The papers preserved by her secretary, Valant, show that she maintained an extensive correspondence with persons of various rank and character; that her pen was untiring in the interest of others; that men made her the depositary of their thoughts, women of their sorrows; that her friends were as impatient, when she secluded herself, as if they had been rival lovers and she a youthful beauty. It is into her ear that Madame de Longueville pours her troubles and difficulties, and that Madame de La Fayette communicates her little alarms, lest young Count de St. Paul should have detected her intimacy with La Roche-foucauld.[10] The few of Madame de Sablé's letters which survive show that she excelled in that epistolary style which was the speciality of the Hôtel de Rambouillet; one to Madame de Montausier, in favour of M. Périer, the brother-in-law of Pascal, is a happy mixture of good taste and good sense; but amongst them all we prefer quoting one to the Duchess de la Tremouille. It is light and pretty, and made out of almost nothing, like soap-bubbles.

> Je crois qu'il n'y a que moi qui face si bien tout le contraire de ce que je veux faire, car il est vrai qu'il n'y a personne que j'honore plus que vous, et j'ai si bien fait qu'il est quasi impossible que vous le puissiez croire. Ce n'estoit pas assez pour vous persuader que je suis indigne de vos bonnes grâces et de votre souvenir que d'avoir manqué fort longtemps à vous écrire; il falloit encore retarder quinze jours à me donner l'honneur de répondre à votre lettre. En vérité, Madame, cela me fait parôître si coupable, que vers tout autre que vous j'aimerois mieux l'etre en effet que d'entreprendre une chose si

[10] The letter to which we allude has this charming little touch;—'Je hais comme la mort que les gens de son age puissent croire que j'ai des galanteries. Il semble qu'on leur parait cent ans des qu'on est plus vielle qu'eux, et ils sont tout propre à s'étonner qu'il y ait encore question des gens' [George Eliot's note.]

difficile qu'est celle de me justifier. Mais je me sens si innocente dans mon âme, et j'ai tant d'estime, de respect et d'affection pour vous, qu'il me semble que vous devez le connôitre à cent lieues de distance d'ici, encore que je ne vous dise pas un mot. C'est ce que me donne le courage de vous écrire à cette heure, mais non pas ce qui m'en a empêché si longtemps. J'ai commencé à faillir par force, ayant eu beaucoup de maux, et depuis je l'ai fait par honte, et je vous avoue que si je n'avois à cette heure la confiance que vous m'avez donnée en me rassurant, et celle que je tire de mes propres sentimens pour vous, je n'oserois jamais entreprendre de vous faire souvenir de moi; mais je m'assure que vous oublierez tout, sur la protestation que je vous fais de ne me laisser plus endurcir en mes fautes et de demeurer inviolablement, Madame, votre, &c.[11]

Was not the woman, who could unite the ease and grace indicated by this letter, with an intellect that men thought worth consulting on matters of reasoning and philosophy, with warm affections, untiring activity for others, no ambition as an authoress, and an insight into *confitures* and *ragoûts*, a rare combination? No wonder that her *salon* at Port-Royal was the favourite resort of such women as Madame de La Fayette, Madame de Montausier, Madame de Longueville, and Madame de Hautefort; and of such men as Pascal, La Rochefoucauld, Nicole, and Domat. The collections of Valant contain papers which show what were the habitual subjects of conversation in this salon. Theology, of course, was a chief topic; but physics and metaphysics had their turn, and still more frequently morals, taken in their widest sense. There were *Conferences on Calvinism*, of which an abstract is preserved. When Rohault invented his glass tubes to serve for the barometrical experiments, in which Pascal had roused a strong interest, the Marquis de Sourdis entertained the society with a paper, entitled *Why Water mounts in a Glass Tube*. Cartesianism was an exciting topic here, as well as everywhere else in France; it had its partisans and opponents; and papers were read, containing *Thoughts on the Opinions of M. Descartes*. These lofty matters were varied by discussions on love and friendship, on the drama, and on most of the things in heaven and earth which the philosophy of that day

[11] A number of minor errors—omitted accents, changes in punctuation, variant spellings, misspellings, and occasional words omitted—have crept into most of George Eliot's longer quotations from the French; whether these are owing to her carelessness in transcribing, to the compositors or to both, is not always clear.

dreamt of. Morals—generalizations on human affections, sentiments, and conduct—seem to have been the favourite theme; and
the aim was to reduce these generalizations to their briefest form of
expression, to give them the epigrammatic turn which made them
portable in the memory. This was the speciality of Madame de
Sablé's circle, and was, probably, due to her own tendency. As the
Hôtel de Rambouillet was the nursery of graceful letter-writing,
and the Luxembourg of 'portraits' and 'characters', so Madame
de Sablé's *salon* fostered that taste for the sententious style, to
which we owe, probably, some of the best *Pensées* of Pascal, and,
certainly, the Maxims of La Rochefoucauld. Madame de Sablé
herself wrote maxims, which were circulated among her friends;
and, after her death, were published by the Abbé d'Ailly. They
have the excellent sense and nobility of feeling which we should
expect in everything of hers; but they have no stamp of genius or
individual character: they are, to the Maxims of La Rochefoucauld, what the vase moulded in dull, heavy clay, is to the vase
which the action of fire has made light, brittle, and transparent.
She also wrote a treatise on Education, which is much praised by
La Rochefoucauld and M. d'Andilly; but which seems no longer
to be found: probably it was not much more elaborate than her so-
called 'Treatise on Friendship', which is but a short string of
maxims. Madame de Sablé's forte was evidently not to write herself, but to stimulate others to write; to show that sympathy and
appreciation which are as genial and encouraging as the morning
sunbeams. She seconded a man's wit with understanding—one of
the best offices which womanly intellect has rendered to the
advancement of culture; and the absence of originality made her
all the more receptive towards the originality of others.

The manuscripts of Pascal show that many of the *Pensées*,
which are commonly supposed to be raw materials for a great work
on religion, were remodelled again and again, in order to bring
them to the highest degree of terseness and finish, which would
hardly have been the case if they had only been part of a quarry
for a greater production. Thoughts which are merely collected as
materials, as stones out of which a building is to be erected, are
not cut into facets, and polished like amethysts or emeralds. Since
Pascal was from the first in the habit of visiting Madame de Sablé
at Port-Royal, with his sister, Madame Périer (who was one of
Madame de Sablé's dearest friends), we may well suppose that he

would throw some of his jewels among the large and small coin of maxims, which were a sort of subscription-money there. Many of them have an epigrammatic piquancy, which was just the thing to charm a circle of vivacious and intelligent women; they seem to come from a La Rochefoucauld, who has been dipped over again in philosophy and wit, and received a new layer. But whether or not Madame de Sablé's influence served to enrich the *Pensées* of Pascal, it is clear that but for her influence the 'Maxims' of La Rochefoucauld would never have existed. Just as in some circles the effort is, who shall make the best puns, (*horribile dictu*!) or the best charades, in the *salon* of Port-Royal the amusement was to fabricate maxims. La Rochefoucauld said, 'L'envie de faire des maximes se gagne comme le rhume.' So far from claiming for himself the initiation of this form of writing, he accuses Jacques Esprit, another *habitué* of Madame de Sablé's *salon*, of having excited in him the taste for maxims, in order to trouble his repose. The said Esprit was an academician, and had been a frequenter of the Hôtel de Rambouillet. He had already published 'Maxims in Verse', and he subsequently produced a book called *La Fausseté des Vertus Humaines*, which seems to consist of Rochefoucauldism become flat with an infusion of sour Calvinism. Nevertheless, La Rochefoucauld seems to have prized him, to have appealed to his judgment, and to have concocted maxims with him, which he afterwards begs him to submit to Madame de Sablé. He sends a little batch of maxims to her himself, and asks for an equivalent in the shape of good eatables: 'Voilà tout ce que j'ai de maximes; mais comme je ne donne rien pour rien, je vous demande un potage aux carottes, un ragoût de mouton,' &c. The taste and the talent enhanced each other; until, at last, La Rochefoucauld began to be conscious of his pre-eminence in the circle of maxim-mongers, and thought of a wider audience. Thus grew up the famous 'Maxims', about which little need be said. Every one is now convinced, or professes to be convinced, that, as to form, they are perfect, and that as to matter, they are at once undeniably true and miserably false; true as applied to that condition of human nature in which the selfish instincts are still dominant, false if taken as a representation of all the elements and possibilities of human nature. We think La Rochefoucauld himself wavered as to their universality, and that this wavering is indicated in the qualified form of some of the maxims; it occasionally struck him

75

that the shadow of virtue must have a substance, but he had never grasped that substance—it had never been present to his consciousness.

It is curious to see La Rochefoucauld's nervous anxiety about presenting himself before the public as an author; far from rushing into print, he stole into it, and felt his way by asking private opinions. Through Madame de Sablé he sent manuscript copies to various persons of taste and talent, both men and women, and many of the written opinions which she received in reply are still in existence. The women generally find the maxims distasteful, but the men write approvingly. These men, however, are for the most part ecclesiastics who decry human nature that they may exalt divine grace. The coincidence between Augustinianism or Calvinism, with its doctrine of human corruption, and the hard cynicism of the maxims, presents itself in quite a piquant form in some of the laudatory opinions on La Rochefoucauld. One writer says: 'On ne pourroit faire une instruction plus propre à un catechumène pour convertir à Dieu son esprit et sa volonté. . . Quand il n'y auroit que cet escrit au monde et l'Evangile je voudrois etre chrétien. L'un m'apprendroit à connoistre mes misères, et l'autre à implorer mon libérateur.' Madame de Maintenon sends word to La Rochefoucauld, after the publication of his work, that the Book of Job and the Maxims are her only reading!

That Madame de Sablé herself had a tolerably just idea of La Rochefoucauld's character, as well as of his maxims, may be gathered not only from the fact that her own maxims are as full of the confidence in human goodness which La Rochefoucauld wants, as they are empty of the style which he possesses, but also from a letter in which she replies to the criticism of Madame de Schomberg. 'The author,' she says, 'derived the maxim on indolence from his own disposition, for never was there so great an indolence as his, and I think that his heart, inert as it is, owes this defect as much to his idleness as his will. It has never permitted him to do the least action for others; and I think that, amidst all his great desires and great hopes, he is sometimes indolent even on his own behalf.' Still she must have felt a hearty interest in the 'Maxims', as in some degree her foster-child, and she must also have had considerable affection for the author, who was lovable enough to those who observed the rule of Helvetius,[12]

[12] An allusion to the hedonistic morality of Helvétius' *De l'esprit* (1758).

and expected nothing from him. She not only assisted him, as we have seen, in getting criticisms, and carrying out the improvements suggested by them, but when the book was actually published, she prepared a notice of it for the only journal then existing—the *Journal des Savants*. This notice was originally a brief statement of the nature of the work, and the opinions which had been formed for and against it, with a moderate eulogy, in conclusion, on its good sense, wit, and insight into human nature. But when she submitted it to La Rochefoucauld he objected to the paragraph which stated the adverse opinion, and requested her to alter it. She, however, was either unable or unwilling to modify her notice, and returned it with the following note:

> Je vous envoie ce que j'ai pu tirer de ma teste pour mettre dans le *Journal des Savants*. J'y ai mis cet endroit qui vous est le plus sensible, afin que cela vous fasse surmonter la mauvaise honte qui vous fit mettre la préface sans y rien retrancher; et je n'ai pas craint de le mettre, parce que je suis assurée que vous ne le ferez pas imprimer, quand même le reste vous plairoit. Je vous assure aussi que je vous serai plus obligée, si vous en usez comme d'une chose qui servit à vous pour le corriger ou pour le jeter au feu. Nous autres grands auteurs, nous sommes trop riches pour craindre de rien perdre de nos productions. Mandez-moi ce qu'il vous semble de ce dictum.

La Rochefoucauld availed himself of this permission, and 'edited' the notice, touching up the style, and leaving out the blame. In this revised form it appeared in the *Journal des Savants*. In some points, we see, the youth of journalism was not without promise of its future.

While Madame de Sablé was thus playing the literary confidante to La Rochefoucauld, and was the soul of a society whose chief interest was the *belles lettres*, she was equally active in graver matters. She was in constant intercourse or correspondence with the devout women of Port-Royal, and of the neighbouring convent of the Carmelites, many of whom had once been the ornaments of the court; and there is a proof that she was conscious of being highly valued by them in the fact that when the Princess Marie-Madeline, of the Carmelites, was dangerously ill, not being able or not daring to visit her, she sent her youthful portrait to be hung up in the sick-room, and received from the same Mère Agnès whose grave admonition we have quoted above, a charming note, describing the pleasure which the picture had given in the infirmary of 'Notre bonne Mère'. She was interesting herself deeply in the translation of the New Testament, which was the work of Sacy, Arnauld, Nicole, Le Maître and the Duc de Luynes conjointly, Sacy having the principal share. We have mentioned that Arnauld asked her opinion on the Discourse prefixed to his *Logic*, and we may conclude from this that he had found her judgment valuable in many other cases. Moreover, the persecution of the Port-Royalists had commenced, and she was uniting with Madame de Longueville in aiding and protecting her pious friends. Moderate in her Jansenism, as in everything else, she held that the famous formulary denouncing the Augustinian doctrine, and declaring it to have been originated by Jansenius, should be signed without reserve, and, as usual, she had faith in conciliatory measures; but her moderation was no excuse for inaction. She was at one time herself threatened with the necessity of abandoning her residence at Port-Royal, and had thought of retiring to a religious house at Auteuil, a village near Paris. She did, in fact, pass some summers there, and she sometimes took refuge with her brother, the Commandeur de Souvré, with Madame de Montausier or Madame de Longueville. The last was much bolder in her partisanship than her friend, and her superior wealth and position enabled her to give the Port-Royalists more efficient aid. Arnauld and Nicole resided five years in her house; it was under her protection that the translation of the New Testament was carried on and completed, and it was chiefly through her efforts that, in 1669, the persecution was brought to an end. Madame de Sablé co-operated with all her talent and interest in the same direction; but here, as elsewhere, her influence was chiefly valuable in what she stimulated others to do, rather than in what she did herself. It was by her that Madame de Longueville was first won to the cause of Port-Royal; and we find this ardent brave woman constantly seeking the advice and sympathy of her more timid and self-indulgent, but sincere and judicious friend.

In 1669, when Madame de Sablé had at length rest from these anxieties, she was at the good old age of seventy, but she lived nine years longer—years, we may suppose, chiefly dedicated to her spiritual concerns. This gradual, calm decay allayed the fear of death which had tormented her more vigorous days; and she died with tranquillity and trust. It is a beautiful trait of these last moments, that she desired not to be buried with her family, or even at Port-Royal, among her saintly and noble companions, but in the cemetery of her parish, like one of the people, without pomp or ceremony.

It is worth while to notice, that with Madame de Sablé, as with some other remarkable Frenchwomen, the part of her life which is richest in interest and results, is that which is looked forward to by most of her sex with melancholy as the period of decline. When between fifty and sixty, she had philosophers, wits, beauties, and saints clustering around her; and one naturally cares to know what was the elixir which gave her this enduring and general attraction. We think it was, in a great degree, that well-balanced development of mental powers which gave her a comprehension of varied intellectual processes, and a tolerance for varied forms of character, which is still rarer in women than in men. Here was one point of distinction between her and Madame de Longueville; and an amusing passage, which Saint-Beuve has disinterred from the writings of the Abbé St. Pierre, so well serves to indicate, by contrast, what we regard as the great charm of Madame de Sablé's mind, that we shall not be wandering from our subject in quoting it.

I one day asked M. Nicole what was the character of Mme de Longueville's intellect; he told me it was very subtle and delicate in the penetration of character, but very small, very feeble; and that her comprehension was extremely narrow in matters of science and reasoning, and on all speculations that did not concern matters of sentiment. For example, he added, I one day said to her that I could wager and demonstrate that there were in Paris, at least two inhabitants who had the same numbers of hairs, although I could not point out who these two men were. She told me, I could never be sure of it until I had counted the hairs of these two men. Here is my demonstration, I said:—I take it for granted that the head which is most amply supplied with hairs has not more than 200,000, and the head which is least so has but one hair. Now, if you suppose that 200,000 heads have each a different number of hairs, it necessarily follows that they have each one of the numbers of hairs which form the series from 1 to 200,000; for if it were supposed that there were two among these 200,000 who had the same number of hairs, I should have gained my wager. Supposing, then, that these 200,000 inhabitants have all a different number of hairs, if I add a single inhabitant who has hairs, and who has not more than 200,000, it necessarily follows that this number of hairs, whatever it may be, will be contained in the series from 1 to 200,000, and consequently will be equal to the number of hairs on one of the previous 200,000 inhabitants. Now as, instead of one inhabitant more than 200,000, there are nearly 800,000 inhabitants in Paris, you see clearly that there must be many heads which have an equal number of hairs, though I have not counted them. Still Mme de Longueville could never comprehend that this equality of hairs could be demonstrated, and always maintained that the only way of proving it was to count them.[13]

Surely, the most ardent admirer of feminine shallowness must have felt some irritation when he found himself arrested by this dead wall of stupidity, and have turned with relief to the larger intelligence of Madame de Sablé, who was not the less graceful, delicate, and feminine, because she could follow a train of reasoning, or interest herself in a question of science. In this combination consisted her pre-eminent charm: she was not a genius, not a heroine, but a woman whom men could more than love—whom they could make their friend, confidante, and counsellor; the sharer, not of their joys and sorrows only, but of their ideas and aims.

Such was Madame de Sablé, whose name is, perhaps, new to some of our readers, so far does it lie from the surface of literature and history. We have seen, too, that she was only one amongst a crowd—one in a firmament of feminine stars which, when once the biographical telescope is turned upon them, appear scarcely less remarkable and interesting. Now, if the reader recollects what was the position and average intellectual character of women in the high society of England during the reigns of James the First and the two Charleses—the period through which Madame de Sablé's career extends—we think he will admit our position as to the early superiority of womanly development in France: and this fact, with its causes, has not merely an historical interest, it has an important bearing on the culture of women in the present day. Women become superior in France by being admitted to a common fund of ideas, to common objects of interest with men; and this must ever be the essential condition at once of true womanly culture and of true social well-being. We have no faith in feminine conversazioni, where ladies are eloquent on Apollo and Mars; though we sympathize with the yearning activity of faculties which, deprived of their proper material, waste themselves in weaving fabrics out

[13] *Portraits de femmes*, Nouvelle Édition (Paris, 1862), pp. 313–314.

of cobwebs. Let the whole field of reality be laid open to woman as well as to man, and then that which is peculiar in her mental modification, instead of being, as it is now, a source of discord and repulsion between the sexes, will be found to be a necessary complement to the truth and beauty of life. Then we shall have that marriage of minds which alone can blend all the hues of thought and feeling in one lovely rainbow of promise for the harvest of human happiness.

5

THREE MONTHS IN WEIMAR

Fraser's Magazine, LI (June, 1855), 699–706

'Three Months in Weimar' is an account worked up from the 'Recollections of Weimar' that George Eliot wrote in her Journal shortly after she and Lewes came to Berlin from Weimar in November, 1854. A comparison of the article with the Journal, part of which is published in Cross, *Life*, I, 333–349, shows that in revising her 'Recollections' for publication George Eliot did little more than rearrange her material and omit the personal references (most of which Cross, too, omitted in his selection from the Journal).

Since the object of the three months she and Lewes spent in Weimar was to gather information for his biography of Goethe, it is not surprising that her impressions of the town are dominated by the idea of its connection with Goethe. The article, though far less intimate than the 'Recollections', allows us to see how thoroughly George Eliot, in this more successful than her Dorothea, joined in the pursuits of her husband. For further evidence of how she and Lewes may have shared their observations the reader should compare George Eliot's article with Lewes's description of Weimar in Book IV, Ch. 1, of *The Life of Goethe*.

'Three Months in Weimar' was begun about a month after George Eliot's return to England on 13 March 1855, and finished, according to her Journal, on 28 April. Together with its companion article, 'Liszt, Wagner, and Weimar', it is the only work she did for *Fraser's*, a magazine traditionally friendly to German subjects, and with which Lewes had a long history of association.

The article has never been reprinted as George Eliot wrote it. When she revised a selection of her essays for reprinting at the end of her life she combined 'Three Months in Weimar' with 'Liszt, Wagner, and Weimar', making one article of two and omitting from the second the account of Liszt and of Wagner and his operas.

*   *   *

т was between three and four o'clock, on a fine morning in August, that, after a ten hours' journey from Frankfort, I awoke at the Weimar station.[1] No tipsiness can be more dead to all appeals than that which comes from fitful draughts of sleep on a railway journey by night. To the disgust of your wakeful companions, you are totally insensible to the existence of your umbrella, and to the fact that your carpet bag is stowed under your seat, or that you have borrowed books and tucked them behind the cushion. 'What's the odds, so long as one can sleep?' is your [*formule de la vie*][2], and it is not until you have begun to shiver on the platform in the early morning air that you become alive to property and its duties, *i.e.*, to the necessity of keeping a fast grip upon it. Such was my condition when I reached the station at Weimar. The ride to the town thoroughly roused me, all the more because the glimpses I caught from the carriage window were in startling contrast with my preconceptions. The lines of houses looked rough and straggling, and were often interrupted by trees peeping out from the gardens behind. At last we stopped before the Erbprinz, an inn of long standing in the heart of the town, and were ushered along heavy-looking in-and-out corridors, such as are found only in German inns, into rooms which overlooked a garden just like one you may see at the back of a farmhouse in many an English village.

A walk in the morning in search of lodgings confirmed the impression that Weimar was more like a market town than the precinct of a court. 'And this is the Athens of the North!' we said. Materially speaking, it is more like Sparta. The blending of rustic and civic life, the indications of a central government in the midst of very primitive-looking objects, has some distant analogy with the condition of old Lacedæmon. The shops are most of them such as you would see in the back streets of an English provincial town, and the commodities on sale are often chalked on the doorposts. A loud rumbling of vehicles may indeed be heard now and then; but the rumbling is loud not because the vehicles are many, but because the springs are few. The inhabitants seemed to us to have more than the usual heaviness of *Germanity*; even their stare was slow, like that of herbivorous quadrupeds. We set out with the

---

[1] Leaving London on 20 July 1854, George Eliot and Lewes travelled by way of Antwerp, Brussels, Cologne, and Frankfort, arriving in Weimar on 2 August, where they remained until 4 November.

[2] 'philosophic formula', 1884.

intention of exploring the town, and at every other turn we came into a street which took us *out* of the town, or else into one that led us back to the market from which we set out. One's first feeling was—how could Goethe live here in this dull, lifeless village? The reproaches cast on him for his worldliness and attachment to court splendour seemed ludicrous enough, and it was inconceivable that the stately Jupiter [*en redingote*]³ so familiar to us all through Rauch's statuette, could have habitually walked along these rude streets and among these slouching mortals. Not a picturesque bit of building was to be seen; there was no quaintness, nothing to remind one of historical associations, nothing but the most arid prosaism.

This was the impression produced by a first morning's walk in Weimar, an impression which very imperfectly represents what Weimar is, but which is worth recording, because it is true as a sort of back view. Our ideas were considerably modified when, in the evening, we found our way to the Belvedere chaussée, a splendid avenue of chestnut trees, two miles in length, reaching from the town to the summer residence of Belvedere; when we saw the Schloss, and discovered the labyrinthine beauties of the park; indeed, every day opened to us fresh charms in this quiet little valley and its environs. To any one who loves Nature in her gentle aspects, who delights in the chequered shade on a summer morning, and in a walk on the corn-clad upland at sunset, within sight of a little town nestled among the trees below, I say—come to Weimar. And if you are weary of English unrest, of that society of 'eels in a jar', where each is trying to get his head above the other, the somewhat stupid [*bien-être*]⁴ of the Weimarians will not be an unwelcome contrast, for a short time at least. If you care nothing about Goethe and Schiller and Herder and Wieland, why, so much the worse for you—you will miss many interesting thoughts and associations; still, Weimar has a charm independent of these great names.

First among all its attractions is the Park, which would be remarkably beautiful even among English parks, and it has one advantage over all these, namely, that it is without a fence. It runs

³ 'in a frock coat', 1884. The allusion is to the statuette of Goethe made in 1828 by Christian Daniel Rauch (1777–1857). George Eliot twice visited Rauch's atelier in Berlin on this trip to Germany (Cross, *Life*, I, 359–361).

⁴ 'well-being', 1884.

up to the houses, and far out into the corn fields and meadows, as
if it had a 'sweet will'[5] of its own, like a river or a lake, and had not
been planned and planted by human will. Through it flows the
Ilm—not a clear stream, it must be confessed, but like all water,
as Novalis says, 'an eye to the landscape'.[5a] Before we came to
Weimar we had had dreams of boating on the Ilm, and we were
not a little amused at the difference between this vision of our own
and the reality. A few water-fowl are the only navigators of the
river, and even they seem to confine themselves to one spot, as if
they were there purely in the interest of the picturesque. The real
extent of the park is small, but the walks are so ingeniously
arranged, and the trees are so luxuriant and various, that it takes
weeks to learn the turnings and windings by heart, so as no longer
to have the sense of novelty. In the warm weather our great
delight was the walk which follows the course of the Ilm, and is
over-arched by tall trees with patches of dark moss on their
trunks, in rich contrast with the transparent green of the delicate
leaves, through which the golden sunlight played, and chequered
the walk before us. On one side of this walk the rocky ground rises
to the height of twenty feet or more, and is clothed with mosses
and rock plants; on the other side there are, every now and then,
openings—breaks in the continuity of shade, which show you a
piece of meadow land, with fine groups of trees; and at every such
opening a seat is placed under the rock, where you may sit and
chat away the sunny hours, or listen to those delicate sounds which
one might fancy came from tiny bells worn on the garment of
Silence to make us aware of her invisible presence. It is along this
walk that you come upon a truncated column with a serpent
wined round it, devouring cakes, placed on the column as
offerings—a bit of rude sculpture in stone. The inscription—
Genio loci—enlightens the learned as to the significance of this
symbol, but the people of Weimar, unedified by classical allusions,
have explained the sculpture by a story which is an excellent
example of a modern myth. Once on a time, say they, a huge serpent infested the park, and evaded all attempts to exterminate him,
until at last a cunning baker made some appetizing cakes which
contained an effectual poison, and placed them in the serpent's

[5] Wordsworth, 'Composed upon Westminster Bridge', 12.
[5a] 'Die Ströme sind die Augen einer Landschaft', *Heinrich von
Ofterdingen*, Part I, Ch. 7.

reach, thus meriting a place with Hercules, Theseus, and other monster-slayers. Weimar, in gratitude, erected this column as a memorial of the baker's feat, and its own deliverance. A little farther on is the Borkenhaus, where Carl August[6] used to play the hermit for days together, and from which he used to telegraph to Goethe in his Gartenhaus. Sometimes we took our shady walk in the *Stern*, the oldest part of the park plantations, on the opposite side of the river, lingering on our way to watch the crystal brook which hurries on, like a foolish young maiden, to wed itself with the muddy Ilm. The Stern (Star), a large circular opening amongst the trees, with walks radiating from it, has been thought of as the place for the projected statues of Goethe and Schiller. In Rauch's model for these statues the poets are draped in togas, Goethe, who was considerably the shorter of the two, resting his hand on Schiller's shoulder; but it has been wisely determined to represent them in their 'habit as they lived',[7] so Rauch's design is rejected. Of classical idealising in portrait sculpture, Weimar has already a sufficient [*exemplar ad evitandum*][8] in the colossal statue of Goethe, executed after Bettina's design, which the readers of the 'Correspondence with a Child' may see engraved as a frontispiece to the second volume.[9] This statue is locked up in an odd structure standing in the park, and looking like a compromise between a church and a summer-house (Weimar does *not* shine in its buildings!) How little real knowledge of Goethe must the mind have that could wish to see him represented as a naked Apollo, with a Psyche at his knee! The execution is as feeble as the sentiment is false; the Apollo-Goethe is a caricature, and the Psyche is simply vulgar. The statue was executed under Bettina's encouragement in the hope that it would be bought by the King of Prussia; but a breach having taken place between her and her royal friend, a purchaser was sought in the Grand Duke of Weimar, who, after transporting it at enormous expense from Italy, wisely shut it up where it is seen only by the curious.

As autumn advanced and the sunshine became precious, we preferred the broad walk on the higher grounds of the park, where the masses of trees are finely disposed, leaving wide spaces of

[6] Carl August, Duke of Weimar (1757–1828), Goethe's patron.
[7] Cf. *Hamlet*, III, iv, 135.   [8] 'warning', 1884.
[9] Elisabeth (Bettina) von Arnim, *Goethe's Correspondence with a Child* (1835). The statue was by Karl Steinhäusser (1813–1879).

eadow which extend on one side to the Belvedere allée with its
venue of chesnut trees, and on the other to the little cliffs which
have already described as forming a wall by the walk along the
m. Exquisitely beautiful were the graceful forms of the plane
ees, thrown in golden relief on a back-ground of dark pines. Here
e used to turn and turn again in the autumn afternoons, at first
right and warm, then sombre with low-lying, purple clouds, and
ill with winds that sent the leaves raining from the branches.
he eye here welcomes, as a contrast, the white façade of a
uilding looking like a small Greek temple, placed on the edge of
ie cliff, and you at once conclude it to be a bit of pure ornament
-a device to set off the landscape; but you presently see a porter
ated near the door of the basement story, beguiling the *ennui* of
is sinecure by a book and a pipe, and you learn with surprise that
iis is another retreat for ducal dignity to unbend and philosophize
. Singularly ill-adapted to such a purpose it seems to beings not
ucal. On the other side of the Ilm the park is bordered by the road
ading to the little village of Ober Weimar, another sunny walk
hich has the special attraction of taking one by Goethe's Garten-
aus, his first residence at Weimar. Inside, this Gartenhaus is a
omely sort of cottage such as many an English nobleman's
ardener lives in; no furniture is left in it, and the family wish to
ell it. Outside, its aspect became to us like that of a dear friend
hose irregular features and rusty clothes have a peculiar charm.
t stands, with its bit of garden and orchard, on a pleasant slope,
onting the west; before it the park stretches one of its meadowy
penings to the trees which fringe the Ilm, and between this
ieadow and the garden hedge lies the said road to Ober Weimar.
. grove of weeping birches sometimes tempted us to turn out of
iis road up to the fields at the top of the slope, on which not only
ie Gartenhaus, but several other modest villas are placed. From
his little height one sees to advantage the plantations of the park
i their autumnal colouring; the town, with its steep-roofed
hurch, and castle clock-tower, painted a gay green; the bushy line
f the Belvedere chaussée, and Belvedere itself peeping on an
minence from its nest of trees. Here, too, was the place for seeing
lovely sunset—such a sunset as September sometimes gives us,
vhen the western horizon is like a rippled sea of gold, sending over
he whole hemisphere golden vapours, which, as they near the east,
re subdued to a deep rose-colour.

The Schloss is rather a stately, ducal-looking building, forming three sides of a quadrangle. Strangers are admitted to see a suite of rooms called the Dichter-Zimmer (Poets' Rooms), dedicated to Goethe, Schiller, and Wieland. The idea of these rooms is really a pretty one: in each of them there is a bust of the poet who is its presiding genius, and the walls of the Schiller and Goethe rooms are covered with frescoes representing scenes from their works. The Wieland room is much smaller than the other two, and serves as an antechamber to them; it is also decorated more sparingly, but the arabesques on the walls are very tastefully designed, and satisfy one better than the ambitious compositions from Goethe and Schiller. A more interesting place to visitors is the library, which occupies a large building not far from the Schloss. The principal Saal, surrounded by a broad gallery, is ornamented with some very excellent busts and some very bad portraits. Of the busts, the most remarkable is that of Gluck, by Houdon—a striking specimen of the *real* in art. The sculptor has given every scar made by the small-pox; he has left the nose as pug and insignificant, and the mouth as common, as Nature made them; but then he has done what, doubtless, Nature also did—[he has made one feel in those coarsely-cut features the presence of the genius *qui divinise la laideur*].[10] A specimen of the opposite style in art is Trippel's bust of Goethe as the young Apollo, also fine in its way. It was taken when Goethe was in Italy; and in the *Italiänische Reise*, mentioning the progress of the bust, he says that he sees little likeness to himself, but is not discontented that he should go forth to the world as such a *hübscher Bursch*—a good-looking fellow.[11] This bust, however, is a frank idealization; when an artist tells us that the ideal of a Greek god divides his attention with his immediate subject, we are warned [to take his representation *cum grano*.][12] But one gets rather irritated with idealization in portrait when, as in Dannecker's bust of Schiller,[13] one has been misled into supposing that Schiller's brow was square and massive, while, in fact, it was receding. We say this partly on the evidence of his

[10] 'he has spread over those coarsely cut features the irradiation of genius', 1884.
[11] Alexander Trippel (1744–1793) did the bust of Goethe in 1787. See the *Italiänische Reise*, 12 September 1787 (*Hamburger Ausgabe*, XI, 397).
[12] Omitted, 1884.
[13] Johann Heinrich von Dannecker (1758–1841); bust of Schiller, 1794

kull, a cast of which is kept in the library, so that we could place
t in juxtaposition with the bust. The story of this skull is curious.
When it was determined to disinter Schiller's remains, that they
might repose in company with those of Carl August and Goethe,
the question of identification was found to be a difficult one, for
his bones were mingled with those of ten insignificant fellow
mortals. When, however, the eleven skulls were placed in juxta-
position, a large number of persons who had known Schiller,
separately and successively fixed upon the same skull as his, and
their evidence was clenched by the discovery that the teeth of this
skull corresponded to the statement of Schiller's servant, that his
master had lost no teeth, except one, which he specified. Accordingly it was decided that this was Schiller's skull, and the comparative anatomist, Loder, was sent for from Jena, to select the bones
which completed the skeleton.[14] The evidence certainly leaves
room for a doubt; but the [*front fuyant*][15] of the skull agrees with
the testimony of persons who knew Schiller, that he had, as Rauch
said to us, a 'miserable forehead';[16] it agrees, also, with a beautiful
miniature of Schiller, taken when he was about twenty. This
miniature is deeply interesting; it shows us a youth whose clearly
cut features, with the mingled fire and melancholy of their
expression, could hardly have been passed with indifference; it has
the *langer gänsehals* (long goose-neck), which he gives to his Karl
Moor;[17] but instead of the black, sparkling eyes, and the gloomy,
overhanging, bushy eyebrows he chose for his robber hero, it has
the fine wavy, auburn locks, and the light-blue eyes, which belong
to our idea of pure German race. We may be satisfied that we
know at least the *form* of Schiller's features, for in this particular
his busts and portraits are in striking accordance; unlike the busts
and portraits of Goethe, which are a proof, if any were wanted,
how inevitably subjective art is, even when it professes to be
purely imitative—how the most active perception gives us rather a
reflex of what we think and feel, than the real sum of objects
before us. The Goethe of Rauch or of Schwanthaler is widely

[14] I tell this story from my recollection of Stahr's account in his *Weimar und Jena*, an account which was confirmed to me by residents in Weimar; but as I have not the book by me, I cannot test the accuracy of my memory. [George Eliot's note.] See Adolf Stahr, *Weimar und Jena*, 2nd ed. (Berlin, 1871), pp. 51–60.
[15] 'receding forehead', 1884.
[16] See Cross, *Life*, I, 340.   [17] *Die Räuber*, IV, ii.

different in form, as well as expression, from the Goethe of Stieler;[18] and Winterberger, the actor, who knew Goethe intimately, told us that to him not one of all the likenesses, sculptured or painted, seemed to have more than a faint resemblance to their original. There is, indeed, one likeness, taken in his old age, and preserved in the library, which is startling from the conviction it produces of close resemblance, and Winterberger admitted it to be the best he had seen. It is a tiny miniature painted on a small cup of Dresden china, and is so wonderfully executed, that a magnifying-glass exhibits the perfection of its texture as if it were a flower or a butterfly's wing. It is more like Stieler's portrait than any other; the massive neck, unbent though withered, rises out of his dressing-gown, and supports majestically a head, from which one might imagine (though, alas! it never is so in reality) that the discipline of seventy years had purged away all meaner elements than those of the sage and the poet—a head which might serve as a type of sublime old age. Amongst the collection of toys and trash, melancholy records of the late Grand Duke's eccentricity, which occupy the upper rooms of the library, there are some precious relics hanging together in a glass case, which almost betray one into sympathy with 'holy coat' worship. They are—Luther's gown, the coat in which Gustavus Adolphus was shot, and Goethe's court coat and schlafrock. What a rush of thoughts from the mingled memories of the passionate reformer, the heroic warrior, and the wise singer!

The only one of its great men to whom Weimar has at present erected a statue in the open air is Herder. His statue, inaugurated in 1850, stands in what is called the Herder Platz, with its back to the church in which he preached; in the right hand is a roll bearing his favourite motto—*Licht, Liebe, Leben* (Light, Love, Life), and on the pedestal is the inscription—*von Deutscher aller* [*lande*][19] (from Germans of all lands). This statue, which is by Schaller of Munich, is very much admired; but, remembering the immortal description in the *Dichtung und Wahrheit*,[20] of Herder's appearance when Goethe saw him for the first time at Strasburg,

---

[18] George Eliot and Lewes saw the statue of Goethe by Ludwig Michael Schwanthaler (1802–1848) in Frankfort (Journal, 1 August 1854). The portrait of Goethe by Josef Stieler (1781–1858), painted in 1828, is reproduced as the frontispiece of Lewes's *Life of Goethe*.

[19] 'Länder', 1884.   [20] Part II, Book X.

was disappointed with the parsonic appearance of the statue, as
well as of the bust in the library. The part of the town which
imprints itself on the memory, next to the Herder Platz, is the
Markt, a cheerful square, made smart by a new Rath-haus. Twice
a week it is crowded with stalls and country people, and it is the
very pretty custom for the band to play in the balcony of the Rath-
haus about twenty minutes every market-day to delight the ears of
the peasantry. A head-dress worn by many of the old women, and
here and there by a young one, is, I think, peculiar to Thuringia.
Let the fair reader imagine half-a-dozen of her broadest French
sashes dyed black, and attached as streamers to the back of a stiff
black skullcap, ornamented in front with a large bow, which stands
out like a pair of donkey's ears; let her further imagine, mingled
with the streamers of ribbon, equally broad pendents of a thick
woollen texture, something like the fringe of an urn-rug, and she
will have an idea of the head-dress in which I have seen a Thuring-
an damsel figure on a hot summer's day. Two houses in the Markt
are pointed out as those from which Tetzel published his indulgences and Luther thundered against them; but it is difficult to
one's imagination to conjure up scenes of theological controversy
in Weimar, where, from princes down to pastry-cooks, rationalism
is taken as a matter of course.

Passing along the Schiller-strasse, a broad, pleasant street, one
is thrilled by the inscription, *Hier wohnte Schiller*, over the door
of a small house with casts in its bow window. Mount up to the
second story and you will see Schiller's study very nearly as it was
when he worked in it. It is a cheerful room with three windows,
two towards the street and one looking on a little garden which
divides his house from the neighbouring one. The writing-table,
which he notes as an important purchase in one of his letters to
Körner, and in one of the drawers of which he used to keep rotten
apples for the sake of their scent, stands near the last-named window, so that its light would fall on his left hand. On another side
of the room is his piano, with his guitar lying upon it, and above
these hangs an ugly print of an Italian scene, which has a [*pendant*][21] equally ugly on another wall. Strange feelings it awakened
in me to run my fingers over the keys of the little piano and call
forth its tones, now so queer and feeble, like those of an invalided
old woman whose voice could once make a heart beat with fond

[21] 'companion', 1884.

passion or soothe its angry pulses into calm. The bedstead on which Schiller died has been removed into the study, from the small bedroom behind, which is now empty. A little table is placed close to the head of the bed with his drinking glass upon it, and on the wall above the bedstead there is a beautiful sketch of him lying dead. He used to occupy the whole of the second floor. It contains, besides the study and bedroom, an ante-chamber, now furnished with casts and prints on sale, in order to remunerate the custodiers of the house, and a *salon* tricked out, since his death, with a symbolical cornice, statues, and a carpet worked by the ladies of Weimar.

Goethe's house is much more important looking, but, to English eyes, far from being the palatial residence which might be expected, from the descriptions of German writers. The entrance hall is indeed rather imposing, with its statues in niches, and its broad staircase, but the rest of the house is not proportionately spacious and elegant. The only part of the house open to the public—and this only on a Friday—is the principal suite of rooms which contain his collection of casts, pictures, cameos, &c. This collection is utterly insignificant, except as having belonged to him, and one turns away from bad pictures and familiar casts, to linger over the manuscript of the wonderful *Römische Elegien*, written by himself in the Italian character. It is to be regretted that a large sum offered for this house by the German Diet, was refused by the Goethe family in the hope, it is said, of obtaining a still larger sum from that mythical English Crœsus always ready to turn fabulous sums into dead capital, who haunts the imagination of continental people. One of the most fitting tributes a nation can pay to its great dead, is to make their habitation, like their works, a public possession, a shrine where affectionate reverence may be more vividly reminded that the being who has bequeathed to us immortal thoughts or immortal deeds, had to endure the daily struggle with the petty details, perhaps with the sordid cares, of this working-day world;[22] and it is a sad pity that Goethe's study, bedroom, and library, so fitted to call up that kind of sympathy, because they are preserved just as he left them, should be shut out from all but the specially privileged. We were happy enough to be amongst these,—to look through the mist of rising tears at the dull study with its two small windows, and without a single object

[22] See 'Silly Novels by Lady Novelists', note 6.

chosen for the sake of luxury or beauty; at the dark little bedroom with the bed on which he died, and the arm-chair where he took his morning coffee as he read; at the library with its common deal shelves, and books containing his own paper marks. In the presence of this hardy simplicity, the contrast suggests itself of the study of Abbotsford, with its elegant gothic fittings, its delicious easy chair, and its oratory of painted glass.[23]

We were very much amused at the privacy with which people keep their shops at Weimar. Some of them have [no kind of *enseigne*][24]—not so much as their names written up; and there is so much [*nonchalance*][25] towards customers, that one might suppose every shopkeeper was a salaried functionary employed by government. The distribution of commodities, too, is carried on according to a peculiar Weimarian logic: we bought our lemons at a [*seiler's*, or][26] ropemaker's, and should not have felt ourselves very unreasonable if we had asked for shoes at a stationer's. As to competition, I should think a clever tradesman or artificer is almost as free from it at Weimar as Æsculapius or Vulcan in the days of old Olympus. Here is an illustration. Our landlady's husband was called the '*süsser* Rabenhorst',[27] by way of distinguishing him from a brother of his who was the reverse of sweet. This Rabenhorst, who was not sweet, but who nevertheless dealt in sweets, for he was a confectioner, was so utter a rogue that any transaction with him was avoided almost as much as if he had been the Evil One himself, yet so clever a rogue that he always managed to keep on the windy side of the law. Nevertheless, he had so many dainties in the confectionery line—*so viel Süssigkeiten und Lecker-bissen*—that people bent on giving a fine entertainment were at last constrained to say, 'After all, I must go to Rabenhorst'; and so he got abundant custom, in spite of general detestation.

A very fair dinner is to be had at several *tables d'hôte* in Weimar for ten or twelve groschen (a shilling or fifteen-pence). The Germans certainly excel us in their *mehlspeise*, or farinaceous puddings, and in their mode of cooking vegetables; they are bolder and more imaginative in their combination of sauces, fruits and

[23] George Eliot visited Abbotsford with the Brays and Sara Hennell in 1845 (*Letters*, I, 200).
[24] Omitted, 1884.
[25] 'indifference of manner', 1884.   [26] Omitted, 1884.
[27] The name of their landlady was Münderloh (Journal).

vegetables with animal food, and they are faithful to at least one principle of dietetics—variety. The only thing at table we have any pretext for being supercilious about is the quality and dressing of animal food. The meat at a *table d'hôte* in Thuringia, and even at Berlin, except in the very first hotels, bears about the same relation to ours as [cat or][28] horse-flesh probably bears to German beef and mutton; and an Englishman with a bandage over his eyes would often be sorely puzzled to guess the kind of flesh he was eating. For example, the only flavour we could ever discern in hare, which is a very frequent dish, was that of the more or less disagreeable fat which predominated in the dressing; and roast meat seems to be considered an extravagance rarely admissible. A melancholy sight is a flock of Weimarian sheep, followed or led by their shepherd. They are as dingy as London sheep, and far more skinny; indeed, an Englishman[29] who dined with us said the sight of the sheep had set him against mutton. Still, the variety of dishes you get for ten groschen is something marvellous to those who have been accustomed to English charges, and among the six courses it is not a great evil to find a dish or two the reverse of appetizing. I suppose, however, that the living at *tables d'hôte* gives one no correct idea of the mode in which the people live at home. The basis of the national food seems to be raw ham and sausage, with a copious superstratum of blaukraut, sauerkraut, and black bread. Sausage (*wurst*) seems to be to the German what potatoes were to the Irish—the *sine quâ non* of bodily sustenance. Goethe asks the Frau von Stein to send him *so eine wurst* when he wants to have a make-shift dinner away from home; and in his letters to Kestner he is enthusiastic about the delights of dining on *blaukraut* and *leberwurst* (blue cabbage and liver sausage). If *kraut* and *wurst* may be called the solid prose of Thuringian diet, fish and *kuchen* (generally a heavy kind of fruit tart) are the poetry: the German appetite disports itself with these as the English appetite does with ices and whipped creams.

At the beginning of August, when we arrived in Weimar, almost every one was away—'at the Baths', of course—except the tradespeople. As birds nidify in the spring, so Germans wash themselves in the summer; their *waschungstrieb* acts strongly only at a particu-

[28] Omitted, 1884.

[29] Probably Lewes's friend Arthur Helps, who spent 29 August with them in Weimar (*Letters*, II, 174).

lar time of the year; during all the rest, apparently, a decanter and a sugar-basin or pie-dish, are an ample toilette service for them. We were quite contented, however, that it was not yet the Weimar 'season', fashionably speaking, since it was the very best time for enjoying something far better than Weimar gaieties—the lovely park and environs. It was pleasant, too, to see the good bovine [*bourgeoisie*][30] enjoying life in their quiet fashion. Unlike our English people, they take pleasure into their calculations, and seem regularly to set aside part of their time for recreation. It is understood that something is to be done in life besides business and housewifery: the women take their children and their knitting to the *Erholung*, or walk with their husbands to Belvedere, or in some other direction, where a cup of coffee is to be had. The *Erholung*, by the way, is a pretty garden, with shady walks, abundant seats, an orchestra, a ball-room, and a place for refreshments. The higher classes are subscribers and visitors here as well as the *bourgeoisie;* but there are several resorts of a similar kind frequented by the latter exclusively. The reader of Goethe will remember his little poem, *Die Lustigen von Weimar*, which still indicates the round of amusements in this simple capital: the walk to Belvedere or Tiefurt; the excursion to Jena, or some other trip, not made expensive by distance; the round game at cards; the dance; the theatre; and so many other enjoyments to be had by a people not bound to give dinner parties and 'keep up a position'.

[Another time I will tell what we saw of these recreations, rural and theatrical; of lovely walks along *chaussées* bordered by plum-trees laden with purple fruit, or by the mountain ash, lifting its bunches of coral against the sky, to country seats where no gate or padlock obstructs your entrance, and no gardener haunts you, expectant of a fee, and to happy-looking villages:

> Each with its little patch of fields
> And little lot of hills;

of excursions to the classic Jena and the romantic Ilmenau; and, for a variety, of Weimar fairs and target-shooting, and Wagner presided over by Liszt.][31]

[30] 'citizens', 1884.   [31] Omitted, 1884.

6

LISZT, WAGNER, AND WEIMAR

Fraser's Magazine, LII (July, 1855), 48–62

'Liszt, Wagner, and Weimar' is the article promised at the end of 'Three Months in Weimar' and like its predecessor is an expansion of George Eliot's Journal 'Recollections of Weimar'. To her personal observations she has added a lengthy discussion of Wagner and a summary of three of his operas, giving the article a special historical interest. Before 1855, Wagner as a composer was almost totally unknown in England. In that year, however, he came at the invitation of the London Philharmonic to conduct a series of eight concerts, from 12 March to 25 June, and included a number of his own works in the concert programmes. Though Victoria and Albert attended the seventh concert, hearing the overture to *Tannhäuser*, Wagner was very roughly handled by the London press, and it was no doubt the sensation stirred up by his appearance before English audiences that prompted George Eliot to add an account of Wagner to the otherwise personal recollections of her German trip.[1]

If not the first, George Eliot's article is certainly one of the earliest friendly comments on Wagner in the English press. Despite her tone of conscientious forbearance, she never came to like Wagner's music. Not until 1870, in Berlin, did she hear any of his operas again, when, after a performance of *Tannhäuser*, Lewes wrote: 'We came to the conclusion that Wagner's music is not for us.'[2]

According to George Eliot's Journal 'Liszt, Wagner, and Weimar' was finished on 9 June 1855, while Wagner was still in England. For its reprinting history, see the headnote to 'Three Months in Weimar'.

*   *   *

[THE Weimar theatre opens about the middle of September. A

---

[1] For this period in Wagner's life, see Ernest Newman, *The Life of Richard Wagner*, II (New York, 1937), Ch. 22. [2] *Letters*, V, 85.

very pretty theatre it is, and all its appointments show that the Grand Duke does not grudge expense for the sake of keeping up its traditional reputation. The opera here, as every one knows, has two special attractions: it is superintended by Liszt; and Wagner's operas, in many places consigned to the *Index Expurgatorius* of managers, are a standing part of the Weimar *répertoire*. Most London concert-goers, for whom Liszt has 'blazed the comet of a season',[3] think of him as certainly the archimagus of pianists, but as otherwise a man of no particular significance; as merely an erratic, flighty, artistic genius, who has swept through Europe, the Napoleon of the *salon*, carrying devastation into the hearts of countesses.[4] A single morning's interview with him is enough to show the falsity of this conception.[5] In him Nature has not sacrificed the man to the artist; rather, as the blossom of the acacia is a glorious ornament to the tree, but we see it fall without regret because the tree itself is grand and beautiful, so if Liszt the pianist were unknown to you, or even did not exist, Liszt the man would win your admiration and love. See him for a few hours and you will be charmed by the originality of his conversation and the brilliancy of his wit; know him for weeks or months, and you will discern in him a man of various thought, of serious purpose, and of a moral nature which, in its mingled strength and gentleness, has the benignest influence on those about him.

The lovers of characteristic heads could hardly have a more interesting study than the head of Liszt. No wonder Ary Scheffer[6]

[3] Byron, 'Churchill's Grave', 1–2.

[4] According to Ernest Newman, *Life of Wagner*, II, 465–466, Liszt in the England of 1855 was known only as 'the Liszt who had mingled so much that was shoddy with the brilliance of his virtuosity as a pianist, and the Liszt whose name stank in the nostrils of thousands of quiet, sober people because it had so often been associated with the escapades of the boudoir and the bedchamber'.

[5] For George Eliot's first impressions of Liszt, see her Journal for 10 August 1854 in *Letters*, II, 169–170. Liszt is usually named as the original of Klesmer in *Daniel Deronda*, but as Gordon S. Haight has observed, 'aside from genius and talent, their characters are not similar'. ('George Eliot's Originals', in *From Jane Austen to Joseph Conrad*, ed. Rathburn and Steinmann [Minneapolis, 1958], p. 193).

[6] Dutch painter (1795–1858): portrait of Liszt, 1838. The picture referred to below is Scheffer's 'Les Rois Mages' (1841); something of the ideal type of Liszt's head may also be seen in Scheffer's 'Christ au Jardin des Oliviers' (1839) and 'L'Annonciation aux Bergers' (1841).

is fond of painting him, and that the type of Liszt's face seems to haunt this artist in so many of his compositions. I never saw features having at once so strong and clear an outline and so rich a gamut of expression; at one moment you think what a capital face he has for a witch in *Macbeth*, with knitted brow and preternatural grey light in his eyes; at another, with head thrown back and nostril dilated, he suggests a prophet in the moment of inspiration: and then again, seated placidly silent amidst a group of gay talkers, he is a perfect model of a St. John. Scheffer has seized something of the second expression in a picture in which he expressly intended to introduce an idealization of Liszt. The picture represents the three Magi, two of whom are venerable bearded sages watching with bent head the third—a young man in the likeness of Liszt— who is gazing in ecstasy at the guiding light above them. In Liszt, of course, there is baser metal mingled with the fine gold; and besides this natural alloy, there is the tarnish contracted in a life spent in the midst of adulation. Even an ordinary man has to pass through so many 'mud baths' before he reaches his fortieth year, and some of the mud will become ingrained in the process. But, take him all in all, he is a glorious creature—one of those men whom the ancients would have imagined the son of a god or goddess, from their superiority to the common clay of humanity.

It seems to be understood that we may write the more freely of our personal admiration for musical and dramatic artists, because their fame does not live after them, except for a few short years in the eulogies of their superannuated contemporaries, who are listened to with an incredulous smile as *laudatores temporis acti*. It is this fact which gives a character of justice to the apparently excessive tribute of adoration paid to a great actor, a great singer, or a great instrumentalist; they have but their 'one crowded hour of glorious life',[7] while the genius who can leave permanent creations behind him knows that he shall live for the next age more emphatically than for his own—an ideal life, if you will, but happily one which is felt to be more real by many a noble soul than the pudding and praise of the present hour. Fame is but another word for the sympathy of mankind with individual genius, and the great poet or the great composer is sure that that sympathy will be given some day, though his Paradise Lost will fetch only five

[7] Scott, verse motto to Ch. 34 of *Old Mortality*.

pounds, and his symphony is received with contemptuous laughter, so he can transport himself from the present and live by anticipation in that future time when he will be thrilling men's minds and ravishing their ears. But the artist whose genius can only act through his physical presence has not this reversionary life; the memory of the *prima donna* scarcely outlives the flowers that are flung at her feet on her farewell night, and even the fame of a Garrick or a Siddons is simply a cold acquiescence in the verdict of the past. It is possible, however, that Liszt will turn out to be something more than one of those coruscating meteors, who come, are seen, and are extinguished in darkness; he is now devoting himself principally to composition, and may perhaps produce something perennial, though the opponents of the Wagner sect, of which Liszt is the great apostle, will not believe that any good can come out of Nazareth.

Liszt, indeed, has devoted himself with the enthusiasm of earnest conviction to the propaganda of Wagnerism: he has not only used his personal influence to get Wagner's operas put on the stage, but he has also founded a musical newspaper (*Neue Zeitschrift für Musik*),[8] which is the organ of the Romantic School in music, and derives its chief value from the contributions of his pen. Much cheap ridicule has been spent on the 'music of the future';[9] a ridicule excused, perhaps, by the more than ordinary share Herr Wagner seems to have of a quality which is common to almost all innovators and heretics, and which their converts baptize as profound conviction, while the adherents of the old faith brand it as arrogance. It might be well, however, if the ridicule were arrested by the consideration that there never was an innovating movement which had not some negative value as a criticism of the prescriptive, if not any positive value as a lasting creation. The attempt at an innovation reveals a want that has not hitherto been met, and if the productions of the innovator are exaggerated symbols of the want, rather than symmetrical creations which have within them the conditions, of permanence—like an Owenite parallelogram,[10] an early poem of Wordsworth's, or

[8] Founded not by Liszt but by Robert Schumann in 1834.

[9] The term, most often used derisively, had been current since the publication of Wagner's *Das Kunstwerk der Zukunft* in 1850.

[10] A communal building in the form of a parallelogram, suggested by Robert Owen in 1817 as a device to remedy pauperism.

an early picture of Overbeck's[11]—still they are protests which it is wiser to accept as strictures than to hiss down as absurdities. Without pretending to be a musical critic, one may be allowed to give an opinion as a person with an ear and a mind susceptible to the direct and indirect influences of music. In this character I may say that, though unable to recognize Herr Wagner's compositions as the ideal of the opera, and though, with a few slight exceptions, not deeply affected by his music on a first hearing, it is difficult to me to understand how any one who finds deficiencies in the opera as it has existed hitherto, can give fair attention to Wagner's theory, and his exemplification of it in his operas, without admitting that he has pointed out the direction in which the lyric drama must develope itself, if it is to be developed at all. Moreover, the musician who writes librettos for himself, which can be read with interest as dramatic poems, must be a man of no ordinary mind and accomplishments, and such a man, even when he errs, errs with ingenuity, so that his mistakes are worth studying.

Wagner would make the opera a perfect musical drama, in which feelings and situations spring out of *character*, as in the highest order of tragedy, and in which no dramatic probability or poetic beauty is sacrificed to musical effect. The drama must not be a mere pretext for the music; but music, drama, and spectacle must be blended, like the coloured rays in the sunbeam, so as to produce one undivided impression. The controversy between him and his critics is the old controversy between Gluck and Piccini,[12] between the declamatory and melodic schools of music, with the same difference in comprehensiveness as between the disputes of La Motte and the Daciers[13] about the value of the classics, and the disputes of the classical and romantic schools of literature in our own day. In its first period the opera aimed simply at the expression of feeling through melody; the second period, which has its

[11] Johann Friedrich Overbeck (1789–1869), founder of the 'Nazarene' or 'Pre-Raphaelite' school of German painters in Rome, devoted to reviving a Christian art. George Eliot and Lewes missed seeing Overbeck's 'picture of Xtianity triumphing over the Arts' in Frankfort, but saw his 'The Marriage of Joseph and Mary' in Berlin (Journal).

[12] Nicola Piccini (1728–1800), Gluck's rival in Paris as composer of operas, representing the 'melodic' against Gluck's 'declamatory' style.

[13] The second (1714–1716) and lesser of the quarrels of the Ancients and Moderns, between Antoine Houdar de la Motte for the Moderns and André and Mme. Dacier for the Ancients.

culmination in the joint productions of Meyerbeer and Scribe, added the search for effective situations and a heightening of dramatic movement, which has led more and more to the predominance of the declamatory style and the subordination of melody. But in Meyerbeer's operas the grand object is to produce a climax of spectacle, situation, and orchestral effects; there is no attempt at the evolution of these from the true workings of human character and human passions; on the contrary, the characters seem to be a second thought, and with a few exceptions, such as Alice and Marcel,[14] are vague and uninteresting. Every opera-goer has remarked that *Robert* is a mere nose of wax; or has laughed at the pathos with which the fiend Bertram invites his son to go to the bottomless pit with him, instead of settling into respectability above ground;[15] or has felt that *Jean, the Prophet*, is a feeble sketch, completely lost in the blaze of spectacle. Yet what a progress is there in the libretto of these operas compared with the libretto of *Der Freischütz*, which, nevertheless, was thought so good in its day that Goethe said Weber ought to divide the merit of success with Kind.[16] Even Weber's enchanting music cannot overcome the sense of absurdity when, in a drinking party of two, one of whom is sunk in melancholy, a man gets up and bursts into a rolling song which seems the very topmost wave in the high tide of bacchanalian lyrism; or when Caspar climbs a tree apparently for no other reason than because the *dénouement* requires him to be shot.[17]

Now, says Wagner,[18] this ascent from the warbling puppets of the early opera to the dramatic effects of Meyerbeer, only serves to bring more clearly into view the unattained summit of the true

[14] From *Robert le Diable* and *Les Huguenots*, respectively.

[15] *Robert le Diable*, Act V.

[16] Johann Peter Eckermann, *Gespräche mit Goethe*, ed. H. H. Houben (Leipzig, 1925), p. 229, under date of Thursday, 9 October 1828. Friedrich Kind was librettist for Weber's *Der Freischütz* (1821). George Eliot heard the opera for the first time in Weimar (Journal).

[17] Act I; Act III, scene ii.

[18] Though Wagner had published extensively by 1854, there is no reason to suppose that George Eliot had consulted his writings for this article. Her discussion of the history of opera is mostly a paraphrase of an article by Liszt in the *Neue Zeitschrift für Musik*, 16 June 1854, that she translated for publication in the *Leader*, where it appeared as one of Lewes's 'Vivian' letters under the title of 'The Romantic School of Music', 28 October 1854.

musical drama. An opera must be no mosaic of melodies stuck together with no other method than is supplied by accidental contrast, no mere succession of ill-prepared crises, but an organic whole, which grows up like a palm, its earliest portion containing the germ and prevision of all the rest. He will write no *part* to suit a *primo tenore*, and interpolate no *cantata* to show off the powers of a *prima donna assoluta*; those who sing his operas must be content with the degree of prominence which falls to them in strict consonance with true dramatic development and ordonnance. Such, so far as I understand it, is Wagner's theory of the opera—surely a theory worth entertaining, and one which he has admirably exemplified so far as the libretto of his operas is concerned.

But it is difficult to see why this theory should entail the exclusion of melody to the degree at which he has arrived in *Lohengrin*,[19] unless we accept one of two suppositions: either that Wagner is deficient in melodic inspiration, or that his inspiration has been overridden by his system, which opposition has pushed to exaggeration. Certainly his *Fliegender Holländer*—a transition work, in which, as Liszt says,[20] he only seeks to escape from the idols to which he has hitherto sacrificed, and has not yet reached the point of making war against them—is a charming opera; and *Tannhäuser* too is still the music of men and women, as well of Wagnerites;[21] but *Lohengrin* to us ordinary mortals seemed something like the whistling of the wind through the keyholes of a cathedral, which has a dreamy charm for a little while, but by and bye you long for the sound even of a street organ to rush in and break the monotony. It may be safely said, that whatever the music of the future may be, it will not be a music which is in contradiction with a permanent element in human nature—the need for a frequent alternation of sensations or emotions; and this need is *not* satisfied in *Lohengrin*.

As to melody—who knows? It is just possible that melody, as we conceive it, is only a transitory phase of music, and that the musicians of the future may read the airs of Mozart and Beethoven

[19] George Eliot and Lewes went to hear *Lohengrin* on 22 October 1854. 'G. however had not patience to sit out more than two acts of Lohengrin, & indeed I too was weary.' (Journal.)

[20] *Neue Zeitschrift für Musik*, XLI (1854), 122.

[21] '. . . we went to hear Tannhäuser. The overture & the first & second acts thrilled me, but the third I felt rather wearisome.' (Journal, 3 October 1854.)

and Rossini as scholars read the *Stabreim* and assonance of early poetry. We are but in 'the morning of the times',[22] and must learn to think of ourselves as tadpoles unprescient of the future frog. Still the tadpole is limited to tadpole pleasures; and so, in our state of development, we are swayed by melody. When, a little while after hearing *Lohengrin*, we happened to come on a party of musicians who were playing exquisitely a quartette of Beethoven's, it was like returning to the pregnant speech of men after a sojourn among glums and gowries.

This is a purely individual impression, produced even in spite of favourable prepossessions derived from hearing the *Fliegender Holländer* and *Tannhäuser*, and only accidentally in agreement with the judgment of anti-Wagner critics, who are certainly in the majority at present. Still, those who are familiar with the history of music during the last forty or fifty years, should be aware that the reception of new music by the majority of musical critics, is not at all a criterion of its ultimate success. A man of high standing, both as a composer and executant, told a friend of mine, that when a symphony of Beethoven's was first played at the Philharmonic, there was a general titter among the musicians in the orchestra, of whom he was one, at the idea of sitting seriously to execute such music! And as a proof that professed musicians are sometimes equally unfortunate in their predictions about music which begins by winning the ear of the public, he candidly avowed that when Rossini's music was first fascinating the world of opera-goers, he had joined in pronouncing it a mere passing fashion, that tickled only by its novelty. Not indeed that the contempt of musicians and the lash of critics is a pledge of future triumph: St. Paul five times received forty stripes save one, but so did many a malefactor; and unsuccessful composers before they take consolation from the pooh-poohing or 'damnation' of good music, must remember how much bad music has had the same fate, from the time when Jean Jacques' oratorio set the teeth of all hearers on edge.[23]

If it were admissible for a person entirely without technical qualifications for judgment, to give an opinion on Wagner as a musician, I should say that his musical inspiration is not sufficiently predominant over his thinking and poetical power, for him to have the highest creative genius in music. So far as music is an art, one

[22] Tennyson, 'The Day Dream, L'Envoi.'
[23] *Confessions*, Part I, Book IV (1732).

would think that the same rule applied to musicians as to other artists. Now, the greatest painters and sculptors have surely not been those who have been inspired through their intellect, who have first thought and then chosen a plastic symbol for their thought; rather, the symbol rushes in on their imagination before their slower reflection has seized any abstract idea embodied in it. Nay, perhaps the artist himself *never* seizes that idea, but his picture or his statue stands there an immortal symbol nevertheless. So the highest degree of musical inspiration must overmaster all other conceptions in the mind of the musical genius; and music will be great and ultimately triumphant over men's ears and souls in proportion as it is less a studied than an involuntary symbol. Of course in composing an oratorio or an opera, there is a prior conception of a theme; but while the composer in whom other mental elements outweigh his musical power will be preoccupied with the idea, the *meaning* he has to convey, the composer who is pre-eminently a musical genius, on the slightest hint of a passion or an action, will have all other modes of conception merged in the creation of music, which is for him the supreme language, the highest order of representation. All this may be wrong, and so may be my conjecture that Wagner is a composer of the reflective kind. We often enough mistake our own negations for a negation out of ourselves, as purblind people are apt to think the sun gives but a feeble light.

Certainly Wagner has admirably fulfilled his own requisition of organic unity in the opera. In his operas there is a gradual unfolding and elaboration of that fundamental contrast of emotions, that collision of forces, which is the germ of the tragedy; just as the leaf of the plant is successively elaborated into branching stem and compact bud and radiant corolla. The artifice, however, of making certain contrasted strains of melody run like coloured threads through the woof of an opera, and also the other dramatic device of using a particular melody or musical phrase as a sort of Ahnung or prognostication of the approach or action of a particular character, are not altogether peculiar to Wagner, though he lays especial stress on them as his own. No one can forget the recurring hymn of Marcel in the *Huguenots*, or the strain of the Anabaptists in the *Prophète*, which is continually contrasted with the joyous song or dance of the rustics. Wagner, however, has carried out these devices much more completely, and, in the *Fliegender Holländer* and *Tannhäuser*, with very impressive effect. With all my inability at present to enjoy his music as I have enjoyed that of Mozart, or Beethoven, or Mendelssohn, these two operas left in me a real desire to hear them again.

Wagner has wisely gone for the themes of his operas to the fresh and abundant source of early German poetry and legend, and the mode in which he expands and works up these themes shows a deep and refined poetic feeling. He was led to choose the story of the *Fliegender Holländer*—familiar to English ears as the 'Flying Dutchman'—by happening to read Heine's beautiful version of the legend on a sea voyage, when a storm occurred and gave vividness to his conception of the doomed mariner's fate. The legend tells how, long, long ago, a Dutch vessel, making for the Cape of Good Hope, was encountered by an obstinate storm; how, when the sailors entreated the captain to put back, he exclaimed, 'Not if I must live on the sea to all eternity!' and how, as a punishment for this blasphemy, he was condemned to wander about the ocean until the last day, and bring destruction to all ships which met him on their way. The angel of mercy, however, announced to him that he should be permitted to go on shore every seven years and marry: if the wife he chose proved untrue to him, she too would become the prey of the Evil One; but if he found a wife who would love him till death, her truth would expiate his guilt, and would open to him the gates of salvation. It is Heine's version of this legend which Wagner has expanded into a beautiful drama.

The first scene represents the rocky coast of Norway. It is night, and the sea is violent. A merchant ship is struggling with the storm, but at length manages to cast anchor. Daland, the captain, comes ashore to reconnoitre, and finds that the storm has thrown him seven miles from the accustomed haven, whither he was returning after a long absence. As the wind begins to be laid, he and his men go to rest, leaving a young pilot as a watch. The pilot tries to keep himself awake by singing a song to the south wind; but presently sleep conquers him so completely that he is undisturbed by the reawakening of the storm, through which glides in doomed safety, accompanied by mournful, mysterious music, the Hollander's black ship, with its red sails and ghastly crew. As the Hollander slowly descends to land, a strain that rises from the orchestra sounds like a sentence of doom, and recurs throughout the opera whenever his terrible fate is immediately operative. Leaning against a rock, the pale man soliloquizes on this new crisis in his destiny. Meanwhile morning breaks and rouses Daland, who, seeing the newly-arrived ship, hails it through the speaking-trumpet; but, to his amazement, receives no answer. Descrying the Hollander, he goes up to him, and asks him whence he comes. Then follows a scene in which the Hollander tells that he is a weary wanderer, and that he carries in his ship treasures from all climes, which he is ready to offer Daland if he will give him a home for a short time beneath his roof. Chests of precious things are brought from the ship; and the cupidity of Daland is so strongly excited, that when the Hollander asks to have his daughter as a wife, he persuades himself, with ready sophistry, that he is consulting his daughter's interest in consenting, and that the Hollander's open-handedness is a sign that he has a good heart. The storm is now allayed, and the ships weigh anchor. Daland's ship leads the way amid the joyous song of the sailors, and after it glides in dread silence the black ship with red sails.

The scene of the second act is a room in Daland's house, where his daughter Senta is sitting in dreamy sadness, gazing at a portrait of the unhappy Hollander which hangs on the wall; while round her a company of sprightly Norwegian maidens, presided over by Senta's nurse, are seated at their wheels, which mark the time of a charming song sung by them in chorus. The nurse becomes uneasy at Senta's rapt silence, and chides her for dwelling continually on this picture. The maidens join in her complaint, and jokingly tell Senta that her lover Eric will be jealous. Senta, disturbed in her reverie, asks the nurse to sing her the ballad about the Dutch captain; and when the nurse refuses, telling her to let the Dutch captain alone, she herself sings the wild and thrilling ballad; and by and bye, her companions, carried away by sympathy, join in the melancholy *refrain*. Exhausted by her emotion, she sinks fainting into her chair, while the maidens involuntarily sing *pianissimo* the conclusion of the ballad, asking where the 'pale man' will find the woman who will save him by her truth. Suddenly Senta rises, and singing in piercing tones, 'I am she!':

> Ich sei's die Dich durch ihre Treu erlöse!
> Mög' Gottes Engel mich Dir zeigen:
> Durch mich sollst Du das Heil erreichen!

she rushes with outstretched arms to the picture. While all are trembling at this outburst, Eric enters, and announces the arrival

f Senta's father, with his ship; the maidens rush out to greet their
overs and relatives, and Senta is left alone with Eric, who tenderly
urges her to ask her father's sanction for their speedy marriage.
Unsatisfied by her answers, he accuses her of dwelling on the
image of the legendary captain, and when these reproaches only
call out stronger evidence of Senta's absorption in this ideal being,
he exclaims that Satan has ensnared her, and that he has been
admonished of this in a dream. Senta sinks into her chair, eager to
hear the dream, but exhausted by her emotions, and during Eric's
narration, seems gradually to enter into a state of *clairvoyance*, in
which the objects he describes as having appeared to him in a
dream are actually present to her inward vision—the approach of
the dark ship, the entrance of her father into their dwelling with
the *pale man*, whom she runs to meet, and who passionately
embraces her. 'And then', continues Eric, 'I saw you flee away on
the sea'. At these words Senta, her cheek pale, and her eyes fixed,
exclaims, 'I must be lost with him!'

> Er sucht mich auf, ich muss ihn sehn,
> Mit ihm muss ich zu grunde gehn!

Eric, horror-struck at what he believes to be madness, rushes
out. Senta turns again towards the portrait with affectionate
gestures, as if it were a living being. While she is sunk in contemplation the door opens, and the *pale man* stands within its
frame like a Vandyck picture. At this sight Senta gives a cry, but
fixes her eye steadily on the apparition, as if gathering up her
resolution to follow it till death. The Hollander returns her gaze
with equal fixedness, and slowly advances into the room. Daland
follows, puzzled at his daughter's astonishment, and asking her
why she does not come to meet him. She embraces her father
without turning away her eyes from the countenance of the
stranger. In reply to her question, Daland tells her that the
stranger possesses immense riches, that he is a banished wanderer,
and hopes to find a new home with them. In a charming *aria* he
exhorts her to receive the stranger well, and at length tells her that
he has promised him her hand. Senta accepts this information with
a melancholy gesture of acquiescence, and will not even turn her
head to look at the casket of jewels which her father shows as a
proof that he has consulted her welfare. At length Daland leaves
them to make acquaintance with each other. They break silence by

speaking apart of their amazement at the sudden realization of a long presentiment. At last the Hollander approaches Senta, and asks her if she will fulfil her father's promise. She replies, without revealing her knowledge of his secret, that whoever he may be, and whatever may be her lot in accepting him, she will obey her father. The unhappy man kneels at her feet, adoring her as a messenger from heaven, and they join in a duet of yearning desire that Senta may be the being who will bring him release. Then, with a movement of pride and generosity, unwilling to allow this self-sacrifice for his sake, the Hollander rises, and pointing out to Senta the sad lot to which she would unite herself in the bloom of youth, seeks to deter her from such an act of devotion. But Senta answers, that she knows woman's sacred duties, and will be true till death.:

> Wohl kenn ich Weibes heil'ge Pflichten,
> Sei d'rum getrost, unsel'ger Mann!
> Lass' über Die das Schicksal richten
> Die seinem Spruche trotzen kann!
> Kenn' ich der Treue Hochgebot:—
> Wem ich sie weih', schenk ich die Eine,
> *Die Treue bis zum Tod!*

Exquisitely beautiful is Senta's declamation of these verses. The Hollander seems to drink hope and new life from her words, and both join in a glorious duet of triumphant love and confidence.

The third act opens with a sailors' festival. The scene is the haven where two ships lie at anchor. Daland's ship is decked with streamers, garlands, and lamps, and the crew are feasting and dancing; the mysterious ship meanwhile remaining in darkness and silence. Presently women come with fresh provisions, and the sailors playfully attempt to get possession of the baskets, but the women will not allow this, wishing to reserve some for the sailors of the rich bridegroom. Seeing none of these among the merry-makers, they go to the edge of the quay and call to the Dutch ship. The deck is empty, and no sign is made in answer. The women repeat their call again and again, the sailors joining in with jeers and laughter, but the same deathlike stillness continuing to reign in the mysterious ship, they begin to be alarmed, and hurry from the quay, trying to drown their terrors in new gaiety. When the women have left the scene, the fun becomes more riotous, and the sailors take up their original joyous song. In the moment when the bacchanalian shout of the refrain *Hussassahe! Johollohe!* is at its

height, there floats on the Dutch ship a bluish flame, the crew
suddenly rise out of the darkness, and, assembled round the masts,
fill the air with a demoniacal chorus. At first Daland's crew are too
much deafened by their own song to perceive this outburst of
satanic harmony—this terrific response to their gay *refrain*; but
by and bye they become aware of it, and ask each other whether
it may not be a delusion of their wine-heated brains, or the work of
evil spirits. To banish their fears, they continue their song,
pitching it higher and higher, but are each time interrupted by the
hellish *Huissa! Johohoe! Johohoe!* till at length they are reduced to
complete silence by a tremendous *fortissimo*. The pale, white-
bearded phantoms continue their unearthly chorus, until the
swelling flood of diabolical song bursts into a torrent of still more
diabolical laughter. The Norwegians cross themselves and rush
from the spot in a panic. The whole scene is wonderfully effective,
and the climax of the hellish chorus and hideous laughter is, I
should think, not surpassed in its kind. In the stillness that
succeeds, Senta appears, already attired in the pretty dress of the
Norwegian bride. She is pursued by the importunities of Eric, who
is visiting her with tender reproaches. The Hollander approaches
and overhears him. In vain Senta tries to end the dialogue; Eric
reminds her of all the tokens of kindness she has given him, tokens
which he has interpreted as promises. Thus the Hollander learns
that Senta has already loved, and thinks that she will perhaps one
day regret the loss of this peaceful love, and repent her self-sacrifice, that she will at last forget her plighted truth, break her
oath, and so fall to perdition. He loves her too well to expose her
to this danger; he hastens to her, takes leave of her, and rushing
towards his ship, calls to his sailors, 'To sea! To sea! for ever! all
is over with thy truth and my salvation!' Senta rushes after him,
holds him by the arm, and reproaches him for so lightly doubting
her truth. Then the Hollander tells her the doom she would incur
by being faithless to him, and that he is determined to renounce
the hope of salvation, so that at all events *she* may be saved. In vain
Senta assures him that she knows him, and the duties she has
sworn to fulfil—that she will save *him*. He tells her she does not
know him, and exclaiming that he is the Flying Hollander:

> Der Fliengender Holländer nennt man mich!

he breaks loose from her, springs on board and pushes off from

land. Senta struggles out of the hands of her friends, whom Eric
has summoned in his alarm, and, springing to the edge of a jutting
rock, calls to the Hollander, to behold that she is true till death,
and throws herself into the sea. In the same moment the Hollander's ship sinks into the waves, and presently the forms of Senta
and her rescued lover are seen hovering above the waters in light
and glory.[24]

In *Tannhäuser* the dramatic situations are more striking than in
the *Fliegender Holländer*; indeed, I never saw an opera which had
a more interesting succession of well-contrasted effects. The libretto is founded on the old German *saga* of the Venusberg and the
knightly minstrel Tannhäuser. On the introduction of Christianity
into Germany, the clergy, finding it impossible to eradicate from
the minds of the people the faith in their old gods, resorted to the
plan of representing them as demons, and transforming the benign
influences formerly attributed to them into malignant ones. Thus
Holda, the genial goddess, whose yearly procession through the
land made the meadows flourish, was thrust down into subterranean caverns, and her appearance above ground was represented as unpropitious. Later, by a not uncommon blending of
names and ideas, Holda was merged into a Germanized conception
of Venus, and she was made the symbol of seductive sensuality.
Her chief dwelling was supposed to be in Thüringia, in the
interior of the Hörselberg, near Eisenach, thence called the
Venusberg. Here she held open court in a fairy palace, surrounded
by her nymphs, naiads, and syrens, whose song was heard in the
distance, and seduced mortals, who were the prey of impure
desires, along unknown paths, to this grotto, where hell lay concealed under ensnaring ravishments, enticing them to everlasting
destruction. Tannhäuser, the knight and minstrel, had, in one of
the contests for the palm in song, won a brilliant victory, and with
it the heart of the Princess Elizabeth of Thüringia. A short time

[24] My recollection of Wagner's three greatest operas has been assisted
by Liszt's charming analysis or rather paraphrase of them—that of the
Fliegender Holländer, contained in five numbers of the *Neue Zeitschrift für
Musik*, and that of *Tannhäuser* and *Lohengrin*, in his little work entitled,
Richard Wagner's Lohengrin und Tannhäuser. [George Eliot's note.] The
references are to Liszt's 'Wagners Fliegender Holländer', *Neue Zeitschrift für Musik*, XLI (1854), 121–125; 133–140; 145–150; 157–165;
169–178; and to the pamphlet first published in French as 'Lohengrin et
Tannhäuser de R. Wagner' (Leipzig, 1851.)

after this he disappears, and no one can explain his absence. It is after the lapse of a year from this disappearance that the opera is supposed to commence. The curtain is drawn up on the interior of the Venusberg, with its nymphs and syrens dancing in rosy twilight, Venus lying on her couch, and Tannhäuser at her feet, with his harp in his hand. He has become weary of hectic sensualism, and tells her that he longs once more for the free air of the field and forest under the blue arch of heaven:

> —Sterblich, ach! bin ich geblieben,
> Un übergross ist mir dein Lieben;
> Wenn stets ein Gott geniessen kann,
> Bin ich dem Wechsel unterthan;
> Nicht Lust allein liegt mir am Herzen,
> *Aus Freuden sehn' ich mich nach schmerzen!*

Venus starts up enraged, and reminds him with bitter sarcasm that he is accursed through his residence with her, and that the world he desires to return to would reject him with horror. Then she attempts to lull his awakened conscience by blandishments; but he breaks loose at once from her threats and her fascinations, by an appeal to the Virgin, on whom his salvation depends. At the mention of this sacred name the whole scene of enchantment vanishes. Instead of the grotto we see the landscape round the Wartburg in the pure air of a spring morning. To the deafening sounds of the preceding scene follows a complete silence of the orchestra, and the soft, dreamy song of a shepherd seated on a neighbouring rock. Before Tannhäuser is awakened to complete consciousness of his deliverance, we hear in the distance the chorus of a band of pilgrims. In the pauses of their song the voice of the shepherd who recommends himself to their prayers forms a fresh contrast. The pilgrims approach, and pause before an image of the Virgin. Tannhäuser on hearing their song throws himself on his knees, and overwhelmed with gratitude for the mercy which has rescued him, repeats the penitent words of the pilgrims. The bells of the neighbouring church call believers to morning prayer, and at the same time the signals of a hunting horn heard, at various distances, heighten the impression of rural peace and sylvan loneliness. Soon after arrives the Landgrave with his hunt, and perceiving a knight who seems to be standing apart from the train of courtiers, approaches him, and recognizes Tannhäuser.

Wolfram von Eschenbach, Tannhäuser's rival in the poetic art, and also in love for the Princess Elizabeth, at last by speaking of her prevails on Tannhäuser to take his old place among the minstrels, whom he had so often conquered, and who nevertheless mourned his absence. The name of Elizabeth is like a sunbeam to Tannhäuser, and he breaks into a song of joy, ending 'To her! To her!' As soon as his voice unites with the others, the septett commences a joyous allegro, the finale of which, interrupted by the sound of the hunting horn, forms the close of the first act.

The second act opens with the meeting between Elizabeth and Tannhäuser, generously brought about by Wolfram, and we have a duet of happy greeting. Elizabeth is dressed for the festival, which is about to commence—the contest of minstrels. During the entrance of the Landgrave and his guests, a fine march is played by the orchestra. A second march in another key accompanies the entrance of the minstrels. As soon as the guests have ranged themselves and the minstrels have entered, there is a deep silence. Wolfram rises first, his name having been drawn from the urn by Elizabeth. Like all the other minstrels he carries his harp in his hand, and the songs are all accompanied by this instrument in the orchestra. He sings in praise of spiritual love. Tannhäuser replies, intimating that true love demands something more than mere contemplation. Walther von der Vogelweide then rises, and admonishes Tannhäuser that his idea of love is too sensuous. Tannhäuser starts up, and sings again in ardent vindication of his former strain—that distant worship belongs to the stars, and other incomprehensible glories, but that which is near to us, and of like nature with us, is to be the object of tender love:

> Dem ziemt Genuss in freud'gem Triebe,
> Und im Genuss nur kenn' ich Liebe.

He is interrupted by Biterolf, who impetuously and scornfully challenges Tannhäuser to a strife of weapons instead of song. Biterolf, like the other opponents of Tannhäuser, is encouraged with loud signs of applause, and Tannhäuser, provoked, answers him with scornful bitterness. Immediately there is a tumult and a clashing of swords. Wolfram tries to restore peace, and sings with new enthusiasm in honour of pure, exalted love. Tannhäuser, beside himself with indignation at the scorn and bitterness of which he is the object, scarcely hears Wolfram, and bursts into a song in praise of Venus, declaring that he alone knows what love is who has been in the Venusberg:

> Armsel'ge, die ihr Liebe nie genossen,
> Zieht hin, zieht in der Berg der Venus ein!

A cry of horror arises at the mention of this unhallowed name. The noble ladies, shocked at this insult to their delicacy, flee from the hall; the men draw their swords and fall on the bold sinner, whose long absence is now explained. But Elizabeth, who on this fearful avowal is at first completely overwhelmed, suddenly throws herself as a shield before her lover. All are amazed that she can defend one who has so betrayed her, but she exclaims, 'What of me! But he—his salvation! Will you rob him of eternal salvation?' Overcome by her noble devotion, all retire, and Tannhäuser, melted into penitence and hope by this sublime love, rushes to unite himself with the pilgrims to Rome, whose chant is now heard without, there to seek forgiveness for his dreadful sin.

The third act opens with the return of pilgrims, whose procession winds through the same valley, near the Wartburg, where the Landgrave found Tannhäuser. Elizabeth, who has been awaiting his return through long days and nights of prayer and weeping, is wandering through this valley in the evening. A thrilling moment in the drama is that when Elizabeth scrutinizes the faces of all the pilgrims as they kneel before the image of the Virgin, in the hope of finding her lover among them. He is not there. As the pilgrims pass on, she sinks down before the image, and pours forth the anguish of her heart in a prayer for her lover. When she rises to return to the castle, Wolfram, who has approached in the interval, offers to accompany her, but in vain. Meanwhile the evening deepens, and in the gloom of twilight Tannhäuser, transformed from the brilliant knight and minstrel into a withered and ragged pilgrim, returns in solitude. Wolfram with difficulty recognizes him, and eagerly questions him concerning his fate, on which hangs the peace of Elizabeth. Tannhäuser only answers ironically, inquiring the way to the Venus Grotto. Struck with horror, Wolfram nevertheless will not give up the man who is beloved by Elizabeth; he continues his questions, and Tannhäuser at length gives him a description of his pilgrimage —how, full of penitence and thirsting for reconciliation, he had inflicted every possible penance on himself on his way to Rome;

how, on the confession of his sin, the bishop had denied him
absolution, declaring that the man who had been in the Venusberg
could no more win pardon than the pastoral staff in his hand could
bud with fresh green; and how, hopeless on earth and in heaven,
he was now returning to the goddess who had predicted to him
this rejection. (According to the legend, the bishop, after Tannhäuser had departed, found his pastoral staff had actually budded,
as a reproof to his inexorable severity.) Tannhäuser now rises to
take his way to the Venusberg, and the voices of the syrens are
heard singing their old strain of enticement. Wolfram holds him
back with all his force, but can only succeed in neutralizing the
unholy charm by uttering the name of Elizabeth. Once more this
name exercises its saving power. Immediately the seductive
melodies are silenced, and Tannhäuser repeats the beloved name
with the same rapture and hope as ever. At this moment a funeral
procession approaches, bearing Elizabeth to the grave. He falls
down beside the corpse, and exclaiming, 'Holy Elizabeth, pray for
me!' dies. As soon as the long procession, led by the Landgrave,
has filled the scene, the sun rises over the valley, and in the same
moment all break into a chorus, 'Alleluja! he is saved!'—joined in
by a band of pilgrims who have just come from Rome, bringing
news of the salvation which has been announced to the inexorable
bishop by the budding of his staff.

The theme of *Lohengrin*, which I must only allow myself to
sketch very rapidly, is taken from the romantic poetry of the
middle ages. To understand it we must know the legend of the
Holy Graal. This was a dish made of a precious stone which fell
from the crown of Lucifer on his expulsion from heaven. In this
dish the Saviour blessed the bread and wine at the Last Supper,
and Joseph of Arimathea received the blood that streamed from
the wounded side of Jesus on the cross. Joseph of Arimathea
brought the Holy Graal to the West, where it at length came under
the charge of King Arthur and the Knights of the Round Table.
A glorious temple was built for it on Mont Salvage, a mountain in
Biscay, encircled with a forest of cedars and cypresses. Here it was
served by loyal and brave knights, chosen by the Holy Graal
itself, which, like the high priest's breastplate, had a mode of
giving revelations. One of the bravest and most devout of these
knights was Lohengrin, and the pathetic story of his championship
and love for Elsa of Brabant forms the theme of the opera.

The scene of the first act is on the shores of the Scheldt. Henry the Fowler, the German King, has come into Brabant to summon its nobles to aid him, their feudal lord, in his war against the Hungarians. Frederic of Telramund, a rejected lover of Elsa or Alice, who by her brother's mysterious death has become Duchess of Brabant, seizes this occasion, under the instigation of his wife Ortruda, who is a sorceress, to accuse Elsa of her brother's murder. The truth is, that Ortruda herself has by her sorceries changed the brother into a swan, and that by this accusation of Elsa she means to clear the way for her own hereditary pretensions to the duchy. When Elsa denies the charge, Henry the Fowler decrees that an appeal shall be made to heaven by single combat, if Elsa can find a champion. She declares that she has seen a knight in a vision, who will come and defend her, and on the double summons of the trumpet, a boat is seen approaching along the Scheldt, drawn by a swan. From it lands a knight in silver armour, with a golden horn at his side, as seen by Elsa in her vision; while the swan sails slowly away again. Elsa recognises the knight with rapture, and in reply to his wish, promises to be his for ever, when he has cleared her fame. Telramund is overthrown in the combat, and the act ends with the raising of Lohengrin and Elsa on shields, in sign that they are accepted rulers.

The second act opens in the town of Antwerp. It is night, and Frederic of Telramund, and his wife Ortruda, now sunk in disgrace and condemned to banishment, are seated on the steps of the cathedral, opposite the palace, which is lighted up. Ortruda, with stinging sarcasms, reproaches Frederic for his deep debasement, informs him that if the stranger knight is required to tell his name, and whence he comes, his power will be at an end, and suggests to him to betray Elsa into making this demand. At length, Elsa appears in the balcony, Frederic retires, and Ortruda, by her feigned penitence, induces Elsa to take her into the palace, so that in the morning she presents herself in the marriage-train. Her insinuations to Elsa, and the public accusation of Frederic that Lohengrin has won the combat by foul magic, which will be evident if he be required to disclose his name and origin, though repelled for the moment, prepare the way for the tragic *dénoue-ment*. The act closes with the entrance of the marriage procession into the cathedral.

The third act is divided into two parts. In the first part we have an exquisitely pathetic scene between Lohengrin and Elsa in their bridal chamber. The doubts with which Frederic and Ortruda have poisoned her mind, are heightened when Lohengrin tells her that he has come from a glorious and happy lot, for which her love only is a full compensation. She dreads that he will yearn for that lot again—that he will one day forsake her, and in spite of his assurance that her doubt alone can separate them, she is led on to utter the fatal demand that he should tell her his name and whence he comes. The words Lohengrin has dreaded have scarcely passed her lips, when she sees Telramund and four other nobles, lurking with drawn swords near the door. Uttering a cry of terror, she calls to Lohengrin to seize his sword, and in a moment he is fallen on by Frederic, whom, however, he lays dead at his feet, to the dismay of the other nobles, who fall on their knees before him. Lohengrin tells them to carry the corpse before the king's judgment-seat, and with tender sadness summons Elsa to robe herself, that she too may appear in the king's presence, where he will reveal to her his name and origin. Then follows the second part of the act, which takes place on the banks of the Scheldt. Here Lohengrin declares, before the assembled court, that he is a knight of the Holy Graal, and that it is one of the laws of their society, that in whatever deed of virtuous valour a knight engages, he shall be triumphant so long as his office remains concealed, but the secret once betrayed, he must flee from the eyes of the uninitiated, and return to the temple on Mont Salvage. Complaining tones had been wafted to the Graal, revealing that a maiden was in distress, and while the knights were preparing to inquire of the sacred vessel whither one of them should be sent to relieve this distress, a swan came, leading a boat on the waters. Parcival, Lohengrin's father, knew this swan, that it was under an enchantment, and in obedience to a command of the sacred vessel, took it into the service of the Graal, that service being, after the lapse of a year, a means of dissolving every evil charm. Lohengrin was chosen as the champion of the distressed maiden, and committing himself to the guidance of the swan, was brought, as had been seen, to the shores of Brabant. But now, his bride having been seduced by guile to demand the betrayal of his name and office, he must part from her for ever. While Elsa and the rest are entreating him to stay, the swan is seen approaching once more along the Scheldt. Lohengrin turns to Elsa, and giving her his horn, his sword, and his ring, which she is to present to her brother when he shall return, released from enchantment by the power of the Holy Graal, he embraces her, and says a sad, lingering farewell:

Leb wohl! leb wohl! leb wohl, mein süsses Weib!
Leb wohl! mir zürnt der Graal wenn ich noch bleib!

He has reached the shore, and is ready to step into the boat, when, hearing the scornful voice of Ortruda rejoicing that he is going without restoring Elsa's brother, he kneels down in silent prayer. Suddenly a white dove descends on his neck; he rises joyfully, and loosens the chain that holds the swan, which instantly sinks into the water, and in its place appears the youth Gottfried, Elsa's brother. Lohengrin springs into the boat, which is now guided by the dove instead of the swan, and glides away. Elsa casts one last look of joy on her brother, then turns to the water, exclaiming, 'My husband! my husband!'—sees that Lohengrin is already in the distance, and uttering a cry of anguish, sinks lifeless into the arms of her brother. At this moment the curtain falls.

Of these three operas, we heard the *Fliegender Holländer* to the greatest advantage, from the fact that the principal man's part, being a baritone, was filled by an excellent artist—Herr Milde.[25] His wife sang admirably, as the heroine in each of the operas; but *Tannhäuser* and *Lohengrin* absolutely demand a tenor with a voice, and the first tenor at Weimar had only 'intentions.'][26]

It is charming to see how real an amusement the theatre is to the Weimar people. The greater number of places are occupied by subscribers, and there is no fuss about toilette or escort. The ladies come alone, and slip quietly into their places without need of 'protection'—a proof of civilization perhaps more than equivalent to our preeminence in patent locks and carriage springs—and after the performance is over, you may see the same ladies following their servants, with lanterns, through streets innocent of gas, in which an oil lamp, suspended from a rope slung across from house to house, occasionally reveals to you the shafts of a cart or omnibus, conveniently placed for you to run upon them.

A yearly autumn festival at Weimar is the *Vogelschiessen*, or

[25] Hans Feodor von Milde (1821–1899), brought to Weimar by Liszt; created the role of Telramund in *Lohengrin*.
[26] The whole of the article to this point omitted, 1884.

Bird-shooting; but the reader must not let his imagination wander
at this word into fields and brakes. The bird here concerned is of
wood, and the shooters, instead of wandering over breezy down
and common, are shut up, day after day, in a room clouded with
tobacco smoke, that they may take their turn at shooting with the
rifle from the window of a closet about the size of a sentinel's box.
However, this is a mighty enjoyment to the Thüringian yeomanry
and an occasion of profit to our friend Punch, and other itinerant
performers; for while the *Vogelschiessen* lasts, a sort of fair is held
in the field where the marksmen assemble.

Among the quieter every-day pleasures of the Weimarians,
perhaps the most delightful is a stroll on a bright afternoon or
evening to Belvedere, one of the Duke's summer residences, about
two miles from Weimar. [A glorious][27] avenue of chestnut trees
leads all the way from the town to the entrance of the grounds,
which are open to all the world as much as to the Duke himself.
Close to the palace and its subsidiary buildings there is an inn,
for the accommodation of the good people who come to take
dinner, or any other meal here, by way of holiday making. A sort
of pavilion stands on a spot commanding a lovely view of Weimar
and its valley, and here the Weimarians constantly come on
summer and autumn evenings to smoke a cigar, or drink a cup of
coffee. In one wing of the little palace, which is made smart by
wooden cupolas, with gilt pinnacles, there is a saloon, which I
recommend to the imitation of tasteful people in their country
houses. It has no decoration but that of natural foliage: ivy is
trained at regular intervals up the pure white walls, and all round
the edge of the ceiling, so as to form pilasters and a cornice; ivy
again, trained on trellis-work, forms a blind to the window, which
looks towards the entrance-court; and beautiful ferns, arranged in
tall baskets, are placed here and there against the walls. The
furniture is of light cane-work. Another pretty thing here is the
Natur-Theater—a theatre constructed with living trees, trimmed
into walls and side scenes. We pleased ourselves for a little while
with thinking that this was one of the places where Goethe acted
in his own dramas, but we afterwards learned that it was not made
until his acting days were over. The inexhaustible charm of
Belvedere, however, is the grounds, which are laid out with a
taste worthy of a first-rate landscape gardener. The tall and grace-

[27] 'As I have said, a glorious . . .', 1884.

ul limes, plane trees, and weeping birches, the little basins of water here and there, with fountains playing in the middle of them, and with a fringe of broad-leaved plants, or other tasteful bordering round them, the gradual descent towards the river, and the hill clothed with firs and pines on the opposite side, forming a fine dark background for the various and light foliage of the trees that ornament the gardens—all this we went again and again to enjoy, from the time when everything was of a vivid green until the Virginian creepers which festooned the silver stems of the birches were bright scarlet, and the touch of autumn had turned all the green to gold. One of the spots to linger in is at a semicircular seat against an artificial rock, on which are placed large glass globes of different colours. It is wonderful to see with what minute perfection the scenery around is painted in these globes. Each is like a pre-Rafaelite picture, with every little detail of gravelly walk, mossy bank, and delicately-leaved, interlacing boughs, presented in accurate miniature.

In the opposite direction to Belvedere lies Tiefurt, with its small park and tiny chateau, formerly the residence of the Duchess Amalia, the mother of Carl August, and the friend and patroness of Wieland, but now apparently serving as little else than a receptacle for the late Duke Carl Friederich's rather childish collections. In the second story there is a suite of rooms, so small that the largest of them does not take up as much space as a good dining table, and each of these doll-house rooms is crowded with prints, old china, and all sorts of knick-knacks and rococo wares. The park is a little paradise. The Ilm is seen here to the best advantage: it is clearer than at Weimar, and winds about gracefully between the banks, on one side steep, and curtained with turf and shrubs, or fine trees. It was here, at a point where the bank forms a promontory into the river, that Goethe and his court friends got up the performance of an operetta—*Die Fischerin*, by torchlight.[28] On the way to Tiefurt lies the Webicht, a beautiful wood, through which run excellent carriage roads and grassy footpaths. It was a rich enjoyment to skirt this wood along the Jena road, and see the sky arching grandly down over the open fields on the other side of us, the evening red flushing the west over the town, and the stars coming out as if to relieve the sun in its watch; or to take the winding road through the wood, under its tall overarching trees,

[28] Described in Lewes's *Life of Goethe*, Book IV, Ch. 5.

now bending their mossy trunks forward, now standing with the
stately erectness of lofty pillars; or to saunter along the grassy
footpaths where the sunlight streamed through the fairy-like
foliage of the silvery barked birches.

Stout pedestrians who go to Weimar will do well to make a
walking excursion, as we did, to Ettersburg, a more distant summer
residence of the Grand Duke, interesting to us beforehand as the
scene of private theatricals and *sprees* in the Goethe days. We set
out on one of the brightest and hottest mornings that August ever
bestowed, and it required some resolution to trudge along the
shadeless *chaussée*, which formed the first two or three miles of our
way. One compensating pleasure was the sight of the beautiful
mountain ash trees in full berry, which, alternately with cherry
trees, border the road for a considerable distance. At last we rested
from our broiling walk on the borders of a glorious pine wood, so
extensive that the trees in the distance form a complete wall with
their trunks, and so give one a twilight very welcome on a summer's
noon. Under these pines you tread on a carpet of the softest moss,
so that you hear no sound of a footstep, and all is as solemn and
still as in the crypt of a cathedral. Presently we passed out of the
pine wood into one of limes, beeches, and other trees of transparent and light foliage, and from this again we emerged into the
open space of the Ettersburg Park in front of the *Schloss*, which is
finely placed on an eminence commanding a magnificent view of
the far-reaching woods. Prince Pückler Muskau[29] has been of
service here by recommending openings to be made in the woods,
in the taste of the English parks. The Schloss, which is a favourite
residence of the Grand Duke, is a house of very moderate size, and
no pretension of any kind. Its stuccoed walls, and doors long
unacquainted with fresh paint, would look distressingly shabby to
the owner of a villa at Richmond or Twickenham; but much beauty
is procured here at slight expense, by the tasteful disposition of
creepers on the balustrades, and pretty vases full of plants ranged
along the steps, or suspended in the little piazza beneath them. A

---

[29] Hermann Ludwig Heinrich von Pückler-Muskau (1785–1871), whose
Briefe eines Verstorbenen were translated in 1832 as a *Tour in England,
Ireland, and France, in the Years 1826, 1827, and 1829.* . . . Pückler-
Muskau, who is supposed to have been in part Dickens' model for Count
Smorltork, *Pickwick Papers*, Ch. 15, was at one time attached to the court
at Weimar.

walk through a beech wood took us to the Mooshütte, in front of which stands the famous beech from whence Goethe denounced Jacobi's *Woldemar*.[30] The bark is covered with initials cut by him and his friends.

People who only allow themselves to be idle under the pretext of hydropathizing, may find all the apparatus necessary to satisfy their conscience at Bercka, a village seated in a lovely valley about six miles from Weimar. Now and then a Weimar family takes lodgings here for the summer, retiring from the quiet of the capital to the deeper quiet of Bercka; but generally the place seems not much frequented. It would be difficult to imagine a more peace-inspiring scene than this little valley. The hanging woods— the soft colouring and graceful outline of the uplands—the village, with its roofs and spire of a reddish violet hue, muffled in luxuriant trees—the white *Kurhaus* glittering on a grassy slope—the avenue of poplars contrasting its pretty primness with the wild bushy out-line of the wood-covered hill, which rises abruptly from the smooth, green meadows—the clear winding stream, now sparkling in the sun, now hiding itself under soft grey willows—all this makes an enchanting picture. The walk to Bercka and back was a favourite expedition with us and a few Weimar friends, for the road thither is a pleasant one, leading at first through open cultivated fields, dotted here and there with villages, and then through wooded hills—the outskirts of the Thüringian Forest. We used not to despise the fine plums which hung in tempting abundance by the roadside; but we afterwards found that we had been deceived in supposing ourselves free to pluck them, as if it were the golden age, and that we were liable to a penalty of ten groschen for our depredations.

But I must not allow myself to be exhaustive on pleasures which seem monotonous when told, though in enjoying them one is as far from wishing them to be more various as from wishing for any change in the sweet sameness of successive summer days. I will only advise the reader who has yet to make excursions in Thüringia to visit Jena, less for its traditions than for its fine scenery, which makes it, as Goethe says, [*ein allerliebster ort—*][31] a delicious place,

---

[30] Goethe 'denounced' Friedrich Heinrich Jacobi's *Woldemar* (1779), a novel in the style of *Werther*, by nailing it to a beech tree in the park at Ettersburg.

[31] Omitted, 1884.

in spite of its dull, ugly streets; and exhort him, above all, to brave
the discomforts of a postwagen for the sake of getting to Ilmenau.
Here he will find the grandest pineclad hills, with endless walks
under their solemn shades; beech woods where every tree is a
picture; an air that he will breathe with as conscious a pleasure as
if he were taking iced water on a hot day; baths *ad libitum*, with a
douche lofty and tremendous enough to invigorate the giant
Cormoran;[32] and, more than all, one of the most interesting relics
of Goethe, who had a great love for Ilmenau. This is the small
wooden house, on the height called the Kickelhahn, where he often
lived in his long retirements here, and where you may see written
by his own hand, near the windowframe, those wonderful lines—
perhaps the finest expression yet given to the sense of resignation
inspired by the sublime calm of Nature:

> Ueber allen Gipfeln
> Ist Ruh,
> In allen Wipfeln
> Spürest du
> Kaum einen Hauch;
> Die Vögelein schweigen im Walde.
> Warte nur, balde
> Ruhest du auch.

[32] In 'Jack the Giant Killer'.

7

[WESTWARD HO! AND CONSTANCE HERBERT]

Westminster Review, LXIV (July, 1855), 288–296

Charles Kingsley's *Westward Ho!* (1855) was reviewed twice by George Eliot. The first review, finished on 9 May 1855 according to her Journal, appeared in the *Leader*, 19 May 1855, pp. 474–475. Half of it consists of extracts from the novel, and in her own comment George Eliot is nicely balanced between praise and disapproval. She concludes that:

> the preacher overcomes the painter often, which, though creditable to the writer's earnestness and honesty, injures his work as a mere work of art. It is as if a painter in colour were to write 'Oh, you villain!' under his Jesuits or murderers; or to have a strip flowing from a hero's mouth, with 'Imitate me, my man!' on it. No doubt the villain is to be hated, and the hero loved; but we ought to see that sufficiently in the figures of them. We don't want a man with a wand, going about the gallery and haranguing us. Art is art, and tells its own story. We do not think *Westward Ho!* equal, for instance, to Thackeray's *Esmond*, where the illusion of living in a past age is so delightfully kept up. This is our only literary objection to the book; it by no means prevents our most fully recognising the manly earnestness, the glowing vivacity, the hearty humanity, the glorious bits of vivid painting.

The second review of the book opens the first of the seven 'Belles Lettres' sections George Eliot contributed to the *Westminster* between July, 1855 and January, 1857, and appears to have been written in place of a separate article she thought of writing on Kingsley.[1] In general, her judgment of the novel in the two reviews is much the same,

---

[1] *Letters*, II, 198.

but in the *Westminster* she develops in detail and at length the objections only summarized in the *Leader*, producing a much more hostile tone and emphasis than she had at first allowed herself.

Kingsley himself was typically less moderate about George Eliot than she about him. Writing in 1857 to Frederick Denison Maurice, who had been unfavourably reviewed in the *Westminster*, Kingsley said:

> I do hope you will not bother your soul about what the Westminster says. The woman who used to insult you therein[2]—& who I suppose does so now—is none other than Miss Evans, the infidel esprit forte, who is now G. H. Lewes's concubine—I met him yesterday, & lucky for me that I had not had your letter when I did so; or I certainly should have given him (he probably being the co-sinner for he pretends to know all about the philosophers, & don't) a queer piece of my mind to carry home to his lady. Let them be.[3]

When *Adam Bede* appeared, Kingsley was one of the seven people to whom George Eliot had copies of the novel sent,[4] but it does not appear whether he ever connected George Eliot with Miss Evans, or what response he made to the gift. He did not receive any more such presentations from George Eliot, and her last comment on him is harsh. When she read Newman's *Apologia* in 1864 she told Sara Hennell that 'I have been made so indignant by Kingsley's mixture of arrogance, coarse impertinence and unscrupulousness with real intellectual *in*competence, that my first interest in Newman's answer arose from a wish to see what I consider thoroughly vicious writing thoroughly castigated.'[5]

The review of Geraldine Jewsbury's *Constance Herbert* (1855), which follows that of *Westward Ho!* in the *Westminster*, may be usefully compared with the analysis of renunciation in *The Mill on the Floss*, Book IV, Ch. 3 and Book V, Ch. 3. The theme is a favourite one in George Eliot's work—it is fundamental to *The Spanish Gypsy* and

---

[2] George Eliot perhaps wrote the review of Maurice's *The Old Testament* in the *Westminster*, LVII (January, 1852), 282–283, and it may be that Kingsley is referring to that notice. More likely, Kingsley simply means that George Eliot, as editor of the *Westminster*, was responsible for its reviews. Books by Maurice were also reviewed in the *Westminster* in April, 1853; October, 1854; January, 1855; and January, 1857. None of these reviews, so far as is known, is George Eliot's.

[3] Robert Bernard Martin, *The Dust of Combat: A Life of Charles Kingsley* (London, 1959), p. 181.

[4] *Letters*, III, 6.

[5] *Letters*, IV, 158–159.

Daniel Deronda—and justifies G. M. Young's description of her as 'the moralist of the Victorian revolution' with its 'Evangelical faith in duty and renunciation'.[6]

* * *

EVERY one who was so happy as to go mushrooming in his early days, remembers his delight when, after picking up and throwing away heaps of dubious fungi, dear to naturalists but abhorred of cooks, he pounces on an unmistakeable mushroom, with its delicate fragrance and pink lining tempting him to devour it there and then, to the prejudice of the promised dish for breakfast. We speak in parables, after the fashion of the wise, amongst whom Reviewers are always to be reckoned. The plentiful dubious fungi are the ordinary quarter's crop of novels, not all poisonous, but generally not appetizing, and certainly not nourishing; and the unmistakeable mushroom is a new novel by Charles Kingsley. It seemed too long since we had any of that genuine description of external nature, not done after the poet's or the novelist's recipe, but flowing from spontaneous observation and enjoyment [;] any of that close, vigorous painting of out-door life, which serves as myrrh and rich spices to embalm much perishable theorizing and offensive objurgation—too long since we had a taste of that exquisite lyrical inspiration to which we owe:

> O, Mary! go and call the cattle home
> Along the sands of Dee.[7]

After courses of 'psychological' novels (very excellent things in their way), where life seems made up of talking and journalizing, and men are judged almost entirely on 'carpet consideration',[8] we are ready to welcome a stirring historical romance, by a writer who, poet and scholar and social reformer as he is, evidently knows the points of a horse and has followed the hounds, who betrays a

---

[6] *Victorian England: Portrait of an Age*, 2nd ed. (London, New York, Toronto, 1953), p. 4.

[7] 'The Sands of Dee', misquoted from stanza 1:

> 'O Mary, go and call the cattle home,
> And call the cattle home,
> And call the cattle home
> Across the sands of Dee.'

[8] *Twelfth Night*, III, iv, 258.

fancy for pigs, and becomes dithyrambic on the virtues of tobacco. After a surfeit of Hebes and Psyches, or Madonnas and Magdalens, it is a refreshment to turn to Kiss's Amazon.[9] But this ruddy and, now and then, rather ferocious barbarism, which is singularly compounded in Mr. Kingsley with the susceptibility of the poet and the warm sympathy of the philanthropist, while it gives his writings one of their principal charms, is also the source of their gravest fault. The battle and the chase seem necessary to his existence; and this Red Man's nature, planted in a pleasant rectory among corn fields and pastures, takes, in default of better game, to riding down capitalists and Jesuits, and fighting with that Protean personage—'the devil'. If, however, Mother Nature has made Mr. Kingsley very much of a poet and philanthropist, and a little of a savage, her dry-nurse Habit has made him superlatively a preacher: he drops into the homily as readily as if he had been 'to the manner born;'[10] and while by his artistic faculty he can transplant you into whatever scene he will, he can never trust to the impression that scene itself will make on you, but, true to his cloth, must always 'improve the occasion'. In these two points— his fierce antagonism and his perpetual hortative tendency—lie, to our thinking, the grand mistakes which enfeeble the effect of all Mr. Kingsley's works, and are too likely to impede his production of what his high powers would otherwise promise—a fiction which might be numbered among our classics. Poet and artist in a rare degree, his passionate impetuosity and theological prepossessions inexorably forbid that he should ever be a philosopher; he sees, feels, and paints vividly, but he theorizes illogically and moralizes absurdly. If he would confine himself to his true sphere, he might be a teacher in the sense in which every great artist is a teacher— namely, by giving us his higher sensibility as a medium, a delicate acoustic or optical instrument, bringing home to our coarser senses what would otherwise be unperceived by us. But Mr. Kingsley, unhappily, like so many other gifted men, has two steeds —his Pegasus and his hobby: the one he rides with a graceful *abandon*, to the admiration of all beholders; but no sooner does he

[9] The German sculptor August Kiss (1802–1865) exhibited his monumental 'Mounted Amazon Attacked by a Tiger' at the Great Exhibition in 1851, where it divided popular honours with Hiram Powers's 'Greek Slave'.
[10] *Hamlet*, I, iv, 15.

get astride the other, than he becomes a feeble imitator of Carlyle's
manège, and attempts to put his wooden toy to all the wonderful
paces of the great Scotchman's fiery Tartar horse. This imitation
is probably not a conscious one, but arises simply from the fact,
that Mr. Kingsley's impetuosity and Boanerges' vein give him an
affinity for Carlyle's faults--his one-sided judgment of character
and his undiscriminating fulminations against the men of the
present as tried by some imaginary standard in the past. Carlyle's
great merits Mr. Kingsley's powers are not fitted to achieve; his
genius lies in another direction. He has not that piercing insight
which every now and then flashes to the depth of things, and
alternating as it does with the most obstinate one-sidedness,
makes Carlyle a wonderful paradox of wisdom and wilfulness; he
has not that awful sense of the mystery of existence which continually checks and chastens the denunciations of the Teufelsdröckh; still less has he the rich humour, the keen satire, and the
tremendous word-missiles, which Carlyle hurls about as Milton's
angels hurl the rocks. But Mr. Kingsley *can* scold; he *can* select
one character for unmixed eulogy and another for unmitigated
vituperation; he *can* undertake to depict a past age and try to make
out that it was the pattern of all heroisms now utterly extinct; he
can sneer at actual doings which are only a new form of the sentiments he vaunts as the peculiar possession of his pet period; he
can call his own opinion God, and the opposite opinion the Devil.
Carlyle's love of the concrete makes him prefer any proper name
rather than an abstraction, and we are accustomed to smile at this
in him, knowing it to be mere Carlylian rhetoric; but with Mr.
Kingsley, who has publicly made a vehement disclaimer of all
heterodoxy, and wishes to be understood as believing 'all the
doctrines of the Catholic Church',[11] we must interpret such
phraseology more literally. But enough of general remarks. Let us
turn to the particular work before us, where we shall find all the

[11] In 1851 Kingsley defended himself in a letter to the *Guardian*
against an anonymous review (by Lord Coleridge) attacking the morality
of *Yeast*. Kingsley asserted that 'whosoever henceforth, either explicitly
or by insinuation, says that I do not hold and believe *ex animo*, and in the
simple and literal sense, all the doctrines of the Catholic and Apostolic
Church of England, as embodied in her Liturgy or Articles, shall have no
answer from me but Father Valerian's *Mentiris impudentissimé*'. (*Charles
Kingsley, His Letters and Memories of His Life, Edited by His Wife*,
abridged from the London Edition [New York, 1877], p. 142.)

writer's merits and faults in full blow. We abstain on principle
from telling the story of novels, which seems to us something like
stealing geraniums from your friend's flower-pot to stick in your
own button-hole: you spoil the effect of his plant, and you secure
only a questionable ornament for yourself. We shall therefore be
careful to give the reader no hint of the domestic story around
which Mr. Kingsley has grouped the historical scenes and characters of 'Westward Ho!'

Hardly any period could furnish a happier subject for an
historical fiction than the one Mr. Kingsley has here chosen. It is
unhackneyed, and it is unsurpassed in the grandeur of its moral
elements, and the picturesqueness and romance of its manners and
events. Mr. Kingsley has not brought only genius but much labour
to its illustration. He has fed his strong imagination with all
accessible material, and given care not only to the grand figures
and incidents but to small details. One sees that he knows and
loves his Devonshire at first hand, and he has evidently lingered
over the description of the forests and savannahs and rivers of the
New World, until they have become as vividly present to him as if
they were part of his own experience. We dare not pronounce on
the merit of his naval descriptions, but to us, landlubbers as we
are, they seem wonderfully real, and not to smack at all of tech-
nicalities learned by rote over the desk. He has given a careful
and loving study to the history and literature of the period, and
whatever misrepresentation there is in the book, is clearly not due
to ignorance but to prepossession: if he misrepresents, it is not
because he has omitted to examine, but because he has examined
through peculiar spectacles. In the construction of a story Mr.
Kingsley has never been felicitous; and the feebleness of his
dénouements have [*sic*] been matter of amazement, even to his
admirers. In this respect, 'Westward Ho!' though by no means
criticism-proof, is rather an advance on his former works, especially
in the winding-up. It is true, this winding-up reminds us a little of
Jane Eyre, but we prefer a partially borrowed beauty to an
original bathos, which was what Mr. Kingsley achieved in the later
chapters of 'Alton Locke' and 'Yeast'. Neither is humour his forte.
His Jack Brimblecombe is too much like a piece of fun *obligato*,
after the manner of Walter Scott, who remains the unequalled
model of historical romancists, however they may criticize him.
Mr. Kingsley's necessity for strong loves and strong hatreds, and

his determination to hold up certain persons as models, is an obstacle to his successful delineation of character, in which he might otherwise excel. As it is, we can no more believe in and love his men and women than we could believe in and love the pattern-boy at school, always cited as a rebuke to our aberrations. Amyas Leigh would be a real, loveable fellow enough if he were a little less exemplary, and if Mr. Kingsley would not make him a text to preach from, as we suppose he is accustomed to do with Joshua, Gideon, and David. Until he shakes off this parsonic habit he will not be able to create truly human characters, or to write a genuine historical romance. Where his prepossessions do not come into play, where he is not dealing with his model heroes, or where the drama turns on a single passion or motive, he can scarcely be rivalled in truthfulness and beauty of presentation; for in clothing passion with action and language, and in the conception of all that gives local colouring, he has his best gifts to aid him. Beautiful is that episode of Mr. Oxenham's love, told by Salvation Yeo! Very admirable, too, is the felicity with which Mr. Kingsley has seized the style and spirit of the Elizabethan writers, and reproduced them in the poetry and supposed quotations scattered through his story. But above all other charms in his writings, at least to us, is his scene-painting. Who does not remember the scene by the wood in 'Alton Locke',[12] or that of the hunt at the beginning of 'Yeast'? And 'Westward Ho!' is wealthy in still greater beauties of the same kind.   Here is a perfect gem.   After a description of the old house at Stow, the residence of Sir Richard Grenvile, we read:

> From the house on three sides, the hill sloped steeply down, and the garden where Sir Richard and Amyas were walking gave a truly English prospect. At one turn they could catch, over the western walls, a glimpse of the blue ocean flecked with passing sails; and at the next, spread far below them, range on range of fertile park, stately avenue, yellow autumn woodland, and purple heather moors, lapping over and over each other up the valley to the old British earthwork, which stood black and furze-grown on its conical peak; and standing out against the sky on the highest bank of hill which closed the valley to the east, the lofty tower of Kilkhampton church, rich with the monuments and offerings of five centuries of Grenviles. A yellow

---

[12] Ch. 11. George Eliot also praises this scene in 'The Natural History of German Life'. See below, p. 270.

eastern haze hung soft over park, and wood, and moor; the red cattle lowed to each other as they stood brushing away the flies in the rivulet far below; the colts in the horse-park close on their right whinnied as they played together, and their sires from the Queen's park, on the opposite hill, answered them in fuller though fainter voices. A rutting stag made the still woodland rattle with his hoarse thunder, and a rival far up the valley gave back a trumpet note of defiance, and was himself defied from heathery brows which quivered far away above, half seen through the veil of eastern mist. And close at home, upon the terrace before the house, amid romping spaniels and golden-haired children, sat Lady Grenvile herself, the beautiful St. Leger of Annery, the central jewel of all that glorious place, and looked down at her noble children, and then up at her more noble husband, and round at that broad paradise of the west, till life seemed too full of happiness, and heaven of light.

It is pleasanter to linger over beauties such as these, than to point out faults; but unhappily, Mr. Kingsley's faults are likely to do harm in other ways than in subtracting from the lustre of his fame, and faithful reviewer must lift up his voice against them, whether men 'will hear, or whether they will forbear'.[13] Who that has any knowledge of our history and literature—that has felt his heart beat high at the idea of great crises and great deeds—that has any true recognition of the greatest poetry, and some of the greatest thoughts enshrined in our language, is not ready to pay the tribute of enthusiastic reverence to the Elizabethan age? In his glowing picture of that age, Mr. Kingsley would have carried with him all minds in which there is a spark of nobleness, if he could have freed himself from the spirit of the partisan, and been content to admit that in the Elizabethan age, as in every other, human beings, human parties, and human deeds are made up of the most subtly intermixed good and evil. The battle of Armageddon in which all the saints are to fight on one side, has never yet come.   It is perfectly true that, at certain epochs, the relations and tendencies of ideas and events are so clearly made out to minds of any superiority, that the best and ablest men are for the most part ranged under one banner: there was a point at which it must have become disgraceful to a cultivated mind not to accept the Copernican system, and in these days we are unable to draw any favourable inference concerning the intellect or morals

[13] Ezekiel 2:5; 2:7; 3:11.

of a man who advocates capital punishment for sheep-stealing or forgery. But things have never come to this pass with regard to Catholicism and Protestantism; and even supposing they had, Mr. Kingsley's ethics seem to resemble too closely those of his bugbears the Dominicans, when he implies that it is a holy work for the 'Ayes' to hunt down the 'Noes' like so many beasts of prey. His view of history seems not essentially to differ from that we have all held in our childish days, when it seemed perfectly easy to us to divide mankind into the sheep and the goats, when we devoutly believed that our favourite heroes, Wallace and Bruce, and all who fought on their side, were 'good,' while Edward and his soldiers were all 'wicked'; that all the champions of the Reformation were of unexceptionable private character, and all the adherents of Popery consciously vicious and base. Doubtless the Elizabethan age bore its peculiar fruit of excellence, as every age has done which forms a nodus, a ganglion, in the historical development of humanity—as the age of Pericles produced the divinest sculptures, or the age of the Roman Republic the severe grandeur of Roman law and Roman patriotism, or as the core of the Middle Ages held the germ of chivalrous honour and reverential love. Doubtless the conquest of the Spanish Armada was virtually the triumph of light and freedom over darkness and bondage. What then? Is this a reason why Mr. Kingsley should seem almost angry with us for not believing with the men of that day in the golden city of Manoa and the Gulf-stream, or scold by anticipation any one who shall dare to congratulate himself on being undeceived in these matters? Doubtless Drake, Hawkins, Frobisher, and the rest, were brave, energetic men—men of great will and in some sort of great faculty; but like all other human agents, they 'builded better than they knew';[14] and it would be as rational to suppose that the bee is an entomological Euclid, interested only in the solution of a problem, as to suppose that the motives of these mariners were as grand as the results of their work.

We had marked several passages as specimens of the small success which attends Mr. Kingsley in his favourite exercise of deducing a moral, but our want of space obliges us to renounce the idea of quoting them, with the exception of one, which, we think, will in some degree justify our low estimate of Mr. Kingsley's gifts as a philosophizer. Here is the passage:

[14] Emerson, 'The Problem', st. 2: 'He builded better than he knew.'

Humboldt has somewhere a curious passage; in which, looking on some wretched group of Indians, squatting stupidly round their fires, besmeared with grease and paint, and devouring ants and clay, he somewhat naively remarks, that were it not for science, which teaches us that such is the crude material of humanity, and this the state from which we all have risen, he should have been tempted rather to look upon those hapless beings as the last degraded remnants of some fallen and dying race. One wishes that the great traveller had been bold enough to yield to that temptation, which his own reason and common sense presented to him as the real explanation of the sad sight, instead of following the dogmas of a so-called science, which has not a fact whereon to base its wild notion, and must ignore a thousand facts in asserting it. His own good sense, it seems, coincided instinctively with the Bible doctrine, that man in a state of nature is a fallen being, doomed to death—a view which may be a sad one, but still one more honourable to poor humanity than the theory, that we all began as some sort of two-handed apes. It is surely more hopeful to believe that those poor Otomacs or Guahibas were not what they ought to be, than to believe that they were. It is certainly more complimentary to them, to think that they had been somewhat nobler and more prudent in centuries gone by, than that they were such blockheads as to have dragged on, the son after the father, for all the thousands of years which have elapsed since man was made, without having had wit enough to discover any better food than ants and clay.

Our voyagers, however, like those of their time, troubled their heads with no such questions. Taking the Bible story as they found it, they agreed with Humboldt's reason, and not with his science; or, to speak correctly, agreed with Humboldt's self, and not with the shallow anthropologic theories which happened to be in vogue fifty years ago; and their new hosts were in their eyes immortal souls like themselves, 'captivated by the devil at his will,' lost there in the pathless forests, likely to be lost hereafter.

Note the accuracy of Mr. Kingsley's reasoning. Humboldt observes that, but for scientific data leading to an opposite conclusion, he could have imagined that a certain group of Indians were the remnants of a race which had sunk from a state of well-being to one of almost helpless barbarism. Hereupon, Mr. Kingsley is sorry that Humboldt did not reject 'the dogmas of a so-called science', and rest in this conception which 'coincided with the Bible doctrine'; and he urges as one of his reasons for this regret, that it would be complimentary to the Otomacs and Guahibas to suppose that in centuries gone by, they had been nobler and more prudent. Now, so far as we are acquainted with the third chapter of Genesis, and with the copious exegeses of that chapter from St. Paul downwards, the 'Bible doctrine' is *not* that man multiplied on the earth and formed communities and nations—amongst the rest, noble and prudent societies of Otomacs and Guahibas—in a state of innocence, and that *then* came the Fall. We have always understood that for the Fall 'we may thank Adam', and that consequently the very first Otomac or Guahiba was already 'captived by the devil', and 'likely to be lost hereafter.' Hence, what the question of the Otomacs and Guahibas having been nobler and more prudent in centuries gone by, can have to do with the doctrine of the Fall, we are at a loss to perceive. We will do no more than point to Mr. Kingsley's cool arrogance in asserting that a man like Humboldt, the patriarch of scientific investigators, is 'misled by the dogmas of a so-called science, which has *not a fact* whereon to base its wild notions.' Indeed it is rather saddening to dwell on the occasional absurdities into which anomalous opinions can betray a man of real genius; and after all, the last word we have to say of 'Westward Ho!' is to thank Mr. Kingsley for the great and beautiful things we have found in it, as our dominant feeling towards his works in general is that of high admiration.

Next in interest to 'Westward Ho!' at least among the English novels of the quarter, is 'Constance Herbert'. Miss Jewsbury has created precedents for herself which make critics exacting towards her. We measure her work by her own standard, and find it deficient; when if measured by the standard of ordinary feminine novelists, it would perhaps seem excellent. We meet with some beauties in it which, coming from the author of the 'Half Sisters', we take as a matter of course, but we miss other beauties which she has taught us to expect; we feel that she is not equal to herself; and it is a tribute to her well-attested powers if we dwell on what has disappointed us, rather than on what has gratified us. An easy, agreeable style of narrative, some noble sentiments expressed in the quiet, unexaggerated way that indicates their source to be a deep spring of conviction and experience, not a mere rain-torrent of hearsay enthusiasm, with here and there a trait of character or conduct painted with the truthfulness of close observation, are merits enough to raise a book far above the common run of circulating library fiction; but they are not enough to make a good novel, or one worthy of Miss Jewsbury's reputation. 'Constance Herbert' is a *Tendenz-roman;* the characters and incidents are selected with a view to the enforcement of a principle. The general principle meant to be enforced is the unhesitating, uncompromising sacrifice of inclination to duty, and the special case to which this principle is applied in the novel, is the abstinence from marriage where there is an inheritance of insanity. So far, we have no difference of opinion with Miss Jewsbury. But the *mode* in which she enforces the principle, both theoretically in the *Envoi* and illustratively in the story of her novel, implies, we think, a false view of life, and virtually nullifies the very magnanimity she inculcates. 'If', she says in the *Envoi*, 'we have succeeded in articulating any principle in this book, it is to entreat our readers to have boldness to act up to the sternest requirements that duty claims as right. Although it may at the time seem to slay them, it will in the end prove life. *Nothing they renounce for the sake of a higher principle, will prove to have been worth the keeping*'. The italics are ours, and we use them to indicate what we think false in Miss Jewsbury's moral. This moral is illustrated in the novel by the story of three ladies, who, after renouncing their lovers, or being renounced by them, have the satisfaction of feeling in the end that these lovers were extremely 'good-for-nothing', and that they (the ladies) have had an excellent riddance. In all this we can see neither the true doctrine of renunciation, nor a true representation of the realities of life; and we are sorry that a writer of Miss Jewsbury's insight and sincerity should have produced three volumes for the sake of teaching such copy-book morality. It is not the fact that what duty calls on us to renounce, will invariably prove 'not worth the keeping'; and if it *were* the fact, renunciation would cease to be moral heroism, and would be simply a calculation of prudence. Let us take the special case which Miss Jewsbury has chosen as her illustration. It might equally happen that a woman in the position of Constance Herbert, who renounces marriage because she will not entail on others the family heritage of insanity, had fixed her affections, not on an egotistic, shallow worldling like Philip Marchmont, but on a man who was fitted to make the happiness of a woman's life, and whose subsequent career would only impress on her more and more deeply the extent of the sacrifice she had made in refusing him. And it is this very perception that the thing we renounce is precious, is something never to be compensated to us, which constitutes the beauty and heroism of renunciation. The only motive that renders such a resolution as Constance Herbert's noble, is that keen sympathy with human misery which makes a woman prefer to suffer for the term of her own life, rather than run the risk of causing misery to an indefinite number of other human beings; and a mind influenced by such a motive will find no support in the very questionable satisfaction of discovering that objects once cherished were in fact worthless. The notion that duty looks stern, but all the while has her hand full of sugar-plums, with which she will reward us by-and-by, is the favourite cant of optimists, who try to make out that this tangled wilderness of life has a plan as easy to trace as that of a Dutch garden; but it really undermines all true moral development by perpetually substituting something extrinsic as a motive to action, instead of the immediate impulse of love or justice, which alone makes an action truly moral. This is a grave question to enter on *à propos* of a novel; but Miss Jewsbury is so emphatic in the enunciation of her moral, that she forces us to consider her book rather in the light of a homily than of a fiction—to criticise her doctrine rather than her story. On another point, too, we must remonstrate with her a little, chiefly because we value her influence, and should like to see it always in what seems to us the right scale. With the exception of Mr. Harrop, who is simply a cipher awaiting a wife to give him any value, there is not a man in her book who is not either weak, perfidious, or rascally, while almost all the women are models of magnanimity and devotedness. The lions, *i.e.*, the ladies, have got the brush in their hands with a vengeance now, and are retaliating for the calumnies of men from Adam downwards. Perhaps it is but fair to allow them a little exaggeration. Still we must meekly suggest that we cannot accept an *ex parte* statement, even from that paragon Aunt Margaret, as altogether decisive. Aunt Margaret tells us that in the bloom of youth and beauty, with virtues and accomplishments to correspond, she alienated her husband by pure devotion to him. 'No man,' she says, 'can bear entire devotion.' This reminds us of a certain toper, who after drinking a series of glasses of brandy-and-water one night, complained the next morning that the water did not agree with him. We are inclined to think that it is less frequently devotion which alienates men, than something infused in the devotion—a certain amount of silliness, or temper, or *exigeance*, for example, which, though given in small doses, will, if persevered in, have a strongly alterative effect. Men, in fact, are in rather a difficult position: in one ear a Miss Grace Lee, or some such strong-minded woman, thunders that they demand to be worshipped, and abhor a woman who has any self-dependence; on the other, a melancholy Viola complains that they never appreciate devotion, that they care only for a woman who treats them with indifference. A discouraging view of the case for both sexes! Seriously, we care too much for the attainment of a better understanding as to woman's true position, not to be sorry when a writer like Miss Jewsbury only adds her voice to swell the confusion on this subject.

8

LORD BROUGHAM'S
LITERATURE

Leader, VI (7 July 1855), 652–653

In her Journal for 21 June 1855 George Eliot recorded her review of the 1855 reprint of Lord Brougham's *Lives of Men of Letters and Science, Who Flourished in the Time of George III*, 2 vols., first published in 1845–1846. Two days after finishing the review she wrote to Sara Hennell, saying 'I have written a castigation of Lord Brougham for the *Leader*, and shall be glad if your sympathy goes along with it.'[1] The sympathy of her friends at Coventry was apparently less than perfect, however, for on 16 July she wrote to Charles Bray, explaining that:

> The article on Lord Brougham was written conscientiously, and you seem to have misunderstood its purpose, in taking it for mere word quibbling. I consider it criminal in a man to prostitute Literature for the purposes of his own vanity and this is what Lord Brougham has done. A man who has something vitally important to mankind to say, may be excused for saying it in bad English. In such a case criticism of style is irrelevant. But Literature is Fine Art, and the man who writes mere literature with insolent slovenliness is as inexcusable as a man who gets up in a full drawing-room to sing Rossini's music in a cracked voice and out of tune. Because Lord Brougham has done some services to the public it does not follow that he is to be treated with anything else than justice when he is doing injury to the public, and I consider his 'Lives' *bad* and *injurious*. I say thus much in vindication of my view of right, not at all in vindication of my article.[2]

*   *   *

IT is matter of very common observation that members of the 'privileged classes,' who, either from want of work or want of ability to do their proper work, find their time hang rather heavily

[1] *Letters*, II, 205.   [2] *Letters*, II, 210.

on their hands, try to get rid of it by employments which, if not self-imposed, they would think rather pitiable. Kings and emperors have turned their hands to making locks and sealing-wax; ambassadresses have collected old stockings for the sake of darning them; and we knew a wealthy old gentleman who devoted himself to making pokers, which he presented to all the ladies of his acquaintance. It is generally presumed of such people that if they had brains to enable them to do anything better, they would prosecute this voluntary artisanship with less zeal; still, the case of these incapables is one to be charitably smiled at or sighed over, not gravely rebuked; we graciously accept the present of their lock or their poker and say no more about it. But it would be a different affair if these voluntary artisans were to set up shop—if, for example, Lord A, or Sir B.C., or any other of the tribe of wealthy Englishmen to whom foreigners give the generic title of *milord*, were not only to amuse himself with making boots, but were to hire a shop frontage, with plate glass, and exhibit his clumsy wares to the public with as much pomp and circumstance as if he were a very Hoby,[3] thereby inducing snobbish people to set the fashion of wearing and crying up Lord A's boots, to the depreciation of really well-made articles, and to the great detriment both of human candour and the human foot. Political economists and bootmakers, lady-loves and orthopœdists, science and æsthetics, would vote the aristocratic Crispin[4] a nuisance.

A sufficiently close parallel to this hypothetic case is suggested by Lord Brougham's *Lives of Men of Letters*, the sight of which, republished in a cheap form, has, we confess, roused our critical gall. Relieved from the labours of his chancellorship, Lord Brougham, we suppose, found a good deal of leisure on his hands; and how did he employ it? By taking to what we may call literary lock and poker-making—by writing third-rate biographies in the style of a literary hack! Biographies, too, of men whose lives had already been depicted in all sorts of ways, and presented to us in all sorts of lights—like Prince Albert's face and legs. If we had found these 'Lives of Men of Letters' in a biographical dictionary we should perhaps have thought them about up to the average of the piece-work usually to be met with in such compilations; finding

---

[3] 'Geo. Hoby, boot and shoe maker, 48 St. James's St., Pall Mall.' (*Post Office London Directory*, 1842.)

[4] Patron saint of shoemakers.

them, as we did more than ten years ago, in an *édition de luxe* adorned with portraits, and with Lord Brougham's name on the title-page, we felt some simmering indignation at such gratuitous mediocrities in a pretentious garb; and now that we see them in a cheaper reissue—as if there were any demand for these clumsy superfluities, these amateur locks and pokers—our indignation fairly boils over. We have not the slightest wish to be disrespectful to Lord Brougham. His name is connected with some of the greatest movements in the last half century, and in general, is on the side of the liberal and the just. But he has been a successful man; his reputation is fully equal to his merit; society is unanimous in pronouncing that he has done many things well and wisely; and there is, therefore, no reason why we should be reticent of our criticism where, in our opinion, he has done some things less wisely and *not* well.

The first thing that strikes us in these *Lives* is the slovenliness of their style, which is thrown almost ludicrously into relief by the fact that many of Lord Brougham's pages are occupied with criticism of other men's style. The hard-run literary man, who is every moment expecting the knock of the printer's boy, has reason enough to renounce fastidiousness; but his lordship, in the elegant ease of his library, with no call impending but that of the lunch or dinner-bell, might at least atone for the lack of originality by finish —might, if he has no jewels to offer us, at least polish his pebbles. How far he has done this we will let the reader judge by giving some specimens of the manner in which Lord Brougham contrives

To blunt a moral and to spoil a tale.[5]

One of his reproaches against Gibbon's style is, that it is 'prone to adopt false and mixed metaphors'; but we doubt whether the *Decline and Fall* could furnish us with a more typical specimen of that kind than one which he himself gives us in his life of Voltaire. 'Proofs also remain,' says Lord Brougham, 'which place beyond all doubt his (Voltaire's) kindness to several worthless men, who repaid it with the black ingratitude so commonly used as their *current coin* by the base and spiteful, who thus repay their benefactors and *salve their own wounded pride by pouring venom on the hand that saved or served them.*' Again, in the life of Johnson, we read: 'Assuredly, we may in vain search all the Mantuan *tracery of*

[5] Samuel Johnson, 'The Vanity of Human Wishes', 222: 'To point a moral, or adorn a tale.'

sweets for any to excel them in the beauty of numbers.' It may be our ignorance of confectionery that prevents us from perceiving what 'tracery' can have to do with 'sweets'; as it is, however, we can only explain his lordship's metaphor by supposing *tracery* to be a misprint for *tea-tray*, since misprints abound in this volume. Lord Brougham is very frequently quite as infelicitous in his phrases, and in the structure of his sentences, as in his metaphors. For example: 'It is none of the least absurd *parts* of Condorcet's work, that he, being so well versed in physical and mathematical science, passes without any particular observation the writings of Voltaire on physical subjects, when he was so competent to pronounce an opinion upon their merits.' 'Condorcet was a man of science, no doubt, a good mathematician; but he was *in other respects* of a middling understanding and *violent feelings*.' 'The lady treated him with kindness, apparently as a child; his friend St. Lambert did not much relish the matter, being unable to adopt his singular *habit* of *several lovers at one and the same time intimate* with one mistress'. The style of Rousseau's *Confessions*, we are told, is 'so exquisitely graphic without any effort, and so accommodated to its subject without any baseness, *that there hardly exists another example of the miracles which composition can perform*'. In the labour of turning his heavy sentences, his lordship is sometimes oblivious of logic. Speaking of Johnson's Latin verses to Mrs. Thrale, he says: 'Such offences as "Littera Skaiæ" ' (*sic*—a misprint, of course, for *littora*),[6] 'for an Adonian in his Sapphics to "Thralia dulcis", would have called down his severe censure on any luckless wight of Paris or Edinburgh who should peradventure have perpetrated them; nor would his being the countryman of Polignac or of by far the finest of modern Latinists, Buchanan, have operated except as an aggravation of the fault'. Why should it?

Remembering Sydney Smith's verdict on Scotch 'wut',[7] we

[6] The last line of Johnson's ode reads 'Littora Skiae'. (Boswell, *Journal of a Tour to the Hebrides*, 7 September 1773.)

[7] 'Their only idea of wit, or rather that inferior variety of this electric talent which prevails occasionally in the North, and which, under the name of WUT, is so infinitely distressing to people of good taste, is laughing immoderately at stated intervals.' (*A Memoir of the Reverend Sydney Smith, by His Daughter, Lady Holland* . . . , 2 vols. [New York, 1855], I, 25.) George Eliot's Journal for 13 June 1855 notes that 'We are reading in the evening now Sydney Smith's letters.' Lewes reviewed the *Memoir* in the *Leader*, 16 June 1855.

are not very much surprised to find that Lord Brougham has some anticipation of a Millennium when men will cease to perpetrate witticisms—when not only will the lion eat straw like the ox, but latter-day Voltaires will be as heavy as Scotch lawyers. At least, this is the only way in which we can interpret his peroration to the Life of Voltaire. After an allusion in the previous sentence to 'the graces of his style', and 'the spirit of his *immortal* wit', we read: 'But if ever the time shall arrive when men, intent solely on graver matters, and bending their whole minds to things of solid import-ance, shall be careless of such light accomplishments, and the writings which now have so great a relish more or less openly tasted, shall pass into oblivion, then', &c., &c. We confess that we shudder at such a Millennium as much as at one predicted by Dr. Cumming, or planned by Robert Owen.[8]

Another striking characteristic of these *Lives of Men of Letters* is the way in which the writer ignores what is not only notorious to all the educated world, but notoriously well known to Lord Brougham. The long-faced gravity with which he discourses on Voltaire's ridicule of religious dogmas, and on Hume's abstinence from such ridicule, might lead a very ignorant reader to suppose that Lord Brougham had led a retired life, chiefly in clerical and senile society, and could only with difficulty imagine a man passing a joke on the Trinity. He says of Hume that 'occasionally his opinions were perceivable' in his conversation, and that one day the inscription on the staircase of the college library, *Christo et Musis has ædes sacrarunt cives Edinenses*, actually 'drew from the unbeliever an irreverent observation on the junction which the piety rather than the classical purity of the good town had made between the worship of the heathen and our own'. Astounding! Even this distant allusion to such irreverence might have had a pernicious effect by exciting in us an unhealthy desire to know what the irreverent observation was, had we not remembered that Hume had no wit, but only 'wut', so that his joke was probably a feeble one. . . . A still more surprising example of Lord Brougham's ignoring system as a writer is his comment on Voltaire's relation to

[8] George Eliot had begun reading the books of the Evangelical preacher Dr. John Cumming on 13 June 1855 in preparation for her attack on him in 'Evangelical Teaching: Dr. Cumming'. She had met the socialist Robert Owen (1771–1858) and had no great opinion of him. See *Letters*, I, 161.

Madame du Châtelet. He thinks that on the whole there is no sufficient reason for questioning that it was Platonic, and the chief grounds he alleges for this conclusion are: that the laws of French society at *that* time, as well as now, were exceedingly rigorous, that the relation was recognised by all their friends, that Voltaire mentions Madame du Châtelet in his letters, and that Frederick II. sent his regards to her! One would think it did not require Lord Brougham's extensive acquaintance with the history of French society in the days of Voltaire and Rousseau to know that, whatever may be the truth of his conclusion, the grounds by which he supports it must sound like irony rather than like a grave statement of fact; and, indeed, he himself, on another page, having laid aside his ignoring spectacles, talks of Grimm being the 'professed lover of Madame d'Epinay,' and of St. Lambert being 'the avowed lover' of Madame d'Houdetot.

We had marked several other points for notice, especially that very remarkable criticism of Lord Brougham's on the *Nouvelle Heloïse*, in which he implies, that for a lover to remind his mistress that she had allowed him to kiss her, is to tell her what a 'forward, abandoned wanton she proved', and his supposition, that because Johnson was sometimes wandering all night in the streets with Savage he must necessarily have indulged in certain vices 'in their more crapulous form' (an unfortunate suggestion to come from the Brougham of Jeffrey's letters, who is described as 'roaming the streets with the sons of Belial').[9] But we must remember that when indignation makes reviews instead of Juvenalian verses, the result is not equally enjoyable by the reader. So we restrain our noble rage, and say good-by now and for ever to Lord Brougham's *Lives of Men of Letters*, hoping that the next time we meet with any production of his we may be able to express admiration as strongly as we have just now expressed the reverse.

[9] Lord Cockburn, *Life of Lord Jeffrey, with a Selection from His Correspondence* (Edinburgh, 1852), II, 67.

9

THE MORALITY OF
WILHELM MEISTER

Leader, VI (21 July 1855), 703

In the year before this article appeared Goethe was part of George Eliot's daily life as Lewes brought to completion his pioneer biography of the poet. In November, 1854, while she and Lewes were in Berlin to gather material for the *Life*, her Journal records that between the 8th and the 29th of the month they were reading *Wilhelm Meister* aloud in the evenings. A comparison between her article and Lewes's remarks in the *Life* on the question of the morality of *Wilhelm Meister* shows considerable similarity in the principles of the two discussions. Lewes, while conceding that '*Wilhelm Meister* is not a moral story', appeals to the principle of realistic presentation: 'All that can be said is that the Artist has been content to paint scenes of life, *without comment*; and that some of these scenes belong to an extensive class of subjects, familiar indeed to the experience of all but children, yet by general consent not much talked of in society.' Though the book is 'in no respect a Moral Tale,' Lewes adds, 'I am bound to declare that deep and healthy moral meaning lies in it, pulses through it, speaking in many tones to him who hath ears to hear it. As Wordsworth says of *Tam o' Shanter*, "I pity him who cannot perceive that in all this, though there was no moral purpose, there is a moral effect." What each reader will see in it, will depend on his insight and experience.'[1]

How close the agreement between George Eliot and Lewes is on this point may be seen from the article printed below (it would be dangerous to decide whether the grounds for the defence of *Wilhelm Meister* are originally hers or his). But George Eliot's own distinctive note is heard in the *Leader* article in her assertion of the artist's right to 'place before us every aspect of human life where there is some trait of love, or

[1] *The Life of Goethe*, 3rd ed. (London, 1875), pp. 404–405.

endurance, or helplessness to call forth our best sympathies': such passages anticipate the famous statements of her realistic theory in Ch. 5 of *Amos Barton* and Ch. 17 of *Adam Bede*.

The translation of *Wilhelm Meister's Apprenticeship* by R. Dillon Boylan (1855), ostensibly the occasion for the article, was also noticed by George Eliot in the *Westminster Review*, LXIV (October, 1855), 613, where she observes of it that, 'though the translation is tolerably executed so far as the prose is concerned, the rendering of the poetry is as atrocious a case of literary murder as we happen to have met with'.

The authorship of the article is attested by an entry in George Eliot's Journal for 8 July 1855: 'Wilhelm Meister & Art. on Gruppe for the Leader.' It has been reprinted once, in *Essays and Uncollected Papers*.

*   *   *

PERHAPS Mr. Lewes's *Life of Goethe*, which we now see adver-tised,[2] may throw some new light on the structure and purpose of the much-debated novel—*Wilhelm Meister's Apprenticeship*. In the meantime, we are tempted by the appearance of a new translation to give the opinion which our present knowledge enables us to form on one or two aspects of this many-sided work.

Ask nineteen out of twenty moderately educated persons what they think of *Wilhelm Meister*, and the answer will probably be— 'I think it an immoral book; and besides, it is awfully dull: I was not able to read it'. Whatever truth there may be in the first half of this judgment, the second half is a sufficient guarantee that the book is not likely to do any extensive injury in English society. Parents may let it lie on the drawing-room table without scruple, in the confidence that for youthful minds of the ordinary cast it will have no attractions, and that the exceptional youthful mind which is strongly arrested by it is of too powerful and peculiar a character to be trained according to educational dogmas.

But is *Wilhelm Meister* an immoral book? We think not: on the contrary, we think that it appears immoral to some minds because its morality has a grander orbit than any which can be measured by the calculations of the pulpit and of ordinary literature. Goethe, it is sometimes said, seems in this book to be almost destitute of moral bias: he shows no hatred of bad actions, no warm sympathy with good ones; he writes like a passionless Mejnour, to whom all

[2] It was published on 30 October 1855 and reviewed by George Eliot in the *Leader*, VI (3 November 1855), 1058–1061.

uman things are interesting only as objects of intellectual con-
emplation. But we question whether the direct exhibition of a
noral bias in the writer will make a book really moral in its in-
luence. Try this on the first child that asks you to tell it a story.
As long as you keep to an apparently impartial narrative of facts
ou will have earnest eyes fixed on you in rapt attention, but no
ooner do you begin to betray symptoms of an intention to
noralise, or to turn the current of facts towards a personal applica-
ion, than the interest of your hearer will slacken, his eyes will
vander, and the moral dose will be doubly distasteful from the
ery sweet-meat in which you have attempted to insinuate it. One
grand reason of this is, that the child is aware you are talking *for it*
nstead of *from yourself*, so that instead of carrying it along in a
tream of sympathy with your own interest in the story, you give it
he impression of contriving coldly and talking artificially. Now,
he moralising novelist produces the same effect on his mature
eaders; an effect often heightened by the perception that the
noralising is rather intended to make his book eligible for family
eading than prompted by any profound conviction or enthusiasm.
ust as far from being really moral is the so-called moral *dénoue-
ment*, in which rewards and punishments are distributed according
o those notions of justice on which the novel-writer would have
ecommended that the world should be governed if he had been
onsulted at the creation. The emotion of satisfaction which a
eader feels when the villain of the book dies of some hideous
lisease, or is crushed by a railway train, is no more essentially
noral than the satisfaction which used to be felt in whipping
ulprits at the cart-tail. So we dismiss the charge of immorality
gainst *Wilhelm Meister* on these two counts—the absence of
noral bias in the mode of narration, and the comfortable issues
llowed to questionable actions and questionable characters.

But there is another ground for the same accusation which
nvolves deeper considerations. It is said that some of the scenes
nd incidents are such as the refined moral taste of these days will
ot admit to be proper subjects for art, that to depict irregular
elations in all the charms they really have for human nature, and
o associate lovely qualities with vices which society makes a brand
of outlawry, implies a toleration which is at once a sign and a
ource of perverted moral sentiment. Wilhelm's relation to
Mariana, and the charm which the reader is made to feel in the

145

lawless Philina, many incidents that occur during Wilhelm's life with the players, and the stories of Lothario's loves in the present, preterite, and future, are shocking to the prevalent English. It is no answer to this objection to say—what is the fact—that Goethe's pictures are truthful, that the career of almost every young man brings him in contact with far more vitiating irregularities than any presented in the experience of Wilhelm Meister; for no one can maintain that *all* fact is a fit subject for art. The sphere of the artist has its limit somewhere, and the first question is, Has Goethe overstepped this limit, so that the mere fact of artistic representation is a mistake? The second: If his subjects are within the legitimate limits of art, is his mode of treatment such as to make his pictures pernicious? Surely the sphere of art extends wherever there is beauty either in form, or thought, or feeling. A ray of sunlight falling on the dreariest sandbank will often serve the painter for a fine picture; the tragedian may take for his subject the most hideous passions if they serve as the background for some divine deed of tenderness or heroism, and so the novelist may place before us every aspect of human life where there is some trait of love, or endurance, or helplessness to call forth our best sympathies. Balzac, perhaps the most wonderful writer of fiction the world has ever seen,[3] has in many of his novels overstepped this limit. He drags us by his magic force through scene after scene of unmitigated vice, till the effect of walking among this human carrion is a moral nausea. But no one can say that Goethe has sinned in this way.

Everywhere he brings us into the presence of living, generous humanity—mixed and erring, and self-deluding, but saved from utter corruption by the salt of some noble impulse, some disinterested effort, some beam of good nature, even though grotesque or homely. And his mode of treatment seems to us precisely that which is really moral in its influence. It is without exaggeration; he is in no haste to alarm readers into virtue by melodramatic consequences; he quietly follows the stream of fact and of life; and

[3] George Eliot's earliest reference to Balzac is in 1854 (*Letters*, II, 149), though perhaps Balzac is indicated in a letter of 1847 saying that she 'has been *guanoing* her mind with French novels' (*Letters*, I, 234). Lewes had contributed an article on Balzac to the *Monthly Magazine* in 1842 and another to the *Foreign Quarterly* in 1844. According to Anna T. Kitchel, *George Lewes and George Eliot*, pp. 134–135, he also translated Balzac's comedy *Mercadet* (1848).

waits patiently for the moral processes of nature as we all do for her material processes. The large tolerance of Goethe, which is markedly exhibited in *Wilhelm Meister*, is precisely that to which we point as the element of moral superiority. We all begin life by associating our passions with our moral prepossessions, by mistaking indignation for virtue, and many go through life without awaking from this illusion. These are the 'insupportables justes, qui du haut de leurs chaises d'or narguent les misères et les souffrances de l'humanité.' But a few are taught by their own falls and their own struggles, by their experience of sympathy, and help and goodness in the 'publicans and sinners' of these modern days, that the line between the virtuous and vicious, so far from being a necessary safeguard to morality, is itself an immoral fiction. Those who have been already taught this lesson will at once recognise the true morality of Goethe's works. Like *Wilhelm Meister*, they will be able to love the good in a Philina, and to reverence the far-seeing efforts of a Lothario.

10

THE FUTURE OF GERMAN
PHILOSOPHY

Leader, VI (28 July 1855), 723–724

Otto Friedrich Gruppe (1804–1876), whose *Gegenwart und Zukunf der Philosophie in Deutschland* (1855) is the subject of this review, wa one of the learned circle George Eliot and Lewes had known durin their stay in Berlin in 1854–1855. She seems to have been fascinated b Gruppe, in whom she found a curious type of the German *Gelehrte* fully developed. Describing him in a letter to Sara Hennell, she wrote

'He has written books on everything—on the Greek drama—a grea book on the Cosmic Systems of the Greeks—an epic, numberless lyric poems etc.—he has a philosophical work and a history of literature in the press—is professor of philosophy at the University—has invented a mode of staining paper beautifully for bookcovers—is enthusiastic about Boar-hunting, and has written a volume of hunting-poems—and *ich weiss nicht was*. Withal he is as simple as a child.'[1]

Though Gruppe the man was an amusing puzzle to her, George Eliot had no difficulty in agreeing with Gruppe the philosopher. As her approving review of his book shows, his positivistic assumptions were entirely sympathetic to her own choice of the hard '*à posteriori* path' and its secular promise.

The review is entered in her Journal for 8 July 1855.

*　　　*　　　*

'THE age of systems is passed. . . . System is the childhood of philosophy; the manhood of philosophy is investigation.' So says Professor Gruppe in the work of which we have given the title above, and we quote this dictum at the outset in order to propitiate

[1] *Letters*, II, 192. George Eliot also set down her impressions of Gruppe in 'Recollections of Berlin', Cross, *Life*, I, 354–356.

ʌose readers who might otherwise turn away with disgust from ʌe mention of German philosophy, having registered a vow to ʇrouble themselves no more with those spinners of elaborate ɔcoons—German system-mongers.

Perhaps, however, there are some of our readers who would not equire any such password from Professor Gruppe; for although ʇe is better known in England as a writer on classical literature ʇhan as a philosopher, still it is likely that many German scholars ɯmongst us are acquainted with his two philosophical works, *Intæus*, published in 1831, and *Wendepunkt der Philosophie im ʃeunzehnten Jahrhundert*, published in 1834. He is a man of very ʌarious accomplishments, and throws his active intellect with qual fervour and facility into many channels—into poetry and ʇolitics as well as into classical literature and philosophy. This ʌersatility in authorship is rare among erudite Germans, and is ɥeld rather in suspicion by them, in spite of the fact that some of ʇheir greatest men—Lessing, Herder, Goethe, and Schiller—were ʇroductive in several departments. Those who decry versatility— ɯnd there are many who do so in other countries besides Germany —seem to forget the immense service rendered by the *suggestive- ʇess* of versatile men, who come to a subject with fresh, unstrained ɯinds. You have perhaps been spending much time and ingenuity ɩn planning a house or in spinning a theory which seems to you to ɯccount satisfactorily for many things: an intelligent neighbour ɔomes in, and you show him your plan, or explain to him your ʇheory. He is not an accomplished architect, but he sees at once ʇhat you have put a door and a chimney in incompatible positions; ʌe is not, perhaps, a profound thinker, but he makes an observa- ʇion on your theory which directly shows you that it will not 'hold ʌvater'. Such is the service which the versatile man will often ʇender to the patient, exclusive inquirer. To return to Professor Gruppe: he has vindicated his versatility by achieving more than ɑn average success in more than one department; his *Ariadne* is ɔne of the best books, if not the very best, we have on the Greek Drama; his *Cosmic System of the Greeks* is an ingenious application ɔf scholarship; many of his lyrical poems have considerable merit;[2]

[2] The books referred to are *Ariadne, Die tragische Kunst der Griechen* ʁ1834) and *Die kosmischen Systeme der Griechen* (1851). George Eliot ɦeard Gruppe read many of his poems, but she may also have looked at ɦis *Gedichte* (1835).

and his *Wendepunkt der Philosophie* is a striking philosophical
work, showing much acumen and independent thought. In the
work now before us, which was originally intended to be a mere
pamphlet, but which has swelled to a volume of nearly three
hundred pages, he rapidly (and somewhat too allusively for the
general reader) restates the views contained in his earlier philosophical works, the *Antæus* and the *Wendepunkt*—views which
twenty years of additional study and considerable experience as a
professor of Moral Philosophy in the University of Berlin have
served to confirm and make clearer.

The object towards which Herr Gruppe chiefly directs his
consideration is the Reformation of Logic, or the rectification of
the *method* of philosophical inquiry, which, as he justly insists, is
the essential preliminary to all true progress. It is, he says, simply
to a reform in method that we owe all the splendid achievements
of modern natural science, and it is only by the extension of that
reform to every department of philosophical inquiry that here also
any of what Bacon calls 'fruit' can be obtained. In fact, the gist of
his philosophical labours is partly to map out the road which John
Mill (to whose work he seems to have given imperfect attention)[3]
has actually wrought out and made available. It is curious that while
Locke is, on the one hand, accused of being the originator of the
French Sensational Philosophy, he is, on the other hand, as in the
present work, reproached for having formed a step towards the
speculative systems of Germany, in admitting *ideas of reflection*,
thus severing *ideas* from *things*. This, says Professor Gruppe, is the
fundamental error of philosophy, and, from Parmenides downwards, has issued in nothing but the bewilderment of the human
intellect. Kant's classification of Infinity and Universality as ideas
à priori, and of Space and Time as purely subjective forms of the
intelligence, is a further elaboration of this fundamental error.
These abstract terms on which speculation has built its huge
fabrics are simply the x and y by which we mark the boundary of
our knowledge; they have no value except in connexion with the
concrete. The abstract is derived from the concrete: what, then,
can we expect from a philosophy the essence of which is the

[3] George Eliot first mentions Mill's *A System of Logic* (1843) in 1849
(*Letters*, I, 310). Her Journal for 7 March 1866 notes that she is 'reading
Mill's Logic again'; and in a letter of 1875 she acknowledges having
studied the book 'with much benefit'. (*Letters*, VI, 163.)

erivation of the concrete from the abstract? The chief argument
ι favour of *à priori* ideas, as insisted on by Leibnitz and Kant is,
ιat they can never be arrived at by induction; that induction may
:ad to the *general* but never to the *universal*, and that, neverthe-
:ss, this idea of universality is found in speech and in thought with
ιe mark of necessity. But this argument will not bear a rigid
xamination. The language of all peoples soon attains to the
xpressions *all*, *universal*, *necessary*, but these expressions have
ιeir origin purely in the observations of the senses; they are
imply a practical expedient, and are valued only under certain
ιell-known and presupposed conditions. To isolate such expres-
ions, to operate with them apart from experience, to exalt their
ιlative value into an absolute value, to deduce knowledge from
ιem alone, and to make them a standing point higher than all
xperience—this, which is what Parmenides and all speculative
ιhilosophers since him have done, is an attempt to poise the
ιniverse on one's head, and no wonder if dizziness and delusion
ιre the consequence.

These views are familiar enough to us in England, but to find
ιhem urged by a German professor is not so familiar.

A system of logic, says Herr Gruppe, which assigns the first
ιlace to general ideas, and makes them prior to judgment, inverts
ιhe true order of things. The true object of investigation is the
ιormation of ideas from judgments, and in order to ascertain the
ιaw of their formation, we must direct our observation to those
:ases in which a new judgment or perception occurs, and is
ιmbodied in language, to the mental process which takes a dis-
:overy in natural science is made and is expressed in words, to the
ιlace when development of language, and to the application of
ιanguage by children.[4] In these three ways the formation of general
ιdeas is daily carried forward. According to these tests, every judg-
ιnent exhibits itself as a comparison, or perception of likeness
ι the midst of difference: the metaphor is no mere ornament
ιf speech, but belongs to its essence, though usage gradually

---

[4] A possible reading of this garbled passage is: 'we must direct our
ιbservation to those cases in which a new judgment or perception occurs,
ιnd is embodied in language, to the mental process which takes place
ιhen a discovery in natural science is made and is expressed in words, to
ιhe development of language, and to the application of language by
ιhildren'.

dispenses with it. When we say the evening sky is red, the lily is white, it may seem as if red and white were independent, immediate ideas; not so, when we say the sky is rose-red or rosy, the lily snow-white or snowy. Again, when we hear a child call the neighbour's dog, not a dog, but *Caro*, because its own dog is named Caro, we see the origin of the idea of species, or of general ideas; this is the first step towards the remotest abstractions. A consideration of examples, taken from the doctrines of natural science, shows, what has hitherto been overlooked by logicians, that every true judgment inevitably alters the idea both of the subject and predicate. Thus, when we say granite is volcanic, we modify both the idea of granite and of the predicate volcanic: a new quality is attributed to granite, and the predicate volcanic receives a wider extension. Kant, then, was mistaken in regarding synthetical and analytical judgments as two distinct classes. The true statement is, that every analytical judgment has previously been synthetic, and every synthetic judgment is such only once, and immediately becomes analytic. By a synthetic judgment, the idea of the predicate passes into that of the subject, and is incorporated with it, so that when I repeat this judgment it is necessarily analytic. Thus, from the simple act of judgment we ascend to the formation of ideas, to their modification, and their generalisation. And by a series of ascending generalisations we are led to the most comprehensive, abstract ideas. But by the side of these abstract ideas, to which we attain by an ascent from positive particulars, there is another set of ideas which owe their origin to unprecise expressions and mere devices of language, by which we bridge over our ignorance or eke out our limitation, and singularly enough these are the very ideas which have been enthroned as the *absolute*.

Professor Gruppe, in common with many before him, makes war against the syllogism as a *petitio principii*, and even seems to reject it altogether as an instrument. He seems to us not to have rightly apprehended Mill's analysis of the syllogism[5] and the function he assigns to it, since he makes it an objection to that writer's views that he gives an important place to deduction in his method. Deduction, as Mill shows, is not properly opposed to induction but to experiment, and is a means of registering and using the results of induction, indispensable to any great progress in

[5] In Book II of *A System of Logic*.

science. But these are questions which this is not the place to discuss.

What then, asks Herr Gruppe in conclusion, is the future sphere of Philosophy? It must renounce metaphysics: it must renounce the ambitious attempt to form a theory of the universe, to know things in their causes and first principles. But in its function of determining logic or method, it is still the centre and heart of human knowledge, and it has to apply this method to the investigation of Psychology, with its subordinate department Æsthetics; to Ethics; and to the principles of Jurisprudence. A sufficient task!

These are rather abstruse subjects to enter on in a short space, but we have at least been able to present one point of interest to our readers, in the fact that a German professor of philosophy renounces the attempt to climb to heaven by the rainbow bridge of 'the high *priori* road', and is content humbly to use his muscles in treading the uphill *à posteriori* path which will lead, not indeed to heaven, but to an eminence whence we may see very bright and blessed things on earth.

11

LIFE AND OPINIONS OF MILTON

Leader, VI (4 August 1855), 750

Thomas Keightley (1789–1872), who compiled or edited many historical and literary texts during his long life, among them a still useful edition of Milton (1859), published in 1855 *An Account of the Life, Opinions, and Writings of John Milton, with an Introduction to Paradise Lost*. George Eliot reviewed the book twice, first in the *Leader* then in the *Westminster*, LXIV (October, 1855), 602–604. In the *Westminster* she chose Milton's plan of education—calling it a 'magnificent impossibility'—for particular discussion; in the *Leader* review she dwells on Milton's doctrine of divorce. Thornton Hunt, the man with whom Lewes was associated in the founding of the *Leader*, and who was responsible for breaking up Lewes's marriage, was then still with the paper, though what effect George Eliot may have designed her remarks to have on him it is difficult to conceive.

The article is entered in George Eliot's Journal for 1 August 1855.

* * *

THIS volume on Milton has been a labour of love to Mr. Keightley, and, as with all such labours where there is ability as well as love, the result is valuable. The biographical part is full without being prolix; all the accessible materials are well digested, and the evidence for questionable details carefully sifted: there are no bookmaking digressions from the history of Milton's life to the history of his period, but the reader finds as much illustrative information as is necessary. Those who are unacquainted with Milton's prose works may get a very fair idea of them from Mr. Keightley's analysis and extracts: they may learn what were Milton's opinions, how he argued, and in what style he wrote prose;

and perhaps in these days, when the chief place of study is the railway carriage, the majority of readers will be satisfied with this rapid *coup d'œil*. Mr. Keightley does not seem to us to be always felicitous in his criticism of Milton's poems, but his comments, especially in the introduction to *Paradise Lost*, contain much that is highly suggestive.

The principal phases and incidents of Milton's life are familiar to us all: the sentence of rustication passed on him at the university; the bright, idyllic days at Horton when his early poems were produced; the journey to Italy where he 'found and visited the famous Galileo, grown old, a prisoner';[1] the prosaic transition to school-keeping in London City and inharmonious marriage with Mary Powell; his Latin secretaryship; his second and third ventures in matrimony, and small satisfaction in his daughters; the long days of blindness in which the *Paradise Lost* was poured forth by thirty lines at a time when a friendly pen happened to be near; and the quiet closing years when he might be seen 'to sit in a coarse grey cloth coat at the door of his house in Bunhill Fields, in warm, sunny weather, to enjoy the fresh air, and so, as well as in his room, to receive the visits of people of distinguished parts as well as quality.'[2]

Less familiar, because less generally interesting, are Milton's religious opinions, which were not fully known until 1823, when Mr. Lemon, during his researches in the Old State Paper-office, happened to lay his hands on a Latin manuscript which proved to be the Treatise on Christian Doctrine, known to have been written by Milton. In this treatise, we have a complete statement of Milton's theological and ethical views. That he was an Arian, a believer in free-will and in the universal efficacy of Christ's death, had been already apparent to the understanding reader in the pages of *Paradise Lost*; the Calvinists, it was evident, could not claim him as their own. His famous work, too, on the *Doctrine and Discipline of Divorce*, had sufficiently announced his departure from the prevalent opinion on that subject. The more unexpected points in the treatise on Christian doctrine are the position that polygamy is permitted by the law of Christ; the rejection of infant baptism; and the materialistic view of the human soul, that 'man

[1] From 'Areopagitica', quoted by Keightley, pp. 14–15.
[2] Jonathan Richardson's life of Milton (1734), slightly misquoted from Keightley, p. 71.

is not, according to the common opinion, made up and framed of two distinct and different natures, as of soul and body, but that the whole man is soul and the soul man.' Milton was anti-Puritan in his view of the Sabbath, concurring with Luther in regarding the Christian day of rest as a matter of expediency to be regulated by the civil government, not as a matter of divine authority.

When Milton wrote his *Doctrine and Discipline of Divorce* he was pleading his own cause as well as urging a general argument, just as, two centuries later, Mrs. Norton has recently done, and is doing in her *Letter to the Queen*.[3] There is much unreasonable prejudice against this blending of personal interest with a general protest. If we waited for the impulse of abstract benevolence or justice, we fear that most reforms would be postponed to the Greek Kalends, and in all matters where popular alarms and prejudices do not come into play, personal experience is considered the next qualification for bearing witness to an evil. The Athenians, so far from sharing this ultra-delicate notion of ours, that a man is not to appear in a cause for the very reason that he has an interest in it, would allow no man to bring a case of litigation into court unless he had a personal concern in that case: they distrusted all disinterested officiousness as much as we should distrust a man who set up shop purely for the good of the community. The personal interest may lead to exaggeration, and may be unwisely thrust into prominence, but *in* itself it is assuredly not a ground for silence but for speech, until we have reached that stage in which the work of this world will be all done vicariously, everybody acting for some one else, and nobody for himself.

Milton's plea for divorce, of course, drew down on him plenty of Presbyterian vituperation: his book was 'a wicked book', his error 'too gross for refutation'.[4] Yet his style is singularly calm and dignified. He desires 'not that licence and levity and unconsented breach of faith should herein be countenanced, but that some conscionable and tender pity might be had of those who have unwarily, in a thing they never practised before, made themselves

---

[3] Caroline Norton (1808–1877) had in 1853 been involved in a sensational public quarrel with her estranged husband over his refusal to pay her allowance. 'A letter to the Queen on Lord Cranworth's Marriage and Divorce Bill' (1855) was an attack on both the existing divorce law and the bill to amend it.

[4] Slightly misquoted from Keightley, p. 37.

the bondmen of a luckless and helpless matrimony'. We seem to see a trace of his own experience when he says, 'Who knows not that the bashful muteness of a virgin may ofttimes hide all the unliveliness and natural sloth which is really unfit for conversation?'—and when he speaks of a 'sober man' discovering that the appearance of modesty in the woman he has chosen hides a nature 'to all the more estimable and superior purposes of matrimony useless and almost lifeless.' There is pathos as well as force in the following passage:

> And yet there follows upon this a worse temptation. For if he (the husband) be such as hath spent his youth unblamably, and laid up his chiefly earthly comforts in the enjoyment of a contented marriage, nor did neglect the furtherance which was to be obtained therein by constant prayers, when he shall find himself bound fast to an uncomplying discord of nature, or, as it oft happens, to an image of earth and phlegm, with whom he looked to be the copartner of a sweet and gladsome society; and sees withal that his bondage is now inevitable: though he be almost the strongest Christian, he will be ready to despair in virtue, and mutiny against Divine Providence.

A picture, alas! too often realised since the year 1644, when it was thus powerfully drawn. For want of a more modern pendant to Mrs. Norton's plea, it is worth while to take up Milton's, and consider what such a mind as his had to urge on the husband's side of this painful subject.

Before taking leave of Mr. Keightley's volume, let us say that it is the best introduction we have seen to the study of Milton, and that we recommend it to our readers as a fund of knowledge at once instructive and delightful.

12

EVANGELICAL TEACHING: DR. CUMMING

Westminster Review, LXIV (October, 1855), 436–462

George Eliot's article on Dr. Cumming, begun on 13 June, was finished on 24 August 1855 (Journal). With its Macaulayesque exordium and its impassioned appeal to the God who 'sympathizes with all we feel and endure for our fellow-men', it is certainly the most energetic of her several attacks upon the religious spirit she had known in her youth. According to Charles Lewes, 'it was after reading this article that his father was prompted to say to George Eliot, whilst walking one day with her in Richmond Park, that it convinced him of the true genius in her writing. . . . Up to this time he had not been quite sure of anything beyond great talent in her productions.'[1]

Dr. John Cumming (1807–1881), the subject of the article, was minister of the Scottish National Church, Crown Court, Covent Garden, from 1832 to 1879. He was best known as an interpreter of Biblical prophecy, and was especially notorious for his belief that the seventh vial of the Apocalypse was to be poured out between 1848 and 1867. According to the *DNB* he wrote 'more than a hundred publications of various kinds'; their character is evident from their titles, as *Rome the Babylon of the Apocalypse* (1851); *Genesis and Geology* (1852); *The End: or, the Proximate Signs of the Close of this Dispensation* (1855); and *Moses Right, and Bishop Colenso Wrong* (1863).

In a letter to her friend Charles Bray written two weeks after the appearance of the article George Eliot asks him not to reveal that she is the author: 'The article appears to have produced a strong impression, and that impression would be a little counteracted if the author were known to be a *woman*. . . . I have had a letter addressed to "the author of article No. 4." begging me to print it separately for "the good of mankind in general." '[2] Though 'Evangelical Teaching' is written from

---

[1] Cross, *Life*, I, 384–385.   [2] *Letters*, II, 218.

the viewpoint of a Radical, informed by the study of historical criticism, and influenced by the theology of Feuerbach, George Eliot's attitude toward Cumming was shared by some Victorians of quite different intellectual character. Writing to his mother a few months before the article appeared, Thackeray said of Cumming: 'I think him a bigot, a blasphemer; that the world would be horrible if he & his could have his way. . . .'[3] Tennyson, whose mother's favourite reading was Cumming's books, held quite as low an opinion of Cumming as George Eliot did, and expressed himself in a passage from his idyl 'Sea Dreams', describing a chapel service where

> a heated pulpiteer
> Not preaching simple Christ to simple men,
> Announced the coming doom, and fulminated
> Against the Scarlet Woman and her creed.

As Jerome Hamilton Buckley has pointed out,[4] the poem recalls the terms of George Eliot's attack on Cumming. Since, in addition, there is clear evidence that Tennyson had seen the October, 1855, issue of the *Westminster*,[5] it is probable that he had read her article before writing 'Sea Dreams'.

At the head of the article George Eliot lists the following titles by Cumming as the sources of her information: *The Church before the Flood* (1853); *Occasional Discourses*, 2 vols. (1850); *Signs of the Times* (1854); *The Finger of God* (1853); *Is Christianity from God? or, a Manual of Christian Evidence, for Scripture-Readers, City Missionaries, Sunday-School Teachers, &c.* (1847); *Apocalyptic Sketches; or, Lectures on the Book of Revelation*, 1st and 2nd Series (1848–1849); and *Prophetic Studies; or Lectures on the Book of Daniel* (1850).

'Evangelical Teaching' has been reprinted in Nathan Sheppard, *The Essays of 'George Eliot', Complete;* and in *Essays and Leaves from a Note-Book*.

*   *   *

GIVEN, a man with moderate intellect, a moral standard not higher than the average, some rhetorical affluence and great glibness of speech, what is the career in which, without the aid of birth or money, he may most easily attain power and reputation in English society? Where is that Goshen of mediocrity in which a smattering of science and learning will pass for profound instruction, where

[3] *The Letters and Private Papers of William Makepeace Thackeray*, ed. Gordon N. Ray, III (Cambridge, 1946), 439.
[4] *Tennyson, The Growth of a Poet* (Cambridge, 1960), pp. 139–140.
[5] See 'Tennyson's *Maud*', note 7.

platitudes will be accepted as wisdom, bigoted narrowness as holy zeal, unctuous egoism as God-given piety? Let such a man become an evangelical preacher; he will then find it possible to reconcile small ability with great ambition, superficial knowledge with the prestige of erudition, a middling morale with a high reputation for sanctity. Let him shun practical extremes and be ultra only in what is purely theoretic: let him be stringent on predestination, but latitudinarian on fasting; unflinching in insisting on the Eternity of punishment, but diffident of curtailing the substantial comforts of Time; ardent and imaginative on the pre-millennial advent of Christ, but cold and cautious towards every other infringement of the *status quo*. Let him fish for souls not with the bait of inconvenient singularity, but with the dragnet of comfortable conformity. Let him be hard and literal in his interpretation only when he wants to hurl texts at the heads of unbelievers and adversaries, but when the letter of the Scriptures presses too closely on the genteel Christianity of the nineteenth century, let him use his spiritualizing alembic and disperse it into impalpable ether. Let him preach less of Christ than of Antichrist; let him be less definite in showing what sin is than in showing who is the Man of Sin,[6] less expansive on the blessedness of faith than on the accursedness of infidelity. Above all, let him set up as an interpreter of prophecy, and rival Moore's Almanack[7] in the prediction of political events, tickling the interest of hearers who are but moderately spiritual by showing how the Holy Spirit has dictated problems and charades for their benefit, and how, if they are ingenious enough to solve these, they may have their Christian graces nourished by learning precisely to whom they may point as the 'horn that had eyes', 'the lying prophet', and the 'unclean spirits'.[8] In this way he will draw men to him by the strong cords of their passions, made reason-proof by being baptized with the name of piety. In this way he may gain a metropolitan pulpit; the avenues to his church will be as crowded as the passages to the opera; he has but to print his prophetic sermons and bind them in lilac and gold, and they will adorn the drawing-room table of all evangelical ladies, who will regard as a sort of pious 'light reading' the demonstration that the

[6] An allusion to Cumming's *The Pope, the Man of Sin* (1851).
[7] A prophetic almanac, published from 'about 1680 to 1835 (?)' (*Allibone*).
[8] Cf. Daniel 7:8; Revelation 16:13.

prophecy of the locusts whose sting is in their tail,[9] is fulfilled in the fact of the Turkish commander's having taken a horse's tail for his standard, and that the French are the very frogs predicted in the Revelations.

Pleasant to the clerical flesh under such circumstances is the arrival of Sunday! Somewhat at a disadvantage during the week, in the presence of working-day[10] interests and lay splendours, on Sunday the preacher becomes the cynosure of a thousand eyes, and predominates at once over the Amphitryon with whom he dines, and the most captious member of his church or vestry. He has an immense advantage over all other public speakers. The platform orator is subject to the criticism of hisses and groans. Counsel for the plaintiff expects the retort of counsel for the defendant. The honourable gentleman on one side of the House is liable to have his facts and figures shown up by his honourable friend on the opposite side. Even the scientific or literary lecturer, if he is dull or incompetent, may see the best part of his audience quietly slip out one by one. But the preacher is completely master of the situation: no one may hiss, no one may depart. Like the writer of imaginary conversations, he may put what imbecilities he pleases into the mouths of his antagonists, and swell with triumph when he has refuted them. He may riot in gratuitous assertions, confident that no man will contradict him; he may exercise perfect free-will in logic, and invent illustrative experience; he may give an evangelical edition of history with the inconvenient facts omitted:—all this he may do with impunity, certain that those of his hearers who are not sympathizing are not listening. For the Press has no band of critics who go the round of the churches and chapels, and are on the watch for a slip or defect in the preacher, to make a 'feature' in their article: the clergy are, practically, the most irresponsible of all talkers. For this reason, at least, it is well that they do not always allow their discourses to be merely fugitive, but are often induced to fix them in that black and white in which they are open to the criticism of any man who has the courage and patience to treat them with thorough freedom of speech and pen.

It is because we think this criticism of clerical teaching desirable for the public good, that we devote some pages to Dr. Cumming. He is, as every one knows, a preacher of immense popularity, and

[9] Revelation 9:10.   [10] See 'Silly Novels by Lady Novelists', note 6.

of the numerous publications in which he perpetuates his pulpit labours, all circulate widely, and some, according to their title-page, have reached the sixteenth thousand. Now our opinion of these publications is the very opposite of that given by a newspaper eulogist: we do *not* 'believe that the repeated issues of Dr. Cumming's thoughts are having a beneficial effect on society,' but the reverse; and hence, little inclined as we are to dwell on his pages, we think it worth while to do so, for the sake of pointing out in them what we believe to be profoundly mistaken and pernicious. Of Dr. Cumming personally we know absolutely nothing: our acquaintance with him is confined to a perusal of his works, our judgment of him is founded solely on the manner in which he has written himself down on his pages. We know neither how he looks nor how he lives. We are ignorant whether, like St. Paul, he has a bodily presence that is weak and contemptible, or whether his person is as florid and as prone to amplification as his style. For aught we know, he may not only have the gift of prophecy, but may bestow the profits of all his works to feed the poor,[11] and be ready to give his own body to be burned with as much alacrity as he infers the everlasting burning of Roman-catholics and Puseyites. Out of the pulpit he may be a model of justice, truthfulness, and the love that thinketh no evil; but we are obliged to judge of his charity by the spirit we find in his sermons, and shall only be glad to learn that his practice is, in many respects, an amiable *non sequitur* from his teaching.

Dr. Cumming's mind is evidently not of the pietistic order. There is not the slightest leaning towards mysticism in his Christianity—no indication of religious raptures, of delight in God, or spiritual communion with the Father. He is most at home in the forensic view of Justification, and dwells on salvation as a scheme rather than as an experience. He insists on good works as the sign of justifying faith, as labours to be achieved to the glory of God, but he rarely represents them as the spontaneous, necessary outflow of a soul filled with Divine love. He is at home in the external, the polemical, the historical, the circumstantial, and is only episodically devout and practical. The great majority of his

[11] Since Cumming was well known for his philanthropic activities, this is perhaps George Eliot's attempt to forestall an obvious objection to her criticism.

published sermons are occupied with argument or philippic against Romanists and unbelievers, with 'vindications' of the Bible, with the political interpretation of prophecy, or the criticism of public events; and the devout aspiration, or the spiritual and practical exhortation, is tacked to them as a sort of fringe in a hurried sentence or two at the end. He revels in the demonstration that the Pope is the Man of Sin; he is copious on the downfall of the Ottoman empire; he appears to glow with satisfaction in turning a story which tends to show how he abashed an 'infidel'; it is a favourite exercise with him to form conjectures of the process by which the earth is to be burned up, and to picture Dr. Chalmers and Mr. Wilberforce[12] being caught up to meet Christ in the air, while Romanists, Puseyites, and infidels are given over to gnashing of teeth. But of really spiritual joys and sorrows, of the life and death of Christ as a manifestation of love that constrains the soul, of sympathy with that yearning over the lost and erring which made Jesus weep over Jerusalem, and prompted the sublime prayer, 'Father, forgive them', of the gentler fruits of the Spirit, and the peace of God which passeth understanding—of all this, we find little trace in Dr. Cumming's discourses.

His style is in perfect correspondence with this habit of mind. Though diffuse, as that of all preachers must be, it has rapidity of movement, perfect clearness, and some aptness of illustration. He has much of that literary talent which makes a good journalist— the power of beating out an idea over a large space, and of introducing far-fetched à propos. His writings have, indeed, no high merit: they have no originality or force of thought, no striking felicity of presentation, no depth of emotion. Throughout nine volumes we have alighted on no passage which impressed us as worth extracting, and placing among the 'beauties' of evangelical writers, such as Robert Hall, Foster the Essayist, or Isaac Taylor.[13] Everywhere there is commonplace cleverness, nowhere a spark of

[12] Thomas Chalmers (1780–1847), professor of divinity at Edinburgh and a leader in the movement that ended in the formation of the Scottish Free Church. William Wilberforce (1759–1833), the great Evangelical and abolitionist.
[13] Robert Hall (1764–1831) and John Foster (1770–1843), Baptist preachers. Isaac Taylor (1787–1846), though a member of the Church of England, was strongly Evangelical. His *Ancient Christianity and the Doctrines of the Oxford Tracts for the Times* (1839–1840) influenced George Eliot's views of early Christian history.

rare thought, of lofty sentiment, or pathetic tenderness. We feel ourselves in company with a voluble retail talker, whose language is exuberant but not exact, and to whom we should never think of referring for precise information, or for well-digested thought and experience. His argument continually slides into wholesale assertion and vague declamation, and in his love of ornament he frequently becomes tawdry. For example, he tells us (Apoc. Sketches, p. 265), that 'Botany weaves around the cross her amaranthine garlands; and Newton comes from his starry home— Linnæus from his flowery resting-place—and Werner and Hutton from their subterranean graves at the voice of Chalmers, to acknowledge that all they learned and elicited in their respective provinces, has only served to show more clearly that Jesus of Nazareth is enthroned on the riches of the universe': —and so prosaic an injunction to his hearers as that they should choose a residence within an easy distance of church, is magnificently draped by him as an exhortation to prefer a house 'that basks in the sunshine of the countenance of God'. Like all preachers of his class, he is more fertile in imaginative paraphrase than in close exposition, and in this way he gives us some remarkable fragments of what we may call the romance of Scripture, filling up the outline of the record with an elaborate colouring quite undreamed of by more literal minds. The serpent, he informs us, said to Eve, 'Can it be so? Surely you are mistaken, that God hath said you shall die, a creature so fair, so lovely, so beautiful. It is impossible. *The laws of nature and physical science tell you that my interpretation is correct*; you shall not die. I can tell you by my own experience as an angel that you shall be as gods, knowing good and evil'. (Apoc. Sketches, p. 294). Again, according to Dr. Cumming, Abel had so clear an idea of the Incarnation and Atonement, that when he offered his sacrifice 'he must have said, "I feel myself a guilty sinner, and that in myself I cannot meet thee alive; I lay on thine altar this victim, and I shed its blood as my testimony that mine should be shed; and I look for forgiveness and undeserved mercy through Him who is to bruise the serpent's head, and whose atonement this typifies"'.' (Occas. Disc. vol. i, p. 23.) Indeed, his productions are essentially ephemeral; he is essentially a journalist, who writes sermons instead of leading articles, who, instead of venting diatribes against her Majesty's Ministers, directs his power of invective against Cardinal Wiseman and the Puseyites,—

instead of declaiming on public spirit, perorates on the 'glory of God'. We fancy he is called, in the more refined evangelical circles, an 'intellectual preacher'; by the plainer sort of Christians, a 'flowery preacher'; and we are inclined to think that the more spiritually-minded class of believers, who look with greater anxiety for the kingdom of God within them than for the visible advent of Christ in 1864, will be likely to find Dr. Cumming's declamatory flights and historico-prophetical exercitations as little better than 'clouts o' cauld parritch'.[13a]

Such is our general impression from his writings after an attentive perusal. There are some particular characteristics which we shall consider more closely, but in doing so we must be understood as altogether declining any doctrinal discussion. We have no intention to consider the grounds of Dr. Cumming's dogmatic system, to examine the principles of his prophetic exegesis, or to question his opinion concerning the little horn, the river Euphrates, or the seven vials. We identify ourselves with no one of the bodies whom he regards it as his special mission to attack: we give our adhesion neither to Romanism, Puseyism, nor to that anomalous combination of opinions which he introduces to us under the name of Infidelity. It is simply as spectators that we criticize Dr. Cumming's mode of warfare, and we concern ourselves less with what he holds to be Christian truth than with his manner of enforcing that truth, less with the doctrines he teaches than with the moral spirit and tendencies of his teaching.

One of the most striking characteristics of Dr. Cumming's writings is *unscrupulosity of statement*. His motto apparently is, *Christianitatem, quocunque modo, Christianitatem*;[14] and the only system he includes under the term Christianity is Calvinistic Protestantism. Experience has so long shown that the human brain is a congenial nidus for inconsistent beliefs, that we do not pause to inquire how Dr. Cumming, who attributes the conversion of the unbelieving to the Divine Spirit, can think it necessary to co-operate with that Spirit by argumentative white lies. Nor do we for a moment impugn the genuineness of his zeal for Christianity, or the sincerity of his conviction that the doctrines he preaches are

---

[13a] In Scott, *Rob Roy*, Ch. 17, "clauts o' cauld parritch" is Andrew Fairservice's phrase for degenerate preaching.

[14] Cf. Horace, Ep. I, i, 66: 'rem facias, rem / Recte, si possis, si non, quocunque modo rem'.

necessary to salvation; on the contrary, we regard the flagrant
unveracity that we find on his pages as an indirect result of that
conviction—as a result, namely, of the intellectual and moral
distortion of view which is inevitably produced by assigning to
dogmas, based on a very complex structure of evidence, the place
and authority of first truths. A distinct appreciation of the value
of evidence—in other words, the intellectual perception of truth
—is more closely allied to truthfulness of statement, or the moral
quality of veracity, than is generally admitted. There is not a more
pernicious fallacy afloat in common parlance, than the wide
distinction made between intellect and morality. [Amiable impulses without intellect, man may have in common with dogs
and horses; but morality, which is specifically human, is dependent
on the regulation of feeling by intellect. All human beings who
can be said to be in any degree moral have their impulses
guided, not indeed always by their own intellect, but by the
intellect of human beings who have gone before them, and created
traditions and associations which have taken the rank of laws.
Now][15] that highest moral habit, the constant preference of truth
both theoretically and practically, preeminently demands the co-
operation of the intellect with the impulses; as is indicated by
the fact that it is only found in anything like completeness in the
highest class of minds. [In accordance with this we think it is
found that, in proportion as religious sects exalt feeling above
intellect, and believe themselves to be guided by direct inspiration
rather than by a spontaneous exertion of their faculties—that is, in
proportion as they are removed from rationalism—their sense of
truthfulness is misty and confused.][16] No one can have talked to
the more enthusiastic Methodists and listened to their stories of
miracles without perceiving that they require no other passport to
a statement than that it accords with their wishes and their general
conception of God's dealings; nay, they regard as a symptom of
sinful scepticism an inquiry into the evidence for a story which
they think unquestionably tends to the glory of God, and in
retailing such stories, new particulars, further tending to his

[15] Omitted, 1884.

[16] 'And it is commonly seen that, in proportion as religious sects
believe themselves to be guided by direct inspiration rather than by a
spontaneous exertion of their faculties, their sense of truthfulness is
misty and confused.' 1884.

glory, are 'borne in' upon their minds. Now, Dr. Cumming, as we have said, is no enthusiastic pietist: within a certain circle—within the mill of evangelical orthodoxy, his intellect is perpetually at work; but that principle of sophistication which our friends the Methodists derive from the predominance of their pietistic feelings, is involved for him in the doctrine of verbal inspiration; what is for them a state of emotion submerging the intellect, is with him a formula imprisoning the intellect, depriving it of its proper function—the free search for truth—and making it the mere servant-of-all-work to a foregone conclusion. Minds fettered by this doctrine no longer inquire concerning a proposition whether it is attested by sufficient evidence, but whether it accords with Scripture; they do not search for facts, as such, but for facts that will bear out their doctrine. They become accustomed to reject the more direct evidence in favour of the less direct, and where adverse evidence reaches demonstration they must resort to devices and expedients in order to explain away contradiction. It is easy to see that this mental habit blunts not only the perception of truth, but the sense of truthfulness, and that the man whose faith drives him into fallacies, treads close upon the precipice of falsehood.

We have entered into this digression for the sake of mitigating the inference that is likely to be drawn from that characteristic of Dr. Cumming's works to which we have pointed. He is much in the same intellectual condition as that Professor of Padua, who, in order to disprove Galileo's discovery of Jupiter's satellites, urged that as there were only seven metals there could not be more than seven planets[17]—a mental condition scarcely compatible with candour. And we may well suppose that if the Professor had held the belief in seven planets, and no more, to be a necessary condition of salvation, his mental vision would have been so dazed that even if he had consented to look through Galileo's telescope, his eyes would have reported in accordance with his inward alarms rather than with the external fact. So long as a belief in propositions is regarded as indispensable to salvation, the pursuit of truth *as such* is not possible, any more than it is possible for a man who is swimming for his life to make meteorological observations on the storm which threatens to overwhelm him. The sense

[17] The Florentine astronomer Francesco Sizi employed this argument in his attack upon Galileo in *Dianoia astronomia* (1610).

of alarm and haste, the anxiety for personal safety, which Dr. Cumming insists upon as the proper religious attitude, unmans the nature, and allows no thorough, calm-thinking, no truly noble, disinterested feeling. Hence, we by no means suspect that the unscrupulosity of statement with which we charge Dr. Cumming, extends beyond the sphere of his theological prejudices; [we do not doubt that, religion apart, he appreciates and practises veracity.][18]

A grave general accusation must be supported by details, and in adducing these, we purposely select the most obvious cases of misrepresentation—such as require no argument to expose them, but can be perceived at a glance. Among Dr. Cumming's numerous books, one of the most notable for unscrupulosity of statement is the 'Manual of Christian Evidences', written, as he tells us in his Preface, not to give the deepest solutions of the difficulties in question, but to furnish Scripture-Readers, City Missionaries, and Sunday School Teachers, with a 'ready reply' to sceptical arguments. This announcement that *readiness* was the chief quality sought for in the solutions here given, modifies our inference from the other qualities which those solutions present; and it is but fair to presume, that when the Christian disputant is not in a hurry, Dr. Cumming would recommend replies less ready and more veracious. Here is an example of what in another place[19] he tells his readers is 'change in their pocket. . . . a little ready argument which they can employ, and therewith answer a fool according to his folly.' From the nature of this argumentative small coin, we are inclined to think Dr. Cumming understands answering a fool according to his folly to mean, giving him a foolish answer. We quote from the 'Manual of Christian Evidences', p. 62.

> Some of the gods which the heathen worshipped were among the greatest monsters that ever walked the earth. Mercury was a thief; and because he was an expert thief, he was enrolled among the gods. Bacchus was a mere sensualist and drunkard; and therefore he was enrolled among the gods. Venus was a dissipated and abandoned courtezan; and therefore she was enrolled among the goddesses. Mars was a savage, that gloried in battle and in blood; and therefore he was deified and enrolled among the gods.

Does Dr. Cumming believe the purport of these sentences? If so, this passage is worth handing down as his theory of the Greek

[18] 'religion apart, he probably appreciates and practises veracity.' 1884.
[19] Lect. on Daniel, p. 6 [George Eliot's note].

myth—as a specimen of the astounding ignorance which was possible in a metropolitan preacher, A.D. 1854. And if he does not believe them. . . . The inference must then be, that he thinks delicate veracity about the ancient Greeks is not a Christian virtue, but only a 'splendid sin' of the unregenerate. This inference is rendered the more probable by our finding, a little further on, that he is not more scrupulous about the moderns, if they come under his definition of 'Infidels'. But the passage we are about to quote in proof of this has a worse quality than its discrepancy with fact. Who that has a spark of generous feeling, that rejoices in the presence of good in a fellow-being, has not dwelt with pleasure on the thought that Lord Byron's unhappy career was ennobled and purified towards its close by a high and sympathetic purpose, by honest and energetic efforts for his fellow-men? Who has not read with deep emotion those last pathetic lines, beautiful as the after-glow of sunset, in which love and resignation are mingled with something of a melancholy heroism?[20] Who has not lingered with compassion over the dying scene at Missolonghi—the sufferer's inability to make his farewell messages of love intelligible, and the last long hours of silent pain? Yet for the sake of furnishing his disciples with a 'ready reply', Dr. Cumming can prevail on himself to inoculate them with a bad-spirited falsity like the following:

> We have one striking exhibition of *an infidel's brightest thoughts*, in some lines *written in his dying moments* by a man, gifted with great genius, capable of prodigious intellectual prowess, but of worthless principle, and yet more worthless practices—I mean the celebrated Lord Byron. He says—

> 'Though gay companions o'er the bowl
>   Dispel awhile the sense of ill
> Though pleasure fills the maddening soul,
>   The heart—*the heart* is lonely still.

> 'Ay, but to die, and go, alas!
>   Where all have gone and all must go;
> To be the *Nothing* that I was,
>   Ere born to life and living woe!

[20] George Eliot means 'On This Day I Complete My Thirty-Sixth Year', then supposed to be Byron's last poem.

'Count o'er the joys thine hours have seen,
  Count o'er thy days from anguish free,
And know, whatever thou hast been,
  'Tis *something better* not to be.

'Nay, for myself, so dark my fate
  Through every turn of life hath been,
Man and the *world* so much *I hate*
  I care not when I quit the scene.'

It is difficult to suppose that Dr. Cumming can have been so grossly imposed upon—that he can be so ill-informed as really to believe that these lines were 'written' by Lord Byron in his dying moments; but, allowing him the full benefit of that possibility, how shall we explain his introduction of this feebly rabid doggrel as 'an infidel's brightest thoughts'?

In marshalling the evidences of Christianity, Dr. Cumming directs most of his arguments against opinions that are either totally imaginary, or that belong to the past rather than to the present, while he entirely fails to meet the difficulties actually felt and urged by those who are unable to accept Revelation. There can hardly be a stronger proof of misconception as to the character of free-thinking in the present day, than the recommendation of Leland's[21] 'Short and Easy Method with the Deists'—a method which is unquestionably short and easy for preachers disinclined to reconsider their stereotyped modes of thinking and arguing, but which has quite ceased to realize those epithets in the conversion of Deists. Yet Dr. Cumming not only recommends this book, but takes the trouble himself to write a feebler version of its arguments. For example, on the question of the genuineness and authenticity of the New Testament writings, he says:—'If, therefore, at a period long subsequent to the death of Christ, a number of men had appeared in the world, drawn up a book which they christened by the name of Holy Scripture, and recorded these things which appear in it as facts when they were only the fancies of their own imagination, surely the *Jews* would have instantly reclaimed that no such events transpired, that no such person as Jesus Christ appeared in their capital, and that *their* crucifixion of Him, and their alleged evil treatment of his apostles, were mere fictions'.[22]

[21] I.e., Charles Leslie (1650–1722), *A Short and Easie Method with the Deists . . . in a Letter to a Friend* (1698).

[22] Man. of Ev. p. 81 [George Eliot's note].

It is scarcely necessary to say that, in such argument as this, Dr. Cumming is beating the air. He is meeting a hypothesis which no one holds, and totally missing the real question. The only type of 'infidel' whose existence Dr. Cumming recognises is that fossil personage who 'calls the Bible a lie and a forgery'. He seems to be ignorant—or he chooses to ignore the fact—that there is a large body of eminently instructed and earnest men who regard the Hebrew and Christian Scriptures as a series of historical documents, to be dealt with according to the rules of historical criticism, and that an equally large number of men, who are not historical critics, find the dogmatic scheme built on the letter of the Scriptures opposed to their profoundest moral convictions. Dr. Cumming's infidel is a man who, because his life is vicious, tries to convince himself that there is no God, and that Christianity is an imposture, but who is all the while secretly conscious that he is opposing the truth, and cannot help 'letting out' admissions 'that the Bible is the Book of God'. We are favoured with the following 'Creed of the Infidel':

> I believe that there is no God, but that matter is God, and God is matter; and that it is no matter whether there is any God or not. I believe also that the world was not made, but that the world made itself, or that it had no beginning, and that it will last for ever. I believe that man is a beast; that the soul is the body, and that the body is the soul; and that after death there is neither body nor soul. I believe that there is no religion, that *natural religion is the only religion, and all religion unnatural.* I believe not in Moses; I believe in the first philosophers. I believe not in the evangelists; I believe in Chubb, Collins, Toland, Tindal, and Hobbes. I believe in Lord Bolingbroke, and I believe not in St. Paul. I believe not in revelation; *I believe in tradition; I believe in the Talmud: I believe in the Korân;* I believe not in the Bible. I believe in Socrates; I believe in Confucius; I believe in Mahomet; I believe not in Christ. And lastly, *I believe* in all unbelief.

The intellectual and moral monster whose creed is this complex web of contradictions, is, moreover, according to Dr. Cumming, a being who unites much simplicity and imbecility with his Satanic hardihood—much tenderness of conscience with his obdurate vice. Hear the 'proof':

> I once met with an acute and enlightened infidel, with whom I reasoned day after day, and for hours together; I submitted to him

the internal, the external, and the experimental evidences, but made no impression on his scorn and unbelief. At length I entertained a suspicion that there was something morally, rather than intellectually wrong, and that the bias was not in the intellect, but in the heart; one day therefore I said to him—'I must now state my conviction, and you may call me uncharitable, but duty compels me; you are living in some known and gross sin.' *The man's countenance became pale; he bowed and left me.—Man. of Evidences*, p. 254.

Here we have the remarkable psychological phenomenon of an 'acute and enlightened' man who, deliberately purposing to indulge in a favourite sin, and regarding the Gospel with scorn and unbelief, is, nevertheless, so much more scrupulous than the majority of Christians, that he cannot 'embrace sin and the Gospel simultaneously'; who is so alarmed at the Gospel in which he does not believe, that he cannot be easy without trying to crush it; whose acuteness and enlightenment suggest to him, as a means of crushing the Gospel, to argue from day to day with Dr. Cumming; and who is withal so naïve that he is taken by surprise when Dr. Cumming, failing in argument, resorts to accusation, and so tender in conscience that, at the mention of his sin, he turns pale and leaves the spot. If there be any human mind in existence capable of holding Dr. Cumming's 'Creed of the Infidel', of at the same time believing in tradition and 'believing in all unbelief', it must be the mind of the infidel just described, for whose existence we have Dr. Cumming's *ex officio* word as a theologian; and to theologians we may apply what Sancho Panza says of the bachelors of Salamanca, that they never tell lies—except when it suits their purpose.[23]

The total absence from Dr. Cumming's theological mind of any demarcation between fact and rhetoric is exhibited in another passage, where he adopts the dramatic form:

Ask the peasant on the hills—*and I have asked amid the mountains of Braemar and Dee-side*,—'How do you know that this book is Divine, and that the religion you profess is true? You never read Paley?' 'No, I never heard of him.'—'You have never read Butler?' 'No, I have never heard of him.'—'Nor Chalmers?' 'No, I do not know him.'—'You have never read any books on evidence?' 'No, I have read no such books.'—'Then, how do you know this book is

[3] *Don Quixote*, Part II, Ch. 33.

true?' 'Know it! Tell me that the Dee, the Clunie, and the Garrawalt, the streams at my feet, do not run; that the winds do not sigh amid the gorges of these blue hills; that the sun does not kindle the peaks of Loch-na-Gar; tell me my heart does not beat, and I will believe you; but do not tell me the Bible is not Divine. I have found its truth illuminating my footsteps; its consolations sustaining my heart. May my tongue cleave to my mouth's roof, and my right hand forget its cunning, if I ever deny what is my deepest inner experience, that this blessed book is the book of God.'—*Church before the Flood*, p. 35.

Dr. Cumming is so slippery and lax in his mode of presentation, that we find it impossible to gather whether he means to assert, that this is what a peasant on the mountains of Braemar *did* say, or that it is what such a peasant *would* say: in the one case, the passage may be taken as a measure of his truthfulness; in the other, of his judgment.

His own faith, apparently, has not been altogether intuitive, like that of his rhetorical peasant, for he tells us (Apoc. Sketches, p. 405) that he has himself experienced what it is to have religious doubts. 'I was tainted while at the University by this spirit of scepticism. I thought Christianity might not be true. The very possibility of its being true was the thought I felt I must meet and settle. Conscience could give me no peace till I had settled it. I read, and I have read from that day, for fourteen or fifteen years, till this, and now I am as convinced, upon the clearest evidence, that this book is the book of God as that I now address you.' This experience, however, instead of impressing on him the fact that doubt may be the stamp of a truth-loving mind—that *sunt quibus non credidisse honor est, et fidei futuræ pignus*—seems to have produced precisely the contrary effect. It has not enabled him even to conceive the condition of a mind 'perplext in faith but pure in deeds',[24] craving light, yearning for a faith that will harmonize and cherish its highest powers and aspirations, but unable to find that faith in dogmatic Christianity. His own doubts apparently were of a different kind. Nowhere in his pages have we found a humble, candid, sympathetic attempt to meet the difficulties that may be felt by an ingenuous mind. Everywhere he supposes that the doubter is hardened, conceited, consciously shutting his eyes to the light—a fool who is to be answered according to his folly—

[24] Tennyson, *In Memoriam*, xcvi, 9.

that is, with ready replies made up of reckless assertions, of apocryphal anecdotes, and, where other resources fail, of vituperative
imputations. As to the reading which he has prosecuted for fifteen
years—*either* it has left him totally ignorant of the relation which
his own religious creed bears to the criticism and philosophy of
the nineteenth century, *or* he systematically blinks that criticism
and that philosophy; and instead of honestly and seriously
endeavouring to meet and solve what he knows to be the real
difficulties, contents himself with setting up popinjays to shoot at,
for the sake of confirming the ignorance and winning the cheap
admiration of his evangelical hearers and readers. Like the
Catholic preacher who, after throwing down his cap and apostro-
phizing it as Luther, turned to his audience and said, 'You see this
heretical fellow has not a word to say for himself', Dr. Cumming,
having drawn his ugly portrait of the infidel, and put arguments of
a convenient quality into his mouth, finds a 'short and easy
method' of confounding this 'croaking frog'.

In his treatment of infidels, we imagine he is guided by a mental
process which may be expressed in the following syllogism:
Whatever tends to the glory of God is true; it is for the glory of
God that infidels should be as bad as possible; therefore, whatever
tends to show that infidels are as bad as possible is true. All
infidels, he tells us, have been men of 'gross and licentious lives'.
Is there not some well-known unbeliever, David Hume, for
example, of whom even Dr. Cumming's readers may have heard
as an exception? No matter. Some one suspected that he was *not* an
exception, and as that suspicion tends to the glory of God, it is
one for a Christian to entertain. (See 'Man. of Ev.' p. 73.)—If we
were unable to imagine this kind of self-sophistication, we should
be obliged to suppose that, relying on the ignorance of his evangelical disciples, he fed them with direct and conscious falsehoods.
'Voltaire', he informs them, 'declares there is no God'; he was 'an
antitheist, that is, one who deliberately and avowedly opposed and
hated God; who swore in his blasphemy that he would dethrone
him;' and 'advocated the very depths of the lowest sensuality'.
With regard to many statements of a similar kind, equally at
variance with truth, in Dr. Cumming's volumes, we presume that
he has been misled by hearsay or by the secondhand character of
his acquaintance with free-thinking literature. An evangelical
preacher is not obliged to be well-read. Here, however, is a case

which the extremest supposition of educated ignorance will not reach. Even books of 'evidences' quote from Voltaire the line—

> Si Dieu n'existait pas, il faudrait l'inventer;

even persons fed on the mere whey and buttermilk of literature, must know that in philosophy Voltaire was nothing if not a theist —must know that he wrote not against God, but against Jehovah, the God of the Jews, whom he believed to be a false God—must know that to say Voltaire was an atheist on this ground is as absurd as to say that a Jacobite opposed hereditary monarchy, because he declared the Brunswick family had no title to the throne. That Dr. Cumming should repeat the vulgar fables about Voltaire's death, is merely what we might expect from the specimens we have seen of his illustrative stories. A man whose accounts of his own experience are apocryphal, is not likely to put borrowed narratives to any severe test.

The alliance between intellectual and moral perversion is strikingly typified by the way in which he alternates from the unveracious to the absurd, from misrepresentation to contradiction. Side by side with the adduction of 'facts' such as those we have quoted, we find him arguing on one page that the Trinity was too grand a doctrine to have been conceived by man, and was *therefore* Divine; and on another page, that the Incarnation *had* been pre-conceived by man, and is *therefore* to be accepted as Divine. But we are less concerned with the fallacy of his 'ready replies', than with their falsity; and even of this we can only afford space for a very few specimens. Here is one: 'There is a *thousand times* more proof that the gospel of John was written by him than there is that the Ἀναβασις was written by Xenophon, or the Ars Poetica by Horace'. If Dr. Cumming had chosen Plato's Epistles or Anacreon's Poems, instead of the Anabasis or the Ars Poetica, he would have reduced the extent of the falsehood, and would have furnished a ready reply which would have been equally effective with his Sunday-school teachers and their disputants. Hence we conclude this prodigality of misstatement, this exuberance of mendacity, is an effervescence of zeal *in majorem gloriam Dei.* Elsewhere he tells us that 'the idea of the author of the "Vestiges" is, that man is the development of a monkey, that the monkey is the embryo man, so that *if you keep a baboon long enough, it will develope itself into a man*'. How well Dr. Cumming has qualified himself to judge of the ideas in 'that very unphilosophical book', as he pronounces it, may be inferred from the fact that he implies the author of the 'Vestiges'[25] to have *originated* the nebular hypothesis.

In the volume from which the last extract is taken, even the hardihood of assertion is surpassed by the suicidal character of the argument. It is called 'The Church before the Flood', and is devoted chiefly to the adjustment of the question between the Bible and Geology. Keeping within the limits we have prescribed to ourselves, we do not enter into the matter of this discussion; we merely pause a little over the volume in order to point out Dr. Cumming's mode of treating the question. He first tells us that 'the Bible has not a single scientific error in it'; that *'its slightest intimations of scientific principles or natural phenomena have in every instance been demonstrated to be exactly and strictly true'*, and he asks:

> How is it that Moses, with no greater education than the Hindoo or the ancient philosopher, has written his book, touching science at a thousand points, so accurately, that scientific research has discovered no flaws in it; and yet in those investigations which have taken place in more recent centuries, it has not been shown that he has committed one single error, or made one solitary assertion which can be proved by the maturest science, or by the most eagle-eyed philosopher, to be incorrect, scientifically or historically?

According to this, the relation of the Bible to Science should be one of the strong points of apologists for Revelation: the scientific accuracy of Moses should stand at the head of their evidences; and they might urge with some cogency, that since Aristotle, who devoted himself to science, and lived many ages after Moses, does little else than err ingeniously, this fact, that the Jewish Lawgiver, though touching science at a thousand points, has written nothing that has not been 'demonstrated to be exactly and strictly true', is an irrefragable proof of his having derived his knowledge from a supernatural source. How does it happen, then, that Dr. Cumming forsakes this strong position? How is it that we find him, some pages further on, engaged in reconciling Genesis with the discoveries of science, by means of imaginative hypotheses and feats of 'interpretation'? Surely, that which has been demonstrated to

[25] The authorship of Robert Chambers's *Vestiges of Creation* (1844) was not acknowledged until 1884, thirteen years after the death of Chambers.

be exactly and strictly true does not require hypothesis and critical argument, in order to show that it may *possibly* agree with those very discoveries by means of which its exact and strict truth has been demonstrated. And why should Dr. Cumming suppose, as we shall presently find him supposing, that men of science hesitate to accept the Bible, because it appears to contradict their discoveries? By his own statement, that appearance of contradiction does not exist; on the contrary, it has been demonstrated that the Bible precisely agrees with their discoveries. Perhaps, however, in saying of the Bible that its 'slightest intimations of scientific principles or natural phenomena have in every instance been demonstrated to be exactly and strictly true', Dr. Cumming merely means to imply that theologians have found out a way of explaining the biblical text so that it no longer, in their opinion, appears to be in contradiction with the discoveries of science. One of two things, therefore: either, he uses language without the slightest appreciation of its real meaning; or, the assertions he makes on one page are directly contradicted by the arguments he urges on another.

Dr. Cumming's principles—or, we should rather say, confused notions—of biblical interpretation, as exhibited in this volume, are particularly significant of his mental calibre. He says ('Church before the Flood', p. 93): 'Men of science, who are full of scientific investigation and enamoured of scientific discovery, will hesitate before they accept a book which, they think, contradicts the plainest and the most unequivocal disclosures they have made in the bowels of the earth, or among the stars of the sky. To all these we answer, as we have already indicated, there is not the least dissonance between God's written book and the most mature discoveries of geological science. One thing, however, there may be; *there may be a contradiction between the discoveries of geology and our preconceived interpretations of the Bible.* But this is not because the Bible is wrong, but because our interpretation is wrong'. (The italics in all cases are our own.)

Elsewhere he says: 'It seems to me plainly evident that the record of Genesis, when read fairly, and not in the light of our prejudices,—*and mind you, the essence of Popery is to read the Bible in the light of our opinions, instead of viewing our opinions in the light of the Bible, in its plain and obvious sense,*—falls in perfectly with the assertion of geologists'.

On comparing these two passages, we gather that when Dr. Cumming, under stress of geological discovery, assigns to the biblical text a meaning entirely different from that which, on his own showing, was universally ascribed to it for more than three thousand years, he regards himself as 'viewing his opinions in the light of the Bible in its plain and obvious sense'! Now he is reduced to one of two alternatives: either, he must hold that the 'plain and obvious meaning' [of the whole Bible differs from age to age, so that the criterion of its meaning][26] lies in the sum of knowledge possessed by each successive age—the Bible being an elastic garment for the growing thought of mankind; or, he must hold that some portions are amenable to this criterion, and others not so. In the former case, he accepts the principle of interpretation adopted by the early German rationalists; in the latter case, he has to show a further criterion by which we can judge what parts of the Bible are elastic and what rigid. If he says that the interpretation of the text is rigid wherever it treats of doctrines necessary to salvation, we answer, that for doctrines to be necessary to salvation they must first be true; and in order to be true, according to his own principle, they must be founded on a correct interpretation of the biblical text. Thus he makes the necessity of doctrines to salvation the criterion of infallible interpretation, and infallible interpretation the criterion of doctrines being necessary to salvation. He is whirled round in a circle, having, by admitting the principle of novelty in interpretation, completely deprived himself of a basis. That he should seize the very moment in which he is most palpably betraying that he has no test of biblical truth beyond his own opinion, as an appropriate occasion for flinging the rather novel reproach against Popery that its essence is to 'read the Bible in the light of our opinions', would be an almost pathetic self-exposure, if it were not disgusting. Imbecility that is not even meek, ceases to be pitiable and becomes simply odious.

Parenthetic lashes of this kind against Popery are very frequent with Dr. Cumming, and occur even in his more devout passages, where their introduction must surely disturb the spiritual exercises of his hearers. Indeed, Roman-catholics fare worse with him even than infidels. Infidels are the small vermin—the mice to be bagged *en passant*. The main object of his chace—the rats which

[26] Omitted, 1884.

are to be nailed up as trophies—are the Roman-catholics. Romanism is the master-piece of Satan; but re-assure yourselves! Dr. Cumming has been created. Antichrist is enthroned in the Vatican; but he is stoutly withstood by the Boanerges of Crown-court. The personality of Satan, as might be expected, is a very prominent tenet in Dr. Cumming's discourses; those who doubt it are, he thinks, 'generally specimens of the victims of Satan as a triumphant seducer'; and it is through the medium of this doctrine that he habitually contemplates Roman-catholics. They are the puppets of which the devil holds the strings. It is only exceptionally that he speaks of them as fellow-men, acted on by the same desires, fears, and hopes as himself; his *rule* is to hold them up to his hearers as foredoomed instruments of Satan, and vessels of wrath. If he is obliged to admit that they are 'no shams', that they are 'thoroughly in earnest'—that is because they are inspired by hell, because they are under an 'infra-natural' influence. If their missionaries are found wherever Protestant missionaries go, this zeal in propagating their faith is not in them a consistent virtue, as it is in Protestants, but a 'melancholy fact', affording additional evidence that they are instigated and assisted by the devil. And Dr. Cumming is inclined to think that they work miracles, because that is no more than might be expected from the known ability of Satan who inspires them.[27] He admits, indeed, that 'there is a fragment of the Church of Christ in the very bosom of that awful apostasy',[28] and that there are members of the Church of Rome in glory; but this admission is rare and episodical—is a declaration, *pro formâ*, about as influential on the general disposition and habits as an aristocrat's profession of democracy.

This leads us to mention another conspicuous characteristic of Dr. Cumming's teaching—the *absence of genuine charity*. It is true that he makes large profession of tolerance and liberality within a certain circle; he exhorts Christians to unity; he would have Churchmen fraternize with Dissenters, and exhorts these two branches of God's family to defer the settlement of their differences till the millennium. But the love thus taught is the love of the *clan*, which is the correlative of antagonism to the rest of mankind. It is not sympathy and helpfulness towards men as men, but towards men as Christians, and as Christians in the sense of a small

[27] Signs of the Times, p. 38 [George Eliot's note].
[28] Apoc. Sketches, p. 243 [George Eliot's note].

minority. Dr. Cumming's religion may demand a tribute of love, but it gives a charter to hatred; it may enjoin charity, but it fosters all uncharitableness. If I believe that God tells me to love my enemies, but at the same time hates His own enemies and requires me to have one will with Him, which has the larger scope, love or hatred? And we refer to those pages of Dr. Cumming's in which he opposes Roman-catholics, Puseyites, and infidels—pages which form the larger proportion of what he has published—for proof that the idea of God which both the logic and spirit of his discourses keep present to his hearers, is that of a God who hates his enemies, a God who teaches love by fierce denunciations of wrath —a God who encourages obedience to his precepts by elaborately revealing to us that his own government is in precise opposition to those precepts. We know the usual evasions on this subject. We know Dr. Cumming would say that even Roman-catholics are to be loved and succoured as men; that he would help even that 'unclean spirit', Cardinal Wiseman, out of a ditch. But who that is in the slightest degree acquainted with the action of the human mind, will believe that any genuine and large charity can grow out of an exercise of love which is always to have an *arrière-pensée* of hatred? Of what quality would be the conjugal love of a husband who loved his spouse as a wife, but hated her as a woman? It is reserved for the regenerate mind, according to Dr. Cumming's conception of it, to be 'wise, amazed, temperate and furious, loyal and neutral, in a moment'. Precepts of charity uttered with faint breath at the end of a sermon are perfectly futile, when all the force of the lungs has been spent in keeping the hearer's mind fixed on the conception of his fellow-men, not as fellow-sinners and fellow-sufferers, but as agents of hell, as automata through whom Satan plays his game upon earth,—not on objects which call forth their reverence, their love, their hope of good even in the most strayed and perverted, but on a minute identification of human things with such symbols as the scarlet whore, the beast out of the abyss, scorpions whose sting is in their tails, men who have the mark of the beast, and unclean spirits like frogs. You might as well attempt to educate a child's sense of beauty by hanging its nursery with the horrible and grotesque pictures in which the early painters represented the Last Judgment, as expect Christian graces to flourish on that prophetic interpretation which Dr. Cumming offers as the principal nutriment of his flock. Quite apart from the critical basis of that interpretation, quite apart from the degree of truth there may be in Dr. Cumming's prognostications—questions into which we do not choose to enter—his use of prophecy must be *à priori* condemned in the judgment of right-minded persons, by its results as testified in the net moral effect of his sermons. The best minds that accept Christianity as a divinely inspired system, believe that the great end of the Gospel is not merely the saving but the educating of men's souls, the creating within them of holy dispositions, the subduing of egoistical pretensions, and the perpetual enhancing of the desire that the will of God—a will synonymous with goodness and truth—may be done on earth. But what relation to all this has a system of interpretation which keeps the mind of the Christian in the position of a spectator at a gladiatorial show, of which Satan is the wild beast in the shape of the great red dragon, and two-thirds of mankind the victims—the whole provided and got up by God for the edification of the saints? The demonstration that the Second Advent is at hand, if true, can have no really holy, spiritual effect; the highest state of mind inculcated by the Gospel is resignation to the disposal of God's providence—'Whether we live, we live unto the Lord; whether we die, we die unto the Lord'[29]—not an eagerness to see a temporal manifestation which shall confound the enemies of God and give exaltation to the saints; it is to dwell in Christ by spiritual communion with his nature, not to fix the date when He shall appear in the sky. Dr. Cumming's delight in shadowing forth the downfall of the Man of Sin, in prognosticating the battle of Gog and Magog, and in advertizing the pre-millennial Advent, is simply the transportation of political passions on to a so-called religious platform; it is the anticipation of the triumph of 'our party', accomplished by our principal men being 'sent for' into the clouds. Let us be understood to speak in all seriousness. If we were in search of amusement, we should not seek for it by examining Dr. Cumming's works in order to ridicule them. We are simply discharging a disagreeable duty in delivering our opinion that, judged by the highest standard even of orthodox Christianity, they are little calculated to produce:

A closer walk with God,
A calm and heavenly frame;[30]

[29] Romans 14:8.
[30] Cowper, *Olney Hymns*, 'Walking with God', 1–2.

but are more likely to nourish egoistic complacency and pretension, a hard and condemnatory spirit towards one's fellow-men, and a busy occupation with the minutiæ of events, instead of a reverent contemplation of great facts and a wise application of great principles. It would be idle to consider Dr. Cumming's theory of prophecy in any other light,—as a philosophy of history or a specimen of biblical interpretation; it bears about the same relation to the extension of genuine knowledge as the astrological 'house' in the heavens bears to the true structure and relations of the universe.

The slight degree in which Dr. Cumming's faith is imbued with truly human sympathies, is exhibited in the way he treats the doctrine of Eternal Punishment. *Here* a little of that readiness to strain the letter of the Scriptures which he so often manifests when his object is to prove a point against Romanism, would have been an amiable frailty if it had been applied on the side of mercy. When he is bent on proving that the prophecy concerning the Man of Sin, in the Second Epistle to the Thessalonians,[31] refers to the Pope, he can extort from the innocent word καθισαι the meaning *cathedrize*, though why we are to translate 'He as God cathedrizes in the temple of God', any more than we are to translate 'cathedrize here, while I go and pray yonder',[32] it is for Dr. Cumming to show more clearly than he has yet done. But when rigorous literality will favour the conclusion that the greater proportion of the human race will be eternally miserable—*then* he is rigorously literal.

He says: 'The Greek words, εἰς τους αἰῶνας των αἰῶνων here translated "everlasting", signify literally "unto the ages of ages"; αἰεὶ ὢν, "always being", that is, everlasting, ceaseless existence. Plato uses the word in this sense when he says, "The gods that live for ever". *But I must also admit*, that this word is used several times in a limited extent,—as for instance, "The everlasting hills". Of course, this does not mean that there never will be a time when the hills will cease to stand; the expression here is evidently figurative, but it implies eternity. The hills shall remain as long as the earth lasts, and no hand has power to remove them but that Eternal One which first called them into being; *so the state of the soul* remains the same after death as long as the soul exists, and no one has power to alter it. The same word is often applied to denote the existence of God—"the Eternal God". Can

[31] 2:4.   [32] Matthew 26:36.

182

we limit the word when applied to Him? Because occasionally used in a limited sense, we must not infer it is always so. "Everlasting" plainly means in Scripture "without end"; it is only to be explained figuratively when it is evident it cannot be interpreted in any other way.'

We do not discuss whether Dr. Cumming's interpretation accords with the meaning of the New Testament writers: we simply point to the fact that the text becomes elastic for him when he wants freer play for his prejudices, while he makes it an adamantine barrier against the admission that mercy will ultimately triumph,—that God, *i.e.*, Love, will be all in all. He assures us that he does not 'delight to dwell on the misery of the lost': and we believe him. That misery does not seem to be a question of feeling with him, either one way or the other. He does not merely resign himself to the awful mystery of eternal punishment; he contends for it. Do we object, he asks,[33] to everlasting happiness? then why object to everlasting misery?—reasoning which is perhaps felt to be cogent by theologians who anticipate the everlasting happiness for themselves, and the everlasting misery for their neighbours.

The compassion of some Christians has been glad to take refuge in the opinion, that the Bible allows the supposition of annihilation for the impenitent: but the rigid sequence of Dr. Cumming's reasoning will not admit of this idea. He sees that flax is made into linen, and linen into paper; that paper, when burnt, partly ascends as smoke and then again descends in rain, or in dust and carbon. 'Not one particle of the original flax is lost, although there may be not one particle that has not undergone an entire change: annihilation is not, but change of form is. *It will be thus with our bodies at the resurrection.* The death of the body means not annihilation. *Not one feature of the face* will be annihilated'. Having established the perpetuity of the body by this close and clear analogy, namely, that *as* there is a total change in the particles of flax in consequence of which they no longer appear as flax, *so* there will *not* be a total change in the particles of the human body, but they will re-appear as the human body, he does not seem to consider that the perpetuity of the body involves the perpetuity of the soul, but requires separate evidence for this, and finds such evidence by begging the very question at issue; namely, by asserting that the text of the Scriptures implies 'the perpetuity of

[33] Man. of Christ. Ev. p. 184 [George Eliot's note].

the punishment of the lost, and the consciousness of the punishment which they endure'. Yet it is drivelling like this which is listened to and lauded as eloquence by hundreds, and which a Doctor of Divinity can believe that he has his 'reward as a saint' for preaching and publishing!

One more characteristic of Dr. Cumming's writings, and we have done. This is the *perverted moral judgment* that everywhere reigns in them. Not that this perversion is peculiar to Dr. Cumming: it belongs to the dogmatic system which he shares with all evangelical believers. But the abstract tendencies of systems are represented in very different degrees, according to the different characters of those who embrace them; just as the same food tells differently on different constitutions: and there are certain qualities in Dr. Cumming that cause the perversion of which we speak to exhibit itself with peculiar prominence in his teaching. A single extract will enable us to explain what we mean:

The 'thoughts' are evil. If it were possible for human eye to discern and to detect the thoughts that flutter round the heart of an unregenerate man—to mark their hue and their multitude, it would be found that they are indeed 'evil.' We speak not of the thief, and the murderer, and the adulterer, and such like, whose crimes draw down the cognizance of earthly tribunals, and whose unenviable character it is to take the lead in the paths of sin; but we refer to the men who are marked out by their practice of many of the seemliest moralities of life—by the exercise of the kindliest affections, and the interchange of the sweetest reciprocities—and of these men, if unrenewed and unchanged, we pronounce that their thoughts are evil. To ascertain this, we must refer to the object around which our thoughts ought continually to circulate. The Scriptures assert that this object is *the glory of God*; that for this we ought to think, to act, and to speak; and that in thus thinking, acting, and speaking, there is involved the purest and most endearing bliss. Now it will be found true of the most amiable men, that with all their good society and kindliness of heart, and all their strict and unbending integrity, they never or rarely think of the glory of God. The question never occurs to them—Will this redound to the glory of God? Will this make his name more known, his being more loved, his praise more sung? And just inasmuch as their every thought comes short of this lofty aim, in so much does it come short of good, and entitle itself to the character of evil. If the glory of God is not the absorbing and the influential aim of their thoughts, then they are evil; but God's glory never enters into their minds. They are amiable, because it chances to be one of the constitutional tendencies of their individual character, left uneffaced by the Fall; and *they are just and upright, because they have perhaps no occasion to be otherwise, or find it subservient to their interests to maintain such a character.*—(Occ. Disc. vol. i. p. 8). . . . Again we read (Ibid. p. 236), There are traits in the Christian character which the mere worldly man cannot understand. He can understand the outward morality, but he cannot understand the inner spring of it; he can understand Dorcas' liberality to the poor, but he cannot penetrate the ground of Dorcas' liberality. *Some men give to the poor because they are ostentatious, or because they think the poor will ultimately avenge their neglect; but the Christian gives to the poor, not only because he has sensibilities like other men,* but because inasmuch as ye did it to the least of these my brethren ye did it unto me.

Before entering on the more general question involved in these quotations, we must point to the clauses we have marked with italics, where Dr. Cumming appears to express sentiments which, we are happy to think, are not shared by the majority of his brethren in the faith. Dr. Cumming, it seems, is unable to conceive that the natural man can have any other motive for being just and upright than that it is useless to be otherwise, or that a character for honesty is profitable; according to his experience, between the feelings of ostentation and selfish alarm and the feeling of love to Christ, there lie no sensibilities which can lead a man to relieve want. Granting, as we should prefer to think, that it is Dr. Cumming's exposition of his sentiments which is deficient rather than his sentiments themselves, still, the fact that the deficiency lies precisely here, and that he can overlook it not only in the haste of oral delivery but in the examination of proof-sheets, is strongly significant of his mental bias—of the faint degree in which he sympathizes with the disinterested elements of human feeling, and of the fact, which we are about to dwell upon, that those feelings are totally absent from his religious theory. Now, Dr. Cumming invariably assumes that, in fulminating against those who differ from him, he is standing on a moral elevation to which they are compelled reluctantly to look up; that his theory of motives and conduct is in its loftiness and purity a perpetual rebuke to their low and vicious desires and practice. It is time he should be told that the reverse is the fact; that there are men who do not merely cast a superficial glance at his doctrine, and fail to see its beauty or justice, but who, after a close consideration of that doctrine, pronounce it to be subversive of true moral development, and therefore positively noxious. Dr. Cumming is fond of showing-up the teaching of Romanism, and accusing it of undermining true morality: it is time he should be told that there is a large body both of thinkers and practical men, who hold precisely the same opinion of his own teaching—with this difference, that they do not regard it as the inspiration of Satan, but as the natural crop of a human mind where the soil is chiefly made up of egoistic passions and dogmatic beliefs.

Dr. Cumming's theory, as we have seen, is that actions are good or evil according as they are prompted or not prompted by an exclusive reference to the 'glory of God'. God, then, in Dr. Cumming's conception, is a being who has no pleasure in the exercise of love and truthfulness and justice, considered as effecting the well-being of his creatures; He has satisfaction in us only in so far as we exhaust our motives and dispositions of all relation to our fellow-beings, and replace sympathy with men by anxiety for the 'glory of God'. The deed of Grace Darling, when she took a boat in the storm to rescue drowning men and women,[34] was not good if it was only compassion that nerved her arm and impelled her to brave death for the chance of saving others; it was only good if she asked herself—Will this redound to the glory of God? The man who endures tortures rather than betray a trust, the man who spends years in toil in order to discharge an obligation from which the law declares him free, must be animated not by the spirit of fidelity to his fellow-man, but by a desire to make 'the name of God more known'. The sweet charities of domestic life—the ready hand and the soothing word in sickness, the forbearance towards frailties, the prompt helpfulness in all efforts and sympathy in all joys, are simply evil if they result from a 'constitutional tendency', or from dispositions disciplined by the experience of suffering and the perception of moral loveliness. A wife is not to devote herself to her husband out of love to him and a sense of the duties implied by a close relation—she is to be a faithful wife for the glory of God; if she feels her natural affections welling up too strongly, she is to repress them; it will not do to act from natural affection—she must think of the glory of God. A man is to guide his affairs with energy and discretion, not from an honest desire to fulfil his responsibilities as a member of society and a father, but—that 'God's

[34] In 1838, off the coast of Northumberland.

praise may be sung'. Dr. Cumming's Christian pays his debts for the glory of God; were it not for the coercion of that supreme motive, it would be evil to pay them. A man is not to be just from a feeling of justice; he is not to help his fellow-men out of good-will to his fellow-men; he is not to be a tender husband and father out of affection: all these natural muscles and fibres are to be torn away and replaced by a patent steel-spring—anxiety for the 'glory of God'.

Happily, the constitution of human nature forbids the complete prevalence of such a theory. Fatally powerful as religious systems have been, human nature is stronger and wider than religious systems, and though dogmas may hamper, they cannot absolutely repress its growth: build walls round the living tree as you will, the bricks and mortar have by and bye to give way before the slow and sure operation of the sap. But next to that hatred of the enemies of God which is the principle of persecution, there perhaps has been no perversion more obstructive of true moral development than this substitution of a reference to the glory of God for the direct promptings of the sympathetic feelings. Benevolence and justice are strong only in proportion as they are directly and inevitably called into activity by their proper objects: pity is strong only because we are strongly impressed by suffering; and only in proportion as it is compassion that speaks through the eyes when we soothe, and moves the arm when we succour, is a deed strictly benevolent. If the soothing or the succour be given because another being wishes or approves it, the deed ceases to be one of benevolence, and becomes one of deference, of obedience, of self-interest, or vanity. Accessory motives may aid in producing an *action*, but they pre-suppose the weakness of the direct motive; and conversely, when the direct motive is strong, the action of accessory motives will be excluded. If then, as Dr. Cumming inculcates, the glory of God is to be 'the absorbing and the influential aim' in our thoughts and actions, this must tend to neutralize the human sympathies; the stream of feeling will be diverted from its natural current in order to feed an artificial canal. The idea of God is really moral in its influence—it really cherishes all that is best and loveliest in man—only when God is contemplated as sympathizing with the pure elements of human feeling, as possessing infinitely all those attributes which we recognize to be moral in humanity. In this light, the idea of God and the sense of His presence intensify all noble feeling, and encourage all noble effort, on the same principle that human sympathy is found a source of strength: the brave man feels braver when he knows that another stout heart is beating time with his; the devoted woman who is wearing out her years in patient effort to alleviate suffering or save vice from the last stages of degradation, finds aid in the pressure of a friendly hand which tells her that there is one who understands her deeds, and in her place would do the like. The idea of a God who not only sympathizes with all we feel and endure for our fellow-men, but who will pour new life into our too languid love, and give firmness to our vacillating purpose, is an extension and multiplication of the effects produced by human sympathy; and it has been intensified for the better spirits who have been under the influence of orthodox Christianity, by the contemplation of Jesus as 'God manifest in the flesh'. But Dr. Cumming's God is the very opposite of all this: he is a God who instead of sharing and aiding our human sympathies, is directly in collision with them; who instead of strengthening the bond between man and man, by encouraging the sense that they are both alike the objects of His love and care, thrusts himself between them and forbids them to feel for each other except as they have relation to Him. He is a God, who, instead of adding his solar force to swell the tide of those impulses that tend to give humanity a common life in which the good of one is the good of all, commands us to check those impulses, lest they should prevent us from thinking of His glory. It is in vain for Dr. Cumming to say that we are to love man for God's sake: with the conception of God which his teaching presents, the love of man for God's sake involves, as his writings abundantly show, a strong principle of hatred. We can only love one being for the sake of another when there is an habitual delight in associating the idea of those two beings—that is, when the object of our indirect love is a source of joy and honour to the object of our direct love: but, according to Dr. Cumming's theory, the majority of mankind—the majority of his neighbours—are in precisely the opposite relation to God. His soul has no pleasure in them, they belong more to Satan than to Him, and if they contribute to His glory, it is against their will. Dr. Cumming then can only love *some* men for God's sake; the rest he must in consistency *hate* for God's sake.

There must be many, even in the circle of Dr. Cumming's admirers, who would be revolted by the doctrine we have just exposed, if their natural good sense and healthy feeling were not early stifled by dogmatic beliefs, and their reverence misled by pious phrases. But as it is, many a rational question, many a generous instinct, is repelled as the suggestion of a supernatural enemy, or as the ebullition of human pride and corruption. This state of inward contradiction can be put an end to only by the conviction that the free and diligent exertion of the intellect, instead of being a sin, is a part of their responsibility—that Right and Reason are synonymous. The fundamental faith for man is faith in the result of a brave, honest, and steady use of all his faculties:

> Let knowledge grow from more to more
>> But more of reverence in us dwell;
>> That mind and soul according well
> May make one music as before,
>> But vaster.[35]

Before taking leave of Dr. Cumming, let us express a hope that we have in no case exaggerated the unfavourable character of the inferences to be drawn from his pages. His creed often obliges him to hope the worst of men, and to exert himself in proving that the worst is true; but thus far we are happier than he. We have no theory which requires us to attribute unworthy motives to Dr. Cumming, no opinions, religious or irreligious, which can make it a gratification to us to detect him in delinquencies. On the contrary, the better we are able to think of him as a man, while we are obliged to disapprove him as a theologian, the stronger will be the evidence for our conviction, that the tendency towards good in human nature has a force which no creed can utterly counteract, and which ensures the ultimate triumph of that tendency over all dogmatic perversions.

[35] Tennyson, *In Memoriam*, Prologue, st. 7.

13

[TENNYSON'S 'MAUD']

Westminster Review, LXIV (October, 1855), 596–601

George Eliot's review of *Maud, and Other Poems* (1855) opens the October 'Belles Lettres' section of the *Westminster*, which was finished, according to her Journal, on 15 September 1855. Her response to the poem was by no means remarkable, for, as Sir Charles Tennyson says, 'Poor *Maud* was received with almost universal reprobation', and 'the Liberal press was incensed by the poet's political attitude'.[1]

That Tennyson read her review we know on his own showing (see note 7, below), but that he ever discovered her authorship is extremely unlikely. It is amusing to know that in the 1870's George Eliot heard Tennyson read *Maud* on at least three different occasions.[2] Though the poem was Tennyson's favourite, and though he is said to have read it with impressive effect, it is not recorded whether these experiences succeeded in softening her attitude towards *Maud*.

*　　　*　　　*

IF we were asked who among contemporary authors is likely to live in the next century, the name that would first and most unhesitatingly rise to our lips is that of Alfred Tennyson. He, at least, while belonging emphatically to his own age, while giving a voice to the struggles and the far-reaching thoughts of this nineteenth century, has those supreme artistic qualities which must make him a poet for all ages. As long as the English language is spoken, the word-music of Tennyson must charm the ear; and when English has become a dead language, his wonderful concentration of thought into luminous speech, the exquisite pictures in which he

---

[1] *Alfred Tennyson* (New York, 1949), p. 286.
[2] See *Letters*, V, 181; VI, 360; VII, 21.

oughtorms for
themselves, but once condense them into the diamonds of poetry,
and the form, as well as the element, will be lasting. This is the
sublime privilege of the artist—to be present with future generations, not merely through the indirect results of his work, but
through his immediate creations; and of all artists the one whose
works are least in peril from the changing conditions of humanity,
is the highest order of poet, who has received—

> Aus Morgenduft gewebt und Sonnenklarheit
> Der Dichtung Schleier aus der Hand der Wahrheit.[3]

Such a poet, by the suffrage of all competent judges among his
countrymen, is Tennyson. His 'Ulysses' is a pure little ingot of the
same gold that runs through the ore of the Odyssey. It has the
'large utterance' of the early epic, with that rich fruit of moral
experience which it has required thousands of years to ripen. The
'Morte d'Arthur' breathes the intensest spirit of chivalry in the
pure and serene air of unselfish piety; and it falls on the ear with
the rich, soothing melody of a *Dona nobis* swelling through the
aisles of a cathedral. 'Locksley Hall' has become, like Milton's
minor poems, so familiar that we dare not quote it; it is the object
of a sort of family affection which we all cherish, but think it is not
good taste to mention. Then there are his idyls, such as the
'Gardener's Daughter',—works which in their kind have no rival,
either in the past or present. But the time would fail us to tell of
all we owe to Tennyson, for, with two or three exceptions, every
poem in his two volumes is a favourite. The 'Princess', too, with
all that criticism has to say against it, has passages of inspiration
and lyrical gems inbedded in it, which make it a fresh claim on our
gratitude. But, last and greatest, came 'In Memoriam', which to
us enshrines the highest tendency of this age, as the Apollo
Belvedere expressed the presence of a free and vigorous human
spirit amidst a decaying civilization. Whatever was the immediate
prompting of 'In Memoriam', whatever the form under which the
author represented his aim to himself, the deepest significance of
the poem is the sanctification of human love as a religion. If, then,
the voice that sang all these undying strains had remained for ever

² Goethe, 'Zueignung', 95–96.

191

after mute, we should have had no reason to reproach Tennyson with gifts inadequately used; we should rather have rejoiced in the thought that one who has sown for his fellow-men so much—

generous seed,
Fruitful of further thought and deed,[4]

should at length be finding rest for his wings in a soft nest of home affections, and be living idyls, instead of writing them.

We could not prevail on ourselves to say what we think of 'Maud', without thus expressing our love and admiration of Tennyson. For that optical law by which an insignificant object, if near, excludes very great and glorious things that lie in the distance, has its moral parallel in the judgments of the public: men's speech is too apt to be exclusively determined by the unsuccessful deed or book of to-day, the successful doings and writings of past years being for the moment lost sight of. And even seen in the light of the most reverential criticism, the effect of 'Maud' cannot be favourable to Tennyson's fame. Here and there only it contains a few lines in which he does not fall below himself. With these slight exceptions, he is everywhere saying, if not something that would be better left unsaid, something that he had already said better; and the finest sentiments that animate his other poems are entirely absent. We have in 'Maud' scarcely more than a residuum of Alfred Tennyson; the wide-sweeping intellect, the mild philosophy, the healthy pathos, the wondrous melody, have almost all vanished, and left little more than a narrow scorn which piques itself on its scorn of narrowness, and a passion which clothes itself in exaggerated conceits. While to his other poems we turn incessantly with new distress that we cannot carry them all in our memory, of 'Maud' we must say, if we say the truth, that excepting only a few passages, we wish to forget it as we should wish to forget a bad opera. And this not only because it wants the charms of mind and music which belong to his other poetry, but because its tone is throughout morbid; it opens to us the self revelations of a morbid mind, and what it presents as the cure for this mental disease is itself only a morbid conception of human relations.

But we will abstain from general remarks, and make the reader acquainted with the plan and texture of the poem. It opens, like the gates of Pandemonium, 'with horrible discord and jarring

[4] Tennyson, 'The Two Voices', 143–144.

sound',[5]—with harsh and rugged hexameters, in which the hero, who is throughout the speaker, tells us something of his history and his views of society. It is impossible to suppose that, with so great a master of rhythm as Tennyson, this harshness and rugged- ness are otherwise than intentional; so we must conclude that it is a device of his art thus to set our teeth on edge with his verses when he means to rouse our disgust by his descriptions; and that, writing of disagreeable things, he has made it a rule to write disagreeably. These hexameters, weak in logic and grating in sound, are undeniably strong in expression, and eat themselves with phosphoric eagerness into our memory, in spite of our will. The hero opens his story by telling us how 'long since' his father was found dead in 'the dreadful hollow behind the little wood', supposed to have committed suicide in despair at the ruin entailed on him by the failure of a great speculation; and he paints with terrible force that crisis in his boyhood:

I remember the time, for the roots of my hair were stirr'd
By a shuffled step, by a dead weight trail'd, by a whisper'd fright,
And my pulses closed their gates with a shock on my heart as I heard
The shrill-edged shriek of a mother divide the shuddering night.

An old neighbour 'dropt off gorged' from that same speculation, and is now lord of the broad estate and the hall. These family sorrows and mortifications the hero regards as a direct result of the anti-social tendencies of Peace, which he proceeds to expose to us in all its hideousness; looking to war as the immediate curative for unwholesome lodging of the poor, adulteration of provisions, child- murder, and wife-beating—an effect which is as yet by no means visible in our police reports. It seems indeed that, in the opinion of our hero, nothing short of an invasion of our own coasts is the consummation devoutly to be wished:

For I trust if an enemy's fleet came yonder round by the hill,
And the rushing battle-bolt sang from the three-decker out of the
    foam,
That the smoothfaced snubnosed rogue would leap from his counter
    and till,
And strike, if he could, were it but with his cheating yardwand, home.

[5] Apparently George Eliot's recollection of *Paradise Lost*, Book II, 880: 'With impetuous recoil and jarring sound.'

From his deadly hatred of retail traders and susceptibility as to the adulteration of provisions, we were inclined to imagine that this modern Conrad, with a 'devil in his sneer', but not a 'laughing devil',[6] had in his reduced circumstances taken a London lodging and endured much peculation in the shape of weekly bills, and much indigestion arising from unwholesome bread and beer. But no: we presently learn that he resides in a lone house not far from the Hall, and can still afford to keep 'a man and a maid.' And now, he says, the family is coming home to the Hall; the old bloodsucker, with his son and a daughter, Maud, whom he remembers as a little girl, 'with her sweet purse-mouth, when my father dangled the grapes.' He is determined not to fall in love with her, and the glance he gets of her as she passes in her carriage, assures him that he is in no danger from her 'cold and clear-cut face',—

> Faultily faultless, icily regular, splendidly null,
> Dead perfection, no more.

However, he does not escape from this first glance without the 'least little touch of the spleen', which the reader foresees is the germinal spot that is to develop itself into love. The first lines of any beauty in the poem are those in which he describes the 'cold and clear-cut face,' breaking his sleep, and haunting him 'starsweet on a gloom profound,' till he gets up and walks away the wintry night in his own dark garden. Then Maud seems to look haughtily on him as she returns his bow, and he makes fierce resolves to flee from the cruel madness of love, and more especially from the love of Maud, who is 'all unmeet for a wife;' but presently he hears her voice, which has a more irresistible magic even than her face. By-and-bye she looks more benignantly on him, but his suspicious heart dares not sun itself in her smile, lest her brother—

> That jewell'd mass of millinery,
> That oil'd and curl'd Assyrian Bull,

may have prompted her to this benignity as a mode of canvassing for a vote at the coming election. A fresh circumstance is now added in the form of a new-made lord, apparently a suitor of Maud's—

> a captain, a padded shape,
> A bought commission, a waxen face,
> A rabbit mouth that is ever agape.

[6] Byron, *The Corsair*, Canto I, 223, where it is said of the hero, Conrad, that 'There was a laughing devil in his sneer.'

Very indignant is our hero with this lord's grand-father, for having made his fortune by a coal-mine, though the consideration that the said grandfather is now in 'a blacker pit', is somewhat soothing to his chafed feelings. In the denunciations we have here of new-made fortunes, new titles, new houses, and new suits of clothes, it is evidently Mr. Tennyson's aversion, and not merely his hero's morbid mood, that speaks; and we must say, that this immense expenditure of gall on trivial social phases, seems to us intrinsically petty and snobbish. The gall presently overflows, as gall is apt to do, without any visible sequence of association, on Mr. Bright,[7] who is denounced as—

> This broad-brimm'd hawker of holy things,
> Whose ear is stuft with his cotton, and rings
> Even in dreams to the chink of his pence.

In a second edition of 'Maud', we hope these lines will no longer appear on Tennyson's page: we hope he will by that time have recovered the spirit in which he once wrote how the 'wise of heart'

> Would love the gleams of good that broke
> From either side, nor veil his eyes.[8]

On the next page, he gives us an agreeable change of key in a little lyric, which will remind the German reader of Thekla's song. Here is the second stanza:

> Let the sweet heavens endure
>   Not close and darken above me,
> Before I am quite, quite sure
>   That there is one to love me;
> Then let come what come may
>   To a life that has been so sad,
> I shall have had my day.

[7] In the outline of *Maud* that Tennyson drew up for his son Hallam he says of Part I, section X, of the poem: 'The *Westminster Review* said this was an attack on John Bright. I did not know at the time that he was a Quaker. (It was not against Quakers but against peace-at-all-price men that the hero fulminates.)' (Hallam Tennyson, *Alfred Lord Tennyson, A Memoir*, one-vol. ed. [London, 1899], p. 340.)

[8] 'Love Thou Thy Land', 81; 89–90.

At length, after many alternations of feeling and metre, our hero becomes assured that he is Maud's accepted lover, and atones for rather a silly outburst, in which he requests the sky to

> Blush from West to East
>> Blush from East to West,
> Till the West is East,
>> Blush it thro' the West,

by some very fine lines, of which we can only afford to quote the concluding ones:

> Is that enchanted moan only the swell
> Of the long waves that roll in yonder bay?
> And hark the clock within, the silver knell
> Of twelve sweet hours that past in bridal white,
> And died to live, long as my pulses play;
> But now by this my love has closed her sight
> And given false death her hand, and stol'n away
> To dreamful wastes where footless fancies dwell
> Among the fragments of the golden day.
> May nothing there her maiden grace affright!
> Dear heart, I feel with thee the drowsy spell.
> My bride to be, my evermore delight,
> My own heart's heart and ownest own, farewell.
> It is but for a little space I go:
> And ye meanwhile far over moor and fell
> Beat to the noiseless music of the night!
> Has our whole earth gone nearer to the glow
> Of your soft splendours that you look so bright?
> I have climb'd nearer out of lonely Hell.
> Beat, happy stars, timing with things below,
> Beat with my heart more blest than heart can tell,
> Blest, but for some dark undercurrent woe
> That seems to draw—but it shall not be so:
> Let all be well, be well.

We are now approaching the crisis of the story. A grand dinner and a dance are to be held at the Hall, and the hero, not being invited, waits in the garden till the festivities are over, that Maud may then come out and show herself to him in all the glory of her ball-dress. Here occurs the invocation, which has been deservedly admired and quoted by every critic:

Come into the garden, Maud,
  For the black bat, night, has flown,—
Come into the garden, Maud,
  I am here at the gate alone;
And the woodbine spices are wafted abroad,
  And the musk of the roses blown.

For a breeze of morning moves,
  And the planet of Love is on high,
Beginning to faint in the light that she loves
  On a bed of daffodil sky,—
To faint in the light of the sun she loves,
  To faint in his light, and to die.

Very exquisite is that descriptive bit, in the second stanza, where the music of the verse seems to faint and die like the star. Still the whole poem, which is too long for us to quote, is very inferior, as a poem of the Fancy, to the 'Talking Oak'. We do not, for a moment, believe in the sensibility of the roses and lilies in Maud's garden, as we believe in the thrills felt to his 'inmost ring' by the 'Old Oak of Summer Chace.'[9] This invocation is the topmost note of the lover's joy. The interview in the garden is disturbed by the 'Assyrian Bull', and the 'padded shape'. A duel follows, in which the brother is killed. And now we find the hero an exile on the Breton coast, where, from delivering some stanzas of Natural Theology *à propos* of a shell, he proceeds to retrace the sad memories of his love, until he becomes mad. We have then a Bedlam soliloquy, in which he fancies himself dead, and mingles with the images of Maud, her father, and her brother, his early-fixed idea—the police reports. From this madness he is recovered by the news that the Allies have declared war against Russia; whereupon he bursts into a pæan, that

the long, long canker of Peace is over and done.

It is possible, no doubt, to allegorize all this into a variety of edifying meanings; but it remains true, that the ground-notes of the poem are nothing more than hatred of peace and the Peace Society, hatred of commerce and coal-mines, hatred of young gentlemen with flourishing whiskers and padded coats, adoration of a clear-cut face, and faith in War as the unique social regenerator. Such are the sentiments, and such is the philosophy embodied

[9] 'The Talking Oak', 30, reads: 'Broad Oak of Sumner-chace'.

in 'Maud'; at least, for plain people not given to allegorizing; and it, perhaps, speaks well for Tennyson's genius, that it has refused to aid him much on themes so little worthy of his greatest self. Of the smaller poems, which, with the well-known 'Ode', make up the volume, 'The Brook' is rather a pretty idyl, and 'The Daisy' a graceful, unaffected recollection of Italy; but no one of them is remarkable enough to be ranked with the author's best poems of the same class.

14

MARGARET FULLER AND MARY WOLLSTONECRAFT

Leader, VI (13 October 1855), 988-989

There are many signs of George Eliot's interest in the life and personality of Margaret Fuller, with whom, especially in the days before her union with Lewes, she apparently felt a strong sense of identification. In a letter of 1852 she confided that 'It is a help to read such a life as Margaret Fuller's. How inexpressibly touching that passage from her journal—"I shall always reign through the intellect, but the life! the life! O my God! shall that never be sweet?" I am thankful, as if for myself, that it was sweet at last'.[1] The review of the *Memoirs of Margaret Fuller Ossoli* that appeared in the *Westminster* of April, 1852, is perhaps by George Eliot, and in July of 1852 she wrote to Chapman of her wish to write a full-scale article on Margaret Fuller's life.[2] This was never done, but George Eliot later wrote, in addition to the article reprinted below, notices of Margaret Fuller's *At Home and Abroad* for both the *Westminster* (July, 1856) and the *Leader* (17 May 1856).

The solitary allusion to Mary Wollstonecraft in the *Letters*, though written in 1871, throws light on the melancholy attraction such anomalous women as she and Margaret Fuller had for the young George Eliot:

Hopelessness has been to me, all through my life, but especially in painful years of my youth, the chief source of wasted energy with all the consequent bitterness of regret. Remember, it has happened to many to be glad they did not commit suicide, though they once ran for the final leap, or as Mary Wolstonecraft did, wetted their garments well in the rain hoping to sink the better when they plunged. She tells how it occurred to her as she was walking in this damp shroud, that she might live to be glad that she had not put an end to herself—and

[1] *Letters*, II, 15.   [2] *Letters*, II, 48.

so it turned out. She lived to know some real joys, and death came in time to hinder the joys from being spoiled.[3]

'Margaret Fuller and Mary Wollstonecraft' is entered in George Eliot's Journal for 9 October 1855. It has been reprinted once, in *Essays and Uncollected Papers*.

*   *   *

THE dearth of new books just now gives us time to recur to less recent ones which we have hitherto noticed but slightly; and among these we choose the late edition of Margaret Fuller's *Woman in the Nineteenth Century*,[4] because we think it has been unduly thrust into the background by less comprehensive and candid productions on the same subject. Notwithstanding certain defects of taste and a sort of vague spiritualism and grandiloquence which belong to all but the very best American writers, the book is a valuable one: it has the enthusiasm of a noble and sympathetic nature, with the moderation and breadth and large allowance of a vigorous and cultivated understanding. There is no exaggeration of woman's moral excellence or intellectual capabilities; no injudicious insistance on her fitness for this or that function hitherto engrossed by men; but a calm plea for the removal of unjust laws and artificial restrictions, so that the possibilities of her nature may have room for full development, a wisely stated demand to disencumber her of the

> Parasitic forms
> That seem to keep her up, but drag her down—
> And leave her field to burgeon and to bloom
> From all within her, make herself her own
> To give or keep, to live and learn and be
> All that not harms distinctive womanhood[5].

It is interesting to compare this essay of Margaret Fuller's published in its earliest form in 1843,[6] with a work on the position of woman, written between sixty and seventy years ago—we mean

[3] *Letters*, V, 160–161.

[4] *Woman in the Nineteenth Century, and Kindred Papers Relating to the Sphere, Condition, and Duties of Woman* (1855).

[5] Tennyson, *The Princess*, VII, 253–258. George Eliot is quoting, slightly inaccurately, from the 1847 text of this passage, the phrasing of which was altered in later editions.

[6] *Woman in the Nineteenth Century* was revised and expanded from an article entitled 'The Great Lawsuit, Man versus Men: Woman versus Women' in the *Dial*, July, 1843.

Mary Wollstonecraft's *Rights of Woman*.[7] The latter work was not continued beyond the first volume; but so far as this carries the subject, the comparison, at least in relation to strong sense and loftiness of moral tone, is not at all disadvantageous to the woman of the last century. There is in some quarters a vague prejudice against the *Rights of Woman* as in some way or other a reprehensible book, but readers who go to it with this impression will be surprised to find it eminently serious, severely moral, and withal rather heavy—the true reason, perhaps, that no edition has been published since 1796, and that it is now rather scarce. There are several points of resemblance, as well as of striking difference, between the two books. A strong understanding is present in both; but Margaret Fuller's mind was like some regions of her own American continent, where you are constantly stepping from the sunny 'clearings' into the mysterious twilight of the tangled forest —she often passes in one breath from forcible reasoning to dreamy vagueness; moreover, her unusually varied culture gives her great command of illustration. Mary Wollstonecraft, on the other hand, is nothing if not rational; she has no erudition, and her grave pages are lit up by no ray of fancy. In both writers we discern, under the brave bearing of a strong and truthful nature, the beating of a loving woman's heart, which teaches them not to undervalue the smallest offices of domestic care or kindliness. But Margaret Fuller, with all her passionate sensibility, is more of the literary woman, who would not have been satisfied without intellectual production; Mary Wollstonecraft, we imagine, wrote not at all for writing's sake, but from the pressure of other motives. So far as the difference of date allows, there is a striking coincidence in their trains of thought; indeed, every important idea in the *Rights of Woman*, except the combination of home education with a common day-school for boys and girls, reappears in Margaret Fuller's essay.

One point on which they both write forcibly is the fact that, while men have a horror of such faculty or culture in the other sex as tends to place it on a level with their own, they are really in a state of subjection to ignorant and feeble-minded women. Margaret Fuller says:

Wherever man is sufficiently raised above extreme poverty or brutal stupidity, to care for the comforts of the fireside, or the bloom

[7] *A Vindication of the Rights of Woman* (1792).

and ornament of life, woman has always power enough, if she choose to exert it, and is usually disposed to do so, in proportion to her ignorance and childish vanity. Unacquainted with the importance of life and its purposes, trained to a selfish coquetry and love of petty power, she does not look beyond the pleasure of making herself felt at the moment, and governments are shaken and commerce broken up to gratify the pique of a female favourite. The English shop-keeper's wife does not vote, but it is for her interest that the politician canvasses by the coarsest flattery.

Again:

All wives, bad or good, loved or unloved, inevitably influence their husbands from the power their position not merely gives, but necessitates of colouring evidence and infusing feelings in hours when the—patient, shall I call him?—is off his guard.

Hear now what Mary Wollstonecraft says on the same subject:

Women have been allowed to remain in ignorance and slavish dependence many, very many years, and still we hear of nothing but their fondness of pleasure and sway, their preference of rakes and soldiers, their childish attachment to toys, and the vanity that makes them value accomplishments more than virtues. History brings forward a fearful catalogue of the crimes which their cunning has produced, when the weak slaves have had sufficient address to over-reach their masters. . . . When, therefore, I call women slaves, I mean in a political and civil sense; for indirectly they obtain too much power, and are debased by their exertions to obtain illicit sway. . . . The libertinism, and even the virtues of superior men, will always give women of some description great power over them; and these weak women, under the influence of childish passions and selfish vanity, *will throw a false light over the objects which the very men view with their eyes who ought to enlighten their judgment.* Men of fancy, and those sanguine characters who mostly hold the helm of human affairs in general, relax in the society of women; and surely I need not cite to the most superficial reader of history the numerous examples of vice and oppression which the private intrigues of female favourites have produced; not to dwell on the mischief that naturally arises from the blundering interposition of well-meaning folly. *For in the transactions of business it is much better to have to deal with a knave than a fool, because a knave adheres to some plan, and any plan of reason may be seen through sooner than a sudden flight of folly.* The power which vile and foolish women have had over wise men who possessed sensibility is notorious.

There is a notion commonly entertained among men that an instructed woman, capable of having opinions, is likely to prove an impracticable yoke-fellow, always pulling one way when her husband wants to go the other, oracular in tone, and prone to give curtain lectures on metaphysics. But surely, so far as obstinacy is concerned, your unreasoning animal is the most unmanageable of creatures, where you are not allowed to settle the question by a cudgel, a whip and bridle, or even a string to the leg. For our own parts, we see no consistent or commodious medium between the old plan of corporal discipline and that thorough education of women which will make them rational beings in the highest sense of the word. Wherever weakness is not harshly controlled it must *govern*, as you may see when a strong man holds a little child by the hand, how he is pulled hither and thither, and wearied in his walk by his submission to the whims and feeble movements of his companion. A really cultured woman, like a really cultured man, will be ready to yield in trifles. So far as we see, there is no indissoluble connexion between infirmity of logic and infirmity of will, and a woman quite innocent of an opinion in philosophy, is as likely as not to have an indomitable opinion about the kitchen. As to airs of superiority, no woman ever had them in consequence of true culture, but only because her culture was shallow or unreal, only as a result of what Mrs. Malaprop well calls 'the ineffectual qualities in a woman'[8]—mere acquisitions carried about, and not knowledge thoroughly assimilated so as to enter into the growth of the character.

To return to Margaret Fuller, some of the best things she says are on the folly of absolute definitions of woman's nature and absolute demarcations of woman's mission. 'Nature,' she says, 'seems to delight in varying the arrangements, as if to show that she will be fettered by no rule; and we must admit the same varieties that she admits.' Again: 'If nature is never bound down, nor the voice of inspiration stifled, that is enough. We are pleased that women should write and speak, if they feel need of it, from having something to tell; but silence for ages would be no misfortune, if that silence be from divine command, and not from man's tradition.' And here is a passage, the beginning of which has been often quoted:

If you ask me what offices they (women) may fill, I reply—any. I do not care what case you put; let them be sea-captains if you will. I

[8] Sheridan, *The Rivals*, III, iii.

do not doubt there are women well fitted for such an office, and, if so, I should be as glad as to welcome the Maid of Saragossa, or the Maid of Missolonghi, or the Suliote heroine, or Emily Plater. I think women need, especially at this juncture, a much greater range of occupation than they have, to rouse their latent powers. . . . In families that I know, some little girls like to saw wood, others to use carpenter's tools. Where these tastes are indulged, cheerfulness and good-humour are promoted. Where they are forbidden, because 'such things are not proper for girls,' they grow sullen and mischievous. Fourier had observed these wants of women, as no one can fail to do who watches the desires of little girls, or knows the *ennui* that haunts grown women, except where they make to themselves a serene little world by art of some kind. He, therefore, in proposing a great variety of employments, in manufactures or the care of plants and animals, allows for one-third of women as likely to have a taste for masculine pursuits, one-third of men for feminine. . . . I have no doubt, however, that a large proportion of women would give themselves to the same employments as now, because there are circumstances that must lead them. Mothers will delight to make the nest soft and warm. Nature would take care of that; no need to clip the wings of any bird that wants to soar and sing, or finds in itself the strength of pinion for a migratory flight unusual to its kind. The difference would be that *all* need not be constrained to employments for which *some* are unfit.

A propos of the same subject, we find Mary Wollstonecraft offering a suggestion which the women of the United States have already begun to carry out. She says:

> Women, in particular, all want to be ladies, Which is simply to have nothing to do, but listlessly to go they scarcely care where, for they cannot tell what. But what have women to do in society? I may be asked, but to loiter with easy grace; surely you would not condemn them all to suckle fools and chronicle small beer. No. *Women might certainly study the art of healing, and be physicians as well as nurses.* . . . Business of various kinds they might likewise pursue, if they were educated in a more orderly manner. . . . Women would not then marry for a support, as men accept of places under government, and neglect the implied duties.

Men pay a heavy price for their reluctance to encourage self-help and independent resources in women. The precious meridian years of many a man of genius have to be spent in the toil of routine, that an 'establishment' may be kept up for a woman who can understand none of his secret yearnings, who is fit for nothing but to sit in her drawing-room like a doll-Madonna in her shrine. No matter. Anything is more endurable than to change our established formulæ about women, or to run the risk of looking up to our wives instead of looking down on them. *Sit divus, dummodo non sit vivus* (let him be a god, provided he be not living), said the Roman magnates of Romulus; and so men say of women, let them be idols, useless absorbents of precious things, provided we are not obliged to admit them to be strictly fellow-beings, to be treated, one and all, with justice and sober reverence.

On one side we hear that woman's position can never be improved until women themselves are better; and, on the other, that women can never become better until their position is improved—until the laws are made more just, and a wider field opened to feminine activity. But we constantly hear the same difficulty stated about the human race in general. There is a perpetual action and reaction between individuals and institutions; we must try and mend both by little and little—the only way in which human things can be mended. Unfortunately, many over-zealous champions of women assert their actual equality with men —nay, even their moral superiority to men—as a ground for their release from oppressive laws and restrictions. They lose strength immensely by this false position. If it were true, then there would be a case in which slavery and ignorance nourished virtue, and so far we should have an argument for the continuance of bondage. But we want freedom and culture for woman, because subjection and ignorance have debased her, and with her, Man; for—

> If she be small, slight-natured, miserable,
> How shall men grow?[9]

Both Margaret Fuller and Mary Wollstonecraft have too much sagacity to fall into this sentimental exaggeration. Their ardent hopes of what women may become do not prevent them from seeing and painting women as they are. On the relative moral excellence of men and women Mary Wollstonecraft speaks with the most decision:

Women are supposed to possess more sensibility, and even humanity, than men, and their strong attachments and instantaneous emotions of compassion are given as proofs; but the clinging affection

[9] Tennyson, *The Princess*, VII, 249–250.

of ignorance has seldom anything noble in it, and may mostly be resolved into selfishness, as well as the affection of children and brutes. I have known many weak women whose sensibility was entirely engrossed by their husbands; and as for their humanity, it was very faint indeed, or rather it was only a transient emotion of compassion. Humanity does not consist 'in a squeamish ear,' says an eminent orator. 'It belongs to the mind as well as to the nerves.' But this kind of exclusive affection, though it degrades the individual, should not be brought forward as a proof of the inferiority of the sex, because it is the natural consequence of confined views; for even women of superior sense, having their attention turned to little employments and private plans, rarely rise to heroism, unless when spurred on by love! and love, as an heroic passion, like genius, appears but once in an age. I therefore agree with the moralist who asserts 'that women have seldom so much generosity as men;' and that their narrow affections, to which justice and humanity are often sacrificed, render the sex apparently inferior, especially as they are commonly inspired by men; but I contend that the heart would expand as the understanding gained strength, if women were not depressed from their cradles.

We had marked several other passages of Margaret Fuller's for extract, but as we do not aim at an exhaustive treatment of our subject, and are only touching a few of its points, we have, perhaps, already claimed as much of the reader's attention as he will be willing to give to such desultory material.

15

TRANSLATIONS AND TRANSLATORS

Leader, VI (20 October 1855), 1014–1015

As the translator of Strauss's *Life of Jesus*, Feuerbach's *Essence of Christianity*, and Spinoza's *Ethics*, George Eliot could speak with special authority on the subject of this article. The desultory remarks of 'Translation and Translators' only suggest the articulate theory she might have presented had she conceived her role of reviewer differently and had the conditions of her writing for the *Leader* allowed. Nevertheless, the article is the fullest published statement George Eliot made of her views on the matter, and indicates that her own considerable experience had not injured her belief in either the possibility or the value of translation.

Kant's *Critique of Pure Reason*, translated by J. M. D. Meiklejohn, and *Specimens of the Choicest Lyrical Productions of the Most Celebrated German Poets*, 2nd ed., 2 vols., translated by Mary Anne Burt, both appeared in 1855. George Eliot recorded her review of them in her Journal for 15 and 16 October 1855.

*   *   *

A CLERGYMAN (of the Charles Honeyman[1] species) once told us that he never set about preparing his sermons till Saturday evening, for he 'trusted to Providence.' A similar kind of trust, we suppose, must be prevalent among translators, for many of them are evidently relying on some power which

> Can teach all people to translate,
> Though out of languages in which
> They understand no part of speech—[2]

[1] In Thackeray's *The Newcomes*. George Eliot and Lewes were reading ' "The Newcomes" as light fare after dinner' (Journal, 16 October 1855).

[2] Butler, *Hudibras*, I, i, 660–662: 'And teach all people . . .'.

a *Nachklang*, or resonance, perhaps, of the famous legend about those early translators, the Seventy who turned the Old Testament into Greek, which legend tells how Ptolemy shut them up in separate cells to do their work, and how, when they came to compare their renderings, there was perfect agreement! We are convinced, however, that the translators of the Septuagint had some understanding of their business to begin with, or this supernatural aid would not have been given, for in the matter of translation, at least, we have observed, that 'God helps them who help themselves'.[3] A view of the case, which we commend to all young ladies and some middle-aged gentlemen, who consider a very imperfect acquaintance with their own language, and an anticipatory acquaintance with the foreign language, quite a sufficient equipment for the office of translator.

It is perfectly true that, though geniuses have often undertaken translation, translation does not often demand genius. The power required in the translation varies with the power exhibited in the original work: very modest qualifications will suffice to enable a person to translate a book of ordinary travels, or a slight novel, while a work of reasoning or science can be adequately rendered only by means of what is at present exceptional faculty and exceptional knowledge. Among books of this latter kind, Kant's *Critique of Pure Reason* is perhaps the very hardest nut—the peachstone—for a translator to crack so as to lay open the entire uninjured kernel of meaning, and we are glad at last to believe that a translator of adequate power has been employed upon it. For so far as we have examined the version placed at the head of our article, it appears to us very different indeed from the many renderings of German metaphysical works, in which the translator, having ventured into deep waters without learning to swim, clings to the dictionary, and commends himself to Providence. Mr. Meiklejohn's translation—so far, we must again observe, as we have examined it—indicates a real mastery of his author, and, for the first time, makes Kant's *Critik der reinen Vernunft* accessible to English readers.[4]

It may seem odd that we should associate with this mighty book

[3] *Poor Richard's Almanac:* one of Adam Bede's favourite texts (*Adam Bede*, Ch. 19).

[4] Meiklejohn's translation is still in print in Everyman's Library and in the *Encyclopædia Britannica* edition of the 'Great Books'.

—this terrible ninety-gun ship—such a little painted pleasure-boat
is Miss (or Mrs.) Burt's miscellaneous collection of translations
from German lyric poets. But we are concerning ourselves here
simply with translation—not at all with Kant's Philosophy or with
German Lyrics considered in themselves, and these two volumes
happen to be the specimens of translation most recently presented
to our notice. With regard to prose, we may very generally use
Goldsmith's critical recipe,[5] and say that the translation would
have been better if the translator had taken more pains; but of
poetical attempts we are often sure that no amount of pains would
produce a satisfactory result. And so it is with Miss Burt's
Specimens of the German Poets. She appears to have the knowledge
and the industry which many translators want, but she has not the
poetic power which makes poetical translations endurable to those
acquainted with the originals. Amongst others, however, who have
no such acquaintance, Miss Burt's translations seem to have been
in some demand, since they have reached a second edition. She has
been bold enough to attempt a version of Goethe's exquisite
Zueignung (Dedication), and here is a specimen of her rendering.
Goethe sings with divine feeling and music:

> Für andre wächst in mir das edle Gut,
> Ich kann und will das Pfund nicht mehr vergraben,
> Warum sucht' ich den Weg so sehnsuchtsvoll,
> Wenn ich ihn nicht den Brüdern zeigen soll?

Miss Burt follows him much as a Jew's harp would follow a
piano—

> Entombed no longer shall my *talent* be,
> That treasure I amass, shall other's share?
> To find the road—oh, why such zeal display,
> If I guide not my brethren on their way?

A version like this bears about the same relation to the original
as the portraits in an illustrated newspaper bear to the living face
of the distinguished gentleman they misrepresent; and considering
how often we hear opinions delivered on foreign poets by people
who only know those poets at second hand, it becomes the
reviewer's duty to insist again and again on the inadequacy of
poetic translations.

[5] *The Vicar of Wakefield*, Ch. 20.

The Germans render our poetry better than we render theirs, for their language, as slow and unwieldly as their own post-horses in prose, becomes in poetry graceful and strong and flexible as an Arabian war-horse. Besides, translation among them is more often undertaken by men of genius. We remember, for example, some translations of Burns, by Freiligrath,[6] which would have arrested us by their beauty if we had seen the poems, for the first time, in this language. It is true the Germans think a little too highly of their translations, and especially are under the illusion, encouraged by some silly English people, that Shakspeare according to Schlegel is better than Shakspeare himself—not simply to a German as being easier for him to understand, but absolutely better as poetry. A very close and admirable rendering Schlegel's assuredly is, and it is a high pleasure to track it in its faithful adherence to the original,[7] just as it is to examine a fine engraving of a favourite picture. Sometimes the German is as good as the English—the same music played on another but as good an instrument. But more frequently the German is a feeble echo, and here and there it breaks down in a supremely fine passage. An instance of this kind occurs in the famous speech of Lorenzo to Jessica. Shakspeare says—

> Soft stillness and the night
> Become the touches of sweet harmony.[8]

This Schlegel renders—

> Saufte Still und Nacht
> Sie werden *Tasten* süsser Harmonie.

That is to say, 'Soft stillness and the night *are* the *finger-board* of sweet harmony.' A still worse blunder is made by Tieck (whose

---

[6] Ferdinand Freiligrath (1810–1876) published translations of Burns's songs in *Gedichte* (1838).

[7] '. . . we compared several scenes of Hamlet in Schlegel's translation with the original. It is generally very close & often admirably well done, but Shakspear's strong concrete language is almost always weakened. For example, "Though this hand were *thicker than* itself in brother's blood" is rendered "auch *um und um* in Bruder's Blut *getauchnet*." The prose speeches of Hamlet lose all their felicity in the translation' (Journal, 7 January 1855).

[8] *Merchant of Venice*, V, i, 56–57.

translation is the rival of Schlegel's) in the monologue of Macbeth. In the lines—

> That but this blow
> Might be the be-all and the end-all here—
> But here upon this bank and shoal of time,
> I'd jump the life to come—[9]

Tieck renders, 'Upon this bank and shoal of time,' 'Auf dieser *Schülerbank* der Gegenwart,' that is 'On this *school-bench* of the present!' These are cases of gross inaccuracy arising from an imperfect understanding of the original. Here is an instance of feebleness. Coriolanus says—

> And like an eagle in the dovecote, I
> Flutter'd the Volscians in Corioli.[10]

For the admirably descriptive word 'fluttered', Schlegel gives '*schlug*', which simply means *slew*. Weak renderings of this kind are abundant.

Such examples of translators' fallibility in men like Schlegel and Tieck might well make less accomplished persons more backward in undertaking the translation of great poems, and by showing the difficulty of the translator's task, might make it an object of ambition to real ability. Though a good translator is infinitely below the man who produces *good* original works, he is infinitely above the man who produces *feeble* original works. We had meant to say something of the moral qualities especially demanded in the translator—the patience, the rigid fidelity, and the sense of responsibility in interpreting another man's mind. But we have gossiped on this subject long enough.

[9] I, vii, 4–7: 'We'ld jump the life to come.' 'Shoal' in this passage is Theobald's conjecture in place of the Folio's 'schoole'. Tieck followed the Folio reading, which numbered Pope among its advocates.

[10] V, vi, 115–116: 'That, like an eagle in a dovecote, I / Fluttered your Volscians . . .'.

16

THOMAS CARLYLE

Leader, VI (27 October 1855), 1034–1035

Thomas Ballantyne (1806–1871), whose *Passages Selected from th* *Writings of Thomas Carlyle: With a Biographical Memoir* is the occasio of this review, was a member of the original company that formed th *Leader*, though that partnership had long been dissolved by the tim George Eliot's notice was written.

Her description in this short article of Carlyle's influence upon th 'superior and active' minds of his generation may be taken as a acknowledgment of her own sense of indebtedness. As early as 1841 sh wrote her old school-fellow Martha Jackson, asking 'have you . . . rea any of T. Carlyle's books? He is a grand favourite of mine, and I ventur to recommend to you his "Sartor Resartus." . . . His soul is a shrine o the brightest and purest philanthropy, kindled by the live coal o gratitude and devotion to the Author of all things. I should observe tha he is not "orthodox." '[1] Seven years later she wrote John Sibree tha 'you and Carlyle . . . are the only two people who feel just as I woul have them—who can glory in what is actually great and beautiful with out putting forth any cold reservations and incredulities to save thei credit for wisdom.'[2] When *Adam Bede* was published, George Eliot sen a copy, as she had done before with *Scenes of Clerical Life*, to Mrs Carlyle, hoping that Carlyle himself could be induced to break his rul against novels and read her work. As she wrote to Blackwood, 'I shoul like, if possible, to give him the same sort of pleasure he has given me i the early chapters of *Sartor*, where he describes little Diogenes eatin his porridge on the wall in sight of the sunset, and gaining deep wisdo from the contemplation of the pigs and other "higher animals" o Entepfuhl.'[3] Lewes, too, was an early and ardent admirer of Carlyle, an his *Life of Goethe*, published three days after George Eliot's notice o

[1] *Letters*, I, 122-123.   [2] *Letters*, I, 252-253.
[3] *Letters*, III, 23.

Ballantyne's selections from Carlyle, bears the following dedication: 'To Thomas Carlyle, who first taught England to appreciate Goethe, his work is inscribed as a memorial of esteem for rare and noble qualities.'

According to George Eliot's Journal, the review of Ballantyne's selections was finished 12 October 1855; it has been reprinted once, in *Essays and Uncollected Papers*.

*　　*　　*

IT has been well said that the highest aim in education is analogous to the highest aim in mathematics, namely, to obtain not *results* but *powers*, not particular solutions, but the means by which endless solutions may be wrought. He is the most effective educator who aims less at perfecting specific acquirements than at producing that mental condition which renders acquirements easy, and leads to their useful application; who does not seek to make his pupils moral by enjoining particular courses of action, but by bringing into activity the feelings and sympathies that must issue in noble action. On the same ground it may be said that the most effective writer is not he who announces a particular discovery, who convinces men of a particular conclusion, who demonstrates that this measure is right and that measure wrong; but he who rouses in others the activities that must issue in discovery, who awakes men from their indifference to the right and the wrong, who nerves their energies to seek for the truth and live up to it at whatever cost. The influence of such a writer is dynamic. He does not teach men how to use sword and musket, but he inspires their souls with courage and sends a strong will into their muscles. He does not, perhaps, enrich your stock of data, but he clears away the film from your eyes that you may search for data to some purpose. He does not, perhaps, convince you, but he strikes you, undeceives you, animates you. You are not directly fed by his books, but you are braced as by a walk up to an alpine summit, and yet subdued to calm and reverence as by the sublime things to be seen from that summit.

Such a writer is Thomas Carlyle. It is an idle question to ask whether his books will be read a century hence: if they were all burnt as the grandest of Suttees on his funeral pile, it would be only like cutting down an oak after its acorns have sown a forest. For there is hardly a superior or active mind of this generation that has not been modified by Carlyle's writings; there has hardly been

an English book written for the last ten or twelve years that would
not have been different if Carlyle had not lived. The character of
his influence is best seen in the fact that many of the men who have
the least agreement with his opinions are those to whom the
reading of *Sartor Resartus* was an epoch in the history of their
minds. The extent of his influence may be best seen in the fact that
ideas which were startling novelties when he first wrote them are
now become common-places. And we think few men will be found
to say that this influence on the whole has not been for good.
There are plenty who question the justice of Carlyle's estimates of
past men and past times, plenty who quarrel with the exaggerations of the *Latter-Day Pamphlets*, and who are as far as possible
from looking for an amendment of things from a Carlylian theo-
cracy with the 'greatest man', as a Joshua who is to smite the
wicked (and the stupid) till the going down of the sun. But for any
large nature, those points of difference are quite incidental. It is
not as a theorist, but as a great and beautiful human nature, that
Carlyle influences us. You may meet a man whose wisdom seems
unimpeachable, since you find him entirely in agreement with
yourself; but this oracular man of unexceptionable opinions has a
green eye, a wiry hand, and altogether a *Wesen*, or demeanour, that
makes the world look blank to you, and whose unexceptionable
opinions become a bore; while another man who deals in what you
cannot but think 'dangerous paradoxes', warms your heart by the
pressure of his hand, and looks out on the world with so clear and
loving an eye, that nature seems to reflect the light of his glance
upon your own feeling. So it is with Carlyle. When he is saying the
very opposite of what we think, he says it so finely, with so hearty
conviction—he makes the object about which we differ stand out
in such grand relief under the clear light of his strong and honest
intellect—he appeals so constantly to our sense of the manly and
the truthful—that we are obliged to say 'Hear! hear'! to the writer
before we can give the decorous 'Oh! oh'! to his opinions.

Much twaddling criticism has been spent on Carlyle's style.
Unquestionably there are some genuine minds, not at all given to
twaddle, to whom his style is antipathetic, who find it as unendurable as an English lady finds peppermint. Against antipathies
there is no arguing; they are misfortunes. But instinctive repulsion
apart, surely there is no one who can read and relish Carlyle without feeling that they could no more wish him to have written in

nother style than they could wish Gothic architecture not to be
othic, or Raffaelle not to be Raffaellesque. It is the fashion to
peak of Carlyle almost exclusively as a philosopher; but, to our
inking, he is yet more of an artist than a philosopher. He glances
eep down into human nature, and shows the causes of human
ctions; he seizes grand generalisations, and traces them in the
articular with wonderful acumen; and in all this he is a philoso-
her. But, perhaps, his greatest power lies in concrete presentation.
o novelist has made his creations live for us more thoroughly than
arlyle has made Mirabeau and the men of the French Revolution,
romwell and the Puritans. What humour in his pictures! Yet
hat depth of appreciation, what reverence for the great and god-
ke under every sort of earthly mummery!

It is several years now since we read a work of Carlyle's *seriatim*,
ut this our long-standing impression of him as a writer we find
onfirmed by looking over Mr. Ballantyne's Selections. Such a
olume as this is surely a benefit to the public, for alas! Carlyle's
orks are still dear, and many who would like to have them are
bliged to forego the possession of more than a volume or two.
hrough this good service of Mr. Ballantyne's, however, they may
ow obtain for a moderate sum a large collection of extracts—if
ot the best that could have been made, still very precious ones.

To make extracts from a book of extracts may at first seem easy,
nd to make extracts from a writer so well known may seem
uperfluous. The *embarras de richesses* and the length of the
assages make the first not easy; and as to the second, why, we
ave reread these passages so often in the volumes, and now again
n Mr. Ballantyne's selection, that we cannot suppose any amount
f repetition otherwise than agreeable. We will, however, be
paring.[4]

---

[4] The rest of the article consists of three extracts taken from *On Heroes,
Hero-Worship and the Heroic in History*, Centenary Edition, Lecture II,
The Hero as Prophet', pp. 46-47; Lecture V, 'The Hero as Man of
Letters', pp. 180-181; *Past and Present*, Centenary Edition, Book III,
Ch. 3, pp. 152-153.

17

GERMAN WIT: HEINRICH HEINE

Westminster Review, LXV (January, 1856), 1–33

The second and longest of four articles on Heine that George Eliot wrote in 1855–1856, 'German Wit' is an expansion of her brief review of the *Reisebilder* in the *Leader*, 1 September 1855.[1] Her interest in Heine apparently dates from her first trip to Germany with Lewes in 1854. During their winter in Berlin, when they were in touch with a circle of German writers and artists, including Heine's sympathetic friend Varnhagen von Ense, she had many opportunities to learn of Heine's life and work. The publication of Heine's *Geständnisse* in 1854, which George Eliot read during this time, would have provided a special occasion for talk about Heine among her Berlin acquaintances, and a few of the biographical details included in her article are apparently recollections of the gossip she then heard about him.

The article, published a month before Heine's death, is another evidence of George Eliot's position as one of the leading sponsors of German thought and art in nineteenth-century England. Appearing seven years before Matthew Arnold's more famous essay, it is one of the earliest discussions of Heine in English and, according to S. L. Wormley 'probably did more than any other single work in introducing to English-speaking peoples the genius that was Heine's'.[2]

The titles reviewed in the article are the first volumes of Heine's *Sämmtliche Werke*, Philadelphia, 1855, the earliest collected edition of Heine in German; and the three volumes of Heine's *Vermischte Schriften*, Hamburg, 1854, which include the brief *Geständnisse* to which George Eliot frequently refers.

According to George Eliot's Journal 'German Wit' was commissioned by John Chapman on 12 October 1855 and finished on

[1] The two other articles are 'Heine's Book of Songs', *Saturday Review*, 26 April 1856, pp. 523–524; and 'Recollections of Heine', *Leader*, 23 August 1856, pp. 811–812.

[2] *Heine in England* (Chapel Hill, 1943), p. 113.

28 November. It has been reprinted in Nathan Sheppard, *The Essays of George Eliot'*, *Complete;* and in *Essays and Leaves from a Note-Book.*

*   *   *

NOTHING,' says Goethe, 'is more significant of men's character than what they find laughable.'[3] The truth of this observation would perhaps have been more apparent if he had said *culture* instead of character. The last thing in which the cultivated man can have community with the vulgar is their jocularity; and we can hardly exhibit more strikingly the wide gulf which separates him from them, than by comparing the object which shakes the diaphragm of a coal-heaver with the highly complex pleasure derived from a real witticism. That any high order of wit is exceedingly complex, and demands a ripe and strong mental development, has one evidence in the fact that we do not find it in boys at all in proportion to their manifestation of other powers. Clever boys generally aspire to the heroic and poetic rather than the comic, and the crudest of all their efforts are their jokes. Many a witty man will remember how in his school days a practical joke, more or less Rabelaisian, was for him the *ne plus ultra* of the ludicrous. It seems to have been the same with the boyhood of [human race.][4] [The history and literature of the ancient Hebrews gives the idea of a people who went about their business and their pleasure as gravely as a society of beavers; the smile and the laugh are often mentioned metaphorically, but the smile is one of complacency, the laugh is one of scorn. Nor can we imagine that the facetious element was very strong in the Egyptians; no laughter lurks in the wondering eyes and the broad calm lips of their statues. Still less can the Assyrians have had any genius for the comic: the round eyes and simpering satisfaction of their ideal faces belong to a type which is not witty, but the cause of wit in others.][5] The fun of [these] early races was, we fancy, of the after-dinner kind—loud-throated laughter over the wine-cup, taken too little account of in sober moments to enter as an element into their Art, and differing as much from the laughter of a Chamfort[6] or a Sheridan as the

[3] *Die Wahlverwandschaften*, Part II, Ch. 4: 'Aus Ottiliens Tagebuche.'
[4] 'mankind', 1884.
[5] Omitted, 1884, causing the omission of 'these' in the next sentence.
[6] Sebastian Roch Nicolas Chamfort (1741–1794), French wit and man of letters, celebrated for his conversation.

gastronomic enjoyment of an ancient Briton, whose dinner had no other 'removes' than from acorns to beech-mast and back again to acorns, differed from the subtle pleasures of the palate experienced by his turtle-eating descendant. [In fact they had to live seriously through the stages which to subsequent races][7] were to become comedy, as those amiable-looking pre-Adamite amphibia which Professor Owen has restored for us in effigy at Sydenham, [took perfectly *au sérieux*][8] the grotesque physiognomies of their kindred. Heavy experience in their case as in every other, was the base from which the salt of future wit was to be made.

Humour is of earlier growth than Wit, and it is in accordance with this earlier growth that it has more affinity with the poetic tendencies, while Wit is more nearly allied to the ratiocinative intellect. Humour draws its materials from situations and characteristics; Wit seizes on unexpected and complex relations. Humour is chiefly representative and descriptive; it is diffuse, and flows along without any other law than its own fantastic will; or it flits about like a will-o'-the-wisp, amazing us by its whimsical transitions. Wit is brief and sudden, and sharply defined as a crystal; it does not make pictures, it is not fantastic; but it detects an unsuspected analogy or suggests a startling or confounding inference. Every one who has had the opportunity of making the comparison will remember that the effect produced on him by some witticisms is closely akin to the effect produced on him by subtle reasoning which lays open a fallacy or absurdity, and there are persons whose delight in such reasoning always manifests itself in laughter. This affinity of Wit with ratiocination is the more obvious in proportion as the species of wit is higher and deals less with words and with superficialities than with the essential qualities of things. Some of Johnson's most admirable witticisms consist in the suggestion of an analogy which immediately exposes the absurdity of an action or proposition; and it is only their ingenuity, condensation, and instantaneousness which lift them from reasoning into Wit—they are *reasoning raised to a higher power*. On the other hand, Humour,

[7] 'It was their lot to live seriously through stages which to later generations . . .', 1884.

[8] 'doubtless took seriously', 1884. Richard Owen (1804–1892), naturalist, Hunterian Professor of Comparative Anatomy, directed 'the restorations of the megatherium and other extinct animals in the geological section of the grounds of the Crystal Palace at Sydenham'. (Richard Owen, *The Life of Richard Owen*, 2 vols. [New York, 1894], I, 397.)

in its higher forms, and in proportion as it associates itself with the sympathetic emotions, continually passes into poetry: nearly all great modern humorists may be called prose poets.

Some confusion as to the nature of Humour has been created by the fact, that those who have written most eloquently on it have dwelt almost exclusively on its higher forms, and have defined humour in general as the *sympathetic* presentation of incongruous elements in human nature and life; a definition which only applies to its later development. A great deal of humour may co-exist with a great deal of barbarism, as we see in the Middle Ages; but the strongest flavour of the humour in such cases will come, not from sympathy, but more probably from triumphant egoism or intolerance; at best it will be the love of the ludicrous exhibiting itself in illustrations of successful cunning and of the *lex talionis*, as in *Reineke Fuchs*, or shaking off in a holiday mood the yoke of a too exacting faith, as in the old Mysteries. Again, it is impossible to deny a high degree of humour to many practical jokes, but no sympathetic nature can enjoy them. Strange as the genealogy may seem, the original parentage of that wonderful and delicious mixture of fun, fancy, philosophy, and feeling which constitutes modern humour, was probably the cruel mockery of a savage at the writhings of a suffering enemy—such is the tendency of things towards the [good and beautiful on this earth!][9] Probably the reason why high culture demands more complete harmony with its moral sympathies in humour than in wit, is that humour is in its nature more prolix— that it has not the direct and irresistible force of wit. Wit is an electric shock, which takes us by violence, quite independently of our predominant mental disposition; but humour approaches us more deliberately and leaves us masters of ourselves. Hence it is, that while coarse and cruel humour has almost disappeared from contemporary literature, coarse and cruel wit abounds: even refined men cannot help laughing at a coarse *bon mot* or a lacerating personality, if the 'shock' of the witticism is a powerful one; while mere fun will have no power over them if it jar on their moral taste. Hence, too, it is, that while wit is perennial, humour is liable to become superannuated.

As is usual with definitions and classifications, however, this distinction between wit and humour does not exactly represent the

[9] 'better and more beautiful', 1884. The revision is an amusingly fastidious instance of George Eliot's meliorism.

actual fact. Like all other species, Wit and Humour over-lap and blend with each other. There are *bon mots*, like many of Charles Lamb's, which are a sort of facetious hybrids, we hardly know whether to call them witty or humourous; there are rather lengthy descriptions or narratives, which, like Voltaire's 'Micromégas', would be humourous if they were not so sparkling and antithetic, so pregant with suggestion and satire, that we are obliged to call them witty. We rarely find wit untempered by humour, or humour without a spice of wit; and sometimes we find them both united in the highest degree in the same mind, as in Shakspeare and Molière. A happy conjunction this, for wit is apt to be cold, and thin-lipped, and Mephistophelean in men who have no relish for humour, whose lungs do never crow like Chanticleer at fun and drollery;[10] and broad-faced, rollicking humour needs the refining influence of wit. Indeed, it may be said that there is no really fine writing in which wit has not an implicit, if not an explicit action. The wit may never rise to the surface, it may never flame out into a witticism; but it helps to give brightness and transparency, it warns off from flights and exaggerations which verge on the ridiculous—in every *genre* of writing it preserves a man from sinking into the *genre ennuyeux*. And it is eminently needed for this office in humorous writing; for as humour has no limits imposed on it by its material, no law but its own exuberance, it is apt to become preposterous and wearisome unless checked by wit, which is the enemy of all monotony, of all lengthiness, of all exaggeration.

Perhaps the nearest approach Nature has given us to a complete analysis, in which wit is as thoroughly exhausted of humour as possible, and humour as bare as possible of wit, is in the typical Frenchman and the typical German. Voltaire, the intensest example of pure wit, fails in most of his fictions from his lack of humour. *Micromégas* is a perfect tale, because, as it deals chiefly with philosophic ideas and does not touch the marrow of human feeling and life, the writer's wit and wisdom were all-sufficient for his purpose. Not so with *Candide*. Here Voltaire had to give pictures of life as well as to convey philosophic truth and satire, and here we feel the want of humour. The sense of the ludicrous is continually defeated by disgust, and the scenes, instead of presenting us with an amusing or agreeable picture, are only the frame for a witticism. On the other hand, German humour generally shows

[10] Cf. *As You Like It*, II, vii, 30.

no sense of measure, no instinctive tact; it is either floundering and clumsy as the antics of a leviathan, or laborious and interminable as a Lapland day, in which one loses all hope that the stars and quiet will ever come. For this reason, Jean Paul, the greatest of German humorists, is unendurable to many readers, and frequently tiresome to all. Here, as elsewhere, the German shows the absence of that delicate perception, that sensibility to gradation, which is the essence of tact and taste, and the necessary concomitant of wit. All his subtlety is reserved for the region of metaphysics. For *Identität* in the abstract, no one can have an acuter vision, but in the concrete he is satisfied with a very loose approximation. He has the finest nose for *Empirismus* in philosophical doctrine, but the presence of more or less tobacco-smoke in the air he breathes is imperceptible to him. To the typical German —*Vetter Michel*—it is indifferent whether his door-lock will catch, whether his tea-cup be more or less than an inch thick; whether or not his book have every other leaf unstitched; whether his neighbour's conversation be more or less of a shout; whether he pronounce *b* or *p*, *t* or *d*; whether or not his adored one's teeth be few and far between. He has the same sort of insensibility to gradations in time. A German comedy is like a German sentence: you see no reason in its structure why it should ever come to an end, and you accept the conclusion as an arrangement of Providence rather than of the author. We have heard Germans use the word *Langeweile*, the equivalent for ennui, and we have secretly wondered *what* it can be that produces ennui in a German. Not the longest of long tragedies, for we have known him to pronounce that *höchst fesselnd* [(so enchaining!);][11] not the heaviest of heavy books, for he delights in that as *gründlich* [(deep, Sir, deep!);] not the slowest of journeys in a *Post-wagen*, for the slower the horses, the more cigars he can smoke before he reaches his journey's end. German ennui must be something as superlative as Barclay's treble X, which, we suppose, implies an extremely unknown quantity of stupefaction.

It is easy to see that this national deficiency in nicety of perception must have its effect on the national appreciation and exhibition of Humour. You find in Germany ardent admirers of Shakspeare, who tell you that what they think most admirable in him is his *Wortspiel*, his verbal quibbles; [and one of these, a man of no

[11] This and the following parenthesis omitted, 1884.

slight culture and refinement, once cited to a friend of ours
Proteus's joke in 'The Two Gentlemen of Verona'—'Nod, I? why
that's Noddy', as a transcendent specimen of Shakspearian wit.
German facetiousness is seldom comic to foreigners, and an
Englishman with a swelled cheek might take up *Kladderadatsch*,
the German Punch, without any danger of agitating his facial
muscles. Indeed,][12] it is a remarkable fact that, among the five
great races concerned in modern civilization, the German race is
the only one which, up to the present century, had contributed
nothing classic to the common stock of European wit and humour;
[for *Reineke Fuchs* cannot be regarded][13] as a peculiarly Teutonic
product. Italy was the birth-place of Pantomime and the immortal
Pulcinello; Spain had produced Cervantes; France had produced
Rabelais and Molière, and classic wits innumerable; England had
yielded Shakespeare and a host of humorists. But Germany had
borne no great comic dramatist, no great satirist, and she has not
yet repaired the omission; she had not even produced any
humorist of a high order. Among her great writers, Lessing is
the one who is the most specifically witty. We feel the implicit
influence of wit—the 'flavour of mind'—throughout his writings;
and it is often concentrated into pungent satire, as every reader of
the *Hamburgische Dramaturgie* remembers. Still, Lessing's name
has not become European through his wit, and his charming
comedy, 'Minna von Barnhelm', has won no place on a foreign
stage. Of course, we do not pretend to an exhaustive acquaintance
with German literature; we not only admit—we are sure, that it
includes much comic writing of which we know nothing. We
simply state the fact, that no German production of that kind,
before the present century, ranked as European; a fact which does
not, indeed, determine the *amount* of the national facetiousness,
but which is quite decisive as to its *quality*. Whatever may be the
stock of fun which Germany yields for home consumption, she has
provided little for the palate of other lands.—All honour to her for
the still greater things she has done for us! She has fought the
hardest fight for freedom of thought, has produced the grandest

[12] Omitted, 1884. The illustration is from George Eliot's stay in Berlin,
where one evening she heard the Graf York praise Shakespeare's '*Wortspiel*. ' "For example," he said, "I nod—noddy! Das ist vortrefflich." '
(Journal, miscellaneous notes on Weimar and Berlin.)
[13] 'unless "Reineke Fuchs" can be fairly claimed . . .', 1884.

inventions, has made magnificent contributions to science, has given us some of the divinest poetry, and quite the divinest music, in the world. [No one reveres and treasures the products of the German mind more than we do.][14] To say that that mind is not fertile in wit, is only like saying that excellent wheat land is not rich pasture; to say that we do not enjoy German facetiousness, is no more than to say, that though the horse is the finest of quadrupeds, we do not like him to lay his hoof playfully on our shoulder. Still, as we have noticed that the pointless puns and stupid jocularity of the boy may ultimately be developed into the epigrammatic brilliancy and polished playfulness of the man; as we believe that racy wit and chastened delicate humour are inevitably the results of invigorated and refined mental activity; we can also believe that Germany will, one day, yield a crop of wits and humorists.

Perhaps there is already an earnest of that future crop in the existence of HEINRICH HEINE, a German born with the present century, who, to Teutonic imagination, sensibility, and humour, adds an amount of *esprit* that would make him brilliant among the most brilliant of Frenchmen. True, this unique German wit is half a Hebrew; but he and his ancestors spent their youth in German air, and were reared on *Wurst* and *Sauerkraut*, so that he is as much a German as a pheasant is an English bird, or a potato an Irish vegetable. But whatever else he may be, Heine is one of the most remarkable men of this age: no echo, but a real voice, and therefore, like all genuine things in this world, worth studying; a surpassing lyric poet, who has uttered our feelings for us in delicious song; a humorist, who touches leaden folly with the magic wand of his fancy, and transmutes it into the fine gold of art —who sheds his sunny smile on human tears, and makes them a beauteous rainbow on the cloudy background of life; a wit, who holds in his mighty hand the most scorching lightnings of satire; an artist in prose literature, who has shown even more completely than Goethe the possibilities of German prose; and—in spite of all charges against him, true as well as false—a lover of freedom, who has spoken wise and brave words on behalf of his fellow-men. He is, moreover, a suffering man, who, with all the highly-wrought sensibility of genius, has to endure terrible physical ills; and as such he calls forth more than an intellectual interest. It is true,

[14] 'We revere and treasure the products of the German mind', 1884.

alas! that there is a heavy weight in the other scale—that Heine's magnificent powers have often served only to give electric force to the expression of debased feeling, so that his works are no Phidian statue of gold, and ivory, and gems, but have not a little brass, and iron, and miry clay mingled with the precious metal. The audacity of his occasional coarseness and personality is unparalleled in contemporary literature, and has hardly been exceeded by the licence of former days. Hence, before his volumes are put within the reach of immature minds, there is need of a friendly penknife to exercise a strict censorship. Yet, when all coarseness, all scurrility, all Mephistophelean contempt for the reverent feelings of other men, is removed, there will be a plenteous remainder of exquisite poetry, of wit, humour, and just thought. It is apparently too often a congenial task to write severe words about the transgressions committed by men of genius, especially when the censor has the advantage of being himself a man of *no* genius, so that those transgressions seem to him quite gratuitous; *he*, forsooth, never lacerated any one by his wit, or gave irresistible piquancy to a coarse allusion, and his indignation is not mitigated by any knowledge of the temptation that lies in transcendent power. We are also apt to measure what a gifted man has done by our arbitrary conception of what he might have done, rather than by a comparison of his actual doings with our own or those of other ordinary men. We make ourselves over-zealous agents of heaven, and demand that our brother should bring usurious interest for his five Talents, forgetting that it is less easy to manage five Talents than two. Whatever benefit there may be in denouncing the evil, it is after all more edifying, and certainly more cheering, to appreciate the good. Hence, in endeavouring to give our readers some account of Heine and his works, we shall not dwell lengthily on his failings; we shall not hold the candle up to dusty, vermin-haunted corners, but let the light fall as much as possible on the nobler and more attractive details. Our sketch of Heine's life, which has been drawn from various sources, will be free from everything like intrusive gossip, and will derive its colouring chiefly from the autobiographical hints and descriptions scattered through his own writings. Those of our readers who happen to know nothing of Heine, will in this way be making their acquaintance with the writer while they are learning the outline of his career.

We have said that Heine was born with the present century; but this statement is not precise, for we learn that, according to his certificate of baptism, he was born December 12, 1799.[15] However, as he himself says, the important point is, that he was born, and born on the banks of the Rhine, at Düsseldorf, where his father was a merchant. In his 'Reisebilder' he gives us some recollections, in his wild poetic way, of the dear old town where he spent his childhood, and of his schoolboy troubles there. We shall quote from these in butterfly fashion, sipping a little nectar here and there, without regard to any strict order:

I first saw the light on the banks of that lovely stream, where Folly grows on the green hills, and in autumn in plucked, pressed, poured into casks, and sent into foreign lands. Believe me, I yesterday heard some one utter folly which, in anno 1811, lay in a bunch of grapes I then saw growing on the Johannisberg. . . . Mon Dieu! if I had only such faith in me that I could remove mountains, the Johannisberg would be the very mountain I should send for wherever I might be; but as my faith is not so strong, imagination must help me, and it transports me at once to the lovely Rhine. . . . I am again a child, and playing with other children on the Schlossplatz, at Düsseldorf on the Rhine. Yes, madam, there was I born; and I note this expressly, in case, after my death, seven cities—Schilda, Krähwinkel, Polkwitz, Bockum, Dülken, Göttingen, and Schöppenstädt—should contend for the honour of being my birthplace. Düsseldorf is a town on the Rhine; sixteen thousand men live there, and many hundred thousand men besides lie buried there. . . . Among them, many of whom my mother says, that it would be better if they were still living; for example, my grandfather and my uncle, the old Herr von Geldern and the young Herr von Geldern, both such celebrated doctors, who saved so many men from death, and yet must die themselves. And the pious Ursula, who carried me in her arms when I was a child, also lies buried there, and a rosebush grows on her grave; she loved the scent of roses so well in life, and her heart was pure rose-incense and goodness. The knowing old Canon, too, lies buried there. Heavens, what an object he looked when I last saw him! *He was made up of nothing but mind and plasters*, and nevertheless studied day and night,

[15] I.e., 1797. I do not know the source of the error, which was not corrected in the reprint. The early articles on Heine in England are naturally liable to error: George Eliot is also mistaken in calling Heine only 'half a Hebrew', while Matthew Arnold, writing after George Eliot, has Heine born in Hamburg.

as if he were alarmed lest the worms should find an idea too little in his head. And the little William lies there, and for this I am to blame. We were school-fellows in the Franciscan monastery, and were playing on that side of it where the Düssel flows between stone walls, and I said—'William, fetch out the kitten that has just fallen in'— and merrily he went down on to the plank which lay across the brook, snatched the kitten out of the water, but fell in himself, and was dragged out dripping and dead. *The kitten lived to a good old age. . . .* Princes in that day were not the tormented race as they are now; the crown grew firmly on their heads, and at night they drew a nightcap over it, and slept peacefully, and peacefully slept the people at their feet; and when the people waked in the morning, they said—'Good morning, father!'—and the princes answered—'Good morning, dear children!' But it was suddenly quite otherwise; for when we awoke one morning at Düsseldorf, and were ready to say—'Good morning, father!'—lo! the father was gone away; and in the whole town there was nothing but dumb sorrow, everywhere a sort of funeral disposition; and people glided along silently to the market, and read the long placard placed on the door of the Town Hall. It was dismal weather; yet the lean tailor, Kilian, stood in his nankeen jacket which he usually wore only in the house, and his blue worsted stockings hung down so that his naked legs peeped out mournfully, and his thin lips trembled while he muttered the announcement to himself. And an old soldier read rather louder, and at many a word a crystal tear trickled down to his brave old moustache. I stood near him and wept in company, and asked him—'*Why we wept?*' He answered—'The Elector has abdicated.' And then he read again, and at the words, 'for the long-manifested fidelity of my subjects,' and 'hereby set you free from your allegiance,' he wept more than ever. It is strangely touching to see an old man like that, with faded uniform and scarred face, weep so bitterly all of a sudden. While we were reading, the electoral arms were taken down from the Town Hall; everything had such a desolate air, that it was as if an eclipse of the sun were expected. . . . I went home and wept, and wailed out—'The Elector has abdicated!' In vain my mother took a world of trouble to explain the thing to me. I knew what I knew; I was not to be persuaded, but went crying to bed, and in the night dreamed that the world was at an end.

The next morning, however, the sun rises as usual, and Joachim Murat is proclaimed Grand Duke, whereupon there is a holiday at the public school, and Heinrich (or Harry, for that was his baptismal name, which he afterwards had the good taste to change), perched on the bronze horse of the Electoral statue, sees quite a different scene from yesterday's:

The next day the world was again all in order, and we had school as before, and things were got by heart as before—The Roman emperors, chronology, the nouns in *im*, the *verba irregularia*, Greek, Hebrew, geography, mental arithmetic!—heavens! my head is still dizzy with it—all must be learned by heart! And a great deal of this came in very conveniently for me in after life. For if I had not known the Roman kings by heart, it would subsequently have been quite indifferent to me whether Niebuhr had proved or had not proved that they never really existed. . . . But oh! the trouble I had at school with the endless dates. And with arithmetic it was still worse. What I understood best was subtraction, for that has a very practical rule: 'Four can't be taken from three, therefore I must borrow one.' But I advise every one in such a case to borrow a few extra pence, for no one can tell what may happen. . . . As for Latin, you have no idea, Madam, what a complicated affair it is. The Romans would never have found time to conquer the world if they had first had to learn Latin. Luckily for them, they already knew in their cradles what nouns have their accusative in *im*. I, on the contrary, had to learn them by heart in the sweat of my brow; nevertheless, it is fortunate for me that I know them . . . and the fact that I have them at my finger-ends if I should ever happen to want them suddenly, affords me much inward repose and consolation in many troubled hours of life. . . . Of Greek I will not say a word, I should get too much irritated. The monks in the middle ages were not so far wrong when they maintained that Greek was an invention of the devil. God knows the suffering I endured over it. . . . With Hebrew it went somewhat better, for I had always a great liking for the Jews, though to this very hour they crucify my good name; but I could never get on so far in Hebrew as my watch, which had much familiar intercourse with pawnbrokers, and in this way contracted many Jewish habits—for example, it wouldn't go on Saturdays.

Heine's parents were apparently not wealthy, but his education was cared for by his uncle, Solomon Heine, a great banker in Hamburg, so that he had no early pecuniary disadvantages to struggle with. He seems to have been very happy in his mother, who was not of Hebrew, but of Teutonic blood; he often mentions her with reverence and affection, and in the 'Buch der Lieder' there are two exquisite sonnets addressed to her, which tell how his proud spirit was always subdued by the charm of her presence,

and how her love was the home of his heart after restless weary
wanderings:

> Wie mächtig auch mein stolzer Muth sich blähe,
> In deiner selig süssen, trauten Nähe
> Ergreift mich oft ein demuthvolle Zagen.
>
> .   .   .   .
>
> Und immer irrte ich nach Liebe, immer
> Nach Liebe, doch die Liebe fand ich nimmer,
> Und kehrte un mach Hause, krank und trübe.
> Doch da bist du entgegen mir gekommen,
> Und ach! was da in deinem Aug' geschwommen,
> Das war die süsse, langgesuchte Liebe.

He was at first destined for a mercantile life, but Nature
declared too strongly against this plan. 'God knows,' he has lately
said in conversation with his brother, 'I would willingly have
become a banker, but I could never bring myself to that pass. I
very early discerned that bankers would one day be the rulers of
the world.' So commerce was at length given up for law, the study
of which he began in 1819 at the University of Bonn. He had
already published some poems in the corner of a newspaper, and
among them was one on Napoleon, the object of his youthful
enthusiasm. This poem, he says in a letter to St. René Taillandier,
was written when he was only sixteen. It is still to be found in the
'Buch der Lieder' under the title 'Die Grenadiere', and it proves
that even in its earliest efforts his genius showed a strongly specific
character.

It will be easily imagined that the germs of poetry sprouted too
vigorously in Heine's brain for jurisprudence to find much room
there. Lectures on history and literature, we are told, were more
diligently attended than lectures on law. He had taken care, too, to
furnish his trunk with abundant editions of the poets, and the poet
he especially studied at that time was Byron. At a later period we
find his taste taking another direction, for he writes, 'Of all
authors, Byron is precisely the one who excites in me the most
intolerable emotion; whereas Scott, in every one of his works,
gladdens my heart, soothes and invigorates me.' Another indication
of his bent in these Bonn days, was a newspaper essay, in which he
attacked the Romantic school; and here also he went through that
chicken-pox of authorship—the production of a tragedy. Heine's

tragedy—'Almansor'—is, as might be expected, better than the majority of these youthful mistakes. The tragic collision lies in the conflict between natural affection and the deadly hatred of religion and of race—in the sacrifice of youthful lovers to the strife between Moor and Spaniard, Moslem and Christian. Some of the situations are striking, and there are passages of considerable poetic merit; but the characters are little more than shadowy vehicles for the poetry, and there is a want of clearness and probability in the structure. It was published two years later, in company with another tragedy, in one act, called 'William Ratcliffe', in which there is rather a feeble use of the Scotch second-sight after the manner of the Fate in the Greek tragedy. We smile to find Heine saying of his tragedies, in a letter to a friend soon after their publication: 'I know they will be terribly cut up, but I will confess to you in confidence that they are very good, better than my collection of poems, which are not worth a shot.' Elsewhere he tells us, that when, after one of Paganini's concerts, he was passionately complimenting the great master on his violin-playing, Paganini interrupted him thus: 'But how were you pleased with my *bows*?'

In 1820 Heine left Bonn for Göttingen. He there pursued his omission of law studies; and at the end of three months he was rusticated for a breach of the laws against duelling. While there, he had attempted a negotiation with Brockhaus for the printing of a volume of poems, and had endured that first ordeal of lovers and poets—a refusal. It was not until a year after, that he found a Berlin publisher for his first volume of poems, subsequently transformed, with additions, into the 'Buch der Lieder'. He remained between two and three years at Berlin, and the society he found there seems to have made these years an important epoch in his culture. He was one of the youngest members of a circle which assembled at the house of the poetess Elise von Hohenhausen, the translator of Byron—a circle which included Chamisso, Varnhagen, and Rahel (Varnhagen's wife). For Rahel, Heine had a profound admiration and regard; he afterwards dedicated to her the poems included under the title 'Heimkehr'; and he frequently refers to her or quotes her in a way that indicates how he valued her influence. According to his friend, F. von Hohenhausen,[16] the opinions concerning Heine's talent were very various among his

[16] F. von Hohenhausen, 'Der kranke Dichter in Paris', *Magazin für die Literatur des Auslandes*, No. 34 (Berlin, 1853).

Berlin friends, and it was only a small minority that had any presentiment of his future fame. In this minority was Elise von Hohenhausen, who proclaimed Heine as the Byron of Germany; but her opinion was met with much head-shaking and opposition. We can imagine how precious was such a recognition as hers to the young poet, then only two or three and twenty, and with by no means an impressive personality for superficial eyes. Perhaps even the deep-sighted were far from detecting in that small, blond, pale young man, with quiet, gentle manners, the latent powers of ridicule and sarcasm—the terrible talons that were one day to be thrust out from the velvet paw of the young leopard.

It was apparently during this residence in Berlin that Heine united himself with the Lutheran Church. He would willingly, like many of his friends, he tells us, have remained free from all ecclesiastical ties if the authorities there had not forbidden residence in Prussia, and especially in Berlin, to every one who did not belong to one of the positive religions recognised by the State.

> As Henri IV. once laughingly said, '*Paris vaut bien une messe,*' so I might with reason say, '*Berlin vaut bien une prêche;*' and I could afterwards, as before, accommodate myself to the very enlightened Christianity, filtrated from all superstition, which could then be had in the churches of Berlin, and which was even free from the divinity of Christ, like turtle-soup without turtle.

At the same period, too, Heine became acquainted with Hegel. In his lately published 'Geständnisse' (Confessions), he throws on Hegel's influence over him the blue light of demoniacal wit, and confounds us by the most bewildering double-edged sarcasms; but that influence seems to have been at least more wholesome than the one which produced the mocking retractations of the 'Geständnisse'. Through all his self-satire, we discern that in those days he had something like real earnestness and enthusiasm, which are certainly not apparent in his present theistic confession of faith.

> On the whole, I never felt a strong enthusiasm for this philosophy, and conviction on the subject was out of the question. I never was an abstract thinker, and I accepted the synthesis of the Hegelian doctrine without demanding any proof, since its consequences flattered my vanity. I was young and proud, and it pleased my vainglory when I learned from Hegel that the true God was not, as my grandmother believed, the God who lives in heaven, but myself here upon earth. This foolish pride had not in the least a pernicious influence on my feelings,

on the contrary, it heightened these to the pitch of heroism. I was at that time so lavish in generosity and self-sacrifice, that I must assuredly have eclipsed the most brilliant deeds of those good *bourgeois* of virtue who acted merely from a sense of duty, and simply obeyed the laws of morality.

His sketch of Hegel is irresistibly amusing; but we must warn the reader that Heine's anecdotes are often mere devices of style by which he conveys his satire or opinions. The reader will see that he does not neglect an opportunity of giving a sarcastic lash or two, in passing, to Meyerbeer, for whose music he has a great contempt. The sarcasm conveyed in the substitution of *reputation* for *music* and *journalists* for *musicians*, might perhaps escape any one unfamiliar with the sly and unexpected turns of Heine's ridicule.

To speak frankly, I seldom understood him, and only arrived at the meaning of his words by subsequent reflection. I believe he wished not to be understood; and hence his practice of sprinkling his discourse with modifying parentheses; hence, perhaps, his preference for persons of whom he knew that they did not understand him, and to whom he all the more willingly granted the honour of his familiar acquaintance. Thus every one in Berlin wondered at the intimate companionship of the profound Hegel with the late Heinrich Beer, a brother of Giacomo Meyerbeer, who is universally known by his reputation, and who has been celebrated by the cleverest journalists. This Beer, namely Heinrich, was a thoroughly stupid fellow, and indeed was afterwards actually declared imbecile by his family, and placed under guardianship, because instead of making a name for himself in art or in science by means of his great fortune, he squandered his money on childish trifles; and, for example, one day bought six thousand thalers' worth of walking sticks. This poor man, who had no wish to pass either for a great tragic dramatist, or for a great star-gazer, or for a laurel-crowned musical genius, a rival of Mozart and Rossini, and preferred giving his money for walking-sticks—this degenerate Beer enjoyed Hegel's most confidential society; he was the philosopher's bosom friend, his Pylades, and accompanied him everywhere like his shadow. The equally witty and gifted Felix Mendelssohn once sought to explain this phenomenon, by maintaining that Hegel did not understand Heinrich Beer. I now believe, however, that the real ground of that intimacy consisted in this— Hegel was convinced that no word of what he said was understood by Heinrich Beer; and he could therefore, in his presence, give himself up to all the intellectual outpourings of the moment. In general,

Hegel's conversation was a sort of monologue, sighed forth by starts in a noiseless voice; the odd roughness of his expressions often struck me, and many of them have remained in my memory. One beautiful starlight evening we stood together at the window, and I, a young man of one-and-twenty, having just had a good dinner and finished my coffee, spoke with enthusiasm of the stars, and called them the habitations of the departed. But the master muttered to himself, 'The stars! hum! hum! The stars are only a brilliant leprosy on the face of the heavens.' 'For God's sake,' I cried, 'is there, then, no happy place above, where virtue is rewarded after death?' But he, staring at me with his pale eyes, said, cuttingly, 'So you want a bonus for having taken care of your sick mother, and refrained from poisoning your worthy brother?' At these words he looked anxiously round, but appeared immediately set at rest when he observed that it was only Heinrich Beer, who had approached to invite him to a game at whist.

In 1823, Heine returned to Göttingen to complete his career as a law-student, and this time he gave evidence of advanced mental maturity, not only by producing many of the charming poems subsequently included in the 'Reisebilder', but also by prosecuting his professional studies diligently enough to leave Göttingen, in 1825, as *Doctor juris*. Hereupon he settled at Hamburg as an advocate, but his profession seems to have been the least pressing of his occupations. In those days, a small blond young man, with the brim of his hat drawn over his nose, his coat flying open, and his hands stuck in his trouser-pockets, might be seen stumbling along the streets of Hamburg, staring from side to side, and appearing to have small regard to the figure he made in the eyes of the good citizens. Occasionally an inhabitant, more literary than usual, would point out this young man to his companion as *Heinrich Heine*; but in general, the young poet had not to endure the inconveniences of being a lion. His poems were devoured, but he was not asked to devour flattery in return. Whether because the fair Hamburghers acted in the spirit of Johnson's advice to Hannah More—to 'consider what her flattery was worth before she choked him with it'[17]—or for some other reason, Heine, according to the testimony of August Lewald,[18] to whom we owe these particulars of his Hamburgh life, was left free from the persecution

[17] Mrs. Piozzi, *Anecdotes of Samuel Johnson*, ed. S. C. Roberts (Cambridge, 1932), p. 119.

[18] Lewald published recollections of Heine in *Aquarelle aus dem Leben*, 4 vols. (1836–1837), vols. II and IV.

of tea-parties. Not, however, from another persecution of genius nervous headaches, which some persons, we are told, regarded as an improbable fiction, intended as a pretext for raising a delicate white hand to his forehead. It is probable that the sceptical persons alluded to were themselves untroubled with nervous headache, and that their hands were *not* delicate. Slight details these, but worth telling about a man of genius, because they help us to keep in mind that he is, after all, our brother, having to endure the petty everyday ills of life as we have; with this difference, that his heightened sensibility converts what are mere insect stings for us into scorpion stings for him.

It was, perhaps, in these Hamburg days that Heine paid the visit to Goethe, of which he gives us this charming little picture:

> When I visited him in Weimar, and stood before him, I involuntarily glanced at his side to see whether the eagle was not there with the lightning in his beak. I was nearly speaking Greek to him; but, as I observed that he understood German, I stated to him in German, that the plums on the road between Jena and Weimar were very good. I had for so many long winter nights thought over what lofty and profound things I would say to Goethe, if ever I saw him. And when I saw him at last, I said to him, that the Saxon plums were very good! And Goethe smiled.

During the next few years, Heine produced the most popular of all his works—those which have won him his place as the greatest of living German poets and humorists. Between 1826 and 1829,[19] appeared the four volumes of the 'Reisebilder' (Pictures of Travel), and the 'Buch der Lieder' (Book of Songs)—a volume of lyrics, of which it is hard to say whether their greatest charm is the lightness and finish of their style, their vivid and original imaginativeness, or their simple, pure sensibility. In his 'Reisebilder', Heine carries us with him to the Harz, to the isle of Norderney, to his native town Düsseldorf, to Italy, and to England, sketching scenery and character, now with the wildest, most fantastic humour, now with the finest idyllic sensibility,—letting his thoughts wander from poetry to politics, from criticism to dreamy reverie, and blending fun, imagination, reflection, and satire in a sort of exquisite, ever-varying shimmer, like the hues of the opal.

Heine's journey to England did not at all heighten his regard for the English. He calls our language the 'hiss of egoism' (*Zisch-*

[19] I.e., 1826–1831.

laute des Egoismus); and his ridicule of English awkwardness is as merciless as—English ridicule of German awkwardness. His antipathy towards us seems to have grown in intensity, like many of his other antipathies; and in his 'Vermischte Schriften' he is more bitter than ever. Let us quote one of his philippics; since bitters are understood to be wholesome.

> It is certainly a frightful injustice to pronounce sentence of condemnation on an entire people. But with regard to the English, momentary disgust might betray me into this injustice; and on looking at the mass, I easily forget the many brave and noble men who distinguished themselves by intellect and love of freedom. But these, especially the British poets, were always all the more glaringly in contrast with the rest of the nation; they were isolated martyrs to their national relations; and, besides, great geniuses do not belong to the particular land of their birth: they scarcely belong to this earth, the Golgotha of their sufferings. The mass—the English blockheads, God forgive me!—are hateful to me in my inmost soul; and I often regard them not at all as my fellow-men, but as miserable automata —machines, whose motive power is egoism. In these moods, it seems to me as if I heard the whizzing wheel-work by which they think, feel, reckon, digest, and pray: their praying, their mechanical Anglican church-going, with the gilt Prayer-book under their arms, their stupid, tiresome Sunday, their awkward piety, is most of all odious to me. I am firmly convinced that a blaspheming Frenchman is a more pleasing sight for the Divinity than a praying Englishman.

On his return from England, Heine was employed at Munich in editing the *Allgemeinen Politischen Annalen*, but in 1830 he was again in the north, and the news of the July Revolution surprised him on the island of Heligoland. He has given us a graphic picture of his democratic enthusiasm in those days in some letters, apparently written from Heligoland, which he has inserted in his book on Börne. We quote some passages, not only for their biographic interest as showing a phase of Heine's mental history, but because they are a specimen of his power in that kind of dithyrambic writing which, in less masterly hands, easily becomes ridiculous:

> The thick packet of newspapers arrived from the Continent with these warm, glowing-hot tidings. They were sunbeams wrapped up in packing-paper, and they inflamed my soul till it burst into the wildest conflagration. . . . It is all like a dream to me; especially the

name, Lafayette, sounds to me like a legend out of my earliest child-hood. Does he really sit again on horseback, commanding the National Guard? I almost fear it may not be true, for it is in print. I will myself go to Paris, to be convinced of it with my bodily eyes. . . . It must be splendid, when he rides through the streets, the citizen of two worlds, the god-like old man, with his silver locks streaming down his sacred shoulder. . . . He greets, with his dear old eyes, the grand-children of those who once fought with him for freedom and equality. . . . It is now sixty years since he returned from America with the Declaration of Human Rights, the decalogue of the world's new creed, which was revealed to him amid the thunders and light-nings of cannon. . . . And the tri-coloured flag waves again on the towers of Paris, and its streets resound with the Marseillaise! . . . It is all over with my yearning for repose. I now know again what I will do, what I ought to do, what I must do. . . . I am the son of the Revolution, and seize again the hallowed weapons on which my mother pronounced her magic benediction. . . . Flowers! flowers! I will crown my head for the death-fight. And the lyre too, reach me the lyre, that I may sing a battle-song. . . . Words like flaming stars, that shoot down from the heavens, and burn up the palaces, and illuminate the huts. . . . Words like bright javelins, that whirr up to the seventh heaven and strike the pious hypocrites who have skulked into the Holy of Holies. . . . I am all joy and song, all sword and flame! Perhaps, too, all delirium. . . . One of those sunbeams wrapped in brown paper has flown to my brain, and set my thoughts aglow. In vain I dip my head into the sea. No water extinguishes this Greek fire. . . . Even the poor Heligolanders shout for joy, although they have only a sort of dim instinct of what has occurred. The fisherman who yesterday took me over to the little sand island, which is the bathing-place here, said to me smilingly, 'The poor people have won!' Yes; instinctively the people comprehend such events, perhaps better than we, with all our means of knowledge. Thus Frau von Varnhagen once told me that when the issue of the Battle of Leipzig was not yet known, the maid-servant suddenly rushed into the room with the sorrowful cry, 'The nobles have won!'. . . . This morning another packet of newspapers is come. I devour them like manna. Child that I am, affecting details touch me yet more than the momentous whole. Oh, if I could but see the dog Medor. . . . The dog Medor brought his master his gun and cartridge-box, and when his master fell, and was buried with his fellow-heroes in the Court of the Louvre, there stayed the poor dog like a monument of faithfulness, sitting motion-less on the grave, day and night, eating but little of the food that was offered him—burying the greater part of it in the earth, perhaps as nourishment for his buried master!

The enthusiasm which was kept thus at boiling heat by imagination, cooled down rapidly when brought into contact with reality. In the same book he indicates, in his caustic way, the commencement of that change in his political *temperature*—for it cannot be called a change in opinion—which has drawn down on him immense vituperation from some of the patriotic party, but which seems to have resulted simply from the essential antagonism between keen wit and fanaticism.

On the very first days of my arrival in Paris, I observed that things wore, in reality, quite different colours from those which had been shed on them, when in perspective, by the light of my enthusiasm. The silver locks which I saw fluttering so majestically on the shoulders of Lafayette, the hero of two worlds, were metamorphosed into a brown perruque, which made a pitiable covering for a narrow skull. And even the dog Medor, which I visited in the Court of the Louvre, and which, encamped under tri-coloured flags and trophies, very quietly allowed himself to be fed—he was not at all the right dog, but quite an ordinary brute, who assumed to himself merits not his own, as often happens with the French; and, like many others, he made a profit out of the glory of the Revolution. . . . He was pampered and patronized, perhaps promoted to the highest posts, while the true Medor, some days after the battle, modestly slunk out of sight, like the true people who created the Revolution.

That it was not merely interest in French politics which sent Heine to Paris in 1831, but also a perception that German air was not friendly to sympathizers in July revolutions, is humorously intimated in the 'Geständnisse'.

I had done much and suffered much, and when the sun of the July Revolution arose in France, I had become very weary, and needed some recreation. Also, my native air was every day more unhealthy for me, and it was time I should seriously think of a change of climate. I had visions: the clouds terrified me, and made all sorts of ugly faces at me. It often seemed to me as if the sun were a Prussian cockade; at night I dreamed of a hideous black eagle, which gnawed my liver; and I was very melancholy. Add to this, I had become acquainted with an old Berlin Justizrath, who had spent many years in the fortress of Spandau, and he related to me how unpleasant it is when one is obliged to wear irons in winter. For myself I thought it very unchristian that the irons were not warmed a trifle. If the irons were warmed a little for us they would not make so unpleasant an impression, and even chilly natures might then bear them very well; it would be only proper consideration, too, if the fetters were perfumed with essence of roses and laurels, as is the case in this country (France). I asked my Justizrath whether he often got oysters to eat at Spandau? He said, No; Spandau was too far from the sea. Moreover, he said meat was very scarce there, and there was no kind of *volaille* except flies, which fell into one's soup. . . . Now, as I really needed some recreation, and, as Spandau is too far from the sea for oysters to be got there, and the Spandau fly-soup did not seem very appetizing to me, as, besides all this, the Prussian chains are very cold in winter, and could not be conducive to my health, I resolved to visit Paris.

Since this time Paris has been Heine's home, and his best prose works have been written either to inform the Germans on French affairs or to inform the French on German philosophy and literature. He became a correspondent of the *Allgemeine Zeitung*, and his correspondence, which extends, with an interruption of several years, from 1831 to 1844, forms the volume entitled 'Französische Zustände' (French Affairs), and the second and third volumes of his 'Vermischte Schriften.' It is a witty and often wise commentary on public men and public events: Louis Philippe, Casimir Périer, Thiers, Guizot, Rothschild, the Catholic party, the Socialist party, have their turn of satire and appreciation, for Heine deals out both with an impartiality which made his less favourable critics—Börne, for example—charge him with the rather incompatible sins of reckless caprice and venality. Literature and art alternate with politics: we have now a sketch of George Sand, or a description of one of Horace Vernet's pictures,—now a criticism of Victor Hugo, or of Liszt,—now an irresistible caricature of Spontini, or Kalkbrenner,—and occasionally the predominant satire is relieved by a fine saying or a genial word of admiration. And all is done with that airy lightness, yet precision of touch, which distinguishes Heine beyond any living writer. The charge of venality was loudly made against Heine in Germany: first, it was said that he was paid to write; then, that he was paid to abstain from writing; and the accusations were supposed to have an irrefragable basis in the fact that he accepted a stipend from the French government. He has never attempted to conceal the reception of that stipend, and we think his statement (in the 'Vermischte Schriften') of the circumstances under which it was offered and received, is a sufficient vindication of himself and M. Guizot from any dishonour in the matter.

It may be readily imagined that Heine, with so large a share of the Gallic element as he has in his composition, was soon at his ease in Parisian society, and the years here were bright with intellectual activity and social enjoyment. 'His wit,' wrote August Lewald, 'is a perpetual gushing fountain; he throws off the most delicious descriptions with amazing facility, and sketches the most comic characters in conversation.' Such a man could not be neglected in Paris, and Heine was sought on all sides—as a guest in distinguished salons, as a possible proselyte in the circle of the Saint Simonians. His literary productiveness seems to have been furthered by this congenial life, which, however, was soon to some extent embittered by the sense of exile; for since 1835 both his works and his person have been the object of denunciation by the German governments. Between 1833 and 1845 appeared the four volumes of the 'Salon', 'Die Romantische Schule' (both written, in the first instance, in French), the book on Börne, 'Atta Troll,' a romantic poem, 'Deutschland,' an exquisitely humorous poem, describing his last visit to Germany, and containing some grand passages of serious writing; and the 'Neue Gedichte,' a collection of lyrical poems. Among the most interesting of his prose works are the second volume of the 'Salon,' which contains a survey of religion and philosophy in Germany, and the 'Romantische Schule,' a delightful introduction to that phase of German literature known as the Romantic school. The book on Börne, which appeared in 1840, two or three years after the death of that writer, excited great indignation in Germany, as a wreaking of vengeance on the dead, an insult to the memory of a man who had worked and suffered in the cause of freedom—a cause which was Heine's own. Börne, we may observe parenthetically for the information of those who are not familiar with recent German literature, was a remarkable political writer of the ultra-liberal party in Germany, who resided in Paris at the same time with Heine: a man of stern, uncompromising partisanship and bitter humour. Without justifying Heine's production of this book, we see excuses for him which should temper the condemnation passed on it. There was a radical opposition of nature between him and Börne; to use his own distinction, Heine is a Hellene—sensuous, realistic, exquisitely alive to the beautiful; while Börne was a Nazarene—ascetic, spiritualistic, despising the pure artist as destitute of earnestness. Heine has too keen a perception of

238

practical absurdities and damaging exaggerations ever to become a thorough-going partisan; and with a love of freedom, a faith in the ultimate triumph of democratic principles, of which we see no just reason to doubt the genuineness and consistency, he has been unable to satisfy more zealous and one-sided liberals by giving his adhesion to their views and measures, or by adopting a denunciatory tone against those in the opposite ranks. Börne could not forgive what he regarded as Heine's epicurean indifference and artistic dalliance, and he at length gave vent to his antipathy in savage attacks on him through the press, accusing him of utterly lacking character and principle, and even of writing under the influence of venal motives. To these attacks Heine remained absolutely mute—from contempt according to his own account; but the retort, which he resolutely refrained from making during Börne's life, comes in this volume published after his death with the concentrated force of long-gathering thunder. The utterly inexcusable part of the book is the caricature of Börne's friend, Madame Wohl, and the scurrilous insinuations concerning Börne's domestic life. It is said, we know not with how much truth, that Heine had to answer for these in a duel with Madame Wohl's husband, and that, after receiving a serious wound, he promised to withdraw the offensive matter from a future edition. That edition, however, has not been called for. Whatever else we may think of the book, it is impossible to deny its transcendent talent—the dramatic vigour with which Börne is made present to us, the critical acumen with which he is characterized, and the wonderful play of wit, pathos, and thought which runs through the whole. But we will let Heine speak for himself, and first we will give part of his graphic description of the way in which Börne's mind and manners grated on his taste:

> To the disgust which, in intercourse with Börne, I was in danger of feeling towards those who surrounded him, was added the annoyance I felt from his perpetual talk about politics. Nothing but political argument, and again political argument, even at table, where he managed to hunt me out. At dinner, when I so gladly forget all the vexations of the world, he spoiled the best dishes for me by his patriotic gall, which he poured as a bitter sauce over everything. Calf's feet, *à la maître d'hôtel*, then my innocent *bonne bouche*, he completely spoiled for me by Job's tidings from Germany, which he scraped together out of the most unreliable newspapers. And then

his accursed remarks, which spoiled one's appetite! . . . This was a
sort of table-talk which did not greatly exhilarate me, and I avenged
myself by affecting an excessive, almost impassioned indifference for
the objects of Börne's enthusiasm. For example, Börne was indignant
that immediately on my arrival in Paris, I had nothing better to do
than to write for German papers a long account of the Exhibition of
Pictures. I omit all discussion as to whether that interest in Art
which induced me to undertake this work was so utterly irreconcilable
with the revolutionary interests of the day: but Börne saw in it a
proof of my indifference towards the sacred cause of humanity, and I
could in my turn spoil the taste of his patriotic *sauerkraut* for him by
talking all dinner-time of nothing but pictures, of Robert's 'Reapers,'
Horace Vernet's 'Judith,' and Scheffer's 'Faust.' . . . That I never
thought it worth while to discuss my political principles with him it is
needless to say; and once when he declared that he had found a
contradiction in my writings, I satisfied myself with the ironical
answer, 'You are mistaken, *mon cher*; such contradictions never occur
in my works, for always before I begin to write, I read over the
statement of my political principles in my previous writings, that I
may not contradict myself, and that no one may be able to reproach
me with apostacy from my liberal principles.'

And here is his own account of the spirit in which the book was
written:

I was never Börne's friend, nor was I ever his enemy. The dis-
pleasure which he could often excite in me was never very important,
and he atoned for it sufficiently by the cold silence which I opposed
to all his accusations and raillery. While he lived I wrote not a line
against him, I never thought about him, I ignored him completely;
and that enraged him beyond measure. If I now speak of him, I do so
neither out of enthusiasm nor out of uneasiness; I am conscious of
the coolest impartiality. I write here neither an apology nor a
critique, and as in painting the man I go on my own observation, the
image I present of him ought perhaps to be regarded as a real portrait.
And such a monument is due to him—to the great wrestler who, in
the arena of our political games, wrestled so courageously, and
earned, if not the laurel, certainly the crown of oak leaves. I give an
image with his true features, without idealization—the more like him
the more honourable for his memory. He was neither a genius nor a
hero; he was no Olympian god. He was a man, a denizen of this
earth; he was a good writer and a great patriot. . . . Beautiful delicious
peace, which I feel at this moment in the depths of my soul! Thou
rewardest me sufficiently for everything I have done and for everything I have despised. . . . I shall defend myself neither from the

reproach of indifference nor from the suspicion of venality. I have for years, during the life of the insinuator, held such self-justification unworthy of me; now even decency demands silence. That would be a frightful spectacle!—polemics between Death and Exile! Dost thou stretch out to me a beseeching hand from the grave? Without rancour I reach mine towards thee. . . . See how noble it is and pure! It was never soiled by pressing the hands of the mob, any more than by the impure gold of thy people's enemy. In reality thou hast never injured me. . . . In all thy insinuations there is not a *louis-d'or's* worth of truth.

In one of these years Heine was married, and, in deference to the sentiments of his wife, married according to the rites of the Catholic Church. On this fact busy rumour afterwards founded the story of his conversion to Catholicism, and could of course name the day and the spot on which he abjured Protestantism. In his 'Geständnisse' Heine publishes a denial of this rumour; less, he says, for the sake of depriving the Catholics of the solace they may derive from their belief in a new convert, than in order to cut off from another party the more spiteful satisfaction of bewailing his instability:

That statement of time and place was entirely correct. I was actually on the specified day in the specified church, which was, moreover, a Jesuit church, namely St. Sulpice; and I then went through a religious act. But this act was no odious abjuration, but a very innocent conjugation; that is to say, my marriage, already performed according to the civil law, there received the ecclesiastical consecration, because my wife, whose family are staunch Catholics, would not have thought her marriage sacred enough without such a ceremony. And I would on no account cause this beloved being any uneasiness or disturbance in her religious views.

For sixteen years—from 1831 to 1847—Heine lived that rapid concentrated life which is known only in Paris; but then, alas! stole on the 'days of darkness,' and they were to be many. In 1847 he felt the approach of the terrible spinal disease which has for seven years chained him to his bed in acute suffering. The last time he went out of doors, he tells us, was in May, 1848:

With difficulty I dragged myself to the Louvre, and I almost sank down as I entered the magnificent hall where the ever-blessed goddess of beauty, our beloved Lady of Milo, stands on her pedestal. At her feet I lay long, and wept so bitterly that a stone must have pitied me. The goddess looked compassionately on me, but at the same time disconsolately, as if she would say: Dost thou not see, then, that I have no arms, and thus cannot help thee?

Since 1848, then, this poet, whom the lovely objects of Nature have always 'haunted like a passion,'[20] has not descended from the second story of a Parisian house; this man of hungry intellect has been shut out from all direct observation of life, all contact with society, except such as is derived from visitors to his sick-room. The terrible nervous disease has affected his eyes; the sight of one is utterly gone, and he can only raise the lid of the other by lifting it with his finger. Opium alone is the beneficent genius that stills his pain. We hardly know whether to call it an alleviation or an intensification of the torture that Heine retains his mental vigour, his poetic imagination, and his incisive wit; for if this intellectual activity fills up a blank, it widens the sphere of suffering. His brother described him in 1851 as still, in moments when the hand of pain was not too heavy on him, the same Heinrich Heine, poet and satirist by turns. In such moments, he would narrate the strangest things in the gravest manner. But when he came to an end, he would roguishly lift up the lid of his right eye with his finger to see the impression he had produced; and if his audience had been listening with a serious face, he would break into Homeric laughter. We have other proof than personal testimony that Heine's disease allows his genius to retain much of its energy, in the 'Romanzero', a volume of poems published in 1851, and written chiefly during the first three years of his illness; and in the first volume of the 'Vermischte Schriften', also the product of recent years. Very plaintive is the poet's own description of his condition, in the epilogue to the 'Romanzero':

Do I really exist? My body is so shrunken that I am hardly anything but a voice; and my bed reminds me of the singing grave of the magician Merlin, which lies in the forest of Brozeliand, in Brittany, under tall oaks whose tops soar like green flames towards heaven. Alas! I envy thee those trees and the fresh breeze that moves their branches, brother Merlin, for no green leaf rustles about my mattress-grave in Paris, where early and late I hear nothing but the rolling of vehicles, hammering, quarrelling, and piano-strumming. A grave without repose, death without the privileges of the dead, who have no debts to pay, and need write neither letters nor books—that is a piteous condition. Long ago the measure has been taken for my coffin

[20] Wordsworth, 'Tintern Abbey', 77.

and for my necrology, but I die so slowly, that the process is tedious for me as well as my friends. But patience; everything has an end. You will one day find the booth closed where the puppet-show of my humour has so often delighted you.

As early as 1850, it was rumoured that since Heine's illness a change had taken place in his religious views; and as rumour seldom stops short of extremes, it was soon said that he had become a thorough pietist, Catholics and Protestants by turns claiming him as a convert. Such a change in so uncompromising an iconoclast, in a man who had been so zealous in his negations as Heine, naturally excited considerable sensation in the camp he was supposed to have quitted, as well as in that he was supposed to have joined. In the second volume of the 'Salon', and in the 'Romantische Schule', written in 1834 and '35, the doctrine of Pantheism is dwelt on with a fervour and unmixed seriousness which show that Pantheism was then an animating faith to Heine, and he attacks what he considers the false spiritualism and asceticism of Christianity as the enemy of true beauty in Art, and of social well being. Now, however, it was said that Heine had recanted all his heresies; but from the fact that visitors to his sick-room brought away very various impressions as to his actual religious views, it seemed probable that his love of mystification had found a tempting opportunity for exercise on this subject, and that, as one of his friends said, he was not inclined to pour out unmixed wine to those who asked for a sample out of mere curiosity. At length, in the epilogue to the 'Romanzero', dated 1851, there appeared, amidst much mystifying banter, a declaration that he had embraced Theism and the belief in a future life, and what chiefly lent an air of seriousness and reliability to this affirmation, was the fact that he took care to accompany it with certain negations:

As concerns myself, I can boast of no particular progress in politics; I adhered (after 1848) to the same democratic principles which had the homage of my youth, and for which I have ever since glowed with increasing fervour. In theology, on the contrary, I must accuse myself of retrogression, since, as I have already confessed, I returned to the old superstition—to a personal God. This fact is, once for all, not to be stifled, as many enlightened and well-meaning friends would fain have had it. But I must expressly contradict the report that my retrograde movement has carried me as far as to the threshold of a Church, and that I have even been received into her lap. No: my religious convictions and views have remained free from any tincture of ecclesiasticism; no chiming of bells has allured me, no altar-candles have dazzled me. I have dallied with no dogmas, and have not utterly renounced my reason.

This sounds like a serious statement. But what shall we say to a convert who plays with his newly-acquired belief in a future life, as Heine does in the very next page? He says to his reader:

Console thyself; we shall meet again in a better world, where I also mean to write thee better books. I take for granted that my health will there be improved, and that Swedenborg has not deceived me. He relates, namely, with great confidence, that we shall peacefully carry on our old occupations in the other world, just as we have done in this; that we shall there preserve our individuality unaltered, and that death will produce no particular change in our organic development. Swedenborg is a thoroughly honourable fellow, and quite worthy of credit in what he tells us about the other world, where he saw with his own eyes the persons who had played a great part on our earth. Most of them, he says, remained unchanged, and busied themselves with the same things as formerly; they remained stationary, were old-fashioned, *rococo*—which now and then produced a ludicrous effect. For example, our dear Dr. Martin Luther kept fast by his doctrine of Grace, about which he had for three hundred years daily written down the same mouldy arguments—just in the same way as the Baron Ekstein, who during twenty years printed in the *Allgemeine Zeitung* one and the same article, perpetually chewing over again the old cud of jesuitical doctrine. But, as we have said, all persons who once figured here below were not found by Swedenborg in such a state of fossil immutability: many had considerably developed their character, both for good and evil, in the other world; and this gave rise to some singular results. Some who had been heroes and saints on earth had *there* sunk into scamps and good-for-nothings; and there were examples, too, of a contrary transformation. For instance, the fumes of self-conceit mounted to Saint Anthony's head when he learned what immense veneration and adoration had been paid to him by all Christendom; and he who here below withstood the most terrible temptations, was now quite an impertinent rascal and dissolute gallows-bird, who vied with his pig in rolling himself in the mud. The chaste Susanna, from having been excessively vain of her virtue, which she thought indomitable, came to a shameful fall, and she who once so gloriously resisted the two old men, was a victim to the seductions of the young Absalom, the son of David. On the contrary, Lot's daughters had in the lapse of time become very virtuous, and passed in the other world for models of propriety: the old man, alas! had stuck to the wine-flask.

In his 'Geständnisse', the retractation of former opinions and profession of Theism are renewed, but in a strain of irony that repels our sympathy and baffles our psychology. Yet what strange, deep pathos is mingled with the audacity of the following passage:

> What avails it me, that enthusiastic youths and maidens crown my marble bust with laurel, when the withered hands of an aged nurse are pressing Spanish flies behind my ears? What avails it me, that all the roses of Shiraz glow and waft incense for me? Alas! Shiraz is two thousand miles from the Rue d'Amsterdam, where, in the wearisome loneliness of my sick room, I get no scent except it be, perhaps, the perfume of warmed towels. Alas! God's satire weighs heavily on me. The great Author of the universe, the Aristophanes of Heaven, was bent on demonstrating, with crushing force, to me, the little, earthly, German Aristophanes, how my wittiest sarcasms are only pitiful attempts at jesting in comparison with His, and how miserably I am beneath Him in humour, in colossal mockery.

For our own part, we regard the paradoxical irreverence with which Heine professes his theoretical reverence as pathological, as the diseased exhibition of a predominant tendency urged into anomalous action by the pressure of pain and mental privation— as the delirium of wit starved of its proper nourishment. It is not for us to condemn, who have never had the same burthen laid on us; it is not for pigmies at their ease to criticize the writhings of the Titan chained to the rock.

On one other point we must touch before quitting Heine's personal history. There is a standing accusation against him in some quarters of wanting political principle, of wishing to de-nationalize himself, and of indulging in insults against his native country. Whatever ground may exist for these accusations, that ground is not, so far as we see, to be found in his writings. He may not have much faith in German revolutions and revolutionists; experience, in his case as in that of others, may have thrown his millennial anticipations into more distant perspective; but we see no evidence that he has ever swerved from his attachment to the principles of freedom, or written anything which to a philosophic mind is incompatible with true patriotism. He has expressly denied the report that he wished to become naturalized in France; and his yearning towards his native land and the accents of his native language is expressed with a pathos the more reliable from the fact that he is sparing in such effusions. We do not see why Heine's satire of the blunders and foibles of his fellow-countrymen should be denounced as the crime of *lèse-patrie*, any more than the political caricatures of any other satirist. The real offences of Heine are his occasional coarseness and his unscrupulous personalities, which are reprehensible, not because they are directed against his fellow-countrymen, but because they are *personalities*. That these offences have their precedents in men whose memory the world delights to honour does not remove their turpitude, but it is a fact which should modify our condemnation in a particular case; unless, indeed, we are to deliver our judgments on a principle of compensation—making up for our indulgence in one direction by our severity in another. On this ground of coarseness and personality, a true bill may be found against Heine; *not*, we think, on the ground that he has laughed at what is laughable in his compatriots. Here is a specimen of the satire under which we suppose German patriots wince:

> Rhenish Bavaria was to be the starting-point of the German revolution. Zweibrücken was the Bethlehem in which the infant Saviour—Freedom—lay in the cradle, and gave whimpering promise of redeeming the world. Near his cradle bellowed many an ox, who afterwards, when his horns were reckoned on, showed himself a very harmless brute. It was confidently believed that the German revolution would begin in Zweibrücken, and everything was there ripe for an outbreak. But, as has been hinted, the tender-heartedness of some persons frustrated that illegal undertaking. For example, among the Bipontine conspirators there was a tremendous braggart, who was always loudest in his rage, who boiled over with the hatred of tyranny, and this man was fixed on to strike the first blow, by cutting down a sentinel who kept an important post. . . . 'What!' cried the man, when this order was given him—'What!—me! Can you expect so horrible, so bloodthirsty an act of me?—I—*I*, kill an innocent sentinel? I, who am father of a family! And this sentinel is perhaps also father of a family. One father of a family kill another father of a family? Yes! Kill—murder!'

In political matters, Heine, like all men whose intellect and taste predominate too far over their impulses to allow of their becoming partisans, is offensive alike to the aristocrat and the democrat. By the one he is denounced as a man who holds incendiary principles, by the other as a half-hearted 'trimmer'. He has no sympathy, as he says, with 'that vague, barren pathos, that useless effervescence of enthusiasm, which plunges, with the spirit of a martyr, into an ocean of generalities, and which always reminds me of the American sailor, who had so fervent an enthusiasm for General Jackson, that he at last sprang from the top of a mast into the sea, crying, *I die for General Jackson!*'

But thou liest, Brutus, thou liest, Cassius, and thou, too, liest, Asinius, in maintaining that my ridicule attacks those ideas which are the precious acquisition of Humanity, and for which I myself have so striven and suffered. No! for the very reason that those ideas constantly hover before the poet in glorious splendour and majesty, he is the more irresistibly overcome by laughter when he sees how rudely, awkwardly, and clumsily those ideas are seized and mirrored in the contracted minds of contemporaries. . . . There are mirrors which have so rough a surface that even an Apollo reflected in them becomes a caricature, and excites our laughter. *But we laugh then only at the caricature, not at the god.*

For the rest, why should we demand of Heine that he should be a hero, a patriot, a solemn prophet, any more than we should demand of a gazelle that it should draw well in harness? Nature has not made him of her sterner stuff—not of iron and adamant, but of pollen of flowers, the juice of the grape, and Puck's mischievous brain, plenteously mixing also the dews of kindly affection and the gold-dust of noble thoughts. It is, after all, a *tribute* which his enemies pay him when they utter their bitterest dictum, namely, that he is '*nur Dichter*'—only a poet. Let us accept this point of view for the present, and, leaving all consideration of him as a man, look at him simply as a poet and literary artist.

Heine is essentially a lyric poet. The finest products of his genius are

> Short swallow flights of song that dip
> Their wings in tears, and skim away;[21]

and they are so emphatically songs that, in reading them, we feel as if each must have a twin melody born in the same moment and by the same inspiration. Heine is too impressible and mercurial for any sustained production; even in his short lyrics his tears sometimes pass into laughter and laughter into tears; and his longer

[21] Tennyson, *In Memoriam*, xlviii, st. 4.

poems, 'Atta Troll' and 'Deutschland', are full of Ariosto-like
transitions. His song has a wide compass of notes: he can take us to
the shores of the Northern Sea and thrill us by the sombre sublimity of his pictures and dreamy fancies; he can draw forth our
tears by the voice he gives to our own sorrows, or to the sorrows of
'Poor Peter'; he can throw a cold shudder over us by a mysterious
legend, a ghost story, or a still more ghastly rendering of hard
reality; he can charm us by a quiet idyl, shake us with laughter at
his over-flowing fun, or give us a piquant sensation of surprise by
the ingenuity of his transitions from the lofty to the ludicrous.
This last power is not, indeed, essentially poetical; but only a poet
can use it with the same success as Heine, for only a poet can poise
our emotion and expectation at such a height as to give effect to
the sudden fall. Heine's greatest power as a poet lies in his simple
pathos, in the ever varied but always natural expression he has
given to the tender emotions. We may perhaps indicate this phase
of his genius by referring to Wordsworth's beautiful little poem,
'She dwelt among the untrodden ways'; the conclusion—

> She dwelt alone, and few could know
>   When Lucy ceased to be;
> But she is in her grave, and, oh!
>   The difference to me—[22]

is entirely in Heine's manner; and so is Tennyson's poem of a
dozen lines, called 'Circumstance'. Both these poems have Heine's
pregnant simplicity. But, lest this comparison should mislead, we
must say that there is no general resemblance between either
Wordsworth, or Tennyson, and Heine. Their greatest qualities lie
quite away from the light, delicate lucidity, the easy, rippling
music, of Heine's style. The distinctive charm of his lyrics may
best be seen by comparing them with Goethe's. Both have the
same masterly, finished simplicity and rhythmic grace; but there is
more thought mingled with Goethe's feeling—his lyrical genius is
a vessel that draws more water than Heine's, and, though it seems
to glide along with equal ease, we have a sense of greater weight
and force accompanying the grace of its movement. But, for this
very reason, Heine touches our hearts more strongly; his songs are
all music and feeling—they are like birds that not only enchant us

[22] Wordsworth reads: 'She lived unknown . . .'.

with their delicious notes, but nestle against us with their soft
breasts, and make us feel the agitated beating of their hearts. He
indicates a whole sad history in a single quatrain: there is not an
image in it, not a thought; but it is beautiful, simple, and perfect
as a 'big round tear'[23]—it is pure feeling breathed in pure
music:

> Anfangs wollt' ich fast verzagen
> Und ich glaubt' ich trug es nie,
> Und ich hab' es doch getragen,—
> Aber fragt mich nur nicht, wie.[24]

He excels equally in the more imaginative expression of feeling:
he represents it by a brief image, like a finely-cut cameo; he
expands it into a mysterious dream, or dramatizes it in a little
story, half ballad, half idyl; and in all these forms his art is so
perfect, that we never have a sense of artificiality or of unsuccessful
effort; but all seems to have developed itself by the same beautiful
necessity that brings forth vine-leaves and grapes and the natural
curls of childhood.   Of Heine's humorous poetry, 'Deutschland'
is the most charming specimen—charming, especially, because its
wit and humour grow out of a rich loam of thought. 'Atta Troll' is
more original, more various, more fantastic; but it is too great a
strain on the imagination to be a general favourite. We have said,
that feeling is the element in which Heine's poetic genius habitually
floats; but he can occasionally soar to a higher region, and impart
deep significance to picturesque symbolism; he can flash a sublime
thought over the past and into the future; he can pour forth a lofty
strain of hope or indignation. Few could forget, after once hearing
them, the stanzas at the close of 'Deutschland', in which he warns
the King of Prussia not to incur the irredeemable hell which the
injured poet can create for him—the *singing flames* of a Dante's
terza rima!

> Kennst du die Hölle des Dante nicht,
> Die schrecklichen Terzetten?
> Wen da der Dichter hineingesperrt
> Den kann kein Gott mehr retten.

[23] *As You Like It*, II, i, 38.
[24] At first I was almost in despair, and I thought I could never bear it,
and yet I have borne it—only do not ask me *how*? [George Eliot's note.]

Kein Gott, kein Heiland, erlöst ihn je
Aus diesen singenden flammen!
Nimm dich in Acht, das wir dich nicht
Zu solcher Hölle verdammen.[25]

As a prosaist, Heine is, in one point of view, even more distinguished than as a poet. The German language easily lends
itself to all the purposes of poetry; like the ladies of the Middle
Ages, it is gracious and compliant to the Troubadours. But as these
same ladies were often crusty and repulsive to their unmusical
mates, so the German language generally appears awkward and
unmanageable in the hands of prose writers. Indeed, the number
of really fine German prosaists before Heine, would hardly have
exceeded the numerating powers of a New Hollander, who can
count three and no more. Persons the most familiar with German
prose testify that there is an extra fatigue in reading it, just as we
feel an extra fatigue from our walk when it takes us over ploughed
clay. But in Heine's hands German prose, usually so heavy, so
clumsy, so dull, becomes, like clay in the hands of the chemist,
compact, metallic, brilliant; it is German in an *allotropic* condition.
No dreary, labyrinthine sentences in which you find 'no end in
wandering mazes lost';[26] no chains of adjectives in linked harshness long drawn out; no digressions thrown in as parentheses; but
crystalline definiteness and clearness, fine and varied rhythm, and
all that delicate precision, all those felicities of word and cadence,
which belong to the highest order of prose. And Heine has proved
—what Madame de Staël seems to have doubted[27]—that it is
possible to be witty in German; indeed, in reading him, you

[25] It is not fair to the English reader to indulge in German quotations,
but in our opinion poetical translations are usually worse than valueless.
For those who think differently, however, we may mention that Mr. Stores
Smith has published a modest little book, containing 'Selections from the
Poetry of Heinrich Heine', and that a meritorious (American) translation
of Heine's complete works, by Charles Leland, is now appearing in
shilling numbers. [George Eliot's note.] John Stores Smith ('John
Ackerlos'), *Selections from the Poetry of Heinrich Heine*, 1854; Charles G.
Leland, *Heine's Pictures of Travel*, 1855. Leland translated eight of the
twelve volumes in *The Works of Heine*, London, 1892–1905. George
Eliot favourably reviewed his translation of the *Reisebilder* in the *Leader*,
1 September 1855.
[26] *Paradise Lost*, II, 561; for the next phrase, cf. Milton's 'L'Allegro',
140.
[27] In *De L'Allemagne*, Part I, Ch. 12.

might imagine that German was pre-eminently the language of wit, so flexible, so subtle, so piquant does it become under his management. He is far more an artist in prose than Goethe. He has not the breadth and repose, and the calm development which belong to Goethe's style, for they are foreign to his mental character; but he excels Goethe in susceptibility to the manifold qualities of prose, and in mastery over its effects. Heine is full of variety, of light and shadow: he alternates between epigrammatic pith, imaginative grace, sly allusion, and daring piquancy; and athwart all these there runs a vein of sadness, tenderness, and grandeur which reveals the poet. He continually throws out those finely-chiselled sayings which stamp themselves on the memory, and become familiar by quotation. For example: 'The People have time enough, they are immortal; kings only are mortal'.—'Wherever a great soul utters its thoughts, there is Golgotha'.—'Nature wanted to see how she looked, and she created Goethe'.—'Only the man who has known bodily suffering is truly a *man*; his limbs have their Passion-history, they are spiritualized'. He calls Rubens 'this Flemish Titan, the wings of whose genius were so strong that he soared as high as the sun, in spite of the hundred weight of Dutch cheeses that hung on his legs.' Speaking of Börne's dislike to the calm creations of the true artist, he says, 'He was like a child which, insensible to the glowing significance of a Greek statue, only touches the marble and complains of the cold.'

The most poetic and specifically humorous of Heine's prose writings are the 'Reisebilder'. The comparison with Sterne is inevitable here; but Heine does not suffer from it, for if he falls below Sterne in raciness of humour, he is far above him in poetic sensibility and in reach and variety of thought. Heine's humour is never persistent, it never flows on long in easy gaiety and drollery; where it is not swelled by the tide of poetic feeling, it is continually dashing down the precipice of a witticism. It is not broad and unctuous; it is aërial and sprite-like, a momentary resting-place between his poetry and his wit. In the 'Reisebilder' he runs through the whole gamut of his powers, and gives us every hue of thought, from the wildly droll and fantastic to the sombre and the terrible. Here is a passage almost Dantesque in conception:

Alas! one ought in truth to write against no one in this world. Each of us is sick enough in this great lazaretto, and many a polemical writing reminds me involuntarily of a revolting quarrel, in a little hospital at Cracow, of which I chanced to be a witness, and where it was horrible to hear how the patients mockingly reproached each other with their infirmities: how one who was wasted by consumption jeered at another who was bloated by dropsy; how one laughed at another's cancer in the nose, and this one again at his neighbour's locked-jaw or squint, until at last the delirious fever-patient sprang out of bed and tore away the coverings from the wounded bodies of his companions, and nothing was to be seen but hideous misery and mutilation.

And how fine is the transition in the very next chapter, where, after quoting the Homeric description of the feasting gods, he says:

Then suddenly approached, panting, a pale Jew, with drops of blood on his brow, with a crown of thorns on his head, and a great cross laid on his shoulders; and he threw the cross on the high table of the gods, so that the golden cups tottered, and the gods became dumb and pale, and grew ever paler, till they at last melted away into vapour.

The richest specimens of Heine's wit are perhaps to be found in the works which have appeared since the 'Reisebilder'. The years, if they have intensified his satirical bitterness, have also given his wit a finer edge and polish. His sarcasms are so subtly prepared and so slily allusive, that they may often escape readers whose sense of wit is not very acute; but for those who delight in the subtle and delicate flavours of style, there can hardly be any wit more irresistible than Heine's. We may measure its force by the degree in which it has subdued the German language to its purposes, and made that language brilliant in spite of a long hereditary transmission of dulness. As one of the most harmless examples of his satire, take this on a man who has certainly had his share of adulation:

Assuredly it is far from my purpose to depreciate M. Victor Cousin. The titles of this celebrated philosopher even lay me under an obligation to praise him. He belongs to that living pantheon of France, which we call the peerage, and his intelligent legs rest on the velvet benches of the Luxembourg. I must indeed sternly repress all private feelings which might seduce me into an excessive enthusiasm. Otherwise I might be suspected of servility; for M. Cousin is very influential in the State by means of his position and his tongue. This consideration might even move me to speak of his faults as frankly as of his virtues. Will he himself disapprove of this? Assuredly not. I know that we cannot do higher honour to great minds than when we throw as strong a light on their demerits as on their merits. When we sing the praises of a Hercules, we must also mention that he once laid aside the lion's skin and sat down to the distaff: what then? he remains notwithstanding a Hercules! So when we relate similar circumstances concerning M. Cousin, we must nevertheless add, with discriminating eulogy: *M. Cousin, if he has sometimes sat twaddling at the distaff, has never laid aside the lion's skin. . . .* It is true that, having been suspected of demagogy, he spent some time in a German prison, just as Lafayette and Richard Cœur de Lion. But that M. Cousin there in his leisure hours studied Kant's 'Critique of Pure Reason' is to be doubted on three grounds. First, this book is written in German. Secondly, in order to read this book, a man must understand German. Thirdly, M. Cousin does not understand German. . . . I fear I am passing unawares from the sweet waters of praise into the bitter ocean of blame. Yes, on one account I cannot refrain from bitterly blaming M. Cousin; namely, that he who loves truth far more than he loves Plato and Tenneman, is unjust to himself when he wants to persuade us that he has borrowed something from the philosophy of Schelling and Hegel. Against this self-accusation, I must take M. Cousin under my protection. On my word and conscience! this honourable man has not stolen a jot from Schelling and Hegel, and if he brought home anything of theirs, it was merely their friendship. That does honour to his heart. But there are many instances of such false self-accusation in psychology. I knew a man who declared that he had stolen silver spoons at the king's table; and yet we all knew that the poor devil had never been presented at court, and accused himself of stealing these spoons to make us believe that he had been a guest at the palace. No! In German philosophy M. Cousin has always kept the sixth commandment; here he has never pocketed a single idea, not so much as a salt-spoon of an idea. All witnesses agree in attesting that in this respect M. Cousin is honour itself. . . . I prophesy to you that the renown of M. Cousin, like the French Revolution, will go round the world! I hear some one wickedly add: Undeniably the renown of M. Cousin is going round the world, and *it has already taken its departure from France.*

The following 'symbolical myth' about Louis Philippe is very characteristic of Heine's manner:

I remember very well that immediately on my arrival (in Paris) I hastened to the Palais Royal to see Louis Philippe. The friend who conducted me told me that the king now appeared on the terrace only at stated hours, but that formerly he was to be seen at any time for five francs. 'For five francs!' I cried, with amazement; 'does he then show himself for money?' 'No; but he is shown for money, and it happens in this way:—There is a society of *claqueurs, marchands de contremarques*, and such riff-raff, who offered every foreigner to show him the king for five francs: if he would give ten francs, he might see the king raise his eyes to heaven, and lay his hand pro-testingly on his heart; if he would give twenty francs, the king would sing the Marseillaise. If the foreigner gave five francs, they raised a loud cheering under the king's windows, and his Majesty appeared on the terrace, bowed and retired. If ten francs, they shouted still louder, and gesticulated as if they had been possessed, when the King appeared, who then, as a sign of silent emotion, raised his eyes to heaven, and laid his hand on his heart. English visitors, however, would sometimes spend as much as twenty francs, and then the enthusiasm mounted to the highest pitch; no sooner did the King appear on the terrace, than the Marseillaise was struck up and roared out frightfully, until Louis Philippe, perhaps only for the sake of putting an end to the singing, bowed, laid his hand on his heart, and joined in the Marseillaise. Whether, as is asserted, he beat time with his foot, I cannot say.'

[One more quotation, and it must be our last:

O the women! We must forgive them much, for they love much—and many. Their hate is properly only love turned inside out. Some-times they attribute some delinquency to us, because they think they can in this way gratify another man. When they write, they have always one eye on the paper and the other on a man; and this is true of all authoresses, except the Countess Hahn-Hahn, who has only one eye.][28]

18

INTRODUCTION TO GENESIS

Leader, VII (12 January 1856), 41–42

As a dispassionate and informed description of the grounds for the mid-nineteenth-century intellectual's heterodoxy, George Eliot's 'Introduction to Genesis' could hardly be bettered. The effects on her mind of the historical, scientific, and philosophical criticism of the Old Testament are all summarized or implied in this succinct account of the 'various answers' to the question of Biblical inspiration.

James Heywood's edition of *Introduction to the Book of Genesis*, 2 vols. (1855), is an abridged translation of *Die Genesis, historisch-kritisch erläutert* (1835) by Peter Von Bohlen (1796–1840). According to her Journal, George Eliot began her review of the book on 1 January 1856.

*   *   *

WHAT is the office of the Biblical critic in relation to the Old Testament? There are various answers to this question.

Extreme orthodoxy says, that since there is irrefragable external evidence for the Divine origin and direct verbal inspiration of the Hebrew Scriptures, the critic has simply to interpret the meaning of the text: any record which is in contradiction with the text, if not reconcileable by hypothesis, is to be pronounced false; but if an undeniable fact turns out to be in contradiction with the text, the received interpretation is to be reconsidered and altered so as to agree with the undeniable fact. According to this theory the critic has not to examine the Hebrew writings in order to ascertain their origin, but having beforehand settled their origin, he has to explain everything so as to make it accord with this premiss. He is not an inquirer, but an advocate. He has not to weigh evidence in order to arrive at a conclusion, but having arrived at a conclusion, he has to make it the standard by which he accepts or rejects evidence. His criticism is a deductive process, which has for its axiom, the Hebrew writings are from beginning to end revealed truth. And it is only while orthodoxy strictly adheres to this point of view that it is on safe and consistent ground; for if we are to examine a book for proof—though it be only confirmatory proof—of its origin, we must have some criteria to judge it by, and we can only obtain such criteria by borrowing them from pure historical criticism, an ally that must be ultimately incompatible with rigid orthodoxy. As long as we rely implicitly on testimony as evidence of a man's health, we have no need to examine the indications of health in his person; but the moment we feel the testimony insufficient, we must have recourse to physiological criteria, which are common to every human organism.

The first symptom that orthodoxy begins to feel the pressure of historical criticism is shown in an extension of the 'accommodation' theory. As the Deity, it is said, in speaking to human beings, must use human language, and consequently anthropomorphic expressions, such as the 'eye of God,' the 'arm of God,' the 'laughter and jealousy of God,' which we have no difficulty in understanding figuratively, so he must adapt the form of His revelations to the degree of culture, which belongs to men at the period in which His revelations are made. He teaches them as a father teaches his children, by adapting the information he gives to their narrow stock of ideas. It was in this way that the candid Dr. Pye Smith[1] explained the narratives of the Creation and the Deluge, to the great scandal of his Evangelical brethren. It is easy to see that this system of interpretation is very elastic, and that it may soon amount to little more than a theological formula for the history of human development. The relation between the theory of *accommodation* and that of *development* is analogous to the relation between the doctrine that the brain is the organ of mind, and the doctrine that mind is the function of the brain; in both cases the manifestation of mind is determined by the conditions of the body. And thus the 'accommodation' theory necessarily leads to what may be called a

---

[1] John Pye Smith (1774–1851), nonconformist divine. His *Relation Between the Holy Scriptures and Some Parts of Geological Science* (1839), an attempt to harmonize Genesis and geological fact, was commended by Whewell, Herschel, and others.

mitigated orthodoxy or a mild heterodoxy, which allows the presence of mythical and legendary elements in the Hebrew records, and renounces the idea that they are from beginning to end infallible, but still regards them as the medium of a special revelation, as the shell that held a kernel of peculiarly Divine truth, by which a monotheistic faith was preserved, and the way prepared for the Christian dispensation. They who hold this theory believe that the Hebrew nation was the grandest instrument of Providence—the Hebrew writings, the vehicle of superhuman truth; but they do not believe in talking serpents and talking asses, or in divine commands to butcher men wholesale; and they hold that, to identify a belief in such fables with the faith of a Christian, is as dangerous to reverence as it would be to fix an absurd popinjay on the divine symbol of the Cross. The laws of Moses are something more to them than the laws of Menu[2]—a Hebrew prophet something more than a religious and patriotic poet; a chapter of Isaiah something more than the Hymn of Cleanthes. They do not feel about the Hebrew temple and the Hebrew worship as they feel about a temple of Isis or the Eleusinian mysteries: the history of Israel is a sacred precinct to them—they take their shoes from off their feet, for it is holy ground. To them, therefore, the Old Testament is still an exceptional book; they only use historical criticism as a winnowing fan to carry away all demands on their belief, which are not strictly involved in their acceptance of Christianity as a special revelation.

Extreme heterodoxy, on the contrary, holds no conviction that removes the Hebrew scriptures from the common category of early national records, which are a combination of myth and legend, gradually clarifying at their later stages into genuine history. It enters on the examination of the Old Testament with as perfect a freedom from pre-suppositions, as unreserved a submission to the guidance of historical criticism, as if it were examining the Vedas or the Zendavesta, or the fragments of Manetho and Sanchoniathon.[3] On thus looking at the Hebrew records by the 'light of common day,'[4] without the lamp of faith, heterodoxy finds in them

[2] Variant of Manu, the progenitor of the human race and author of laws in Hindu myth.

[3] Respectively, the sacred writings of the Hindus and the Parsees; early chroniclers of Egypt and Phoenicia.

[4] Wordsworth, 'Ode, Intimations of Immortality', 76.

no evidence of anything exceptionally divine, but sees in them simply the history and literature of a barbarous tribe that gradually rose from fetichism to a ferocious polytheism, offering human sacrifices, and ultimately, through the guidance of their best men, and contact with more civilised nations, to Jehovistic monotheism. It finds in them, as in other early records, a mythical cosmogony, an impossible chronology, and extravagant marvels tending to flatter national vanity, or to aggrandise a priesthood; it finds discrepant conceptions of Deity in documents attributed to one and the same source; it finds legislative enactments, springing from an advanced period, stamped with the sanction of primeval names, or of mythical crises in the national history; in short, it not only finds in the Hebrew writings nothing which cannot be accounted for on grounds purely human, but it finds them of a character which it would be monstrous to attribute to any other than a human origin.

These are results arrived at in the present day by very grave and competent scholars, and whatever opinion may be held concerning them, no educated person can dispense with some knowledge of the evidence on which they are based. There are few books, at least in English, better adapted to give such knowledge in a concise form than the *Introduction to Genesis* by Von Bohlen, named at the head of our article. Von Bohlen's was a thoroughly earnest and reverent mind, and orthodox believers need never be shocked by his manner, if they are inevitably pained by his matter. To this admirable qualification he added that of immense learning, especially in the department of Hindoo literature, his fame having been first won by a work on 'Ancient India.'[5] We have only to regret that Mr. Heywood did not heighten the value of his disinterested labour in editing the *Introduction to Genesis*, by publishing it in a cheaper and more portable form.

The first volume is chiefly occupied with considerations on the origin and character of the Pentateuch, or five books of Moses, generally, considerations which embrace the course of Hebrew history until after the Captivity, or transplantation to Babylon. Every important particular is discussed clearly and briefly, but not scantily, and the reader, though he may not accept Von Bohlen's conclusions, is placed in an excellent position for pursuing the investigation by a closer study of the Scriptures themselves. Mr. Heywood has added in an appendix to this volume the valuable

[5] *Das alte Indien* (1830–1831).

remarks of Von Bohlen on the Week, extracted from his *Ancient India*.

The second volume contains a commentary on the opening portion of Genesis. Von Bohlen wrote a commentary on the whole book, but the translation is limited to the first ten chapters which comprise the important narratives of the Creation, the Fall, the Flood, and the Dispersion of mankind. Mr. Heywood has enriched this volume by notes and by additional remarks on the flood; he has also inserted some interesting extracts on this subject and on the Paradisaic myth from Professor Tuck's Commentary on Genesis.[6]

Instead of quoting from the more argumentative and critical portion of the volumes, which would not be effective in the cursory reading usually given to newspapers, we will borrow from them an admirable Hebrew myth which has arisen since the Christian era. We cannot agree with Von Bohlen that it is 'true to the spirit of antiquity.' The tolerance it breathes is unknown to the Books of the Law:

> Pococke is said to have actually found this chapter in a manuscript at Cairo. The Talmud too is supposed to have been acquainted with it. Saadi alludes to it in his 'Bustan' (see Asiat. Journ. iii. 315). Taylor cites it in the middle of the seventeenth century, and it has now become generally known through the means of Franklin [by whom it was communicated to Lord Kames], who quotes it in his 'Sketches' as a parable against intolerance. It runs as follows:
>
> 1. Now it came to pass that Abraham sat at the door of his tent in the heat of the day. 2. And behold a man drew nigh from the wilderness, and he was bowed down with age, and his white beard hung down even to his girdle, and he leant upon his staff. 3. And when Abraham saw him he stood up, and ran to meet him from the door of his tent, and said, 4. Friend, come in; water shall be brought thee to wash thy feet, and thou shalt eat and tarry the night, and on the morrow thou mayest go on thy way. 5. But the wayfaring man answered and said, Let me, I pray thee, remain under the tree. 6. And Abraham pressed him sore; then he turned and went into the tent. 7. And Abraham set before him cream and milk and cake, and they eat and were satisfied. 8. And when Abraham saw that the man blessed not God, he said to him, Wherefore dost thou not honour the Almighty, the Creator of the heavens and the earth? 9. And the man answered, I worship not thy God, neither do I

[6] Johann Christian Friedrich Tuch (1806–1867), *Kommentar über die Genesis* (1838).

call upon his name; for I have made gods for myself that dwell in my house, and hear me when I call upon them. 10. Then the wrath of Abraham was kindled against the man, and he stood up and fell upon him, and drove him forth into the wilderness. 11. And God cried, Abraham! Abraham! and Abraham answered, Here am I. 12. And God said, where is the stranger that was with thee? 13. Then answered Abraham and said, Lord, he would not reverence thee nor call upon thy name, and therefore have I driven him from before my face into the wilderness. 14. And the Lord said unto Abraham, Have I borne with the man these hundred and ninety-eight years, and given him food and raiment although he has rebelled against me, and canst thou not bear with him one night? 15. And Abraham said, Let not the wrath of my Lord be kindled against his servant, behold I have sinned! forgive me. 16. And Abraham stood up and went forth into the wilderness, and cried and sought the man, and found him and led him back into his tent, and dealt kindly by him, and the next morning he let him go in peace.

19

THE ANTIGONE AND ITS MORAL

Leader, VII (29 March 1856), 306

Ostensibly a notice of *The Antigone of Sophocles: Text with Short English Notes for the Use of Schools* (Oxford, 1855), 'The Antigone and Its Moral' was begun, according to George Eliot's Journal, on 25 March 1856. In her high estimate of the tragedy and her analysis of it as the 'antagonism of valid claims' she follows the lead of the German critics of the play, but there is an intense personal note in her argument for the universality of the conflict: 'Wherever the strength of a man's intellect, or moral sense, or affection brings him into opposition with the rules which society has sanctioned, *there* is renewed the conflict between Antigone and Creon'. Her own life, before the days of success as a novelist, could be resolved into a series of such conflicts, and if they were not strictly tragic, they were at least intensely painful to a mind like hers, in which the principles of intellectual independence and of piety were equally strong.

*   *   *

'L O! here a little volume but great Book'[1]—a volume small enough to slip into your breast pocket, but containing in fine print one of the finest tragedies of the single dramatic poet who can be said to stand on a level with Shakspeare. Sophocles is the crown and flower of the classic tragedy as Shakspeare is of the romantic: to borrow Schlegel's comparison, which cannot be improved upon, they are related to each other as the Parthenon to Strasburg Cathedral.[2]

[1] Crashaw, 'On a Prayer-Book Sent to Mrs. M. R.' (1648 text.)
[2] 'The Pantheon is not more different from Westminster Abbey or the church of St. Stephen at Vienna, than the structure of a tragedy of Sophocles from a drama of Shakspeare'. A. W. Schlegel, *A Course of Lectures on Dramatic Art and Literature*, trans. John Black, rev. A. J. W. Morrison (London, 1871), p. 23.

The opinion which decried all enthusiasm for Greek literature as 'humbug,' was put to an excellent test some years ago by the production of the Antigone at Drury Lane.[3] The translation then adopted was among the feeblest by which a great poet has ever been misrepresented; yet so completely did the poet triumph over the disadvantages of his medium and of a dramatic motive foreign to modern sympathies, that the Pit was electrified, and Sophocles, over a chasm of two thousand years, once more swayed the emotions of a popular audience. And no wonder. The Antigone has every quality of a fine tragedy, and fine tragedies can never become mere mummies for Hermanns and Böckhs[4] to dispute about: they must appeal to perennial human nature, and even the ingenious dulness of translators cannot exhaust them of their passion and their poetry.

E'en in their ashes live their wonted fires.[5]

We said that the dramatic motive of the Antigone was foreign to modern sympathies, but it is only superficially so.[6] It is true we no longer believe that a brother, if left unburied, is condemned to wander a hundred years without repose on the banks of the Styx; we no longer believe that to neglect funeral rites is to violate the claims of the infernal deities. But these beliefs are the accidents and not the substance of the poet's conception. The turning point of the tragedy is not, as it is stated to be in the argument prefixed to this

[3] I May 1850: Mr. Vandenhoff as Creon, Miss Vandenhoff as Antigone; Mendelssohn's music was sung by the chorus of the Italian Opera. 'The representation was quite successful'. (Athenæum, 4 May 1850, p. 482). I have found no mention of the translation used. Since George Eliot was at Meriden from 24 April until she went to Rosehill on 4 May 1850 (Letters, I, 336) she could not have seen this production of Antigone. Perhaps her information was from Lewes.

[4] Johann Gottfried Jacob Hermann (1772–1848); August Böckh (1785–1867), rival German philologians representing opposite methodological and critical schools.

[5] Gray, 'Elegy Written in a Country Churchyard', st. 23: 'E'en in our ashes. . .'.

[6] What follows is perhaps a deliberate reply to Matthew Arnold's assertion in the 1853 preface to his poems that the action of Antigone 'is no longer one in which it is possible that we should feel a deep interest'. George Eliot's familiarity with Arnold's 1853 volume is evident from her review of his Poems: Second Series in the Westminster Review, LXIV (July, 1855), 297–298.

edition, 'reverence for the dead and the importance of the sacred rites of burial', but the *conflict* between these and obedience to the State. Here lies the dramatic collision: the impulse of sisterly piety which allies itself with reverence for the Gods, clashes with the duties of citizenship; two principles, both having their validity, are at war with each. Let us glance for a moment at the plot.

Eteocles and Polynices, the brothers of Antigone, have slain each other in battle before the gates of Thebes, the one defending his country, the other invading it in conjunction with foreign allies. Hence Creon becomes, by the death of these two sons of Œdipus, the legitimate ruler of Thebes, grants funeral honours to Eteocles, but denies them to Polynices, whose body is cast out to be the prey of beasts and birds, a decree being issued that death will be the penalty of an attempt to bury him. In the second scene of the play Creon expounds the motive of his decree to the Theban elders, insisting in weighty words on the duty of making all personal affection subordinate to the well-being of the State. The impulses of affection and religion which urge Antigone to disobey this proclamation are strengthened by the fact that in her last interview with her brother he had besought her not to leave his corpse unburied. She determines to brave the penalty, buries Polynices, is taken in the act and brought before Creon, to whom she does not attempt to deny that she knew of the proclamation, but declares that she deliberately disobeyed it, and is ready to accept death as its consequence. It was not Zeus, she tells him—it was not eternal Justice that issued that decree. The proclamation of Creon is not so authoritative as the unwritten law of the Gods, which is neither of to-day nor of yesterday, but lives eternally, and none knows its beginning.

> Οὐ γάρ τι νῦν γε κἀχθές, ἀλλ᾽ ἀεὶ ποτε
> Ζῇ ταῦτα, κοὐδεὶς οἶδεν ἐξότου 'φάνη.[7]

Creon, on his side, insists on the necessity to the welfare of the State that he should be obeyed as legitimate ruler, and becomes exasperated by the calm defiance of Antigone. She is condemned to death. Hæmon, the son of Creon, to whom Antigone is betrothed, remonstrates against this judgment in vain. Teiresias also, the blind old soothsayer, alarmed by unfavourable omens, comes to warn Creon against persistence in a course displeasing to the

[7] *Antigone*, 456–457.

Gods. It is not until he has departed, leaving behind him the denunciation of coming woes, that Creon's confidence begins to falter, and at length, persuaded by the Theban elders, he reverses his decree, and proceeds with his followers to the rocky tomb in which Antigone has been buried alive, that he may deliver her. It is too late. Antigone is already dead; Hæmon commits suicide in the madness of despair, and the death of his mother Eurydice on hearing the fatal tidings, completes the ruin of Creon's house.

It is a very superficial criticism which interprets the character of Creon as that of a hypocritical tyrant, and regards Antigone as a blameless victim. Coarse contrasts like this are not the materials handled by great dramatists. The exquisite art of Sophocles is shown in the touches by which he makes us feel that Creon, as well as Antigone, is contending for what he believes to be the right, while both are also conscious that, in following out one principle, they are laying themselves open to just blame for transgressing another; and it is this consciousness which secretly heightens the exasperation of Creon and the defiant hardness of Antigone. The best critics have agreed with Böckh[8] in recognising this balance of principles, this antagonism between valid claims; they generally regard it, however, as dependent entirely on the Greek point of view, as springing simply from the polytheistic conception, according to which the requirements of the Gods often clashed with the duties of man to man.

But, is it the fact that this antagonism of valid principles is peculiar to polytheism? Is it not rather that the struggle between Antigone and Creon represents that struggle between elemental tendencies and established laws by which the outer life of man is gradually and painfully being brought into harmony with his inward needs. Until this harmony is perfected, we shall never be able to attain a great right without also doing a wrong. Reformers, martyrs, revolutionists, are never fighting against evil only; they are also placing themselves in opposition to a good—to a valid principle which cannot be infringed without harm. Resist the payment of ship-money, you bring on civil war; preach against

[8] According to R. C. Jebb, *Sophocles, the Plays and Fragments*, III (Cambridge, 1888), xxi, Böckh was the 'chief representative' of the view later identified with Hegel, that *Antigone* presents the conflict of one-sided truths. Böckh's edition of *Antigone* was reviewed by Lewes in the *Foreign Quarterly Review*, April, 1845.

false doctrines, you disturb feeble minds and send them adrift on a sea of doubt; make a new road, and you annihilate vested interests; cultivate a new region of the earth, and you exterminate a race of men. Wherever the strength of a man's intellect, or moral sense, or affection brings him into opposition with the rules which society has sanctioned, *there* is renewed the conflict between Antigone and Creon; such a man must not only dare to be right, he must also dare to be wrong—to shake faith, to wound friendship, perhaps, to hem in his own powers. Like Antigone, he may fall a victim to the struggle, and yet he can never earn the name of a blameless martyr any more than the society—the Creon he has defied, can be branded as a hypocritical tyrant.

Perhaps the best moral we can draw is that to which the Chorus points—that our protest for the right should be seasoned with moderation and reverence, and that lofty words—$\mu\epsilon\gamma\acute{\alpha}\lambda o\iota$ $\lambda\acute{o}\gamma o\iota$[9] —are not becoming to mortals.

[9] *Antigone,* 1350.

20

THE NATURAL HISTORY
OF GERMAN LIFE

Westminster Review, LXVI (July, 1856), 51–79

George Eliot spent the summer of 1856, when the article on Riehl was written, at Ilfracombe and Tenby with Lewes, helping him in the work that resulted in his *Sea-Side Studies* (1858), and thereby increasing her respect for the value of scientific observation and the weight of fact. At the same time she kept a journal of their life at Ilfracombe in which she set down a number of minute and finished descriptions of the surrounding countryside, inspired by her desire 'to escape from all vagueness and inaccuracy into the daylight of distinct, vivid ideas. The mere fact of naming an object tends to give definiteness to our conception of it— we have then a sign that at once calls up in our minds the distinctive qualities which mark out for us that particular object from all others.'[1] Her 'Recollections of Ilfracombe' are in fact an exercise in the manner of Ruskin, whose 'doctrine that all truth and beauty are to be attained by a humble and faithful study of nature' she had praised in her review of *Modern Painters*, III, in the *Westminster* of April, 1856. Finally, it was during this summer that she was planning her first attempt at fiction, and in consequence was redefining for her own guidance her ideas about the nature and value of realism in art.

The signs of all these activities and preoccupations of her summer in Ilfracombe are apparent in her article on Riehl, whose carefully observed studies of German life satisfied many of the conditions she was laying down for her own work: his *Land und Leute*, she says, 'would be fascinating as literature, if it were not important for its facts and philosophy'. George Eliot made literature of just such material in *Adam Bede*, several details of which are anticipated in her review of Riehl's account of peasant life.

[1] *Letters*, II, 251.

Two other points about the article are worth noting: it provides the best statement, through its sympathetic comment on Riehl's position, of the grounds for George Eliot's conservatism, and should be read as a commentary on the political beliefs expressed in 'Address to Working Men, by Felix Holt'; it also makes clear the Wordsworthian conviction, dramatized especially in her early novels, that the highest function of art is 'the extension of our sympathies' towards 'the life of the People'.

'The Natural History of German Life' reviews new editions of two books by Wilhelm Heinrich von Riehl, *Die burgerliche Gesellschaft* (1851) and *Land und Leute* (1853), which form the first two parts of Riehl's *Naturgeschichte des Volks*, a pioneering work in the foundation of *Kulturgeschichte*. The article was begun, according to George Eliot's Journal, on 13 May and finished on 5 June 1856. It has been reprinted in Sheppard, *The Essays of 'George Eliot', Complete*; and in *Essays and Leaves from a Note-Book*.

*   *   *

IT is an interesting branch of psychological observation to note the images that are habitually associated with abstract or collective terms—what may be called the picture-writing of the mind, which it carries on concurrently with the more subtle symbolism of language. Perhaps the fixity or variety of these associated images would furnish a tolerably fair test of the amount of concrete knowledge and experience which a given word represents, in the minds of two persons who use it with equal familiarity. The word *railways*, for example, will probably call up, in the mind of a man who is not highly locomotive, the image either of a 'Bradshaw', or of the station with which he is most familiar, or of an indefinite length of tram-road; he will alternate between these three images, which represent his stock of concrete acquaintance with railways. But suppose a man to have had successively the experience of a 'navvy', an engineer, a traveller, a railway director and shareholder, and a landed proprietor in treaty with a railway company, and it is probable that the range of images which would by turns present themselves to his mind at the mention of the *word* 'railways', would include all the essential facts in the existence and relations of the *thing*. Now it is possible for the first-mentioned personage to entertain very expanded views as to the multiplication of railways in the abstract, and their ultimate function in civilization. He may talk of a vast net-work of railways stretching over the globe, of future 'lines' in Madagascar, and elegant refreshment-rooms in the Sandwich Islands, with none the less glibness because his distinct conceptions on the subject do not extend beyond his one station and his indefinite length of tram-road. But it is evident that if we want a railway to be made, or its affairs to be managed, this man of wide views and narrow observation will not serve our purpose.

Probably, if we could ascertain the images called up by the terms 'the people,' 'the masses,' 'the proletariat,' 'the peasantry,' by many who theorize on those bodies with eloquence, or who legislate for them without eloquence, we should find that they indicate almost as small an amount of concrete knowledge—that they are as far from completely representing the complex facts summed up in the collective term, as the railway images of our non-locomotive gentleman. How little the real characteristics of the working-classes are known to those who are outside them, how little their natural history has been studied, is sufficiently disclosed by our Art as well as by our political and social theories. Where, in our picture exhibitions, shall we find a group of true peasantry? What English artist even attempts to rival in truthfulness such studies of popular life as the pictures of Teniers or the ragged boys of Murillo? Even one of the greatest painters of the pre-eminently realistic school,[2] while, in his picture of 'The Hireling Shepherd,' he gave us a landscape of marvellous truthfulness, placed a pair of peasants in the foreground who were not much more real than the idyllic swains and damsels of our chimney ornaments. Only a total absence of acquaintance and sympathy with our peasantry, could give a moment's popularity to such a picture as 'Cross Purposes,'[3] where we have a peasant girl who looks as if she knew L.E.L.'s[4] poems by heart, and English rustics, whose costume seems to indicate that they are meant for ploughmen, with exotic features that remind us of a handsome *primo tenore*. Rather than such cockney sentimentality as this, as an education for the taste and sympathies, we prefer the most crapulous group of boors that Teniers ever painted. But even those among our painters who aim at giving the rustic type of features, who are far above the effeminate feebleness of the 'Keepsake' style, treat their subjects under

[2] Holman Hunt's 'The Hireling Shepherd' was exhibited at the Royal Academy in 1852.

[3] Not identified.

[4] Letitia Elizabeth Landon (1802–1838), whose sentimental verses were familiar in the fashionable literary annuals such as the 'Keepsake'. Rosamond Vincy liked L.E.L.'s poetry (*Middlemarch*, Ch. 27).

the influence of traditions and prepossessions rather than of direct observation. The notion that peasants are joyous, that the typical moment to represent a man in a smock-frock is when he is cracking a joke and showing a row of sound teeth, that cottage matrons are usually buxom, and village children necessarily rosy and merry, are prejudices difficult to dislodge from the artistic mind, which looks for its subjects into literature instead of life. The painter is still under the influence of idyllic literature, which has always expressed the imagination of the cultivated and town-bred, rather than the truth of rustic life. Idyllic ploughmen are jocund when they drive their team afield; idyllic shepherds make bashful love under hawthorn bushes; idyllic villagers dance in the chequered shade and refresh themselves, not immoderately, with spicy nut-brown ale. But no one who has seen much of actual ploughmen thinks them jocund; no one who is well acquainted with the English peasantry can pronounce them merry. The slow gaze, in which no sense of beauty beams, no humour twinkles,—the slow utterance, and the heavy slouching walk, remind one rather of that melancholy animal the camel, than of the sturdy countryman, with striped stockings, red waistcoat, and hat aside, who represents the traditional English peasant. Observe a company of haymakers. When you see them at a distance, tossing up the forkfuls of hay in the golden light, while the wagon creeps slowly with its increasing burthen over the meadow, and the bright green space which tells of work done gets larger and larger, you pronounce the scene 'smiling,' and you think these companions in labour must be as bright and cheerful as the picture to which they give animation. Approach nearer, and you will certainly find that haymaking time is a time for joking, especially if there are women among the labourers; but the coarse laugh that bursts out every now and then, and expresses the triumphant taunt, is as far as possible from your conception of idyllic merriment. That delicious effervescence of the mind which we call fun, has no equivalent for the northern peasant, except tipsy revelry; the only realm of fancy and imagination for the English clown exists at the bottom of the third quart pot.

The conventional countryman of the stage, who picks up pocket-books and never looks into them, and who is too simple even to know that honesty has its opposite, represents the still lingering mistake, that an unintelligible dialect is a guarantee for ingenuousness, and that slouching shoulders indicate an upright disposition. It is quite true that a thresher is likely to be innocent of any adroit arithmetical cheating, but he is not the less likely to carry home his master's corn in his shoes and pocket;[5] a reaper is not given to writing begging-letters, but he is quite capable of cajolling the dairymaid into filling his small-beer bottle with ale. The selfish instincts are not subdued by the sight of buttercups, nor is integrity in the least established by that classic rural occupation, sheep-washing. To make men moral, something more is requisite than to turn them out to grass.

Opera peasants, whose unreality excites Mr. Ruskin's indignation,[6] are surely too frank an idealization to be misleading; and since popular chorus is one of the most effective elements of the opera, we can hardly object to lyric rustics in elegant laced boddices and picturesque motley, unless we are prepared to advocate a chorus of colliers in their pit costume, or a ballet of char-women and stocking-weavers. But our social novels profess to represent the people as they are, and the unreality of their representations is a grave evil. The greatest benefit we owe to the artist, whether painter, poet, or novelist, is the extension of our sympathies. Appeals founded on generalizations and statistics require a sympathy ready-made, a moral sentiment already in activity; but a picture of human life such as a great artist can give, surprises even the trivial and the selfish into that attention to what is apart from themselves, which may be called the raw material of moral sentiment. When Scott takes us into Luckie Mucklebackit's cottage,[7] or tells the story of 'The Two Drovers,'—when Wordsworth sings to us the reverie of 'Poor Susan,'—when Kingsley shows us Alton Locke gazing yearningly over the gate which leads from the highway into the first wood he ever saw,[8]—when Hornung paints a group of chimney-sweepers,[9]—more is done towards linking the higher classes with the lower, towards obliterating the vulgarity of exclusiveness, than by hundreds of sermons and philosophical

[5] As did Ben Tholoway, 'detected more than once in carrying away his master's corn in his pockets'. (*Adam Bede*, Ch. 53.)

[6] *Modern Painters*, III, Ch. 5, section 13.

[7] *The Antiquary*, Ch. 31.

[8] *Alton Locke*, Ch. 11.

[9] 'The Little Chimney-sweep' is among the paintings of Joseph Hornung (1792–1870), Swiss painter of popular life and historical subjects.

dissertations. Art is the nearest thing to life; it is a mode of amplifying experience and extending our contact with our fellow-men beyond the bounds of our personal lot. All the more sacred is the task of the artist when he undertakes to paint the life of the People. Falsification here is far more pernicious than in the more artificial aspects of life. It is not so very serious that we should have false ideas about evanescent fashions—about the manners and conversation of beaux and duchesses; but it *is* serious that our sympathy with the perennial joys and struggles, the toil, the tragedy, and the humour in the life of our more heavily-laden fellow-men, should be perverted, and turned towards a false object instead of the true one.

This perversion is not the less fatal because the misrepresentation which gives rise to it has what the artist considers a moral end. The thing for mankind to know is, not what are the motives and influences which the moralist thinks *ought* to act on the labourer or the artisan, but what are the motives and influences which *do* act on him. We want to be taught to feel, not for the heroic artisan or the sentimental peasant, but for the peasant in all his coarse apathy, and the artisan in all his suspicious selfishness.

We have one great novelist who is gifted with the utmost power of rendering the external traits of our town population; and if he could give us their psychological character—their conceptions of life, and their emotions—with the same truth as their idiom and manners, his books would be the greatest contribution Art has ever made to the awakening of social sympathies. But while he can copy Mrs. Plornish's[10] colloquial style with the delicate accuracy of a sun-picture, while there is the same startling inspiration in his description of the gestures and phrases of 'Boots',[11] as in the speeches of Shakspeare's mobs or numbskulls, he scarcely ever passes from the humorous and external to the emotional and tragic, without becoming as transcendent in his unreality as he was a moment before in his artistic truthfulness. But for the precious salt of his humour, which compels him to reproduce external traits that serve, in some degree, as a corrective to his frequently false psychology, his preternaturally virtuous poor children and

[10] In *Little Dorrit*, at the time of George Eliot's article appearing in monthly parts.
[11] Of the several 'Bootses' in Dickens, George Eliot probably means Cobbs, the boots of the 'Holly-Tree' in the Christmas story of that name.

artisans, his melodramatic boatmen and courtezans, would be as noxious as Eugène Sue's idealized proletaires in encouraging the miserable fallacy that high morality and refined sentiment can grow out of harsh social relations, ignorance, and want; or that the working-classes are in a condition to enter at once into a millennial state of *altruism*, wherein everyone is caring for everyone else, and no one for himself.

If we need a true conception of the popular character to guide our sympathies rightly, we need it equally to check our theories, and direct us in their application. The tendency created by the splendid conquests of modern generalization, to believe that all social questions are merged in economical science, and that the relations of men to their neighbours may be settled by algebraic equations,—the dream that the uncultured classes are prepared for a condition which appeals principally to their moral sensibilities,—the aristocratic dilettantism which attempts to restore the 'good old times' by a sort of idyllic masquerading, and to grow feudal fidelity and veneration as we grow prize turnips, by an artificial system of culture,[12]—none of these diverging mistakes can co-exist with a real knowledge of the People, with a thorough study of their habits, their ideas, their motives. The landholder, the clergyman, the mill-owner, the mining-agent, have each an opportunity for making precious observations on different sections of the working-classes, but unfortunately their experience is too often not registered at all, or its results are too scattered to be available as a source of information and stimulus to the public mind generally. If any man of sufficient moral and intellectual breadth, whose observations would not be vitiated by a foregone conclusion, or by a professional point of view, would devote himself to studying the natural history of our social classes, especially of the small shop-keepers, artisans, and peasantry,—the degree in which they are influenced by local conditions, their maxims and habits, the points of view from which they regard their religious teachers, and the degree in which they are influenced by religious doctrines, the interaction of the various classes on each other, and what are the

[12] An allusion to the 'Young England' movement, whose text was Disraeli's *Coningsby* (1844). In 1848 George Eliot wrote: 'Young Englandism is almost as remote from my sympathies as Jacobitism as far as its form is concerned, though I love and respect it as an effort on behalf of the people'. (*Letters*, I, 246.)

tendencies in their position towards disintegration or towards development,—and if, after all this study, he would give us the result of his observations in a book well nourished with specific facts, his work would be a valuable aid to the social and political reformer.

What we are desiring for ourselves has been in some degree done for the Germans by Riehl, the author of the very remarkable books the titles of which are placed at the head of this article; and we wish to make these books known to our readers, not only for the sake of the interesting matter they contain and the important reflections they suggest, but also as a model for some future or actual student of our own people. By way of introducing Riehl to those who are unacquainted with his writings, we will give a rapid sketch from his picture of the German Peasantry, and perhaps this indication of the mode in which he treats a particular branch of his subject may prepare them to follow us with more interest when we enter on the general purpose and contents of his works.

In England, at present, when we speak of the peasantry, we mean scarcely more than the class of farm-servants and farm-labourers; and it is only in the most primitive districts, as in Wales, for example, that farmers are included under the term. In order to appreciate what Riehl says of the German peasantry, we must remember what the tenant-farmers and small proprietors were in England half a century ago, when the master helped to milk his own cows, and the daughters got up at one o'clock in the morning to brew,—when the family dined in the kitchen with the servants, and sat with them round the kitchen fire in the evening. In those days, the quarried parlour was innocent of a carpet, and its only specimens of art were a framed sampler and the best tea-board; the daughters even of substantial farmers had often no greater accomplishment in writing and spelling than they could procure at a dame-school; and, instead of carrying on sentimental correspondence, they were spinning their future table-linen, and looking after every saving in butter and eggs that might enable them to add to the little stock of plate and china which they were laying in against their marriage. In our own day, setting aside the superior order of farmers, whose style of living and mental culture are often equal to that of the professional class in provincial towns, we can hardly enter the least imposing farm-house without finding a bad piano in the 'drawing-room', and some old annuals, disposed with a symmetrical imitation of negligence, on the table; though the daughters may still drop their *h's*, their vowels are studiously narrow; and it is only in very primitive regions that they will consent to sit in a covered vehicle without springs, which was once thought an advance in luxury on the pillion.

The condition of the tenant-farmers and small proprietors in Germany is, we imagine, about on a par, not, certainly, in material prosperity, but in mental culture and habits, with that of the English farmers who were beginning to be thought old-fashioned nearly fifty years ago, and if we add to these the farm servants and labourers, we shall have a class approximating in its characteristics to the *Bauernthum*, or peasantry, described by Riehl.

In Germany, perhaps more than in any other country, it is among the peasantry that we must look for the historical type of the national *physique*. In the towns this type has become so modified to express the personality of the individual, that even 'family likeness' is often but faintly marked. But the peasants may still be distinguished into groups by their physical peculiarities. In one part of the country we find a longer-legged, in another a broader-shouldered race, which has inherited these peculiarities for centuries. For example, in certain districts of Hesse are seen long faces, with high foreheads, long, straight noses, and small eyes with arched eyebrows and large eyelids. On comparing these physiognomies with the sculptures in the church of St. Elizabeth, at Marburg, executed in the thirteenth century, it will be found that the same old Hessian type of face has subsisted unchanged, with this distinction only, that the sculptures represent princes and nobles, whose features then bore the stamp of their race, while that stamp is now to be found only among the peasants. A painter who wants to draw mediæval characters with historic truth, must seek his models among the peasantry. This explains why the old German painters gave the heads of their subjects a greater uniformity of type than the painters of our day: the race had not attained to a high degree of individualization in features and expression. It indicates, too, that the cultured man acts more as an individual; the peasant, more as one of a group. Hans drives the plough, lives, and thinks just as Kunz does; and it is this fact, that many thousands of men are as like each other in thoughts and habits as so many sheep or oysters, which constitutes the weight of the peasantry in the social and political scale.

In the cultivated world each individual has his style of speaking and writing. But among the peasantry it is the race, the district, the province, that has its style; namely, its dialect, its phraseology, its proverbs and its songs, which belong alike to the entire body of the people. This provincial style of the peasant is again, like his *physique*, a remnant of history to which he clings with the utmost tenacity. In certain parts of Hungary, there are still descendants of German colonists of the twelfth and thirteenth centuries, who go about the country as reapers, retaining their old Saxon songs and manners, while the more cultivated German emigrants in a very short time forget their own language, and speak Hungarian. Another remarkable case of the same kind is that of the Wends, a Sclavonic race settled in Lusatia, whose numbers amount to 200,000, living either scattered among the German population or in separate parishes. They have their own schools and churches, and are taught in the Sclavonic tongue. The Catholics among them are rigid adherents of the Pope; the Protestants not less rigid adherents of Luther, or *Doctor* Luther, as they are particular in calling him—a custom which, a hundred years ago, was universal in Protestant Germany. The Wend clings tenaciously to the usages of his Church, and perhaps this may contribute not a little to the purity in which he maintains the specific characteristics of his race. German education, German law and government, service in the standing army, and many other agencies, are in antagonism to his national exclusiveness; but the *wives* and *mothers* here, as elsewhere, are a conservative influence, and the habits temporarily laid aside in the outer world are recovered by the fireside. The Wends form several stout regiments in the Saxon army; they are sought far and wide, as diligent and honest servants; and many a weakly Dresden or Leipzig child becomes thriving under the care of a Wendish nurse. In their villages they have the air and habits of genuine, sturdy peasants, and all their customs indicate that they have been, from the first, an agricultural people. For example, they have traditional modes of treating their domestic animals. Each cow has its own name, generally chosen carefully, so as to express the special qualities of the animal; and all important family events are narrated to the *bees*—a custom which is found also in Westphalia. Whether by the help of the bees or not, the Wend farming is especially prosperous; and when a poor Bohemian peasant has a son born to him, he binds him to the end of a long pole and turns his face towards Lusatia, that he may be as lucky as the Wends who live there.

The peculiarity of the peasant's language consists chiefly in his retention of historical peculiarities, which gradually disappear under the friction of cultivated circles. He prefers any proper name that may be given to a day in the calendar, rather than the abstract date, by which he very rarely reckons. In the baptismal names of his children he is guided by the old custom of the country, not at all by whim and fancy. Many old baptismal names, formerly common in Germany, would have become extinct but for their preservation among the peasantry, especially in North Germany; and so firmly have they adhered to local tradition in this matter, that it would be possible to give a sort of topographical statistics of proper names, and distinguish a district by its rustic names as we do by its Flora and Fauna. The continuous inheritance of certain favourite proper names in a family, in some districts, forces the peasant to adopt the princely custom of attaching a numeral to the name, and saying, when three generations are living at once, Hans I., II., and III.; or—in the more antique fashion—Hans the elder, the middle, and the younger. In some of our English counties there is a similar adherence to a narrow range of proper names, and as a mode of distinguishing collateral branches in the same family, you will hear of Jonathan's Bess, Thomas's Bess, and Samuel's Bess—the three Bessies being cousins.[13]

The peasant's adherence to the traditional has much greater inconvenience than that entailed by a paucity of proper names. In the Black Forest and in Hüttenberg you will see him in the dog-days wearing a thick fur cap, because it is an historical fur cap—a cap worn by his grandfather. In the Wetterau, that peasant girl is considered the handsomest who wears the most petticoats. To go to field-labour in seven petticoats can be anything but convenient or agreeable, but it is the traditionally correct thing, and a German peasant girl would think herself as unfavourably conspicuous in an untraditional costume, as an English servant-girl would now think herself in a 'linsey-woolsey' apron or a thick muslin cap. In many districts no medical advice would induce the rustic to renounce the tight leather belt with which he injures his digestive functions; you could more easily persuade him to smile on a new communal system than on the unhistorical invention of braces. In the

[13] Cf. Chad's Bess and Timothy's Bess in *Adam Bede*, Ch. 2.

eighteenth century, in spite of the philanthropic preachers of potatoes, the peasant for years threw his potatoes to the pigs and the dogs, before he could be persuaded to put them on his own table. However, the unwillingness of the peasant to adopt innovations has a not unreasonable foundation in the fact, that for him experiments are practical, not theoretical, and must be made with expense of money instead of brains—a fact that is not, perhaps, sufficiently taken into account by agricultural theorists, who complain of the farmer's obstinacy. The peasant has the smallest possible faith in theoretic knowledge; he thinks it rather dangerous than otherwise, as is well indicated by a Lower Rhenish proverb—'One is never too old to learn, said an old woman; so she learned to be a witch.'

Between many villages an historical feud, once perhaps the occasion of much bloodshed, is still kept up under the milder form of an occasional round of cudgelling, and the launching of traditional nicknames. An historical feud of this kind still exists, for example, among many villages on the Rhine and more inland places in the neighbourhood. *Rheinschnacke* (of which the equivalent is perhaps 'water-snake') is the standing term of ignominy for the inhabitant of the Rhine village, who repays it in kind by the epither 'karst' (mattock) or 'kukuk' (cuckoo), according as the object of his hereditary hatred belongs to the field or the forest. If any Romeo among the 'mattocks' were to marry a Juliet among the 'water-snakes', there would be no lack of Tybalts and Mercutios to carry the conflict from words to blows, though neither side knows a reason for the enmity.

A droll instance of peasant conservatism is told of a village on the Taunus, whose inhabitants, from time immemorial, had been famous for impromptu cudgelling. For this historical offence the magistrates of the district had always inflicted the equally historical punishment of shutting up the most incorrigible offenders, not in prison, but in their own pig-sty. In recent times, however, the government, wishing to correct the rudeness of these peasants, appointed an 'enlightened' man as magistrate, who at once abolished the original penalty above-mentioned. But this relaxation of punishment was so far from being welcome to the villagers, that they presented a petition praying that a more energetic man might be given them as a magistrate, who would have the courage to punish according to law and justice, 'as had been beforetime.'

And the magistrate who abolished incarceration in the pig-sty could never obtain the respect of the neighbourhood. This happened no longer ago than the beginning of the present century.

But it must not be supposed that the historical piety of the German peasant extends to anything not immediately connected with himself. He has the warmest piety towards the old tumble-down house which his grandfather built, and which nothing will induce him to improve, but towards the venerable ruins of the old castle that overlooks his village he has no piety at all, and carries off its stones to make a fence for his garden, or tears down the gothic carving of the old monastic church, which is 'nothing to him,' to mark off a foot-path through his field. It is the same with historical traditions. The peasant has them fresh in his memory so far as they relate to himself. In districts where the peasantry are unadulterated, you discern the remnants of the feudal relations in innumerable customs and phrases, but you will ask in vain for historical traditions concerning the empire, or even concerning the particular princely house to which the peasant is subject. He can tell you what 'half people and whole people' mean; in Hesse you will still hear of 'four horses making a whole peasant,' or of 'four-day and three-day peasants;' but you will ask in vain about Charlemagne and Frederic Barbarossa.

Riehl well observes that the feudal system, which made the peasant the bondman of his lord, was an immense benefit in a country, the greater part of which had still to be colonized,—rescued the peasant from vagabondage, and laid the foundation of persistency and endurance in future generations. If a free German peasantry belongs only to modern times, it is to his ancestor who was a serf, and even, in the earliest times, a slave, that the peasant owes the foundation of his independence, namely, his capability of a settled existence,—nay, his unreasoning persistency, which has its important function in the development of the race.

Perhaps the very worst result of that unreasoning persistency is the peasant's inveterate habit of litigation. Every one remembers the immortal description of Dandie Dinmont's importunate application to Lawyer Pleydell to manage his 'bit lawsuit,' till at length Pleydell consents to help him ruin himself, on the ground that Dandie may fall into worse hands.[14] It seems, this is a scene which has many parallels in Germany. The farmer's lawsuit is his

[14] Scott, *Guy Mannering*, Ch. 38.

point of honour; and he will carry it through, though he knows from the very first day that he shall get nothing by it. The litigious peasant piques himself, like Mr. Saddletree,[15] on his knowledge of the law, and this vanity is the chief impulse to many a lawsuit. To the mind of the peasant, law presents itself as the 'custom of the country,' and it is his pride to be versed in all customs. *Custom with him holds the place of sentiment, of theory, and in many cases of affection.* Riehl justly urges the importance of simplifying law proceedings, so as to cut off this vanity at its source, and also of encouraging, by every possible means, the practice of arbitration.

The peasant never begins his lawsuit in summer, for the same reason that he does not make love and marry in summer,—because he has no time for that sort of thing. Anything is easier to him than to move out of his habitual course, and he is attached even to his privations. Some years ago, a peasant youth, out of the poorest and remotest region of the Westerwald, was enlisted as a recruit, at Weilburg in Nassau. The lad, having never in his life slept in a bed, when he had to get into one for the first time began to cry like a child; and he deserted twice because he could not reconcile himself to sleeping in a bed, and to the 'fine' life of the barracks: he was homesick at the thought of his accustomed poverty and his thatched hut. A strong contrast, this, with the feeling of the poor in towns, who would be far enough from deserting because their condition was too much improved! The genuine peasant is never ashamed of his rank and calling; he is rather inclined to look down on every one who does not wear a smock-frock, and thinks a man who has the manners of the gentry is likely to be rather windy and unsubstantial. In some places, even in French districts, this feeling is strongly symbolized by the practice of the peasantry, on certain festival days, to dress the images of the saints in peasant's clothing. History tells us of all kinds of peasant insurrections, the object of which was to obtain relief for the peasants from some of their many oppressions; but of an effort on their part to step out of their hereditary rank and calling, to become gentry, to leave the plough and carry on the easier business of capitalists or government-functionaries, there is no example.

The German novelists who undertake to give pictures of peasant-life fall into the same mistake as our English novelists; they transfer their own feelings to ploughmen and woodcutters, and

[15] In Scott, *The Heart of Midlothian.*

give them both joys and sorrows of which they know nothing. The peasant never questions the obligation of family-ties—he questions *no custom*,—but tender affection, as it exists amongst the refined part of mankind, is almost as foreign to him as white hands and filbert-shaped nails. That the aged father who has given up his property to his children on condition of their maintaining him for the remainder of his life, is very far from meeting with delicate attentions, is indicated by the proverb current among the peasantry —'Don't take your clothes off before you go to bed'.[16] Among rustic moral tales and parables, not one is more universal than the story of the ungrateful children, who made their grey-headed father, dependent on them for a maintenance, eat at a wooden trough, because he shook the food out of his trembling hands. Then these same ungrateful children observed one day that their own little boy was making a tiny wooden trough; and when they asked him what it was for, he answered—that his father and mother might eat out of it, when he was a man and had to keep them.

Marriage is a very prudential affair, especially among the peasants who have the largest share of property. Politic marriages are as common among them as among princes; and when a peasant-heiress in Westphalia marries, her husband adopts her name, and places his own after it with the prefix *geborner* (*né*). The girls marry young, and the rapidity with which they get old and ugly is one among the many proofs that the early years of marriage are fuller of hardships than of conjugal tenderness. 'When our writers of village stories,' says Riehl, 'transferred their own emotional life to the peasant, they obliterated what is precisely his most predominant characteristic, namely, that with him general custom holds the place of individual feeling.'

We pay for greater emotional susceptibility too often by nervous diseases of which the peasant knows nothing. To him headache is the least of physical evils, because he thinks head-work the easiest and least indispensable of all labour. Happily, many of the younger sons in peasant families, by going to seek their living in the towns, carry their hardy nervous system to amalgamate with the over-wrought nerves of our town population, and refresh them with a little rude vigour. And a return to the habits of peasant life is the best remedy for many moral as well as physical diseases

[16] This proverb is common among the English farmers also. [George Eliot's note, 1884.]

induced by perverted civilization. Riehl points to colonization as presenting the true field for this regenerative process. On the other side of the ocean, a man will have the courage to begin life again as a peasant, while at home, perhaps, opportunity as well as courage will fail him. *Apropos* of this subject of emigration, he remarks the striking fact, that the native shrewdness and mother-wit of the German peasant seem to forsake him entirely when he has to apply them under new circumstances, and on relations foreign to his experience. Hence it is that the German peasant who emigrates, so constantly falls a victim to unprincipled adventurers in the preliminaries to emigration; but if once he gets his foot on the American soil, he exhibits all the first-rate qualities of an agricultural colonist; and among all German emigrants, the peasant class are the most successful.

But many disintegrating forces have been at work on the peasant character, and degeneration is unhappily going on at a greater pace than development. In the wine districts especially, the inability of the small proprietors to bear up under the vicissitudes of the market, or to ensure a high quality of wine by running the risks of a late vintage, and the competition of beer and cider with the inferior wines, have tended to produce that uncertainty of gain which, with the peasant, is the inevitable cause of demoralization. The small peasant proprietors are not a new class in Germany, but many of the evils of their position are new. They are more dependent on ready money than formerly; thus, where a peasant used to get his wood for building and firing from the common forest, he has now to pay for it with hard cash; he used to thatch his own house, with the help perhaps of a neighbour, but now he pays a man to do it for him; he used to pay taxes in kind, he now pays them in money. The chances of the market have to be discounted, and the peasant falls into the hands of money-lenders. Here is one of the cases in which social policy clashes with a purely economical policy.

Political vicissitudes have added their influence to that of economical changes in disturbing that dim instinct, that reverence for traditional custom, which is the peasant's principle of action. He is in the midst of novelties for which he knows no reason— changes in political geography, changes of the government to which he owes fealty, changes in bureaucratic management and police regulations. He finds himself in a new element before an apparatus for breathing in it is developed in him. His only knowledge of modern history is in some of its results—for instance, that he has to pay heavier taxes from year to year. His chief idea of a government is of a power that raises his taxes, opposes his harmless customs, and torments him with new formalities. The source of all this is the false system of 'enlightening' the peasant which has been adopted by the bureaucratic governments. A system which disregards the traditions and hereditary attachments of the peasant and appeals only to a logical understanding which is not yet developed in him, is simply disintegrating and ruinous to the peasant character. The interference with the communal regulations has been of this fatal character. Instead of endeavouring to promote to the utmost the healthy life of the Commune, as an organism the conditions of which are bound up with the historical characteristics of the peasant, the bureaucratic plan of government is bent on improvement by its patent machinery of state-appointed functionaries and off-hand regulations in accordance with modern enlightenment. The spirit of communal exclusiveness—the resistance to the indiscriminate establishment of strangers, is an intense traditional feeling in the peasant. 'This gallows is for us and our children,' is the typical motto of this spirit. But such exclusiveness is highly irrational and repugnant to modern liberalism; therefore a bureaucratic government at once opposes it, and encourages to the utmost the introduction of new inhabitants in the provincial communes. Instead of allowing the peasants to manage their own affairs, and, if they happen to believe that five and four make eleven, to unlearn the prejudice by their own experience in calculation, so that they may gradually understand processes, and not merely see results, bureaucracy comes with its 'Ready Reckoner' and works all the peasant's sums for him—the surest way of maintaining him in his stupidity, however it may shake his prejudice.

Another questionable plan for elevating the peasant, is the supposed elevation of the clerical character by preventing the clergyman from cultivating more than a trifling part of the land attached to his benefice; that he may be as much as possible of a scientific theologian, and as little as possible of a peasant. In this, Riehl observes, lies one great source of weakness to the Protestant Church as compared with the Catholic, which finds the great majority of its priests among the lower orders; and we have had the opportunity of making an analogous comparison in England, where many of us can remember country districts in which the great mass of the people were christianized by illiterate Methodist and Independent ministers, while the influence of the parish clergyman among the poor did not extend much beyond a few old women in scarlet cloaks, and a few exceptional church-going labourers.

Bearing in mind the general characteristics of the German peasant, it is easy to understand his relation to the revolutionary ideas and revolutionary movements of modern times. The peasant, in Germany as elsewhere, is a born grumbler. He has always plenty of grievances in his pocket, but he does not generalize those grievances; he does not complain of 'government' or 'society,' probably because he has good reason to complain of the burgomaster. When a few sparks from the first French Revolution fell among the German peasantry, and in certain villages of Saxony the country people assembled together to write down their demands, there was no glimpse in their petition of the 'universal rights of man,' but simply of their own particular affairs as Saxon peasants. Again, after the July revolution of 1830, there were many insignificant peasant insurrections; but the object of almost all was the removal of local grievances. Toll-houses were pulled down; stamped paper was destroyed; in some places there was a persecution of wild boars, in others, of that plentiful tame animal, the German *Rath*, or councillor who is never called into council. But in 1848, it seemed as if the movements of the peasants had taken a new character; in the small western states of Germany, it seemed as if the whole class of peasantry was in insurrection. But in fact, the peasant did not know the meaning of the part he was playing. He had heard that everything was being set right in the towns, and that wonderful things were happening there, so he tied up his bundle and set off. Without any distinct object or resolution, the country people presented themselves on the scene of commotion, and were warmly received by the party leaders. But, seen from the windows of ducal palaces and ministerial hotels, these swarms of peasants had quite another aspect, and it was imagined that they had a common plan of co-operation. This, however, the peasants have never had. Systematic co-operation implies general conceptions, and a provisional subordination of egoism, to which even the artisans of towns have rarely shown themselves equal, and which are as foreign to the mind of the peasant as logarithms or the doctrine of chemical proportions. And the revolutionary fervour of the peasant was soon cooled. The old mistrust of the towns was reawakened on the spot. The Tyrolese peasants saw no great good in the freedom of the press and the constitution, because these changes 'seemed to please the gentry so much'. Peasants who had given their voices stormily for a German parliament, asked afterwards, with a doubtful look, whether it were to consist of infantry or cavalry. When royal domains were declared the property of the State, the peasants in some small principalities rejoiced over this, because they interpreted it to mean that every one would have his share in them, after the manner of the old common and forest rights.

The very practical views of the peasants, with regard to the demands of the people, were in amusing contrast with the abstract theorizing of the educated townsmen. The peasant continually withheld all State payments until he saw how matters would turn out, and was disposed to reckon up the solid benefit, in the form of land or money, that might come to him from the changes obtained. While the townsman was heating his brains about representation on the broadest basis, the peasant asked if the relation between tenant and landlord would continue as before, and whether the removal of the 'feudal obligations' meant that the farmer should become owner of the land?

It is in the same *naïve* way that Communism is interpreted by the German peasantry. The wide spread among them of communistic doctrines, the eagerness with which they listened to a plan for the partition of property, seemed to countenance the notion, that it was a delusion to suppose the peasant would be secured from this intoxication by his love of secure possession and peaceful earnings. But, in fact, the peasant contemplated 'partition' by the light of an historical reminiscence rather than of novel theory. The golden age, in the imagination of the peasant, was the time when every member of the commune had a right to as much wood from the forest as would enable him to sell some, after using what he wanted in firing,—in which the communal possessions were so profitable that, instead of his having to pay rates at the end of the year, each member of the commune was something in pocket. Hence the peasants in general understood by 'partition', that the State lands, especially the forests, would be divided among the communes, and that, by some political legerdemain or other, everybody would have free fire-wood, free grazing for his cattle, and over and above that, a piece of gold without working for it. That he should give up a single clod of his own to further the general 'partition,' had never entered the mind of the peasant communist; and the perception that this was an essential preliminary to 'partition', was often a sufficient cure for his Communism.

In villages lying in the neighbourhood of large towns, however, where the circumstances of the peasantry are very different, quite another interpretation of Communism is prevalent. Here the peasant is generally sunk to the position of the proletaire, living from hand to mouth; he has nothing to lose, but everything to gain by 'partition.' The coarse nature of the peasant has here been corrupted into bestiality by the disturbance of his instincts, while he is as yet incapable of principles; and in this type of the degenerate peasant is seen the worst example of ignorance intoxicated by theory.

A significant hint as to the interpretation the peasants put on revolutionary theories, may be drawn from the way they employed the few weeks in which their movements were unchecked. They felled the forest trees and shot the game; they withheld taxes; they shook off the imaginary or real burdens imposed on them by their mediatized princes, by presenting their 'demands' in a very rough way before the ducal or princely 'Schloss;' they set their faces against the bureaucratic management of the communes, deposed the government functionaries who had been placed over them as burgomasters and magistrates, and abolished the whole bureaucratic system of procedure, simply by taking no notice of its regulations, and recurring to some tradition—some old order or disorder of things. In all this it is clear that they were animated not in the least by the spirit of modern revolution, but by a purely narrow and personal impulse towards reaction.

The idea of constitutional government lies quite beyond the range of the German peasant's conceptions. His only notion of representation is that of a representation of ranks—of classes; his only notion of a deputy is of one who takes care, not of the national welfare, but of the interests of his own order. Herein lay the great mistake of the democratic party, in common with the bureaucratic governments, that they entirely omitted the peculiar character of the peasant from their political calculations. They talked of the 'people,' and forgot that the peasants were included in the term. Only a baseless misconception of the peasant's character could induce the supposition that he would feel the slightest enthusiasm about the principles involved in the re-constitution of the Empire, or even about that re-constitution itself. He has no zeal for a written law, as such, but only so far as it takes the form of a living law—a tradition. It was the external authority which the revolutionary party had won in Baden that attracted the peasants into a participation in the struggle.

Such, Riehl tells us, are the general characteristics of the German peasantry—characteristics which subsist amidst a wide variety of circumstances. In Mecklenburg, Pomerania, and Brandenburg, the peasant lives on extensive estates; in Westphalia he lives in large isolated homesteads; in the Westerwald and in Sauerland, in little groups of villages and hamlets; on the Rhine, land is for the most part parcelled out among small proprietors, who live together in large villages. Then, of course, the diversified physical geography of Germany gives rise to equally diversified methods of land-culture; and out of these various circumstances grow numerous specific differences in manner and character. But the generic character of the German peasant is everywhere the same: in the clean mountain hamlet and in the dirty fishing village on the coast; in the plains of North Germany and in the backwoods of America. 'Everywhere he has the same historical character—everywhere custom is his supreme law. Where religion and patriotism are still a naïve instinct—are still a sacred *custom*, there begins the class of the German Peasantry.'

Our readers will perhaps already have gathered from the foregoing portrait of the German peasant, that Riehl is not a man who looks at objects through the spectacles either of the doctrinaire or the dreamer; and they will be ready to believe what he tells us in his Preface, namely, that years ago he began his wanderings over the hills and plains of Germany for the sake of obtaining, in immediate intercourse with the people, that completion of his historical, political, and economical studies which he was unable to find in books. He began his investigations with no party prepossessions, and his present views were evolved entirely from his own gradually amassed observations. He was, first of all, a pedestrian, and only in the second place a political author. The views at which he has arrived by this inductive process, he sums up in the term—*social-political-conservatism*; but his conservatism is, we conceive, of a thoroughly philosophical kind. He sees in European society *incarnate history*, and any attempt to disengage it from its historical elements must, he believes, be simply destructive of social vitality.[17] What has grown up historically can only die out historically, by the gradual operation of necessary laws. The external conditions which society has inherited from the past are but the manifestation of inherited internal conditions in the human beings who compose it; the internal conditions and the external are related to each other as the organism and its medium, and development can take place only by the gradual consentaneous development of both. Take the familiar example of attempts to abolish titles, which have been about as effective as the process of cutting off poppy-heads in a corn-field. *Jedem Menschen*, says Riehl, *ist sein Zopf angeboren, warum soll denn der sociale Sprachgebrauch nicht auch sein Zopf haben?*—which we may render—'as long as snobbism runs in the blood, why should it not run in our speech?' As a necessary preliminary to a purely rational society, you must obtain purely rational men, free from the sweet and bitter prejudices of hereditary affection and antipathy; which is as easy as to get running streams without springs, or the leafy shade of the forest without the secular growth of trunk and branch.

The historical conditions of society may be compared with those of language. It must be admitted that the language of cultivated nations is in anything but a rational state; the great sections of the civilized world are only approximately intelligible to each other, and even that, only at the cost of long study; one word stands for many things, and many words for one thing; the subtle shades of meaning, and still subtler echoes of association, make language an instrument which scarcely anything short of genius can wield with definiteness and certainty. Suppose, then, that the effort which has been again and again made to construct a universal language on a rational basis has at length succeeded, and that you have a language which has no uncertainty, no whims of idiom, no cumbrous forms, no fitful shimmer of many-hued significance, no hoary archaisms

[17] Throughout this article, in our statement of Riehl's opinions, we must be understood not as quoting Riehl, but as interpreting and illustrating him. [George Eliot's note.]

'familiar with forgotten years'[18]—a patent de-odorized and non resonant language, which effects the purpose of communication as perfectly and rapidly as algebraic signs. Your language may be a perfect medium of expression to science, but will never express *life*, which is a great deal more than science. With the anomalies and inconveniences of historical language, you will have parted with its music and its passion, with its vital qualities as an expression of individual character, with its subtle capabilities of wit, with everything that gives it power over the imagination; and the next step in simplification will be the invention of a talking watch, which will achieve the utmost facility and dispatch in the communication of ideas by a graduated adjustment of ticks, to be represented in writing by a corresponding arrangement of dots. A melancholy 'language of the future!' The sensory and motor nerves that run in the same sheath, are scarcely bound together by a more necessary and delicate union than that which binds men's affection, imagination, wit, and humour, with the subtle ramifications of historical language. Language must be left to grow in precision, completeness, and unity, as minds grow in clearness, comprehensiveness, and sympathy. And there is an analogous relation between the moral tendencies of men and the social conditions they have inherited. The nature of European men has its roots intertwined with the past, and can only be developed by allowing those roots to remain undisturbed while the process of development is going on, until that perfect ripeness of the seed which carries with it a life independent of the root. This vital connexion with the past is much more vividly felt on the Continent than in England, where we have to recal it by an effort of memory and reflection; for though our English life is in its core intensely traditional, Protestantism and commerce have modernized the face of the land and the aspects of society in a far greater degree than in any continental country:

> Abroad, [says Ruskin], a building of the eighth or tenth century stands ruinous in the open street; the children play round it, the peasants heap their corn in it, the buildings of yesterday nestle about it, and fit their new stones in its rents, and tremble in sympathy as it trembles. No one wonders at it, or thinks of it as separate, and of another time; we feel the ancient world to be a real thing, and one with the new; antiquity is no dream; it is rather the children playing

[18] Wordsworth, *The Excursion*, I, 276.

about the old stones that are the dream. But all is continuous; and the words 'from generation to generation', understandable here.[19]

This conception of European society as incarnate history, is the fundamental idea of Riehl's books. After the notable failure of revolutionary attempts conducted from the point of view of abstract democratic and socialistic theories, after the practical demonstration of the evils resulting from a bureaucratic system which governs by an undiscriminating, dead mechanism, Riehl wishes to urge on the consideration of his countrymen, a social policy founded on the special study of the people as they are—on the natural history of the various social ranks. He thinks it wise to pause a little from theorizing, and see what is the material actually present for theory to work upon. It is the glory of the Socialists— in contrast with the democratic doctrinaires who have been too much occupied with the general idea of 'the people' to inquire particularly into the actual life of the people—that they have thrown themselves with enthusiastic zeal into the study at least of one social group, namely, the factory operatives; and here lies the secret of their partial success. But unfortunately, they have made this special study of a single fragment of society the basis of a theory which quietly substitutes for the small group of Parisian proletaires or English factory-workers, the society of all Europe— nay, of the whole world. And in this way they have lost the best fruit of their investigations. For, says Riehl, the more deeply we penetrate into the knowledge of society in its details, the more thoroughly we shall be convinced that a *universal social policy has no validity except on paper*, and can never be carried into successful practice. The conditions of German society are altogether different from those of French, of English, or of Italian society; and to apply the same social theory to these nations indiscriminately, is about as wise a procedure as Triptolemus Yellowley's application of the agricultural directions in Virgil's 'Georgics' to his farm in the Shetland Isles.[20]

It is the clear and strong light in which Riehl places this important position, that in our opinion constitutes the suggestive value of his books for foreign as well as German readers. It has not been sufficiently insisted on, that in the various branches of Social

[19] *Modern Painters*, IV, Part V, Ch. 1, section 5: the last word in the original is 'there'.
[20] Scott, *The Pirate*, Ch. 4.

Science there is an advance from the general to the special, from the simple to the complex, analogous with that which is found in the series of the sciences, from Mathematics to Biology. To the laws of quantity comprised in Mathematics and Physics are superadded, in Chemistry, laws of quality; to these again are added, in Biology, laws of life; and lastly, the conditions of life in general, branch out into its special conditions, or Natural History, on the one hand, and into its abnormal conditions, or Pathology, on the other. And in this series or ramification of the sciences, the more general science will not suffice to solve the problems of the more special. Chemistry embraces phenomena which are not explicable by Physics; Biology embraces phenomena which are not explicable by Chemistry; and no biological generalization will enable us to predict the infinite specialities produced by the complexity of vital conditions. So Social Science, while it has departments which in their fundamental generality correspond to mathematics and physics, namely, those grand and simple generalizations which trace out the inevitable march of the human race as a whole, and, as a ramification of these, the laws of economical science, has also, in the departments of government and jurisprudence, which embrace the conditions of social life in all their complexity, what may be called its Biology, carrying us on to innumerable special phenomena which outlie the sphere of science, and belong to Natural History.[21] And just as the most thorough acquaintance with physics, or chemistry, or general physiology will not enable you at once to establish the balance of life in your private vivarium, so that your particular society of zoophytes, molluscs, and echinoderms may feel themselves, as the Germans say, at ease in their skin; so the most complete equipment of theory will not enable a statesman or a political and social reformer to adjust his measures wisely, in the absence of a special acquaintance with the section of society for which he legislates, with the peculiar characteristics of the nation, the province, the class whose well-being he has to consult. In other words, a wise social policy must be based not simply on abstract social science, but on the Natural History of social bodies.

[21] In this analysis George Eliot follows the classification of the sciences set forth by Comte in his *Cours de philosophie positive*. Compare Lewes's brief account of Comte's hierarchy of the sciences in *A Biographical History of Philosophy*, IV (London, 1846), 258–261.

Riehl's books are not dedicated merely to the argumentative maintenance of this or of any other position; they are intended chiefly as a contribution to that knowledge of the German people on the importance of which he insists. He is less occupied with urging his own conclusions than with impressing on his readers the facts which have led him to those conclusions. In the volume entitled *Land und Leute*, which, though published last, is properly an introduction to the volume entitled *Die Bürgerliche Gesellschaft*, he considers the German people in their physical-geographical relations; he compares the natural divisions of the race, as determined by land and climate, and social traditions, with the artificial divisions which are based on diplomacy; and he traces the genesis and influences of what we may call the ecclesiastical geography of Germany—its partition between Catholicism and Protestantism. He shows that the ordinary antithesis of North and South Germany represents no real ethnographical distinction, and that the natural divisions of Germany, founded on its physical geography, are threefold; namely, the low plains, the middle mountain region, and the high mountain region, or Lower, Middle, and Upper Germany; and on this primary natural division all the other broad ethnographical distinctions of Germany will be found to rest. The plains of North or Lower Germany include all the seaboard the nation possesses; and this, together with the fact that they are traversed to the depth of 600 miles by navigable rivers, makes them the natural seat of a trading race. Quite different is the geographical character of Middle Germany. While the northern plains are marked off into great divisions, by such rivers as the Lower Rhine, the Weser, and the Oder, running almost in parallel lines, this central region is cut up like a mosaic by the capricious lines of valleys and rivers. Here is the region in which you find those famous roofs from which the rain-water runs towards two different seas, and the mountain-tops from which you may look into eight or ten German States. The abundance of water-power and the presence of extensive coal-mines allow of a very diversified industrial development in Middle Germany. In Upper Germany, or the high mountain region, we find the same symmetry in the lines of the rivers as in the north; almost all the great Alpine streams flow parallel with the Danube. But the majority of these rivers are neither navigable nor available for industrial objects, and instead of serving for communication, they shut off one great tract from another. The slow development, the simple peasant life of many districts is here determined by the mountain and the river. In the south-east, however, industrial activity spreads through Bohemia towards Austria, and forms a sort of balance to the industrial districts of the Lower Rhine. Of course, the boundaries of these three regions cannot be very strictly defined; but an approximation to the limits of Middle Germany may be obtained by regarding it as a triangle, of which one angle lies in Silesia, another in Aix-la-Chapelle, and a third at Lake Constance.

This triple division corresponds with the broad distinctions of climate. In the northern plains the atmosphere is damp and heavy; in the southern mountain region it is dry and rare, and there are abrupt changes of temperature, sharp contrasts between the seasons, and devastating storms; but in both these zones men are hardened by conflict with the roughnesses of the climate. In Middle Germany, on the contrary, there is little of this struggle; the seasons are more equable, and the mild, soft air of the valleys tends to make the inhabitants luxurious and sensitive to hardships. It is only in exceptional mountain districts that one is here reminded of the rough, bracing air on the heights of Southern Germany. It is a curious fact that, as the air becomes gradually lighter and rarer from the North German coast towards Upper Germany, the average of suicides regularly decreases. Mecklenburg has the highest number, then Prussia, while the fewest suicides occur in Bavaria and Austria.

Both the northern and southern regions have still a large extent of waste lands, downs, morasses, and heaths; and to these are added, in the south, abundance of snowfields and naked rock; while in Middle Germany culture has almost overspread the face of the land, and there are no large tracts of waste. There is the same proportion in the distribution of forests. Again, in the north we see a monotonous continuity of wheat-fields, potato-grounds, meadow lands, and vast heaths, and there is the same uniformity of culture over large surfaces in the southern table-lands and the Alpine pastures. In Middle Germany, on the contrary, there is a perpetual variety of crops within a short space; the diversity of land surface and the corresponding variety in the species of plants are an invitation to the splitting up of estates, and this again encourages to the utmost the motley character of the cultivation.

According to this threefold division, it appears that there are certain features common to North and South Germany in which they differ from Central Germany, and the nature of this difference Riehl indicates by distinguishing the former as *Centralized Land* and the latter as *Individualized Land;* a distinction which is well symbolized by the fact that North and South Germany possess the great lines of railway which are the medium for the traffic of the world, while Middle Germany is far richer in lines for local communication, and possesses the greatest length of railway within the smallest space. Disregarding superficialities, the East Frieslanders, the Schleswig-Holsteiners, the Mecklenburghers, and the Pomeranians are much more nearly allied to the old Bavarians, the Tyrolese, and the Styrians, than any of these are allied to the Saxons, the Thuringians, or the Rhinelanders. Both in North and South Germany original races are still found in large masses, and popular dialects are spoken; you still find there thoroughly peasant districts, thorough villages, and also, at great intervals, thorough cities; you still find there a sense of rank. In Middle Germany, on the contrary, the original races are fused together or sprinkled hither and thither; the peculiarities of the popular dialects are worn down or confused; there is no very strict line of demarcation between the country and the town population, hundreds of small towns and large villages being hardly distinguishable in their characteristics; and the sense of rank, as part of the organic structure of society, is almost extinguished. Again, both in the north and south there is still a strong ecclesiastical spirit in the people, and the Pomeranian sees Antichrist in the Pope as clearly as the Tyrolese sees him in Doctor Luther; while in Middle Germany the confessions are mingled, they exist peaceably side by side in very narrow space, and tolerance or indifference has spread itself widely even in the popular mind. And the analogy, or rather the causal relation, between the physical geography of the three regions and the development of the population goes still further:

> For [observes Riehl], the striking connexion which has been pointed out between the local geological formations in Germany and the revolutionary disposition of the people has more than a metaphorical significance. Where the primeval physical revolutions of the globe have been the wildest in their effects, and the most multiform strata have been tossed together or thrown one upon the other, it is a very

intelligible consequence that on a land surface thus broken up, the population should sooner develop itself into small communities, and that the more intense life generated in these smaller communities, should become the most favourable nidus for the reception of modern culture, and with this a susceptibility for its revolutionary ideas; while a people settled in a region where its groups are spread over a large space will persist much more obstinately in the retention of its original character. The people of Middle Germany have none of that exclusive one-sidedness which determines the peculiar genius of great national groups, just as this one-sidedness or uniformity is wanting to the geological and geographical character of their land.

This ethnographical outline Riehl fills up with special and typical descriptions, and then makes it the starting-point for a criticism of the actual political condition of Germany. The volume is full of vivid pictures, as well as penetrating glances into the maladies and tendencies of modern society. It would be fascinating as literature, if it were not important for its facts and philosophy. But we can only commend it to our readers, and pass on to the volume entitled *Die Bürgerliche Gesellschaft*, from which we have drawn our sketch of the German peasantry. Here Riehl gives us a series of studies in that natural history of the people, which he regards as the proper basis of social policy. He holds that, in European society, there are *three natural ranks or estates*: the hereditary landed aristocracy, the citizens or commercial class, and the peasantry or agricultural class. By *natural ranks* he means ranks which have their roots deep in the historical structure of society, and are still, in the present, showing vitality above ground; he means those great social groups which are not only distinguished externally by their vocation, but essentially by their mental character, their habits, their mode of life,—by the principle they represent in the historical development of society. In his conception of the 'Fourth Estate' he differs from the usual interpretation, according to which it is simply equivalent to the Proletariat, or those who are dependent on daily wages, whose only capital is their skill or bodily strength—factory operatives, artisans, agricultural labourers, to whom might be added, especially in Germany, the day-labourers with the quill, the literary proletariat. This, Riehl observes, is a valid basis of economical classification, but not of social classification. In his view, the Fourth Estate is a stratum produced by the perpetual abrasion of the other great social groups; it is the sign and result of the decomposition which is commencing in the organic constitution of society. Its elements are derived alike from the aristocracy, the bourgeoisie, and the peasantry. It assembles under its banner the deserters of historical society, and forms them into a terrible army, which is only just awaking to the consciousness of its corporate power. The tendency of this Fourth Estate, by the very process of its formation, is to do away with the distinctive historical character of the other estates, and to resolve their peculiar rank and vocation into a uniform social relation founded on an abstract conception of society. According to Riehl's classification, the day-labourers, whom the political economist designates as the Fourth Estate, belong partly to the peasantry or agricultural class, and partly to the citizens or commercial class.

Riehl considers, in the first place, the peasantry and aristocracy as the 'Forces of social persistence,' and in the second, the bourgeoisie and the 'fourth estate' as the 'Forces of social movement.'

The aristocracy, he observes, is the only one among these four groups which is denied by others besides Socialists to have any natural basis as a separate rank. It is admitted that there was once an aristocracy which had an intrinsic ground of existence, but now, it is alleged, this is an historical fossil, an antiquarian relic, venerable because grey with age. In what, it is asked, can consist the peculiar vocation of the aristocracy, since it has no longer the monopoly of the land, of the higher military functions, and of government offices, and since the service of the court has no longer any political importance? To this Riehl replies that in great revolutionary crises, the 'men of progress' have more than once 'abolished' the aristocracy. But remarkably enough, the aristocracy has always re-appeared. This measure of abolition showed that the nobility were no longer regarded as a real class, for to abolish a real class would be an absurdity. It is quite possible to contemplate a voluntary breaking-up of the peasant or citizen class in the socialistic sense, but no man in his senses would think of straight-way 'abolishing' citizens and peasants. The aristocracy, then, was regarded as a sort of cancer, or excrescence of society. Nevertheless, not only has it been found impossible to annihilate an heredi-tary nobility by decree; but also, the aristocracy of the eighteenth century outlived even the self-destructive acts of its own perversity. A life which was entirely without object, entirely destitute of functions, would not, says Riehl, be so persistent. He has an acute criticism of those who conduct a polemic against the idea of an hereditary aristocracy while they are proposing an 'aristocracy of talent,' which after all is based on the principle of inheritance. The Socialists are, therefore, only consistent in declaring against an aristocracy of talent. 'But when they have turned the world into a great Foundling Hospital, they will still be unable to eradicate the "privileges of birth."' We must not follow him in his criticism, however; nor can we afford to do more than mention hastily his interesting sketch of the mediæval aristocracy, and his admonition to the German aristocracy of the present day, that the vitality of their class is not to be sustained by romantic attempts to revive mediæval forms and sentiments, but only by the exercise of functions as real and salutary for actual society as those of the mediæval aristocracy were for the feudal age. 'In modern society the divisions of rank indicate *division of labour*, according to that distribution of functions in the social organism which the historical constitution of society has determined. In this way the principle of differentiation and the principle of unity are identical.'

The elaborate study of the German bourgeoisie, which forms the next division of the volume, must be passed over, but we may pause a moment to note Riehl's definition of the social *Philister* (Philistine), an epithet for which we have no equivalent, not at all, however, for want of the object it represents.[22] Most people, who read a little German, know that the epithet *Philister* originated in the *Burschen-leben*, or Student-life of Germany, and that the antithesis of *Bursch* and *Philister* was equivalent to the antithesis of 'gown' and 'town;' but since the word has passed into ordinary language, it has assumed several shades of significance which have not yet been merged in a single, absolute meaning; and one of the questions which an English visitor in Germany will probably take an opportunity of asking is, 'What is the strict meaning of the word *Philister*?' Riehl's answer is, that the *Philister* is one who is indifferent to all social interests, all public life, as distinguished

[22] Though there are scattered instances of the term in English, especially in Carlyle, before George Eliot wrote, it was Matthew Arnold's essay on Heine (1863) which gave currency to 'Philistine'. His introduction of the word recalls George Eliot's language: 'Philistinism!—we have not the expression in English. Perhaps we have not the word because we have so much of the thing'. (*Essays in Criticism*, First Series [London, 1921], p. 162.)

from selfish and private interests; he has no sympathy with political and social events except as they affect his own comfort and prosperity, as they offer him material for amusement or opportunity for gratifying his vanity. He has no social or political creed, but is always of the opinion which is most convenient for the moment. He is always in the majority, and is the main element of unreason and stupidity in the judgment of a 'discerning public.' It seems presumptuous in us to dispute Riehl's interpretation of a German word, but we must think that, in literature, the epithet *Philister* has usually a wider meaning than this—includes his definition and something more. We imagine the *Philister* is the personification of the spirit which judges everything from a lower point of view than the subject demands—which judges the affairs of the parish from the egotistic or purely personal point of view— which judges the affairs of the nation from the parochial point of view, and does not hesitate to measure the merits of the universe from the human point of view. At least, this must surely be the spirit to which Goethe alludes in a passage cited by Riehl himself, where he says that the Germans need not be ashamed of erecting a monument to him as well as to Blucher; for if Blucher had freed them from the French, he (Goethe) had freed them from the nets of the *Philister*:

> Ihr mögt mir immer ungescheut
> Gleich Blüchern Denkmal setzen!
> Von Franzosen hat er euch befreit,
> Ich von Philister-netzen.[23]

Goethe could hardly claim to be the apostle of public spirit; but he is eminently the man who helps us to rise to a lofty point of observation, so that we may see things in their relative proportions.

The most interesting chapters in the description of the 'Fourth Estate,' which concludes the volume, are those on the 'Aristocratic Proletariat' and the 'Intellectual Proletariat'. The Fourth Estate in Germany, says Riehl, has its centre of gravity not, as in England and France, in the day labourers and factory operatives, and still less in the degenerate peasantry. In Germany, the *educated* proletariat is the leaven that sets the mass in fermentation; the dangerous classes there go about, not in blouses, but in frock-coats; they begin with the impoverished prince and end in the

[23] Number 112 of Goethe's *Sprüche* (*Hamburger Ausgabe*, I, 322), slightly misquoted.

hungriest *littérateur.* The custom that all the sons of a nobleman shall inherit their father's title, necessarily goes on multiplying that class of aristocrats who are not only without function but without adequate provision, and who shrink from entering the ranks of the citizens by adopting some honest calling. The younger son of a prince, says Riehl, is usually obliged to remain without any vocation; and however zealously he may study music, painting, literature, or science, he can never be a regular musician, painter, or man of science; his pursuit will be called a 'passion', not a 'calling', and to the end of his days he remains a dilettante. 'But the ardent pursuit of a fixed practical calling can alone satisfy the active man.' Direct legislation cannot remedy this evil. The inheritance of titles by younger sons is the universal custom, and custom is stronger than law. But if all government preference for the 'aristocratic proletariat' were withdrawn, the sensible men among them would prefer emigration, or the pursuit of some profession, to the hungry distinction of a title without rents.

The intellectual proletaires Riehl calls the 'church militant' of the Fourth Estate in Germany. In no other country are they so numerous; in no other country is the trade in material and industrial capital so far exceeded by the wholesale and retail trade, the traffic and the usury, in the intellectual capital of the nation. *Germany yields more intellectual produce than it can use and pay for.*

> This over-production, which is not transient but permanent, nay, is constantly on the increase, evidences a diseased state of the national industry, a perverted application of industrial powers, and is a far more pungent satire on the national condition than all the poverty of operatives and peasants. . . . Other nations need not envy us the preponderance of the intellectual proletariat over the proletaires of manual labour. For man more easily becomes diseased from overstudy than from the labour of the hands; and it is precisely in the intellectual proletariat that there are the most dangerous seeds of disease. This is the group in which the opposition between earnings and wants, between the ideal social position and the real, is the most hopelessly irreconcilable.

We must unwillingly leave our readers to make acquaintance for themselves with the graphic details with which Riehl follows up this general statement; but before quitting these admirable volumes, let us say, lest our inevitable omissions should have left room for a different conclusion, that Riehl's conservatism is not in the least tinged with the partisanship of a class, with a poetic fanaticism for the past, or with the prejudice of a mind incapable of discerning the grander evolution of things to which all social forms are but temporarily subservient. It is the conservatism of a clear-eyed, practical, but withal large-minded man—a little caustic, perhaps, now and then in his epigrams on democratic doctrinaires who have their nostrum for all political and social diseases, and on communistic theories which he regards as 'the despair of the individual in his own manhood, reduced to a system,' but nevertheless able and willing to do justice to the elements of fact and reason in every shade of opinion and every form of effort. He is as far as possible from the folly of supposing that the sun will go backward on the dial, because we put the hands of our clock backward; he only contends against the opposite folly of decreeing that it shall be mid-day, while in fact the sun is only just touching the mountain-tops, and all along the valley men are stumbling in the twilight.

21

SILLY NOVELS BY LADY NOVELISTS

Westminster Review, LXVI (October, 1856), 442–461

The origin of this article can be traced back to a letter from George Eliot to John Chapman on 5 July 1856 in which she wrote, 'I wonder what the story called "Compensation" is. I have long wanted to fire away at the doctrine of Compensation, which I detest, considered as a way of life'.[1] The article that grew from this germ turned out to be not an attack on false moral doctrine but on the class of silly novels represented by *Compensation*. Two weeks after the first letter George Eliot noted in her Journal for 20 July that Chapman had invited her to contribute to the October number of the *Westminster*, and on the same day she wrote to him saying, 'I think an article on "Silly Women's Novels" might be made the vehicle of some wholesome truth as well as of some amusement. I mentioned this to Mr. Lewes last night and he thought the idea a good one.'[2]

The resulting article, 'Silly Novels', is of special interest as a record of George Eliot's thoughts about the writing of fiction made just at the time when she began her first story. Throughout the summer before she wrote the article Lewes had been pressing her to try her hand at fiction, and when Chapman's request for a contribution arrived she had already resolved to make the attempt: the Journal entry noting Chapman's offer adds that '*I am anxious to begin my fiction writing* and so am not

---

[1] *Letters*, II, 258. Cf. *Theophrastus Such*, 'Looking Inward', p. 11 (Cabinet Ed.): 'At one time I dwelt much on the idea of compensation; trying to believe that I was all the wiser for my bruised vanity, that I had the higher place in the true spiritual scale, and even that a day might come when some visible triumph would place me in the French heaven of having the laughers on my side. But I presently perceived that this was a very odious sort of self-cajolery'.

[2] *Letters*, II, 258.

inclined to undertake an article that will give me much trouble. . . .'
'Silly Novels' was completed on 12 September;[3] on 23 September
George Eliot began *The Sad Fortunes of the Reverend Amos Barton*,
the story she had been meditating throughout the time of writing her
article.

Since more than one attempt has been made to derive the critical
views of 'Silly Novels' from Lewes's 'The Lady Novelists' (*Westminster
Review*, July, 1852), it is worth pointing out that George Eliot's article
is a restatement of the principles she applied in her very earliest
reviewing for the *Westminster*. In January, 1852, she had complained
that few women writers 'exhibit the subtle penetration into feeling and
character, and the truthful delineation of manners which can alone
compensate for the want of philosophic breadth in their views of men
and things, and for their imperfect knowledge of life outside the
drawing-room'.[4] And she condemned a whole class of religious novels
for aiming 'at a didactic effect by an inflated style of reflection, and by
melodramatic incident, instead of faithfully depicting life and leaving
it to teach its own lesson, as the stars do theirs'.[5] 'Silly Novels' reaffirms
at the beginning of her novelist's career the position she had long
since arrived at in her work as a reviewer.

'Silly Novels' has been reprinted in Nathan Sheppard, *The Essays of
'George Eliot', Complete*; in Mrs. S. B. Herrick, *Essays and Reviews of
George Eliot*; and in *Essays and Uncollected Papers*.

*   *   *

SILLY novels by Lady Novelists are a genus with many species,
determined by the particular quality of silliness that predominates
in them—the frothy, the prosy, the pious, or the pedantic. But it
is a mixture of all these—a composite order of feminine fatuity,
that produces the largest class of such novels, which we shall
distinguish as the *mind-and-millinery* species. The heroine is
usually an heiress, probably a peeress in her own right, with
perhaps a vicious baronet, an amiable duke, and an irresistible
younger son of a marquis as lovers in the foreground, a clergyman
and a poet sighing for her in the middle distance, and a crowd of

[3] Journal, 12 September 1856; for the date on which *Amos Barton* was
begun, see *Letters*, II, 407, note 3.
[4] *Westminster Review*, LXII, 283. The attribution of this review to
George Eliot was made by Gordon S. Haight 'on the basis of style alone'
in 'George Eliot's Theory of Fiction', *Victorian Newsletter*, 10 (Autumn,
1956), 1–3.
[5] *Westminster Review*, LXII, 284.

undefined adorers dimly indicated beyond. Her eyes and her wit
are both dazzling; her nose and her morals are alike free from any
tendency to irregularity; she has a superb *contralto* and a superb
intellect; she is perfectly well-dressed and perfectly religious; she
dances like a sylph, and reads the Bible in the original tongues. Or
it may be that the heroine is not an heiress—that rank and wealth
are the only things in which she is deficient; but she infallibly gets
into high society, she has the triumph of refusing many matches
and securing the best, and she wears some family jewels or other
as a sort of crown of righteousness at the end. Rakish men either
bite their lips in impotent confusion at her repartees, or are
touched to penitence by her reproofs, which, on appropriate
occasions, rise to a lofty strain of rhetoric; indeed, there is a
general propensity in her to make speeches, and to rhapsodize at
some length when she retires to her bedroom. In her recorded
conversations she is amazingly eloquent, and in her unrecorded
conversations, amazingly witty. She is understood to have a depth
of insight that looks through and through the shallow theories of
philosophers, and her superior instincts are a sort of dial by which
men have only to set their clocks and watches, and all will go well.
The men play a very subordinate part by her side. You are con-
soled now and then by a hint that they have affairs, which keeps
you in mind that the working-day[6] business of the world is some-
how being carried on, but ostensibly the final cause of their
existence is that they may accompany the heroine on her 'starring'
expedition through life. They see her at a ball, and are dazzled; at
a flower-show, and they are fascinated; on a riding excursion, and
they are witched by her noble horsemanship; at church, and they
are awed by the sweet solemnity of her demeanour. She is the ideal
woman in feelings, faculties, and flounces. For all this, she as often
as not marries the wrong person to begin with, and she suffers
terribly from the plots and intrigues of the vicious baronet; but
even death has a soft place in his heart for such a paragon, and
remedies all mistakes for her just at the right moment. The vicious

[6] 'Working day': the phrase, originally from *As You Like It*, I, iii, 12,
is a key term in George Eliot's conception of realism. She uses it in the
essays on 'Evangelical Teaching' and 'Three Months in Weimar'; in
Adam Bede, Chs. 27 and 50; *Felix Holt*, Introduction; and *Middlemarch*,
Ch. 56. See also *Letters*, I, 44; 66. The *OED*, which cites the *Middlemarch* passage, glosses the term as equivalent to 'workaday' in the sense
of 'ordinary humdrum everyday life'.

baronet is sure to be killed in a duel, and the tedious husband dies in his bed requesting his wife, as a particular favour to him, to marry the man she loves best, and having already dispatched a note to the lover informing him of the comfortable arrangement. Before matters arrive at this desirable issue our feelings are tried by seeing the noble, lovely, and gifted heroine pass through many *mauvais moments*, but we have the satisfaction of knowing that her sorrows are wept into embroidered pocket-handkerchiefs, that her fainting form reclines on the very best upholstery, and that whatever vicissitudes she may undergo, from being dashed out of her carriage to having her head shaved in a fever, she comes out of them all with a complexion more blooming and locks more redundant than ever.

We may remark, by the way, that we have been relieved from a serious scruple by discovering that silly novels by lady novelists rarely introduce us into any other than very lofty and fashionable society. We had imagined that destitute women turned novelists, as they turned governesses, because they had no other 'lady-like' means of getting their bread. On this supposition, vacillating syntax and improbable incident had a certain pathos for us, like the extremely supererogatory pincushions and ill-devised nightcaps that are offered for sale by a blind man. We felt the commodity to be a nuisance, but we were glad to think that the money went to relieve the necessitous, and we pictured to ourselves lonely women struggling for a maintenance, or wives and daughters devoting themselves to the production of 'copy' out of pure heroism,— perhaps to pay their husband's debts, or to purchase luxuries for a sick father. Under these impressions we shrank from criticising a lady's novel: her English might be faulty, but, we said to ourselves, her motives are irreproachable; her imagination may be uninventive, but her patience is untiring. Empty writing was excused by an empty stomach, and twaddle was consecrated by tears. But no! This theory of ours, like many other pretty theories, has had to give way before observation. Women's silly novels, we are now convinced, are written under totally different circumstances. The fair writers have evidently never talked to a tradesman except from a carriage window; they have no notion of the working-classes except as 'dependents'; they think five hundred a-year a miserable pittance; Belgravia and 'baronial halls' are their primary truths; and they have no idea of feeling interest in any man who is not at least a great landed proprietor, if not a prime minister. It is clear that they write in elegant boudoirs, with violet-coloured ink and a ruby pen; that they must be entirely indifferent to publishers' accounts, and inexperienced in every form of poverty except poverty of brains. It is true that we are constantly struck with the want of verisimilitude in their representations of the high society in which they seem to live; but then they betray no closer acquaintance with any other form of life. If their peers and peeresses are improbable, their literary men, tradespeople, and cottagers are impossible; and their intellect seems to have the peculiar impartiality of reproducing both what they *have* seen and heard, and what they have *not* seen and heard, with equal unfaithfulness.

There are few women, we suppose, who have not seen something of children under five years of age, yet in 'Compensation',[7] a recent novel of the mind-and-millinery species, which calls itself a 'story of real life', we have a child of four and a half years old talking in this Ossianic fashion—

> 'Oh, I am so happy, dear gran'mamma;—I have seen,—I have seen such a delightful person: he is like everything beautiful,—like the smell of sweet flowers, and the view from Ben Lomond;—or no, *better than that*—he is like what I think of and see when I am very, very happy; and he is really like mamma, too, when she sings; and his forehead is like *that distant sea*,' she continued, pointing to the blue Mediterranean; 'there seems no end—no end; or like the clusters of stars I like best to look at on a warm fine night.... Don't look so ... your forehead is like Loch Lomond, when the wind is blowing and the sun is gone in; I like the sunshine best when the lake is smooth. ... So now—I like it better than ever ... it is more beautiful still from the dark cloud that has gone over it, *when the sun suddenly lights up all the colours of the forests and shining purple rocks, and it is all reflected in the waters below.*'

We are not surprised to learn that the mother of this infant phenomenon, who exhibits symptoms so alarmingly like those of adolescence repressed by gin, is herself a phœnix. We are assured, again and again, that she had a remarkably original mind, that she was a genius, and 'conscious of her originality,' and she was fortunate enough to have a lover who was also a genius, and a man of 'most original mind.'

This lover, we read, though 'wonderfully similar' to her 'in

[7] [Henrietta Georgiana Marcia Lascelles, Lady Chatterton], '*Compensation*'. *A Story of Real Life Thirty Years Ago*, 2 vols., 1856.

powers and capacity,' was 'infinitely superior to her in faith and development,' and she saw in him the ' "Agape"—so rare to find —of which she had read and admired the meaning in her Greek Testament; having, *from her great facility in learning languages*, read the Scriptures in their original *tongues*.' Of course! Greek and Hebrew are mere play to a heroine; Sanscrit is no more than *a b c* to her; and she can talk with perfect correctness in any language except English. She is a polking polyglott, a Creuzer[8] in crinoline. Poor men! There are so few of you who know even Hebrew; you think it something to boast of if, like Bolingbroke, you only 'understand that sort of learning, and what is writ about it;'[8a] and you are perhaps adoring women who can think slightingly of you in all the Semitic languages successively. But, then, as we are almost invariably told, that a heroine has a 'beautifully small head,' and as her intellect has probably been early invigorated by an attention to costume and deportment, we may conclude that she can pick up the Oriental tongues, to say nothing of their dialects, with the same aërial facility that the butterfly sips nectar. Besides, there can be no difficulty in conceiving the depth of the heroine's erudition, when that of the authoress is so evident.

In 'Laura Gay,'[9] another novel of the same school, the heroine seems less at home in Greek and Hebrew, but she makes up for the deficiency by a quite playful familiarity with the Latin classics— with the 'dear old Virgil,' 'the graceful Horace, the humane Cicero, and the pleasant Livy;' indeed, it is such a matter of course with her to quote Latin, that she does it at a pic-nic in a very mixed company of ladies and gentlemen, having, we are told, 'no conception that the nobler sex were capable of jealousy on this subject. And if, indeed,' continues the biographer of Laura Gay, 'the wisest and noblest portion of that sex were in the majority, no such sentiment would exist; but while Miss Wyndhams and Mr. Redfords abound, great sacrifices must be made to their existence.' Such sacrifices, we presume, as abstaining from Latin quotations, of extremely moderate interest and applicability, which the wise and noble minority of the other sex would be quite as willing to

---

[8] Georg Friedrich Creuzer, author of *Symbolik*. See 'The Progress of the Intellect', note 11.

[8a] Pope's answer to the question whether Bolingbroke knew Hebrew, reported in Spence, *Anecdotes*, ed. S. W. Singer (1820), p. 178.

[9] 2 vols., 1856.

dispense with as the foolish and ignoble majority. It is as little the custom of well-bred men as of well-bred women to quote Latin in mixed parties; they can contain their familiarity with 'the humane Cicero' without allowing it to boil over in ordinary conversation, and even references to 'the pleasant Livy' are not absolutely irrepressible. But Ciceronian Latin is the mildest form of Miss Gay's conversational power. Being on the Palatine with a party of sightseers, she falls into the following vein of well-rounded remark: 'Truth can only be pure objectively, for even in the creeds where it predominates, being subjective, and parcelled out into portions, each of these necessarily receives a hue of idiosyncrasy, that is, a taint of superstition more or less strong; while in such creeds as the Roman Catholic, ignorance, interest, the bias of ancient idolatries, and the force of authority, have gradually accumulated on the pure truth, and transformed it, at last, into a mass of superstition for the majority of its votaries; and how few are there, alas! whose zeal, courage, and intellectual energy are equal to the analysis of this accumulation, and to the discovery of the pearl of great price which lies hidden beneath this heap of rubbish.' We have often met with women much more novel and profound in their observations than Laura Gay, but rarely with any so inopportunely long winded. A clerical lord, who is half in love with her, is alarmed by the daring remarks just quoted, and begins to suspect that she is inclined to free-thinking. But he is mistaken; when in a moment of sorrow he delicately begs leave to 'recal to her memory, a *depôt* of strength and consolation under affliction, which, until we are hard pressed by the trials of life, we are too apt to forget,' we learn that she really has 'recurrence to that sacred depôt,' together with the tea-pot. There is a certain flavour of orthodoxy mixed with the parade of fortunes and fine carriages in 'Laura Gay', but it is an orthodoxy mitigated by study of the humane Cicero,' and by an 'intellectual disposition to analyse.'

'Compensation' is much more heavily dosed with doctrine, but then it has a treble amount of snobbish worldliness and absurd incident to tickle the palate of pious frivolity. Linda, the heroine, is still more speculative and spiritual than Laura Gay, but she has been 'presented,' and has more, and far grander, lovers; very wicked and fascinating women are introduced—even a French *lionne*; and no expense is spared to get up as exciting a story as you will find in the most immoral novels. In fact, it is a wonderful *pot pourri* of Almack's, Scotch second-sight, Mr. Rogers's breakfasts, Italian brigands, death-bed conversions, superior authoresses, Italian mistresses, and attempts at poisoning old ladies, the whole served up with a garnish of talk about 'faith and development,' and 'most original minds.' Even Miss Susan Barton, the superior authoress, whose pen moves in a 'quick decided manner when she is composing,' declines the finest opportunities of marriage; and though old enough to be Linda's mother (since we are told that she refused Linda's father), has her hand sought by a young earl, the heroine's rejected lover. Of course, genius and morality must be backed by eligible offers, or they would seem rather a dull affair; and piety, like other things, in order to be *comme il faut*, must be in 'society,' and have admittance to the best circles.

'Rank and Beauty'[10] is a more frothy and less religious variety of the mind-and-millinery species. The heroine, we are told, 'if she inherited her father's pride of birth and her mother's beauty of person, had in herself a tone of enthusiastic feeling that perhaps belongs to her age even in the lowly born, but which is refined into the high spirit of wild romance only in the far descended, who feel that it is their best inheritance.' This enthusiastic young lady, by dint of reading the newspaper to her father, falls in love with the *prime minister*, who, through the medium of leading articles and 'the *resumé* of the debates,' shines upon her imagination as a bright particular star, which has no parallax for her, living in the country as simple Miss Wyndham. But she forthwith becomes Baroness Umfraville in her own right, astonishes the world with her beauty and accomplishments when she bursts upon it from her mansion in Spring Gardens, and, as you foresee, will presently come into contact with the unseen *objet aimé*. Perhaps the words 'prime minister' suggest to you a wrinkled or obese sexagenarian; but pray dismiss the image. Lord Rupert Conway has been 'called while still almost a youth to the first situation which a subject can hold in the *universe*,' and even leading articles and a *resumé* of the debates have not conjured up a dream that surpasses the fact.

The door opened again, and Lord Rupert Conway entered. Evelyn gave one glance. It was enough; she was not disappointed. It seemed as if a picture on which she had long gazed was suddenly instinct with life, and had stepped from its frame before her. His tall figure, the

[10] *Rank and Beauty, or the Young Baroness*, 3 vols., 1856.

distinguished simplicity of his air—it was a living Vandyke, a cavalier, one of his noble cavalier ancestors, or one to whom her fancy had always likened him, who long of yore had, with an Umfraville, fought the Paynim far beyond sea. Was this reality?

Very little like it, certainly.

By-and-by, it becomes evident that the ministerial heart is touched. Lady Umfraville is on a visit to the Queen at Windsor, and,

> The last evening of her stay, when they returned from riding, Mr. Wyndham took her and a large party to the top of the Keep, to see the view. She was leaning on the battlements, gazing from that 'stately height' at the prospect beneath her, when Lord Rupert was by her side. 'What an unrivalled view!' exclaimed she.
>
> 'Yes, it would have been wrong to go without having been up here. You are pleased with your visit?'
>
> 'Enchanted! A Queen to live and die under, to live and die for!'
>
> 'Ha!' cried he, with sudden emotion, and with a *eureka* expression of countenance, as if he had *indeed found a heart in unison with his own*.

The '*eureka* expression of countenance,' you see at once to be prophetic of marriage at the end of the third volume; but before that desirable consummation, there are very complicated misunderstandings, arising chiefly from the vindictive plotting of Sir Luttrell Wycherley, who is a genius, a poet, and in every way a most remarkable character indeed. He is not only a romantic poet, but a hardened rake and a cynical wit; yet his deep passion for Lady Umfraville has so impoverished his epigrammatic talent, that he cuts an extremely poor figure in conversation. When she rejects him, he rushes into the shrubbery, and rolls himself in the dirt; and on recovering, devotes himself to the most diabolical and laborious schemes of vengeance, in the course of which he disguises himself as a quack physician, and enters into general practice, foreseeing that Evelyn will fall ill, and that he shall be called in to attend her. At last, when all his schemes are frustrated, he takes leave of her in a long letter, written, as you will perceive from the following passage, entirely in the style of an eminent literary man:

> 'Oh, lady, nursed in pomp and pleasure, will you ever cast one thought upon the miserable being who addresses you? Will you ever, as your gilded galley is floating down the unruffled stream of pros-

perity, will you ever, while lulled by the sweetest music—thine own praises,—hear the far-off sigh from that world to which I am going?'

On the whole, however, frothy as it is, we rather prefer 'Rank and Beauty' to the other two novels we have mentioned. The dialogue is more natural and spirited; there is some frank ignorance, and no pedantry; and you are allowed to take the heroine's astounding intellect upon trust, without being called on to read her conversational refutations of sceptics and philosophers, or her rhetorical solutions of the mysteries of the universe.

Writers of the mind-and-millinery school are remarkably unanimous in their choice of diction. In their novels, there is usually a lady or gentleman who is more or less of a upas tree: the lover has a manly breast; minds are redolent of various things; hearts are hollow; events are utilized; friends are consigned to the tomb; infancy is an engaging period; the sun is a luminary that goes to his western couch, or gathers the rain-drops into his refulgent bosom; life is a melancholy boon; Albion and Scotia are conversational epithets. There is a striking resemblance, too, in the character of their moral comments, such, for instance, as that 'It is a fact, no less true than melancholy, that all people, more or less, richer or poorer, are swayed by bad example;' that 'Books, however trivial, contain some subjects from which useful information may be drawn;' that 'Vice can too often borrow the language of virtue;' that 'Merit and nobility of nature must exist, to be accepted, for clamour and pretension cannot impose upon those too well read in human nature to be easily deceived;' and that, 'In order to forgive, we must have been injured.' There is, doubtless, a class of readers to whom these remarks appear peculiarly pointed and pungent; for we often find them doubly and trebly scored with the pencil, and delicate hands giving in their determined adhesion to these hardy novelties by a distinct *très vrai*, emphasized by many notes of exclamation. The colloquial style of these novels is often marked by much ingenious inversion, and a careful avoidance of such cheap phraseology as can be heard every day. Angry young gentlemen exclaim—"'Tis ever thus, methinks;' and in the half-hour before dinner a young lady informs her next neighbour that the first day she read Shakspeare she 'stole away into the park, and beneath the shadow of the greenwood tree, devoured with rapture the inspired page of the great magician.'

But the most remarkable efforts of the mind-and-millinery writers lie in their philosophic reflections. The authoress of 'Laura Gay,' for example, having married her hero and heroine, improves the event by observing that 'if those sceptics, whose eyes have so long gazed on matter that they can no longer see aught else in man, could once enter with heart and soul into such bliss as this, they would come to say that the soul of man and the polypus are not of common origin, or of the same texture.' Lady novelists, it appears, can see something else besides matter; they are not limited to phenomena, but can relieve their eyesight by occasional glimpses of the *noumenon*, and are, therefore, naturally better able than any one else to confound sceptics, even of that remarkable, but to us unknown school, which maintains that the soul of man is of the same texture as the polypus.

The most pitiable of all silly novels by lady novelists are what we may call the *oracular* species—novels intended to expound the writer's religious, philosophical, or moral theories. There seems to be a notion abroad among women, rather akin to the superstition that the speech and actions of idiots are inspired, and that the human being most entirely exhausted of common sense is the fittest vehicle of revelation. To judge from their writings, there are certain ladies who think that an amazing ignorance, both of science and of life, is the best possible qualification for forming an opinion on the knottiest moral and speculative questions. Apparently, their recipe for solving all such difficulties is something like this: Take a woman's head, stuff it with a smattering of philosophy and literature chopped small, and with false notions of society baked hard, let it hang over a desk a few hours every day, and serve up hot in feeble English, when not required. You will rarely meet with a lady novelist of the oracular class who is diffident of her ability to decide on theological questions,—who has any suspicion that she is not capable of discriminating with the nicest accuracy between the good and evil in all church parties,—who does not see precisely how it is that men have gone wrong hitherto,—and pity philosophers in general that they have not had the opportunity of consulting her. Great writers, who have modestly contented themselves with putting their experience into fiction, and have thought it quite a sufficient task to exhibit men and things as they are, she sighs over as deplorably deficient in the application of their powers. 'They have solved no great questions'—and she is ready to remedy their omission by setting before you a complete theory of life and manual of divinity, in a love story, where ladies and gentlemen of good family go through genteel vicissitudes, to the utter confusion of Deists, Puseyites, and ultra-Protestants, and to the perfect establishment of that particular view of Christianity which either condenses itself into a sentence of small caps, or explodes into a cluster of stars on the three hundred and thirtieth page. It is true, the ladies and gentlemen will probably seem to you remarkably little like any you have had the fortune or misfortune to meet with, for, as a general rule, the ability of a lady novelist to describe actual life and her fellow-men, is in inverse proportion to her confident eloquence about God and the other world, and the means by which she usually chooses to conduct you to true ideas of the invisible is a totally false picture of the visible.

As typical a novel of the oracular kind as we can hope to meet with, is 'The Enigma: a Leaf from the Chronicles of the Wolchorley House.'[11] The 'enigma' which this novel is to solve, is certainly one that demands powers no less gigantic than those of· a lady novelist, being neither more nor less than the existence of evil. The problem is stated, and the answer dimly foreshadowed on the very first page. The spirited young lady, with raven hair, says, 'All life is an inextricable confusion;' and the meek young lady, with auburn hair, looks at the picture of the Madonna which she is copying, and—'*There* seemed the solution of that mighty enigma.' The style of this novel is quite as lofty as its purpose; indeed, some passages on which we have spent much patient study are quite beyond our reach, in spite of the illustrative aid of italics and small caps; and we must await further 'development' in order to understand them. Of Ernest, the model young clergyman, who sets every one right on all occasions, we read, that 'he held not of marriage in the marketable kind, after a social desecration;' that, on one eventful night, 'sleep had not visited his divided heart, where tumultuated, in varied type and combination, the aggregate feelings of grief and joy;' and that, 'for the *marketable* human article he had no toleration, be it of what sort, or set for what value it might, whether for worship or class, his upright soul abhorred it, whose ultimatum, the self-deceiver, was to him THE *great spiritual lie*, "living in a vain show, deceiving and being

[11] The title according to the *English Catalogue* is *The Enigma*: *A Leaf from the Archives of Wolchorley House*, 1856.

deceived;" since he did not suppose the phylactery and enlarged border on the garment to be *merely* a social trick.' (The italics and small caps are the author's, and we hope they assist the reader's comprehension.) Of Sir Lionel, the model old gentleman, we are told that 'the simple ideal of the middle age, apart from its anarchy and decadence, in him most truly seemed to live again, when the ties which knit men together were of heroic cast. The first-born colours of pristine faith and truth engraven on the common soul of man, and blent into the wide arch of brotherhood, where the primæval law of *order* grew and multiplied, each perfect after his kind, and mutually inter-dependent.' You see clearly, of course, how colours are first engraven on a soul, and then blent into a wide arch, on which arch of colours—apparently a rainbow—the law of order grew and multiplied, each—apparently the arch and the law —perfect after his kind? If, after this, you can possibly want any further aid towards knowing what Sir Lionel was, we can tell you, that in his soul 'the scientific combinations of thought could educe no fuller harmonies of the good and the true, than lay in the primæval pulses which floated as an atmosphere around it!' and that, when he was sealing a letter, 'Lo! the responsive throb in that good man's bosom echoed back in simple truth the honest witness of a heart that condemned him not, as his eye, bedewed with love, rested, too, with something of ancestral pride, on the undimmed motto of the family—"LOIAUTÉ".'

The slightest matters have their vulgarity fumigated out of them by the same elevated style. Commonplace people would say that a copy of Shakspeare lay on a drawing-room table; but the authoress of 'The Enigma,' bent on edifying periphrasis, tells you that there lay on the table, 'that fund of human thought and feeling, which teaches the heart through the little name, "Shakspeare."' A watchman sees a light burning in an upper window rather longer than usual, and thinks that people are foolish to sit up late when they have an opportunity of going to bed; but, lest this fact should seem too low and common, it is presented to us in the following striking and metaphysical manner: 'He marvelled—as man *will* think for others in a necessarily separate personality, consequently (though disallowing it) in false mental premise,—how differently *he* should act, how gladly *he* should prize the rest so lightly held of within.' A footman—an ordinary Jeames, with large calves and aspirated vowels—answers the door-bell, and the opportunity is seized to tell you that he was a 'type of the large class of pampered menials, who follow the curse of Cain—"vagabonds" on the face of the earth, and whose estimate of the human class varies in the graduated scale of money and expenditure. . . . These, and such as these, O England, be the false lights of thy morbid civilization!' We have heard of various 'false lights,' from Dr. Cumming to Robert Owen,[12] from Dr. Pusey to the Spirit-rappers, but we never before heard of the false light that emanates from plush and powder.

In the same way very ordinary events of civilized life are exalted into the most awful crises, and ladies in full skirts and *manches à la Chinoise*, conduct themselves not unlike the heroines of sanguinary melodramas. Mrs. Percy, a shallow woman of the world, wishes her son Horace to marry the auburn-haired Grace, she being an heiress; but he, after the manner of sons, falls in love with the raven-haired Kate, the heiress's portionless cousin; and, moreover, Grace herself shows every symptom of perfect indifference to Horace. In such cases, sons are often sulky or fiery, mothers are alternately manœuvring and waspish, and the portionless young lady often lies awake at night and cries a good deal. We are getting used to these things now, just as we are used to eclipses of the moon, which no longer set us howling and beating tin kettles. We never heard of a lady in a fashionable 'front' behaving like Mrs. Percy under these circumstances. Happening one day to see Horace talking to Grace at a window, without in the least knowing what they are talking about, or having the least reason to believe that Grace, who is mistress of the house and a person of dignity, would accept her son if he were to offer himself, she suddenly rushes up to them and clasps them both, saying, 'with a flushed countenance and in an excited manner'—'This is indeed happiness; for, may I not call you so, Grace?—my Grace—my Horace's Grace!—my dear children!' Her son tells her she is mistaken, and that he is engaged to Kate, whereupon we have the following scene and tableau:

> Gathering herself up to an unprecedented height,(!) her eyes lightning forth the fire of her anger:—
>
> 'Wretched boy!' she said, hoarsely and scornfully, and clenching her hand, 'Take then the doom of your own choice! Bow down your miserable head and let a mother's—'

[12] See 'Lord Brougham's Literature', note 8.

'Curse not!' spake a deep low voice from behind, and Mrs. Percy started, scared, as though she had seen a heavenly visitant appear, to break upon her in the midst of her sin.

Meantime, Horace had fallen on his knees at her feet, and hid his face in his hands.

Who, then, is she—who! Truly his 'guardian spirit' hath stepped between him and the fearful words, which, however unmerited, must have hung as a pall over his future existence;—a spell which could not be unbound—which could not be unsaid.

Of an earthly paleness, but calm with the still, iron-bound calmness of death—the only calm one there,—Katherine stood; and her words smote on the ear in tones whose appallingly slow and separate intonation rung on the heart like the chill, isolated tolling of some fatal knell.

'He would have plighted me his faith, but I did not accept it; you cannot, therefore—you *dare* not curse him. And here,' she continued, raising her hand to heaven, whither her large dark eyes also rose with a chastened glow, which, for the first time, *suffering* had lighted in those passionate orbs,—'here I promise, come weal, come woe, that Horace Wolchorley and I do never interchange vows without his mother's sanction—without his mother's blessing'!

Here, and throughout the story, we see that confusion of purpose which is so characteristic of silly novels written by women. It is a story of quite modern drawing-room society—a society in which polkas are played and Puseyism discussed; yet we have characters, and incidents, and traits of manner introduced, which are mere shreds from the most heterogeneous romances. We have a blind Irish harper 'relic of the picturesque bards of yore,' startling us at a Sunday-school festival of tea and cake in an English village; we have a crazy gipsy, in a scarlet cloak, singing snatches of romantic song, and revealing a secret on her deathbed which, with the testimony of a dwarfish miserly merchant, who salutes strangers with a curse and a devilish laugh, goes to prove that Ernest, the model young clergyman, is Kate's brother; and we have an ultra-virtuous Irish Barney, discovering that a document is forged, by comparing the date of the paper with the date of the alleged signature, although the same document has passed through a court of law, and occasioned a fatal decision. The 'Hall' in which Sir Lionel lives is the venerable country-seat of an old family, and this, we suppose, sets the imagination of the authoress flying to donjons and battlements, where 'lo! the warder blows his horn;' for, as the inhabitants are in their bedrooms on a night certainly within the recollection of Pleaceman X., and a breeze springs up, which we are at first told was faint, and then that it made the old cedars bow their branches to the greensward, she falls into this mediæval vein of description (the italics are ours): 'The banner *unfurled it* at the sound, and shook its guardian wing above, while the startled owl *flapped her* in the ivy; the firmament looking down through her "argus eyes,"—

'Ministers of heaven's mute melodies'.
And lo! two strokes tolled from out the warder tower, and "Two o'clock" re-echoed its interpreter below.'

Such stories as this of 'The Enigma' remind us of the pictures clever children sometimes draw 'out of their own head', where you will see a modern villa on the right, two knights in helmets fighting in the foreground, and a tiger grinning in a jungle on the left, the several objects being brought together because the artist thinks each pretty, and perhaps still more because he remembers seeing them in other pictures.

But we like the authoress much better on her mediæval stilts than on her oracular ones,—when she talks of the *Ich* and of 'subjective' and 'objective', and lays down the exact line of Christian verity, between 'right-hand excesses and left-hand declensions.' Persons who deviate from this line are introduced with a patronizing air of charity. Of a certain Miss Inshquine she informs us, with all the lucidity of italics and small caps, that '*function*, not *form*, AS *the inevitable outer expression of the spirit in this tabernacled age*, weakly engrossed her.' And *à propos* of Miss Mayjar, an evangelical lady who is a little too apt to talk of her visits to sick women and the state of their souls, we are told that the model clergyman is 'not one to disallow, through the *super* crust, the undercurrent towards good in the *subject*, or the positive benefits, nevertheless, to the *object*.' We imagine the double-refined accent and protrusion of chin which are feebly represented by the italics in this lady's sentences! We abstain from quoting any of her oracular doctrinal passages, because they refer to matters too serious for our pages just now.

The epithet 'silly' may seem impertinent, applied to a novel which indicates so much reading and intellectual activity as 'The Enigma;' but we use this epithet advisedly. If, as the world has long agreed, a very great amount of instruction will not make a wise man, still less will a very mediocre amount of instruction make a wise woman. And the most mischievous form of feminine silliness is the literary form, because it tends to confirm the popular prejudice against the more solid education of women. When men see girls wasting their time in consultations about bonnets and ball dresses, and in giggling or sentimental love-confidences, or middle-aged women mismanaging their children, and solacing themselves with acrid gossip, they can hardly help saying, 'For Heaven's sake, let girls be better educated; let them have some better objects of thought—some more solid occupations.' But after a few hours' conversation with an oracular literary woman, or a few hours' reading of her books, they are likely enough to say, 'After all, when a woman gets some knowledge, see what use she makes of it! Her knowledge remains acquisition, instead of passing into culture; instead of being subdued into modesty and simplicity by a larger acquaintance with thought and fact, she has a feverish consciousness of her attainments; she keeps a sort of mental pocket-mirror, and is continually looking in it at her own "intellectuality"; she spoils the taste of one's muffin by questions of metaphysics; "puts down" men at a dinner table with her superior information; and seizes the opportunity of a *soirée* to catechise us on the vital question of the relation between mind and matter. And then, look at her writings! She mistakes vagueness for depth, bombast for eloquence, and affectation for originality; she struts on one page, rolls her eyes on another, grimaces in a third, and is hysterical in a fourth. She may have read many writings of great men, and a few writings of great women; but she is as unable to discern the difference between her own style and theirs as a Yorkshireman is to discern the difference between his own English and a Londoner's: rhodomontade is the native accent of her intellect. No—the average nature of women is too shallow and feeble a soil to bear much tillage; it is only fit for the very lightest crops.'

It is true that the men who come to such a decision on such very superficial and imperfect observation may not be among the wisest in the world; but we have not now to contest their opinion—we are only pointing out how it is unconsciously encouraged by many women who have volunteered themselves as representatives of the feminine intellect. We do not believe that a man was ever strengthened in such an opinion by associating with a woman of true culture, whose mind had absorbed her knowledge instead of being absorbed by it. A really cultured woman, like a really cultured man, is all the simpler and the less obtrusive for her knowledge; it has made her see herself and her opinions in something like just proportions; she does not make it a pedestal from which she flatters herself that she commands a complete view of men and things, but makes it a point of observation from which to form a right estimate of herself. She neither spouts poetry nor quotes Cicero on slight provocation; not because she thinks that a sacrifice must be made to the prejudices of men, but because that mode of exhibiting her memory and Latinity does not present itself to her as edifying or graceful. She does not write books to confound philosophers, perhaps because she is able to write books that delight them. In conversation she is the least formidable of women, because she understands you, without wanting to make you aware that you *can't* understand her. She does not give you information, which is the raw material of culture,—she gives you sympathy, which is it subtlest essence.

A more numerous class of silly novels than the oracular, (which are generally inspired by some form of High Church, or transcendental Christianity,) is what we may call the *white neck-cloth* species, which represent the tone of thought and feeling in the Evangelical party. This species is a kind of genteel tract on a large scale, intended as a sort of medicinal sweetmeat for Low Church young ladies; an Evangelical substitute for the fashionable novel, as the May Meetings[13] are a substitute for the Opera. Even Quaker children, one would think, can hardly have been denied the indulgence of a doll; but it must be a doll dressed in a drab gown and a coal-scuttle bonnet—not a wordly doll, in gauze and spangles. And there are no young ladies, we imagine,—unless they belong to the Church of the United Brethren, in which people are married without any love-making—who can dispense with love stories. Thus, for Evangelical young ladies there are Evangelical love stories, in which the vicissitudes of the tender passion are sanctified by saving views of Regeneration and the Atonement. These novels differ from the oracular ones, as a Low Church-woman often differs from a High Churchwoman: they are a little less supercilious, and a great deal more ignorant, a little less correct in their syntax, and a great deal more vulgar.

[13] The Church of England Missionary Society's annual May Meetings at Exeter Hall.

The Orlando of Evangelical literature is the young curate, looked at from the point of view of the middle class, where cambric bands are understood to have as thrilling an effect on the hearts of young ladies as epaulettes have in the classes above and below it. In the ordinary type of these novels, the hero is almost sure to be a young curate, frowned upon, perhaps, by worldly mammas, but carrying captive the hearts of their daughters, who can 'never forget *that* sermon;' tender glances are seized from the pulpit stairs instead of the opera-box; *tête-à-têtes* are seasoned with quotations from Scripture, instead of quotations from the poets; and questions as to the state of the heroine's affections are mingled with anxieties as to the state of her soul. The young curate always has a background of well-dressed and wealthy, if not fashionable society;—for Evangelical silliness is as snobbish as any other kind of silliness; and the Evangelical lady novelist, while she explains to you the type of the scapegoat on one page, is ambitious on another to represent the manners and conversation of aristocratic people. Her pictures of fashionable society are often curious studies considered as efforts of the Evangelical imagination; but in one particular the novels of the White Neck-cloth School are meritoriously realistic,—their favourite hero, the Evangelical young curate is always rather an insipid personage.

The most recent novel of this species that we happen to have before us, is 'The Old Grey Church.'[14] It is utterly tame and feeble; there is no one set of objects on which the writer seems to have a stronger grasp than on any other; and we should be entirely at a loss to conjecture among what phases of life her experience has been gained, but for certain vulgarisms of style which sufficiently indicate that she has had the advantage, though she has been unable to use it, of mingling chiefly with men and women whose manners and characters have not had all their bosses and angles rubbed down by refined conventionalism. It is less excusable in an Evangelical novelist, than in any other, gratuitously to seek her subjects among titles and carriages. The real drama of Evangelicalism—and it has abundance of fine drama for any one who has genius enough to discern and reproduce it—lies among the middle and lower classes; and are not Evangelical opinions understood to give an especial interest in the weak things of the earth, rather than in the mighty? Why then, cannot our Evangelical lady novelists

[14] [By Lady Caroline Lucy Scott], 3 vols., 1856.

show us the operation of their religious views among people (there really are many such in the world) who keep no carriage, 'not so much as a brassbound gig,' who even manage to eat their dinner without a silver fork, and in whose mouths the authoress's questionable English would be strictly consistent? Why can we not have pictures of religious life among the industrial classes in England, as interesting as Mrs. Stowe's pictures of religious life among the negroes?[15] Instead of this, pious ladies nauseate us with novels which remind us of what we sometimes see in a worldly woman recently 'converted';—she is as fond of a fine dinner table as before, but she invites clergymen instead of beaux; she thinks as much of her dress as before, but she adopts a more sober choice of colours and patterns; her conversation is as trivial as before, but the triviality is flavoured with gospel instead of gossip. In 'The Old Grey Church,' we have the same sort of Evangelical travesty of the fashionable novel, and of course the vicious, intriguing baronet is not wanting. It is worth while to give a sample of the style of conversation attributed to this high-born rake—a style that in its profuse italics and palpable innuendoes, is worthy of Miss Squeers.[16] In an evening visit to the ruins of the Colosseum, Eustace, the young clergyman, has been withdrawing the heroine, Miss Lushington, from the rest of the party, for the sake of a *tête-à-tête*. The baronet is jealous, and vents his pique in this way:

There they are, and Miss Lushington, no doubt, quite safe; for she is under the holy guidance of Pope Eustace the First, who has, of course, been delivering to her an edifying homily on the wickedness of the heathens of yore, who, as tradition tells us, in this very place let loose the wild *beastises* on poor St. Paul!—Oh, no! by-the-bye, I believe I am wrong, and betraying my want of clergy, and that it was not at all St. Paul, nor was it here. But no matter, it would equally serve as a text to preach from, and from which to diverge to the degenerate *heathen* Christians of the present day, and all their naughty practices, and so end with an exhortation to 'come out from among them, and be separate;'—and I am sure, Miss Lushington, you have most scrupulously conformed to that injunction this evening, for we have seen nothing of you since our arrival. But every one seems agreed it has been a *charming party of pleasure*, and I am sure we all feel *much*

[15] George Eliot's review of Mrs. Stowe's *Dred* appeared in the same number of the *Westminster* containing 'Silly Novels'.
[16] See her letter in Ch. 15 of *Nicholas Nickleby*.

indebted to Mr. Grey for having *suggested* it; and as he seems so capital a cicerone, I hope he will think of something else equally agreeable to *all*.

This drivelling kind of dialogue, and equally drivelling narrative, which, like a bad drawing, represents nothing, and barely indicates what is meant to be represented, runs through the book; and we have no doubt is considered by the amiable authoress to constitute an improving novel, which Christian mothers will do well to put into the hands of their daughters. But everything is relative; we have met with American vegetarians[17] whose normal diet was dry meal, and who, when their appetite wanted stimulating, tickled it with *wet* meal; and so, we can imagine that there are Evangelical circles in which 'The Old Grey Church' is devoured as a powerful and interesting fiction.

But, perhaps, the least readable of silly women's novels, are the *modern-antique* species, which unfold to us the domestic life of Jannes and Jambres,[18] the private love affairs of Sennacherib, or the mental struggles and ultimate conversion of Demetrius the silversmith.[19] From most silly novels we can at least extract a laugh; but those of the modern antique school have a ponderous, a leaden kind of fatuity, under which we groan. What can be more demonstrative of the inability of literary women to measure their own powers, than their frequent assumption of a task which can only be justified by the rarest concurrence of acquirement with genius? The finest effort to reanimate the past is of course only approximative—is always more or less an infusion of the modern spirit into the ancient form,

> Was ihr den Geist der Zeiten heisst,
> Das ist im Grund der Herren eigner Geist,
> In dem die Zeiten sich bespiegeln.[20]

Admitting that genius which has familiarized itself with all the relics of an ancient period can sometimes, by the force of its sympathetic divination, restore the missing notes in the 'music of

[17] No doubt the original of the American 'vegetarian seer, / By name Elias Baptist Butterworth', in George Eliot's 'A Minor Prophet'.

[18] St. Paul's names for the Egyptian magicians who contended against Moses at the court of Pharaoh (2 Tim. 3:8).

[19] Acts 19:24 ff.

[20] Goethe, *Faust I*, 'Nacht', 577–579.

humanity,'[21] and reconstruct the fragments into a whole which will really bring the remote past nearer to us, and interpret it to our duller apprehension,—this form of imaginative power must always be among the very rarest, because it demands as much accurate and minute knowledge as creative vigour. Yet we find ladies constantly choosing to make their mental mediocrity more conspicuous, by clothing it in a masquerade of ancient names; by putting their feeble sentimentality into the mouths of Roman vestals or Egyptian princesses, and attributing their rhetorical arguments to Jewish high-priests and Greek philosophers. A recent example of this heavy imbecility is, 'Adonijah, a Tale of the Jewish Dispersion,'[22] which forms part of a series, 'uniting,' we are told, 'taste, humour, and sound principles.'[22a] 'Adonijah,' we presume, exemplifies the tale of 'sound principles;' the taste and humour are to be found in other members of the series. We are told on the cover, that the incidents of this tale are 'fraught with unusual interest,' and the preface winds up thus: 'To those who feel interested in the dispersed of Israel and Judea, these pages may afford, perhaps, information on an important subject, as well as amusement.' Since the 'important subject' on which this book is to afford information is not specified, it may possibly lie in some esoteric meaning to which we have no key; but if it has relation to the dispersed of Israel and Judea at any period of their history, we believe a tolerably well-informed school-girl already knows much more of it than she will find in this 'Tale of the Jewish Dispersion.' 'Adonijah' is simply the feeblest kind of love story, supposed to be instructive, we presume, because the hero is a Jewish captive, and the heroine a Roman vestal; because they and their friends are converted to Christianity after the shortest and easiest method approved by the 'Society for Promoting the Conversion of the Jews;' and because, instead of being written in plain language, it is adorned with that peculiar style of grandiloquence which is held by some lady novelists to give an antique colouring, and which we recognise at once in such phrases as these: 'the splendid regnal

[21] Wordsworth, 'Tintern Abbey', 91.

[22] [By Jane Margaret Strickland?], 1856.

[22a] *Adonijah* appeared in the 'Run and Read Library', whose preliminary announcement stated that '*Taste, sprightliness, humour and command of diction, combined with sound principles*, will be the leading qualification of the works admitted into this Series' (Michael Sadleir, *XIX Century Fiction*, 2 vols. [London and Berkeley, 1951], II, 70).

talents undoubtedly possessed by the Emperor Nero'—'the expiring scion of a lofty stem'—'the virtuous partner of his couch'—'ah, by Vesta!'—and 'I tell thee, Roman.' Among the quotations which serve at once for instruction and ornament on the cover of this volume, there is one from Miss Sinclair,[23] which informs us that 'Works of imagination are *avowedly* read by men of science, wisdom, and piety'; from which we suppose the reader is to gather the cheering inference that Dr. Daubeny,[24] Mr. Mill, or Mr. Maurice, may openly indulge himself with the perusal of 'Adonijah', without being obliged to secrete it among the sofa cushions, or read it by snatches under the dinner table.

'Be not a baker if your head be made of butter,' says a homely proverb, which, being interpreted, may mean, let no woman rush into print who is not prepared for the consequences. We are aware that our remarks are in a very different tone from that of the reviewers who, with a perennial recurrence of precisely similar emotions, only paralleled, we imagine, in the experience of monthly nurses, tell one lady novelist after another that they 'hail' her productions 'with delight.' We are aware that the ladies at whom our criticism is pointed are accustomed to be told, in the choicest phraseology of puffery, that their pictures of life are brilliant, their characters well drawn, their style fascinating, and their sentiments lofty. But if they are inclined to resent our plainness of speech, we ask them to reflect for a moment on the chary praise, and often captious blame, which their panegyrists give to writers whose works are on the way to become classics. No sooner does a woman show that she has genius or effective talent, than she receives the tribute of being moderately praised and severely criticised. By a peculiar thermometric adjustment, when a woman's talent is at zero, journalistic approbation is at the boiling pitch; when she attains mediocrity, it is already at no more than summer heat; and if ever she reaches excellence, critical enthusiasm drops to the freezing point. Harriet Martineau, Currer Bell, and Mrs. Gaskell have been treated as cavalierly as if they had been men. And every critic who forms a high estimate of the share women may ultimately take in literature, will, on principle, abstain from any exceptional indulgence towards the productions of literary women. For it must be plain to every one

[23] Catherine Sinclair (1800–1864), novelist and philanthropist.
[24] Charles Giles Bridle Daubeny (1795–1867), chemist and naturalist.

who looks impartially and extensively into feminine literature, that its greatest deficiencies are due hardly more to the want of intellectual power than to the want of those moral qualities that contribute to literary excellence—patient diligence, a sense of the responsibility involved in publication, and an appreciation of the sacredness of the writer's art. In the majority of women's books you see that kind of facility which springs from the absence of any high standard; that fertility in imbecile combination or feeble imitation which a little self-criticism would check and reduce to barrenness; just as with a total want of musical ear people will sing out of tune, while a degree more melodic sensibility would suffice to render them silent. The foolish vanity of wishing to appear in print, instead of being counter balanced by any consciousness of the intellectual or moral derogation implied in futile authorship, seems to be encouraged by the extremely false impression that to write *at all* is a proof of superiority in a woman. On this ground, we believe that the average intellect of women is unfairly represented by the mass of feminine literature, and that while the few women who write well are very far above the ordinary intellectual level of their sex, the many women who write ill are very far below it. So that, after all, the severer critics are fulfilling a chivalrous duty in depriving the mere fact of feminine authorship of any false prestige which may give it a delusive attraction, and in recommending women of mediocre faculties—as at least a negative service they can render their sex—to abstain from writing.

The standing apology for women who become writers without any special qualification is, that society shuts them out from other spheres of occupation. Society is a very culpable entity, and has to answer for the manufacture of many unwholesome commodities, from bad pickles to bad poetry. But society, like 'matter,' and Her Majesty's Government, and other lofty abstractions, has its share of excessive blame as well as excessive praise. Where there is one woman who writes from necessity, we believe there are three women who write from vanity; and, besides, there is something so antiseptic in the mere healthy fact of working for one's bread, that the most trashy and rotten kind of feminine literature is not likely to have been produced under such circumstances. 'In all labour there is profit;'[25] but ladies' silly novels, we imagine, are less the result of labour than of busy idleness.

[25] Proverbs 14:23.

Happily, we are not dependent on argument to prove that Fiction is a department of literature in which women can, after their kind, fully equal men. A cluster of great names, both living and dead, rush to our memories in evidence that women can produce novels not only fine, but among the very finest;—novels, too, that have a precious speciality, lying quite apart from masculine aptitudes and experience. No educational restrictions can shut women out from the materials of fiction, and there is no species of art which is so free from rigid requirements. Like crystalline masses, it may take any form, and yet be beautiful; we have only to pour in the right elements—genuine observation, humour, and passion. But it is precisely this absence of rigid requirement which constitutes the fatal seduction of novel-writing to incompetent women. Ladies are not wont to be very grossly deceived as to their power of playing on the piano; here certain positive difficulties of execution have to be conquered, and incompetence inevitably breaks down. Every art which has its absolute *technique* is, to a certain extent, guarded from the intrusions of mere left-handed imbecility. But in novel-writing there are no barriers for incapacity to stumble against, no external criteria to prevent a writer from mistaking foolish facility for mastery. And so we have again and again the old story of La Fontaine's ass, who puts his nose to the flute, and, finding that he elicits some sound, exclaims, 'Moi, aussi, je joue de la flute;'[26]—a fable which we commend, at parting, to the consideration of any feminine reader who is in danger of adding to the number of 'silly novels by lady novelists.'

[26] George Eliot was thoroughly familiar with La Fontaine's fables, and quotes them several times in her writings; but this story is in none of the editions of La Fontaine that I have seen.

22

[THREE NOVELS]

Westminster Review, LXVI (October, 1856), 571–578

The three novels reviewed below are Mrs. Stowe's *Dred: A Tale of the Great Dismal Swamp* (1856); Charles Reade's *It is Never Too Late to Mend: A Matter of Fact Romance* (1856); and *Hertha* (1856), by the Swedish novelist Fredrika Bremer. The 'Belles Lettres' section of which these reviews form a part was finished, according to George Eliot's Journal, on 19 September, and appeared in the same number of the *Westminster* containing her 'Silly Novels by Lady Novelists'.

*   *   *

AT length we have Mrs. Stowe's new novel, and for the last three weeks there have been men, women, and children reading it with rapt attention—laughing and sobbing over it—lingering with delight over its exquisite landscapes,[1] its scenes of humour, and tenderness, and rude heroism—and glowing with indignation at its terrible representation of chartered barbarities. Such a book is an uncontrollable power, and critics who follow it with their objections and reservations—who complain that Mrs. Stowe's plot is defective, that she has repeated herself, that her book is too long and too full of hymns and religious dialogue, and that it creates an unfair bias—are something like men pursuing a prairie fire with desultory watering-cans. In the meantime, 'Dred' will be devoured by the million, who carry no critical talisman against the enchant-

---

[1] Writing to Mrs. Stowe sixteen years later George Eliot remembered that she had 'dwelt on the descriptions in "Dred" with much enjoyment'. (*Letters*, V, 280.)

325

ments of genius. We confess ourselves to be among the million, and quite unfit to rank with the sage minority of Fadladeens.[2] We have been too much moved by 'Dred' to determine with precision how far it is inferior to 'Uncle Tom;' too much impressed by what Mrs. Stowe *has* done to be quite sure that we can tell her what she ought to have done. Our admiration of the book is quite distinct from any opinions or hesitations we may have as to the terribly difficult problems of Slavery and Abolition—problems which belong to quite other than 'polite literature.' Even admitting Mrs. Stowe to be mistaken in her views, and partial or exaggerated in her representations, 'Dred' remains not the less a novel inspired by a rare genius—rare both in intensity and in range of power.

Looking at the matter simply from an artistic point of view, we see no reason to regret that Mrs. Stowe should keep to her original ground of negro and planter life, any more than that Scott should have introduced Highland life into 'Rob Roy' and 'The Fair Maid of Perth,' when he had already written 'Waverley.' Mrs. Stowe has *invented* the Negro novel, and it is a novel not only fresh in its scenery and its manners, but possessing that *conflict of races* which Augustin Thierry has pointed out[3] as the great source of romantic interest—witness 'Ivanhoe.' Inventions in literature are not as plentiful as inventions in the paletôt and waterproof department, and it is rather amusing that we reviewers, who have, for the most part, to read nothing but imitations of imitations, should put on airs of tolerance towards Mrs. Stowe because she has written a second Negro novel, and make excuses for her on the ground that she perhaps would not succeed in any other kind of fiction. Probably she would not; for her genius seems to be of a very special character: her 'Sunny Memories'[4] were as feeble as her novels are powerful. But whatever else she may write, or may not write, 'Uncle Tom' and 'Dred' will assure her a place in that highest rank of novelists who can give us a national life in all its phases—popular and aristocratic, humorous and tragic, political and religious.

[2] Fadladeen, 'Great Nazir or Chamberlain of the Harem' to Aurungzebe in Moore's *Lalla Rookh*, was 'a judge of everything—from the pencillings of a Circassian's eyelids to the deepest questions of science and literature'.

[3] Beginning with his *Histoire de la conquête de l'Angleterre par les Normands* (1825). Thierry's notion of racial conflict was influenced by his reading of *Ivanhoe*. See Emery Neff, *The Poetry of History*, pp. 119–120.

[4] *Sunny Memories of Foreign Lands*, 2 vols., 1854.

But Mrs. Stowe's novels have not only that grand element—conflict of races; they have another element equally grand, which she also shares with Scott, and in which she has, in some respects, surpassed him. This is the exhibition of a people to whom what we may call Hebraic Christianity is still a reality, still an animating belief, and by whom the theocratic conceptions of the Old Testament are literally applied to their daily life. Where has Scott done anything finer than the character of Balfour of Burley, the battles of Drumclog and Bothwell Brigg, and the trial of Ephraim MacBriar?[5] And the character of Dred, the death scenes in the Swamp, and the Camp Meeting of Presbyterians and Methodists, will bear comparison—if we except the fighting—with the best parts of 'Old Mortality'. The strength of Mrs. Stowe's own religious feeling is a great artistic advantage to her here; she never makes you feel that she is coldly calculating an effect, but you see that she is all a-glow for the moment with the wild enthusiasm, the unreasoning faith, and the steady martyr-spirit of Dred, or Tiff, or of Father Dickson. But with this, she has the keen sense of humour which preserves her from extravagance and monotony; and though she paints her religious negroes *en beau*, they are always specifically negroes—she never loses hold of her characters, and lets dramatic dialogue merge into vague oratory. Indeed, here is her strongest point: her dramatic instinct is always awake; and whether it is the grotesque Old Tiff or the aërial Nina, the bluff sophist Father Bonim or the gentlemanly sophist Frank Russell, her characters are always like themselves; a quality which is all the more remarkable in novels animated by a vehement polemical purpose.

The objection which is patent to every one who looks at Mrs. Stowe's novels in an argumentative light, is also, we think, one of their artistic defects; namely, the absence of any proportionate exhibition of the negro character in its less amiable phases. Judging from her pictures, one would conclude that the negro race was vastly superior to the mass of whites, even in other than slave countries—a state of the case which would singularly defeat Mrs. Stowe's sarcasms on the cant of those who call Slavery a 'Christianizing Institution.' If the negroes are really so very good, slavery has answered as moral discipline. But apart from the argumentative suicide involved in this one-sidedness, Mrs. Stowe loses by it the most terribly tragic element in the relation of the two races—the

[5] All from *Old Mortality*.

Nemesis lurking in the vices of the oppressed. She alludes to demoralization among the slaves, but she does not depict it; and yet why should she shrink from this, since she does not shrink from giving us a full-length portrait of a Legree or a Tom Gordon?

It would be idle to tell anything about the story of a work which is, or soon will be, in all our readers' hands; we only render our tribute to it as a great novel, leaving to others the task of weighing it in the political balance.

Close upon 'Dred' we have read Mr. Charles Reade's novel— 'It is Never Too Late to Mend;' also a remarkable fiction, and one that sets vibrating very deep chords in our nature, yet presenting a singular contrast with 'Dred,' both in manner and in the essential qualities it indicates in the writer. Mr. Reade's novel opens with some of the true pathos to be found in English country life: the honest young farmer, George Fielding, unable to struggle against 'bad times' and an exhausted farm, is driven to Australia to seek the fortune that will enable him to marry Susan Merton, the woman he loves. It then carries us, with a certain Robinson, a clever thief, who has been rusticating as George Fielding's lodger, to the gaol, and makes us shudder at the horrors of the separate and silent system, administered by an ignorant and brutal gaoler, while we follow with keen interest the struggle of the heroic chaplain against this stupid iniquity—thus bringing home the tragedy of Birmingham gaol[6] to people whose sympathies are more easily roused by fiction than by bare fact. Then it takes us to Australia, and traces George Fielding's fortunes and misfortunes—first through the vicissitudes of the Australian 'sheep-run', and then through the fierce drama of gold-digging—bringing him home at last with four thousand pounds in his pocket, in time to prevent his Susan from marrying his worst enemy.

In all the three 'acts' of this novel, so to speak, there are fine situations, fine touches of feeling, and much forcible writing; especially while the scene is in the Gaol, the best companion who drops in you will probably regard as a bore, and will become earnest in inviting to remain only when you perceive he is determined to go. Again, honest George Fielding's struggles, renewed

[6] In 1855 William Austin, former governor of Birmingham gaol, was sentenced to three months' imprisonment for cruelties to a 16-year-old prisoner named Edward Andrewes, who had committed suicide in the gaol in 1853 (*Annual Register*).

at the antipodes, and lightened by the friendship of Carlo the dog —of the reformed thief, Robinson—and of the delightful 'Jacky', the Australian native—are a thread of interest which you pursue with eagerness to the *dénouement*. 'Jacky' is a thoroughly fresh character, entirely unlike any other savage *frotté de civilisation*, and drawn with exquisite yet sober humour. In the English scenes every one who has seen anything of life amongst our farmers will recognise many truthful, well-observed touches: the little 'tiff' between the brothers George and William Fielding, old Merton's way of thinking, and many traits of manner in the heroine, Susan Merton. In short, 'It is Never Too Late to Mend' is one of the exceptional novels to be read not merely by the idle and the half-educated, but by the busy and the thoroughly informed.

Nevertheless, Mr. Reade's novel does not rise above the level of cleverness: we feel throughout the presence of remarkable talent, which makes effective use of materials, but nowhere of the genius which absorbs material, and reproduces it as a living whole, in which you do not admire the ingenuity of the workman, but the vital energy of the producer. Doubtless there is a great deal of nonsense talked about genius and inspiration, as if genius did not and must not labour; but, after all, there remains the difference between the writer who thoroughly possesses you by his creation, and the writer who only awakens your curiosity and makes you recognise his ability; and this difference may as well be called 'genius' as anything else. Perhaps a truer statement of the difference is, that the one writer is himself thoroughly possessed by his creation—he lives *in* his characters; while the other remains outside them, and dresses them up. Here lies the fundamental contrast between Mrs. Stowe's novel and Mr. Reade's. Mrs. Stowe seems for the moment to glow with all the passion, to quiver with all the fun, and to be inspired with all the trust that belong to her different characters; she attains her finest dramatic effects by means of her energetic sympathy, and not by conscious artifice. Mr. Reade, on the contrary, seems always self-conscious, always elaborating a character after a certain type, and carrying his elaboration a little too far—always working up to situations, and over-doing them. The habit of writing for the stage misleads him into seeking after those exaggerated contrasts and effects which are accepted as a sort of rapid symbolism by a theatrical audience, but are utterly out of place in a fiction, where the time and means for attaining a result are less limited, and an impression of character or purpose may be given more nearly as it is in real life—by a sum of less concentrated particulars. In Mr. Reade's dialogue we are constantly imagining that we see a theatrical gentleman, well 'made-up,' delivering a repartee in an emphatic voice, with his eye fixed on the pit. To mention one brief example: Hawes, the gaoler, tells Fry, the turnkey, after Mr. Eden's morning sermon on *theft*, that he approves of preaching *at* people. The same day there is an afternoon sermon on *cruelty*; whereupon Hawes remarks again to Fry, 'I'll teach him to preach at people from the pulpit'. 'Well', answers Fry, 'that is what I say, Sir: but you said you liked him to preach at folk?' 'So I do', replied Hawes, angrily, 'but not at me, ye fool!' This would produce a roar on the stage, and would seem a real bit of human nature; but in a novel one has time to be sceptical as to this extreme *naïveté* which allows a man to make palpable epigrams on himself.

In everything, Mr. Reade seems to distrust the effect of moderation and simplicity. His picture of gaol life errs by excess, and he wearies our emotion by taxing it too repeatedly; the admirable inspiration which led him to find his hero and heroine among Berkshire homesteads, is counteracted by such puerile and incongruous efforts at the romantic and diabolical, as the introduction of the Jew, Isaac Levi, who is a mosaic character in more senses than one, and the far-seeing Machiavelianism of the top-booted Mr. Meadows; and even when he is speaking in his own person, he lashes himself into fury at human wrongs, and calls on God and man to witness his indignation, apparently confounding the importance of the effect with the importance of the cause. But the most amazing foible in a writer of so much power as Mr. Reade, is his reliance on the magic of typography. We had imagined that the notion of establishing a relation between magnitude of ideas and magnitude of type was confined to the literature of placards, but we find Mr. Reade endeavouring to impress us with the Titanic character of modern events by suddenly bursting into capitals at the mention of 'THIS GIGANTIC AGE!' It seems ungrateful in us to notice these minor blemishes in a work which has given us so much pleasure, and roused in us so much healthy feeling as 'It is Never Too Late to Mend;' but it is our very admiration of Mr. Reade's talent which makes these blemishes vexatious to us, and which induces us to appeal against their introduction in the many other books we hope to have from his pen.[7]

The appearance of a new novel by Miss Bremer, revives the impressions of ten years ago, when all the novel-reading world was discussing the merits of 'The Neighbours,' 'The President's Daughters,' 'The H——— Family,' and the rest of the 'Swedish novels,' which about that time were creating a strong current in the literary and bookselling world.[8] The discussion soon died out; and perhaps there is hardly another instance of fictions so eagerly read in England which have left so little trace in English literature as Miss Bremer's. No one quotes them, no one alludes to them: and grave people who have entered on their fourth decade, remember their enthusiasm for the Swedish novels among those intellectual 'wild oats' to which their mature wisdom can afford to give a pitying smile. And yet, how is this? For Miss Bremer had not only the advantage of describing manners which were fresh to the English public; she also brought to the description unusual gifts—lively imagination, poetic feeling, wealth of language, a quick eye for details, and considerable humour, of that easy, domestic kind which throws a pleasant light on every-day things. The perusal of 'Hertha' has confirmed in our minds the answer we should have previously given to our own question. One reason, we think, why Miss Bremer's novels have not kept a high position among us is, that her luxuriant faculties are all overrun by a rank growth of sentimentality, which, like some faint-smelling creeper on the boughs of an American forest, oppresses us with the sense that the air is unhealthy. Nothing can be more curious than the combination in her novels of the vapourishly affected and unreal with the most solid Dutch sort of realism. In one page we have

[7] Less than two years later George Eliot's tone towards Reade expresses more than vexation. She described his *White Lies* (1857) as 'the inflated plagiarisms of a man gone mad with restless vanity and unveracity'. (*Letters*, II, 422.)

[8] Mary Howitt began the translation of Miss Bremer's works in 1843: 'In England and America they immediately met with wide recognition. . . . Such became the rage for them, that our translations were seized by a publisher, altered, and reissued as new ones'. (Mary Howitt, *Auto-biography* [Boston, 1889], II, 23.) George Eliot had read the Swedish novels by 1847 (see *Letters*, I, 240). During the early days of her residence at John Chapman's establishment in London she met Miss Bremer and found her at first a 'repulsive person' but later began to 'repent of my repugnance'. (*Letters*, I, 366; 377.)

copious sausage sandwiches and beer posset, and on another
rhapsodies or wildly improbable incidents that seem rather to
belong to sylphs and salamanders, than to a race of creatures who
are nourished by the very excellent provisions just mentioned.
Another reason why Miss Bremer's novels are not likely to take
rank among the permanent creations of art, is the too confident
tone of the religious philosophy which runs through them. When
a novelist is quite sure that she has a theory which suffices to
illustrate all the difficulties of our earthly existence, her novels are
too likely to illustrate little else than her own theory.

These two characteristics of sentimentality and dogmatic confidence are very strongly marked in 'Hertha', while it has less of the
attention to detail, less of the humorous realism, which was the
ballast of Miss Bremer's earlier novels. It has been written not
simply from an artistic impulse, but with the object of advocating
the liberation of woman from those legal and educational restrictions which limit her opportunities of a position and a sphere of
usefulness to the chance of matrimony; and we think there are few
well-judging persons who will not admire the generous energy
with which Miss Bremer, having long ago won fame and independence for herself, devotes the activity of her latter years to the
cause of women who are less capable of mastering circumstance.
Many wise and noble things she says in 'Hertha,' but we cannot
help regretting that she has not presented her views on a difficult
and practical question in the 'light of common day,'[9] rather than
in the pink haze of visions and romance. The story is very briefly
this:

Hertha, who has lost her mother in childhood, is, at the age of
seven-and-twenty, becoming more and more embittered by her
inactive bondage to a narrow-minded, avaricious father, who
demands obedience to the pettiest exactions. Her elder sister, Alma,
is slowly dying in consequence of the same tyranny, which has
prevented her from marrying the man she loves. We meet our
heroine, with her gloomy and bitter expression of face, first of all,
at the rehearsal of a fancy ball, which is to take place in a few days
in the good town of Kungsköping; and after being introduced to
the various *dramatis personæ*—among the rest, to a young man
named Yngve Nordin, who interests Hertha by his agreement in
her opinions about women, we accompany her to her cheerless

[9] Wordsworth, 'Ode, Intimations of Immortality', 76.

home, where she is roughly chid by her father, the rigid old Director, for being later than the regulation-hour of eight; and where, by the bedside of her sister Alma, she pours out all the bitterness of her soul, all her hatred and smothered rebellion towards her father for his injustice towards them. She and Alma have inherited a share in their mother's fortune, but according to the Swedish law they are still minors, and unable to claim their property. This very night, however, a fire breaks out, and lays waste a large district of the town. The Director's house is consumed, and he himself is only saved by the heroic exertions of Hertha, who rushes to his room, and carries his meagre, feeble body through the flames. This act of piety, and the death of Alma, who, in her last moments, extracts from her father a promise to give Hertha independence, win some ungracious concessions from the crabbed Director towards his daughter. He still withholds her property and a declaration of her majority; but she has power in the household, and greater freedom of action out of doors. A Ladies' Society has been organized for relieving the sufferers from the fire, and Hertha is one of those whose department is the care of the sick and wounded. The patient who falls to her share is no other than Yngve Nordin, who has been severely hurt in his benevolent efforts on the fatal night, and is now lodged in the house of the good pastor, who is at the head of the 'Society.' Here is an excellent opportunity for discovering that Yngve is just the friend she needs to soothe and invigorate her mind, by his sympathy and riper experience; and the feeling which is at first called friendship, is at last confessed to be love. After certain jealousies and suspicions, which are satisfactorily cleared up, Yngve asks the Director for Hertha's hand, but is only accepted prospectively, on condition of his attaining an assured position. Yngve goes abroad, and for seven years Hertha submits to the procrastination of her marriage, rather than rebel against her father in his last years. It is only when Yngve is hopelessly ill that she sacrifices her scruples and marries him. In the mean time she has made her seven years of separation rich in active usefulness, by founding and superintending two schools—one in which girls are instructed in the ordinary elements of education, forming a sort of nursery-garden for the other, in which voluntary pupils are to be led to a higher order of thought and purpose by Hertha's readings, conversation, and personal influence. Her schools are successful; but after

333

Yngve's death she begins to sink under her long trial, and follows him rapidly to the grave.

This bare outline of the story can only suggest and not fully explain the grounds of our objection to 'Hertha.' Our objection is, that it surrounds questions, which can only be satisfactorily solved by the application of very definite ideas to specific facts, with a cloudy kind of eloquence and flighty romance. Take, for example, the question whether it will not be well for women to study and practise medicine. It can only tend to retard the admission that women may pursue such a career with success, for a distinguished authoress to imply that they may be suitably prepared for effective activity by lectures on such a very nebulous thesis as this—'The consciousness of thought ought to be a living observation and will,' or to associate the attendance of women by the sick bed, not with the hard drudgery of real practice, but with the vicissitudes of a love-story. Women have not to prove that they can be emotional, and rhapsodic, and spiritualistic; every one believes that already. They have to prove that they are capable of accurate thought, severe study, and continuous self-command. But we say all this with reluctance, and should prefer noticing the many just and pathetic observations that Miss Bremer puts into the mouth of her heroine. We can only mention, and have not space to quote, a passage where Hertha complains of the ignorance in which women are left of Natural Science. 'In my youth,' she concludes, 'I used to look at the rocks, the trees, the grass, and all objects of nature, with unspeakable longing, wishing to know something about their kinds, their life, and their purpose. But the want of knowledge, the want of opportunity to acquire it, has caused nature to be to me a sealed book, and still to this moment it is to me a tantalizing, enticing, and ever-retreating wave, rather than a life-giving fountain which I can enjoy, and enjoying, thank the Creator.'

23

WORLDLINESS AND OTHER-WORLDLINESS: THE POET YOUNG

Westminster Review, LXVII (January, 1857), 1-42

George Eliot's attack on Young in 'Worldliness and Other-Worldliness' may be regarded as an episode in the long history of the nineteenth century's revolt from the eighteenth. The *Night Thoughts*, a poem that Boswell thought 'a mass of the grandest and richest poetry that human genius has ever produced',[1] and large parts of which Burke is said to have memorized, appeared to George Eliot as vicious rhetoric inculcating a low morality. Her criticism was accepted by her contemporaries, for, according to J. W. Mackail, the 'able and acrid' essay on Young 'dealt what for the time was a fatal blow to his reputation'.[2]

The history of 'Worldliness and Other-Worldliness' goes back to some point before 5 April 1856, when George Eliot noted in her Journal that Chapman 'accepted my proposition to write an article on Young'. She began it on 22 April, but laid it aside to write her article on 'The Natural History of German Life', published in the *Westminster* for July, 1856. On 5 July she wrote to Chapman proposing to finish the article on Young if he still wanted it: 'I didn't think well of what I had written,' she added, 'and so was going to give it up, but when I read it to Mr. Lewes he said he thought it would be the best article I had written.'[3] In the same letter, however, she suggested an idea for an article which resulted in her 'Silly Novels', the writing of which once again deferred the completion of her article on Young. After 'Silly Novels', she turned to her long-meditated project of writing a story, and on 5 November finished 'The Sad Fortunes of the Reverend Amos Barton'. When this

[1] *Life of Johnson*, ed. Hill and Powell, IV, 60 (1781).
[2] *Studies of English Poets* (New York, 1926), pp. 115–116.
[3] *Letters*, II, 258.

was done, she went back to 'Worldliness and Other-Worldliness', which was finally completed, according to her Journal, on 4 December 1856. It was the last of her essays to appear in the *Westminster*.

As its history suggests, the article was a difficult one for George Eliot to write; the reason is found, perhaps, in her confession that her mature judgment of Young is 'entirely opposed to our youthful predilections and enthusiasm'. Her general reluctance to condemn was compounded in this instance by her consciousness of early admiration, for she never liked attacking an object that had once been able to arouse strong and genuine feeling. But it was, ironically, her very respect for the integrity of personal feeling that inspired her criticism of Young: the principle of truth to feeling, an idea of central importance in the ethics and art of George Eliot, is the basis of her argument. As Humphry House has perceptively observed, she brings to the judgment of Young an implicitly Wordsworthian standard: 'She focuses on Young's neglect of the true qualities of objects described or the emotion expressed; on his lack of allusions that carry us "to the lanes, woods, or fields"; and above all on the fact that he is not "true to his own sensibilities or inward vision".'[4]

The sources that George Eliot acknowledged in the list of titles prefixed to the review are *The Works of the Author of the Night Thoughts. Corrected by Himself*, 5 vols., 1767; Johnson's *Lives of the Poets*, ed. Peter Cunningham, 3 vols., 1854; the memoir of Young in *Night Thoughts . . . with a Life of the Author by J[ohn] D[oran]*, 1853; a letter on Young in the *Gentleman's Magazine*, LII (1782); volume I of John Nichols, *Literary Anecdotes of the Eighteenth Century*, 9 vols., 1812–1816; and Joseph Spence, *Anecdotes*, ed. S. W. Singer, 1820. The Cunningham and Doran volumes furnish the slight contemporary occasion for the review.

'Worldliness and Other-Worldliness' has been reprinted in Nathan Sheppard, *The Essays of 'George Eliot', Complete*; and in *Essays and Leaves from a Note-Book*.

*   *   *

THE study of men, as they have appeared in different ages, and under various social conditions, may be considered as the natural history of the race. Let us, then, for a moment imagine ourselves, as students of this natural history, 'dredging' the first half of the eighteenth century in search of specimens. About the year 1730, we have hauled up a remarkable individual of the species *divine—* a surprising name, considering the nature of the animal before us, but we are used to unsuitable names in natural history. Let us

[4] *All in Due Time* (London, 1955), p. 111.

examine this individual at our leisure. He is on the verge of fifty, and has recently undergone his metamorphosis into the clerical form. Rather a paradoxical specimen, if you observe him narrowly: a sort of cross between a sycophant and a psalmist; a poet whose imagination is alternately fired by the 'Last Day' and by a creation of peers, who fluctuates between rhapsodic applause of King George and rhapsodic applause of Jehovah. After spending 'a foolish youth, the sport of peers and poets,'[5] after being a hanger-on of the profligate Duke of Wharton, after aiming in vain at a parliamentary career, and angling for pensions and preferment with fulsome dedications and fustian odes, he is a little disgusted with his imperfect success, and has determined to retire from the general mendicancy business to a particular branch; in other words, he has determined on that renunciation of the world implied in 'taking orders', with the prospect of a good living and an advantageous matrimonial connexion. [And no man can be better fitted for an Established Church. He personifies completely her nice balance of temporalities and spiritualities.][6] He is equally impressed with the momentousness of death and of burial fees; he languishes at once for immortal life and for 'livings'; he has a fervid attachment to patrons in general, but on the whole prefers the Almighty. He will teach, with something more than official conviction, the nothingness of earthly things; and he will feel something more than private disgust if his meritorious efforts in directing men's attention to another world are not rewarded by substantial preferment in this. His secular man believes in cambric bands and silk stockings as characteristic attire for 'an ornament of religion and virtue;'[7] hopes courtiers will never forget to copy Sir Robert Walpole; and writes begging-letters to the King's mistress. His spiritual man recognises no motives more familiar than Golgotha and 'the skies;' it walks in graveyards, or it soars among the stars. His religion exhausts itself in ejaculations and rebukes, and knows no medium between the ecstatic and the sententious. If it were not for the prospect of immortality, he considers, it would be wise and agreeable to be indecent, or to

---

[5] Pope, quoted in Ruffhead's *Life*. George Eliot would have found it in the life of Young contributed by Herbert Croft to Johnson's *Lives of the Poets*, ed. Peter Cunningham, III, 310 (cited hereafter as 'Cunningham').

[6] Omitted, 1884.

[7] Cunningham, III, 310: 'the ornament to religion and morality. . . .'

murder one's father; and, heaven apart, it would be extremely irrational in any man not to be a knave. Man, he thinks, is a compound of the angel and the brute: the brute is to be humbled by being reminded of its 'relation to the stalls,' and frightened into moderation by the contemplation of death-beds and skulls; the angel is to be developed by vituperating this world and exalting the next; and by this double process you get the Christian—'the highest style of man.' With all this, our new-made divine is an unmistakeable poet. To a clay compounded chiefly of the worldling and the rhetorician, there is added a real spark of Promethean fire. He will one day clothe his apostrophes and objurgations, his astronomical religion and his charnel-house morality, in lasting verse, which will stand, like a Juggernaut made of gold and jewels, at once magnificent and repulsive: for this divine is Edward Young, the future author of the 'Night Thoughts'.

[It would be extremely ill-bred in us to suppose that our readers are not acquainted with the facts of Young's life; they are amongst the things that 'every one knows;' but we have observed that, with regard to these universally-known matters, the majority of readers like to be treated after the plan suggested by Monsieur Jourdain. When that distinguished *bourgeois* was asked if he knew Latin, he replied, 'Oui, mais faîtes comme si je ne le savais pas'.[8] Assuming, then, as a polite writer should, that our readers know everything about Young, it will be a direct *sequitur* from that assumption that we should proceed as if they knew nothing, and recal the incidents of his biography with as much particularity as we may, without trenching on the space we shall need for our main purpose—the reconsideration of his character as a moral and religious poet.][9]

Judging from Young's works, one might imagine that the preacher had been organized in him by hereditary transmission through a long line of clerical forefathers,—that the diamonds of the 'Night Thoughts' had been slowly condensed from the charcoal of ancestral sermons. Yet it was not so. His grandfather, apparently, wrote himself *gentleman*, not *clerk*; and there is no evidence that preaching had run in the family blood before it took that turn in the person of the poet's father, who was quadruply clerical, being at once rector, prebendary, court chaplain, and dean. Young was

[8] Molière, *Le Bourgeois Gentilhomme*, II, iv.
[9] Omitted, 1884.

born at his father's rectory of Upham, in 1681.[10] [We may confidently assume that even the author of the 'Night Thoughts' came
into the world without a wig, but, apart from Dr. Doran's authority,
we should not have ventured to state that the excellent rector 'kissed,
with dignified emotion, his only son and intended namesake.'[11] Dr.
Doran doubtless knows this, from his intimate acquaintance with
clerical physiology and psychology. He has ascertained that the
paternal emotions of prebendaries have a sacerdotal quality, and
that the very chyme and chyle of a rector are conscious of the gown
and band.][12]

In due time the boy went to Winchester College, and subsequently, though not till he was twenty-two, to Oxford, where, for
his father's sake, he was befriended by the wardens of two colleges,
and in 1708, three years after his father's death, nominated by
Archbishop Tenison to a law fellowship at All Souls. Of Young's
life at Oxford in these years, hardly anything is known. His
biographer, Croft, has nothing to tell us but the vague report that,
when 'Young found himself independent and his own master at
All Souls, he was not the ornament to religion and morality that he
afterwards became,'[13] and the perhaps apocryphal anecdote, that
Tindal, the atheist, confessed himself embarrassed by the originality of Young's arguments. Both the report and the anecdote,
however, are borne out by indirect evidence. As to the latter,
Young has left us sufficient proof that he was fond of arguing on
the theological side, and that he had his own way of treating old
subjects. As to the former, we learn that Pope, after saying other
things which we know to be true of Young, added, that he passed
'a foolish youth, the sport of peers and poets;' and, from all the
indications we possess of his career till he was nearly fifty, we are
inclined to think that Pope's statement only errs by defect, and
that he should rather have said, 'a foolish youth and *middle age*.'
It is not likely that Young was a very hard student, for he impressed
Johnson, who saw him in his old age, as 'not a great scholar,' and

[10] I.e., 1683. This error in Croft was not corrected until Leslie Stephen's
life of Young in the *DNB*. All of George Eliot's subsequent statements of
Young's age should be adjusted for this mistake.
[11] John Doran, *The Life of Edward Young, LL.D.*, in *The Complete
Works . . . of the Rev. Edward Young*, 2 vols. (London, 1854), I, xiii.
George Eliot's italics.
[12] Omitted, 1884.
[13] See above, note 7.

as surprisingly ignorant of what Johnson thought 'quite common maxims' in literature;[14] and there is no evidence that he filled either his leisure or his purse by taking pupils. His career as an author did not commence till he was nearly thirty, even dating from the publication of a portion of the 'Last Day,' in the *Tatler*; so that he could hardly have been absorbed in composition. But where the fully developed insect is parasitic, we believe the larva is usually parasitic also, and we shall probably not be far wrong in supposing that Young at Oxford, as elsewhere, spent a good deal of his time in hanging about possible and actual patrons, and accommodating himself to their habits with considerable flexibility of conscience and of tongue; being none the less ready, upon occasion, to present himself as the champion of theology, and to rhapsodize at convenient moments in the company of the skies or of skulls. That brilliant profligate, the Duke of Wharton, to whom Young afterwards clung as his chief patron, was at this time a mere boy; and, though it is probable that their intimacy had [commenced,][15] since the Duke's father and mother were friends of the old Dean, that intimacy ought not to aggravate any unfavourable inference as to Young's Oxford life. It is less likely that he fell into any exceptional vice, than that he differed from the men around him chiefly in his episodes of theological advocacy and rhapsodic solemnity. He probably sowed his wild oats after the coarse fashion of his times, for he has left us sufficient evidence that his moral sense was not delicate; but his companions, who were occupied in sowing their own oats, perhaps took it as a matter of course that he should be a rake, and were only struck with the exceptional circumstance that he was a pious and moralizing rake.

There is some irony in the fact that the two first poetical productions of Young, published in the same year, were his 'Epistle to Lord Lansdowne,' celebrating the recent creation of peers—Lord Lansdowne's creation in particular; and the 'Last Day.' Other poets, besides Young, found the device for obtaining a Tory majority by turning twelve insignificant commoners into insignificant lords, an irresistible stimulus to verse; but no other poet showed so versatile an enthusiasm—so nearly equal an ardour for the honour of the new baron and the honour of the Deity. But the

[14] Boswell, *Journal of a Tour to the Hebrides*, under date of 30 September.

[15] 'already begun', 1884.

twofold nature of the sycophant and the psalmist is not more strikingly shown in the contrasted themes of the two poems, than in the transitions from bombast about monarchs, to bombast about the resurrection, in the 'Last Day' itself. The dedication of this poem to Queen Anne, Young afterwards suppressed, for he was always ashamed of having flattered a dead patron. In this dedication, Croft tells us, 'he gives her Majesty praise indeed for her victories, but says that the author is more pleased to see her rise from this lower world, soaring above the clouds, passing the first and second heavens, and leaving the fixed stars behind her; nor will he lose her there, he says, but keep her still in view through the boundless spaces on the other side of creation, in her journey towards eternal bliss, till he behold the heaven of heavens open, and angels receiving and conveying her still onward from the stretch of his imagination, which tires in her pursuit, and falls back again to earth'.[16]

The self-criticism which prompted the suppression of the dedication, did not, however, lead him to improve either the rhyme or the reason of the unfortunate couplet—

> When other Bourbons reign in other lands,
> And, if men's sins forbid not, other Annes.

In the 'Epistle to Lord Lansdowne,' Young indicates his taste for the drama; and there is evidence that his tragedy of 'Busiris' was 'in the theatre' as early as this very year, 1713, though it was not brought on the stage till nearly six years later; so that Young was now very decidedly bent on authorship, for which his degree of B.C.L., taken in this year, was doubtless a magical equipment. Another poem, 'The Force of Religion; or, Vanquished Love,' founded on the execution of Lady Jane Grey and her husband, quickly followed, showing fertility in feeble and tasteless verse; and on the Queen's death, in 1714, Young lost no time in making a poetical lament for a departed patron a vehicle for extravagant laudation of the new monarch. No further literary production of his appeared until 1716, when a Latin oration which he delivered on the foundation of the Codrington Library at All Souls, gave him a new opportunity for displaying his alacrity in inflated panegyric.

In 1717 it is probable that Young accompanied the Duke of Wharton to Ireland, though so slender are the materials for his

---

[16] Cunningham, III, 314.

biography, that the chief basis for this supposition is a passage in his 'Conjectures on Original Composition', written when he was nearly eighty, in which he intimates that he had once been in that country. But there are many facts surviving to indicate that for the next eight or nine years, Young was a sort of *attaché* of Wharton's. In 1719, according to legal records, the Duke granted him an annuity, in consideration of his having relinquished the office of tutor to Lord Burleigh, with a life annuity of £100 a year, on his Grace's assurances that he would provide for him in a much more ample manner. And again, from the same evidence, it appears that in 1721 Young received from Wharton a bond for 600*l.*, in compensation of expenses incurred in standing for Parliament at the Duke's desire, and as an earnest of greater services which his Grace had promised him on his refraining from the spiritual and temporal advantages of taking orders, with a certainty of two livings in the gift of his college. It is clear, therefore, that lay advancement, as long as there was any chance of it, had more attractions for Young than clerical preferment; and that at this time he accepted the Duke of Wharton as the pilot of his career.

A more creditable relation of Young's was his friendship with Tickell, with whom he was in the habit of interchanging criticisms, and to whom in 1719—the same year, let us note, in which he took his doctor's degree—he addressed his 'Lines on the Death of Addison.' Close upon these followed his 'Paraphrase of Part of the Book of Job,' with a dedication to Parker, recently made Lord Chancellor, showing that the possession of Wharton's patronage did not prevent Young from fishing in other waters. He knew nothing of Parker, but that did not prevent him from magnifying the new Chancellor's merits; on the other hand, he *did* know Wharton, but this again did not prevent him from prefixing to his tragedy, 'The Revenge,' which appeared in 1721, a dedication attributing to the Duke all virtues, as well as all accomplishments. In the concluding sentence of this dedication, Young naïvely indicates that a considerable ingredient in his gratitude was a lively sense of anticipated favours. 'My present fortune is his bounty, and my future his care; which I will venture to say will always be remembered to his honour; since he, I know, intended his generosity as an encouragement to merit, though through his very pardonable partiality to one who bears him so sincere a duty and respect, I happen to receive the benefit of it.' Young was

conomical with his ideas and images; he was rarely satisfied with
sing a clever thing once, and this bit of ingenious humility was
fterwards made to do duty in the 'Instalment,' a poem addressed
o Walpole:

> Be this thy partial smile, from censure free,
> 'Twas meant for merit, though it fell on me.

It was probably 'The Revenge,' that Young was writing when,
s we learn from Spence's anecdotes, the Duke of Wharton gave
im a skull with a candle fixed in it, as the most appropriate lamp
y which to write tragedy. According to Young's dedication, the
Duke was 'accessory' to the scenes of this tragedy in a more
mportant way, 'not only by suggesting the most beautiful incident
n them, but by making all possible provision for the success of
he whole.' A statement which is credible, not indeed on the ground
f Young's dedicatory assertion, but from the known ability of the
Duke, who, as Pope tells us, possessed

> each gift of Nature and of Art,
> And wanted nothing but an honest heart.[17]

The year 1722 seems to have been the period of a visit to Mr.
Dodington, at Eastbury, in Dorsetshire—the 'pure Dorsetian
downs,'[18] celebrated by Thomson,—in which Young made the
acquaintance of Voltaire; for in the subsequent dedication of his
'Sea Piece' to 'Mr. Voltaire,' he recals their meeting on 'Dorset
Downs;' and it was in this year that Christopher Pitt, a gentleman-
poet of those days, addressed an 'Epistle to Dr. Edward Young, at
Eastbury, in Dorsetshire,' which has at least the merit of this
biographical couplet—

> While with your Dodington retired you sit,
> Charm'd with his flowing Burgundy and wit.

Dodington, apparently, was charmed in his turn, for he told Dr.
Wharton that Young was 'far superior to the French poet in the
variety and novelty of his *bon-mots* and repartees.'[19] Unfortunately,
the only specimen of Young's wit on this occasion that has been
preserved to us, is the epigram represented as an extempore retort

[17] 'Epistle to Cobham', 192–193, slightly misquoted.
[18] 'Autumn', 657.
[19] Doran's *Life*, xxxiii.

343

(spoken aside, surely) to Voltaire's criticism of Milton's episode of
Sin and Death:

> Thou art so witty, profligate, and thin,
> At once we think thee Milton, Death, and Sin;—[20]

an epigram which, in the absence of 'flowing Burgundy,' does not
strike us as remarkably brilliant. Let us give Young the benefit of
the doubt thrown on the genuineness of this epigram by his own
poetical dedication, in which he represents himself as having
'soothed' Voltaire's 'rage' against Milton 'with gentle rhymes;'
though in other respects that dedication is anything but favourable
to a high estimate of Young's wit. Other evidence apart, we should
not be eager for the after-dinner conversation of the man who wrote,

> Thine is the Drama, how renown'd!
> Thine Epic's loftier trump to sound;—
> *But let Arion's sea-strung harp be mine:*
> *But where's his dolphin? Know'st thou where?*
> *May that be found in thee, Voltaire!*

The 'Satires' appeared in 1725 and 1726,[21] each, of course, with
its laudatory dedication and its compliments insinuated amongst
the rhymes. The seventh and last is dedicated to Sir Robert
Walpole, is very short, and contains nothing in particular except
lunatic flattery of George the First and his prime minister, attributing that [royal hog's][22] late escape from a storm at sea to the
miraculous influence of his grand and virtuous soul—for George,
he says, rivals the angels:

> George, who in foes can soft affections raise,
> And charm envenom'd satire into praise.
> Nor human rage alone his pow'r perceives,
> But the mad winds and the tumultuous waves.
> Ev'n storms (Death's fiercest ministers!) forbear,
> And in their own wild empire learn to spare.
> Thus, Nature's self, supporting Man's decree,
> Styles Britain's sovereign, sovereign of the sea.

As for Walpole, what *he* felt at this tremendous crisis

> No powers of language, but his own, can tell,—
> His own, which Nature and the Graces form,
> At will, to raise, or hush, the civil storm.

[20] Cunningham, III, 328.   [21] I.e., 1725-1728.
[22] 'monarch's', 1884.

It is a coincidence worth noticing,[23] that this seventh Satire was published in 1726, and that the warrant of George the First, granting Young a pension of 200l. a year from Lady-day, 1725, is dated May 3rd, 1726. The gratitude exhibited in this Satire may have been chiefly prospective, but the 'Instalment,' a poem inspired by the thrilling event of Walpole's installation as Knight of the Garter, was clearly written with the double ardour of a man who has got a pension, and hopes for something more. His emotion about Walpole is precisely at the same pitch as his subsequent emotion about the Second Advent. In the 'Instalment' he says,

> With invocations some their hearts inflame;
> *I need no muse, a Walpole is my theme.*

And of God coming to judgment, he says, in the 'Night Thoughts:

> I find my inspiration is my theme;
> *The grandeur of my subject is my muse.*

Nothing can be feebler than this 'Instalment,' except in the strength of impudence with which the writer professes to scorn the prostitution of fair fame, the 'profanation of celestial fire.'

Herbert Croft tells us that Young made more than three thousand pounds by his 'Satires,'—a surprising statement, taken in connexion with the reasonable doubt he throws on the story related in Spence's 'Anecdotes,' that the Duke of Wharton gave Young 2000l. for this work. Young, however, seems to have been tolerably fortunate in the pecuniary results of his publications; and with his literary profits, his annuity from Wharton, his fellowship, and his pension, not to mention other bounties which may be inferred from the high merits he discovers in many men of wealth and position, we may fairly suppose that he now laid the foundation of the considerable fortune he left at his death.

It is probable that the Duke of Wharton's final departure for the Continent and disgrace at Court in 1726, and the consequent cessation of Young's reliance on his patronage, tended not only to heighten the temperature of his poetical enthusiasm for Sir Robert Walpole, but also to turn his thoughts towards the Church again, as the second-best means of rising in the world. On the accession of George the Second, Young found the same transcendent merits

[23] A coincidence of George Eliot's manufacture, brought about by her misdating of the Seventh Satire in 1726, though Croft (Cunningham, III, 321) gives the date correctly.

in him as in his predecessor, and celebrated them in a style of poetry previously unattempted by him—the Pindaric ode, a poetic form which helped him to surpass himself in furious bombast. 'Ocean, an Ode: concluding with a Wish,' was the title of this piece. He afterwards pruned it, and cut off, amongst other things the concluding Wish, expressing the yearning for humble retirement, which, of course, had prompted him to the effusion; but we may judge of the rejected stanzas by the quality of those he has allowed to remain. For example, calling on Britain's dead mariners to rise and meet their 'country's full-blown glory' in the person of the new King, he says,

> What powerful charm
> Can Death disarm?
> Your long, your iron slumbers break?
> *By Jove, by Fame,*
> *By George's name*
> Awake! awake! awake! awake!

Soon after this notable production, which was written with the ripe folly of forty-seven, Young took orders, and was presently appointed chaplain to the King. 'The Brothers,' his third and last tragedy, which was already in rehearsal, he now withdrew from the stage, and sought reputation in a way more accordant with the decorum of his new profession, by turning prose writer. But after publishing 'A True Estimate of Human Life,' with a dedication to the Queen, as one of the 'most shining representatives' of God on earth, and a sermon, entitled 'An Apology for Princes; or, the Reverence due to Government', preached before the House of Commons, his Pindaric ambition again seized him, and he matched his former ode by another, called 'Imperium Pelagi; a Naval Lyric, written in Imitation of Pindar's spirit, occasioned by his Majesty's Return from Hanover, 1729, and the succeeding Peace.' Since he afterwards suppressed this second ode, we must suppose that it was rather worse than the first. Next came his two 'Epistles to Pope, concerning the Authors of the Age,' remarkable for nothing but the audacity of affectation with which the most servile of poets professes to despise servility.

In 1730 Young was presented by his college with the rectory of Welwyn, in Hertfordshire, and, in the following year, when he was just fifty, he married Lady Elizabeth Lee, a widow with two children, who seems to have been in favour with Queen Caroline, and who probably had an income—two attractions which doubtless enhanced the power of her other charms. Pastoral duties and domesticity probably cured Young of some bad habits; but, unhappily, they did not cure him either of flattery or of fustian. Three more odes followed, quite as bad as those of his bachelorhood, except that in the third he announced the wise resolution of never writing another. It must have been about this time, since Young was now 'turned of fifty,' that he wrote the letter to Mrs. Howard (afterwards Lady Suffolk), George the Second's mistress, which proves that he used other engines, besides [Pindaric ones,][24] in 'besieging Court favour'. The letter is too characteristic to be omitted:

Monday Morning.

Madam,—I know his majesty's goodness to his servants, and his love of justice in general, so well, that I am confident, if his Majesty knew my case, I should not have any cause to despair of his gracious favour to me.

Abilities.	Want.	
Good Manners.	Sufferings	⎫
Service.	and	⎬ for his
Age.	Zeal	⎭ majesty.

These, madam, are the proper points of consideration in the person that humbly hopes his majesty's favour.

As to *Abilities*, all I can presume to say is, I have done the best I could to improve them.

As to *Good manners*, I desire no favour, if any just objection lies against them.

As for *Service*, I have been near seven years in his majesty's, and never omitted any duty in it, which few can say.

As for *Age*, I am turned of fifty.

As for *Want*, I have no manner of preferment.

As for *Sufferings*, I have lost 300£. per ann. by being in his majesty's service; as I have shown in a *Representation* which his majesty has been so good as to read and consider.

As for *Zeal*, I have written nothing without showing my duty to their majesties, and some pieces are dedicated to them.

This, madam, is the short and true state of my case. They that make their court to the ministers, and not their majesties, succeed

[24] 'the Pindaric', 1884.

better. If my case deserves some consideration, and you can serve me in it, I humbly hope and believe you will: I shall, therefore, trouble you no farther; but beg leave to subscribe myself, with truest respect and gratitude,

Yours, &c.,

EDWARD YOUNG.

P.S. I have some hope that my Lord Townshend is my friend; if therefore soon, and before he leaves the court, you had an opportunity of mentioning me, with that favour you have been so good to show, I think it would not fail of success; and, if not, I shall owe you more than any.—*Suffolk Letters*, vol. i. p. 285.[25]

Young's wife died in 1741, leaving him one son, born in 1733. That he had attached himself strongly to her two daughters by her former marriage, there is better evidence in the report, mentioned by Mrs. Montagu,[26] of his practical kindness and liberality to the younger, than in his lamentations over the elder as the 'Narcissa' of the 'Night Thoughts.' 'Narcissa' had died in 1735, shortly after marriage to Mr. Temple, the son of Lord Palmerston; and Mr. Temple himself, after a second marriage, died in 1740, a year before Lady Elizabeth Young. These, then, are the three deaths supposed to have inspired 'The Complaint,' which forms the three first books of the 'Night Thoughts':

> Insatiate archer, could not one suffice?
> Thy shaft flew thrice; and thrice my peace was slain;
> And thrice, ere thrice yon moon had fill'd her horn.

Since we find Young departing from the truth of dates, in order to heighten the effect of his calamity, or at least of his climax, we need not be surprised that he allowed his imagination great freedom in other matters besides chronology, and that the character of 'Philander' can, by no process, be made to fit Mr. Temple. The supposition that the much-lectured 'Lorenzo' of the 'Night Thoughts' was Young's own son, is hardly rendered more absurd by the fact that the poem was written when that son was a boy, than by the obvious artificiality of the characters Young introduces as targets for his arguments and rebukes. Among all the trivial efforts of conjectural criticism, there can hardly be one more futile than the attempt to discover the original of those pitiable lay-figures, the 'Lorenzoes' and 'Altamonts' of Young's didactic prose

[25] Quoted from Cunningham, III, 323, note.
[26] In a letter printed by Cunningham, III, 346, note.

and poetry. His muse never stood face to face with a genuine, living human being; she would have been as much startled by such an encounter as a [necromancer][27] whose incantations and blue fire had actually conjured up a demon.

The 'Night Thoughts' appeared between 1741 and 1745.[28] Although he declares in them that he has chosen God for his 'patron' henceforth, this is not at all to the prejudice of some half-dozen lords, duchesses, and right honourables, who have the privilege of sharing finely-turned compliments with their co-patron. The line which closed the Second Night in the earlier editions,

> Wits spare not Heaven, O Wilmington!—nor thee—

is an intense specimen of that perilous juxta-position of ideas by which Young, in his incessant search after point and novelty, unconsciously converts his compliments into sarcasms; and his apostrophe to the moon as more likely to be favourable to his song if he calls her 'fair Portland of the skies', is worthy even of his Pindaric ravings. His ostentatious renunciation of worldly schemes, and especially of his twenty-years' siege of Court favour, are in the tone of one who retains some hope, in the midst of his querulousness.

He descended from the astronomical rhapsodies of his Ninth Night, published in 1745, to more terrestrial strains in his 'Reflections on the Public Situation of the Kingdom', dedicated to the Duke of Newcastle; but in this critical year we get a glimpse of him through a more prosaic and less refracting medium. He spent a part of the year at Tunbridge Wells; and Mrs. Montagu, who was there too, gives a very lively picture of the 'divine Doctor' in her letters to the Duchess of Portland, on whom Young had bestowed the superlative bombast to which we have recently alluded. We shall borrow the quotations from Dr. Doran, in spite of their length, because, to our mind, they present the most agreeable portrait we possess of Young:

'I have great joy in Dr. Young, whom I disturbed in a reverie. At first he started, then bowed, then fell back into a surprise; then began a speech, relapsed into his astonishment two or three times, forgot what he had been saying; began a new subject, and so went on. I told him your grace desired he would write longer letters; to which he cried "Ha"! most emphatically, and I leave you to interpret what it

[27] 'stage necromancer', 1884.   [28] I.e., 1742–1746.

349

meant. He has made a friendship with one person here, whom I believe you would not imagine to have been made for his bosom friend. You would, perhaps, suppose it was a bishop or dean, a prebend, a pious preacher, a clergyman of exemplary life, or, if a layman, of most virtuous conversation, one that had paraphrased St. Matthew, or wrote comments on St. Paul. . . . You would not guess that this associate of the doctor's was—old Cibber! Certainly, in their religious moral, and civil character, there is no relation; but in their dramatic capacity there is some.'—Mrs. Montagu was not aware that Cibber, whom Young had named not disparagingly in his Satires, was the brother of his old school-fellow; but to return to our hero. 'The waters,' says Mrs. Montagu, 'have raised his spirits to a fine pitch, as your grace will imagine, when I tell you how sublime an answer he made to a very vulgar question. I asked him how long he stayed at the Wells: he said, As long as my rival stayed;—as long as the sun did'. Among the visitors at the Wells were Lady Sunderland, (wife of Sir Robert Sutton,) and her sister, Mrs. Tichborne. 'He did an admirable thing to Lady Sunderland: on her mentioning Sir Robert Sutton, he asked her where Sir Robert's lady was; on which we all laughed very heartily, and I brought him off, half ashamed, to my lodgings, where, during breakfast, he assured me he had asked after Lady Sunderland, because he had a great honour for her; and that, having a respect for her sister, he designed to have inquired after her, if we had not put it out of his head by laughing at him. You must know, Mrs. Tichborne sat next to Lady Sunderland. It would have been admirable to have had him finish his compliment in that manner.'

. . . 'His expressions all bear the stamp of novelty, and his thoughts of sterling sense. He practises a kind of philosophical abstinence. . . . He carried Mrs. Rolt and myself to Tunbridge, five miles from hence, where we were to see some fine old ruins. . . . First rode the doctor on a tall steed, decently caparisoned in dark grey; next, ambled Mrs. Rolt on a hackney horse; . . . then followed your humble servant on a milk-white palfrey. I rode on in safety, and at leisure to observe the company, especially the two figures that brought up the rear. The first was my servant, valiantly armed with two uncharged pistols; the last was the doctor's man, whose uncombed hair so resembled the mane of the horse he rode, one could not help imagining they were of kin, and wishing, for the honour of the family, that they had had one comb betwixt them. On his head was a velvet cap, much resembling a black saucepan, and on his side hung a little basket.—At last we arrived at the King's Head, where the loyalty of the doctor induced him to alight; and then, knight-errant-like, he took his damsels from off their palfreys, and courteously handed us into the inn'. . . . The party returned to the Wells; and 'the silver

Cynthia held up her lamp in the heavens' the while. 'The night silenced all but our divine doctor, who sometimes uttered things fit to be spoken in a season when all nature seems to be hushed and hearkening. I followed, gathering wisdom as I went, till I found, by my horse's stumbling, that I was in a bad road, and that the blind was leading the blind. So I placed my servant between the doctor and myself; which he not perceiving, went on in a most philosophical strain, to the great admiration of my poor clown of a servant, who, not being wrought up to any pitch of enthusiasm, nor making any answer to all the fine things he heard, the doctor, wondering I was dumb, and grieving I was so stupid, looked round and declared his surprise'. [29]

Young's oddity and absence of mind are gathered from other sources besides these stories of Mrs. Montagu's, and gave rise to the report that he was the original of Fielding's 'Parson Adams;' but this Croft denies, and mentions another Young, who really sat for the portrait, and who, we imagine, had both more Greek and more genuine simplicity than the poet. His love of chatting with Colley Cibber was an indication that the old predilection for the stage survived, in spite of his emphatic contempt for 'all joys but joys that never can expire;' and the production of 'The Brothers,' at Drury-lane in 1753, after a suppression of fifteen years, was perhaps not entirely due to the expressed desire to give the proceeds to the Society for the Propagation of the Gospel. The author's profits were not more than 400£.—in those days a disappointing sum; and Young, as we learn from his friend Richardson, did not make this the limit of his donation, but gave a thousand guineas to the Society. 'I had some talk with him,' says Richardson, in one of his letters, 'about this great action. "I always", said he, "intended to do something handsome for the Society. Had I deferred it to my demise, I should have given away my son's money. All the world are inclined to pleasure; could I have given myself a greater by disposing of the sum to a different use, I should have done it".'[30] [Surely he took his old friend Richardson for 'Lorenzo!']:[31]

His next work was 'The Centaur not Fabulous; in Six Letters to a Friend, on the Life in Vogue,' which reads very much like the most objurgatory parts of the 'Night Thoughts' reduced to prose. It is preceded by a preface which, though addressed to a lady, is in

[29] Doran's *Life*, lxiii-lxv.
[30] Quoted inaccurately from Cunningham, III, 341, note.
[31] Omitted, 1884.

its denunciations of vice as grossly indecent and almost as flippant as the epilogues written by 'friends', which he allowed to be reprinted after his tragedies in the latest edition of his works. We like much better than 'The Centaur,' 'Conjectures on Original Composition,' written in 1759, for the sake, he says, of communicating to the world the well-known anecdote about Addison's deathbed, and, with the exception of his poem on Resignation, the last thing he ever published.

The estrangement from his son, which must have embittered the later years of his life, appears to have begun not many years after the mother's death. On the marriage of her second daughter, who had previously presided over Young's household, a Mrs. Hallows, understood to be a woman of discreet age, and the daughter (or widow) of a clergyman who was an old friend of Young's, became housekeeper at Welwyn. Opinions about ladies are apt to differ. 'Mrs. Hallows was a woman of piety, improved by reading',[32] says one witness. 'She was a very coarse woman', says Dr. Johnson;[33] and we shall presently find some indirect evidence that her temper was perhaps not quite so much improved as her piety. Servants, it seems, were not fond of remaining long in the house with her; a satirical curate, named Kidgell, hints at 'drops of juniper'[34] taken as a cordial, (but perhaps he was spiteful, and a teetotaler); and Young's son is said to have told his father that 'an old man should not resign himself to the management of anybody'.[35] The result was, that the son was banished from home for the rest of his father's lifetime, though Young seems never to have thought of disinheriting him.

Our latest glimpses of the aged poet are derived from certain letters of Mr. Jones, his curate,—letters preserved in the British Museum, and, happily, made accessible to common mortals in Nichols's 'Anecdotes.'[36] Mr. Jones was a man of some literary activity and ambition,—a collector of interesting documents, and one of those concerned in the 'Free and Candid Disquisitions,'[37]

[32] *Gentleman's Magazine* (1782), p. 71: 'a woman of piety and good sense. . .'.
[33] *Journal of a Tour to the Hebrides*, 30 September.
[34] See Doran's *Life*, lxxi.
[35] *Journal of a Tour to the Hebrides*, 30 September.
[36] I, 585–640. In the quotations that follow the italics are George Eliot's.
[37] *Free and Candid Disquisitions relating to the Church of England, and the means of Advancing Religion therein . . .* (1749).

the design of which was 'to point out such things in our ecclesiastical establishment as want to be reviewed and amended.' On these
and kindred subjects he corresponded with Dr. Birch,[38] occasionally troubling him with queries and manuscripts. We have a
respect for Mr. Jones. [Unlike any person who ever troubled *us*][39]
with queries or manuscripts, he mitigates the infliction by such
gifts as 'a fat pullet', wishing he 'had anything better to send; but
this depauperizing vicarage (of Alconbury) too often checks the
freedom and forwardness of my mind.' Another day comes a
'pound canister of tea', another, a 'young fatted goose.' [Clearly,
Mr. Jones was entirely unlike your literary correspondents of the
present day; he forwarded manuscripts, but he had 'bowels', and
forwarded poultry too.][40] His first letter from Welwyn is dated
June, 1759, not quite six years before Young's death. In June,
1762, he expresses a wish to go to London 'this summer. But,' he
continues,

> My time and pains are almost continually taken up here, and . . . I
> have been (I now find) a considerable loser, upon the whole, by
> continuing here so long. The consideration of this, and the incon-
> veniences I sustained, and do still experience, from my late illness,
> obliged me at last to acquaint the Doctor (Young) with my case, and
> to assure him that I plainly perceived the duty and confinement here
> to be too much for me; for which reason I must (I said) beg to be at
> liberty to resign my charge at Michaelmas. I began to give him these
> notices in February, when I was very ill: and now I perceive, by
> what he told me the other day, that he is in some difficulty: for which
> reason he is at last (he says) resolved to advertise, *and even (which is
> much wondered at) to raise the salary considerably higher.* (What he
> allowed my predecessors was 20£. per annum; and now he proposes
> 50£., as he tells me.) I never asked him to raise it for me, though I
> well knew it was not equal to the duty; nor did I say a word about
> myself when he lately suggested to me his intentions upon this
> subject.

In a postscript to this letter he says,

> I may mention to you farther, as a friend that may be trusted, that,
> in all likelihood, the poor old gentleman will not find it a very easy
> matter, unless by dint of money, *and force upon himself,* to procure
> a man that he can like for his next curate, *nor one that will stay with*

[38] Thomas Birch (1705–1766), historian and biographer.
[39] 'Unlike most persons who trouble others', 1884.
[40] Omitted, 1884. 'His' in the next sentence is changed to 'Mr. Jones's'.

him so long as I have done. Then, his great age will recur to people's thoughts; and if he has any foibles, either in temper or conduct, they will be sure not to be forgotten on this occasion by those who know him; and those who do not, will probably be on their guard. On these and the like considerations, it is by no means an eligible office to be seeking out for a curate for him, as he has several times wished me to do; and would, if he knew that I am now writing to you, wish your assistance also. But my best friends here, *who well foresee the probable consequences,* and wish me well, earnestly dissuade me from complying; and I will decline the office with as much decency as I can: but high salary will, I suppose, fetch in somebody or other, soon.

In the following July, he writes,

The old gentleman here (I may venture to tell you freely) seems to me to be in a pretty odd way of late,—moping, dejected, self-willed, and as if surrounded with some perplexing circumstances. Though I visit him pretty frequently for short intervals, I say very little to his affairs, not choosing to be a party concerned, especially in cases of so critical and tender a nature. There is much mystery in almost all his temporal affairs, as well as in many of his speculative theories. Whoever lives in this neighbourhood to see his exit, will probably see and hear some very strange things. Time will show;—I am afraid, not greatly to his credit. There is thought to be *an irremoveable obstruction to his happiness within his walls, as well as another without them;* but the former is the more powerful, and like to continue so. He has this day been trying anew to engage me to stay with him. No lucrative views can tempt me to sacrifice my liberty or my health, to such measures as are proposed here. *Nor do I like to have to do with persons whose word and honour cannot be depended on.* So much for this very odd and unhappy topic.

In August, Mr. Jones's tone is slightly modified. Earnest entreaties, not lucrative considerations, have induced him to cheer the Doctor's dejected heart by remaining at Welwyn some time longer. The Doctor is, 'in various respects, a very unhappy man,' and few know so much of these respects as Mr. Jones. In September, he recurs to the subject:

My ancient gentleman here is still full of trouble: which moves my concern, though it moves only the secret laughter of many, and some untoward surmises in disfavour of him and his household. The loss of a very large sum of money (about 200£.) is talked of; whereof this vill and neighbourhood is full. Some disbelieve; others say, '*It is no wonder, where about eighteen or more servants are sometimes taken and dismissed in the course of a year.*' The gentleman himself is allowed by all to be far more harmless and easy in his family than some one else who hath too much the lead in it. This, among others, was one reason for my late motion to quit.

No other mention of Young's affairs occurs until April 2, 1765, when he says that Dr. Young is very ill, attended by two physicians.

Having mentioned this young gentleman (Dr. Young's son), I would acquaint you next, that he came hither this morning, having been sent for, as I am told, by the direction of Mrs. Hallows. Indeed, she intimated to me as much herself. And if this be so, I must say, that it is one of the most prudent acts she ever did, or could have done in such a case as this; as it may prove a means of preventing much confusion after the death of the Doctor. I have had some little discourse with the son: he seems much affected, and I believe really is so. He earnestly wishes his father might be pleased to ask after him; for you must know he has not yet done this, nor is, in my opinion, like to do it. And it has been said farther, that upon a late application made to him on the behalf of his son, he desired that no more might be said to him about it. How true this may be, I cannot as yet be certain; all I shall say is, it seems not improbable. . . . I heartily wish the antient man's heart may prove tender towards his son; *though, knowing him so well, I can scarce hope to hear such desirable news.*

Eleven days later, he writes,

I have now the pleasure to acquaint you, that the late Dr. Young, though he had for many years kept his son at a distance from him, yet has now at last left him all his possessions, after the payment of certain legacies; so that the young gentleman (who bears a fair character, and behaves well, as far as I can hear or see) will, I hope, soon enjoy and make a prudent use of a handsome fortune. The father, on his deathbed, and since my return from London, was applied to in the tenderest manner, by one of his physicians, and by another person, to admit the son into his presence, to make submission, entreat forgiveness, and obtain his blessing. As to an interview with his son, he intimated that he chose to decline it, as his spirits were then low, and his nerves weak. With regard to the next particular, he said, '*I heartily forgive him*;' and upon mention of this last, he gently lifted up his hand, and letting it gently fall, pronounced these words, '*God bless him!*'. . . . I know it will give you pleasure to be farther informed, that he was pleased to make respectful mention of me in his will; expressing his satisfaction in my care of his parish, *bequeathing to me a handsome legacy*, and appointing me to be one of his executors.

355

So far Mr. Jones, in his confidential correspondence with a 'friend who may be trusted'. In a letter communicated apparently by him to the *Gentleman's Magazine*, seven years later, namely, in 1782, on the appearance of Croft's biography of Young, we find him speaking of 'the ancient gentleman' in a tone of reverential eulogy, quite at variance with the free comments we have just quoted. But the Rev. John Jones was probably of opinion, with Mrs. Montagu, whose contemporary and retrospective letters are also set in a different key, that 'the interests of religion were connected with the character of a man so distinguished for piety as Dr. Young'.[41] At all events, a subsequent quasi-official statement weighs nothing as evidence against contemporary, spontaneous, and confidential hints.

To Mrs. Hallows, Young left a legacy of 1000£., with the request that she would destroy all his manuscripts. This final request, from some unknown cause, was not complied with, and among the papers he left behind him, was the following letter from Archbishop Secker, which probably marks the date of his latest effort after preferment.

Deanery of St. Paul's, July 8, 1758.
Good Dr. Young,—I have long wondered that more suitable notice of your great merit hath not been taken by persons in power. But how to remedy the omission I see not. No encouragement hath ever been given me to mention things of this nature to his Majesty. And therefore, in all likelihood, the only consequence of doing it would be weakening the little influence which else I may possibly have on some other occasions. *Your fortune and your reputation set you above the need of advancement; and your sentiments above that concern for it, on your own account*, which, on that of the public, is sincerely felt by

Your loving Brother,

THO. CANT.[42]

The loving brother's irony is severe!

Perhaps the least questionable testimony to the better side of Young's character, is that of Bishop Hildesley, who, as the vicar of a parish near Welwyn, had been Young's neighbour for upwards of twenty years. The affection of the clergy for each other, we have observed, is, like that of the fair sex, not at all of a blind and

[41] Cunningham, III, 346, note.
[42] Cunningham, III, 349. George Eliot's italics.

infatuated kind; and we may therefore the rather believe them when they give each other any extra-official praise. Bishop Hildesley, then, writing of Young to Richardson, says,

> The impertinence of my frequent visits to him was amply rewarded; forasmuch as, I can truly say, he never received me but with agreeable open complacency; and I never left him but with profitable pleasure and improvement. He was one or other, the most modest, the most patient of contradiction, and the most informing and entertaining I ever conversed with—at least, of any man who had so just pretensions to pertinacity and reserve.[43]

Mr. Langton, however, who was also a frequent visitor of Young's, informed Boswell—

> That there was an air of benevolence in his manner; but that he could obtain from him less information than he had hoped to receive from one who had lived so much in intercourse with the brightest men of what had been called the Augustan age of England; and that he showed a degree of eager curiosity concerning the common occurrences that were then passing, which appeared somewhat remarkable in a man of such intellectual stores, of such an advanced age, and who had retired from life with declared disappointment in his expectations.[44]

The same substance, we know, will exhibit different qualities under different tests; and, after all, imperfect reports of individual impressions, whether immediate or traditional, are a very frail basis on which to build our opinion of a man. One's character may be very indifferently mirrored in the mind of the most intimate neighbour; it all depends on the quality of that gentleman's reflecting surface.[45]

But, discarding any inferences from such uncertain evidence, the outline of Young's character is too distinctly traceable in the well-attested facts of his life, and yet more in the self-betrayal that runs through all his works, for us to fear that our general estimate of him may be false. For, while no poet seems less easy and spontaneous than Young, no poet discloses himself more completely. Men's minds have no hiding-place out of themselves—their affectations do but betray another phase of their nature. And if, in

[43] Quoted, slightly inaccurately, from Doran's *Life*, lxxii.
[44] *Life of Johnson*, ed. Hill and Powell, IV, 59 (1781).
[45] Cf. *Middlemarch*, Ch. 10: 'even Milton, looking for his portrait in a spoon, must submit to have the facial angle of a bumpkin'.

the present view of Young, we seem to be more intent on laying bare unfavourable facts than on shrouding them in 'charitable speeches,'[46] it is not because we have any irreverential pleasure in turning men's characters 'the seamy side without,' but because we see no great advantage in considering a man as he was *not*. Young's biographers and critics have usually set out from the position that he was a great religious teacher, and that his poetry is morally sublime; and they have toned down his failings into harmony with their conception of the divine and the poet. For our own part, we set out from precisely the opposite conviction—namely, that the religious and moral spirit of Young's poetry is low and false; and we think it of some importance to show that the 'Night Thoughts' are the reflex of a mind in which the higher human sympathies were inactive. This judgment is entirely opposed to our youthful predilections and enthusiasm. The sweet garden-breath of early enjoyment lingers about many a page of the 'Night Thoughts,' and even of the 'Last Day,' giving an extrinsic charm to passages of stilted rhetoric and false sentiment; but the sober and repeated reading of maturer years has convinced us that it would hardly be possible to find a more typical instance than Young's poetry, of the mistake which substitutes interested obedience for sympathetic emotion, and baptizes egoism as religion.

Pope said of Young, that he had 'much of a sublime genius without common sense.'[47] The deficiency Pope meant to indicate was, we imagine, moral rather than intellectual: it was the want of that fine sense of what is fitting in speech and action, which is often eminently possessed by men and women whose intellect is of a very common order, but who have the sincerity and dignity which can never coexist with the selfish preoccupations of vanity or interest. This was the 'common sense' in which Young was conspicuously deficient; and it was partly owing to this deficiency that his genius, waiting to be determined by the highest prizes, fluttered uncertainly from effort to effort, until, when he was more than sixty, it suddenly spread its broad wing, and soared so as to arrest the gaze of other generations besides his own. For he had no versatility of faculty to mislead him. The 'Night Thoughts' only differ from his previous works in the degree and not in the kind of power they

[46] Bacon, 'Last Will', second paragraph.
[47] In Ruffhead's *Life*, quoted from Cunningham, III, 310.

manifest. Whether he writes prose or poetry, rhyme or blank verse, dramas, satires, odes, or meditations, we see everywhere the same Young—the same narrow circle of thoughts, the same love of abstractions, the same telescopic view of human things, the same appetency towards antithetic apothegm and rhapsodic climax. The passages that arrest us in his tragedies are those in which he anticipates some fine passage in the 'Night Thoughts,' and where his characters are only transparent shadows through which we see the bewigged *embonpoint* of the didactic poet, excogitating epigrams or ecstatic soliloquies by the light of a candle fixed in a skull. Thus, in 'The Revenge,' 'Alonzo,' in the conflict of jealousy and love that at once urges and forbids him to murder his wife, says,

> This vast and solid earth, that blazing sun,
> Those skies, through which it rolls, must all have end.
> What then is man? The smallest part of nothing.
> Day buries day; month, month; and year the year!
> Our life is but a chain of many deaths.
> Can then Death's self be feared? Our life much rather:
> *Life is the desert, life the solitude*;
> Death joins us to the great majority:
> 'Tis to be born to Plato and to Cæsar;
> 'Tis to be great for ever;
> 'Tis pleasure, 'tis ambition, then, to die.

His prose writings all read like the 'Night Thoughts,' either diluted into prose, or not yet crystallized into poetry. For example, in his 'Thoughts for Age,' he says,

> Though we stand on its awful brink, such our leaden bias to the world, we turn our faces the wrong way; we are still looking on our old acquaintance, *Time*; though now so wasted and reduced, that we can see little more of him than his wings and his scythe: our age enlarges his wings to our imagination; and our fear of death, his scythe; as Time himself grows less. His consumption is deep; his annihilation is at hand.

This is a dilution of the magnificent image:

> Time in advance behind him hides his wings,
> And seems to creep decrepit with his age.
> Behold him when past by! What then is seen
> But his proud pinions, swifter than the winds?

Again:

> A requesting Omnipotence? What can stun and confound thy reason more? What more can ravish and exalt thy heart? It cannot but

ravish and exalt; it cannot but gloriously disturb and perplex thee, to take in all *that* thought suggests. Thou child of the dust! Thou speck of misery and sin! How abject thy weakness! how great is thy power! Thou crawler on earth, and possible (I was about to say) controller of the skies! Weigh, and weigh well, the wondrous truths I have in view: which cannot be weighed too much; which the more they are weighed, amaze the more; which to have supposed, before they were revealed, would have been as great madness, and to have presumed on as great sin, as, it is now madness and sin not to believe.

Even in his Pindaric odes, in which he made the most violent effort against nature, he is still neither more nor less than the Young of the 'Last Day,' emptied and swept of his genius, and possessed by seven demons of fustian and bad rhyme. Even here, his 'Ercles' vein'[48] alternates with his moral platitudes, and we have the perpetual text of the 'Night Thoughts':

Gold pleasure buys;	Joys felt alone!
But pleasure dies,	Joys asked of none!
For soon the gross fruition	Which Time's and Fortune's
cloys;	arrows miss:
Though raptures court,	Joys that subsist,
The sense is short;	Though fates resist,
But virtue kindles living joys;—	An unprecarious, endless bliss!

Unhappy they!
And falsely gay!
Who bask for ever in success;
A constant feast
Quite palls the taste,
And long enjoyment is distress.

In the 'Last Day', again, which is the earliest thing he wrote, we have an anticipation of all his greatest faults and merits. Conspicuous among the faults is that attempt to exalt our conceptions of Deity by vulgar images and comparisons, which is so offensive in the later 'Night Thoughts.' In a burst of prayer and homage to God, called forth by the contemplation of Christ coming to judgment, he asks, Who brings the change of the seasons? and answers—

Not the great Ottoman, or greater Czar;
Not Europe's arbitress of peace and war!

Conceive the soul in its most solemn moments, assuring God that it doesn't place his power below that of Louis Napoleon or Queen Victoria!

[48] *A Midsummer Night's Dream*, I, ii, 43.

But in the midst of uneasy rhymes, inappropriate imagery, vaulting sublimity that o'erleaps itself,[49] and vulgar emotions, we have in this poem an occasional flash of genius, a touch of simple grandeur, which promises as much as Young ever achieved. Describing the on-coming of the dissolution of all things, he says,

> No sun in radiant glory shines on high;
> *No light but from the terrors of the sky.*

And again, speaking of great armies,

> Whose rear lay wrapt in night, while breaking dawn,
> Rous'd the broad front, and call'd the battle on.

And this wail of the lost souls is fine:

> And this for sin?
> Could I offend if I had never been?
> But still increas'd the senseless, happy mass,
> Flow'd in the stream, *or shiver'd in the grass?*
> Father of mercies! Why from silent earth
> Didst thou awake and curse me into birth?
> Tear me from quiet, ravish me from night,
> And make a thankless present of thy light?
> Push into being a reverse of Thee,
> And *animate a clod with misery?*

But it is seldom in Young's rhymed poems that the effect of a felicitous thought or image is not counteracted by our sense of the constraint he suffered from the necessities of rhyme,—that 'Gothic demon,' as he afterwards called it, 'which modern poetry tasting, became mortal.' In relation to his own power, no one will question the truth of his dictum, that 'blank verse is verse unfallen, uncurst; verse reclaimed, reinthroned in the true language of the gods; who never thundered nor suffered their Homer to thunder in rhyme'.[50] His want of mastery in rhyme is especially a drawback on the effect of his Satires; for epigrams and witticisms are peculiarly susceptible to the intrusion of a superfluous word, or to an inversion which implies constraint. Here, even more than elsewhere, the art that conceals art is an absolute requisite, and to have a witticism presented to us in limping or cumbrous rhythm is as

[49] Cf. *Macbeth*, I, vii, 27.

[50] This and the preceding quotation are slightly misquoted from 'Conjectures on Original Composition', *The Complete Works . . . of the Rev. Edward Young, LL.D.*, II (1854), 566.

counteractive to any electrifying effect, as to see the tentative grimaces by which a comedian prepares a grotesque countenance. We discern the process, instead of being startled by the result.

This is one reason why the Satires, read *seriatim*, have a flatness to us, which, when we afterwards read picked passages, we are inclined to disbelieve in, and to attribute to some deficiency in our own mood. But there are deeper reasons for that dissatisfaction. Young is not a satirist of a high order. His satire has neither the terrible vigour, the lacerating energy of genuine indignation, nor the humour which owns loving fellowship with the poor human nature it laughs at; nor yet the personal bitterness which, as in Pope's characters of Sporus and Atticus, ensures those living touches by virtue of which the individual and particular in Art becomes the universal and immortal. Young could never describe a real complex human being; but what he *could* do with eminent success, was to describe with neat and finished point, obvious *types*, of manners rather than of character,—to write cold and clever epigrams on personified vices and absurdities. There is no more emotion in his satire than if he were turning witty verses on a waxen image of Cupid, or a lady's glove. He has none of those felicitous epithets, none of those pregnant lines, by which Pope's Satires have enriched the ordinary speech of educated men. Young's wit will be found in almost every instance to consist in that antithetic combination of ideas which, of all the forms of wit, is most within reach of clever effort. In his gravest arguments, as well as in his lightest satire, one might imagine that he had set himself to work out the problem, how much antithesis might be got out of a given subject. And there he completely succeeds. His neatest portraits are all wrought on this plan. 'Narcissus,' for example, who—

> Omits no duty; nor can Envy say
> He miss'd, these many years, the Church or Play:
> He makes no noise in Parliament, 'tis true;
> But pays his debts, and visit when 'tis due;
> His character and gloves are ever clean,
> And then he can out-bow the bowing Dean;
> A smile eternal on his lip he wears,
> Which equally the wise and worthless shares.
> In gay fatigues, this most undaunted chief,
> Patient of idleness beyond belief,
> Most charitably lends the town his face

> For ornament in every public place;
> As sure as cards he to th' assembly comes,
> And is the furniture of drawing-rooms:
> When Ombre calls, his hand and heart are free,
> And, joined to two, he fails not—to make three:
> Narcissus is the glory of his race;
> For who does nothing with a better grace?
> To deck my list by nature were designed
> Such shining expletives of human kind,
> Who want, while through blank life they dream along,
> Sense to be right and passion to be wrong.

It is but seldom that we find a touch of that easy slyness which gives an additional zest to surprise; but here is an instance:

> See Tityrus, with merriment possest,
> Is burst with laughter ere he hears the jest.
> What need he stay? for when the joke is o'er,
> His *teeth* will be no whiter than before.

Like Pope, whom he imitated, he sets out with a psychological mistake as the basis of his satire, attributing all forms of folly to one passion—the love of fame, or vanity,—a much grosser mistake, indeed, than Pope's exaggeration of the extent to which the 'ruling passion' determines conduct in the individual. Not that Young is consistent in his mistake. He sometimes implies no more than what is the truth—that the love of fame is the cause, not of all follies, but of many.

Young's satires on women are superior to Pope's, which is only saying that they are superior to Pope's greatest failure. We can more frequently pick out a couplet as successful than an entire sketch. Of the too emphatic 'Syrena,' he says:

> Her judgment just, her sentence is too strong;
> Because she's right, she's ever in the wrong.

Of the diplomatic 'Julia:'

> For her own breakfast she'll project a scheme,
> Nor take her tea without a stratagem.

Of 'Lyce,' the old painted coquette:

> In vain the cock has summoned sprites away;
> She walks at noon, and blasts the bloom of day.

Of the nymph who, 'gratis, clears religious mysteries:'

> 'Tis hard, too, she who makes no use but chat
> Of her religion, should be barr'd in that.

The description of the literary *belle*, 'Daphne,' well prefaces that of 'Stella,' admired by Johnson:

> With legs toss'd high, on her sophee she sits,
> Vouchsafing audience to contending wits:
> Of each performance she's the final test;
> One act read o'er, she prophesies the rest;
> And then, pronouncing with decisive air,
> Fully convinces all the town—*she's fair*.
> Had lovely Daphne Hecatessa's face,
> How would her elegance of taste decrease!
> Some ladies' judgment in their features lies,
> And all their genius sparkles in their eyes.
> But hold, she cries, lampooner! have a care:
> Must I want common sense because I'm fair?
> O no; see Stella: her eyes shine as bright
> As if her tongue was never in the right;
> And yet what real learning, judgment, fire!
> She seems inspir'd, and can herself inspire.
> How then (if malice ruled not all the fair)
> *Could Daphne publish, and could she forbear?*

After all, when we have gone through Young's seven Satires, we seem to have made but an indifferent meal. They are a sort of fricassee, with little solid meat in them, and yet the flavour is not always piquant. It is curious to find him, when he pauses a moment from his satiric sketching, recurring to his old platitudes:

> Can gold calm passion, or make reason shine?
> Can we dig peace or wisdom from the mine?
> Wisdom to gold prefer;—

platitudes which he seems inevitably to fall into, for the same reason that some men are constantly asserting their contempt for criticism—because he felt the opposite so keenly.

The outburst of genius in the earlier books of the 'Night Thoughts' is the more remarkable, that in the interval between them and the Satires, he had produced nothing but his Pindaric odes, in which he fell far below the level of his previous works. Two sources of this sudden strength were the freedom of blank verse and the presence of a genuine emotion. Most persons, in speaking of the 'Night Thoughts,' have in their minds only the two or three first Nights, the majority of readers rarely getting beyond these, unless, as Wilson says, they 'have but few books, are poor, and live in the country.'[51] And in these earlier Nights there is enough genuine sublimity and genuine sadness to bribe us into too favourable a judgment of them as a whole. Young had only a very few things to say or sing—such as that life is vain, that death is imminent, that man is immortal, that virtue is wisdom, that friendship is sweet, and that the source of virtue is the contemplation of death and immortality,—and even in his two first Nights he had said almost all he had to say in his finest manner. Through these first outpourings of 'complaint' we feel that the poet is really sad, that the bird is singing over a rifled nest; and we bear with his morbid picture of the world and of life, as the Job-like lament of a man whom 'the hand of God hath touched.'[52] Death has carried away his best-beloved, and that 'silent land' whither they are gone has more reality for the desolate one than this world which is empty of their love:

> This is the desert, this the solitude;
> How populous, how vital is the grave!

Joy died with the loved one:

> The disenchanted earth
> Lost all her lustre. Where her glitt'ring towers?
> Her golden mountains, where? All darken'd down
> To naked waste; a dreary vale of tears:
> *The great magician's dead!*

Under the pang of parting, it seems to the bereaved man as if love were only a nerve to suffer with, and he sickens at the thought of every joy of which he must one day say—'*it was.*' In its unreasoning anguish, the soul rushes to the idea of perpetuity as the one element of bliss:

> O ye blest scenes of permanent delight!—
> Could ye, so rich in rapture, fear an end,—
> That ghastly thought would drink up all your joy,
> And quite unparadise the realms of light.

In a man under the immediate pressure of a great sorrow, we tolerate morbid exaggerations; we are prepared to see him turn

[51] 'The Man of Ton. A Satire', *The Works of Professor Wilson*, ed. Professor Ferrier, V (1856), 233. First published in *Blackwood's*, XXII (June, 1828).

[52] Job 19:21.

away a weary eye from sunlight and flowers and sweet human faces, as if this rich and glorious life had no significance but as a preliminary of death; we do not criticise his views, we compassionate his feelings. And so it is with Young in these earlier Nights. There is already some artificiality even in his grief, and feeling often slides into rhetoric, but through it all we are thrilled with the unmistakeable cry of pain, which makes us tolerant of egoism and hyperbole:

> In every varied posture, place, and hour,
> How widow'd ev'ry thought of ev'ry joy!
> Thought, busy thought! too busy for my peace!
> Through the dark postern of time long elapsed
> Led softly, by the stillness of the night,—
> Led like a murderer (and such it proves!)
> Strays (wretched rover!) o'er the pleasing past,—
> In quest of wretchedness, perversely strays;
> And finds all desert now; and meets the ghosts
> Of my departed joys.

But when he becomes didactic, rather than complaining,—when he ceases to sing his sorrows, and begins to insist on his opinions,— when that distaste for life which we pity as a transient feeling, is thrust upon us as a theory, we become perfectly cool and critical, and are not in the least inclined to be indulgent to false views and selfish sentiments.

Seeing that we are about to be severe on Young's failings and failures, we ought, if a reviewer's space were elastic, to dwell also on his merits,—on the startling vigour of his imagery,—on the occasional grandeur of his thought,—on the piquant force of that grave satire into which his meditations continually run. But, since our 'limits' are rigorous, we must content ourselves with the less agreeable half of the critic's duty; and we may the rather do so, because it would be difficult to say anything new of Young, in the way of admiration, while we think there are many salutary lessons remaining to be drawn from his faults.

One of the most striking characteristics of Young is his *radical insincerity as a poetic artist*. This, added to the thin and artificial texture of his wit, is the true explanation of the paradox—that a poet who is often inopportunely witty has the opposite vice of bombastic absurdity. The source of all grandiloquence is the want of taking for a criterion the true qualities of the object described, or the emotion expressed. The grandiloquent man is never bent on saying what he feels or what he sees, but on producing a certain effect on his audience; hence he may float away into utter inanity without meeting any criterion to arrest him. Here lies the distinction between grandiloquence and genuine fancy or bold imaginativeness. The fantastic or the boldly imaginative poet may be as sincere as the most realistic: he is true to his own sensibilities or inward vision, and in his wildest flights he never breaks loose from his criterion—the truth of his own mental state. Now, this disruption of language from genuine thought and feeling is what we are constantly detecting in Young; and his insincerity is the more likely to betray him into absurdity, because he habitually treats of abstractions, and not of concrete objects or specific emotions. He descants perpetually on virtue, religion, 'the good man,' life, death, immortality, eternity—subjects which are apt to give a factitious grandeur to empty wordiness. When a poet floats in the empyrean, and only takes a bird's-eye view of the earth, some people accept the mere fact of his soaring for sublimity, and mistake his dim vision of earth for proximity to heaven. Thus:

> His hand the good man fixes on the skies,
> And bids earth roll, nor feels her idle whirl,—

may, perhaps, pass for sublime with some readers. But pause a moment to realize the image, and the monstrous absurdity of a man's grasping the skies, and hanging habitually suspended there, while he contemptuously bids the earth roll, warns you that no genuine feeling could have suggested so unnatural a conception.

[Again,

> See the man immortal: him, I mean,
> Who lives as such; whose heart full bent on heaven,
> Leans all that way, his bias to the stars.

This is worse than the previous example; for you can at least form some imperfect conception of a man hanging from the skies, though the position strikes you as uncomfortable, and of no particular use; but you are utterly unable to imagine how his heart can lean towards the stars.][53] Examples of such vicious imagery, resulting from insincerity, may be found, perhaps, in almost every page of the 'Night Thoughts.' But simple assertions or aspirations,

[53] Omitted, 1884.

undisguised by imagery, are often equally false. No writer whose rhetoric was checked by the slightest truthful intentions, could have said,

> An eye of awe and wonder let me roll,
> And roll for ever.

Abstracting the more poetical associations with the eye, this is hardly less absurd than if he had wished to stand for ever with his mouth open.

Again:

> Far beneath
> A soul immortal is a mortal joy.

Happily for human nature, we are sure no man really believes that. Which of us has the impiety not to feel that our souls are only too narrow for the joy of looking into the trusting eyes of our children, of reposing on the love of a husband or wife,—nay, of listening to the divine voice of music, or watching the calm brightness of autumn afternoons? But Young could utter this falsity without detecting it, because, when he spoke of 'mortal joys,' he rarely had in his mind any object to which he could attach sacredness. He was thinking of bishropics and benefices, of smiling monarchs, patronizing prime ministers, and a 'much indebted muse.' Of anything between these and eternal bliss, he was but rarely and moderately conscious. Often, indeed, he sinks very much below even the bishropic, and seems to have no notion of earthly pleasure, but such as breathes gas-light and the fumes of wine. His picture of life is precisely such as you would expect from a man who has risen from his bed at two o'clock in the afternoon with a headache, and a dim remembrance that he has added to his 'debts of honour':

> What wretched repetition cloys us here!
> What periodic potions for the sick,
> Distemper'd bodies, and distemper'd minds!

And then he flies off to his usual antithesis:

> In an eternity what scenes shall strike!
> Adventures thicken, novelties surprise!

'Earth' means lords and levees, duchesses and Dalilahs, South-Sea dreams and illegal percentage; and the only things distinctly preferable to these are, eternity and the stars. Deprive Young of this antithesis, and more than half his eloquence would be shrivelled up. Place him on a breezy common, where the furze is in its golden bloom, where children are playing, and horses are standing in the sunshine with fondling necks, and he would have nothing to say. Here are neither depths of guilt, nor heights of glory; and we doubt whether in such a scene he would be able to pay his usual compliment to the Creator:

> Where'er I turn, what claim on all applause!

It is true that he sometimes—not often—speaks of virtue as capable of sweetening life, as well as of taking the sting from death and winning heaven; and, lest we should be guilty of any unfairness to him, we will quote the two passages which convey this sentiment the most explicitly. In the one, he gives 'Lorenzo' this excellent recipe for obtaining cheerfulness:

> Go, fix some weighty truth;
> Chain down some passion; do some generous good;
> Teach ignorance to see, or Grief to smile;
> Correct thy friend; befriend thy greatest foe;
> Or, with warm heart, and confidence divine,
> Spring up, and lay strong hold on Him who made thee.

The other passage is vague, but beautiful, and its music has murmured in our minds for many years:

> The cuckoo seasons sing
> The same dull note to such as nothing prize
> But what those seasons from the teeming earth
> To doting sense indulge. But nobler minds,
> Which relish fruit unripen'd by the sun,
> Make their days various; various as the dyes
> On the dove's neck, which wanton in his rays.
> On minds of dove-like innocence possess'd,
> On lighten'd minds that bask in Virtue's beams,
> Nothing hangs tedious, nothing old revolves
> In that for which they long, for which they live.
> Their glorious efforts, wing'd with heavenly hopes,
> Each rising morning sees still higher rise;
> Each bounteous dawn its novelty presents
> To worth maturing, new strength, lustre, fame;
> While Nature's circle, like a chariot wheel,
> Rolling beneath their elevated aims,
> Makes their fair prospect fairer every hour;
> Advancing virtue in a line to bliss.

Even here, where he is in his most amiable mood, you see at what a telescopic distance he stands from mother Earth and simple human joys—'Nature's circle rolls beneath.' Indeed, we remember no mind in poetic literature that seems to have absorbed less of the beauty and the healthy breath of the common land-scape than Young's. His images, often grand and finely presented—witness that sublimely sudden leap of thought,

> Embryos we must be till we burst the shell,
> *Yon ambient azure shell*, and spring to life—

lie almost entirely within that circle of observation which would be familiar to a man who lived in town, hung about the theatres, read the newspaper, and went home often by moon and star light. There is no natural object nearer than the moon that seems to have any strong attraction for him, and even to the moon he chiefly appeals for patronage, and 'pays his court' to her. It is reckoned among the many deficiencies of 'Lorenzo,' that he 'never asked the moon one question'—an omission which Young thinks eminently unbecoming a rational being. He describes nothing so well as a comet, and is tempted to linger with fond detail over nothing more familiar than the day of judgment and an imaginary journey among the stars. Once on Saturn's ring, he feels at home, and his language becomes quite easy:

> What behold I now?
> A wilderness of wonders burning round,
> Where larger suns inhabit higher spheres;
> Perhaps *the villas of descending gods*!

It is like a sudden relief from a strained posture when, in the 'Night Thoughts,' we come on any allusion that carries us to the lanes, woods, or fields. Such allusions are amazingly rare, and we could almost count them on a single hand. That we may do him no injustice, we will quote the three best:

> Like *blossom'd trees o'erturned by vernal storm*,
> Lovely in death the beauteous ruin lay.
>
> . . . .
>
> In the same brook none ever bathed him twice:
> To the same life none ever twice awoke.
> We call the brook the same—the same we think
> Our life, though still more rapid in its flow;

> Nor mark the much irrevocably lapsed,
> And mingled with the sea.
>
> . . . .
>
> The crown of manhood is a winter joy;
> An evergreen that stands the northern blast,
> And blossoms in the rigour of our fate.

The adherence to abstractions, or to the personification of abstractions, is closely allied in Young to the *want of genuine emotion*. He sees Virtue sitting on a mount serene, far above the mists and storms of earth: he sees Religion coming down from the skies, with this world in her left hand and the other world in her right: but we never find him dwelling on virtue or religion as it really exists—in the emotions of a man dressed in an ordinary coat, and seated by his fire-side of an evening, with his hand resting on the head of his little daughter; in courageous effort for unselfish ends, in the internal triumph of justice and pity over personal resentment, in all the sublime self-renunciation and sweet charities which are found in the details of ordinary life. Now, emotion links itself with particulars, and only in a faint and secondary manner with abstractions. An orator may discourse very eloquently on injustice in general, and leave his audience cold; but let him state a special case of oppression, and every heart will throb. The most untheoretic persons are aware of this relation between true emotion and particular facts, as opposed to general terms, and implicitly recognise it in the repulsion they feel towards any one who professes strong feeling about abstractions,—in the interjectional 'humbug!' which immediately rises to their lips. [Wherever abstractions appear to excite strong emotion, this occurs in men of active intellect and imagination, in whom the abstract term rapidly and vividly calls up the particulars it represents, these particulars being the true source of the emotion; and such men, if they wished to express their feeling, would be infallibly prompted to the presentation of details. Strong emotion can no more be directed to generalities apart from particulars, than skill in figures can be directed to arithmetic apart from numbers. Generalities are the refuge at once of deficient intellectual activity and deficient feeling.][54]

If we except the passages in 'Philander,' 'Narcissa,' and 'Lucia,' there is hardly a trace of human sympathy, of self-forgetfulness in

[54] Omitted, 1884.

371

the joy or sorrow of a fellow-being, throughout this long poem, which professes to treat the various phases of man's destiny. And even in the 'Narcissa' Night, Young repels us by the low moral tone of his exaggerated lament. This married step-daughter died at Lyons, and, being a Protestant, was denied burial, so that her friends had to bury her in secret—one of the many miserable results of superstition, but not a fact to throw an educated, still less a Christian man, into a fury of hatred and vengeance, in contemplating it after the lapse of five years. Young, however, takes great pains to simulate a bad feeling:

> Of grief
> And indignation rival bursts I pour'd,
> Half execration mingled with my pray'r;
> Kindled at man, while I his God ador'd;
> Sore grudg'd the savage land her sacred dust;
> Stamp'd the cursed soil; *and with humanity*
> (*Denied Narcissa*) *wish'd them all a grave.*

The odiously bad taste of this last clause makes us hope that it is simply a platitude, and not intended as a witticism, until he removes the possibility of this favourable doubt by immediately asking, 'Flows my resentment into guilt?'[55]

When, by an afterthought, he attempts something like sympathy, he only betrays more clearly his want of it. Thus, in the first Night, when he turns from his private griefs to depict earth as a hideous abode of misery for all mankind, and asks,

> What then am I, who sorrow for myself?

he falls at once into calculating the benefit of sorrowing for others:

> More generous sorrow, while it sinks, exalts;
> *And conscious virtue mitigates the pang.*
> Nor virtue, more than prudence, bids me give
> Swollen thought a second channel.

This remarkable negation of sympathy is in perfect consistency with Young's theory of ethics:

> Virtue is a crime,
> A crime to reason, if it costs us pain
> Unpaid . . .

[55] 'Glows my resentment . . .', *Night Thoughts*, III, 189. Not corrected in 1884.

372

If there is no immortality for man,

> Sense! take the rein; blind Passion, drive us on;
> And Ignorance! befriend us on our way. . . .
> Yes; give the pulse full empire; live the Brute,
> Since as the brute we die. The sum of man,
> Of godlike man, to revel and to rot.

. . . .

> If this life's gain invites him to the deed,
> Why not his country sold, his father slain?

. . . .

> Ambition, avarice, by the wise disdain'd,
> Is perfect wisdom, while mankind are fools,
> And think a turf or tombstone covers all.

. . . .

> Die for thy country, thou romantic fool!
> Seize, seize the plank thyself, and let her sink.

. . . .

> As in the dying parent dies the child,
> Virtue with Immortality expires.
> Who tells me he denies his soul immortal,
> *Whate'er his boast, has told me he's a knave.*
> *His duty 'tis to love himself alone,*
> *Nor care though mankind perish, if he smiles.*

We can imagine the man who 'denies his soul immortal', replying, 'It is quite possible that *you* would be a knave, and love yourself alone, if it were not for your belief in immortality; but you are not to force upon me what would result from your own utter want of moral emotion. I am just and honest, not because I expect to live in another world, but because, having felt the pain of injustice and dishonesty towards myself, I have a fellow-feeling with other men, who would suffer the same pain if I were unjust or dishonest towards them. Why should I give my neighbour short weight in this world, because there is not another world in which I should have nothing to weigh out to him? I am honest, because I don't like to inflict evil on others in this life, not because I'm afraid of evil to myself in another. The fact is, I do *not* love myself alone, whatever logical necessity there may be for that in your mind. I have a tender love for my wife, and children, and friends, and through that love I sympathize with like affections in other men. It is a pang to me to witness the suffering of a fellow-being, and I feel his suffering the more acutely because he is *mortal*—because his life is so short, and I would have it, if possible, filled with happiness and not misery. Through my union and fellowship with the men and women I *have* seen, I feel a like, though a fainter, sympathy with those I have *not* seen; and I am able so to live in imagination with the generations to come, that their good is not alien to me, and is a stimulus to me to labour for ends which may not benefit myself, but will benefit them. It is possible that you might prefer to 'live the brute,' to sell your country, or to slay your father, if you were not afraid of some disagreeable consequences from the criminal laws of another world; but even if I could conceive no motive but by my own worldly interest or the gratification of my animal desires, I have not observed that beastliness, treachery, and parricide, are the direct way to happiness and comfort on earth. [And I should say, that if you feel no motive to common morality but your fear of a criminal bar in heaven, you are decidedly a man for the police on earth to keep their eye upon, since it is matter of world-old experience that fear of distant consequences is a very insufficient barrier against the rush of immediate desire. Fear of consequences is only one form of egoism, which will hardly stand against half-a-dozen other forms of egoism bearing down upon it. And in opposition to your theory that a belief in immortality is the only source of virtue, I maintain that, so far as moral action is dependent on that belief, so far the emotion which prompts it is not truly moral—is still in the stage of egoism, and has not yet attained the higher development of sympathy. In proportion as a man would care less for the rights and the welfare of his fellow, if he did not believe in a future life, in that proportion is he wanting in the genuine feelings of justice and benevolence; as the musician who would care less to play a sonata of Beethoven's finely in solitude than in public, where he was to be paid for it, is wanting in genuine enthusiasm for music'.][56]

[Thus far might answer the man who 'denies himself immortal;' and, allowing for that deficient recognition of the finer and more indirect influences exercised by the idea of immortality which might be expected from one who took up a dogmatic position on such a subject, we think he would have given a sufficient reply to

[56] Omitted, 1884.

374

Young and other theological advocates who, like him, pique themselves on the loftiness of their doctrine when they maintain that
'virtue with immortality expires'.][57] We may admit, indeed, that if
the better part of virtue consists, as Young appears to think, in
contempt for mortal joys, in 'meditation of our own decease,' and
in 'applause' of God in the style of a congratulatory address to Her
Majesty—all which has small relation to the well-being of mankind
on this earth—the motive to it must be gathered from something
that lies quite outside the sphere of human sympathy. But, for
certain other elements of virtue, which are of more obvious
importance to [untheological minds,][58]—a delicate sense of our
neighbour's rights, an active participation in the joys and sorrows
of our fellow-men, a magnanimous acceptance of privation or
suffering for ourselves when it is the condition of good to others,
in a word, [the extension and intensification of our sympathetic
nature,—we think it of some importance to contend, that they have
no more direct relation to the belief in a future state than the
interchange of gases in the lungs has to the plurality of worlds.
Nay, to us it is][59] conceivable that in some minds the deep pathos
lying in the thought of human mortality—that we are here for a
little while and then vanish away, that this earthly life is all that is
given to our loved ones and to our many suffering fellow-men—
lies nearer the fountains of moral emotion than the conception of
extended existence. And surely it ought to be a welcome fact, if the
thought of *mortality*, as well as of immortality, be favourable to
virtue. [Do writers of sermons and religious novels prefer that men
should be vicious in order that there may be a more evident
political and social necessity for printed sermons and clerical
fictions? Because learned gentlemen are theological, are we to have
no more simple honesty and good-will?][60] [We can imagine that
the proprietors of a patent water-supply have a dread of common
springs; but, for our own part, we think there cannot be too great

[57] 'Thus far the man who "denies himself immortal" might give a
warrantable reply to Young's assumption of peculiar loftiness in maintaining that "virtue with immortality expires".' 1884.

[58] 'plain people', 1884.

[59] 'the widening and strengthening of our sympathetic nature,—it is
surely of some moment to contend, that they have no more direct dependence on the belief in a future state than the interchange of gases in the
lungs on the plurality of worlds. Nay, it is . . .', 1884.

[60] Omitted, 1884.

a security against a lack of fresh water or of pure morality. To us it is a matter of unmixed rejoicing that this latter necessary of healthful life is independent of theological ink, and that its evolution is ensured][61] in the interaction of human souls as certainly as the evolution of science or of art, with which, indeed, it is but a twin ray, melting into them with undefinable limits.

To return to Young. We can often detect a man's deficiencies in what he admires more clearly than in what he contemns,—in the sentiments he presents as laudable rather than in those he decries. And in Young's notion of what is lofty he casts a shadow by which we can measure him without further trouble. For example, in arguing for human immortality, he says—

> First, what is *true ambition*? The pursuit
> Of glory *nothing less than man can share.*
>
> . . . .
>
> The Visible and Present are for brutes,
> A slender portion, and a narrow bound!
> These Reason, with an energy divine
> O'erleaps, and claims the Future and Unseen;
> The vast Unseen, the Future fathomless!
> When the great soul buoys up to this high point,
> Leaving gross Nature's sediments below,
> Then, and then only, Adam's offspring quits
> The sage and hero of the fields and woods,
> Asserts his rank, and rises into man.

So, then, if it were certified that, as some benevolent minds have tried to infer, our dumb fellow-creatures would share a future existence, in which it is to be hoped we should neither beat, starve, nor maim them, our ambition for a future life would cease to be 'lofty!' This is a notion of loftiness which may pair off with Dr. Whewell's celebrated observation, that Bentham's moral theory is low, because it includes justice and mercy to brutes.[62]

But, for a reflection of Young's moral personality on a colossal scale, we must turn to those passages where his rhetoric is at its

[61] 'We can imagine that the proprietors of a patent water-supply may have a dread of common springs; but for those who only share the general need there cannot be too great a security against a lack of fresh water—or of pure morality. It should be matter of unmixed rejoicing if this latter necessary of healthful life has its evolution ensured . . .', 1884.

[62] William Whewell, *Lectures on the History of Moral Philosophy in England* (London and Cambridge, 1852), pp. 223–225.

utmost stretch of inflation—where he addresses the Deity, discourses of the Divine operations, or describes the last judgment. As a compound of vulgar pomp, crawling adulation, and hard selfishness, presented under the guise of piety, there are few things in literature to surpass the Ninth Night, entitled 'Consolation,' especially in the pages where he describes the last judgment—a subject to which, with naïve self-betrayal, he applies phraseology favoured by the exuberant penny-a-liner. Thus, when God descends, and the groans of hell are opposed by 'shouts of joy,' much as cheers and groans contend at a public meeting where the resolutions are *not* passed unanimously, the poet completes his climax in this way:

> Hence, in one peal of loud, eternal praise,
> The *charmed spectators* thunder their applause.

In the same taste, he sings—

> Eternity, the various sentence past,
> Assigns the sever'd throng distinct abodes,
> *Sulphureous or ambrosial.*

Exquisite delicacy of indication! He is too nice to be specific as to the interior of the 'sulphureous' abode; but when once half the human race are shut up there, hear how he enjoys turning the key on them!

> What ensues?
> The deed predominant, the deed of deeds!
> Which makes a hell of hell, a *heaven of heaven*!
> The goddess, with determin'd aspect, turns
> Her adamantine key's enormous size
> Through Destiny's inextricable wards,
> *Deep driving every bolt* on both their fates.
> Then, from the crystal battlements of heaven,
> Down, down she hurls it through the dark profound,
> Ten thousand, thousand fathom; there to rust
> And ne'er unlock her resolution more.
> The deep resounds; and Hell, through all her glooms,
> Returns, in groans, the melancholy roar.

This is one of the blessings for which Dr. Young thanks God 'most':

> For all I bless thee, most, for the severe;
> Her death—my own at hand—*the fiery gulf,*
> *That flaming bound of wrath omnipotent!*

> *It thunders;—but it thunders to preserve;*
> . . . . . . its wholesome dread
> Averts the dreaded pain; *its hideous groans*
> *Join Heaven's sweet Hallelujahs in Thy praise,*
> Great Source of good alone! How kind in all!
> In vengeance kind! Pain, Death, Gehenna, *save.* . . .

i.e. save *me*, Dr. Young, who, in return for that favour, promise to
give my divine patron the monopoly of that exuberance in laudatory epithet, of which specimens may be seen at any moment in a
large number of dedications and odes to kings, queens, prime
ministers, and other persons of distinction. *That*, in Young's
conception, is what God delights in. His crowning aim in the
'drama' of the ages, is to vindicate his own renown. The God of
the 'Night Thoughts' is simply Young himself, 'writ large'—a
didactic poet, who 'lectures' mankind in the antithetic hyperbole
of mortal and immortal joys, earth and the stars, hell and heaven;
and expects the tribute of inexhaustible 'applause'. Young has no
conception of religion as anything else than egoism turned heaven-
ward; and he does not merely imply this, he insists on it. Religion,
he tells us, in argumentative passages too long to quote, is
'ambition, pleasure, and the love of gain', directed towards the
joys of the future life instead of the present. And his ethics
correspond to his religion. He vacillates, indeed, in his ethical
theory, and shifts his position in order to suit his immediate
purpose in argument; but he never changes his level so as to see
beyond the horizon of mere selfishness. Sometimes he insists, as
we have seen, that the belief in a future life is the only basis of
morality; but elsewhere he tells us—

In self applause is virtue's golden prize.

Virtue, with Young, must always squint—must never look
straight towards the immediate object of its emotion and effort.
Thus, if a man risks perishing in the snow himself, rather than
forsake a weaker comrade, he must either do this because his hopes
and fears are directed to another world, or because he desires to
applaud himself afterwards! Young, if we may believe him, would
despise the action as folly unless it had these motives. Let us hope
he was not so bad as he pretended to be! The tides of the divine
life in man move under the thickest ice of theory.

Another indication of Young's deficiency in moral, *i.e.*, in sympathetic emotion, is his unintermitting habit of pedagogic moralizing. On its theoretic and preceptive side, morality touches Science; on its emotional side, [Art. Now, the products of Art are great in proportion as they result from the immediate prompting of innate power which we call Genius, and not][63] from laboured obedience to a theory or rule; and the presence of genius or innate prompting is directly opposed to the perpetual consciousness of a rule. The action of faculty is imperious, and [excludes][64] the reflection *why* it should act. In the same way, in proportion as morality is emotional, [*i.e.*, has affinity with Art,][65] it will exhibit itself in direct sympathetic feeling and action, and not as the recognition of a rule. Love does not say, 'I ought to love'—it loves. Pity does not say, 'It is right to be pitiful'—it pities. Justice does not say, 'I am bound to be just'—it feels justly. It is only where moral emotion is comparatively weak that the contemplation of a rule or theory habitually mingles with its action; and in accordance with this, we think experience, both in literature and life, has shown that the minds which are [pre-eminently didactic—which insist on a 'lesson,' and despise everything that will not convey a moral,][66] are deficient in sympathetic emotion. [A certain poet is recorded to have said, that he 'wished everything of his burnt that did not impress some moral; even in love-verses, it might be flung in by the way'.[67] What poet was it who took this medicinal view of poetry? Dr. Watts, or James Montgomery, or some other singer of spotless life and ardent piety? Not at all. It was *Waller*. A significant fact in relation to our position, that the predominant didactic tendency proceeds rather from the poet's perception that it is good for other men to be moral, than from any overflow of moral feeling in himself.][68] [A man who is perpetually thinking in apothegms, who has an unintermittent flux of admonition, can

---

[63] '. . . poetic Art. Now, the products of poetic Art are great in proportion as they result from the immediate prompting of innate power, and not . . .', 1884.

[64] 'supersedes', 1884.

[65] Omitted, 1884.

[66] 'predominantly didactic': the rest omitted, 1884.

[67] Slightly misquoted from Pope as reported by Spence, *Anecdotes*, ed. S. W. Singer, 1820, p. 203.

[68] Omitted, 1884.

have little energy left for simple emotion.][69] And this is the case with Young. In his highest flights of contemplation, and his most wailing soliloquies, he interrupts himself to fling an admonitory parenthesis at 'Lorenzo,' or to hint that 'folly's creed' is the reverse of his own. Before his thoughts can flow, he must fix his eye on an imaginary miscreant, who gives unlimited scope for lecturing, and recriminates just enough to keep the spring of admonition and argument going to the extent of nine books. It is curious to see how this pedagogic habit of mind runs through Young's contemplation of Nature. As the tendency to see our own sadness reflected in the external world has been called by Mr. Ruskin the 'pathetic fallacy,'[70] so we may call Young's disposition to see a rebuke or a warning in every natural object, the 'pedagogic fallacy.' To his mind, the heavens are 'for ever *scolding* as they shine;' and the great function of the stars is to be a 'lecture to mankind.' The conception of the Deity as a didactic author is not merely an implicit point of view with him; he works it out in elaborate imagery, and at length makes it the occasion of his most extraordinary achievement in the 'art of sinking,' by exclaiming, *à propos*, we need hardly say, of the nocturnal heavens,

> Divine Instructor! Thy first volume this
> For man's perusal! all in CAPITALS!

It is this pedagogic tendency, this sermonizing attitude of Young's mind, which produces the wearisome monotony of his pauses. After the first two or three Nights, he is rarely singing, rarely pouring forth any continuous melody inspired by the spontaneous flow of thought or feeling. He is rather occupied with argumentative insistance, with hammering in the proofs of his propositions by disconnected verses, which he puts down at intervals. The perpetual recurrence of the pause at the end of the line throughout long passages, makes them as fatiguing to the ear as a monotonous chant, which consists of the endless repetition of one short musical phrase. For example—

> Past hours,
> If not by guilt, yet wound us by their flight,

[69] 'A man who is perpetually thinking in monitory apothegms, who has an unintermittent flux of rebuke, can have little energy left for simple feeling'. 1884.

[70] George Eliot's review of *Modern Painters*, III, in the *Westminster* for April, 1856, briefly summarizes Ruskin's Ch. 12, 'Of the Pathetic Fallacy'.

> If folly bound our prospect by the grave,
> All feeling of futurity be numb'd,
> All godlike passion for eternals quench'd,
> All relish of realities expired;
> Renounced all correspondence with the skies;
> Our freedom chain'd; quite wingless our desire;
> In sense dark-prison'd all that ought to soar;
> Prone to the centre; crawling in the dust;
> Dismounted every great and glorious aim;
> Enthalled every faculty divine,
> Heart-buried in the rubbish of the world.

How different from the easy, graceful melody of Cowper's blank verse! Indeed, it is hardly possible to criticise Young, without being reminded at every step of the contrast presented to him by Cowper. And this contrast urges itself upon us the more from the fact that there is, to a certain extent, a parallelism between the 'Night Thoughts' and the 'Task.' In both poems, the author achieves his greatest in virtue of the new freedom conferred by blank verse; both poems are professedly didactic, and mingle much satire with their graver meditations; both poems are the productions of men whose estimate of this life was formed by the light of a belief in immortality, and who were intensely attached to Christianity. On some grounds, we might have anticipated a more morbid view of things from Cowper than from Young. Cowper's religion was dogmatically the more gloomy, for he was a Calvinist; while Young was a 'low' Arminian, believing that Christ died for all, and that the only obstacle to any man's salvation lay in his will, which he could change if he chose. There was [real and deep][71] sadness involved in Cowper's personal lot; while Young, apart from his ambitious and greedy discontent, seems to have had no [great][72] sorrow.

Yet, see how a lovely, sympathetic nature manifests itself in spite of creed and circumstance! Where is the poem that surpasses the 'Task' in the genuine love it breathes, at once towards inanimate and animate existence—in truthfulness of perception and sincerity of presentation—in the calm gladness that springs from a delight in objects for their own sake, without self-reference—in divine sympathy with the lowliest pleasures, with the most short-lived capacity for pain? Here is no railing at the earth's 'melan-

[71] 'deep and unusual', 1884.　　　　　[72] 'exceptional', 1884.

choly map,' but the happiest lingering over her simplest scenes with all the fond minuteness of attention that belongs to love; no pompous rhetoric about the inferiority of the 'brutes', but a warm plea on their behalf against man's inconsiderateness and cruelty, and a sense of enlarged happiness from their companionship in enjoyment; no vague rant about human misery and human virtue, but that close and vivid presentation of particular sorrows and privations, of particular deeds and misdeeds, which is the direct road to the emotions. How Cowper's exquisite mind falls with the mild warmth of morning sunlight on the commonest objects, at once disclosing every detail and investing every detail with beauty! No object is too small to prompt his song—not the sooty film on the bars, or the spoutless teapot holding a bit of mignionette that serves to cheer the dingy town-lodging with a 'hint that Nature lives;' and yet his song is never trivial, for he is alive to small objects, not because his mind is narrow, but because his glance is clear and his heart is large. Instead of trying to edify us by supercilious allusions to the 'brutes' and the 'stalls,' he interests us in that tragedy of the hen-roost when the thief has wrenched the door,

> Where Chanticleer amidst his harem sleeps
> *In unsuspecting pomp*;

in the patient cattle, that on the winter's morning

> Mourn in corners where the fence
> Screens them, and seem half petrified to sleep
> *In unrecumbent sadness*;

in the little squirrel, that, surprised by him in his woodland walk,

> At once, swift as a bird,
> Ascends the neighbouring beech; there whisks his brush,
> And perks his ears, and stamps, and cries aloud,
> With all the prettiness of feign'd alarm
> And anger insignificantly fierce.

And then he passes into reflection, not with curt apophthegm and snappish reproof, but with that melodious flow of utterance which belongs to thought when it is carried along in a stream of feeling:

> The heart is hard in nature, and unfit
> For human fellowship, as being void
> Of sympathy, and therefore dead alike

382

> To love and friendship both, that is not pleased
> With sight of animals enjoying life,
> Nor feels their happiness augment his own.

His large and tender heart embraces the most every-day forms of human life—the carter driving his team through the wintry storm; the cottager's wife who, painfully nursing the embers on her hearth, while her infants 'sit cowering o'er the sparks,'

> Retires, content to quake, so they be warm'd;

or the villager, with her little ones, going out to pick

> A cheap but wholesome salad from the brook;

and he compels our colder natures to follow his in its manifold sympathies, not by exhortations, not by telling us to meditate at midnight, to 'indulge' the thought of death, or to ask ourselves how we shall 'weather an eternal night,' *but by presenting to us the object of his compassion truthfully and lovingly.* And when he handles greater themes, when he takes a wider survey, and considers the men or the deeds which have a direct influence on the welfare of communities and nations, there is the same unselfish warmth of feeling, the same scrupulous truthfulness. He is never vague in his remonstrance or his satire; but puts his finger on some particular vice or folly, which excites his indignation or 'dissolves his heart in pity', because of some specific injury it does to his fellow-man or to a sacred cause. And when he is asked why he interests himself about the sorrows and wrongs of others, hear what is the reason he gives. Not, like Young, that the movements of the planets show a mutual dependence, and that

> Thus man his sovereign duty learns in this
> Material picture of benevolence—

or that,

> More generous sorrow while it sinks, exalts,
> And conscious virtue mitigates the pang.

What is Cowper's answer, when he imagines some 'sage erudite, profound,' asking him 'What's the world to you?'—

> Much. *I was born of woman, and drew milk*
> *As sweet as charity from human breasts.*
> I think, articulate, I laugh and weep,

> And exercise all functions of a man.
> How then should I and any man that lives
> Be strangers to each other?

Young is astonished that men can make war on each other—that any one can 'seize his brother's throat,' while

> The Planets cry, 'Forbear.'

Cowper weeps because—

> There is no flesh in man's obdurate heart;
> *It does not feel for man.*

Young applauds God as a monarch with an empire and a court quite superior to the English, or as an author who produces 'volumes for man's perusal.' Cowper sees his Father's love in all the gentle pleasures of the home fire-side, in the charms even of the wintry landscape, and thinks—

> Happy who walks with him! whom what he finds
> Of flavour or of scent in fruit or flower,
> Or what he views of beautiful or grand
> In nature, from the broad, majestic oak
> To the green blade that twinkles in the sun
> *Prompts with remembrance of a present God.*

To conclude—for we must arrest ourselves in a contrast that would lead us beyond our bounds: Young flies for his utmost consolation to the day of judgment, when

> Final Ruin fiercely drives
> Her ploughshare o'er Creation;

when earth, stars, and suns are swept aside,

> And now, all dross removed, Heaven's own pure day
> Full on the confines of our ether, flames:
> While (dreadful contrast!) far (how far!) beneath,
> Hell, bursting, belches forth her blazing seas,
> And storms sulphureous; her voracious jaws
> Expanding wide, and roaring for her prey,—

Dr. Young, and similar 'ornaments of religion and virtue,' passing, of course, with grateful 'applause' into the upper region. Cowper finds his highest inspiration in the Millennium—in the restoration of this our beloved home of earth to perfect holiness and bliss, when the Supreme

> Shall visit earth in mercy; shall descend
> Propitious in his chariot paved with love;
> And what his storms have blasted and defaced
> For man's revolt, shall with a smile repair.

And into what delicious melody his song flows at the thought of that blessedness to be enjoyed by future generations on earth!—

> The dwellers in the vales and on the rocks
> Shout to each other, and the mountain tops
> From distant mountains catch the flying joy;
> Till, nation after nation taught the strain,
> Earth rolls the rapturous Hosanna round!

The sum of our comparison is this—In Young we have the type of that deficient human sympathy, that impiety towards the present and the visible, which flies for its motives, its sanctities, and its religion, to the remote, the vague, and the unknown: in Cowper we have the type of that genuine love which cherishes things in proportion to their nearness, and feels its reverence grow in proportion to the intimacy of its knowledge.

24

A WORD FOR THE GERMANS

Pall Mall Gazette, I (7 March 1865), 201

Late in 1864 the publisher George Smith invited Lewes to act as editorial adviser for the new paper Smith was about to bring out, the *Pall Mall Gazette*. It was apparently in order to support Lewes in this very well-paid but vaguely defined position, which he held until 1868, that George Eliot, then between novels, contributed four articles to the journal between March and May of 1865. 'A Word for the Germans' is the first of these. A further reason for her contributions may have been a sense of indebtedness to Smith, who had lured her away from Blackwood, her regular publisher, with an extravagant offer for *Romola* (1862–1863), and had lost on the transaction.

The writing of the article is noted in George Eliot's Journal for 1 March 1865.

*   *   *

JOHN BULL is open to instruction; slowly, by gentle degrees, he revises his opinions, his habits, and his laws. It is not to be expected that he will ever cease to regard himself as the supreme type of manhood, or to think that the most unmixed truth may always be known by the mark 'British,' which prevents imposture. But he does modify his opinions about other nations. It is no longer his belief that a Frenchman is invariably of the dancing-master type, demanding nothing from existence, but 'his girl, his fiddle, and his frisk',[1] and that if he has a soul at all it is really of too light a quality to be worth saving. The Italian of John Bull's imagination is no longer exclusively that dangerous jesuitical personage, with dark hair and darker intentions, who avails himself of momentary privacy to feel the edge of his stiletto; a personage adorned now

[1] Cowper, 'Table Talk', 237: 'his lass, his fiddle, and his frisk'.

386

with a false title, but in his earlier years nothing better than a small vagrant, who went about exhibiting his white mice and white teeth for casual halfpence.[2]

Having shown himself thus ready to abandon those favourite old portable notions of Frenchmen and Italians, it is a pity he should obstinately retain certain worn-out phrases about the Germans, which hardly imply a more comprehensive estimate. In these days when the excellent Bull is ethnological, and feels himself at home with the widest-grinning 'natives'—nay, shows an eager anxiety as to the personal habits of the gorilla, it might be wished that he would conceive the typical German under some more average aspect than that of 'the cloudy metaphysician.'[3] We venture to suggest that this phrase is quite insufficient to express the *differentia* of the German people. In the first place, only a small proportion of them are metaphysicians; quite as many are bakers, making excellent bread—not inferior, perhaps, to the British in any quality except heaviness. Secondly, the most eminent of German metaphysicians, KANT, is cloudy in no other sense than that in which a mathematician is cloudy to one ignorant of mathematics. What book more nebulous than *Euclid* to a reader acquainted neither with the subject-matter nor with the terminology? What more Laputan and unpractical than algebraic formulæ to one who has never studied algebra? KANT was a rigorous thinker, who, like all other rigorous thinkers, felt the need of terms undefaced by a long currency, free from confusing associations. The recipe for understanding KANT is first to get

[2] Cf. Mrs. Cadwallader's characterization of Ladislaw in *Middlemarch*, Ch. 50: 'an Italian with white mice'.

[3] George Eliot probably has in mind her friend Richard Owen's lecture *On the Gorilla*, delivered at the Royal Institution and published in 1859. The passage perhaps also alludes to the interest in African life generated by the explorations around the headwaters of the Nile in the late '50's and early '60's; and to the growing public discussion of racial and national traits seeking to define on 'ethnological' grounds the essential character of the French, Germans, English, etc. Matthew Arnold's *On the Study of Celtic Literature* (1867), delivered as a series of lectures at Oxford beginning in the spring of 1865, is a good illustration on the then-current fashion for categorizing the moral and intellectual qualities of the nations. That George Eliot, despite her protest against over-simplified conceptions, took in much of the belief in a demonstrable national character, is apparent from this article; later, she made the notion of a determining racial heredity fundamental to *The Spanish Gypsy* and *Daniel Deronda*.

brains capable of following his argument, and next to master his terminology. Observing this recipe, the *Critique of Pure Reason* is not indeed easy reading, but it is not in the least cloudy. It is not fit for the club table. Some gentleman there, turning over the pages and seeing such terms as *synthetic judgments*, *antinomies*, and the like, would be conscious of superior clearness of head, and say: 'Bosh! what dreamers these Germans are!' But possibly, if that clear-headed clubman were imperatively called upon to declare the meaning of *co-efficient* and *hypothenuse* and assured that no smiling would be accepted as legal tender for knowledge, he would discover that these terms also are painfully cloudy. It is one of the interesting weaknesses common to us men to suppose that clearness ends where our own vision fails. The sound British thinker kicks a stone to prove that matter exists, and so confound the metaphysicians; concluding that their arguments are necessaily shallow because he can't see far into them.

Thirdly, we object to 'cloudy metaphysician' as the accepted periphrasis for a German, because it has begotten another habit of speech which the most constant familiarity could not endear to us. Views are set aside by saying that 'they are German.' Doubtless there is a peculiarly German view of things as there is an English view, a French view, a Hindu view, and so on, down to a Patagonian view, perhaps the least metaphysical of all. The English view may be the soundest, and all but born Englishmen may be comparatively pitiable. But the human race has not been educated on a plan of uniformity, and it is precisely that partition of mankind into races and nations, resulting in various national points of view or varieties of national genius, which has been the means of enriching and rendering more and more complete man's knowledge of the inner and outer world.[4] The Seventy who translated the Hebrew Scriptures into Greek are said to have been placed in separate confinement that each might produce his independent version, and their versions, when afterwards compared, were found to be identical. This agreement as to the meaning of a text was highly satisfactory, and some inconvenience might have been saved if subsequent interpretations had been equally harmonious. But it would have been a dreary issue for mankind, if the division into nations had ended in such an identity of mental products, even though the standard had been English.

[4] Cf. Mordecai's apology for Zionism in *Daniel Deronda*, Ch. 42.

And no one who has an acquaintance worth mentioning with the productions of the German mind in any one department, is unaware that the peculiarities of that mind, its characteristic qualities, have been the source of pre-eminently important contributions to the sum of our mental wealth.

The German mind possesses in a high degree two tendencies which are often represented as opposed to each other: namely, largeness of theoretic conception, and thoroughness in the investigation of facts. So undeniable is it that the typical German has these tendencies, that their excess is the very vice he is reproached with by those who know him and don't like him. Your German, it is said, can not write about the drama without going back to the Egyptian mysteries; he sees that everything is related to everything else, and is determined to exhaust you and the subject; his doctrine is all-embracing, and so is his detail. Quite true. No man is less disposed than our German to accept a too slight induction, to let pass an inaccuracy of statement, or to report a conclusion from imperfect observation or experiment; on the other hand, no man is more likely to be contemptuous towards desultory labours which are not *wissenschaftlich* (scientific)—*i.e.* not bound together by a rational doctrine, or conducted in the full sense of a need for such a doctrine. If he is an experimentor, he will be thorough in his experiments; if he is a scholar, he will be thorough in his researches. Accordingly no one in this day really studies any subject without having recourse to German books, or else wishing he knew their language that he might have recourse to them; and the footnotes of every good French or English book that appears, whether in scholarship, history, or natural science, are filled with references to German authors. Without them, historical criticism would have been simply nowhere; take away the Germans, with their patience, their thoroughness, their need for a doctrine which refers all transient and material manifestations to subtler and more permanent causes, and all that we most value in our appreciation of early history would have been wanting to us.

It is true the German rarely writes well, rarely arranges his matter well, or manages it with economy, and therefore seldom produces a good book in the fullest sense of the word. From the necessity his mind is under of looking at a subject in every one of its facets, he is prone to pile one modifying consideration on another, and so perpetually to disappoint a reader who is in a

389

hurry for a conclusion. The German is never in a hurry: for him, art is long, and life, expanded by the absence of adventitious needs, is not so short as for Englishmen making haste to be rich. His writing will sometimes seem to be all stairs and landing-places without any floors. Then the structure of his language lends itself to the formation of involved sentences, like coiled serpents, showing neither head nor tail. Nevertheless, the proportionate badness of German books is much exaggerated. The cumbrousness of the language apart, there is not perhaps a much larger propor-tion of poor books in German than in French or English; it would be nearer the truth to say that there are more books in German of which the matter is valuable, and the style bad, than in any other tongue. Our own literature does not positively swarm with good writers. The difference lies chiefly in this, that when a German author is a blockhead, he is, as HEINE says, *kein oberflächlicher Narr*[5]—no superficial blockhead: his sentences and his book do not come to an end so soon as if he were an Englishman or a French-man. He has a great deal more straw to chop, and he chops it slowly. Still, a blockhead is never exhilarating, though he may have learned to write in epigrams, and to give stupidity the most dapper air of neatness. His sentences may each have a paragraph to itself, and his book may be half white paper, but we decline it as reso-lutely as if it were covered with German print without a break from beginning to end. It is as short work *not* to read one book as another.

In fact, if anyone in the present day can be called cultivated who dispenses with a knowledge of German, it is because the two other greatest literatures of the world are now impregnated with the results of German labour and German genius. Let those who know this have the piety to acknowledge it. Let those who do not know it abstain from pourtraying the typical German until they have made his acquaintance. We have no objection to caricatures; each nation should be content to lend itself to the humour of the world in this passive way. But a caricature to be good, must come from close observation.

---

[5] This may be George Eliot's paraphrase of the passage in *Die Romantische Schule*, Book I (Elster ed., V, 236), in which Heine compares the German Parnassus to a French madhouse, and ironically contrasts the German, with his 'entsetzlichen Gewissenhaftigkeit' to the 'ober-flächlicher französischer Narr.'

25

SERVANTS' LOGIC

Pall Mall Gazette, I (17 March 1865), 310–311

The second of the four articles George Eliot contributed to the newly established *Pall Mall Gazette*, 'Servants' Logic' is noted in her Journal for 25 March 1865, some time after its composition: 'I have written nothing but beginnings since I finished a little article for the Pall Mall on the Logic of Servants.'

*　　　*　　　*

PEOPLE who pride themselves on the correctness of their reasoning have to suffer many mortifications. They are constantly finding that as a means of immediate influence their carefully-drawn conclusions are quite powerless by the side of a good bold fallacy. The majority of minds are no more to be controlled by strong reasons than plum-pudding is to be grasped by sharp pincers. The farther your thinker sees into the real relations of things, the closer he makes his sequences—the farther he will be from the possibility of carrying untrained minds along the path of his argument. Their conclusions are determined, not at all by close sequences, but by vague, habitual impressions and by chance associations. If our experience of this fact had reference only to the affairs of mankind at large, it would, perhaps, be easier to bear. We might smile (bitterly) while platform orators held audiences spell-bound by the triumphant irrelevance of their statements, and console ourselves with the reflection that the life of collective mankind is slowly swayed by the force of truth and not of twaddle; our views may be hissed to-day, but in the next century they will be held too undeniable to be applauded. Unfortunately, our keenest experience of this sort has reference to our own domestic affairs: the fellow-mortals we most need to involve, and whose minds we find our-selves the most incapable of grasping, are our servants, and especially our cooks. We may look to the next century for the triumph of our ideas, but it is impossible to look there for our dinners. When the thing to be achieved by argument is a soup or a dish of vegetables that will not plunge you in the horrors of dyspepsia, the immediateness of the success is everything.

In reasoning with servants we are likely to be thwarted by dis-covering that our axioms are not theirs. For example, they pre-suppose that an effect may exist without a cause, that like causes will constantly produce unlike effects, that *all* may mean only some, that there is no difference between little and none, that any two or more circumstances which can be mentioned will account for a given fact, and that nothing is impossible, except that they can have been in the wrong. Their standard measures, too, are of a private kind; a good lump, a handful, a tea-cup, a littleish basin, as much as will stick on your knife-end, a big spoon, and a good sup. Again, in criticizing them we are liable to use words which, not belonging to their vocabulary, seem to them to be particularly opprobrious, as in the black art gibberish was supposed to have a preternatural strength; or we refer to some fact which happens to have a peculiarily offensive association for them unknown to us; and straightway our quiet attempt to convince rouses as much feeling as if we had fired off a volley of angry rhetoric.

You, gentle madam, discover with some dismay that the scalloped oysters with which you would fain load a friend's plate have their beards on. The beard movement not having yet reached this point, you take an early opportunity of asking your cook whether she is not aware that cooked oysters ought to be bearded. 'Oh, yes, mum, for soup and sauce. I put the beards into that last little saucepan with the liquor, and strain 'em; but there's that little strainer, I must have a new one.' 'Yes, yes, but they must always be bearded, however you may cook them.' 'What, the natives, mum?' 'All oysters; the beards are tough, unfit to be eaten.' 'Well, but what we have from that little fishmonger in Brick-street? I'm sure to pay the same price a dozen for 'em as for the last big ones, it's imposing on them that's got the money; and I did take the knife and just strip a beard or two off the biggest of all—we used to take 'em off at Mrs. Tompkins's, but you've never had scalloped oysters before, and I said to Jane, "Jane, there'll be hardly time for these oysters to be done, and as for that clock, it's beyond everything for losing, it deceives *me*, nobody knows, and the clockmaker a whole hour at it only a week ago",' &c. You depart with a sigh, feeling that to deposit rules in Sally's mind is very much like depositing your thimble in a dust-heap.

You, sir, are perhaps a dyspeptic physiologist, with a weakness for spinach, and you wish to impress on your cook the importance of thoroughly squeezing green vegetables. You tell her the water in which they are boiled is as bad as poison. It follows that the next day they come up only a little less like a soft morass. 'This will not do, Sally; the greens must be squeezed perfectly dry.' 'La, sir, I squeezed 'em ever so long.' 'But you saw there was still water left in them.' 'Well, sir, I'm sure it was very little for any gentleman as can eat greens at all.' You are, perhaps, a little nettled, and you wish to be impressive; your mind goes in search of illustration. 'I tell you, there must be no water. Suppose it was arsenic, instead of poisonous water—should you think there was no difference between little and none?' Fatal ingenuity! Sally fires up; she has heard of cooks being hanged for putting arsenic in food; she feels herself unjustly accused. 'I'm sure I never touched a bit of arsenic —no, not so much as to poison a rat, for at one place where I lived the rats ran about like mice, and the butler, as there wasn't a more respectable man anywhere, he brought some arsenic home, and he said to me, as I might be standing here—' 'Nonsense, what has that to do with the greens? Say no more, I'm in a hurry.' Sally departs, muttering, and spends that morning, not in penitence on account of ill-squeezed spinach, but under a sense of injury from false imputations.

Again, you desire soup, but desire it without fat. You are perhaps a genius; the world is in need of your new poem; or you are evolving a momentous theory, and the evolution of fatty acids within you is a serious impediment. Your mental activity is reduced to the consciousness that interesting facts in animal chemistry are going on within you; you begin to think you can serve mankind only by leaving your body for dissection. At length you ask your wife with hardly suppressed peevishness, and unusual emphasis on 'My dear', to inquire into the making of the soup. Your wife, who is rather frightened at the cook, tells her that Mr. Queasy, in spite of his orders, discerned fatty particles in the soup yesterday. 'It's a thing impossible there can be fat, mum—for skimming and everything—there's nothing neglected in *my* power.' 'Show me your cold stock.' Exit Sally, returning with a vessel in one hand and a spoon in the other. There is a white film of fat over the surface of the stock. 'See, now, Sally, there is fat!' 'La, mum,' says Sally, plunging her spoon in and turning up the jellied soup from beneath as a gardener turns the soil when is he digging for roots, the cold fat getting underneath in the process, 'that's nothing; besides, I take my soup from under, and I take the fat off with the spoon.' (The spoon itself is studded plenteously with fragments of cold fat.) 'But unless you wash your spoon each time you dip it, there will be fat, and, however little, Mr. Queasy suffers from it. Besides'—(Mrs. Q. here exerts all her courage)—'it belongs to a good cook to send up her soup free from fat.' Sally smiles bitterly. 'La, mum, do *you* think, when I was at Nuneham-gate, and there was people of all sorts coming to the house, as I could have give that satisfaction—and Scotch people wanting things you might think no Christian 'ud touch—and Mr. Tooley, the gentleman with the wooden leg, praising my soup and saying he never tasted better? But there's stomachs will *not* stand soup, and that's where it is.' (Here Sally shakes her head and sighs, as is her wont when she is seeing deeply into the causes of things.) 'And as I've said to Jane many and many's the time, if gentlefolks' constitutions are of that sort, it's no wonder what comes. I said so only yesterday, when I was draining the rice, and the cat eating the white sauce all the while, and me not knowing. It's true what I speak—every word.' Here Sally sets down the vessel of stock emphatically, and tapping the outside of it with her finger-ends, looks hard out of the window. Mrs. Queasy is nonplussed. If she says more Sally will give warning; she draws her dress round her crinoline, and rustles upstairs again.

Servants are rich in intuitions. They have a vast number of certainties which are deep by reason of their groundlessness. The postman brings a letter for Maria: she was sure he would—she didn't know from whom it would come, and if you were to knock her down she couldn't tell you why; but this morning when she got out of bed, and drew up the blind and saw the wind blowing the leaves about, she seemed to see the postman coming with the letter in his hand. You make a great mistake if you suggest certain conditions which might have given rise to the expectation. She rejects such low-minded analysis of her certainty. No; there was no reason why she should expect a letter this morning more than any other; but so it was—and it was the same once before, when the dish-cover fell and got bruised; she had said at breakfast something would happen that day, she knew. But as to *your* certainties, for which you allege arguments, the same Maria considers them offensive, unless they are to be overcome by her assertion. If you will not believe that a looking-glass is cloudy and spotty in spite of daily, diligent rubbing, or that the steel of all your variously procured stoves happens to be of so peculiar a quality that it will not 'take' a polish, she thinks she has a right to feel offended. If, however, she happens to be in a good humour, she will perhaps observe, àpropos of the steel, that at one place where she lived there was a bright fender with a sharp edge, and the nurse let the child fall on it and cut itself; and when she has given you all the circumstances attendant on this event, the name of the doctor who was called in and what he said, she will feel that she has readjusted her position as a polisher of stoves.

On the whole, servants are little disposed to think that the opinions of gentlefolks can have any practical value for them. Our remedies, our methods, our explanations, are like the drapery and tailoring we pay so much for; they correspond to the supposed scale of our income; but servants, for their part, get their stuffs and their views from other quarters. The cure for a gentleman's toothache is not likely to suit Sally's molar so well as the cure recommended by the grocer's boy on the authority of his first cousin, who went about with a blue handkerchief round his head for weeks and weeks. And for the probabilities concerning the dryness of the coming summer, or the guilt of the man last taken up for murder, the person to be consulted with the most deference is the laundress who serves very good families, and whose husband is in the carrying line.

The moral of all this is, that wise masters and mistresses will not argue with their servants, will not give them reasons, will not consult them. A mild yet firm authority which rigorously demands that certain things be done, without urging motives or entering into explanations, is both preferred by the servants themselves, and is the best means of educating them into any improvement of their methods and habits. Authority and tradition are the chief, almost the only safe guides of the uninstructed—are the chief means of developing the crude mind, whether childish or adult. Reason about everything with your child, you make him a monster, without reverence, without affections. Reason about things with your servants, consult them, give them the suffrage, and you produce no other effect in them than a sense of anarchy in the house, a suspicion of irresoluteness in you, the most opposed to that spirit of order and promptitude which can alone enable them to fill their places well and make their lives respectable.

26

THE INFLUENCE OF RATIONALISM

Fortnightly Review, I (15 May 1865), 43–55

George Eliot's review of William Edward Hartpole Lecky's *History of the Rise and Influence of the Spirit of Rationalism in Europe*, 2 vols., 1865, was finished, according to her Journal, on 4 May 1865. It appeared in the first number of the *Fortnightly*, a periodical designed in imitation of the *Revue des Deux Mondes* and intended to supply the independent and responsible journalism that its founders, Anthony Trollope among them, felt was lacking in the English periodical press. G. H. Lewes had agreed to edit the magazine, and for this reason, as George Eliot said in a letter, 'it was seemly that I should write a little in it'.[1] In accordance with the *Fortnightly*'s policy against anonymous articles, the review was signed 'George Eliot'.

In the month after her article appeared, George Eliot noted in her Journal for 25 June: 'Tyndal [Sir John Tyndall] told G. [H. Lewes] that he dined with Lecky at Longman's & on going home read my article, which seemed to him to give a thoroughly just conception of the man—to "hit him off exactly." Thinks he will do nothing better. I am glad to have this testimony that I have not in this case done any injustice.'

'The Influence of Rationalism' has been reprinted in Nathan Sheppard, *The Essays of 'George Eliot', Complete*; and in *Essays and Leaves from a Note-Book*.

* * *

THERE is a valuable class of books on great subjects which have something of the character and functions of good popular lecturing. They are not original, not subtle, not of close logical texture,

---

[1] *Letters*, IV, 193.

not exquisite either in thought or style; but by virtue of these negatives they are all the more fit to act on the average intelligence. They have enough of organising purpose in them to make their facts illustrative, and to leave a distinct result in the mind even when most of the facts are forgotten; and they have enough of vagueness and vacillation in their theory to win them ready acceptance from a mixed audience. The vagueness and vacillation are not devices of timidity; they are the honest result of the writer's own mental character, which adapts him to be the instructor and the favourite of 'the general reader.' For the most part, the general reader of the present day does not exactly know what distance he goes; he only knows that he does not go 'too far.' Of any remarkable thinker, whose writings have excited controversy, he likes to have it said that 'his errors are to be deplored,' leaving it not too certain what those errors are; he is fond of what may be called disembodied opinions, that float in vapoury phrases above all systems of thought or action; he likes an undefined Christianity which opposes itself to nothing in particular, as undefined education of the people, an undefined amelioration of all things: in fact, he likes sound views—nothing extreme, but something between the excesses of the past and the excesses of the present. This modern type of the general reader may be known in conversation by the cordiality with which he assents to indistinct, blurred statements: say that black is black, he will shake his head and hardly think it; say that black is not so very black, he will reply, 'Exactly.' He has no hesitation, if you wish it, even to get up at a public meeting and express his conviction that at times, and within certain limits, the radii of a circle have a tendency to be equal; but, on the other hand, he would urge that the spirit of geometry may be carried a little too far. His only bigotry is a bigotry against any clearly-defined opinion; not in the least based on a scientific scepticism, but belonging to a lack of coherent thought—a spongy texture of mind, that gravitates strongly to nothing. The one thing he is staunch for is, the utmost liberty of private haziness.

But precisely these characteristics of the general reader, rendering him incapable of assimilating ideas unless they are administered in a highly diluted form, make it a matter of rejoicing that there are clever, fair-minded men, who will write books for him—men very much above him in knowledge and ability, but not too remote from him in their habits of thinking, and who can thus prepare for him infusions of history and science, that will leave some solidifying deposit, and save him from a fatal softening of the intellectual skeleton. Among such serviceable writers, Mr. Lecky's 'History of the Rise and Influence of the Spirit of Rationalism in Europe' entitles him to a high place. He has prepared himself for its production by an unusual amount of well-directed reading; he has chosen his facts and quotations with much judgment; and he gives proof of those important moral qualifications, impartiality, seriousness, and modesty. This praise is chiefly applicable to the long chapter on the history of Magic and Witchcraft, which opens the work, and to the two chapters on the antecedents and history of Persecution, which occur, the one at the end of the first volume, the other at the beginning of the second. In these chapters Mr. Lecky has a narrower and better-traced path before him than in other portions of his work; he is more occupied with presenting a particular class of facts in their historical sequence, and in their relation to certain grand tide-marks of opinion, than with disquisition; and his writing is freer than elsewhere from an apparent confusedness of thought and an exuberance of approximative phrases, which can be serviceable in no other way than as diluents needful for the sort of reader we have just described.

The history of magic and witchcraft has been judiciously chosen by Mr. Lecky as the subject of his first section on the Declining Sense of the Miraculous, because it is strikingly illustrative of a position with the truth of which he is strongly impressed, though he does not always treat of it with desirable clearness and precision, namely, that certain beliefs become obsolete, not in consequence of direct arguments against them, but because of their incongruity with prevalent habits of thought. Here is his statement of the two 'classes of influences,' by which the mass of men, in what is called civilised society, get their beliefs gradually modified:

> If we ask why it is that the world has rejected what was once so universally and so intensely believed, why a narrative of an old woman who had been seen riding on a broomstick, or who was proved to have transformed herself into a wolf, and to have devoured the flocks of her neighbours, is deemed so entirely incredible, most persons would probably be unable to give a very definite answer to the question. It is not because we have examined the evidence and found it insufficient, for the disbelief always precedes, when it does not prevent, examination.

It is rather because the idea of absurdity is so strongly attached to such narratives, that it is difficult even to consider them with gravity. Yet at one time no such improbability was felt, and hundreds of persons have been burnt simply on the two grounds I have mentioned.

When so complete a change takes place in public opinion, it may be ascribed to one or other of two causes. It may be the result of a controversy which has conclusively settled the question, establishing to the satisfaction of all parties a clear preponderance of argument or fact in favour of one opinion, and making that opinion a truism which is accepted by all enlightened men, even though they have not themselves examined the evidence on which it rests. Thus, if any one in a company of ordinarily educated persons were to deny the motion of the earth, or the circulation of the blood, his statement would be received with derision, though it is probable that some of his audience would be unable to demonstrate the first truth, and that very few of them could give sufficient reasons for the second. They may not themselves be able to defend their position; but they are aware that, at certain known periods of history, controversies on those subjects took place, and that known writers then brought forward some definite arguments or experiments, which were ultimately accepted by the whole learned world as rigid and conclusive demonstrations. It is possible, also, for as complete a change to be effected by what is called the spirit of the age. The general intellectual tendencies pervading the literature of a century profoundly modify the character of the public mind. They form a new tone and habit of thought. They alter the measure of probability. They create new attractions and new antipathies, and they eventually cause as absolute a rejection of certain old opinions as could be produced by the most cogent and definite arguments.

Mr. Lecky proceeds to some questionable views concerning the evidences of witchcraft, which seem to be irreconcilable even with his own remarks later on; but they lead him to the statement, thoroughly made out by his historical survey, that 'the movement was mainly silent, unargumentative, and insensible; that men came gradually to disbelieve in witchcraft, because they came gradually to look upon it as absurd; and that this new tone of thought appeared, first of all, in those who were least subject to theological influences, and soon spread through the educated laity, and, last of all, took possession of the clergy.'

We have rather painful proof that this 'second class of influences' with a vast number go hardly deeper than Fashion, and that witchcraft to many of us is absurd only on the same ground that our grandfathers' gigs are absurd. It is felt preposterous to think of spiritual agencies in connection with ragged beldames soaring on broomsticks, in an age when it is known that mediums of communication with the invisible world are usually unctuous personages dressed in excellent broadcloth, who soar above the curtain-poles without any broomstick, and who are not given to unprofitable intrigues.[2] The enlightened imagination rejects the figure of a witch with her profile in dark relief against the moon and her broomstick cutting a constellation. No undiscovered natural laws, no names of 'respectable' witnesses, are invoked to make us feel our presumption in questioning the diabolic intimacies of that obsolete old woman, for it is known now that the undiscovered laws, and the witnesses qualified by the payment of income-tax, are all in favour of a different conception—the image of a heavy gentlemen in boots and black coat-tails foreshortened against the cornice. Yet no less a person than Sir Thomas Browne once wrote that those who denied there were witches, inasmuch as they thereby denied spirits also, were 'obliquely and upon consequence a sort, not of infidels, but of atheists.'[3] At present, doubtless, in certain circles, unbelievers in heavy gentlemen who float in the air by means of undiscovered laws are also taxed with atheism; illiberal as it is not to admit that mere weakness of understanding may prevent one from seeing how that phenomenon is necessarily involved in the Divine origin of things. With still more remarkable parallelism, Sir Thomas Browne goes on: 'Those that, to refute their incredulity, desire to see apparitions, shall questionless never behold any, nor have the power to be so much as witches.

[2] Here and in the rest of this paragraph George Eliot alludes to the then popular interest in spiritualism, and especially to the famous medium Daniel Dunglas Home (1833–1886), Browning's 'Mr. Sludge', who often performed feats of levitation at his séances. Interest in Home was very keen at the time of this article, for in 1864 he had been expelled from Rome as a sorcerer and had returned to England for redress, where his cause was taken up in Parliament. George Eliot had had 'repeated conversations' with T. A. Trollope on spiritualism, in which Trollope was a hesitant believer (Letters, IV, 81), but her feelings about it are summed up in her phrase describing its phenomena as 'odious trickery' (Letters, III, 359). Lewes wrote a hostile reply in Blackwood's, LXXXVIII (October, 1860), 381–395, to a notorious article [by Robert Bell], 'Stranger than Fiction', Cornhill, II (August, 1860), 211–224. Without attempting to explain the things he was certain he had seen, Bell described various séances, including one at which Home floated up to the ceiling.

[3] Religio Medici, Part I, Section xxx.

The devil hath made them already in a heresy as capital as witch-craft, *and to appear to them were but to convert them*'.[4] It would be difficult to see what has been changed here but the mere drapery of circumstance, if it were not for this prominent difference between our own days and the days of witchcraft, that instead of torturing, drowning, or burning the innocent, we give hospitality and large pay to—the highly-distinguished medium. At least we are safely rid of certain horrors; but if the multitude—that 'farraginous concurrence of all conditions, tempers, sexes, and ages'[5]—do not roll back even to a superstition that carries cruelty in its train, it is not because they possess a cultivated Reason, but because they are pressed upon and held up by what we may call an external Reason—the sum of conditions resulting from the laws of material growth, from changes produced by great historical collisions shattering the structures of ages and making new high-ways for events and ideas, and from the activities of higher minds no longer existing merely as opinions and teaching, but as institu-tions and organisations with which the interests, the affections, and the habits of the multitude are inextricably interwoven. No undis-covered laws accounting for small phenomena going forward under drawing-room tables are likely to affect the tremendous facts of the increase of population, the rejection of convicts by our colonies, the exhaustion of the soil by cotton plantations, which urge even upon the foolish certain questions, certain claims, certain views concerning the scheme of the world, that can never again be silenced. If right reason is a right representation of the co-existences and sequences of things, here are co-existences and sequences that do not wait to be discovered, but press themselves upon us like bars of iron. No séances at a guinea a head for the sake of being pinched by 'Mary Jane' can annihilate railways, steam-ships, and electric telegraphs, which are demonstrating the inter-dependence of all human interests, and making self-interest a duct for sympathy. These things are part of the external Reason to which internal silliness has inevitably to accommodate itself.

Three points in the history of magic and witchcraft are well brought out by Mr. Lecky. First, that the cruelties connected with it did not begin until men's minds had ceased to repose implicitly in a sacramental system which made them feel well armed against

[4] *Ibid.* George Eliot's italics.
[5] Sir Thomas Browne, *Pseudodoxia Epidemica*, Book I, Ch. 3.

evil spirits; that is, until the eleventh century, when there came a sort of morning dream of doubt and heresy, bringing on the one side the terror of timid consciences, and on the other the terrorism of authority or zeal bent on checking the rising struggle. In that time of comparative mental repose, says Mr. Lecky—

All those conceptions of diabolical presence; all that predisposition towards the miraculous, which acted so fearfully upon the imaginations of the fifteenth and sixteenth centuries, existed; but the implicit faith, the boundless and triumphant credulity with which the virtue of ecclesiastical rites was accepted, rendered them comparatively innocuous. If men had been a little less superstitious, the effects of their superstition would have been much more terrible. It was firmly believed that any one who deviated from the strict line of orthodoxy must soon succumb beneath the power of Satan; but as there was no spirit of rebellion or doubt, this persuasion did not produce any extraordinary terrorism.

The Church was disposed to confound heretical opinion with sorcery; false doctrine was especially the devil's work, and it was a ready conclusion that a denier or innovator had held consultation with the father of lies. It is a saying of a zealous Catholic in the sixteenth century, quoted by Maury in his excellent work, 'De la Magie'—'Crescit cum magia hæresis, cum hæresi magia.'[6] Even those who doubted were terrified at their doubts, for trust is more easily undermined than terror. Fear is earlier born than hope, lays a stronger grasp on man's system than any other passion, and remains master of a larger group of involuntary actions. A chief aspect of man's moral development is the slow subduing of fear by the gradual growth of intelligence, and its suppression as a motive by the presence of impulses less animally selfish; so that in relation to invisible Power, fear at last ceases to exist, save in that interfusion with higher faculties which we call awe.

Secondly, Mr. Lecky shows clearly that dogmatic Protestantism, holding the vivid belief in Satanic agency to be an essential of piety, would have felt it shame to be a whit behind Catholicism in severity against the devil's servants. Luther's sentiment was that he would not suffer a witch to live (he was not much more merciful to Jews); and, in spite of his fondness for children, believing a

[6] Louis Ferdinand Alfred Maury, *La magie et l'astrologie dans l'antiquité et au moyen age* (Paris, 1860), p. 192.

certain child to have been begotten by the devil, he recommended
the parents to throw it into the river. The torch must be turned
on the worst errors of heroic minds—not in irreverent ingratitude,
but for the sake of measuring our vast and various debt to all the
influences which have concurred, in the intervening ages, to make
us recognise as detestable errors the honest convictions of men
who, in mere individual capacity and moral force, were very much
above us. Again, the Scotch Puritans, during the comparatively
short period of their ascendency, surpassed all Christians before
them in the elaborate ingenuity of the tortures they applied for the
discovery of witchcraft and sorcery, and did their utmost to prove
that if Scotch Calvinism was the true religion, the chief 'note' of
the true religion was cruelty. It is hardly an endurable task to read
the story of their doings; thoroughly to imagine them as a past
reality is already a sort of torture. One detail is enough, and it is a
comparatively mild one. It was the regular profession of men
called 'prickers' to thrust long pins into the body of a suspected
witch in order to detect the insensible spot which was the infallible
sign of her guilt. On a superficial view one would be in danger of
saying that the main difference between the teachers who sanctioned these things and the much-despised ancestors who offered
human victims inside a huge wicker idol, was that they arrived at
a more elaborate barbarity by a longer series of dependent propositions. [We][7] do not share Mr. Buckle's opinion that a Scotch
minister's groans were a part of his deliberate plan for keeping the
people in a state of terrified subjection;[8] the ministers themselves
held the belief they taught, and might well groan over it. What a
blessing has a little false logic been to the world! Seeing that men
are so slow to question their premises, they must have made each
other much more miserable, if pity 'had not sometimes drawn
tender conclusions not warranted by Major and Minor; if there
had not been people with an amiable imbecility of reasoning which

[7] 'I', 1884.
[8] The whole of Volume III, Ch. 4 of Henry Thomas Buckle's *History
of Civilization in England*, New Edition (London, 1878) is devoted to a
description of the seventeenth-century Scotch clergy's tyranny over the
minds of their congregations: 'All over Scotland, the sermons were, with
hardly an exception, formed after the same plan, and directed to the same
end. To excite fear, was the paramount end' (III, 238). George Eliot,
who had nothing of Buckle's brash confidence in nineteenth-century
progress, called him 'an irreligious, conceited man' (*Letters*, II, 486).

enabled them at once to cling to hideous beliefs, and to be conscientiously inconsistent with them in their conduct. There is nothing like acute deductive reasoning for keeping a man in the dark: it might be called the *technique* of the intellect, and the concentration of the mind upon it corresponds to that predominance of technical skill in art which ends in degradation of the artist's function, unless new inspiration and invention come to guide it.

And of this there is some good illustration furnished by that third node in the history of witchcraft, the beginning of its end, which is treated in an interesting manner by Mr. Lecky. It is worth noticing, that the most important defences of the belief in witchcraft, against the growing scepticism in the latter part of the sixteenth century and in the seventeenth, were the productions of men who in some departments were among the foremost thinkers of their time. One of them was Jean Bodin, the famous writer on government and jurisprudence, whose 'Republic,' Hallam thinks, had an important influence in England, and furnished 'a store of arguments and examples that were not lost on the thoughtful minds of our countrymen.'[9] In some of his views he was original and bold; for example, he anticipated Montesquieu in attempting to appreciate the relations of government and climate. Hallam inclines to the opinion that he was a Jew, and attached Divine authority only to the Old Testament. But this was enough to furnish him with his chief data for the existence of witches and for their capital punishment; and in the account of his 'Republic' given by Hallam, there is enough evidence that the sagacity which often enabled him to make fine use of his learning was also often entangled in it, to temper our surprise at finding a writer on political science of whom it could be said that, along with Montesquieu, he was 'the most philosophical of those who had read so deeply, the most learned of those who had thought so much,'[10] in the van of the forlorn hope to maintain the reality of witchcraft. It should be said that he was equally confident of the unreality of the Copernican hypothesis, on the ground that it was contrary to the tenets of the theologians and philosophers and to common sense, and therefore subversive of the foundations of every science.

[9] Henry Hallam, *Introduction to the Literature of Europe in the Fifteenth, Sixteenth, and Seventeenth Centuries*, 2 vols. (New York, 1847), I, 312, note.

[10] *Ibid.*, I, 320.

Of his work on witchcraft, Mr. Lecky says:

> The 'Démonomanie des Sorciers' is chiefly an appeal to authority, which the author deemed on this subject so unanimous and so conclusive, that it was scarcely possible for any sane man to resist it. He appealed to the popular belief in all countries, in all ages, and in all religions. He cited the opinions of an immense multitude of the greatest writers of pagan antiquity, and of the most illustrious of the Fathers. He showed how the laws of all nations recognised the existence of witchcraft; and he collected hundreds of cases which had been investigated before the tribunals of his own or of other countries. He relates with the most minute and circumstantial detail, and with the most unfaltering confidence, all the proceedings at the witches' Sabbath, the methods which the witches employed in transporting themselves through the air, their transformations, their carnal intercourse with the Devil, their various means of injuring their enemies, the signs that lead to their detection, their confessions when condemned, and their demeanour at the stake.

Something must be allowed for a lawyer's affection towards a belief which had furnished so many 'cases.' Bodin's work had been immediately prompted by the treatise 'De Prestigiis Dæmonum', written by John Wier, a German physician, a treatise which is worth notice as an example of a transitional form of opinion for which many analogies may be found in the history both of religion and science. Wier believed in demons, and in possession by demons, but his practice as a physician had convinced him that the so-called witches were patients and victims, that the devil took advantage of their diseased condition to delude them, and that there was no consent of an evil will on the part of the women. He argued that the word in Leviticus translated 'witch' meant 'poisoner,' and besought the princes of Europe to hinder the further spilling of innocent blood. These heresies of Wier threw Bodin into such a state of amazed indignation that if he had been an ancient Jew instead of a modern economical one, he would have rent his garments. 'No one had ever heard of pardon being accorded to sorcerers;' and probably the reason why Charles IX. died young was because he had pardoned the sorcerer, Trois Echelles! We must remember that this was in 1581, when the great scientific movement of the Renaissance had hardly begun—when Galileo was a youth of seventeen, and Kepler a boy of ten.

But directly afterwards, on the other side, came Montaigne, whose sceptical acuteness could arrive at negatives without any apparatus of method. A certain keen narrowness of nature will secure a man from many absurd beliefs which the larger soul, vibrating to more manifold influences, would have a long struggle to part with. And so we find the charming, chatty Montaigne—in one of the brightest of his essays, 'Des Boiteux,' where he declares that, from his own observation of witches and sorcerers, he should have recommended them to be treated with curative hellebore— stating in his own way a pregnant doctrine, since taught more gravely. It seems to him much less of a prodigy that men should lie, or that their imaginations should deceive them, than that a human body should be carried through the air on a broomstick, or up a chimney by some unknown spirit. He thinks it a sad business to persuade oneself that the test of truth lies in the multitude of believers—'en une presse où les fols surpassent de tant les sages en nombre.'[11] Ordinarily, he has observed, when men have something stated to them as a fact, they are more ready to explain it than to inquire whether it is real: 'ils passent par-dessus les propositions, mais ils examinent les conséquences;[12] *ils laissent les choses, et courent aux causes*'. There is a sort of strong and generous ignorance which is as honourable and courageous as science—'ignorance pour laquelle concevoir il n'y a pas moins de science qu'a concevoir la science'. And *à propos* of the immense traditional evidence which weighed with such men as Bodin, he says—'As for the proofs and arguments founded on experience and facts, I do not pretend to unravel these. What end of a thread is there to lay hold of? I often cut them as Alexander did his knot. *Après tout, c'est mettre ses conjectures à bien haut prix, que d'en faire cuire un homme tout vif.*'

Writing like this, when it finds eager readers, is a sign that the weather is changing; yet much later, namely, after 1665,[13] when

[11] This and the following three quotations are all from Montaigne's 'Des Boiteux', *Essais*, III, ii. The last of them is quoted by Lecky, *History*, 2 vols., Revised Edition (New York, 1878), I, 111, but entirely in English and in a different translation. George Eliot has gone to Montaigne for her text.

[12] Montaigne reads: 'Ils passent par dessus les presuppositions; mais ils examinent curieusement les consequences. . . .'

[13] 1665 is the date of the Society's first *Transactions*. Its charter is 1662.

the Royal Society had been founded, our own Glanvil, the author of the 'Scepsis Scientifica,' a work that was a remarkable advance towards a true definition of the limits of inquiry, and that won him his election as fellow of the society, published an energetic vindication of the belief in witchcraft, of which Mr. Lecky gives the following sketch:

The 'Sadducismus Triumphatus,' which is probably the ablest book ever published in defence of the superstition, opens with a striking picture of the rapid progress of the scepticism in England. Everywhere, a disbelief in witchcraft was becoming fashionable in the upper classes; but it was a disbelief that arose entirely from a strong sense of its antecedent improbability. All who were opposed to the orthodox faith united in discrediting witchcraft. They laughed at it, as palpably absurd, as involving the most grotesque and ludicrous conceptions, as so essentially incredible that it would be a waste of time to examine it. This spirit had arisen since the Restoration, although the laws were still in force, and although little or no direct reasoning had been brought to bear upon the subject. In order to combat it, Glanvil proceeded to examine the general question of the credibility of the miraculous. He saw that the reason why witchcraft was ridiculed was, because it was a phase of the miraculous and the work of the devil; that the scepticism was chiefly due to those who disbelieved in miracles and the devil; and that the instances of witchcraft or possession in the Bible were invariably placed on a level with those that were tried in the law courts of England. That the evidence of the belief was overwhelming, he firmly believed; and this, indeed, was scarcely disputed; but, until the sense of *à priori* improbability was removed, no possible accumulation of facts would cause men to believe it. To that task he accordingly addressed himself. Anticipating the idea and almost the words of modern controversialists, he urged that there was such a thing as a credulity of unbelief; and that those who believed so strange a concurrence of delusions, as was necessary on the supposition of the unreality of witchcraft, were far more credulous than those who accepted the belief. He made his very scepticism his principal weapon; and, analysing with much acuteness the *à priori* objections, he showed that they rested upon an unwarrantable confidence in our knowledge of the laws of the spirit world; that they implied the existence of some strict analogy between the faculties of men and of spirits; and that, as such analogy most probably did not exist, no reasoning based on the supposition could dispense men from examining the evidence. He concluded with a large collection of cases, the evidence of which was, as he thought, incontestible.

We have quoted this sketch because Glanvil's argument against the *à priori* objection of absurdity is fatiguingly urged in relation to other alleged marvels which, to busy people seriously occupied with the difficulties of affairs, of science, or of art, seem as little worthy of examination as aëronautic broomsticks. And also because we here see Glanvil, in combating an incredulity that does not happen to be his own, wielding that very argument of traditional evidence which he had made the subject of vigorous attack in his 'Scepsis Scientifica.' But perhaps large minds have been peculiarly liable to this fluctuation concerning the sphere of tradition, because, while they have attacked its misapplications, they have been the more solicited by the vague sense that tradition is really the basis of our best life. Our sentiments may be called organised traditions; and a large part of our actions gather all their justification, all their attraction and aroma, from the memory of the life lived, of the actions done, before we were born. In the absence of any profound research into psychological functions or into the mysteries of inheritance, in the absence of any comprehensive view of man's historical development and the dependence of one age on another, a mind at all rich in sensibilities must always have had an indefinite uneasiness in an undistinguishing attack on the coercive influence of tradition. And this may be the apology for the apparent inconsistency of Glanvil's acute criticism on the one side, and his indignation at the 'looser gentry,' who laughed at the evidences for witchcraft, on the other. We have already taken up too much space with this subject of witchcraft, else we should be tempted to dwell on Sir Thomas Browne, who far surpassed Glanvil in magnificent incongruity of opinion, and whose works are the most remarkable combination existing, of witty sarcasm against ancient nonsense and modern obsequiousness, with indications of a capacious credulity. After all, we may be sharing what seems to us the hardness of these men, who sat in their studies and argued at their ease about a belief that would be reckoned to have caused more misery and bloodshed than any other superstition, if there had been no such thing as persecution on the ground of religious opinion.

On this subject of Persecution, Mr. Lecky writes his best: with clearness of conception, with calm justice, bent on appreciating the necessary tendency of ideas, and with an appropriateness of illustration that could be supplied only by extensive and intelligent reading. Persecution, he shows, is not in any sense peculiar to the Catholic Church; it is a direct sequence of the doctrines that salvation is to be had only within the Church, and that erroneous belief is damnatory—doctrines held as fully by Protestant sects as by the Catholics; and in proportion to its power, Protestantism has been as persecuting as Catholicism. He maintains, in opposition to the favourite modern notion of persecution defeating its own object, that the Church, holding the dogma of exclusive salvation, was perfectly consequent, and really achieved its end of spreading one belief and quenching another, by calling in the aid of the civil arm. Who will say that governments, by their power over institutions and patronage, as well as over punishment, have not power also over the interests and inclinations of men, and over most of those external conditions into which subjects are born, and which make them adopt the prevalent belief as a second nature? Hence, to a sincere believer in the doctrine of exclusive salvation, governments had it in their power to save men from perdition; and wherever the clergy were at the elbow of the civil arm, no matter whether they were Catholic or Protestant, persecution was the result. 'Compel them to come in'[14] was a rule that seemed sanctioned by mercy, and the horrible sufferings it led men to inflict seemed small to minds accustomed to contemplate, as a perpetual source of motive, the eternal unmitigated miseries of a hell that was the inevitable destination of a majority amongst mankind.

It is a significant fact, noted by Mr. Lecky, that the only two leaders of the Reformation who advocated tolerance were Zuinglius and Socinus, both of them disbelievers in exclusive salvation. And in corroboration of other evidence that the chief triumphs of the Reformation were due to coercion, he commends to the special attention of his readers the following quotation from a work attributed without question to the famous Protestant theologian, Jurieu, who had himself been hindered, as a Protestant, from exercising his professional functions in France, and was settled as pastor at Rotterdam. It should be remembered that Jurieu's labours fell in the latter part of the seventeenth century and in the beginning of the eighteenth, and that he was the contemporary of Bayle, with whom he was in bitter controversial hostility. He wrote, then, at a time when there was warm debate on the question

[14] Luke 14:23.

of Toleration; and it was his great object to vindicate himself and his French fellow-Protestants from all laxity on this point.

> Peut on nier que le paganisme est tombé dans le monde par l'autorité des empereurs Romains? On peut assurer sans temerité que le paganisme seroit encore debout, et que les trois quarts de l'Europe seroit encore payens si Constantin et ses successeurs n'avaient employé leur autorité pour l'abolir. Mais, je vous prie, de quelles voies Dieu s'est il servi dans ces derniers siècles pour rétablir la veritable religion dans l'Occident? *Les rois de Suède, ceux de Danemarck, ceux d'Angleterre, les magistrats souverains de Suisse, des Païs Bas, des villes libres d'Allemagne, les princes électeurs, et autres princes souverains de l'empire, n'ont ils pas emploié leur autorité pour abbattre le Papisme?*

Indeed, wherever the tremendous alternative of everlasting torments is believed in—believed in so that it becomes a motive determining the life—not persecution, but every other form of severity and gloom are the legitimate consequences. There is much ready declamation in these days against the spirit of asceticism and against zeal for doctrinal conversion; but surely the macerated form of a Saint Francis, the fierce denunciations of a Saint Dominic, the groans and prayerful wrestlings of the Puritan who seasoned his bread with tears and made all pleasurable sensation sin, are more in keeping with the contemplation of unending anguish as the destiny of a vast multitude whose nature we share, than the rubicund cheerfulness of some modern divines, who profess to unite a smiling liberalism with a well-bred and tacit but unshaken confidence in the reality of the bottomless pit. But, in fact, as Mr. Lecky maintains, that awful image, with its group of associated dogmas concerning the inherited curse, and the damnation of unbaptised infants, of heathens, and of heretics, has passed away from what he is fond of calling 'the realisations' of Christendom. These things are no longer the objects of practical belief. They may be mourned for in encyclical letters; bishops may regret them; doctors of divinity may sign testimonials to the excellent character of these decayed beliefs; but for the mass of Christians they are no more influential than unrepealed but forgotten statutes. And with these dogmas has melted away the strong basis for the defence of persecution. No man now writes eager vindications of himself and his colleagues from the suspicion of adhering to the principle of toleration. And this momentous change, it is Mr. Lecky's object to show, is due to that con-currence of conditions which he has chosen to call 'the advance of the Spirit of Rationalism.'

In other parts of his work, where he attempts to trace the action of the same conditions on the acceptance of miracles and on other chief phases of our historical development, Mr. Lecky has laid himself open to considerable criticism. The chapters on the Miracles of the Church, the æsthetic, scientific, and moral Develop-ment of Rationalism, the Secularisation of Politics, and the Industrial history of Rationalism, embrace a wide range of diligently gathered facts; but they are nowhere illuminated by a sufficiently clear conception and statement of the agencies at work, or the mode of their action, in the gradual modification of opinion and of life. The writer frequently impresses us as being in a state of hesitation concerning his own standing-point, which may form a desirable stage in private meditation but not in published exposition. Certain epochs in theoretic conception, certain con-siderations, which should be fundamental to his survey, are intro-duced quite incidentally in a sentence or two, or in a note which seems to be an after-thought. Great writers and their ideas are touched upon too slightly and with too little discrimination, and important theories are sometimes characterised with a rashness which conscientious revision will correct. There is a fatiguing use of vague or shifting phrases, such as 'modern civilisation,' 'spirit of the age,' 'tone of thought,' 'intellectual type of the age,' 'bias of the imagination,' 'habits of religious thought,' unbalanced by any precise definition; and the spirit of rationalism is sometimes treated of as if it lay outside the specific mental activities of which it is a generalised expression. Mr. Curdle's famous definition of the dramatic unities as 'a sort of a general oneness,'[15] is not totally false; but such luminousness as it has could only be perceived by those who already knew what the unities were. Mr. Lecky has the advantage of being strongly impressed with the great part played by the emotions in the formation of opinion, and with the high complexity of the causes at work in social evolution; but he frequently writes as if he had never yet distinguished between the complexity of the conditions that produce prevalent states of mind, and the inability of particular minds to give distinct reasons for the preferences or persuasions produced by those states. In

[15] Dickens, *Nicholas Nickleby*, Ch. 24.

412

brief, he does not discriminate, or does not help his reader to discriminate, between objective complexity and subjective confusion. But the most muddle-headed gentleman who represents the spirit of the age by observing, as he settles his collar, that the development-theory is quite 'the thing' is a result of definite processes, if we could only trace them. 'Mental attitudes', and 'predispositions', however vague in consciousness, have not vague causes, any more than the 'blind motions of the spring'[16] in plants and animals.

The word 'Rationalism' has the misfortune, shared by most words in this grey world, of being somewhat equivocal. This evil may be nearly overcome by careful preliminary definition; but Mr. Lecky does not supply this, and the original specific application of the word to a particular phase of Biblical interpretation seems to have clung about his use of it with a misleading effect. Through some parts of his book he appears to regard the grand characteristic of modern thought and civilisation, compared with ancient, as a radiation in the first instance from a change in religious conceptions. The supremely important fact, that the gradual reduction of all phenomena within the sphere of established law, which carries as a consequence the rejection of the miraculous, has its determining current in the development of physical science, seems to have engaged comparatively little of his attention; at least, he gives it no prominence. The great conception of universal regular sequence, without partiality and without caprice—the conception which is the most potent force at work in the modification of our faith, and of the practical form given to our sentiments—could only grow out of that patient watching of external fact, and that silencing of preconceived notions, which are urged upon the mind by the problems of physical science.

[There is not room here to explain and justify the impressions of dissatisfaction which have been briefly indicated, but a serious writer like Mr. Lecky will not find such suggestions altogether useless. The objections, even the misunderstandings, of a reader who is not careless or ill-disposed, may serve to stimulate an author's vigilance over his thoughts as well as his style. It would be gratifying to see some future proof that Mr. Lecky has acquired juster views than are implied in the assertion that philosophers of

[16] Tennyson, 'The Talking Oak', 175.

the sensational school 'can never rise to the conception of the disinterested;' and that he has freed himself from all temptation to that mingled laxity of statement, and ill-pitched elevation of tone, which are painfully present in the closing pages of his second volume.][17]

[17] Omitted, 1884. George Eliot's resentment was provoked by Lecky's concluding suggestion that the decay of religious belief has destroyed the motives to self-sacrifice for an ideal; her own ethics taught that imaginative sympathy is independent of all religious or metaphysical systems.

27

ADDRESS TO WORKING MEN,
BY FELIX HOLT

Blackwood's, CIII (January, 1868), 1–11

After hearing Disraeli's speech on the Reform Bill to the Edinburgh working men in 1867, George Eliot's publisher John Blackwood suggested to her that she too might do 'a first rate address to the Working Men on their new responsibilities'.[1] Begun on 22 November, the 'Address' was finished on 4 December 1867 (Journal); Blackwood expressed himself delighted with its style and sentiment, but added, not surprisingly, 'I wish the poor fellows were capable of appreciating it.'[2]

George Eliot has kept the speech consistent with the character of her hero's politics as they are revealed in *Felix Holt*, but since as a political thinker Felix is only a mouthpiece for his creator this should not have been difficult to do. As Joseph Jacobs has accurately observed, 'Felix Holt the Radical is rather Felix Holt the Conservative; he is not even a Tory-Democrat'.[3] In the tradition of Burke, Scott, and Wordsworth, George Eliot believed that the organic nature of society forbade sudden and violent changes, and her 'radicalism' consisted in her keen sense of the determining function played in human affairs by the root of history.

Another element in her conservatism is indicated by Felix's assertion that 'the nature of things in this world has been determined for us beforehand'. The ideal social attitude which grows from this recognition is realized by such characters as the Garths of *Middlemarch*: Caleb's is the wisdom which respects 'the nature of things' (Ch. 40); Mrs. Garth 'had that rare sense which discerns what is unalterable, and submits to it without murmuring' (Ch. 24). Seen in this light, George Eliot's was the conservatism of Wordsworth's 'Ode to Duty', with its religious perception of the duty enforced by the law inherent in 'the nature of things'.

[1] *Letters*, IV, 395.   [2] *Letters*, IV, 402.
[3] *Literary Studies* (London, 1895), p. xxi.

'Address to Working Men' has been reprinted in Nathan Sheppard, *The Essays of 'George Eliot', Complete*; and in *Essays and Leaves from a Note-Book*.

*   *   *

FELLOW-WORKMEN,—I am not going to take up your time by complimenting you. It has been the fashion to compliment kings and other authorities when they have come into power, and to tell them that, under their wise and beneficent rule, happiness would certainly overflow the land. But the end has not always corresponded to that beginning. If it were true that we who work for wages had more of the wisdom and virtue necessary to the right use of power than has been shown by the aristocratic and mercantile classes, we should not glory much in that fact, or consider that it carried with it any near approach to infallibility.

In my opinion, there has been too much complimenting of that sort; and whenever a speaker, whether he is one of ourselves or not, wastes our time in boasting or flattery, I say, let us hiss him. If we have the beginning of wisdom, which is, to know a little truth about ourselves, we know that as a body we are neither very wise nor very virtuous. And to prove this, I will not point specially to our own habits and doings, but to the general state of the country. Any nation that had within it a majority of men—and we are the majority—possessed of much wisdom and virtue, would not tolerate the bad practices, the commercial lying and swindling, the poisonous adulteration of goods, the retail cheating, and the political bribery which are carried on boldly in the midst of us. A majority has the power of creating a public opinion. We could groan and hiss before we had the franchise: if we had groaned and hissed in the right place, if we had discerned better between good and evil, if the multitude of us artisans, and factory hands, and miners, and labourers of all sorts, had been skilful, faithful, well-judging, industrious, sober—and I don't see how there can be wisdom and virtue anywhere without those qualities—we should have made an audience that would have shamed the other classes out of their share in the national vices. We should have had better members of Parliament, better religious teachers, honester tradesmen, fewer foolish demagogues, less impudence in infamous and brutal men; and we should not have had among us the abomination of men calling themselves religious while living in splendour on ill-gotten gains. I say, it is not possible for any society in which there is a very large body of wise and virtuous men to be as vicious as our society is—to have as low a standard of right and wrong, to have so much belief in falsehood, or to have so degrading, barbarous a notion of what pleasure is, or of what justly raises a man above his fellows. Therefore, let us have done with this nonsense about our being much better than the rest of our countrymen, or the pretence that that was a reason why we ought to have such an extension of the franchise as has been given to us. The reason for our having the franchise, as I want presently to show, lies somewhere else than in our personal good qualities, and does not in the least lie in any high betting chance that a delegate is a better man than a duke, or that a Sheffield grinder is a better man than any one of the firm he works for.

However, we have got our franchise now. We have been sarcastically called in the House of Commons the future masters of the country;[4] and if that sarcasm contains any truth, it seems to me that the first thing we had better think of is, our heavy responsibility; that is to say, the terrible risk we run of working mischief and missing good, as others have done before us. Suppose certain men, discontented with the irrigation of a country which depended for all its prosperity on the right direction being given to the waters of a great river, had got the management of the irrigation before they were quite sure how exactly it could be altered for the better, or whether they could command the necessary agency for such an alteration. Those men would have a difficult and dangerous business on their hands; and the more sense, feeling, and knowledge they had, the more they would be likely to tremble rather than to triumph. Our situation is not altogether unlike theirs. For general prosperity and well-being is a vast crop, that like the corn in Egypt can be come at, not at all by hurried snatching, but only by a well-judged patient process; and whether our political power will be any good to us now we have got it, must depend entirely on the means and materials—the knowledge, ability, and honesty, we have at command. These three things are the only conditions on

---

[4] Robert Lowe, on the passage of Disraeli's Reform Bill in 1867, said 'I believe it will be absolutely necessary to compel our future masters to learn their letters'. (A. Patchett Martin, *Life and Letters of . . . Robert Lowe, Viscount Sherbrooke . . .*, 2 vols. [London and New York, 1893], II, 323.)

which we can get any lasting benefit, as every clever workman among us knows: he knows that for an article to be worth much there must be a good invention or plan to go upon, there must be well-prepared material, and there must be skilful and honest work in carrying out the plan. And by this test we may try those who want to be our leaders. Have they anything to offer us besides indignant talk? When they tell us we ought to have this, that, or the other thing, can they explain to us any reasonable, fair, safe way of getting it? Can they argue in favour of a particular change by showing us pretty closely how the change is likely to work? I don't want to decry a just indignation; on the contrary, I should like it to be more thorough and general. A wise man, more than two thousand years ago, when he was asked what would most tend to lessen injustice in the world, said, ['If every bystander felt][5] as indignant at a wrong as if he himself were the sufferer'. Let us cherish such indignation. But the long-growing evils of a great nation are a tangled business, asking for a good deal more than indignation in order to be got rid of.   Indignation is a fine war-horse, but the war-horse must be ridden by a man: it must be ridden by rationality, skill, courage, armed with the right weapons, and taking definite aim.

We have reason to be discontented with many things, and, looking back either through the history of England to much earlier generations or to the legislation and administrations of later times, we are justified in saying that many of the evils under which our country now suffers are the consequences of folly, ignorance, neglect, or self-seeking in those who, at different times have wielded the powers of rank, office, and money. But the more bitterly we feel this, the more loudly we utter it, the stronger is the obligation we lay on ourselves to beware, lest we also, by a too hasty wresting of measures which seem to promise an immediate partial relief, make a worse time of it for our own generation, and leave a bad inheritance to our children. The deepest curse of wrong doing, whether of the foolish, or wicked sort, is that its effects are difficult to be undone. I suppose there is hardly anything more to be shuddered at than that part of the history of disease which shows how, when a man injures his constitution by a life of vicious excess, his children and grandchildren inherit diseased bodies and minds, and how the effects of that unhappy inheritance continue to spread

[5] 'That every bystander should feel', 1884.

418

ADDRESS TO WORKING MEN, BY FELIX HOLT

beyond our calculation. This is only one example of the law by
which human lives are linked together; another example of what
we complain of when we point to our pauperism, to the brutal
ignorance of multitudes among our fellow countrymen, to the
weight of taxation laid on us by blamable wars, to the wasteful
channels made for the public money, to the expense and trouble
of getting justice, and call these the effects of bad rule. This is the
law that we all bear the yoke of, the law of no man's making, and
which no man can undo. Everybody now sees an example of it in
the case of Ireland. We who are living now are sufferers by the
wrong-doing of those who lived before us; we are sufferers by each
other's wrong doing; and the children who come after us are and
will be sufferers from the same causes. Will any man say he
doesn't care for that law—it is nothing to him—what he wants is to
better himself? With what face then will he complain of any
injury? If he says that in politics or in any sort of social action he
will not care to know what are likely to be the consequences to
others besides himself, he is defending the very worst doings that
have brought about his discontent. He might as well say that there
is no better rule needful for men than that each should tug and
rive for what will please him, without caring how that tugging will
act on the fine widespread network of society in which he is fast
meshed. If any man taught that as a doctrine, we should know him
for a fool. But there are men who act upon it; every scoundrel, for
example, whether he is a rich religious scoundrel who lies and
cheats on a large scale, and will perhaps come and ask you to send
him to Parliament, or a poor pocket-picking scoundrel, who will
steal your loose pence while you are listening round the platform.
None of us are so ignorant as not to know that a society, a nation
is held together by just the opposite doctrine and action—by the
dependence of men on each other and the sense they have of a
common interest in preventing injury. And we working men are,
I think, of all classes the last that can afford to forget this; for if
we did we should be much like sailors cutting away the timbers of
our own ship to warm our grog with. For what else is the meaning
of our Trades-unions? What else is the meaning of every flag we
carry, every procession we make, every crowd we collect for the
sake of making some protest on behalf of our body as receivers of
wages, if not this: that it is our interest to stand by each other, and
that this being the common interest, no one of us will try to make

419

a good bargain for himself without considering what will be good for his fellows? And every member of a union believes that the wider he can spread his union, the stronger and surer will be the effect of it. So I think I shall be borne out in saying that a working man who can put two and two together, or take three from four and see what will be the remainder, can understand that a society, to be well off, must be made up chiefly of men who consider the general good as well as their own.

Well, but taking the world as it is—and this is one way we must take it when we want to find out how it can be improved—no society is made up of a single class: society stands before us like that wonderful piece of life, the human body, with all its various parts depending on one another, and with a terrible liability to get wrong because of that delicate dependence. We all know how many diseases the human body is apt to suffer from, and how difficult it is even for the doctors to find out exactly where the seat or beginning of the disorder is. That is because the body is made up of so many various parts, all related to each other, or likely all to feel the effect if any of them goes wrong. It is somewhat the same with our old nations or societies. No society ever stood long in the world without getting to be composed of different classes. Now, it is all pretence to say that there is no such thing as Class Interest. It is clear that if any particular number of men get a particular benefit from any existing institution, they are likely to band together, in order to keep up that benefit and increase it, until it is perceived to be unfair and injurious to another large number, who get knowledge and strength enough to set up a resistance. And this, again, has been part of the history of every great society since history began. But the simple reason for this being, that any large body of men is likely to have more of stupidity, narrowness, and greed than of farsightedness and generosity, it is plain that the number who resist unfairness and injury are in danger of becoming injurious in their turn. And in this way a justifiable resistance has become a damaging convulsion, making everything worse instead of better. This has been seen so often that we ought to profit a little by the experience. So long as there is selfishness in men; so long as they have not found out for themselves institutions which express and carry into practise the truth, that the highest interest of mankind must at last be a common and not a divided interest; so long as the gradual operation of steady causes has not made that truth a part of every man's knowledge and feeling, just as we now not only know that it is good for our health to be cleanly, but feel that cleanliness is only another word for comfort, which is the under-side or lining of all pleasure; so long, I say as men wink at their own knowingness, or hold their heads high, because they have got an advantage over their fellows; so long Class Interest will be in danger of making itself felt injuriously. No set of men will get any sort of power without being in danger of wanting more than their right share. But, on the other hand, it is just as certain that no set of men will get angry at having less than their right share, and set up a claim on that ground, without falling into just the same danger of exacting too much, and exacting it in wrong ways. It's human nature we have got to work with all round, and nothing else. That seems like saying something very commonplace—nay, obvious; as if one should say that where there are hands there are mouths. Yet, to hear a good deal of the speechifying and to see a good deal of the action that goes forward, one might suppose it was forgotten.

But I come back to this: that, in our old society, there are old institutions, and among them the various distinctions and inherited advantages of classes, which have shaped themselves along with all the wonderful slow-growing system of things made up of our laws, our commerce, and our stores of all sorts, whether in material objects, such as buildings and machinery, or in knowledge, such as scientific thought and professional skill. Just as in that case I spoke of before, the irrigation of a country, which must absolutely have its water distributed or it will bear no crop; there are the old channels, the old banks, and the old pumps, which must be used as they are until new and better have been prepared, or the structure of the old has been gradually altered. But it would be fool's work to batter down a pump only because a better might be made, when you had no machinery ready for a new one: it would be wicked work, if villages lost their crops by it. Now the only safe way by which society can be steadily improved and our worst evils reduced, is not by any attempt to do away directly with the actually existing class distinctions and advantages, as if everybody could have the same sort of work, or lead the same sort of life (which none of my hearers are stupid enough to suppose), but by the turning of Class Interests into Class Functions or duties. What I mean is, that each class should be urged by the surrounding conditions to perform its particular work under the strong pressure of responsibility to the nation at large; that our public affairs should be got into a state in which there should be no impunity for foolish or faithless conduct. In this way, the public judgment would sift out incapability and dishonesty from posts of high charge, and even personal ambition would necessarily become of a worthier sort, since the desires of the most selfish men must be a good deal shaped by the opinions of those around them; and for one person to put on a cap and bells, or to go about dishonest or paltry ways of getting rich that he may spend a vast sum of money in having more finery than his neighbours, he must be pretty sure of a crowd who will applaud him. Now changes can only be good in proportion as they help to bring about this sort of result: in proportion as they put knowledge in the place of ignorance, and fellow-feeling in the place of selfishness. In the course of that substitution class distinctions must inevitably change their character; and represent the varying Duties of men, not their varying Interests. But this end will not come by impatience. 'Day will not break the sooner because we get up before the twilight.' Still less will it come by mere undoing, or change merely as change. And moreover, if we believed that it would be unconditionally hastened by our getting the franchise, we should be what I call superstitious men, believing in magic, or the production of a result by hocus-pocus. Our getting the franchise will greatly hasten that good end in proportion only as every one of us has the knowledge, the foresight, the conscience, that will make him well-judging and scrupulous in the use of it. The nature of things in this world has been determined for us beforehand, and in such a way that no ship can be expected to sail well on a difficult voyage, and reach the right port, unless it is well manned: the nature of the winds and the waves, of the timbers, the sails and the cordage, will not accommodate itself to drunken, mutinous sailors.

You will not suspect me of wanting to preach any cant to you, or of joining in the pretence that everything is in a fine way, and need not be made better. What I am striving to keep in our minds is the care, the precaution, with which we should go about making things better, so that the public order may not be destroyed, so that no fatal shock may be given to this society of ours, this living body in which our lives are bound up. After the Reform Bill of 1832 I was in an election riot,[6] which showed me clearly, on a

[6] The 'I' refers equally to George Eliot and Felix Holt. See Cross, *Life*, I, 27–29; *Felix Holt*, Ch. 33.

small scale, what public disorder must always be; and I have never forgotten that the riot was brought about chiefly by the agency of dishonest men who professed to be on the people's side. Now, the danger hanging over change is great, just in proportion as it tends to produce such disorder by giving any large number of ignorant men, whose notions of what is good are of a low and brutal sort, the belief that they have got power into their hands, and may do pretty much as they like. If any one can look round us and say that he sees no signs of any such danger now, and that our national condition is running along like a clear broadening stream, safe not to get choked with mud, I call him a cheerful man: perhaps he does his own gardening, and seldom takes exercise far away from home. To us who have no gardens, and often walk abroad, it is plain that we can never get into a bit of a crowd but we must rub clothes with a set of Roughs, who have the worst vices of the worst rich—who are gamblers, sots, libertines, knaves, or else mere sensual simpletons and victims. They are the ugly crop that has sprung up while the stewards have been sleeping; they are the multiplying brood begotten by parents who have been left without all teaching save that of a too craving body, without all wellbeing save the fading delusions of drugged beer and gin. They are the hideous margin of society, at one edge drawing towards it the undesigning ignorant poor, at the other darkening imperceptibly into the lowest criminal class. Here is one of the evils which cannot be got rid of quickly, and against which any of us who have got sense, decency, and instruction have need to watch. That these degraded fellow-men could really get the mastery in a persistent disobedience to the laws and in a struggle to subvert order, I do not believe; but wretched calamities would come from the very beginning of such a struggle, and the continuance of it would be a civil war, in which the inspiration on both sides might soon cease to be even a false notion of good, and might become the direct savage impulse of ferocity. We have all to see to it that we do not help to rouse what I may call the savage beast in the breasts of our generation—that we do not help to poison the nation's blood, and make richer provision for bestiality to come. We know well enough that oppressors have sinned in this way— that oppression has notoriously made men mad; and we are determined to resist oppression. But let us, if possible, show that we can keep sane in our resistance, and shape our means more and more reasonably towards the least harmful, and therefore the speediest, attainment of our end. Let us, I say, show that our spirits are too strong to be driven mad, but can keep that sober determination which alone gives mastery over the adaptation of means. And a first guarantee of this sanity will be to act as if we understood that the fundamental duty of a government is to preserve order, to enforce obedience of the laws. It has been held hitherto that a man can be depended on as a guardian of order only when he has much money and comfort to lose. But a better state of things would be, that men who had little money and not much comfort should still be guardians of order, because they had sense to see that disorder would do no good, and had a heart of justice, pity, and fortitude, to keep them from making more misery only because they felt some misery themselves. There are thousands of artisans who have already shown this fine spirit, and have endured much with patient heroism. If such a spirit spread, and penetrated us all, we should soon become the masters of the country in the best sense and to the best ends. For, the public order being preserved, there can be no government in future that will not be determined by our insistance on our fair and practicable demands. It is only by disorder that our demands will be choked, that we shall find ourselves lost amongst a brutal rabble, with all the intelligence of the country opposed to us, and see government in the shape of guns that will sweep us down in the ignoble martyrdom of fools.

It has been a too common notion that to insist much on the preservation of order is the part of a selfish aristocracy and a selfish commercial class, because among these, in the nature of things, have been found the opponents of change. I am a Radical; and, what is more, I am not a Radical with a title, or a French cook, or even an entrance into fine society. I expect great changes, and I desire them. But I don't expect them to come in a hurry, by mere inconsiderate sweeping. A Hercules with a big besom is a fine thing for filthy stable, but not for weeding a seed-bed, where his besom would soon make a barren floor.

That is old-fashioned talk, some one may say. We know all that.

Yes, when things are put in an extreme way, most people think they know them; but, after all, they are comparatively few who see the small degrees by which those extremes are arrived at, or have the resolution and self-control to resist the little impulses by which they creep on surely towards a fatal end. Does anybody set out meaning to ruin himself, or to drink himself to death, or to waste his life so that he becomes a despicable old man, a superannuated nuisance, like a fly in winter? Yet there are plenty, of whose lot this is the pitiable story. Well now, supposing us all to have the best intentions, we working men, as a body, run some risk of bringing evil on the nation in that unconscious manner— half-hurrying, half-pushed in a jostling march towards an end we are not thinking of. For just as there are many things which we know better and feel much more strongly than the richer, softer-handed classes can know or feel them; so there are many things— many precious benefits—which we, by the very fact of our privations, our lack of leisure and instruction, are not so likely to be aware of and take into our account. Those precious benefits form a chief part of what I may call the common estate of society: a wealth over and above buildings, machinery, produce, shipping, and so on, though closely connected with these; a wealth of a more delicate kind, that we may more unconsciously bring into danger, doing harm and not knowing that we do it. I mean that treasure of knowledge, science, poetry, refinement of thought, feeling, and manners, great memories and the interpretation of great records, which is carried on from the minds of one generation to the minds of another. This is something distinct from the indulgences of luxury and the pursuit of vain finery; and one of the hardships in the lot of working men is that they have been for the most part shut out from sharing in this treasure. It can make a man's life very great, very full of delight, though he has no smart furniture and no horses: it also yields a great deal of discovery that corrects error, and of invention that lessens bodily pain, and must at last make life easier for all.

Now the security of this treasure demands, not only the preservation of order, but a certain patience on our part with many institutions and facts of various kinds, especially touching the accumulation of wealth, which from the light we stand in, we are more likely to discern the evil than the good of. It is constantly the task of practical wisdom not to say, 'This is good, and I will have it', but to say, 'This is the less of two unavoidable evils, and I will bear it'. And this treasure of knowledge, which consists in the fine activity, the exalted vision of many minds, is bound up at present with conditions which have much evil in them. Just as in the case of material wealth and its distribution we are obliged to take the selfishness and weaknesses of human nature into account, and however we insist that men might act better, are forced, unless we are fanatical simpletons, to consider how they are likely to act; so in this matter of the wealth that is carried in men's minds, we have to reflect that the too absolute predominance of a class whose wants have been of a common sort, who are chiefly struggling to get better and more food, clothing, shelter, and bodily recreation, may lead to hasty measures for the sake of having things more fairly shared, which, even if they did not fail of their object, would at last debase the life of the nation. Do anything which will throw the classes who hold the treasures of knowledge—nay, I may say, the treasure of refined needs—into the background, cause them to withdraw from public affairs, stop too suddenly any of the sources by which their leisure and ease are furnished, rob them of the chances by which they may be influential and pre-eminent, and you do something as shortsighted as the acts of France and Spain when in jealousy and wrath, not altogether unprovoked, they drove from among them races and classes that held the traditions of handicraft and agriculture. You injure your own inheritance and the inheritance of your children. You may truly say that this which I call the common estate of society has been anything but common to you; but the same may be said, by many of us, of the sunlight and the air, of the sky and the fields, of parks and holiday games. Nevertheless, that these blessings exist makes life worthier to us, and urges us the more to energetic, likely means of getting our share in them; and I say, let us watch carefully, lest we do anything to lessen this treasure which is held in the minds of men, while we exert ourselves first of all, and to the very utmost, that we and our children may share in all its benefits. Yes; exert ourselves to the utmost, to break the yoke of ignorance. If we demand more leisure, more ease in our lives, let us show that we don't deserve the reproach of wanting to shirk that industry which, in some form or other, every man, whether rich or poor, should feel himself as much bound to as he is bound to decency. Let us show that we want to have some time and strength left to us, that we may use it, not for brutal indulgence, but for the rational exercise of the faculties which make us men. Without this no political measures can benefit us. No political institution will alter the nature of Ignorance, or hinder it from producing vice and misery. Let

Ignorance start how it will, it must run the same round of low appetites, poverty, slavery, and superstition. Some us of know this well—nay, I will say, feel it; for knowledge of this kind cuts deep; and to us it is one of the most painful facts belonging to our condition that there are numbers of our fellow-workmen who are so far from feeling in the same way, that they never use the imperfect opportunities already offered them for giving their children some schooling, but turn their little ones of tender age into bread-winners, often at cruel tasks, exposed to the horrible infection of childish vice. Of course, the causes of these hideous things go a long way back. Parents' misery has made parents' wickedness. But we, who are still blessed with the hearts of fathers and the consciences of men—we who have some knowledge of the curse entailed on broods of creatures in human shape, whose enfeebled bodies and dull perverted minds are mere centres of uneasiness, in whom even appetite is feeble and joy impossible—I say we are bound to use all the means at our command to help in putting a stop to this horror. Here, it seems to me, is a way in which we may use extended co-operation among us to the most momentous of all purposes, and make conditions of enrolment that would strengthen all educational measures. It is true enough that there is a low sense of parental duties in the nation at large, and that numbers who have no excuse in bodily hardship seem to think it a light thing to beget children, to bring human beings with all their tremendous possibilities into this difficult world, and then take little heed how they are disciplined and furnished for the perilous journey they are sent on without any asking of their own. This is a sin shared in more or less by all classes; but there are sins which, like taxation, fall the heaviest on the poorest, and none have such galling reasons as we working-men to try and rouse to the utmost the feeling of responsibility in fathers and mothers. We have been urged into co-operation by the pressure of common demands. In war men need each other more; and where a given point has to be defended, fighters inevitably find themselves shoulder to shoulder. So fellowship grows, so grow the rules of fellowship, which gradually shape themselves to thoroughness as the idea of a common good becomes more complete. We feel a right to say, If you will be one of us, you must make such and such a contribution—you must renounce such and such a separate advantage—you must set your face against such and such an infringement. If we have

427

any false ideas about our common good, our rules will be wrong, and we shall be co-operating to damage each other. But now, here is a part of our good, without which everything else we strive for will be worthless—I mean, the rescue of our children. Let us demand from the members of our Unions that they fulfil their duty as parents in this definite matter, which rules can reach. Let us demand that they send their children to school, so as not to go on recklessly breeding a moral pestilence among us, just as strictly as we demand that they pay their contributions to a common fund, understood to be for a common benefit. While we watch our public men, let us watch one another as to this duty, which is also public, and more momentous even than obedience to sanitary regulations. Whilst we resolutely declare against the wickedness in high places, let us set ourselves also against the wickedness in low places, not quarrelling which came first, or which is the worse of the two—not trying to settle the miserable precedence of plague or famine, but insisting unflinchingly on remedies once ascertained, and summoning those who hold the treasure of knowledge to remember that they hold it in trust, and that with them lies the task of searching for new remedies, and finding the right methods of applying them.

To find right remedies and right methods. Here is the great function of knowledge: here the life of one man may make a fresh era straight away, in which a sort of suffering that has existed shall exist no more. For the thousands of years down to the middle of the [sixteenth century][7] that human limbs had been hacked and amputated, nobody knew how to stop the bleeding except by searing the ends of the vessels with red hot iron. But then came a man named Ambrose Paré, and said, 'Tie up the arteries!' That was a fine word to utter. It contained the statement of a method— a plan by which a particular evil was for ever assuaged. Let us try to discern the men whose words carry that sort of kernel, and choose such men to be our guides and representatives—not choose platform swaggerers, who bring us nothing but the ocean to make our broth with.

To get the chief power into the hands of the wisest, which means to get our life regulated according to the truest principles mankind is in possession of, is a problem as old as the very notion of wisdom. The solution comes slowly, because men collectively can only be

[7] 'sixteenth century since Christ', 1884.

made to embrace principles, and to act on them, by the slow stupendous teaching of the world's events. Men will go on planting potatoes, and nothing else but potatoes, till a potatoe-disease comes and forces them to find out the advantage of a varied crop. Selfishness, stupidity, sloth, persist in trying to adapt the world to their desires, till a time comes when the world manifests itself as too decidedly inconvenient to them. Wisdom stands outside of man and urges itself upon him, like the marks of the changing seasons, before it finds a home within him, directs his actions, and from the precious effects of obedience begets a corresponding love.

But while still outside of us, wisdom often looks terrible, and wears strange forms, wrapped in the changing conditions of a struggling world. It wears now the form of wants and just demands in a great multitude of British men: wants and demands urged into existence by the forces of a maturing world. And it is in virtue of this—in virtue of this presence of wisdom on our side as a mighty fact, physical, and moral, which must enter into and shape the thoughts and actions of mankind—that we working men have obtained the suffrage. Not because we are an excellent multitude, but because we are a needy multitude.

But now, for our own part, we have seriously to consider this outside wisdom which lies in the supreme unalterable nature of things, and watch to give it a home within us and obey it. If the claims of the unendowed multitude of working men hold within them principles which must shape the future, it is not less true that the endowed classes, in their inheritance from the past, hold the precious material without which no worthy, noble future can be moulded. Many of the highest uses of life are in their keeping; and if privilege has often been abused, it also has been the nurse of excellence. Here again we have to submit ourselves to the great law of inheritance. If we quarrel with the way in which the labours and earnings of the past have been preserved and handed down, we are just as bigoted, just as narrow, just as wanting in that religion which keeps an open ear and an obedient mind to the teachings of fact, as we accuse those of being, who quarrel with the new truths and new needs which are disclosed in the present. The deeper insight we get into the causes of human trouble, and the ways by which men are made better and happier, the less we shall be inclined to the unprofitable spirit and practice of reproaching classes as such in a wholesale fashion. Not all the evils of our condition are such as we can justly blame others for; and, I repeat, many of them are such as no changes of institutions can quickly remedy. To discern between the evils that energy can remove and the evils that patience must bear, makes the difference between manliness and childishness, between good sense and folly. And more than that, without such discernment, seeing that we have grave duties towards our own body and the country at large, we can hardly escape acts of fatal rashness and injustice.

I am addressing a mixed assembly of workmen, and some of you may be as well or better fitted than I am to take up this office. But they will not think it amiss in me that I have tried to bring together the considerations most likely to be of service to us in preparing ourselves for the use of our new opportunities. I have avoided touching on special questions. The best help towards judging well on these is to approach them in the right temper without vain expectation, and with a resolution which is mixed with temperance.

28

NOTES ON FORM IN ART (1868)

This brief essay, written in a notebook now in the possession of the Yale University Library, is here published for the first time.[1] The date in parentheses after the title is George Eliot's own.

The occasion of 'Notes on Form in Art' is not known, but the date of 1868, the year of *The Spanish Gypsy*, suggests that in speaking of 'Poetry' in the essay George Eliot means, perhaps exclusively, verse rather than prose. Certainly the aesthetic implied by some of the essay's statements—briefly, one which assumes, in nineteenth-century fashion, lyric expression as the poetic norm—is widely different from the doctrines of imaginative realism with which she always described her work as a novelist. Nor is it likely that she would claim for the novel a 'superiority over all other arts' in virtue of the fact that 'its medium, language, is the least imitative', though this is the boast she makes for 'Poetry'. We know that she distinguished sharply between the limits of prose and verse from her letter explaining her choice of prose for the tale of *Silas Marner*: 'I have felt all through', she wrote, 'as if the story would have lent itself best to metrical rather than prose fiction... but, as my mind dwelt on the subject, I became inclined to a more realistic treatment'.[2]

On the other hand, the language of the essay is so general as to make it difficult to say how far its principles are meant to apply. The theory of organic form developed in it is certainly relevant to her novels and the last, detached paragraph describes an action that George Eliot used in the plot of *Felix Holt*.

If the essay is taken as relevant to her theory of the novel it contains important modifications of her earlier conceptions of realism in fiction,

[1] The notebook, which contains another essay entitled 'Versification', some verse, and mottoes for *Felix Holt*, *Middlemarch*, and *Daniel Deronda*, is fully described by Bernard J. Paris, 'George Eliot's Unpublished Poetry', *Studies in Philology*, LVI (July, 1959), 539–558. In his article, which prints the verse from the notebook, Mr. Paris promises to publish the prose, with a commentary, in another article.

[2] *Letters*, III, 382.

which emphasize imitation, and insist upon 'truth' not merely to the feelings of the artist but to the external world. 'Notes on Form in Art' is not, however, irreconcilable with her earlier theory. The supreme social function of art she always held to be the communication of feeling, which in turn depended upon the artist's own power to experience 'admiration, hope, and love'.[3] In this sense, prose as well as verse is 'not only determined by emotion but intended to express it'.

*　　　*　　　*

ABSTRACT words & phrases which have an excellent genealogy are apt to live a little too much on their reputation & even to sink into dangerous imposters that should be made to show how they get their living. For this reason it is often good to consider an old subject as if nothing had yet been said about it; to suspend one's attention even to revered authorities & simply ask what in the present state of our knowledge are the facts which can with any congruity be tied together & labelled by a given abstraction.

For example, to any but those who are under the dire necessity of using the word & cannot afford to wait for a meaning, it must be more fruitful to ask, what relations of things can be properly included under the word Form as applied to artistic composition, than to decide without any such previous inquiry that a particular work is wanting in form, or to take it for granted that the works of any one period or people are the examples of all that is admissible in artistic form.

Plain people, though indisposed to metaphysical subtleties, can yet understand that Form, as an element of human experience, must begin with the perception of separateness, derived principally from touch [of which the other senses are modifications];[4] & that things must be recognized as separate wholes before they can be recognized as wholes composed of parts, or before these wholes again can be regarded as relatively parts of a larger whole.

Form, then, as distinguished from merely massive impression, must first depend on the discrimination of wholes & then on the discrimination of parts. Fundamentally, form is unlikeness, as is seen in the philosophic use of the word Form in distinction from

[3] The phrase, a quotation from Wordsworth's *The Excursion*, IV, 763, occurs in 'Debasing the Moral Currency', *Theophrastus Such*, p. 148 (Cabinet Edition).

[4] Added at the foot of the page in MS.

Matter; & in consistency with this fundamental meaning, every difference is form. Thus, sweetness is a form of sensibility, rage is a form of passion, green is a form both of light & of sensibility. But with this fundamental discrimination is born in necessary antithesis the sense of wholeness or unbroken connexion in space & time: a flash of light is a whole compared with the darkness which precedes & follows it; the taste of sourness is a whole & includes parts or degrees as it subsides. And as knowledge continues to grow by its alternating processes of distinction & combination, seeing smaller & smaller unlikenesses & grouping or associating these under a common likeness, it arrives at the conception of wholes composed of parts more & more multiplied & highly differenced, yet more & more absolutely bound together by various conditions of common likeness or mutual dependence. And the fullest example of such a whole is the highest example of Form: in other words, the relation of multiplex interdependent parts to a whole which is itself in the most varied & therefore the fullest relation to other wholes. Thus, the human organism comprises things as diverse as the finger-nails & tooth-ache, as the nervous stimulus of muscle manifested in a shout, & the discernment of a red spot on a field of snow; but all its different elements or parts of experience are bound together in a more necessary wholeness or more inseparable group of common conditions than can be found in any other existence known to us. The highest Form, then, is the highest organism, that is to say, the most varied group of relations bound together in a wholeness which again has the most varied relations with all other phenomena.

It is only in this fundamental sense that the word Form can be applied to Art in general. Boundary or outline & visual appearance are modes of form which in music & poetry can only have a metaphorical presence. Even in the plastic arts form obviously, in its general application, means something else than mere imitation of outline, more or less correctness of drawing or modelling—just as, with reference to descriptive poetry it means something more than the bare delineation of landscape or figures. Even those who use the phrase with a very dim understanding, always have a sense that it refers to structure or composition, that is, to the impression from a work considered as a whole. And what is a structure but a set of relations selected & combined in accordance with the sequence of mental states in the constructor, or with the preconception of a whole which he has inwardly evolved? Artistic form, as distinguished from mere imitation, begins in sculpture & painting with composition or the selection of attitudes & the formation of groups, let the objects be of what order they may. In music it begins with the adjustment of tones & rhythm to a climax, apart from any direct imitation. But my concern is here chiefly with poetry which I take in its wider sense as including all literary production of which it is the prerogative & not the reproach that the choice & sequence of images & ideas—that is, of relations & groups of relations—are more or less not only determined by emotion but intended to express it. I say more or less; for even the ravings of madness include multitudinous groups & sequences which are parts of common experience; & in the range of poetry we see wide distances of degree in the combination of emotive force with sequences that are not arbitrary & individual but true & universal, just as the guiding emotion varies from an idiosyncracy only short of madness to a profoundly human passion which is or must come to be the heritage of all mankind. Sometimes the wider signification of poetry is taken to be fiction or invention as opposed to ascertained external fact or discovery. But what is fiction other than an arrangement of events or feigned correspondences according to predominant feeling? We find what destiny pleases; we make what pleases us—or what we think will please others.

Even taken in its derivative meaning of outline, what is form but the limit of that difference by which we discriminate one object from another?—a limit determined partly by the intrinsic relations or composition of the object, & partly by the extrinsic action of other bodies upon it. This is true whether the object is a rock or a man; but in the case of the inorganic body, outline is the result of a nearly equal struggle between inner constitution & the outer play of forces; while in the human organism the outline is mainly determined by the intrinsic relation of its parts, & what is called fitness, beauty or harmony in its outline & movements is dependent on the inward balance. The muscular strength which hurls, the muscular grace which gives a rhythmic movement to half a dozen balls, show a moving outline of which the chief factors are relations within the body; but the line with which a rock cuts the sky, or the shape of a boulder, may be more due to outer forces than to inner constitution. In ordinary language, the form of a stone is accidental. But the true expression of the difference is, that the wholeness of the stone depends simply on likeness of crystallization & is merely a wholeness of mass which may be broken up into other wholes; whereas the outline defining the wholeness of the human body is due to a consensus or constant interchange of effects among its parts. It is wholeness not merely of mass but of strict & manifold dependence. The word consensus expresses that fact in a complex organism by which no part can suffer increase or diminution without a participation of all other parts in the effect produced & a consequent modification of the organism as a whole.

By this light, forms of art can be called higher or lower only on the same principle as that on which we apply these words to organisms; viz. in proportion to the complexity of the parts bound up into one indissoluble whole. In Poetry—which has this superiority over all the other arts, that its medium, language, is the least imitative, & is in the most complex relation with what it expresses—Form begins in the choice of rhythms & images as signs of a mental state, for this is a process of grouping or association of a less spontaneous & more conscious order than the grouping or association which constitutes the very growth & natural history of mind. *Poetry* begins when passion weds thought by finding expression in an image; but *poetic form* begins with a choice of elements, however meagre, as the accordant expression of emotional states. The most monotonous burthen chanted by an Arab boatman on the Nile is still a beginning of poetic form.

*   *   *

Poetic Form was not begotten by thinking it out or framing it as a shell which should hold emotional expression, any more than the shell of an animal arises before the living creature; but emotion, by its tendency to repetition, i.e. rhythmic persistence in proportion as diversifying thought is absent, creates a form by the recurrence of its elements in adjustment with certain given conditions of sound, language, action, or environment. Just as the beautiful expanding curves of a bivalve shell are not first made for the reception of the unstable inhabitant, but grow & are limited by the simple rhythmic conditions of its growing life.

It is a stale observation that the earliest poetic forms arose in the same spontaneous unreflecting way—that the rhythmic shouts with clash of metal accompanying the huntsman's or conqueror's course were probably the nucleus of the ballad epic; that the funeral or marriage sing-song, wailing or glad, with more or less violent muscular movement & resonance of wood or metal made the rude beginnings of lyric poetry. But it is still worth emphasis that this spontaneous origin is the most completely demonstrated in relation to a form of art which ultimately came to be treated more reflectively than any other—the tragic & comic drama.

A Form being once started must by & by cease to be purely spontaneous: the form itself becomes the object & material of emotion, & is sought after, amplified and elaborated by discrimination of its elements till at last by the abuse of its refinement it preoccupies the room of emotional thinking; & poetry, from being the fullest expression of the human soul, is starved into an ingenious pattern-work, in which tricks with vocables take the place of living words fed with the blood of relevant meaning, & made musical by the continual intercommunication of sensibility & thought.

*　　　*　　　*

The old phrases should not give way to scientific explanation, for speech is to a great extent like sculpture, expressing observed phenomena & remaining true in spite of Harvey & Bichat.[5]

*　　　*　　　*

In the later development of poetic fable the αναγνωρισις tends to consist in the discernment of a previously unrecognized *character*, & this may also form the περιπατεια, according to Aristotle's notion[6] that in the highest form the two coincide.

---

[5] Marie François Xavier Bichat (1771–1802), French anatomist. His work was Lydgate's inspiration (*Middlemarch*, Ch. 15).

[6] *Poetics*, XI, 3-4. It is interesting to note that this action forms the climax of *Felix Holt*, which, as Fred C. Thomson has shown in his 'Felix Holt as Classic Tragedy', *Nineteenth-Century Fiction*, XVI (June, 1961), 47–58, is in part modelled after Greek tragedy.

29

LEAVES FROM A NOTE-BOOK

These 'Leaves', showing George Eliot at her most ponderously sibylline in thought and manner, were first published by Charles Lee Lewes in the authorized edition of her essays in 1884. The following account of them is taken from his preface to that collection:

> The opportunity afforded by this republication seemed a suitable one for giving to the world some 'notes', as George Eliot simply called them, which belong to a much later period, and which have not been previously published. The exact date of their writing cannot be fixed with any certainty, but it must have been some time between the appearance of 'Middlemarch' and that of 'Theophrastus Such'. They were probably written without any distinct view to publication— some of them for the satisfaction of her own mind; others perhaps as memoranda, and with an idea of working them out more fully at some later time. It may be of interest to know that, besides the 'notes' here given, the note-book contains four which appeared in 'Theophrastus Such', three of them practically as they there stand; and it is not impossible that some of those in the present volume might also have been so utilised had they not happened to fall outside the general scope of the work. The marginal titles are George Eliot's own, but for the general title, 'Leaves from a Note-Book', I am responsible.

*　　*　　*

AUTHORSHIP

TO lay down in the shape of practical moral rules courses of conduct only to be made real by the rarest states of motive and disposition, tends not to elevate but to degrade the general standard, by turning that rare attainment from an object of admiration into an impossible prescription, against which the average nature first rebels and then flings out ridicule. It is for art to present images of a lovelier

437

order than the actual, gently winning the affections, and so determining the taste. But in any rational criticism of the time which is meant to guide a practical reform, it is idle to insist that action ought to be this or that, without considering how far the outward conditions of such change are present, even supposing the inward disposition towards it. Practically, we must be satisfied to aim at something short of perfection—and at something very much further off it in one case than in another. While the fundamental conceptions of morality seem as stationary through ages as the laws of life, so that a moral manual written eighteen centuries ago still admonishes us that we are low in our attainments, it is quite otherwise with the degree to which moral conceptions have penetrated the various forms of social activity, and made what may be called the special conscience of each calling, art or industry. While on some points of social duty public opinion has reached a tolerably high standard, on others a public opinion is not yet born; and there are even some functions and practices with regard to which men far above the line in honourableness of nature feel hardly any scrupulosity, though their consequent behaviour is easily shown to be as injurious as bribery, or any other slowly poisonous procedure which degrades the social vitality.

Among those callings which have not yet acquired anything near a full-grown conscience in the public mind is Authorship. Yet the changes brought about by the spread of instruction and the consequent struggles of an uneasy ambition, are, or at least might well be, forcing on many minds the need of some regulating principle with regard to the publication of intellectual products, which would override the rule of the market: a principle, that is, which should be derived from a fixing of the author's vocation according to those characteristics in which it differs from the other bread-winning professions. Let this be done, if possible, without any cant, which would carry the subject into Utopia away from existing needs. The guidance wanted is a clear notion of what should justify men and women in assuming public authorship, and of the way in which they should be determined by what is usually called success. But the forms of authorship must be distinguished; journalism, for example, carrying a necessity for that continuous production which in other kinds of writing is precisely the evil to be fought against, and judicious careful compilation, which is a great public service, holding in its modest diligence a guarantee against those deductions of vanity and idleness which draw many a young gentleman into reviewing, instead of the sorting and copying which his small talents could not rise to with any vigour and completeness.

A manufacturer goes on producing calicoes as long and as fast as he can find a market for them; and in obeying this indication of demand he gives his factory its utmost usefulness to the world in general and to himself in particular. Another manufacturer buys a new invention of some light kind likely to attract the public fancy, is successful in finding a multitude who will give their testers for the transiently desirable commodity, and before the fashion is out, pockets a considerable sum: the commodity was coloured with a green which had arsenic in it that damaged the factory workers and the purchasers. What then? These, he contends (or does not know or care to contend), are superficial effects, which is folly to dwell upon while we have epidemic diseases and bad government.

The first manufacturer we will suppose blameless. Is an author simply on a par with him, as to the rules of production?

The author's capital is his brain-power—power of invention, power of writing. The manufacturer's capital, in fortunate cases, is being continually reproduced and increased. Here is the first grand difference between the capital which is turned into calico and the brain capital which is turned into literature. The calico scarcely varies in appropriateness of quality, no consumer is in danger of getting too much of it, and neglecting his boots, hats, and flannel-shirts in consequence. That there should be large quantities of the same sort in the calico manufacture is an advantage: the sameness is desirable, and nobody is likely to roll his person in so many folds of calico as to become a mere bale of cotton goods, and nullify his senses of hearing and touch, while his morbid passion for Manchester shirtings makes him still cry 'More!' The wise manufacturer gets richer and richer, and the consumers he supplies have their real wants satisfied and no more.

Let it be taken as admitted that all legitimate social activity must be beneficial to others besides the agent. To write prose or verse as a private exercise and satisfaction is not social activity; nobody is culpable for this any more than for learning other people's verse by heart if he does not neglect his proper business in consequence. If the exercise made him sillier or secretly more self-satisfied, that, to be sure, would be a roundabout way of injuring society; for though a certain mixture of silliness may lighten existence, we have at present more than enough.

But man or woman who publishes writings inevitably assumes the office of teacher or influencer of the public mind. Let him protest as he will that he only seeks to amuse, and has no pretension to do more than while away an hour of leisure or weariness—'the idle singer of an empty day'[1]—he can no more escape influencing the moral taste, and with it the action of the intelligence, than a setter of fashions in furniture and dress can fill the shops with his designs and leave the garniture of persons and houses unaffected by his industry.

For a man who has a certain gift of writing to say, 'I will make the most of it while the public likes my wares—as long as the market is open and I am able to supply it at a money profit—such profit being the sign of liking'—he should have a belief that his wares have nothing akin to the arsenic green in them, and also that his continuous supply is secure from a degradation in quality which the habit of consumption encouraged in the buyers may hinder them from marking their sense of by rejection; so that they complain, but pay, and read while they complain. Unless he has that belief, he is on a level with the manufacturer who gets rich by fancy-wares coloured with arsenic green. He really cares for nothing but his income. He carries on authorship on the principle of the gin-palace.

And bad literature of the sort called amusing is spiritual gin.

A writer capable of being popular can only escape this social culpability by first of all getting a profound sense that literature is good-for-nothing, if it is not admirably good: he must detest bad literature too heartily to be indifferent about producing it if only other people don't detest it. And if he has this sign of the divine afflatus within him, he must make up his mind that he must not pursue authorship as a vocation with a trading determination to get rich by it. It is in the highest sense lawful for him to get as good a price as he honourably can for the best work he is capable of; but not for him to force or hurry his production, or even do over again what has already been done, either by himself or others, so as to render his work no real contribution, for the sake of bringing up his income to the fancy pitch. An author who would keep a

[1] William Morris, *The Earthly Paradise*, 'An Apology', st. 1.

440

pure and noble conscience, and with that a developing instead of degenerating intellect and taste, must cast out of his aims the aim to be rich. And therefore he must keep his expenditure low—he must make for himself no dire necessity to earn sums in order to pay bills.

In opposition to this, it is common to cite Walter Scott's case, and cry, 'Would the world have got as much innocent (and therefore salutary) pleasure out of Scott, if he had not brought himself under the pressure of money-need?' I think it would—and more; but since it is impossible to prove what would have been, I confine myself to replying that Scott was not justified in bringing himself into a position where severe consequences to others depended on his retaining or not retaining his mental competence. Still less is Scott to be taken as an example to be followed in this matter, even if it were admitted that money-need served to press at once the best and the most work out of him: any more than a great navigator who has brought his ship to port in spite of having taken a wrong and perilous route, is to be followed as to his route by navigators who are not yet ascertained to be great.

But after the restraints and rules which must guide the acknowledged author, whose power of making a real contribution is ascertained, comes the consideration, how or on what principle are we to find a check for that troublesome disposition to authorship arising from the spread of what is called Education, which turns a growing rush of vanity and ambition into this current? The well-taught, an increasing number, are almost all able to write essays on given themes, which demand new periodicals to save them from lying in cold obstruction. The ill-taught—also an increasing number—read many books, seem to themselves able to write others surprisingly like what they read, and probably superior, since the variations are such as please their own fancy, and such as they would have recommended to their favourite authors: these ill-taught persons are perhaps idle and want to give themselves 'an object'; or they are short of money, and feel disinclined to get it by a commoner kind of work; or they find a facility in putting sentences together which gives them more than a suspicion that they have genius, which, if not very cordially believed in by private confidants, will be recognised by an impartial public; or finally, they observe that writing is sometimes well paid, and sometimes a ground of fame or distinction, and without any use of punctilious logic, they conclude to become writers themselves.

As to these ill-taught persons, whatever medicines of a spiritual sort can be found good against mental emptiness and inflation—such medicines are needful for *them*. The contempt of the world for their productions only comes after their disease has wrought its worst effects. But what is to be said to the well-taught, who have such an alarming equality in their power of writing 'like a scholar and a gentleman'? Perhaps they, too, can only be cured by the medicine of higher ideals in social duty, and by a fuller representation to themselves of the processes by which the general culture is furthered or impeded.

JUDGMENTS ON AUTHORS

In endeavouring to estimate a remarkable writer who aimed at more than temporary influence, we have first to consider what was his individual contribution to the spiritual wealth of mankind? Had he a new conception? Did he animate long-known but neglected truths with new vigour, and cast fresh light on their relation to other admitted truths? Did he impregnate any ideas with a fresh store of emotion, and in this way enlarge the area of moral sentiment? Did he by a wise emphasis here, and a wise disregard there, give a more useful or beautiful proportion to aims or motives? And even where his thinking was most mixed with the sort of mistake which is obvious to the majority, as well as that which can only be discerned by the instructed, or made manifest by the progress of things, has it that salt of a noble enthusiasm which should rebuke our critical discrimination if its correctness is inspired with a less admirable habit of feeling?

This is not the common or easy course to take in estimating a modern writer. It requires considerable knowledge of what he has himself done, as well as of what others had done before him, or what they were doing contemporaneously; it requires deliberate reflection as to the degree in which our own prejudices may hinder us from appreciating the intellectual or moral bearing of what on a first view offends us. An easier course is to notice some salient mistakes, and take them as decisive of the writer's incompetence; or to find out that something apparently much the same as what he has said in some connection not clearly ascertained, had been said by somebody else, though without great effect, until this new effect of discrediting the other's originality had shown itself as an adequate final cause; or to pronounce from the point of view of individual taste that this writer for whom regard is claimed is repulsive, wearisome, not to be borne except by those dull persons who are of a different opinion.

Elder writers who have passed into classics were doubtless treated in this easy way when they were still under the misfortune of being recent—nay, are still dismissed with the same rapidity of judgment by daring ignorance. But people who think that they have a reputation to lose in the matter of knowledge, have looked into cyclopædias and histories of philosophy or literature, and possessed themselves of the duly balanced epithets concerning the immortals. They are not left to their own unguided rashness, or their own unguided pusillanimity. And it is this sheeplike flock who have no direct impressions, no spontaneous delight, no genuine objection or self-confessed neutrality in relation to the writers become classic—it is these who are incapable of passing a genuine judgment on the living. Necessarily. The susceptibility they have kept active is a susceptibility to their own reputation for passing the right judgment, not the susceptibility to qualities in the object of judgment. Who learns to discriminate shades of colour by considering what is expected of him? The habit of expressing borrowed judgments stupifies the sensibilities, which are the only foundation of genuine judgments, just as the constant reading and retailing of results from other men's observations through the microscope, without ever looking through the lens oneself, is an instruction in some truths and some prejudices, but is no instruction in observant susceptibility; on the contrary, it breeds a habit of inward seeing according to verbal statement, which dulls the power of outward seeing according to visual evidence.

On this subject, as on so many others, it is difficult to strike the balance between the educational needs of passivity or receptivity, and independent selection. We should learn nothing without the tendency to implicit acceptance; but there must clearly be a limit to such mental submission, else we should come to a stand-still. The human mind would be no better than a dried specimen, representing an unchangeable type. When the assimilation of new matter ceases, decay must begin. In a reasoned self-restraining deference there is as much energy as in rebellion; but among the less capable, one must admit that the superior energy is on the side of the rebels. And certainly a man who dares to say that he finds an eminent classic feeble here, extravagant there, and in general over-rated, may chance to give an opinion which has some genuine discrimination in it concerning a new work or a living thinker—an opinion such as can hardly ever be got from the reputed judge who is a correct echo of the most approved phrases concerning those who have been already canonised.

STORY-TELLING

What is the best way of telling a story? Since the standard must be the interest of the audience, there must be several or many good ways rather than one best. For we get interested in the stories life presents to us through divers orders and modes of presentation. Very commonly our first awakening to a desire of knowing a man's past or future comes from our seeing him as a stranger in some unusual or pathetic or humorous situation, or manifesting some remarkable characteristics. We make inquiries in consequence, or we become observant and attentive whenever opportunities of knowing more may happen to present themselves without our search. You have seen a refined face among the prisoners picking tow in gaol; you afterwards see the same unforgetable face in a pulpit: he must be of dull fibre who would not care to know more about a life which showed such contrasts, though he might gather his knowledge in a fragmentary and unchronological way.

Again, we have heard much, or at least something not quite common, about a man whom we have never seen, and hence we look round with curiosity when we are told that he is present; whatever he says or does before us is charged with a meaning due to our previous hearsay knowledge about him, gathered either from dialogue of which he was expressly and emphatically the subject, or from incidental remark, or from general report either in or out of print.

These indirect ways of arriving at knowledge are always the most stirring even in relation to impersonal subjects. To see a chemical experiment gives an attractiveness to a definition of chemistry, and fills it with a significance which it would never have had without the pleasant shock of an unusual sequence such as the transformation of a solid into gas, and *vice versâ*. To see a word for the first time either as substantive or adjective in a connection where we care about knowing its complete meaning, is the way to

444

vivify its meaning in our recollection. Curiosity becomes the more eager from the incompleteness of the first information.[2] Moreover, it is in this way that memory works in its incidental revival of events: some salient experience appears in inward vision, and in consequence the antecedent facts are retraced from what is regarded as the beginning of the episode in which that experience made a more or less strikingly memorable part. 'Ah! I remember addressing the mob from the hustings at Westminster—you wouldn't have thought that I could ever have been in such a position. Well, how I came there was in this way——'; and then follows a retrospective narration.

The modes of telling a story founded on these processes of outward and inward life derive their effectiveness from the superior mastery of images and pictures in grasping the attention —or, one might say with more fundamental accuracy, from the fact that our earliest, strongest impressions, our most intimate convictions, are simply images added to more or less of sensation. These are the primitive instruments of thought. Hence it is not surprising that early poetry took this way—telling a daring deed, a glorious achievement, without caring for what went before. The desire for orderly narration is a later, more reflective birth. The presence of the Jack in the box affects every child: it is the more reflective lad, the miniature philosopher, who wants to know how he got there.

The only stories life presents to us in an orderly way are those of our autobiography, or the career of our companions from our childhood upwards, or perhaps of our own children. But it is a great art to make a connected strictly relevant narrative of such careers as we can recount from the beginning. In these cases the sequence of associations is almost sure to overmaster the sense of proportion. Such narratives *ab ovo* are summer's-day stories for happy loungers; not the cup of self-forgetting excitement to the busy who can snatch an hour of entertainment.

But the simple opening of a story with a date and necessary account of places and people, passing on quietly towards the more rousing elements of narrative and dramatic presentation, without need of retrospect, has its advantages which have to be measured by the nature of the story. Spirited narrative, without more than a

[2] Cf. George Eliot's method in beginning *Daniel Deronda*: 'Was she beautiful or not beautiful?'

touch of dialogue here and there, may be made eminently interest-ing, and is suited to the novelette. Examples of its charm are seen in the short tales in which the French have a mastery never reached by the English, who usually demand coarser flavours than are given by that delightful gaiety which is well described by La Fontaine[3] as not anything that provokes fits of laughter, but a certain charm, an agreeable mode of handling which lends attrac-tiveness to all subjects even the most serious. And it is this sort of gaiety which plays around the best French novelettes. But the opening chapters of the 'Vicar of Wakefield' are as fine as anything that can be done in this way.

Why should a story not be told in the most irregular fashion that an author's idiosyncrasy may prompt, provided that he gives us what we can enjoy? The objections to Sterne's wild way of telling 'Tristram Shandy' lie more solidly in the quality of the interrupting matter than in the fact of interruption. The dear public would do well to reflect that they are often bored from the want of flexibility in their own minds. They are like the topers of 'one liquor.'

HISTORIC IMAGINATION

The exercise of a veracious imagination in historical picturing seems to be capable of a development that might help the judgment greatly with regard to present and future events. By veracious imagination, I mean the working out in detail of the various steps by which a political or social change was reached, using all extant evidence and supplying deficiencies by careful analogical creation. How triumphant opinions originally spread—how institutions arose—what were the conditions of great inventions, discoveries, or theoretic conceptions—what circumstances affecting individual lots are attendant on the decay of long-established systems,—all these grand elements of history require the illumination of special imaginative treatment. But effective truth in this application of art requires freedom from the vulgar coercion of conventional plot, which is become hardly of higher influence on imaginative representation than a detailed 'order' for a picture sent by a rich grocer to an eminent painter—allotting a certain portion of the canvas to a rural scene, another to a fashionable group, with a

[3] 'Je n'appelle pas gayeté ce qui excite le rire, mais un certain charme, un air agréable qu'on peut donner à toutes sortes de sujets, mesme les plus sérieux'.—Preface to Fables. [George Eliot's note.]

request for a murder in the middle distance, and a little comedy to relieve it. A slight approximation to the veracious glimpses of history artistically presented, which I am indicating, but applied only to an incident of contemporary life, is 'Un paquet de lettres'[4] by Gustave Droz. For want of such real, minute vision of how changes come about in the past, we fall into ridiculously inconsistent estimates of actual movements, condemning in the present what we belaud in the past, and pronouncing impossible processes that have been repeated again and again in the historical preparation of the very system under which we live. A false kind of idealisation dulls our perception of the meaning in words when they relate to past events which have had a glorious issue: for lack of comparison no warning image rises to check scorn of the very phrases which in other associations are consecrated.

Utopian pictures help the reception of ideas as to constructive results, but hardly so much as a vivid presentation of how results have been actually brought about, especially in religious and social change. And there is the pathos, the heroism often accompanying the decay and final struggle of old systems, which has not had its share of tragic commemoration. What really took place in and around Constantine before, upon, and immediately after his declared conversion? Could a momentary flash be thrown on Eusebius in his sayings and doings as an ordinary man in bishop's garments? Or on Julian and Libanius?[5] There has been abundant writing on such great turning-points, but not such as serves to instruct the imagination in true comparison. I want something different from the abstract treatment which belongs to grave history from a doctrinal point of view, and something different from the schemed picturesqueness of ordinary historical fiction. I want brief, severely conscientious reproductions, in their concrete incidents, of pregnant movements in the past.

VALUE IN ORIGINALITY

The supremacy given in European cultures to the literatures of Greece and Rome has had an effect almost equal to that of a common religion in binding the Western nations together. It is

[4] 1870. Cross, *Life*, III, 422, says that he and George Eliot read Droz in 1880 on their return from Venice.

[5] George Eliot's reference to these figures from church history in the fourth century recalls her youthful interest in the development of early Christianity.

foolish to be for ever complaining of the consequent uniformity, as if there were an endless power of originality in the human mind. Great and precious origination must always be comparatively rare, and can only exist on condition of a wide massive uniformity. When a multitude of men have learned to use the same language in speech and writing, then and then only can the greatest masters of language arise. For in what does their mastery consist? They use words which are already a familiar medium of understanding and sympathy in such a way as greatly to enlarge the understanding and sympathy. Originality of this order changes the wild grasses into world-feeding grain. Idiosyncrasies are pepper and spices of questionable aroma.

TO THE PROSAIC ALL THINGS ARE PROSAIC

'Is the time we live in prosaic?' 'That depends: it must certainly be prosaic to one whose mind takes a prosaic stand in contemplating it.' 'But it is precisely the most poetic minds that most groan over the vulgarity of the present, its degenerate sensibility to beauty, eagerness for materialistic explanation, noisy triviality.' 'Perhaps they would have had the same complaint to make about the age of Elizabeth, if, living then, they had fixed their attention on its more sordid elements, or had been subject to the grating influence of its everyday meannesses, and had sought refuge from them in the contemplation of whatever suited their taste in a former age.'

'DEAR RELIGIOUS LOVE'

We get our knowledge of perfect Love by glimpses and in fragments chiefly—the rarest only among us knowing what it is to worship and caress, reverence and cherish, divide our bread and mingle our thoughts at one and the same time, under inspiration of the same object. Finest aromas will so often leave the fruits to which they are native and cling elsewhere, leaving the fruit empty of all but its coarser structure!

WE MAKE OUR OWN PRECEDENTS

In the times of national mixture when modern Europe was, as one may say, a-brewing, it was open to a man who did not like to be judged by the Roman law, to choose which of certain other codes he would be tried by. So, in our times, they who openly adopt a higher rule than their neighbours, do thereby make act of choice as to the laws and precedents by which they shall be approved or condemned, and thus it may happen that we see a man morally pilloried for a very customary deed, and yet having no right to complain, inasmuch as in his foregoing deliberative course of life he had referred himself to the tribunal of those higher conceptions, before which such a deed is without question condemnable.

BIRTH OF TOLERANCE

Tolerance first comes through equality of struggle, as in the case of Arianism and Catholicism in the early times—Valens, Eastern and Arian, Valentinian, Western and Catholic, alike publishing edicts of tolerance; or it comes from a common need of relief from an oppressive predominance, as when James II. published his Act of Tolerance towards non-Anglicans, being forced into liberality towards the Dissenters by the need to get it for the Catholics. Community of interest is the root of justice; community of suffering, the root of pity; community of joy, the root of love.

Enveloped in a common mist, we seem to walk in clearness ourselves, and behold only the mist that enshrouds others.

Sympathetic people are often incommunicative about themselves: they give back reflected images which hide their own depths.

The pond said to the ocean, 'Why do you rage so? The wind is not so very violent—nay, it is already fallen. Look at me. I rose into no foaming waves, and am already smooth again'.

FELIX QUI NON POTUIT

Many feel themselves very confidently on safe ground when they say: It must be good for man to know the Truth. But it is clearly not good for a particular man to know some particular truth, as irremediable treachery in one whom he cherishes—better that he should die without knowing it.

Of scientific truth, is it not conceivable that some facts as to the tendency of things affecting the final destination of the race might

449

be more hurtful when they had entered into the human consciousness than they would have been if they had remained purely external in their activity?

DIVINE GRACE A REAL EMANATION

There is no such thing as an impotent or neutral deity, if the deity be really believed in, and contemplated either in prayer or meditation. Every object of thought reacts on the mind that conceives it, still more on that which habitually contemplates it. In this we may be said to solicit help from a generalisation or abstraction. Wordsworth had this truth in his consciousness when he wrote (in the Prelude):

> Nor general truths, which are themselves a sort
> Of elements and agents, Under-powers
> Subordinate helpers of the living mind—[6]

not indeed precisely in the same relation, but with a meaning which involves that wider moral influence.

'A FINE EXCESS.' FEELING IS ENERGY

One can hardly insist too much, in the present stage of thinking, on the efficacy of feeling in stimulating to ardent co-operation, quite apart from the conviction that such co-operation is needed for the achievement of the end in view. Just as hatred will vent itself in private curses no longer believed to have any potency, and joy, in private singing far out among the woods and fields, so sympathetic feeling can only be satisfied by joining in the action which expresses it, though the added 'Bravo!' the added push, the added penny, is no more than a grain of dust on a rolling mass. When students take the horses out of a political hero's carriage, and draw him home by the force of their own muscle, the struggle in each is simply to draw or push, without consideration whether his place would not be as well filled by somebody else, or whether his one arm be really needful to the effect. It is under the same inspiration that abundant help rushes towards the scene of a fire, rescuing imperilled lives, and labouring with generous rivalry in carrying buckets. So the old blind King John of Bohemia at the battle of Creçy begged his vassals to lead him into the fight that he might strike a good blow, though his own stroke, possibly fatal to himself,

[6] I, 151–153.

could not turn by a hair's-breadth the imperious course of victory.[7]

The question, 'Of what use is it for me to work towards an end confessedly good?' comes from that sapless kind of reasoning which is falsely taken for a sign of supreme mental activity, but is really due to languor, or incapability of that mental grasp which makes objects strongly present, and to a lack of sympathetic emotion. In the 'Spanish Gypsy' Fedalma says—

> The grandest death! to die in vain—for Love
> Greater than sways the forces of the world,[8]

referring to the image of the disciples throwing themselves, consciously in vain, on the Roman spears. I really believe and mean this,—not as a rule of general action, but as a possible grand instance of determining energy in human sympathy, which even in particular cases, where it has only a magnificent futility, is more adorable, or as we say divine, than unpitying force, or than a prudent calculation of results. Perhaps it is an implicit joy in the resources of our human nature which has stimulated admiration for acts of self-sacrifice which are vain as to their immediate end. Marcus Curtius was probably not imagined as concluding to himself that he and his horse would so fill up the gap as to make a smooth *terra firma*.[9] The impulse and act made the heroism, not the correctness of adaptation. No doubt the passionate inspiration which prompts and sustains a course of self-sacrificing labour in the light of soberly estimated results gathers the highest title to our veneration, and makes the supreme heroism. But the generous leap of impulse is needed too to swell the flood of sympathy in us beholders, that we may not fall completely under the mastery of calculation, which in its turn may fail of ends for want of energy got from ardour. We have need to keep the sluices open for possible influxes of the rarer sort.

[7] This story, originally from Froissart, is told in John Richard Green, *The History of the English People*, 4 vols. (New York, 1878–1880), I, 419. George Eliot was reading Green's work in 1878 (*Letters*, VII, 6).

[8] *V.* what Demosthenes says (De Coronâ) about Athens pursuing the same course, though she had known from the beginning that her heroic resistance would be in vain. [George Eliot's note]. See *De Corona*, 199–205. The quotation from *The Spanish Gypsy* comes at the end of Book I.

[9] According to the myth, Marcus Curtius, to save his country, leaped into the chasm that opened in the Roman Forum.

APPENDIX A

GEORGE ELIOT'S PERIODICAL ESSAYS AND REVIEWS

THIS list includes only those articles that can be definitely attributed to George Eliot. Though it is complete within the limits of the established evidence, it should not be taken as immutably canonical. Many of the reviews and notices in the 'Contemporary Literature' sections of the *Westminster* between 1852 and 1854 may be her work, but, in the absence of clear external evidence, identifying them is extremely difficult. It is also known that she wrote or collaborated with Lewes on articles for the *Leader* in the first months of 1854, but again these cannot be certainly identified, and for that reason are better left alone.

For further attributions, on the basis of style alone, see Gordon S. Haight, 'George Eliot's Theory of Fiction', *Victorian Newsletter*, 10 (Autumn, 1956), 1–3.

*   *   *

Review of Edgar Quinet, *Christianity in Its Various Aspects*; Jules Michelet and Quinet, *The Jesuits*; Michelet, *Priests, Women, and Families*, trans. by C. Cocks, Coventry *Herald and Observer*, 30 October 1846, p. 2a.

Notice of Gilbert A. À. Beckett, *The Comic History of England*, Coventry *Herald and Observer*, 13 November 1846.

'Poetry and Prose, from the Notebook of an Eccentric', Coventry *Herald and Observer*:

'Introductory', 4 December 1846, p. 2b.
'How to Avoid Disappointment', 15 January 1847, p. 2b.
'The Wisdom of a Child', 5 February 1847, p. 2bc.
'A Little Fable with a Great Moral', 12 February 1847, p. 2ab.
'Hints on Snubbing', 19 February 1847, p. 2ab.

'Vice and Sausages', Coventry *Herald and Observer*, 26 February 1847.

Review of James Anthony Froude, *The Nemesis of Faith*, Coventry *Herald and Observer*, 16 March 1849.

Review of R. W. Mackay, *The Progress of the Intellect*, *Westminster Review*, LIV (January, 1851), 353–368.

'The Creed of Christendom', *Leader*, II (20 September 1851), 897–899.

Review of Carlyle, *Life of John Sterling*, 'Contemporary Literature of England', *Westminster Review*, LVII (January, 1852), 247–251.

'Woman in France: Madame de Sablé', *Westminster Review*, LXII (October, 1854), 448–473.

'The Romantic School of Music', *Leader*, V (28 October 1854), 1027–1028. [A triple collaboration: it is a translation by George Eliot of part of Liszt's 'Scribe's und Meyerbeer's Robert le Diable', *Neue Zeitschrift für Musik*, XL (16 June 1854), 261–269. Lewes added his own comment to the translation and the result was published as a letter to the *Leader* from Weimar].

'The Art of the Ancients', *Leader*, VI (17 March 1855), 257–258.

'Memoirs of the Court of Austria', *Westminster Review*, LXIII (April, 1855), 303–335.

'Westward Ho!', *Leader*, VI (19 May 1855), 474–475.

'Three Months in Weimar', *Fraser's Magazine*, LI (June, 1855), 699–706.

'Menander and the Greek Comedy', *Leader*, VI (16 June 1855), 578–579.

'Liszt, Wagner, and Weimar', *Fraser's Magazine*, LII (July, 1855), 48–62.

'Belles Lettres', *Westminster Review*, LXIV (July, 1855), 288–307.

'Lord Brougham's Literature', *Leader*, VI (7 July 1855), 652–653.

'The Morality of Wilhelm Meister', *Leader*, VI (21 July 1855), 703.

'The Future of German Philosophy', *Leader*, VI (28 July 1855), 723–724.

'Life and Opinions of Milton', *Leader*, VI (4 August 1855), 750.

'Love in the Drama', *Leader*, VI (25 August 1855), 820–821.

'Heine's Poems', *Leader* (1 September 1855), 843–844.

'Michelet on the Reformation', *Leader*, VI (15 September 1855), 892.

'German Mythology and Legend', *Leader*, VI (22 September 1855), 917–918.

'Evangelical Teaching: Dr. Cumming', *Westminster Review*, LXIV (October, 1855), 436–462.

'Belles Lettres', *Westminster Review*, LXIV (October, 1855), 596–615.

'Margaret Fuller and Mary Wollstonecraft', *Leader*, VI (13 October 1855), 988–989.

'Translations and Translators', *Leader*, VI (20 October 1855), 1014–1015.

'Thomas Carlyle', *Leader*, VI (27 October 1855), 1034–1035.

'Life of Goethe', *Leader*, VI (3 November 1855), 1058–1061.

'German Wit: Heinrich Heine', *Westminster Review*, LXV (January, 1856), 1–33.

'Belles Lettres', *Westminster Review*, LXV (January, 1856), 290–312.

'The Shaving of Shagpat', *Leader*, VII (5 January 1856), 15–17.

'Rachel Gray', *Leader*, VII (5 January 1856), 19.

'Introduction to Genesis', *Leader*, VII (12 January 1856), 41–42.

'History of German Protestantism', *Leader*, VII (9 February 1856), 140.

'The Poets and Poetry of America', *Leader*, VII (1 March 1856), 210.

'The Antigone and Its Moral', *Leader*, VII (29 March 1856), 306.

'Art and Belles Lettres', *Westminster Review*, LXV (April, 1856), 625–650.

'Church History of the Nineteenth Century', *Leader*, VII (5 April 1856), 331–332.

'The Court of Austria', *Leader*, VII (12 April 1856), 352–353.

'Who Wrote the Waverley Novels?' *Leader*, VII (19 April 1856), 375–376.

'Story of a Blue-Bottle', *Leader*, VII (26 April 1856), 401–402.

'Heine's Book of Songs', *Saturday Review*, I (26 April 1856), 523–524.

'Margaret Fuller's Letters from Italy', *Leader*, VII (17 May 1856), 475.

'Pictures of Life in French Novels', *Saturday Review*, II (17 May 1856), 69–70.

'The Art and Artists of Greece', *Saturday Review*, II (31 May 1856), 109–110.

'The Natural History of German Life', *Westminster Review*, LXVI (July, 1856), 51–79.

'Belles Lettres and Art', *Westminster Review*, LXVI (July, 1856), 257–278.

'A Tragic Story', *Leader*, VII (19 July 1856), 691.

'The Lover's Seat', *Leader*, VII (2 August 1856), 735–736.

'Ferny Combes', *Leader*, VII (16 August 1856), 787.

'Recollections of Heine', *Leader*, VII (23 August 1856), 811–812.

'Felice Orsini', *Leader*, VII (30 August 1856), 835.

'Sight-seeing in Germany and the Tyrol', *Saturday Review*, II (6 September 1856), 424–425.

'Silly Novels by Lady Novelists', *Westminster Review*, LXVI (October, 1856), 442–461.

'Belles Lettres', *Westminster Review*, LXVI (October, 1856), 566–582.
'Worldliness and Other-Worldliness: The Poet Young', *Westminster Review*, LXVII (January, 1857), 1–42.
'History, Biography, Voyages and Travels', *Westminster Review*, LXVII (January, 1857), 288–306.
'Belles Lettres', *Westminster Review*, LXVII (January, 1857), 306–326.
'A Word for the Germans', *Pall Mall Gazette*, I (7 March 1865), 201.
'Servants' Logic', *Pall Mall Gazette*, I (17 March 1865), 310–311.
'Futile Falsehoods', *Pall Mall Gazette*, I (3 April 1865), 470–471.
'Modern Housekeeping', *Pall Mall Gazette*, I (13 May 1865), 880.
'The Influence of Rationalism', *Fortnightly Review*, I (15 May 1865), 43–55.
'The Grammar of Ornament', *Fortnightly Review*, I (15 May 1865), 124–125.
'Address to Working Men, by Felix Holt', *Blackwood's*, CIII (January, 1868), 1–11.

APPENDIX B

ARTICLES WRONGLY OR DOUBTFULLY ATTRIBUTED TO GEORGE ELIOT

MOST of the mistaken attributions in the list of George Eliot's periodical writings may be traced to two sources. The first is an article by an unidentified writer in the *Academy*, XIX (8 January 1881), 27, which wrongly assigns to George Eliot three articles from the *Westminster Review*: 'The Lady Novelists'; 'George Forster'; and 'Weimar and Its Celebrities'. The second source of confusion is the bibliography by John P. Anderson appended to Oscar Browning's *Life of George Eliot* (London, 1890). Probably through mis-reading certain passages in Cross's *Life*, Anderson made the mistake of attributing to George Eliot two articles from the *Westminster* entitled 'Prussia and Prussian Policy' and 'Dryden and His Times'.

These five wrongly attributed articles are the most persistent errors in the bibliography of George Eliot's writings. I hope that the evidence which follows may lay these ghosts, and the others which have arisen after them. For valuable help in compiling this information I am indebted to Professor Walter E. Houghton and the *Wellesley Index to Victorian Periodicals*.

*   *   *

Notice of *Memoirs of Margaret Fuller* in 'Contemporary Literature of America', *Westminster Review*, LVII (April, 1852), 665–666.

Attributed to George Eliot by Mathilde Blind, *George Eliot* (Boston, 1883), p. 60, 'judging from internal evidence'. The attribution has been generally accepted, and the notice reprinted as George Eliot's in Herrick, *Essays and Reviews of George Eliot* and in *Essays and Uncollected Papers*.

The article refers to the review of Carlyle's *Sterling* in the *Westminster* of January, 1852, in such a way as to indicate that both reviews are by the same author. Since the Carlyle review has long been accepted as George Eliot's, this relationship between it and the review of Margaret Fuller is presumptive evidence for her authorship of both.

Against this must be set the possibility that the 'Contemporary Literature of America' section in the April *Westminster* was written by R. W. Griswold, according to evidence presented in Joy Bayless, *Rufus Wilmot Griswold* (Nashville, 1943), pp. 209–211.

Even if, as seems quite probable, Griswold was responsible for the April 'Contemporary Literature of America', this would not exclude the possibility that George Eliot, as editor of the *Westminster*, added her own contribution to Griswold's. The 'Contemporary Literature' sections in the early numbers of the *Westminster* under Chapman seem to have been of composite authorship, so there would have been clear precedent for such a proceeding. Moreover, the tone of the remarks about Margaret Fuller in the review is quite uncharacteristic of Griswold, who had little or no sympathy for her. But without more conclusive evidence it is unsafe to decide either for or against George Eliot's authorship of the notice.

'The Lady Novelists', *Westminster Review*, LVIII (July, 1852), 129–141.

By G. H. Lewes. His authorship was established by a letter from George Eliot first published in Cross's *Life*, I, 284.

Attributed to George Eliot in the *Academy*, XIX (January, 1881), 27; and in George Willis Cooke, *George Eliot: A Critical Study* (Boston, 1883), Ch. 7.

Reprinted as George Eliot's in Herrick, *Essays and Reviews of George Eliot.*

Review of Nathaniel Hawthorne, *The Blithedale Romance*, *Westminster Review*, LVIII (October, 1852), 592–598.

Perhaps by R. W. Griswold. See Bayless, *Rufus Wilmot Griswold*, p. 210.

Attributed to George Eliot by J. D. Rust, 'George Eliot on the *Blithedale Romance*', *Boston Public Library Quarterly*, VII (October, 1955), 207–215.

The internal, as well as the slight external, evidence is rather against than for George Eliot's authorship. As Richard Stang, *The Theory of the Novel in England, 1850–1870* (New York and London, 1959), p. 176, note, has pointed out, the content of the review contradicts everything known of George Eliot's critical position at that date. The attribution is also questioned, on different grounds, by Gordon S. Haight in

Letters, II, 55, n. 6. It seems worth while to enter at least a strong *caveat* against this attribution, especially since the review is being taken as George Eliot's by students of Hawthorne, e.g., Edward Wagenknecht, *Nathaniel Hawthorne* (New York, 1961), pp. 60–61.

'Prussia and Prussian Policy', *Westminster Review*, LXIII (January, 1855), 53–89.

Probably by Joseph Neuberg. See *The Correspondence of Arthur Hugh Clough*, ed. Frederick L. Mulhauser (Oxford, 1957), II, 502.

Attributed to George Eliot by John P. Anderson in the bibliography to Browning, *Life of George Eliot*. Anderson probably misunderstood the entry from George Eliot's Journal published in Cross, *Life*, I, 377: 'Wrote article on Stahr'. 'Prussia and Prussian Policy' reviews, among other things, *Die Preussische Revolution* by A. Stahr, but George Eliot's reference was to her review of Adolf Stahr's *Torso* in the *Leader*, 17 March 1855.

'Dryden and His Times', *Westminster Review*, LXIII (April, 1855), 336–367.

Probably by William Bodham Donne, to whom it is attributed in Catherine B. Johnson, *W. B. Donne and His Friends* (New York, 1905), Appendix.

Like 'Prussia and Prussian Policy', this too was assigned to George Eliot by John P. Anderson in the bibliography to Browning's *Life of George Eliot*. Anderson perhaps misunderstood the confused summary of George Eliot's Journal given in Cross, *Life*, I, 381–382. Cross prints: 'During this month George Eliot was finishing the translating and revising of Spinoza's Ethics, and was still reading Scherr's book, Schrader's "German Mythology" . . . article on Dryden in the "Westminster". . . .' The Journal entry for 1 April 1855 reads: 'Received Westminster Review . . . Read art. on Dryden in W.R. & looked through the Cont[emporary] Lit[erature]'.

Reprinted as George Eliot's in *Essays and Uncollected Papers*.

'George Forster', *Westminster Review*, LXVI (October, 1856), 360–407.

Author unknown.

Attributed to George Eliot in the *Academy*, XIX (8 January 1881), 27, and in Edith Simcox, 'George Eliot', *Nineteenth Century*, IX (May, 1881), 778–801.

Reprinted as George Eliot's in Herrick, *Essays and Reviews of George Eliot*; and in *Essays and Uncollected Papers*.

Review of George Meredith, *Farina*, *Westminster Review*, LXVIII (October, 1857), 597–599.

By George Meredith, according to evidence published in Gordon S. Haight, 'George Meredith and the Westminster Review', *Modern Language Review*, LIII (January, 1958), 1–16.

Attributed to George Eliot by M. Buxton Forman in his *George Meredith: Some Early Appreciations* (New York, 1909), p. 43; and by J. A. Hammerton, *George Meredith in Anecdote and Criticism* (London and New York, 1909), p. 143. The review is reprinted entire in Forman's book, pp. 43–47, and in part by Hammerton, pp. 143–144.

The knowledge that George Eliot had reviewed Meredith's *The Shaving of Shagpat* in the *Leader*, VII (5 January 1856), 15–17, and in the *Westminster Review*, LXV (April, 1856), 638–639, probably led Forman and Hammerton to believe that the review of *Farina* in the *Westminster* was also hers. But George Eliot had ceased to have any connection with the *Westminster* by the time the review appeared.

'Weimar and Its Celebrities', *Westminster Review*, LXXI (April, 1859), 391–416.

Author unknown.

Attributed to George Eliot in the *Academy*, XIX (8 January 1881), 27, probably through confusing it with the two articles on Weimar that she wrote for *Fraser's* in 1855.

Reprinted as George Eliot's in Herrick, *Essays and Reviews of George Eliot*.

APPENDIX C

EDITIONS OF GEORGE ELIOT'S ESSAYS AND REVIEWS

Nathan Sheppard, ed. *The Essays of 'George Eliot', Complete: Collected and Arranged with an Introduction on Her 'Analysis of Motives'.* New York: Funk and Wagnalls [1883]. Contains: 'The Life of Sterling'; 'Woman in France'; 'Evangelical Teaching'; 'German Wit'; 'The Natural History of German Life'; 'Silly Novels by Lady Novelists'; 'Worldliness and Other-Worldliness'; 'The Influence of Rationalism'; 'The Grammar of Ornament'; 'Felix Holt's Address to Workingmen'.

Essays and Leaves from a Note-Book. Edinburgh and London: Blackwood, 1884. Contains: 'Worldliness and Other-Worldliness'; 'German Wit'; 'Evangelical Teaching'; 'The Influence of Rationalism'; 'The Natural History of German Life'; 'Three Months in Weimar'; 'Address to Working Men, By Felix Holt'; and 'Leaves from a Note-Book'.
[The authorized edition, selected and revised by George Eliot and often reprinted.]

Essays and Reviews of George Eliot, not Hitherto Reprinted, Together With an Introductory Essay on the Genius of George Eliot by Mrs. S. B. Herrick. Boston: Aldine Book Publishing Co., 1887. Contains: 'The Lady Novelists'; 'Weimar and Its Celebrities'; 'Woman in France'; 'Margaret Fuller'; 'George Forster'; 'Silly Novels by Lady Novelists'; 'The Life of Sterling'; 'The Grammar of Ornament'.

Essays and Uncollected Papers, Volume 22 of *The Writings of George Eliot.* Large Paper Edition. 25 vols. Boston and New York: Houghton, Mifflin Company, 1908. Contains: 'Woman in France'; 'Memoirs of the Court of Austria'; 'George Forster'; 'Silly Novels by Lady Novelists'; 'Dryden and His Times'; 'The Progress of the Intellect'; 'The Morality of Wilhelm Meister'; 'Thomas Carlyle'; 'The Life of

Sterling'; 'Margaret Fuller'; 'Margaret Fuller and Mary Wollstone-craft'; 'The Shaving of Shagpat'; 'The Grammar of Ornament'.

Early Essays by George Eliot. Privately printed [by Major George Redway]. Westminster Press, 1919. Contains: 'From the Note-book of an Eccentric'; 'How to Avoid Disappointment'; 'The Wisdom of the Child'; 'A Little Fable with a great Moral'; 'Hints on Snubbing'.

[For the history of this edition see the headnote to 'Poetry and Prose, From the Notebook of an Eccentric'.]

In the bibliography to his *George Eliot: A Critical Study*, 2nd ed. (Boston, 1884), George Willis Cooke describes a volume entitled *The Complete Essays of George Eliot* (Boston: Estes and Lauriat, 1883), containing the 'Life of Sterling'; 'Woman in France'; 'Evangelical Teaching'; 'German Wit'; 'The Natural History of German Life'; 'Silly Novels by Lady Novelists'; 'Worldliness and Other-Worldliness'; 'The Influence of Rationalism'; 'The Grammar of Ornament'; 'Felix Holt's Address to Workingmen'; 'The Lady Novelists'; 'George Foster' [*sic*]; 'Weimar and Its Celebrities'.

Though Cooke's description is quite full, I have been unable to discover a copy of this book or even to find a further mention of it, and suspect that it may be a ghost, perhaps announced but never published.

INDEX

Locke, John, 150
Loder, Justus Christian, 89
London, 83, 94, 97, 155, 331, 353
London Philharmonic, 96, 103
Longman, William, 397
Longueville, Duchesse de, 61, 62, 65, 66–67, 68, 71, 72, 73, 78, 79–80
Louis XIII, King, 62
Louis Phillipe, 237, 253–254
Lowe, Robert, Lord Sherbrooke, 417
Lucian, 36
Lusatia, 275, 276
Luther, Martin, 90, 91, 156, 174, 244, 275, 293, 403
Lutheran Church, 230
Luxembourg, Palais de, 59, 74, 252
Luynes, Duc de, 78
Lyell, Sir Charles, *Principles of Geology*, 31
Lyons, 372

Macarthy, 14–17
Mackail, J. W., *Studies of English Poets*, 335
Mackay, Robert William, 7; *Progress of the Intellect*, 27–45
Madagascar, 267
Madrid, 63
Mahomet, 171
Maintenon, Mme de, 76
Maisons, Seigneur de, 70
Manetho, 257
Manoa, 131
Marburg, 274
Marcus Curtius, 451
Maria, 394–395
Marie-Madeline, Princess, 77
Mars, 80, 168
Martin, Robert Bernard, *The Dust of Combat*, 124
Martineau, Harriet, 322
Massillon, Jean Baptiste, 61
mathematics, 290
Maure, Dona d'Attichy, Comtesse de, 64–65, 67, 71
Maurice, Frederick Denison, 124, 322
Maury, Louis Ferdinand Alfred, *La magie et l'astrologie*, 403
May Meetings, 317
Mazarin, Cardinal, 70, 71
Mecklenburg, 286, 292
Media, 43
mediation, theory of, 44

Medici, Catherine de, 63
Medor, the dog, 235, 236
Meiklejohn, J. M. D., 207, 208
meliorism, 189, 219
Menander, 453
Mendelssohn, Felix, 105, 231, 262
Menu, 257
Mercury, 168
Meredith, George, *Farina*, 458–459; *Shaving of Shagpat*, 4, 459
Meriden, 262
Merlin, 242
Methodists, 166, 167, 283, 327
Meyerbeer, Giacomo, 231; *Jean, the Prophet*, 101, 104; *Les Huguenots*, 101, 104; *Robert le Diable*, 101, 453
Micah, 43
Michael, Archangel, 26
Michelet, Jules, 453; *The Jesuits*, 452; *Les femmes de la révolution*, 52; *Priests, Women, and Families*, 452
Middle Ages, 131, 219
Milde, Hans Feodor von, 117
Mill, John Stuart, 322; *Logic*, 150, 152–153
Milton, John, 127, 154–157, 191, 344, 357, 453; 'Areopagitica,' 155; *Christian Doctrine*, 155–156; *Doctrine of Divorce*, 5, 7, 155–157; 'L'Allegro,' 250; 'On the Morning of Christ's Nativity,' 28; *Paradise Lost*, 98, 155, 193, 250, 344
Mirabeau, Comte de, 215
Misne, Reine de, 67
Missionary Society, Church of England, 317
Missolonghi, 169
Mizraim, 36
Molière, 220, 222; *Bourgeois Gentilhomme*, 338; *Femmes Savantes*, 58; *Précieuses Ridicules*, 58–59
Moloch, 42, 43
Montagu, Elizabeth, 348, 349–351, 356
Montaigne, Michel de, 'Des Boiteux,' 407
Montausier, Julie de Rambouillet, Mme de, 64, 66–67, 72, 73, 78
Montesquieu, Charles Louis de, 405
Montgomery, James, 379
Monthly Magazine, 146

Sinclair, Catherine, 322
Singer, S. W., 336
Sizi, Francesco, 167
slavery, 326, 327
Smith, George, 386
Smith, John Pye, 256
Smith, John Stores ('John Ackerlos'),
    259
Smith, Sydney, *Memoir*, 140
Smithfield, 25
social science, 289–290
Socialist party, 237
Socialists, 289, 295, 296
Society for Promoting the Conversion
    of the Jews, 321
Society for the Propagation of the
    Gospel, 351
Socinus, 410
Socrates, 44, 171
Sophocles, *Antigone*, 261–265, 454
Sourdis, Marquis de, 73
Southey, Robert, 35
Souvré, Commandeur de, 78
Spain and Spanish, 58, 63, 222, 426
Spandau, fortress of, 236–237
Spanish Armada, 131
Spence, Joseph, *Anecdotes*, 305, 336,
    343, 345, 379
Spencer, Herbert, 28
Spinoza, Baruch, *Ethics*, 207
spiritualism, 402
Spontini, Gasparo, 237
Spring Gardens, 307
Staël, Anne-Louise, Mme de, 55; *De
    l'Allemagne*, 250
Stahr, Adolf, *Torso*, 458; *Weimar und
    Jena*, 89
Stang, Richard, 457
Stanley, Arthur Penrhyn, 50
Star-Chamber, 25
Stein, Frau von, 94
Steinhäusser, Karl, 86
Steinmann, Martin, Jr., 97
Stephen, Sir Leslie, 339
Sterling, John, 46–51
Sterne, Laurence, 251; *Tristram
    Shandy*, 446
Stieler, Josef, 90
Stowe, Harriet Beecher, 3; *Dred*, 3,
    319, 325–328, 329; *Sunny Mem-
    ories of Foreign Lands*, 326; *Uncle
    Tom's Cabin*, 326

Strachey, Lytton, *Eminent Victorians*,
    50
Strasburg, 91
Strasburg Cathedral, 261
Strauss, David Friedrich, 6, 30; *Life
    of Jesus*, 48, 207
Strickland, Jane Margaret, 321
Stultus, Rev. Amylatus, 25
Sue, Eugène, 272
Sunderland, Lady, 350
Susanna, 244
Sutton, Sir Robert, 350
Swedenborg, Emanuel, 244
Sydenham, 218
sympathy, morality of, 15–16, 169,
    179, 182–189, 371–385, 450–451

Taillandier, St. René, 228
Talmud, 171
Tatler, 340
Taunus, 277
Taylor, Isaac, 163
Temple, Elizabeth Lee ('Narcissa'),
    348, 372
Temple, Henry, 348
Tenby, 266
Teniers, David, 268
Tenison, Archbishop, 339
Tennemann, Wilhelm, 253
Tennyson, Alfred, Lord, 3, 8, 248;
    'The Brook,' 198; 'Circumstance,'
    248; 'The Day Dream,' 103; 'The
    Daisy,' 198; 'Gardener's Daugh-
    ter,' 191; *In Memoriam*, 173, 189,
    191, 247; 'Locksley Hall,' 191;
    'Love Thou Thy Land,' 195;
    Maud, 3, 4, 190–198; 'Morte
    d'Arthur,' 191; 'Ode on the
    Death of the Duke of Welling-
    ton,' 198; *The Princess*, 191, 200,
    205; 'Sea Dreams,' 159; 'The
    Talking Oak,' 197, 413; 'The
    Two Voices,' 192; 'Ulysses,' 191
Tennyson, Sir Charles, *Alfred Tenny-
    son*, 190
Tennyson, Hallam, Lord, *Alfred
    Lord Tennyson*, 195
Test Act, 25
Tetzel, Johann, 91
Thackeray, William Makepeace, 159;
    Henry Esmond, 123; *The New-
    comes*, 207
Theism, 243, 245